# THE BIRDS OF SIKKIM

# THE BIRDS OF SIKKIM

*By*

**SALIM ALI**

*with coloured plates by*
**David Reid-Henry**
**Robert Scholz** *and* **Paul Barruel**

*and line drawing by*
**Paul Barruel** *and* **Walter Ahrens**

GYAN

*Published by*

GYAN

Gyan Publishing House
5, Ansari Road
Daryaganj, New Delhi-110002
Phone: 011-47034999, 9811692060
E-mail: books@gyanbooks.com

*Distribution Network*
gyanbooks.com
India, USA, Canada, UK, Australia, France



ISBN : 978-81-212-1407-0 (HB)
First Published, 1896

2nd Impression 2021

*Printed at:* Gyan Press, Delhi.



**The Birds of Sikkim**
Author: Sálim Ali

# CONTENTS


LIST OF PLATES xvii
INTRODUCTION xxiii
KEY TO DESCRIPTIVE TERMS xxxi

## *Family* ANATIDAE: Ducks, Geese

The Eastern Goosander, *Mergus merganser orientalis* Gould ... ... 1
The Tufted Pochard, *Aythya fuligula* (Linnaeus) ... ... 2

## *Family* ACCIPITRIDAE: Vultures, Hawks

The Pariah Kite, *Milvus migrans govinda* Sykes ... ... 2
The Blackeared, or Large Indian, Kite, *Milvus migrans lineatus* (Gray) ... 2
The Eastern Goshawk, *Accipiter gentilis schvedowi* (Menzbier) ... 3
The Besra Sparrow-Hawk, *Accipiter virgatus affinis* Hodgson ... 4
The Indian Sparrow-Hawk, *Accipiter nisus melaschistos* Hume ... 5
The Crested Goshawk, *Accipiter trivirgatus indicus* (Hodgson) ... 6
The Longlegged Buzzard, *Buteo rufinus rufinus* (Cretzschmar) ... 6
The Japanese Desert Buzzard, *Buteo buteo burmanicus* Hume ... 7
The Himalayan Hawk-Eagle, *Spizaëtus nipalensis nipalensis* (Hodgson) ... 8
Bonelli's Hawk-Eagle, *Nisaëtus fasciatus fasciatus* (Vieillot) ... ... 9
The Booted Hawk-Eagle, *Hieraëtus pennatus* (Gmelin) ... ... 9
The Black Eagle, *Ictinaëtus malayensis perniger* (Hodgson) ... ... 10
The Ringtailed, or Pallas's, Fishing Eagle, *Haliaëtus leucoryphus* (Pallas) 11
The Black, or King, Vulture, *Torgos calvus* (Scopoli) ... ... 11
The Himalayan Griffon Vulture, *Gyps himalayensis* Hume ... ... 11
The Lämmergeier, or Bearded Vulture, *Gypaëtus barbatus aureus* (Halblizl) ... ... ... ... ... ... 13
The Hen Harrier, *Circus cyaneus cyaneus* (Linnaeus) ... ... 15
The Crested Serpent Eagle, *Spilornis cheela cheela* (Latham) ... 15

## *Family* FALCONIDAE: Falcons

The Himalayan Falconet, *Microhierax caerulescens caerulescens* (Linnaeus) 16
The Shahin Falcon, *Falco peregrinus peregrinator* Sundevall ... 17
The Himalayan Kestrel, *Falco tinnunculus interstinctus* McClelland ... 18

## *Family* PHASIANIDAE: Pheasants, Partridges, Quails

The Snow Partridge, *Lerwa lerwa* (Hodgson) ... ... 20
The Sikkim Snowcock, *Tetraogallus tibetanus aquilonifer* R. & A. Meinertzhagen ... ... ... ... ... 21
The Common Hill Partridge, *Arborophila torqueola torqueola* (Valenciennes) 22
Blyth's, or the Rufousthroated, Hill Partridge, *Arborophila rufogularis rufogularis* (Blyth) ... ... ... ... 23
The Redbreasted Hill Partridge, *Arborophila mandellii* Hume ... 23
The Blood Pheasant, *Ithaginis cruentus affinis* Beebe ... ... 24
The Crimson Horned Pheasant, or Satyr Tragopan, *Tragopan satyra* (Linnaeus) ... ... ... ... ... 25
The Monal, or Impeyan Pheasant, *Lophophorus impejanus* (Latham) ... 26
The Blackbacked Kaleej Pheasant, *Lophura leucomelana melanota* (Hutton) ... ... ... ... ... 27
The Red Junglefowl, *Gallus gallus murghi* Robinson & Kloss ... ... 28

## *Family* CHARADRIIDAE

### *Subfamily* CHARADRIINAE: Plovers

The Spurwinged Plover, *Vanellus spinosus duvaucelii* (Lesson) ... 29
The Pamirs Lesser Sand Plover, *Charadrius mongolus atrifrons* Wagler ... 30

## *Subfamily* Scolopacinae: Sandpipers, Snipe, Woodcock, etc.

The Redshank, *Tringa totanus eurhinus* (Oberholser) ... ... 31
The Green Sandpiper, *Tringa ochropus* Linnaeus ... ... 32
The Common Sandpiper, *Tringa hypoleucos* Linnaeus ... ... 33
The Eastern Solitary Snipe, *Capella solitaria solitaria* (Hodgson) ... 33
The Woodcock, *Scolopax rusticola rusticola* Linnaeus ... ... 34
Temminck's Stint, *Calidris temminckii* (Leisler) ... ... 36
The Ibisbill, *Ibidorhyncha struthersii* Vigors ... ... ... 36

## *Family* Columbidae: Pigeons, Doves

The Pintailed Green Pigeon, *Treron apicauda apicauda* (Blyth) ... 37
The Wedgetailed Green Pigeon, *Treron sphenura sphenura* (Vigors) ... 38
Hodgson's, or the Nepal Maroonbacked, Imperial Pigeon, *Ducula badia insignis* Hodgson ... ... ... ... ... 39
The Snow Pigeon, *Columba leuconota leuconota* Vigors ... ... 40
The Turkestan Hill Pigeon, *Columba rupestris turkestanica* Buturlin ... 41
The Speckled Wood Pigeon, *Columba hodgsonii* Vigors ... ... 42
The Ashy Wood Pigeon, *Columba pulchricollis* Blyth ... ... 43
The Bartailed Cuckoo-Dove, *Macropygia unchall tusalia* (Blyth) ... 43
The Rufous Turtle Dove, *Streptopelia orientalis agricola* (Tickell) ... 44
The Indian Spotted Dove, *Streptopelia chinensis suratensis* (Gmelin) ... 46
The Emerald Dove, *Chalcophaps indica indica* (Linnaeus) ... ... 46

## *Family* Psittacidae: Parrots

The Indian Redbreasted Parakeet, *Psittacula alexandri fasciata* (P.L.S. Müller) ... ... ... ... ... 47
The Himalayan Slatyheaded Parakeet, *Psittacula himalayana himalayana* (Lesson) ... ... ... ... ... 48

## *Family* Cuculidae: Cuckoos

The Large Hawk-Cuckoo, *Cuculus sparverioïdes sparverioïdes* Vigors ... 49
Hodgson's Hawk-Cuckoo, *Cuculus fugax nisicolor* Blyth ... ... 50
The Indian Cuckoo, *Cuculus micropterus micropterus* Gould ... 51
The Khasia Hills Cuckoo, *Cuculus canorus bakeri* Hartert ... ... 52
The Himalayan Cuckoo, *Cuculus saturatus saturatus* Blyth ... ... 53
The Small Cuckoo, *Cuculus poliocephalus poliocephalus* Latham ... 54
The Indian Plaintive Cuckoo, *Cacomantis merulinus passerinus* (Vahl) ... 55
The Emerald Cuckoo, *Chalcites maculatus* (Gmelin) ... ... 56
The Indian Drongo-Cuckoo, *Surniculus lugubris dicruroïdes* (Hodgson) ... 57
The Large Himalayan Greenbilled Malkoha, *Rhopodytes tristis tristis* (Lesson) ... ... ... ... ... 58

## *Family* Strigidae: Owls

### *Subfamily* Tytoninae

The Sikkim Bay Owl, *Phodilus badius saturatus* Robinson ... ... 59

### *Subfamily* Striginae

The Himalayan Collared Scops Owl, *Otus bakkamoena lettia* (Hodgson) 60
The Eastern Spotted Scops Owl, *Otus spilocephalus spilocephalus* (Blyth) 61
The Forest Eagle-Owl, *Bubo nipalensis nipalensis* Hodgson ... 61
The Tawny Fish Owl, *Bubo flavipes* (Hodgson) ... ... ... 62
The Collared Pigmy Owlet, *Glaucidium brodiei brodiei* (Burton) ... 63
The Himalayan Barred Owlet, *Glaucidium cuculoides cuculoides* (Vigors) 64

The Himalayan Brown Wood Owl, *Strix leptogrammica newarensis* (Hodgson) ... ... ... ... ... 65
The Himalayan Wood Owl, *Strix aluco nivicola* (Blyth) ... ... 66
The Shorteared Owl, *Asio flammeus flammeus* (Pontoppidan) ... 67

## *Family* PODARGIDAE: Frogmouths

Hodgson's Frogmouth, *Batrachostomus hodgsoni hodgsoni* (G. R. Gray) ... 67

## *Family* CAPRIMULGIDAE: Nightjars

The Himalayan Jungle Nightjar, *Caprimulgus indicus hazarae* Whistler & Kinnear ... ... ... ... ... 68
The Longtailed Nightjar, *Caprimulgus macrurus albonotatus* Tickell ... 69

## *Family* APODIDAE: Swifts

### *Subfamily* APODINAE

The Himalayan Plainrumped Swiftlet, *Collocalia brevirostris brevirostris* (McClelland) ... ... ... ... ... 70
The Whitethroated Spinetail Swift, *Chaetura caudacuta nudipes* (Hodgson) 71
The Whiterumped Spinetail Swift, *Chaetura sylvatica* (Tickell) ... 72
Blyth's Whiterumped Spinetail Swift, *Apus pacificus leuconyx* (Blyth) ... 72
The Nepal House Swift, *Apus affinis nipalensis* (Hodgson) ... ... 73

## *Family* TROGONIDAE: Trogons

The Redheaded Trogon, *Harpactes erythrocephalus hodgsonii* (Gould) ... 74

## *Family* ALCEDINIDAE: Kingfishers

The West Himalayan Pied Kingfisher, *Ceryle lugubris continentalis* Hartert 75
Blyth's Kingfisher, *Alcedo hercules* Laubmann ... ... ... 76
The Common Indian Kingfisher, *Alcedo atthis bengalensis* Gmelin ... 76
The Assam Blue-eared Kingfisher, *Alcedo meninting coltarti* Baker ... 76
The Threetoed Forest Kingfisher, *Ceyx erithacus erithacus* Linnaeus ... 77
The Brownheaded Storkbilled Kingfisher, *Pelargopsis capensis capensis* (Linnaeus) ... ... ... ... ... 77
The Indian Ruddy Kingfisher, *Halcyon coromanda coromanda* (Latham) 77
The Whitebreasted Kingfisher, *Halcyon smyrnensis smyrnensis* (Linnaeus) 77

## *Family* MEROPIDAE: Bee-eaters

The Bluebearded Bee-eater, *Nyctyornis athertoni athertoni* (Jardine & Selby) 77

## *Family* CORACIIDAE: Rollers or Blue Jays

The Broadbilled Roller, or Dollar Bird, *Eurystomus orientalis cyanicollis* Vieillot .. ... ... ... ... 78

## *Family* UPUPIDAE: Hoopoes

The Tibetan Hoopoe, *Upupa epops saturata* Lönnberg ... ... 79

## *Family* BUCEROTIDAE: Hornbills

The Rufousnecked Hornbill, *Aceros nipalensis* (Hodgson) ... .. 81
The Great Hornbill, *Buceros bicornis homrai* Hodgson ... ... 81

## *Family* Capitonidae: Barbets


The Great Assam Barbet, *Megalaima virens magnifica* Stuart Baker ... 83
The Goldenthroated Barbet, *Megalaima franklinii franklinii* (Blyth) ... 84
The Bluethroated Barbet, *Megalaima asiatica asiatica* (Latham) ... 85


## *Family* Indicatoridae: Honeyguides


The Yellowbacked Honeyguide, *Indicator xanthonotus xanthonotus* Blyth 86


## *Family* Picidae: Woodpeckers


The Himalayan Speckled Piculet, *Picumnus innominatus innominatus* Burton ... ... ... ... 87
The Rufous Piculet, *Sasia ochracea ochracea* Hodgson ... ... 88
The Northern Rufous Woodpecker, *Micropternus brachyurus phaioceps* Blyth ... ... ... ... ... 89
The Assam Blacknaped Woodpecker, *Picus canus gyldenstolpei* Baker ... 90
The Large Yellownaped Woodpecker, *Picus flavinucha flavinucha* Gould ... 91
The East Himalayan Small Yellownaped Woodpecker, *Picus chlorolophus chlorolophus* Vieillot ... ... ... ... 92
The Himalayan Goldenbacked Threetoed Woodpecker, *Dinopium shorii shorii* (Vigors) ... ... ... ... ... 93
The Paleheaded Woodpecker, *Gecinulus grantia grantia* (McClelland) ... 94
The Great Slaty Woodpecker, *Mulleripicus pulverulentus mohun* Ripley ... 95
The Rufousbellied Woodpecker, *Hypopicus hyperythrus hyperythrus* (Vigors) ... ... ... ... ... 95
The Crimsonbreasted Pied Woodpecker, *Dendrocopos cathpharius cathpharius* (Blyth) ... ... ... ... ... 96
The Fulvousbreasted Woodpecker, *Dendrocopos macei macei* (Vieillot) ... 97
The Darjeeling Pied Woodpecker, *Dendrocopos darjellensis darjellensis* (Blyth) ... ... .. ... ... 97
The Pigmy Pied Woodpecker, *Dendrocopos canicapillus semicoronatus* (Malherbe) ... ... ... ... ... 98
The Redeared Bay Woodpecker, *Blythipicus pyrrhotis pyrrhotis* (Hodgson) 99
Tickell's Goldenbacked Woodpecker, *Chrysocolaptes lucidus guttacristatus* (Tickell) ... ... ... ... ... 100


## *Family* Eurylaimidae: Broadbills


Hodgson's, or the Nepal, Collared Broadbill, *Serilophus lunatus rubripygius* (Hodgson) ... ... ... ... ... 101
The Longtailed Broadbill, *Psarisomus dalhousiae dalhousiae* (Jameson) ... 102


## *Family* Pittidae: Pittas


The Bluenaped Pitta, *Pitta nipalensis* (Hodgson) ... ... 103


## *Family* Alaudidae: Larks


The Tibetan Short-toed Lark, *Calandrella acutirostris tibetana* Brooks ... 104
The Rufous Short-toed Lark, *Calandrella cinerea dukhunensis* (Sykes) ... 105
The Skylark, *Alauda arvensis* Linnaeus ... ... ... 105
The Tibetan, or Elwes's, Horned Lark, *Eremophila alpestris elwesi* (Blanford) ... ... ... ... ... 106
The Longbilled Calandra Lark, *Melanocorypha maxima maxima* Gould ... 107


## *Family* Hirundinidae: Swallows, Martins


The Eastern Swallow, *Hirundo rustica gutturalis* Scopoli ... ... 108
The Himalayan Striated Swallow, *Hirundo daurica nipalensis* Hodgson ... 109
The Kashmir House Martin, *Delichon urbica cashmeriensis* (Gould) ... 110
The Nepal House Martin, *Delichon nipalensis nipalensis* Horsfield & Moore 110

## *Family* CAMPEPHAGIDAE: Cuckoo-Shrikes, Minivets


The Brownbacked Pied Flycatcher-Shrike, *Hemipus picatus capitalis* (McClelland) ... ... ... ... ... 111
The Nepal Wood-Shrike, *Tephrodornis virgatus pelvica* (Hodgson) ... 113
The Dark Grey Cuckoo-Shrike, *Coracina melaschista melaschista* (Hodgson) 114
The Scarlet Minivet, *Pericrocotus flammeus speciosus* (Latham) ... 115
The Shortbilled Minivet, *Pericrocotus brevirostris brevirostris* (Vigors) ... 116
The Sikkim Longtailed Minivet, *Pericrocotus ethologus laetus* Mayr ... 116
The Yellowthroated Minivet, *Pericrocotus solaris solaris* Blyth ... 118


## *Family* IRENIDAE: Fairy Bluebird, Chloropses, Ioras


The Goldfronted Chloropsis, *Chloropsis aurifrons aurifrons* (Temminck & Laugier) ... ... ... ... 119
The Orangebellied Chloropsis, *Chloropsis hardwickii hardwickii* Jardine & Selby ... ... ... ... ... 120
The Sikkim Fairy Bluebird, *Irena puella sikkimensis* Whistler & Kinnear ... 121


## *Family* PYCNONOTIDAE: Bulbuls


The Blackcrested Yellow Bulbul, *Pycnonotus melanicterus flaviventris* (Tickell) ... ... ... ... ... 122
The Whitecheeked Bulbul, *Pycnonotus leucogenys leucogenys* (Gray) ... 122
The Redvented Bulbul, *Pycnonotus cafer bengalensis* Blyth ... 123
The Striated Green Bulbul, *Pycnonotus striatus striatus* (Blyth) ... 124
The Whitethroated Bulbul, *Criniger flaveolus flaveolus* (Gould) ... 125
The Rufousbellied Bulbul, *Hypsipetes virescens mcclellandi* Horsfield ... 126
The Browneared Bulbul, *Hypsipetes flavalus flavalus* (Blyth) ... 127
The Himalayan Black Bulbul, *Hypsipetes madagascariensis psaroïdes* Vigors 128


## *Family* MUSCICAPIDAE

### *Subfamily* MUSCICAPINAE: Flycatchers


The Nepal Sooty Flycatcher, *Muscicapa sibirica cacabata* Penard ... 129
The Ferruginous Flycatcher, *Muscicapa ferruginea* (Hodgson) ... 130
The Orangegorgetted Flycatcher, *Muscicapa strophiata strophiata* (Hodgson) ... ... ... ... ... 131
The Sikkim Whitegorgetted Flycatcher, *Muscicapa monileger monileger* (Hodgson) ... ... ... ... ... 132
The Rufousbreasted Blue Flycatcher, *Muscicapa hyperythra hyperythra* Blyth ... ... ... ... ... 133
The Redbreasted Blue, or Slatybacked, Flycatcher, *Muscicapa hodgsonii* (Verreaux) ... ... ... ... ... 134
The Little Pied Flycatcher, *Muscicapa westermanni collini* Rothschild ... 135
The Little Blue-and-White Flycatcher, *Muscicapa superciliaris aestigma* Gray ... ... ... ... ... 136
The Slaty Blue Flycatcher, *Muscicapa leucomelanura leucomelanura* (Hodgson) ... ... ... ... ... 137
The Sapphireheaded Flycatcher, *Muscicapa sapphira* (Blyth) ... 138
The Large Niltava, *Muscicapa grandis grandis* (Blyth) ... ... 139
The Rufousbellied Niltava, *Muscicapa sundara sundara* (Hodgson) ... 140
The Small Niltava, *Muscicapa macgrigoriae* (Burton) ... ... 141
The Pale Blue Flycatcher, *Muscicapa unicolor unicolor* (Blyth) ... 142
The Bluethroated Flycatcher, *Muscicapa rubeculoides rubeculoides* (Vigors) ... ... ... ... ... 143
The Verditer Flycatcher, *Muscicapa thalassina thalassina* Swainson ... 144
The Pigmy Blue Flycatcher, *Muscicapella hodgsoni hodgsoni* (Moore) ... 145
The Greyheaded Flycatcher, *Culicicapa ceylonensis calochrysea* Oberholser 146
The Yellowbellied Fantail Flycatcher, *Rhipidura hypoxantha* Blyth ... 147
The Whitethroated Fantail Flycatcher, *Rhipidura albicollis albicollis* (Vieillot) ... ... ... ... ... 148

## *Subfamily* TIMALIINAE: Babblers

The Sikkim Spotted Babbler, *Pellorneum ruficeps mandellii* Blanford ... 149
The Slatyheaded Scimitar Babbler, *Pomatorhinus schisticeps schisticeps* Hodgson ... ... ... ... ... 150
The Sikkim Rufousnecked Scimitar Babbler, *Pomatorhinus ruficollis godwini* Kinnear ... ... ... ... ... 151
The Sikkim Rustycheeked Scimitar Babbler, *Pomatorhinus erythrogenys haringtoni* Stuart Baker ... ... ... ... 152
The Coralbilled Scimitar Babbler, *Pomatorhinus ferruginosus ferruginosus* Blyth ... ... ... ... ... 153
The Slenderbilled Scimitar Babbler, *Xiphirhynchus superciliaris superciliaris* Blyth ... ... ... ... ... 154
The Longbilled Wren-Babbler, *Rimator malacoptilus malacoptilus* Blyth 155
The Scalybreasted Wren, *Microura albiventer albiventer* (Hodgson) ... 156
The Brown Wren, *Microura pusilla pusilla* (Hodgson) ... ... 157
The Tailed Wren, *Spelaeornis caudatus* (Blyth) ... ... ... 158
The Spotted Wren, *Spelaeornis formosus* (Walden) ... ... 159
Hume's Wedgebilled Wren, *Sphenocichla humei humei* (Mandelli) ... 160
The Assam Redfronted Babbler, *Stachyris rufifrons ambigua* (Harington) 160
The Redheaded Babbler, *Stachyris ruficeps ruficeps* Blyth ... ... 161
The Nepal Goldenheaded Babbler, *Stachyris chrysaea chrysaea* Blyth ... 162
The Sikkim Blackthroated Babbler, *Stachyris nigriceps nigriceps* Blyth ... 163
The Yellowbreasted Babbler, *Macronous gularis rubricapilla* (Tickell) ... 164
The Bengal Redcapped Babbler, *Timalia pileata bengalensis* Godwin-Austen ... ... ... ... ... 164
The Great Parrotbill, *Conostoma aemodium* Hodgson ... ... 165
The Brown Parrotbill, *Paradoxornis unicolor unicolor* (Hodgson) ... 166
The Fulvousfronted Parrotbill, *Paradoxornis fulvifrons fulvifrons* (Hodgson) 167
The Blackfronted Parrotbill, *Paradoxornis nipalensis humii* (Sharpe) ... 168
The Lesser Redheaded Parrotbill, *Paradoxornis atrosuperciliaris oatesi* (Sharpe) ... ... ... ... .. 169
The Redheaded Parrotbill, *Paradoxornis ruficeps ruficeps* Blyth ... 169
The Greyheaded Parrotbill, *Paradoxornis gularis gularis* Gray ... 170
Gould's Parrotbill, *Paradoxornis flavirostris flavirostris* Gould ... ... 171
The Whitethroated Laughing Thrush, *Garrulax albogularis albogularis* (Gould) ... ... ... ... ... 172
The Necklaced Laughing Thrush, *Garrulax moniligerus moniligerus* (Hodgson) ... ... ... ... ... 173
The Blackgorgetted Laughing Thrush, *Garrulax pectoralis melanotis* Blyth 174
The Sikkim Striated Laughing Thrush, *Garrulax striatus sikkimensis* (Ticehurst) ... ... ... ... ... 175
The Himalayan Whitecrested Laughing Thrush, *Garrulax leucolophus leucolophus* (Hardwicke) ... ... ... ... ... 176
The Rufouschinned Laughing Thrush, *Garrulax rufogularis rufogularis* (Gould) ... ... ... ... ... 177
The Whitespotted Laughing Thrush, *Garrulax ocellatus ocellatus* (Vigors) 178
The Sikkim Greysided Laughing Thrush, *Garrulax caerulatus caerulatus* (Hodgson) ... ... ... ... ... 179
The Rufousnecked Laughing Thrush, *Garrulax ruficollis* (Jardine & Selby) 180
The Streaked Laughing Thrush, *Garrulax lineatus setafer* (Hodgson) ... 181
The Bluewinged Laughing Thrush, *Garrulax squamatus* (Gould) ... 182
The Plaincoloured Laughing Thrush, *Garrulax subunicolor subunicolor* (Blyth) ... ... ... ... ... 183
The Blackfaced Laughing Thrush, *Garrulax affinis bethelae* Rand & Fleming ... ... ... ... ... 184
The Sikkim Redheaded Laughing Thrush, *Garrulax erythrocephalus nigrimentum* (Oates) ... ... ... ... ... 185
The Nepal Crimsonwinged Laughing Thrush, *Garrulax phoeniceus phoeniceus* (Gould) ... ... ... ... ... 186
The Silvereared Mesia, *Leiothrix argentauris argentauris* (Hodgson) ... 187
The Redbilled Leiothrix, or 'Pekin Robin', *Leiothrix lutea calipyga* (Hodgson) ... ... ... ... ... 188

The Firetailed Myzornis, *Myzornis pyrrhoura* Blyth ... ... 189
The Nepal Cutia, *Cutia nipalensis nipalensis* Hodgson ... ... 189
The Rufousbellied Shrike-Babbler, *Pteruthius rufiventer rufiventer* Blyth ... 190
The Redwinged Shrike-Babbler, *Pteruthius flaviscapis validirostris* Koelz ... 191
The Green Shrike-Babbler, *Pteruthius xanthochloris xanthochloris* Gray ... 192
The Chestnut-throated Shrike-Babbler, *Pteruthius melanotis melanotis* Hodgson ... ... ... ... ... 193
The Whiteheaded Shrike-Babbler, *Gampsorhynchus rufulus rufulus* Blyth 194
The Nepal Barwing, *Actinodura egertoni egertoni* Gould ... ... 195
The Sikkim Hoary Barwing, *Actinodura nipalensis vinctura* Ripley ... 196
The Redtailed Minla, *Minla ignotincta ignotincta* Hodgson ... ... 197
The Barthroated Siva, *Minla strigula strigula* (Hodgson) ... .. 198
The Nepal Bluewinged Siva, *Minla cyanouroptera cyanouroptera* (Hodgson) 199
The Whitebrowed, or Hume's, Staphida, *Yuhina castaniceps rufigenis* (Hume) ... ... ... ... ... 200
The Chestnut-headed, or Whitenaped, Ixulus, *Yuhina bakeri* Rothschild ... 201
The Yellownaped Ixulus, *Yuhina flavicollis flavicollis* Hodgson ... 202
The Stripedthroated Yuhina, *Yuhina gularis gularis* Hodgson ... ... 203
The Slatyheaded, or Rufousvented, Yuhina, *Yuhina occipitalis occipitalis* Hodgson ... ... ... ... ... 204
The Blackchinned Yuhina, *Yuhina nigrimenta nigrimenta* Hodgson ... 205
The Whitebellied Erpornis, *Yuhina zantholeuca zantholeuca* (Hodgson) ... 206
The Goldenbreasted Babbler, *Alcippe chrysotis chrysotis* (Blyth) ... 207
The Dusky Green, or Yellowthroated, Babbler, *Alcippe cinerea* (Blyth) ... 208
The Chestnut-headed Babbler, *Alcippe castaneceps castaneceps* (Hodgson) 208
The Sikkim Fulvetta, *Alcippe vinipectus chumbiensis* (Kinnear) ... 209
The Nepal White-eyed Quaker Babbler, *Alcippe nipalensis nipalensis* (Hodgson) ... ... ... ... ... 211
The Sikkim Chestnutrumped Sibia, *Heterophasia annectens annectens* (Blyth) ... ... ... ... ... 212
The Blackheaded Sibia, *Heterophasia capistrata bayleyi* (Kinnear) ... 213
The Longtailed Sibia, *Heterophasia picaoides picaoides* (Hodgson) ... 214

## *Subfamily* SYLVIINAE: Warblers

The Slatybellied Wren, *Tesia cyaniventer* Hodgson ... ... 215
The Chestnut-headed Wren, *Tesia castaneocoronata castaneocoronata* (Burton) ... ... ... ... ... 216
The Rufouscapped Bush Warbler, *Cettia brunnifrons brunnifrons* (Hodgson) 217
The Large Bush Warbler, *Cettia major major* (Moore) ... ... 218
Blanford's Bush Warbler, *Cettia pallidipes pallidipes* (Blanford) ... 219
The Strongfooted Bush Warbler, *Cettia fortipes fortipes* (Hodgson) ... 220
Hume's Bush Warbler, *Cettia acanthizoides brunnescens* (Hume) ... 220
The Aberrant Warbler, *Cettia flavolivaceus flavolivaceus* (Hodgson) ... 221
The Brown Bush Warbler, *Bradypterus luteoventris luteoventris* (Hodgson) 222
The Spotted Bush Warbler, *Bradypterus thoracicus thoracicus* (Blyth) ... 223
Tickell's Leaf Warbler, *Phylloscopus affinis* (Tickell) ... ... 224
The Smoky Leaf Warbler, *Phylloscopus fuligiventer fuligiventer* (Hodgson) 225
The Dusky Leaf Warbler, *Phylloscopus fuscatus fuscatus* (Blyth) ... 226
The Greyfaced Leaf Warbler, *Phylloscopus maculipennis maculipennis* (Blyth) ... ... ... ... ... 227
The Orangebarred Leaf Warbler, *Phylloscopus pulcher pulcher* Blyth ... 228
Pallas's Himalayan Leaf Warbler, *Phylloscopus proregulus newtoni* Gaetke 229
The Yellowbrowed Leaf Warber, *Phylloscopus inornatus inornatus* (Blyth) 230
The Dull Green Leaf Warbler, *Phylloscopus trochiloides trochiloides* (Sundevall) ... ... ... ... ... 230
The Largebilled Leaf Warbler, *Phylloscopus magnirostris* Blyth ... 231
Blyth's Crowned Leaf Warbler, *Phylloscopus reguloides reguloides* (Blyth) 232
Temminck's Crowned Leaf Warbler, *Phylloscopus occipitalis coronatus* (Temminck & Schlegel) ... ... ... ... 233
Tickell's, or the Blackbrowed, Leaf Warbler, *Phylloscopus cantator* (Tickell) 234

The Sikkim Goldcrest, *Regulus regulus sikkimensis* R. & A. Meinertzhagen 234
The Allied Flycatcher-Warbler, *Seicercus affinis* (Hodgson) ... ... 235
The Blackbrowed Flycatcher-Warbler, *Seicercus burkii burkii* (Burton) ... 236
The Greyheaded Flycatcher-Warbler, *Seicercus xanthoschistos xanthoschistos* (Gray) ... ... ... ... 237
The Greycheeked Flycatcher-Warbler, *Seicercus poliogenys* (Blyth) ... 238
The Chestnut-headed Flycatcher-Warbler, *Seicercus castaniceps castaniceps* (Hodgson) ... ... ... ... 238
The Yellowbellied Flycatcher-Warbler, *Abroscopus superciliaris albigularis* (Blyth) ... ... ... ... ... 239
The Blackfaced Flycatcher-Warbler, *Abroscopus schisticeps schisticeps* (Gray) ... ... ... ... ... 240
The Broadbilled Flycatcher-Warbler, *Abroscopus hodgsoni hodgsoni* (Moore) ... ... ... ... ... 241
The Goldenheaded Tailor Bird, *Orthotomus cucullatus coronatus* Blyth ... 242
The Tailor Bird, *Orthotomus sutorius patia* Hodgson ... ... 243
The Rufous Wren-Warbler, *Prinia rufescens rufescens* Blyth ... ... 244
The Blackthroated Hill Warbler, *Prinia atrogularis atrogularis* (Moore) ... 245

## *Subfamily* TURDINAE: Chats, Robins, Thrushes

The Indian Blue Chat, *Erithacus brunneus brunneus* (Hodgson) ... 246
The East Himalayan Rubythroat, *Erithacus pectoralis confusus* (Hartert) 247
The Tibet Rubythroat, *Erithacus pectoralis tschebaiewi* (Przevalski) ... 248
The Common Rubythroat, *Erithacus calliope* (Pallas) ... ... 248
The Golden Bush Robin, *Erithacus chrysaeus chrysaeus* (Hodgson) ... 249
The Redflanked Bush Robin, *Erithacus cyanurus rufilatus* (Hodgson) ... 250
The Whitebrowed Bush Robin, *Erithacus indicus indicus* (Vieillot) ... 251
The Rufousbellied Bush Robin, *Erithacus hyperythrus* (Blyth) ... 252
The Whitetailed Blue Bush Robin, *Cinclidium leucurum* (Hodgson) ... 253
The Bluefronted Robin, *Cinclidium frontale frontale* Blyth ... ... 254
Hodgson's Grandala, *Grandala côelicolor côelicolor* Hodgson ... ... 254
Hodgson's Shortwing, *Hodgsonius phœnicuroides phoenicuroides* (Gray) ... 256
The Bluefronted Redstart, *Phoenicurus frontalis* (Vigors) ... ... 257
The Whitethroated Redstart, *Phoenicurus schisticeps schisticeps* (Gray) ... 258
Hodgson's Redstart, *Phoenicurus hodgsoni* (Moore) ... ... 259
The Daurian Redstart, *Phoenicurus auroreus leucopterus* (Blyth) ... 260
The Black Redstart, *Phoenicurus ochruros rufiventris* (Vieillot) ... 261
Güldenstädt's Redstart, *Phoenicurus erythrogaster grandis* (Gould) ... 262
The Blueheaded Robin, *Phoenicurus caeruleocephalus* (Vigors) ... 263
The Whitecapped Redstart, *Chaimarrornis leucocephalus* (Vigors) ... 264
The Plumbeous Redstart, *Rhyacornis fuliginosus fuliginosus* (Vigors) ... 265
The Magpie Robin, *Copsychus saularis saularis* (Linnaeus) ... ... 266
The Shama, *Copsychus malabaricus indicus* (Baker) ... ... 267
The Tibetan Blackbird, *Turdus merula maximus* (Seebohm) ... ... 267
The Whitecollared Blackbird, *Turdus albocinctus* Royle ... ... 268
The Greywinged Blackbird, *Turdus boulboul* (Latham) ... ... 269
The Greyheaded Thrush, *Turdus rubrocanus rubrocanus* Hodgson ... 270
Przevalski's Thrush, *Turdus kessleri* Przevalski ... ... 271
The Redthroated Thrush, *Turdus ruficollis ruficollis* Pallas ... ... 271
The Blackthroated Thrush, *Turdus ruficollis atrogularis* Jarocki ... 272
The Orangeheaded Ground Thrush, *Zoothera citrina citrina* (Latham) ... 273
The Smallbilled Mountain Thrush, *Zoothera dauma dauma* (Latham) ... 274
The Plainbacked Mountain Thrush, *Zoothera mollissima mollissima* (Blyth) 275
The Longtailed Mountain Thrush, *Zoothera dixoni* (Seebohm) ... 276
The Large Brown Thrush, *Zoothera monticola monticola* Vigors ... 277
The Lesser Brown Thrush, *Zoothera marginata marginata* Blyth ... 278
The Chestnutbellied Rock Thrush, *Monticola rufiventris* (Jardine & Selby) 279
The Blueheaded Rock Thrush, *Monticola cinclorhynchus* (Vigors) ... 280
The Blue Rock Thrush, *Monticola solitarius pandoo* (Sykes) ... ... 281
The Collared Bushchat, *Saxicola torquata indica* (Blyth) ... ... 282
Hodgson's Bushchat, *Saxicola insignis* Gray ... ... ... 283

The Dark-Grey Bushchat, *Saxicola ferrea* Gray ... ... ... 283
Gould's Shortwing, *Brachypteryx stellata* Gould ... ... ... 284
The Rustybellied Shortwing, *Brachypteryx hyperythra* Jerdon & Blyth ... 285
The Whitebrowed Shortwing, *Brachypteryx montana cruralis* (Blyth) ... 285
The Nepal Shortwing, *Brachypteryx leucophrys nipalensis* Hodgson ... 286
The Himalayan Whistling Thrush, *Myiophoneus caeruleus temminckii* (Vigors) ... ... ... ... ... ... 287
The Purple Thrush, *Cochoa purpurea* Hodgson ... ... ... 288
The Green Thrush, *Cochoa viridis* Hodgson ... ... ... 289
The Eastern Spotted Forktail, *Enicurus maculatus guttatus* Gould ... 290
The Slatybacked Forktail, *Enicurus schistaceus* (Hodgson) ... ... 292
The Blackbacked Forktail, *Enicurus immaculatus* (Hodgson) ... ... 292
The Blackbreasted Forktail, *Enicurus leschenaulti indicus* Hartert ... 293
The Little Forktail, *Enicurus scouleri* Vigors ... ... ... 293

## *Subfamily* TROGLODYTINAE: Wrens

The Nepal Wren, *Troglodytes troglodytes nipalensis* Blyth ... ... 294

## *Subfamily* CINCLINAE: Dippers

The Whitebreasted Asiatic Dipper, *Cinclus cinclus cinclus* (Linnaeus) ... 296
The Brown Dipper, *Cinclus pallasii tenuirostris* Bonaparte ... ... 297

## *Family* PRUNELLIDAE: Accentors

The Eastern Alpine Accentor, *Prunella collaris nipalensis* (Blyth) ... 298
The Altai, or Rufousbreasted, Accentor, *Prunella himalayana* (Blyth) ... 300
The Maroonbacked Accentor, *Prunella immaculata* (Hodgson) ... 301
The Robin Accentor, *Prunella rubeculoides* (Horsfield & Moore) ... 302
The Rufousbreasted Accentor, *Prunella strophiata strophiata* (Blyth) ... 303

## *Family* MOTACILLIDAE: Wagtails, Pipits

The Kansu Tree-Pipit, *Anthus hodgsoni berezowskii* Zarudny ... 304
The Vinaceousbreasted, or Hodgson's, Pipit, *Anthus roseatus* Blyth ... 305
Blyth's Pipit, *Anthus godlewskii* (Taczanowski) (=*striolatus* Blyth) ... 306
Hodgson's Pied Wagtail, *Motacilla alba alboides* Hodgson ... ... 307
Swinhoe's White Wagtail, *Motacilla alba baicalensis* Swinhoe ... 308
The Large Pied Wagtail, *Motacilla maderaspatensis* Gmelin ... ... 308
The Eastern Grey Wagtail, *Motacilla caspica caspica* (Gmelin) ... 309
The Blackbacked Yellowheaded Wagtail, *Motacilla citreola calcarata* Hodgson ... ... ... ... ... 310

## *Family* LANIIDAE: Shrikes

The Brown Shrike, *Lanius cristatus cristatus* Linnaeus ... ... 311
The Greybacked Shrike, *Lanius tephronotus tephronotus* (Vigors) ... 312
The Blackheaded Shrike, *Lanius schach tricolor* (Hodgson) ... ... 313

## *Family* ARTAMIDAE: Swallow-Shrikes

The Ashy Swallow-Shrike, *Artamus fuscus* Vieillot ... ... 314

## *Family* DICRURIDAE: Drongos

The Himalayan Grey Drongo, *Dicrurus leucophaeus hopwoodi* Baker ... 315
The Bronzed Drongo, *Dicrurus aeneus aeneus* Vieillot ... ... 316

The Haircrested, or Spangled, Drongo, *Dicrurus hottentottus hottentottus* (Linnaeus) ... ... ... ... ... 317
The Indian Lesser Racket-tailed Drongo, *Dicrurus remifer tectirostris* (Hodgson) ... ... ... ... ... 319

## *Family* ORIOLIDAE: Orioles

The Maroon Oriole, *Oriolus traillii traillii* (Vigors) ... ... 320

## *Family* CORVIDAE: Crows, Pies, etc.

The Sikkim Redcrowned Jay, *Garrulus glandarius interstinctus* Hartert ... 321
The Green Magpie, *Kitta chinensis chinensis* (Boddaert) ... ... 322
The Yellowbilled Blue Magpie, *Kitta flavirostris flavirostris* (Blyth) ... 323
The Redbilled Blue Magpie, *Kitta erythrorhyncha occipitalis* Blyth ... 324
The Blackrumped Magpie, *Pica pica bottanensis* Delessert ... ... 324
The Himalayan Tree Pie, *Dendrocitta formosae himalayensis* Blyth ... 324
The Blackbrowed Tree Pie, *Dendrocitta frontalis* Horsfield ... ... 326
Hume's Ground Chough, *Podoces humilis* Hume ... ... 327
The East Himalayan Nutcracker, *Nucifraga caryocatactes macella* Thayer & Bangs ... ... ... ... ... 328
The Himalayan Yellowbilled, or Alpine, Chough, *Pyrrhocorax graculus digitatus* Hemprich & Ehrenberg ... ... ... ... 329
The Himalayan Redbilled Chough, *Pyrrhocorax pyrrhocorax himalayanus* (Gould) ... ... ... ... ... 330
The House Crow, *Corvus splendens splendens* Vieillot ... ... 331
The Jungle Crow, (*a*) *Corvus macrorhynchus intermedius* Adams, (*b*) *Corvus macrorhynchus levaillanti* Lesson (? or *macrorhynchus*) ... 332
The Tibet Raven, *Corvus corax tibetanus* Hodgson ... ... 333

## *Family* STURNIDAE

### *Subfamily* STURNINAE: Starlings, Mynas

The Spottedwinged Stare, *Saroglossa spiloptera* (Vigors) ... ... 334
The Common Myna, *Acridotheres tristis tristis* (Linnaeus) ... ... 335
The North Indian Grackle, *Gracula religiosa intermedia* A. Hay ... 336

## *Family* PARIDAE: Tits

### *Subfamily* PARINAE: True Tits

The Greenbacked Tit, *Parus monticolus monticolus* Vigors ... ... 337
The Himalayan Cole-Tit, *Parus ater aemodius* Hodgson ... ... 338
The Sikkim Black Tit, *Parus rubidiventris beavani* (Jerdon) ... ... 339
The Brown Crested Tit, *Parus dichrous dichrous* Hodgson ... ... 340
The Blackspotted Yellow Tit, *Parus xanthogenys spilonotus* Bonaparte ... 341
The Yellowbrowed Tit, *Parus modestus modestus* (Burton) ... ... 342

### *Subfamily* AEGITHALINAE: Longtailed Tits

The Sikkim Redheaded Tit, *Ægithalos concinnus rubricapillus* (Ticehurst) 343
The Rufousfronted Tit, *Ægithalos iouschistos iouschistos* (Hodgson) ... 344
The Sultan Tit, *Melanochlora sultanea sultanea* (Hodgson) ... ... 345

### *Subfamily* REMIZINAE: Penduline Tits

The Sikkim Firecapped Tit-Warbler, *Cephalopyrus flammiceps olivaceus* Rothschild ... ... ... ... ... 346

## *Family* SITTIDAE

### *Subfamily* TICHODROMADINAE: Wall Creeper, Spotted Grey Creeper

The Wall Creeper, *Tichodroma muraria nepalensis* Bonaparte (Linnaeus) ... 347

### *Subfamily* SITTINAE: Nuthatches

The Whitetailed Nuthatch, *Sitta himalayensis himalayensis* Jardine & Selby 348
The Cinnamonbellied Nuthatch, *Sitta castanea cinnamoventris* Blyth ... 349
The Beautiful Nuthatch, *Sitta formosa* Blyth ... ... ... 350
The Velvetfronted Nuthatch, *Sitta frontalis frontalis* Swainson ... 351

## *Family* CERTHIIDAE: Tree Creepers

The Nepal Tree Creeper, *Certhia familiaris mandellii* Brooks ... 352
The Sikkim Tree Creeper, *Certhia discolor discolor* Blyth ... ... 353
Stoliczka's Tree Creeper, *Certhia nipalensis* Blyth ... ... 354

## *Family* DICAEIDAE: Flowerpeckers

The Firebreasted Flowerpecker, *Dicaeum ignipectus ignipectus* (Blyth) ... 354
The Yellowbellied Flowerpecker, *Dicaeum melanozanthum* (Blyth) ... 356

## *Family* NECTARINIIDAE: Sunbirds

The Firetailed Yellowbacked Sunbird, *Aethopyga ignicauda ignicauda* (Hodgson) ... ... ... ... ... 357
The Blackbreasted Sunbird, *Aethopyga saturata saturata* (Hodgson) ... 358
The Sikkim Yellowbacked Sunbird, *Aethopyga nipalensis koelzi* Ripley ... 359
Mrs Gould's Yellowbacked Sunbird, *Aethopyga gouldiae gouldiae* (Vigors) 360
The Indian Streaked Spiderhunter, *Arachnothera magna magna* (Hodgson) 360

## *Family* ZOSTEROPIDAE: White-eyes

The Indian White-eye, *Zosterops palpebrosa palpebrosa* (Temminck) ... 362

## *Family* PLOCEIDAE: Weaver Finches

### *Subfamily* PASSERINAE: House and Rock Sparrows

The Cinnamon Tree Sparrow, *Passer rutilans schaferi* Stresemann ... 363
The Tree Sparrow, *Passer montanus malaccensis* Dubois ... ... 364
The House Sparrow, *Passer domesticus* (Linnaeus) ssp. ... ... 365
The Tibet Snow Finch, *Montifringilla adamsi adamsi* Adams ... 365
The Rednecked Snow Finch, *Montifringilla ruficollis* Blanford ... 365
Blanford's Snow Finch, *Montifringilla blanfordi blanfordi* Hume ... 365
The Mongolian Snow Finch, *Montifringilla davidiana potanini* (Sushkin) ... 366

### *Subfamily* ESTRILDINAE: Munias

The Spotted Munia, *Lonchura punctulata punctulata* (Linnaeus) ... 366
Hodgson's Munia, *Lonchura striata acuticauda* (Hodgson) ... 367

## *Family* FRINGILLIDAE: Finches

### *Subfamily* EMBERIZINAE: Buntings

The Crested Bunting, *Melophus lathami subcristatus* (Sykes) ... ... 368
The Little Bunting, *Emberiza pusilla* Pallas ... ... ... 369
The Yangtse Blackfaced Bunting, *Emberiza spodocephala sordida* Blyth ... 370

### *Subfamily* CARDUELINAE: Rosefinches, Goldfinches, etc.

The Tibetan Siskin, *Carduelis thibetana thibetana* (Hume) ... ... 370
The Himalayan Greenfinch, *Carduelis spinoïdes spinoïdes* Vigors ... 371
The Sikkim Mountain Finch, *Leucosticte brandti audreyana* Stresemann ... 372
Hodgson's Mountain Finch, *Leucosticte nemoricola nemoricola* (Hodgson) 373
Blanford's Rosefinch, *Carpodacus rubescens* (Blanford) ... ... 374
The Nepal Dark Rosefinch, *Carpodacus nipalensis nipalensis* (Hodgson) ... 375
Severtzov's Rosefinch, *Carpodacus rubicilla severtzovi* Sharpe ... 376
The Great Rosefinch, *Carpodacus rubicilloides lucifer* R. & A. Meinertzhagen 376
The Common Rosefinch, *Carpodacus erythrinus roseatus* (Blyth) ... 377
The Sikkim Large Rosefinch, *Carpodacus edwardsii rubicunda* (Greenway) 378
The Pinkbrowed Rosefinch, *Carpodacus rhodochrous* (Vigors) ... 379
The Beautiful Rosefinch, *Carpodacus pulcherrimus pulcherrimus* (Moore) 379
The Sikkim Whitebrowed Rosefinch, *Carpodacus thura thura* Bonaparte & Schlegel ... ... ... ... ... 380
The Redbreasted Rosefinch, *Carpodacus puniceus puniceus* (Blyth) ... 381
The Redheaded Rosefinch, *Propyrrhula subhimachala* (Hodgson) ... 382
The Himalayan Crossbill, *Loxia curvirostra himalayensis* Blyth ... 383
The Goldenheaded Black Finch, *Pyrrhoplectes epauletta* (Hodgson) ... 384
The Scarlet Finch, *Haematospiza sipahi* (Hodgson) ... ... 385
The Brown Bullfinch, *Pyrrhula nipalensis nipalensis* Hodgson ... 386
Beavan's Bullfinch, *Pyrrhula erythaca erythaca* Blyth ... ... 387
The Redheaded Bullfinch, *Pyrrhula erythrocephala* Vigors ... ... 388
The Spottedwinged Grosbeak, *Mycerobas melanozanthos* (Hodgson) ... 389
The Whitewinged Grosbeak, *Mycerobas carnipes carnipes* (Hodgson) ... 390
The Allied Grosbeak, *Mycerobas affinis* (Blyth) ... ... ... 391

APPENDIX ... ... ... ... ... 393

INDEX ... ... ... ... ... 399

The author and publishers regret that owing to circumstances beyond their control it has been impossible to include a large-scale map of Sikkim.

# LIST OF PLATES

## PHOTOGRAPHS

PLATE 1 (facing p. xxiv)

*a.* Terraced cultivation, from the foothills up to *c.* 6000 ft.
*b.* Junipers and buckthorn scrub, near Thangu, *c.* 13,000 ft.

PLATE 2 (facing p. xxv)

*a.* Deciduous facies of the tropical zone, *c.* 3000 ft. W. Sikkim.
*b.* The fern *Gleichenia* (? *linearis* Cl.), a common feature of the tropical and sub-tropical zones, *c.* 4000-5000 ft.

PLATE 3 (facing p. xxvi)

*a.* Epiphytic ferns, moss, and orchids are characteristic of the tropical and sub-tropical zones.
*b.* The handsome large-leaved *Rhaphidophora* (? *glauca* Schott) and numerous vines and creepers here drape the trunks of the forest trees.

PLATE 4 (facing p. xxvii)

Path along the Teesta River near Dikchu, *c.* 2200 ft. (Note breach caused by flood erosion, and rickety makeshift repair.)

PLATE 5 (facing p. xxx)

Tropical evergreen forest near Temi, 4000-5000 ft.

PLATE 6 (facing p. xxxi)

Moist evergreen sub-tropical forest near Kewzing, *c.* 7000 ft., with heavily moss-covered tree-trunks and boulders, and dense undergrowth of seedlings and ferns. Typical biotope for *Microura* wrens.

PLATE 7 (facing p. xxxii)

*a.* Upland yak pastures near Lachen, *c.* 9500 ft.
*b.* Birch, juniper and dwarf rhododendrons. A good biotope for rosefinches. N. Sikkim, *c.* 13,500 ft.

PLATE 8 (facing p. 1)

*a.* Near Thangu, 13,000-14,000 ft. Temperate Zone. Junipers, conifers, and dwarf rhododendron scrub.
*b.* Upper reaches of Teesta River, Yakthang *c.* 13,000 ft. Shingly islets suitable for Ibisbill nesting.

PLATE 26 (facing p. 337)

Ibisbill (*Ibidorhyncha struthersii*) on nest.

## COLOURED

PLATE 9 (facing p. 80)

1. Sikkim Bay Owl (*Phodilus b. saturatus*)
2. Forest Eagle-Owl (*Bubo n. nipalensis*)
3. Himalayan Collared Scops Owl (*Otus b. lettia*)
4. Collared Pigmy Owlet (*Glaucidium b. brodiei*)
5. Bonelli's Hawk-Eagle (*Nisaëtus f. fasciatus*)
6. Black Eagle (*Ictinaëtus m. perniger*)
7. Himalayan Falconet (*Microhierax c. caerulescens*)

PLATE 10 (facing p. 81)

1. Crimson Horned Pheasant, or Satyr Tragopan (*Tragopan satyra*)
2. Common Hill Partridge (*Arborophila t. torqueola*)
3. Snow Partridge (*Lerwa lerwa*)
4. Blood Pheasant (*Ithaginis c. affinis*)
5. Eastern Goosander (*Mergus m. orientalis*)
6. Ibisbill (*Ibidorhyncha struthersii*)

PLATE 11 (facing p. 96)

1. Indian Redbreasted Parakeet (*Psittacula a. fasciata*)
2. Himalayan Slatyheaded Parakeet (*Psittacula h. himalayana*)
3. Emerald Cuckoo (*Chalcites maculatus*)
4. Redheaded Trogon (*Harpactes e. hodgsonii*)
5. Hodgson's Frogmouth (*Batrachostomus h. hodgsoni*)
6. Pintailed Green Pigeon (*Treron a. apicauda*)
7. Speckled Wood Pigeon (*Columba hodgsonii*)
8. Snow Pigeon (*Columba l. leuconota*)
9. Ashy Wood Pigeon (*Columba pulchricollis*)
10. Bartailed Cuckoo-Dove (*Macropygia u. tusalia*)

PLATE 12 (facing p. 97)

1. Himalayan Goldenbacked Threetoed Woodpecker (*Dinopium s. shorii*)
2. Darjeeling Pied Woodpecker (*Dendrocopos d. darjellensis*)
3. Redeared Bay Woodpecker (*Blythipicus p. pyrrhotis*)
4. Rufous Piculet (*Sasia o. ochracea*)
5. Great Slaty Woodpecker (*Mulleripicus p. mohun*)
6. Large Yellownaped Woodpecker (*Picus f. flavinucha*)
7. Goldenthroated Barbet (*Megalaima f. franklinii*)
8. Great Assam Barbet (*Megalaima v. magnifica*)
9. Yellowbacked Honeyguide (*Indicator x. xanthonotus*)

PLATE 13 (facing p. 144)

1. Mrs Gould's Yellowbacked Sunbird (*Aethopyga g. gouldiae*)
2. Blackbreasted Sunbird (*Aethopyga s. saturata*)
3. Firetailed Yellowbacked Sunbird (*Aethopyga i. ignicauda*)
4. Firebreasted Flowerpecker (*Dicaeum i. ignipectus*)
5. Longtailed Broodbill (*Psarisomus d. dalhousiae*)
6. Hodgson's, or the Nepal, Collared Broadbill (*Serilophus l. rubropygius*)
7. Bluenaped Pitta (*Pitta nipalensis*)

PLATE 14 (facing p. 145)

1. Greybacked Shrike (*Lanius t. tephronotus*)
2. Shortbilled Minivet (*Pericrocotus b. brevirostris*)

3. Yellowthroated Minivet (*Pericrocotus s. solaris*)
4. Maroon Oriole (*Oriolus t. traillii*)
5. Spottedwinged Stare (*Saroglossa spiloptera*)
6. Common Rubythroat (*Erithacus calliope*)
7. Golden Bush Robin (*Erithacus c. chrysaeus*)
8. Whitebrowed Bush Robin (*Erithacus i. indicus*)

PLATE 15 (facing p. 160)

1. Orangebellied Chloropsis (*Chloropsis h. hardwickii*)
2. Redtailed Minla (*Minla i. ignotincta*)
3. Rufousbellied Bulbul (*Hypsipetes v. mcclellandi*)
4. Whitethroated Bulbul (*Criniger f. flaveolus*)
5. Striated Green Bulbul (*Pycnonotus s. striatus*)
6. Beautiful Nuthatch (*Sitta formosa*)
7. Nepal Tree Creeper (*Certhia f. mandellii*)
8. Wall Creeper (*Tichodroma muraria*)

PLATE 16 (facing p. 161)

1. Orangegorgetted Flycatcher (*Muscicapa s. strophiata*)
2. Sapphireheaded Flycatcher (*Muscicapa sapphira*)
3. Slaty Blue Flycatcher (*Muscicapa l. leucomelanura*)
4. Pigmy Blue Flycatcher (*Muscicapella h. hodgsoni*)
5. Large Niltava (*Muscicapa g. grandis*)
6. Yellowbellied Fantail Flycatcher (*Rhipidura hypoxantha*)
7. Collared Bushchat (*Saxicola t. indica*)
8. Whitethroated Redstart (*Phoenicurus s. schisticeps*)
9. Güldenstädt's Redstart (*Phoenicurus e. grandis*)

PLATE 17 (facing p. 208)

1. Bengal Redcapped Babbler (*Timalia p. bengalensis*)
2. Whitethroated Shrike-Babbler (*Gampsorhynchus r. rufulus*)
3. Sikkim Spotted Babbler (*Pellorneum r. mandellii*)
4. Barthroated Siva (*Minla s. strigula*)
5. Longbilled Wren-Babbler (*Rimator m. malacoptilus*)
6. Redwinged Shrike-Babbler (*Pteruthius e. erythropterus=P. f. validirostris*)
7. Rufousbellied Shrike-Babbler (*Pteruthius r. rufiventer*)
8. Sikkim Chestnutrumped Sibia (*Heterophasia a. annectens*)
9. Sikkim Hoary Barwing (*Actinodura n. vinctura*)
10. Nepal Cutia (*Cutia n. nipalensis*)
11. Redbilled Leiothrix, or 'Pekin Robin' (*Leiothrix l. calipyga*)

PLATE 18 (facing p. 209)

1. Spotted Wren (*Spelaeornis formosus*)
2. Tailed Wren (*Spelaeornis caudatus*)
3. Chestnut-headed Wren (*Tesia c. castaneocoronata*)
4. Brown Wren (*Microura p. pusilla*)
5. Sikkim Goldcrest (*Regulus r. sikkimensis*)
6. Sikkim Firecapped Tit-Warbler (*Cephalopyrus f. saturatus*)
7. Spotted Bush Warbler (*Bradypterus t. thoracicus*)
8. Dusky Leaf Warbler (*Phylloscopus f. fuscatus*)
9. Orangebarred Leaf Warbler (*Phylloscopus p. pulcher*)
10. Dull Green Leaf Warbler (*Phylloscopus t. trochiloides*)

PLATE 19 (facing p. 224)

1. Rufousbreasted Accentor (*Prunella s. strophiata*)
2. Allied Grosbeak (*Mycerobas affinis*)

3. Redheaded Bullfinch (*Pyrrhula erythrocephala*)
4. Goldenheaded Black Finch (*Pyrrhoplectes epauletta*)
5. Scarlet Finch (*Haematospiza sipahi*)
6. Sikkim Whitebrowed Rosefinch (*Carpodacus t. thura*)
7. Sikkim Large Rosefinch (*Carpodacus e. rubicunda*)
8. Nepal Dark Rosefinch (*Carpodacus n. nipalensis*)
9. Redbrowed Finch (*Callacanthis burtoni*)
10. Tibetan Siskin (*Carduelis t. thibetana*)
11. Hodgson's Mountain Finch (*Leucosticte n. nemoricola*)

PLATE 20 (facing p. 225)

1. Nepal Crimsonwinged Laughing Thrush (*Garrulax p. phoeniceus*)
2. Sikkim Redheaded Laughing Thrush (*Garrulax c. nigrimentum*)
3. Coralbilled Scimitar Babbler (*Pomatorhinus f. ferruginosus*)
4. Sikkim Striated Laughing Thrush (*Garrulax s. sikkimensis*)
5. Sikkim Rufousnecked Scimitar Babbler (*Pomatorhinus r. godwini*)
6. Rufouschinned Laughing Thrush (*Garrulax r. rufogularis*)
7. Sikkim Greysided Laughing Thrush (*Garrulax c. caerulatus*)
8. Whitespotted Laughing Thrush (*Garrulax o. ocellatus*)
9. Bluewinged Laughing Thrush (*Garrulax squamatus*)
10. Slenderbilled Scimitar Babbler (*Xiphirhynchus s. superciliaris*)

PLATE 21 (facing p. 272)

1. Nepal Goldenheaded Babbler (*Stachyris c. chrysaea*)
2. Firetailed Myzornis (*Myzornis pyrrhoura*)
3. Chestnut-throated Shrike-Babbler (*Pteruthius m. melanotis*)
4. Stripedthroated Yuhina (*Yuhina g. gularis*)
5. Goldenbreasted Babbler (*Alcippe c. chrysotis*)
6. Sikkim Blackthroated Babbler (*Stachyris n. nigriceps*)
7. Assam Redfronted Babbler (*Stachyris r. ambigua*)
8. Nepal White-eyed Quaker Babbler (*Alcippe n. nipalensis*)
9. Yellownaped Ixulus (*Yuhina f. flavicollis*)
10. Whitebrowed, or Hume's, Staphida (*Yuhina c. rufigenis*)
11. Chestnut-headed Babbler (*Alcippe c. castaneceps*)
12. Sikkim Fulvetta (*Alcippe v. chumbiensis*)

PLATE 22 (facing p. 273)

1. Blackbrowed Flycatcher-Warbler (*Seicercus b. burkii*)
2. Chestnut-headed Flycatcher-Warbler (*Seicercus c. castaniceps*)
3. Blackfaced Flycatcher-Warbler (*Abroscopus s. schisticeps*)
4. Blanford's Bush Warbler (*Cettia p. pallidipes*)
5. Goldenheaded Tailor Bird (*Orthotomus c. coronatus*)
6. Firetailed Yellowbacked Sunbird (*Aethopyga i. ignicauda*)
7. Mrs Gould's Yellowbacked Sunbird (*Aethopyga g. gouldiae*)
8. Blackbreasted Sunbird (*Aethopyga s. saturata*)
9. Firebreasted Flowerpecker (*Dicaeum i. ignipectus*)

PLATE 23 (facing p. 288)

1. Blueheaded Robin (*Phoenicurus caeruleocephalus*)
2. Hodgson's Grandala (*Grandala c. côelicolor*)
3. Bluefronted Robin (*Cinclidium f. frontale*)
4. Gould's Shortwing (*Brachypteryx stellata*)
5. Chestnutbellied Rock Thrush (*Monticola rufiventris*)
6. Smallbilled Mountain Thrush (*Zoothera d. dauma*)
7. Purple Thrush (*Cochoa purpurea*)
8. Green Thrush (*Cochoa viridis*)

PLATE 24 (facing p. 289)

1. Blackfronted Parrotbill (*Paradoxornis n. humii*)
2. Fulvousfronted Parrotbill (*Paradoxornis f. fulvifrons*)
3. Sultan Tit (*Melanochlora s. sultanea*)
4. Lesser Redheaded Parrotbill (*Paradoxornis a. oatesi*)
5. Yellowbrowed Tit (*Parus m. modestus*)
6. Himalayan Cole-Tit (*Parus a. aemodius*)
7. Brown Crested Tit (*Parus d. dichrous*)
8. Rufousfronted Tit (*Ægithalos iouschistos*)

PLATE 25 (facing p. 336)

1. Green Magpie (*Kitta c. chinensis*)
2. Sikkim Redcrowned Jay (*Garrulus g. interstinctus*)
3. Yellowbilled Blue Magpie (*Kitta f. flavirostris*)
4. Blackbrowed Tree Pie (*Dendrocitta frontalis*)
5. Great Parrotbill (*Conostoma aemodium*)

# INTRODUCTION

Sikkim is a vertical strip of extremely rugged montane country, 40 to 60 miles broad and about 100 miles deep, wedged in between the Himalayan States of Nepal in the west and Bhutan on the east. It lies between lat. 27° 5′ and 28° 9′ N. and long. 87° 59′ and 88° 56′ E. and covers an area of 2818 square miles. Its northern boundary with Tibet runs more or less parallel with the main Himalayan axis from the Dongkia Mountain westward following the stupendous spur of Kinchinjhau. It is a political demarcation rather than a strictly natural boundary since it admits, within the northernmost section of Sikkim, terrain that is typically Tibetan in physiography possessing a predominantly Palaearctic fauna from about the 28th parallel. The Singalila Ridge or Spur running about 60 miles south to north almost from plains level, separates Sikkim from east Nepal and culminates near its northern extremity in some of the loftiest mountains in the world, the Kinchinjunga massif, which, besides Kinchinjunga itself (28,146 ft.) includes many other peaks, e.g. Pandim, Simvo, Siniolchu, Junnoo and Kabru, all of well over 20,000 ft. The greater part of the eastern boundary of Sikkim is formed by the Chola Range, much loftier than the Singalila, stretching south from the main Himalayan axis at Dongkia Mountain (over 23,000 ft. high). This range is pierced by passes, some of which form the normal trade routes between India (Kalimpong) and Tibet (Lhasa) through the Chumbi Valley. Of these the most frequented are the Tangkar La (16,000 ft.), Natu La (14,200 ft.) and the Jelep La (14,390 ft.). The northern trade route with Tibet, along the Teesta and Lachen Valleys, is through the high Kongra La Pass (16,840 ft.) or eastward from Chungthang up the Lachung Valley through the Dongkia Pass (18,030 ft.). The southern boundary of the State runs with the Darjeeling District of W. Bengal.

The Singalila Ridge on the west, the Chola on the east with the main Himalayan axis across their northern extremities virtually enclose Sikkim in a titanic horseshoe. The horseshoe is the catchment area of the headwaters of the Teesta River, one of the principal physical features of the country, which runs north-south practically throughout its entire length. Its principal feeder streams or affluents —the Lachen, Lachung, Zemu, Talung, Great Rangeet, Rongli and Rangpo—all rise either within the horseshoe or just beyond the political boundaries of the State.

The climate varies between the tropical heat of the valleys and the alpine cold of the snowy ranges. The rainfall, except in the Tibetan facies near the northern boundary, is very heavy, averaging 137 inches annually at Gangtok. From November to February the rainfall is light, and the weather in November and December is normally clear and fine. In March thunderstorms commence, and, growing more and more frequent, usher in the SW. monsoon season which lasts till October.

The main source of the Teesta River is the Chho Lhāmo Lake situated at over 17,000 ft. elevation. From here it descends steeply for some 16,000 ft. down to Rangpo all within a distance of about 50 miles. In its short and torrential course its waters are continually augmented by the concentrated drainage of smaller streams and mountain torrents in addition to its main affluents. It is thus easy to understand how such an insignificant and innocent-looking stream as the Teesta is during the dry season can suddenly swell into the thundering, raging torrent it becomes in the monsoon, causing gigantic landslides all along its course year after year, and widespread floods and devastation where it debouches into the Indian plains.

The level nature of the Gangetic delta and the rest of the country intervening between the mountains and the Bay of Bengal, some 400 miles directly to the south, permits the steady unobstructed inflow from the sea of the moisture-laden currents of the SW. monsoon and renders Sikkim the most humid region of the entire Himalayan chain. The transverse narrow valleys formed by the mass of mountainous spurs criss-crossing one another, heavily forest-clad up to 12,000 ft., give rise to local modifications of exposure, temperature, humidity and luxuriance of vegetation, and affect in varying degree the altitudinal distribution of sedentary birds.

By comparison, the Himalayas to the west of central Nepal are considerably less humid, a feature which is clearly reflected in all their plant and animal life. An analysis of the races of typically Himalayan birds collected along the southern aspect of the entire Himalayan axis suggests that the zoogeographical boundary between the eastern and the western Himalayas lies in the region of the Arun-Kosi River (in Nepal), some 50 miles west of the Sikkim border, the forms inhabiting the moister eastern Himalayas being appreciably darker in coloration as well as somewhat smaller in size.

## Vegetation

In luxuriance and floral composition, the vegetation of Sikkim and the humid eastern Himalayas bears a greater similarity with the Malay Peninsula and Archipelago than with the Himalayas west of central Nepal. Many of the typical orders and families of plants common to the former two regions are totally absent in the western Himalayas.

Broadly speaking, three altitudinal zones of vegetation are recognizable in Sikkim. They are not clear-cut at their boundaries but merge into one another, often showing considerable local encroachments and recessions above and below the line depending upon physical configuration and exposure of the terrain and the resultant ecological factors:

1. The Tropical Zone extends roughly from the foothills of the Outer Himalayas to an altitude of about 4000 ft. It contains deep, steep-sided valleys and gorges, with well-drained flanking slopes clothed in dense evergreen jungle. It is characterized by gigantic trees with buttressed trunks with huge lianas and climbers covering them, intertwining in the foliage canopy and festooning from tree to

PLATE 1

*a.* Terraced cultivation, from the foothills up to *c.* 6,000 ft.

*b.* Junipers and buckthorn scrub, near Thangu, *c.* 13,000 ft.

*a*. Deciduous facies of the tropical zone, *c*. 3,000 ft.
W. Sikkim

*b*. The fern *Gleichenia* (? *linearis* Cl.) a common feature of the tropical and sub-tropical zones, *c*. 4-5,000 ft.

PLATE 2

tree. Orchids of numerous species abound, and the handsome large-leaved *Rhaphidophora* drapes the trunks along with numerous vines and peppers. Wild bananas, straight-stemmed screw-pines (*Pandanus*), nettles, and giant bamboos provide the other features characteristic of this type of moist foothills forest.

2. Above this belt, and up to an elevation of 6500 ft. or so, the vegetation assumes a sub-tropical aspect, passing as it ascends into the Moist Temperate type of Champion's classification: dense tall evergreen forest with oaks and rhododendrons predominating. Near its upper limit (at *c.* 9000 ft.) Silver Fir appears with the oaks, and the forest is mixed with various deciduous trees such as *Magnolia*, *Acer* and *Betula*. The undergrowth consists largely of the high-level 'maling' bamboo (*Arundinaria*) or dwarf rhododendron and other evergreen shrubs. Ferns, epiphytic mosses and many other epiphytes are abundant.

3. Between 9000 ft. and 13,000 ft. comes the Temperate Zone of mixed conifer forest containing hemlock (*Tsuga*) and spruce (*Picea*) with varying amounts of Blue Pine (*Pinus excelsa*), Silver Fir (*Abies webbiana*) and junipers, and with a shrubby undergrowth of rhododendron and *Arundinaria* bamboo.

These three main divisions, which present appreciable gradations and differences in their floristics on the outer ranges and interior of Sikkim as well as locally, are succeeded higher still by Alpine forest and scrub. The former is composed of small crooked trees and large shrubs, interspersed with patches of fir and pine. The stunted forest is mainly of rhododendrons of many species which impart to it an evergreen character. Sikkim is justly renowned for the abundance and lavish variety of its rhododendrons. They range from dwarf bushes growing above the snow line with insignificant tiny white flowers, through dense shrubs with enormous tufts of showy blossoms —white, pink, mauve, crimson and yellow—to large forest trees up to 60 ft. high or more with fiery scarlet blossoms that light up the verdant hillsides from miles away. In May, when most of the high-growing varieties burst into their multi-coloured masses of flowers, they present a spectacle of exquisite and indescribable charm. In spring the ground in the more open patches becomes carpeted with a profusion of flowers, prominent among which are the primulas. Ferns abound in patches, and epiphytic mosses and lichen are common. Vegetation, here dependent largely on snowfall and melting snow, gets progressively dwarfed and scanty towards the upper limits. Low evergreen scrub, 2 or 3 ft. high, of rhododendron, juniper, cotoneaster, etc. predominates, with *Anemone*, *Corydalis* and *Fritillaria* as some of the commonest herbs. Beyond 17,000 ft. or thereabouts vegetation ceases in inner Sikkim, the heights above being covered by rock and snow.

These altitudinal zones of vegetation are of the highest interest to the student of bird ecology inasmuch as each of them harbours a more or less characteristic avifauna of its own. Perhaps nowhere in the world would one find the unique phenomenon of so divergent a range of climates and vegetation telescoped into so circumscribed a space. Hooker gives a good example. He writes: 'From the bed of the Ratong in which grow palms with screw-pine and plantain, it is only seven miles in a direct line to the perpetual ice . . . . In other words the descent is so rapid that in eight miles the Ratong waters every variety of vegetation from the lichen of the Poles to the palm of the Tropics; while throughout the remainder of its mountain course it falls from 4000 ft. to 300 ft. flowing amongst tropical scenery through a valley whose flanks rise from 5000 ft. to 12,000 ft. above its bed.'

This abrupt telescoping of the terrain—from the hot, steamy foothill valleys to the arctic cold of the snow-capped peaks—which has produced the marked altitudinal zonation in the rainfall, humidity, climate and vegetation is also responsible for the great variety and numerical abundance of the resident bird life, making Sikkim perhaps the richest area of its size anywhere in the world. In addition to the 430 species described in the following pages, the Appendix gives a further 97 which have been recorded as occurring or having occurred in Sikkim, bringing the total up to 527 species. This list could easily be enlarged by the inclusion of vagrants, transients on migration and near-certainties, so that a round 550 species would not be an unreasonable overall reckoning for the country. This means about 30 per cent of the aggregate bird species and subspecies found in the entire subcontinent comprising the Indian Union, Pakistan, Nepal and Bhutan together with Ceylon. Many forms of exceptional beauty and rarity are peculiar to this region but also spill over into Nepal on the west and Bhutan on the east.

A curious parallelism exists between the avifauna (and of several other widely differing forms of animal life as well) inhabiting the moist Sikkim Himalayas, Burma and Malaya on the one hand and the far-flung rain forests of the southern Western Ghats on the other. The postulated origin and mechanics of this phenomenon are discussed in my book on the birds of Travancore and Cochin, and it will suffice here merely to draw attention to it again for the benefit of future investigators.

Thanks to the labours of Brian Hodgson and his band of local collectors between 1845 and 1858, and of Mandelli, Blanford and others in the 70's and after, a fairly complete collection of birds from Sikkim territory was built up, which is now available for study chiefly in the British Museum (Natural History), London, but also scattered over various other museums in Europe and in America. In the present century these collections have been enlarged by the contributions of several other ornithologists, notably Col. F. M. Bailey, Herbert Stevens, Frank Ludlow, Col. R. Meinertzhagen, Dr Ernst Schäfer, and lastly by the recent Loke-Sálim Ali bird survey of Sikkim.

It is doubtful if any forms unknown to science still remain undiscovered in this area, though the material relating to several of the rarer and little-known species, e.g. wrens and some of the Timaliinae, is meagre and insufficient for a proper study. But by and large, further general specimen-collecting seems redundant. A review of our

PLATE 3

*a.* Epiphytic ferns, moss, and orchids are characteristic of the tropical and sub-tropical zones.

*b.* The handsome large-leaved *Rhaphidophora* (? *glauca* Schott) and numerous vines and creepers here drape the trunks of the forest trees.

Path along the Teesta River near Dikchu, *c.* 2,200 ft. (Note breach caused by flood erosion, and rickety makeshift repair).

PLATE 4

knowledge of the bionomics of this impressive array of birds, however, reveals a lack that is truly deplorable. In the case of an area that had never been explored before it is understandable that the pioneers should have concentrated their efforts on the amassing of specimens. Unfortunately, they were obliged to do most of their collecting vicariously with the aid of illiterate, local, professional hunters and snarers. Thus, though in the case of Hodgson all the specimens brought to him were carefully measured, weighed and described, and frequently also sketched, many of them are without precise data as to altitude or environment, and even their sexing is often dubious. The published literature dealing with these comprehensive 'classical' collections is largely descriptive and taxonomical; field notes are practically non-existent, excepting those of a very general and diffuse nature, and even that in a few cases only. Of the later investigators B. B. Osmaston, who was posted as a forest officer in Darjeeling District, recorded some very useful notes, especially concerning nidification. Stevens's *Birds of the Sikkim Himalayas* is a commendable attempt to sort out the bird life into 'altitudinal life zones' on the available data. Meinertzhagen with his refreshing tendency to avoid the well-worn ruts of bird study and explore new avenues has provided some model observations on the status and habits of several little-known species of the high altitudes. But perhaps the most thorough and rational collecting of Sikkim birds in recent times has been done by Dr Ernst Schäfer during the two years immediately preceding the Second World War. His collections are particularly valuable since they cover every season of the year, including the monsoon. Anyone acquainted with the depressing conditions prevailing in that period—week after week of gloomy overcast skies, the saturated atmosphere reeking of mildew and dripping with moisture, the incessant relentless downpours with enormous landslides constantly holding up movement, hordes of insatiable leeches for ever after one's blood, and similar other discomforts—will agree that this is no mean achievement and calls for a very high order of dedication to scientific research. Ornithologists familiar with Dr Schäfer's earlier work in Tibet (*Ornithologische Ergebnisse zweier Forschungsreisen nach Tibet, J. f. O.* 1938, Sonderheft) and with his competence and excellence as a field biologist will appreciate the incalculable harm Sikkim ornithology has sustained through tragic loss under war conditions of all his manuscript field notes. Fortunately the collection itself found its way after various vicissitudes to its destination, the Berlin University Zoological Museum, where it was critically studied by Prof. Erwin Stresemann. Through the latter's friendly co-operation I have been privileged to consult and make use of his valuable taxonomical report (in MS.) on Schäfer's material. Stresemann's measurements of these fresh specimens, his notes on ages, moults and other data, together with the dependable sexing, dates and altitudes on their labels have added very considerably to our knowledge of the seasonal local occurrences, altitudinal movements, and nidification of sedentary birds. By filling many of the previous blanks they have helped to make the present account of Sikkim avifauna less incomplete than it must otherwise have been.

## Migration

Certain well-known migrants such as wild ducks and geese can be seen passing over Sikkim regularly in autumn and spring, and some other species are known to spend the winter or a part of that season at lower altitudes. Apart from this, our knowledge of bird migration in Sikkim is on a par with that of their bionomics—in other words practically nil. The Lachen Valley is reputedly a traditional flyway for ducks and geese, at least on northward migration in spring (February/March). But very little authentic data are recorded from the interior of Sikkim because few students of birds have ever been able to stay there, as they have in the more accessible western Himalayas, long enough to carry out adequate observations.

The following is a list of collecting and other localities more commonly mentioned in the text, with their approximate altitudes in feet above sea level. The variants of the spelling, frequently used in maps and publications on Sikkim, are shown in brackets.

| | |
|---|---|
| Ari (Arita) | 4900 |
| Changu (Chhanggu, or Tsomgo) | 12,500 |
| Chungthang (Chumthang) | 5500 |
| Dentam, Great Rangeet Valley | 4500 |
| Dikchu | 2000 |
| Gangtok | 5500 |
| Gayamtashana Tso (Gayum Chhona) | 16,000 |
| Gezing | 5000 |
| Gnatong (Nāthang) | 12,500 |
| Gyagong (Giaogang, or Gyaokong) | 16,000 |
| Jeluk (Jeyluk) | 9000 |
| Kapup (Kupup) | 13,000 |
| Karponang | 9000 |
| Kewzing (Sosing) | 5800 |
| 'Kiang-Lager' (Schäfer's camp) | 16,500 |
| Lachen | 8900 |
| Lachung | 8900 |
| Lingtam | 5500 |
| Manshitang | 6000 |
| Martam | 2000 |
| Pakyong (Pakhyong) | 4400 |
| Pemionche (Pemayangtse) | 6850 |
| Penlom La (Penlong La) | 6000 |
| Rangpo | 1200 |
| Rinchinpong | 5000 |
| Singhik | 4400 |
| Singtam | 1200 |
| Temi | 5200 |
| Thangu (Thanggu) | 13,500 |
| Yumthang (Yeumthang) | 11,500 |

## Some Important Literature on Sikkim Birds

Blanford, W. T. (1871-2): Account of a Visit to the Eastern and Northern frontiers of Independent Sikkim. *Jour. Asiat. Soc. Bengal* 40 : 367; 41 : 30.

—— (1872): Notes on a Collection of Birds from Sikkim. ibid., 152-170 (with plates and descriptions of *Phylloscopus pallidipes, Pellorneum mandellii, Propasser saturatus*).

—— (1877): Notes on some Birds in Mr Mandelli's collection from Sikkim, Bhutan and Tibet. *Stray Feathers* 5: 482-7.

Brooks, W. Edwin (1880): Ornithological Observations in Sikkim, the Punjab and Sind. *Stray Feathers* 8: 464-9.

Gammie, J. A. (1877): Occasional Notes from Sikkim. *Stray Feathers* 5: 380-7.

Ludlow, F., and Kinnear, N. B. (1937): The Birds of Bhutan and adjacent Territories of Sikkim and Tibet. *Ibis*: 1-46, 249-93.

—— —— (1944): The Birds of South-eastern Tibet. *Ibis*: 43-86, 176-208, 348-89.

Meinertzhagen, R. (1927): Systematic Results of Birds collected at High Altitudes in Ladak and Sikkim. *Ibis*: 363-422, 571-633.

Scully, F. (1880): A Contribution to the Ornithology of Nepal. *Stray Feathers* 8: 204-368.

Stevens, Herbert (1923-5): Notes on the Birds of the Sikkim Himalayas. *Jour. Bom. Nat. Hist. Soc.* 29: 503-18, 723-40, 1007-30; 30: 54-71, 353-79, 664-85, 872-98.

A book that is quite indispensable to the proper understanding of the physiography and vegetational characteristics of Sikkim is Sir J. D. Hooker's *Himalayan Journals*, published in 1891. It is a classic of its kind—the enthralling narrative of a most difficult and adventurous pioneering exploration and sojourn between 1848 and 1850 in the then unsettled territories of the Raja of Sikkim. The Appendix to the volume, which deals in some detail with the physical geography and vegetation of the Sikkim Himalayas, east Nepal and adjacent provinces of Tibet, is a masterly account. It is the basis of the description of Sikkim in the *Imperial Gazetteer of India* as well as of practically all other similar accounts, wherever published.

Hooker's description of the vegetation, and the relevant sections of the more recent 'A Preliminary Survey of the Forest Types of India and Burma' by H. G. Champion (*Indian Forest Records,* N. S. Silviculture, Vol. 1, No. 1, 1936) will give even a naturalist with no special training in botany a clear and vivid picture of conditions in Sikkim.

## Acknowledgements

Besides Professor Stresemann and Dr Schäfer, I am indebted to so many for help in various ways that thanking them all individually is not possible. However, special mention must be made of my friend

Loke Wan Tho of Singapore, who with his usual munificence not only kept the Sikkim Ornithological Survey in the field for several months at a time during two separate trips, but by personally taking part in the second expedition, contributed substantially to the field work especially as regards calls and habits, and by his photography.

To the Maharajkumar of Sikkim, Hon. Lt.-Col. P. T. Namgyal, P.V., O.B.E., and the former Dewan, John S. Lall, I.C.S., is due the credit for the original suggestion of a well-illustrated book on the birds of Sikkim which was readily backed up by the State Government with a generous donation towards its production. To Mr Lall as also to his successor Mr K. R. Rustomjee, I.C.S., and to the Chief Secretary Rai Bahadur Densappa and numerous other officials of the Sikkim Government, high and low, I am indebted for their helpful co-operation and the facilities which enabled our prolonged stay and travel in a somewhat difficult country.

Finally my thanks to Dr Biswamoy Biswas of the Zoological Survey of India and Dr S. Dillon Ripley of Yale University's Peabody Museum of Natural History for their continued help and advice, especially in regard to the intricacies of modern fashions in taxonomy and nomenclature, and to the authorities of the Chicago Natural History Museum for permission and facilities to study their rich collections of Himalayan birds, especially the Sikkim material procured by H. Stevens and the Suydam Cutting Expedition, which proved so highly rewarding.

Tropical evergreen forest near Temi, 4-5,000 ft.

PLATE 5

Moist evergreen sub-tropical forest near Kewzing, *c.* 7,000 ft., with heavily moss-covered tree-trunks and boulders, and dense undergrowth of seedlings and ferns. Typical biotope for *Microura* wrens.

PLATE 6

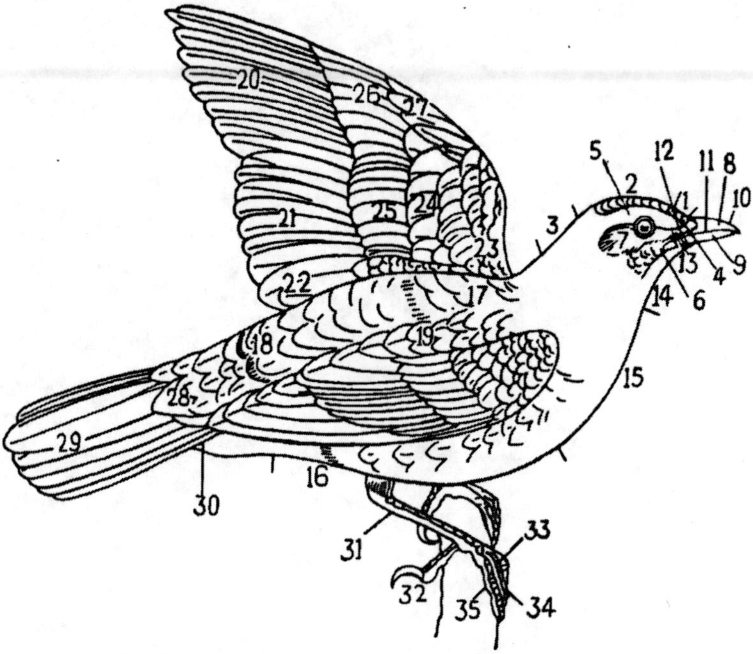


## TERMS USED IN DESCRIPTION OF A BIRD'S PLUMAGE AND PARTS

1. Forehead
2. Crown
3. Nape or occiput; the top end of the hindneck
4. Lores (space in front of eye)
5. Supercilium
6. Cheeks
7. Ear-coverts
8. Upper mandible or maxilla
9. Lower mandible
10. Culmen or upper profile of maxilla
11. Commissure or line of junction of the two mandibles
12. Rictal bristles or vibrissae
13. Chin
14. Throat
15. Breast
16. Abdomen
17. Back
18. Rump
19. Scapulars
20. Primaries (the earlier or outermost 9 or 10 visible quills of the wing)
21. Outer secondaries (wing-quills springing from the radius and ulna)
22. Inner secondaries
23. Lesser wing-coverts
24. Median wing-coverts
25. Greater wing-coverts
26. Primary coverts
27. Winglet or bastard wing
28. Upper tail-coverts
29. Tail-feathers or rectrices
30. Under tail-coverts
31. Tarsus
32. Hind toe or first toe or hallux
33. Inner or second toe
34. Middle or third toe
35. Outer or fourth toe

## STANDARDS OF SIZE EMPLOYED

| | | | | | | | |
|---|---|---|---|---|---|---|---|
| Sparrow | ... | Length about | 6″ | Crow | ... | Length about | 17″ |
| Quail | ... | „ | 7-8″ | Kite | ... | „ | 24″ |
| Bulbul | ... | „ | 8″ | Duck | ... | „ | 24″ |
| Myna | ... | „ | 9″ | Village hen | ... | „ | 18-30″ |
| Pigeon | ... | „ | 13″ | Vulture | ... | „ | 36″ |
| Partridge | ... | „ | 13″ | | | | |

PLATE 7

*a.* Upland yak pastures near Lachen, *c.* 9,500 ft.

*b.* Birch, juniper and dwarf rhododendrons. A good biotope for rosefinches. N. Sikkim, *c.* 13,500 ft.

*a.* Near Thangu, 13-14,000 ft. Temperate Zone. Junipers, conifers, and dwarf rhododendron scrub.

*b.* Upper reaches of Teesta River, Yakthang *c.* 13,000 ft. Shingly islets suitable for Ibisbill nesting.

PLATE 8

## *Family* ANATIDAE: Ducks, Geese

### THE EASTERN GOOSANDER

*Mergus merganser orientalis* Gould

*Mergus Orientalis* Gould, 1845, *Proc. Zool. Soc. London:* 1—Amoy, China.

**Plate 10, fig. 5 (facing p. 81)**

F.B.I. **6**: 472

LOCAL NAME:

SIZE: Domestic duck—. Slimmer.

FIELD CHARACTERS: *Male: Above,* head, neck and crest black, glossed with metallic green and purple. Upper back glossy black; lower back, rump and upper tail-coverts grey, vermiculated with white. Tail silvery brown. Wing primaries blackish; secondaries white. *Below,* from lower neck down, white with a pale rosy salmon tint.

In flight, general aspect black and white with narrow pointed red bill and red legs.

*Female: Above,* head and neck rufous brown; rest of upper parts mottled grey. Primaries blackish; secondaries white and grey. Tail grey-brown. *Below,* sides of neck and underparts white, striped with grey on flanks.

In flight the rufous head, grey back, white underparts, black and white wings and thin pointed red bill and red legs are distinctive.

STATUS AND HABITAT: Uncommon winter visitor. Occasional on the upper reaches of the swift-flowing Teesta River. May breed in the Tibetan facies of N. Sikkim (?).

DISTRIBUTION OUTSIDE SIKKIM: *Summer* (breeding), Afghanistan, Turkestan to Tibet. *Winter,* along the Himalayas and their foothills from Kashmir to Assam.

GENERAL HABITS: Keeps in pairs or small parties of 5 to 8. An expert swimmer and diver, perfectly at home on icy torrential streams. Feeds mainly on fish, for capturing which its bill is especially adapted. Often hunts by concerted effort like cormorants, the birds swimming in a semicircle from bank to bank across fast-flowing streams, driving the fish into the less turbulent shallows near the edge and diving after them. When shifting its hunting grounds, flies low over the stream almost clipping the wavelets and is difficult to see against the background of stones and foam of the rushing water. *Call:* an occasional croak or *krrr.* Said to utter a soft plaintive whistle during the breeding season.

NESTING: Unrecorded within Sikkim limits.

RACIAL CHARACTERISTICS, MEASUREMENTS, ETC: Bill quite unlike a duck's: long, narrow, strongly hooked at tip, and with tooth-like serrations along the edges of the mandibles. Legs very backwardly placed, as in the grebes. The race *orientalis* is smaller than the European *merganser*, with the lower back and rump a paler grey. Wing ♂♂ 243-284 mm.; ♀♀ 189-257 mm. (Fauna).

Iris brown; bill orange-red, dusky at tip and on culmen; lower mandible sometimes fleshy or yellowish red; legs and feet orange-red or orange-brown.

Several other species of duck, and also geese, fly over Sikkim on their autumn and spring migrations, but owing to the absence of suitable shallow jheels very few stop over, and only transitorily. On the deeper mountain lakes and open tarns some of the diving ducks, e.g. Tufted Pochard (*Aythya fuligula*), are more regularly seen in small numbers. In late February and early March, in two successive years, flocks of geese, apparently Barheads (*Anser indicus*), were observed flying northward high over Chungthang. The Lachen valley, above Chungthang, is said by the locals to be a regular flyway for ducks and geese, particularly on the upward migration in March-April.

## *Family* ACCIPITRIDAE: Vultures, Hawks

### THE PARIAH KITE

*Milvus migrans govinda* Sykes

*Milvus Govinda* Sykes, 1832, *Proc. Comm. Zool. Soc. London*: 81—Deccan.

### THE BLACKEARED, or LARGE INDIAN, KITE

*Milvus migrans lineatus* (Gray)

*Haliaëtus lineatus* J. E. Gray, 1831, in Hardwicke, Ill. Ind. Zool. **1** (8): 1, pl. 18—China.

F.B.I. **5**: 122, 124

LOCAL NAME:

SIZE: Vulture—; 24 inches.

FIELD CHARACTERS: *M. m. govinda:* A large, more or less uniformly dark brown hawk, easily distinguished from other similar birds by its forked tail, particularly conspicuous in flight. *M. m. lineatus* differs in being larger, paler and less rufous below, and with much more white in the under wing-coverts which show up as a conspicuous white patch in overhead flight. Sexes alike.

STATUS AND HABITAT: Not common, but small numbers seen locally about the older established villages and habitations (Rangpo, Singtam, Singhik, Gangtok, Chungthang etc.) and the more frequented nomadic yakmen's and muleteers' camp sites. The exact status of the two races in Sikkim is undetermined, though *lineatus* normally is a higher mountain and Palaearctic breeding form. Schäfer collected a specimen of *govinda* at *c.* 9000 ft. (Lachen) on 18 September, and several of *lineatus* at 16,000 and 16,500 ft. (Gayamtashana Tso and his 'Kiang-Lager') in August and October.

DISTRIBUTION OUTSIDE SIKKIM: *M. m. govinda:* Breeds practically throughout India, up to *c.* 7000 ft. in the Himalayas. *M. m. lineatus:* Chiefly Palaearctic; breeds from Siberia, China and Japan south to Ladakh, N. Kashmir and Tibet. Also above *c.* 7000 ft. in the higher hill ranges south of Brahmaputra River (*vide* Baker). Winters in peninsular India etc.

GENERAL HABITS: A scavenger and commensal of man wherever possible. Feeds mainly on carrion and offal; only occasionally takes fledgling or sickly birds. Is a graceful and expert flier capable of astonishing speed and manœuvrability, e.g. when stooping to pick up garbage from the midst of a congested bazaar. *Call:* a shrill whistling *ewe-wir-wir-wir* uttered from a perch as well as on the wing.

NESTING: Neither race specifically recorded in Sikkim. *Season*—*govinda* (W. Himalayas) March-May; *lineatus* (Gyantse) April-May. *Nest*—an untidy platform of twigs, tow, leaves, rags and miscellaneous rubbish high up in a large tree. *Eggs*—2 to 4, variable, commonly dirty pinkish white lightly spotted and blotched with reddish brown. Size: *govinda* about 53×43 mm.; *lineatus* about 58×46 mm.

RACIAL CHARACTERISTICS, MEASUREMENTS, ETC: Schäfer's Sikkim skins measure: *govinda* 1 '♀' ad. Wing 469 mm.; *lineatus* (including specimens from adjoining S. Tibet) 5 ♂♂ ad. 482, 490, 497, 502, 515; 2 ♀♀ ad. 486, 492 mm. (Stresemann).

Iris brown; bill black; cere, gape and extreme base of lower mandible yellow or greenish yellow; legs and feet pale greyish yellow.

## THE EASTERN GOSHAWK

***Accipiter gentilis schvedowi*** (Menzbier)

*Astur palumbarius schvedowi* Menzbier, 1882, Ornith. Geogr. Eur. Russl.: 49—Transbaikalia.

F.B.I. 5: 146

LOCAL NAME:

SIZE: Kite.

FIELD CHARACTERS: *Above,* forehead and supercilium white. Crown, sides of head and neck, and nape greyish black. Rest of upper plumage ashy brown. *Below,* white, narrowly cross-barred with blackish. Sexes alike; female larger.

In overhead aspect the close-barred white body and broad, rather blunt whitish shikra-like wings, barred with brown, are suggestive pointers.

STATUS AND HABITAT: Uncommon winter visitor. Meinertzhagen obtained a specimen at Karponang 8800 ft. on 19 December (1925) and saw two more on that day. On 10 April (1955) I observed three large shikra-shaped hawks circling high above Pakyong which were evidently this species.

DISTRIBUTION OUTSIDE SIKKIM: *Summer* (breeding), Central and

Eastern Asia south to the Tian Shan and the NW. Himalayas. *Winter*, N. India.

GENERAL HABITS: Swoops down on its prey from a look-out post on a leafy branch and strikes it down, or pursues it with speed and determination close to the ground. *Food:* hares and other small mammals, and large game birds such as pheasants and junglefowl.

NESTING: Within Indian limits has only been claimed to breed in Garhwal in precipitous wooded valleys close to the snowy peaks, but very little reliable data available.

RACIAL CHARACTERISTICS, MEASUREMENTS, ETC: Meinertzhagen's Sikkim ♂ has Wing 342 mm.

## THE BESRA SPARROW-HAWK

### *Accipiter virgatus affinis* Hodgson

*Accipiter affinis* Hodgson, 1836, *Bengal Sporting Magazine*, new series, 8: 179 —Nepal.

F.B.I. 5: 161

LOCAL NAME:

SIZE: Pigeon.

FIELD CHARACTERS: Very similar to and easily confused with both the Shikra and the Sparrow-Hawk. Distinguished by a broad black mesial stripe down the white chin and throat. Sexes alike; female larger.

STATUS AND HABITAT: Not common. Meinertzhagen collected specimens at Gangtok, 6600 ft. and Dentam, 4700 ft. in winter (17 December, 9 January), and Schäfer an adult female at Chungthang, 5000 ft. on 25 June. Affects dense forest.

DISTRIBUTION OUTSIDE SIKKIM: The Eastern Himalayas, *c.* 1500 to 7000 ft., from Nepal east to China, south to Manipur; wintering to the south of its breeding range. The adjoining W. Himalayas to Kashmir are inhabited by the paler race *kashmirensis*. A third (smaller) race, *besra*, is resident in the moist forest biotope of S. India and Ceylon.

GENERAL HABITS: Very similar to those of the Sparrow-Hawk and the Shikra of which it is in effect the forest representative. Bold and powerful, often killing birds much larger than itself.

NESTING: Not recorded in Sikkim. *Season* (in W. Himalayas)—chiefly April-May. *Nest*—a platform of sticks high up in a large tree overlooking a forested ravine. *Eggs*—3 to 5, roundish oval, variable, commonly bluish white freckled, blotched and smudged with reddish brown at the broader end. Size about 40×32 mm.

RACIAL CHARACTERISTICS, MEASUREMENTS, ETC: Differs from the W. Himalayan race *kashmirensis* in being much darker, more blackish grey above. Meinertzhagen's Sikkim skins (2 ♀♀) measure Wing 206, 213 mm. An adult female collected by Schäfer has Wing 201 mm.

Iris golden or orange-yellow; bill slate-grey with black tip; cere, legs and feet lemon yellow; claws blackish.

## THE INDIAN SPARROW-HAWK

*Accipiter nisus melaschistos* Hume

*Accipiter Melaschistos* Hume, 1869, Rough Notes, March: 128—Interior of the Himalayas.

F.B.I. 5: 158

LOCAL NAME:

SIZE: Pigeon+.

FIELD CHARACTERS: *Above*, slaty grey, darkest (blackish) on head, palest (grey) on rump. A white supercilium. Tail tipped whitish, with four broad black bands. *Below*, white to pale rufous finely striated with rufous on chin, throat and upper breast; narrowly barred with rufous-brown on rest of underparts. Sexes alike; female larger.

In overhead aspect the whitish narrowly barred underside and rounded shikra-like wings, and the bars on the relatively longish tail, are conspicuous.

Almost indistinguishable from the Shikra (*Accipiter badius*) which Stevens has recorded as generally distributed at moderate altitudes in Sikkim. I also noted it at Rangpo, Singtam, Temi-Kewzing, but in view of possible confusion with the sparrow-hawk sight records are undependable.

STATUS AND HABITAT: Winter visitor? All the Sikkim specimens mentioned by Stevens (Nepal-Sikkim frontier, 10,160 ft.; Rungbong valley 4500 ft.; Lachung) were taken in winter (November to March), Blanford records sparrow-hawks (subspecies?) as common in the Lachen and Lachung valleys after mid-September (1870) evidently on southward migration. He had seen none at the end of August in the Cho La Range. The four specimens in Schäfer's Sikkim collection were also obtained in winter (October, November, December, February)—Lachen, Lachung, Gangtok. Against this, Ludlow collected a female at 11,500 ft. in Bhutan on 16 May with a fully formed oviduct egg (blue, without blotches).

DISTRIBUTION OUTSIDE SIKKIM: Breeds in the Himalayas from Kashmir to Assam and north into Tibet and Yunnan, between 4000 and 10,000 ft. Wanders into the plains in winter. The paler N. Asiatic race *nisosimilis* also winters in India.

GENERAL HABITS: Preys largely on small birds. Glides along at great speed close to the ground, accelerated by spurts of rapid wing beats. Weaves in and out of bushes, hedges and tree-trunks in order to stampede small birds out of cover, whereupon the sparrow-hawk dashes in pursuit and strikes them down.

NESTING: Not recorded in Sikkim. *Season* (W. Himalayas)—April-June. *Nest*—a stick-platform in a tree, usually a disused nest of a crow or other bird. *Eggs*—normally four, roundish ovals, buffy, reddish white or bluish white, spotted and blotched with reddish brown or blackish brown, with secondary markings of pale reddish or lavender grey. Size about 39×33 mm.

RACIAL CHARACTERISTICS, MEASUREMENTS, ETC: In the hand can be told from the Shikra by its much longer and slenderer tarsus and toes, with the middle toe greatly exceeding the others in length.

*Melaschistos* differs from N. Asiatic *nisosimilis* in being much darker above with the lower parts frequently much more rufous, especially in the male. Schäfer's Sikkim examples measure: Wing 2 ♂♂ 210, 215; 2 ♀♀ 242, 245 mm. Stresemann observes that of these the males are definitely *melaschistos*, while it is difficult to decide whether the females are this or *nisosimilis*.

Iris golden yellow or orange; bill slaty blue with black tip; cere, legs and feet yellow; claws black.

THE CRESTED GOSHAWK, *Accipiter trivirgatus indicus* (Hodgson), is apparently a rare resident from the foothills up to *c.* 6500 ft. Meinertzhagen obtained specimens at Dikchu and Gangtok (27 October, 18 December).

FIELD CHARACTERS: *Above,* dark brown, with the forehead, crown and nuchal crest blackish grey. *Below,* white broadly streaked on breast and barred on rest of underparts with rich rufous-brown. Throat and under tail-coverts pure white, the former with a blackish mesial stripe from chin to breast.

Differs from the Besra Sparrow-Hawk (*A. v. affinis*) in its larger size (*c.* Jungle Crow) and the possession of a short but distinct nuchal crest.

A forest hawk, largely predatory on game birds including junglefowl and pheasants.

## THE LONGLEGGED BUZZARD

***Buteo rufinus rufinus*** **(Cretzschmar)**

*Falco rufinus* Cretzschmar, 1829, in Rüppel, Atlas Vögel: 40, pl. 27—Upper Nubia, Schendi & Sennar, and Ethiopia.

F.B.I. 5: 137

LOCAL NAME:

SIZE: Kite.

FIELD CHARACTERS: Similar to next, extremely variable, ranging from dark brown through reddish brown and fulvous to pale sandy.

Buzzards are impossible to identify in the field with certainty as to species. A specimen of the above (determined by Stresemann) was collected by Schäfer at Manshitang 5000 ft. in November.

STATUS AND HABITAT: According to Stresemann only a rare winter visitor to the Eastern Himalayas, probably from its east Turkestan-Mongolian breeding area.

DISTRIBUTION OUTSIDE SIKKIM: The species is found from southern Russia to eastern Asia, and south to N. Africa.

## THE JAPANESE DESERT BUZZARD

### *Buteo buteo burmanicus* Hume

*Buteo burmanicus* Hume, 1875, *Stray Feathers* 3: 30 (in text)—Thayetmyo, Upper Pegu.

F.B.I. 5: 143

LOCAL NAMES: Dan-pang-ti-on, Pang-ti-ong-nok (Lepcha).

SIZE: Kite—.

FIELD CHARACTERS: Like a small eagle or immature Brahminy Kite (*Haliastur indus*). Extremely variable in coloration, from pale buffy brown to dark brown with paler head and neck and broad blackish moustachial stripes. Tail pale creamy rufous with obsolete brown bands, and a broader more distinct subterminal band visible in flight. *Below*, rufous brown except abdomen which is sometimes white barred with brown. Sexes alike.

In overhead aspect the rounded expanded pale coloured tail, and whitish or dark brown half-moon-shaped patch on chestnut-tinged underwing, conspicuous.

STATUS AND HABITAT: Winter visitor. Schäfer obtained specimens at Lachen and Gangtok in September, October, November (juvenile), and February 1938/39. Blanford recorded it at Yumthang *c.* 13,000 ft. in September (1870).

DISTRIBUTION OUTSIDE SIKKIM: *Summer* (breeding), NE. and Central Asia south to Tibet and Ladakh. *Winter,* India, Burma, Ceylon, Malaysia (rare).

Buzzards of uncertain species were frequently observed by the Survey—solos and pairs—between 5000 and 12,000 ft. elevation in winter (November to March) at Temi, Gangtok, Lachen, Lachung and Phalut.

GENERAL HABITS (of buzzards in general): Rather sluggish. Usually seen perched on a stone or mound, or quartering the opener hillsides 50 to 100 ft. up in the air, occasionally hovering head to wind, and pouncing on any small animals moving on the ground below. *Food:* rats, mice, young or sickly birds, lizards, snakes etc. *Call:* a long, wailing kitten-like mewing; particularly noisy in breeding season. Pairs much given to soaring aloft and wheeling in wide circles, playfully darting and stooping at each other at tremendous speed with wings pulled in. One pair (species ?) was observed at this game early one December morning at Phalut, obviously enjoying themselves thoroughly in the face of the icy gale blowing from the snow-clad Makalu Range, with the thermometer at 30° F. in the roofed veranda of the dak bungalow!

RACIAL CHARACTERISTICS, MEASUREMENTS, ETC: Schäfer's Sikkim specimens measure:

*B. r. rufinus:* 1 ♂ Wing 438; tail 242 mm.

*B. b. burmanicus:* Wing 2 ♂♂ 367, 371; 1 ♀ 422; 1 o? 400 mm.

*Buteo r. rufinus* differs from *B. b. burmanicus* chiefly in its longer wing and relatively larger bill and feet.

Iris brown or yellowish brown; cere yellow; bill brownish slate, black at tip, yellowish at base of lower mandible; tarsus partly feathered in front (in *burmanicus* sometimes wholly) and feet dingy lemon yellow; claws black.

## THE HIMALAYAN HAWK-EAGLE

*Spizaëtus nipalensis nipalensis* (Hodgson)

*Nisaëtus nipalensis* Hodgson, 1936, *Jour. Asiat. Soc. Bengal* 5: 229, pl. 7—Nepal.

F.B.I. 5: 89

LOCAL NAME: Kanda-panthiong (Lepcha).

SIZE: Kite+.

FIELD CHARACTERS: A slender, crested, rather variably coloured forest eagle. *Above*, brown, with a prominent crest of a few long black feathers projecting almost horizontally behind hindcrown. Rump and upper tail-coverts barred with white. Tail dark brown, barred with grey and with a broad blackish subterminal bar. *Below*, foreneck and upper breast fulvous white, boldly black-streaked. Prominent blackish moustachial stripes, and a median or gular stripe down throat. Rest of lower plumage brown; posterior flanks and under tail-coverts barred with white. In very old birds black streaks on breast replaced by broken white bars. Sexes alike; female larger.

STATUS AND HABITAT: Resident (?). Not common, but frequent from *c.* 2000 to at least 7000 ft. altitude (Martam, Rinchinpong, Gangtok). Stevens records it at 11,800 ft. (Sandakphu) in March. Affects forested hillsides and valleys.

DISTRIBUTION OUTSIDE SIKKIM: The Himalayas, *c.* 2000 to 7000 ft., from Kashmir to East Assam, south to Cachar and Manipur. Straggling into the plains in winter. The race *kelaarti* is found in S. India and Ceylon. The species ranges east to China and Japan, south through the Indochinese and Malaysian subregions and Sulawesi (Celebes).

GENERAL HABITS: Bold, fierce and powerful. Essentially a hunter, preying on ground game such as pheasants, junglefowl and hares, waiting on them in a leafy branch overlooking a clearing, and pouncing as they come out to feed. *Call:* a shrill metallic whistle.

NESTING: Not recorded in Sikkim. *Season* (in W. Himalayas) —February to April. *Nest*—a large mass of sticks and twigs with a central depression lined with green leaves. Placed in a tall tree in forest, 40 to 80 ft. up. *Eggs*—1 or 2, normally either pale clay or reddish white, stippled and blotched with darker red or red-brown; or white, spotted and blotched with red chiefly at the larger end. Size about 70×54 mm.

RACIAL CHARACTERISTICS, MEASUREMENTS, ETC: In the hand, distinguishable from other hawk-eagles by the feathering of the tarsus running down beyond the first joint of the middle toe.

A specimen (♂ ad.) collected by Schäfer in Sikkim (March) has Wing 453 mm. A ♀ in the British Museum has 502 mm. (*vide* Stuart Baker).

Iris bright golden yellow; cere horny slate, bill horny black; feet dull yellow or yellowish white; claws black.

## BONELLI'S HAWK-EAGLE

### *Nisaëtus fasciatus fasciatus* (Vieillot)

*Aquila fasciata* Vieillot, 1822, *Mem. Soc. Linn. Paris* 2 (2): 152—Montpellier, France.

**Plate 9, fig. 5 (facing p. 80)**

F.B.I. 5: 77

LOCAL NAME:

SIZE: Kite+.

FIELD CHARACTERS: A comparatively slender eagle. *Above*, dark umber brown. Tail dark grey above, whitish below with a broad subterminal black band and others narrower and ill-defined. *Below*, white to rufous-buff, streaked with blackish. Sexes alike; female larger. Young birds rufous underneath.

Black wing-tips slightly upturned in flight. In overhead aspect silvery white body, dark brown underwing with fine greyish barring, and black subterminal tail-band are suggestive pointers.

STATUS AND HABITAT: ? Observed at Gangtok in December. Possibly less uncommon than appears. Affects forested hillsides and valleys.

DISTRIBUTION OUTSIDE SIKKIM: Throughout the Himalayas from Kashmir to Assam, and eastward to S. China. Practically all peninsular India. The species is also found in S. Europe and N. Africa.

GENERAL HABITS: A bold and powerful hunter, preying on junglefowl, kaleej pheasants and other large birds and small mammals, ambushing them from an overlooking leafy tree when they come out to feed in the open. Seldom, if ever, descends to carrion-eating. *Call:* described as a shrill creaking cry.

NESTING: Not recorded in Sikkim. *Nest*—a large stick-platform lined with green leaves, usually on a ledge of a cliff; sometimes in a tall tree.

RACIAL CHARACTERISTICS, MEASUREMENTS, ETC: At rest the closed wings reach almost to end of tail. Wing ♂♂ 482-520; ♀♀ 530-550; tarsus (feathered) 99-102; tail 275-288 mm. (Fauna).

Iris yellowish brown to orange-yellow: cere and gape pale sulphur yellow; bill bluish grey at base, horny black distally; feet pale sulphur yellow; claws horny brown.

THE BOOTED HAWK-EAGLE, *Hieraëtus pennatus* (Gmelin), superficially a smaller edition of Bonelli's, has also been recorded and probably has a similar status in Sikkim.

On the wing the brown immature phase looks very like an immature Brahminy Kite (*Haliastur*), but its relatively longer and markedly square-ended tail (as against rounded) is usually diagnostic.

## THE BLACK EAGLE

*Ictinaëtus malayensis perniger* (Hodgson)

*Aquila Pernigra* Hodgson, 1836, *Jour. Asiat. Soc. Bengal* 5: 227—Nepal.

**Plate 9, fig. 6 (facing p. 80)**

F.B.I. 5: 83

LOCAL NAMES: Laknangbang (Lepcha); Hügong (Bhotia).

SIZE: Kite+.

FIELD CHARACTERS: In overhead aspect the overall black plumage, dark underside of wings with a paler area on the primaries, narrowly grey-barred tail—relatively longer than in most eagles—and bright yellow cere and feet, are diagnostic. At close range a white patch under the eye confirms its identity. In sailing flight the broad wings are held above the line of the back in a wide V, and end in upturned 'splayed fingers' as in a vulture. At rest their tips reach end of tail. Sexes alike; female larger.

STATUS AND HABITAT: Resident (?). Not common, but solos frequent between *c.* 1000 and 6500 ft. elevation in winter (November to April)—Singtam, Martam, Dikchu, Kewzing, Gangtok. Affects forested hillsides and valleys.

DISTRIBUTION OUTSIDE SIKKIM: The Himalayas up to c. 6000 ft. from Chamba to E. Assam. Also in suitable biotope in Bengal, central India, E. and W. Ghats to Travancore, and Ceylon. The species extends through Burma and the Indochinese and Malaysian subregions to Sulawesi (Celebes).

GENERAL HABITS: Mostly seen on the wing quartering the forested hillsides back and forth and along the contours and ravines. Sails gracefully and effortlessly like a harrier skimming the tree-tops, weaving in and out of the canopy foliage, expertly side-slipping and diving through the branches to avoid obstacles. These manœuvres are for stampeding a bird from its nest and giving away its position, for this eagle is a habitual marauder of eggs and nestlings. *Food:* mice, lizards, frogs and large insects in addition to the above. Also kills pheasants and junglefowl. Normally a silent bird, but in courtship aerobatics—stooping, wheeling and tumbling at each other—the pair utter shrill yelping cries.

NESTING: Not recorded in Sikkim. *Season*—March-April. *Nest*—a large twig structure with a central depression lined with green leaves etc. Placed high up in a lofty tree, well concealed in the foliage. *Eggs*—1 or 2, roundish oval, variable in coloration, commonly whitish or pinkish densely stippled and blotched with pale red. Size about 63×50 mm.

RACIAL CHARACTERISTICS, MEASUREMENTS, ETC: Two adult specimens collected by Schäfer in Sikkim (April, June) have Wing '♂' 591; ♀ 605 mm.

Tarsus (feathered to the toes) 69-73; tail 285-313 (Fauna).

Iris dark brown; bill greenish to plumbeous horny with black tip; cere and gape yellow; feet yellow; claws black.

THE RINGTAILED, OR PALLAS'S, FISHING EAGLE, ***Haliaëtus leucoryphus*** (Pallas)

FIELD IDENTIFICATION: A large dark brown eagle (Kite+) with pale golden brown head and a broad white band across the tail, particularly conspicuous in flight.

Recorded by Stevens as being once obtained in the Runghong valley at *c.* 4500 ft. (16 June). On 22 April 1955 an adult-plumaged example was observed by me flying steadily and purposefully due North along the narrow Lachen valley, well above the river and almost on a level with Lachen village (*c.* 9000 ft.). Whether this was merely a vagrant, or the vanguard of the presumptive summer migrants to the high Tibetan plateau is uncertain. Large numbers of this eagle were reported by me[1] on 'tundra bogs' in the Kailas-Manasarowar region of western Tibet in early summer 1945, which, from the bare treeless nature of that country, could conceivably be non-breeding cis-Himalayan visitors. It must be left to future observers to determine whether these river valleys in Sikkim (and elsewhere in the Himalayas) are in fact, and to what extent, used as migration routes by this predominantly fish-eating eagle, and/or by other migratory birds.

THE BLACK, OR KING, VULTURE, *Torgos calvus* (Scopoli)

SIZE: Kite+.

A huge black vulture with deep yellowish red or pinkish scarlet naked head, neck, ear lappets and legs. In overhead aspect a whitish band on the underside of the rather pointed wings, and white patches on upper thighs and at base of neck conspicuous and diagnostic. Met with at low elevations up to *c.* 3000 ft. (Rangpo, Singtam, Martam), though it may wander higher temporarily in search of carrion. Usually solitary or pairs at animal carcases or sailing aloft.

## THE HIMALAYAN GRIFFON VULTURE

### *Gyps himalayensis* Hume

*Gyps himalayensis* Hume, 1869, Rough Notes: 12. 15—Himalayas from Kabul to Bhutan.

F.B.I. 5: 13

LOCAL NAME:

SIZE: Much heavier than the Whitebacked Vulture of the plains. The largest bird in Sikkim.

FIELD CHARACTERS: Old birds sandy white or pale khaki; younger chocolate brown. Long, naked dark scrawny neck and head. In

[1] *Jour. Bombay Nat. Hist. Soc.* **46**: 286-308 (1946).

overhead aspect large size, pale underside, black tail, and black trailing edges to the broad wings ending in 'splayed fingers' diagnostic. Sexes alike.

STATUS AND HABITAT: Common in the mountains and practically the only vulture at 6000 to 16,000 ft. and higher (Gangtok, Lachen, Lachung, Phalut, Gayamtashana Tso). Roosts on cliffs.

DISTRIBUTION OUTSIDE SIKKIM: Mountains of Central Asia, and throughout the higher Himalayas.

GENERAL HABITS: Purely a carrion feeder, with an enormous daily cruising range in search of food. Often seen along the regular trade routes to Tibet attracted by carcases of pack animals and others that have fallen by the wayside. A party of birds will frequently soar and circle majestically on motionless wings at dizzy heights above the mountain-tops, looking like midges in the sky. Such manœuvres can have no connexion with food-finding, and are obviously purely for fun.

Himalayan Griffon Vulture

About one-fourth — About one-twelfth

NESTING: Not specifically recorded in Sikkim. *Season*—January to March/April. Breeds in colonies on cliffs and precipices, using the same sites year after year. *Nest*—a rough untidy pad of sticks and rubbish placed on a ledge. *Egg*—a singleton, white, usually unmarked; sometimes with reddish blotches. Size about 95×70 mm.

RACIAL CHARACTERISTICS, MEASUREMENTS, ETC: Larger than the Fulvous Vulture (*Gyps fulvescens*) and with broader shaft-stripes on the lower plumage. The Fauna gives its measurements as: Wing 755-805; tail 365-402 mm. Schäfer collected 5 specimens at Gayamtashana Tso, *c.* 16,000 feet N. Sikkim, August 1938. They measure (linear under wing) 1 ♂ ad. 765; 1 o? ad. 740; 1 ♂ imm. 755; 2 oo? 735, 750 mm.

Iris dull yellow or pale brown; bill horny green; cere pale brown or greenish brown; legs and feet dingy grey or whitish.

## THE LÄMMERGEIER, or BEARDED VULTURE

*Gypaëtus barbatus aureus* (Halblizl)

*Vulture aureus* Halblizl, 1783, *Neue Nord. Beytr.* 4: 64—Province of Gilan, N. Persia.

F.B.I. 5: 26

LOCAL NAME: Cha-ko (Tibetan).

SIZE: About the same as the Griffon Vulture; less heavy. Wing span *c.* 9 ft.

FIELD CHARACTERS: Eagle-like, with cream-coloured feathered head and neck. *Above,* deep silvery grey and black, streaked with white. *Below,* pale orange-creamy with a broken blackish gorget on breast. A tuft or 'goatee' of hair-like feathers at chin conspicuous in profile. In overhead flight the longish wedge-shaped tail and narrow pointed wings diagnostic. Young birds very dark-plumaged, with head almost black.

STATUS AND HABITAT: Resident. Common, but not abundant, between *c.* 4000 and 16,000 ft., and soaring to over 24,000 ft. (Gangtok, Lachen, Lachung, Langri La, Gyagong, Gayamtashana Tso).

DISTRIBUTION OUTSIDE SIKKIM: SE. Europe to the Himalayas from Kashmir to Assam. The species occurs also in Africa east to S. Arabia.

GENERAL HABITS: A timid carrion-feeder which, in spite of allegations, has never been authenticated to attack living prey. Quarters enormous tracts of mountain and valley in majestic sailing flight, scanning the countryside for food. The primaries produce a loud droning sound as the bird glides past. Apparently the purpose of sailing along a narrow river valley or defile, as so commonly witnessed, is to strike a thermal current upon which the bird immediately spirals upward to considerable heights. It would seem also that this is done to a regular daily chronometer schedule. *Food:* largely bones carried up in the feet and repeatedly dropped on rocks from a height until they are splintered to bits that can be swallowed. Also joins Griffons and ravens at animal carcases. Walks on the ground with a slow dignified eagle-like gait, similar to the Neophron vulture's. Very silent, only rarely uttering a squeal. Indulges in extravagant courtship acrobatics when a sharp guttural cry *koolik, koolik* has been recorded.

NESTING: *Season*—December to February/March. *Nest*—a massive untidy collection of sticks, bones, scraps of mammal skin and other rubbish, on a ledge or in a niche on a precipitous cliff. *Eggs*—1 or 2, pale greyish rusty, blotched and spotted with various reds. Size about 85×68 mm.

RACIAL CHARACTERISTICS, MEASUREMENTS, ETC: Stresemann measures 5 specimens collected by Schäfer in N. Sikkim (linear under wing) as follows: 2 ♂♂ ad. 785, 808; 1 ♂ nearly ad. 805; 1 ♂ imm. 805; 1 o? 793 mm. Two specimens collected in Sikkim by Meinertzhagen measured (in the flesh): Wing ♂ 853 mm., ♀ 812 mm. Expanse ♂ 2,785 mm., ♀ 2,665 mm. Sikkim birds

Lämmergeier or Bearded Vulture
About one-ninth

do not differ in size or colour from the European-W. Asiatic population. The race inhabiting the mountains of Turkestan, Altai etc. is larger: according to Stegmann Wing (50 ♂♂) 813-893 (av. 860) mm. against *aureus* 780-832 (av. 808) mm.

Iris outer ring scarlet, inner khaki; bill horny brown, greenish plumbeous at base; feet grey; claws plumbeous.

Harriers are slender, graceful hawks unmistakable from their habit of gliding buoyantly on motionless outspread pointed wings close to the ground up and down with the contours, skimming the grassy or scrub-covered hillsides. From time to time they drop on lizards, insects, mice and small birds which are disposed of on the spot before resuming the hunt.

Stevens included four species as winter visitors in his list for the Sikkim Himalayas of which he considered 'the commonest' to be—

THE HEN HARRIER, *Circus cyaneus cyaneus* (Linnaeus)

FIELD IDENTIFICATION: ♂ a slender ashy grey hawk with black tips to its narrow wings. ♀ brown with a conspicuous white patch on rump.

The only occasion on which the Survey came across any harrier in Sikkim between November and April was at Phalut, 11,800 ft., in December—a single bird of undetermined species. Neither Meinertzhagen nor Schäfer obtained any specimens; therefore it is evident that the birds are by no means common, and possibly only odd transients occur on passage.

## THE CRESTED SERPENT EAGLE

### *Spilornis cheela cheela* (Latham)

*Falco Cheela* Latham, 1790, Index Ornith. 1: 14—India (=Lucknow *vide* W. L. Sclater).

F.B.I. 5: 96

LOCAL NAME:

SIZE: Kite+; heavier.

FIELD CHARACTERS: A large dark brown eagle with round, full, black-and-white crest (very prominent when erected); a conspicuous yellow patch at base of bill (cere), and unfeathered yellow legs. Underparts pale fulvous brown, ocellated and finely barred with black and white. In overhead aspect the light coloured body, broad rounded wings with a broad white bar along their entire length and a second less defined, a broad whitish band across tail and another ill-defined near its base, are diagnostic pointers. Sexes alike, but coloration very variable individually.

STATUS AND HABITAT: Common and generally distributed in the foothills and up to *c.* 7000 ft. elevation (Rangpo, Singtam, Martam, Kewzing, Singhik, Gangtok). Affects forested hillsides and valleys.

DISTRIBUTION OUTSIDE SIKKIM: W. Pakistan and N. India from Kashmir to Assam north of the Brahmaputra River; wintering south to the Gangetic Plain. Other races in peninsular India and Ceylon. The species extends through the Indochinese and Malaysian subregions to the Riu Kiu Islands and Philippines.

GENERAL HABITS: Sits upright in a high leafy tree overlooking a clearing or stream and pounces on prey moving on the ground—snakes, lizards, frogs; occasionally also small mammals and gamebirds such as junglefowl. Pairs much given to soaring aloft in circles, uttering the characteristic whistling screams *kek-kek-kek-kee.* These are prefaced by a quick-repeated short *whi-whi* or *pu-pu-pu* in undertone, audible only at short range. Particularly noisy when breeding.

NESTING: Not specifically recorded in Sikkim. *Season* (W. Himalayan foothills)—March to May. *Nest*—a large structure of sticks, sometimes lined with green leaves, high up in a tree in or near a forest clearing. *Egg*—a singleton, variable in colour and markings, mostly creamy or yellowish white boldly blotched with reddish brown. Size about 72×56 mm.

RACIAL CHARACTERISTICS, MEASUREMENTS, ETC: The Fauna gives the measurements (♂♀) as: Wing 468-507; tarsus 100-102; tail 295-315 mm.

An adult ♂ collected by Schäfer (Gangtok, 23 March) has Wing 419; in another ♂ recently obtained by Dr Ripley in central Nepal it is 495 mm.

Iris yellow with brownish mottling; supraorbital skin, eyelids and cere yellow, bill basally plumbeous, distally black; legs and feet dirty yellow; claws black.

## *Family* FALCONIDAE: Falcons

### THE HIMALAYAN FALCONET

*Microhierax caerulescens caerulescens* (Linnaeus)

*Falco caerulescens* Linnaeus, 1758, Syst. Nat., ed. 10, 1: 88—Asia=Bengal *ex* Edwards pl. 108.

**Plate 9, fig. 7** (facing p. 80)

F.B.I. 5: 52

LOCAL NAME: Ching-fin-nyel (Lepcha).

SIZE: Between Sparrow and Bulbul.

FIELD CHARACTERS: A diminutive black and white falcon, very shrike-like when perched and in silhouette. Pointed wings and flight—a series of rapid fluttering flaps followed by a graceful glide—reminiscent of the Ashy Swallow-Shrike (*Artamus fuscus*). Tail partly spread in flight, square-ended and rather triangular, with apex at base like a barbet's, but proportionately longer. *Above*, glossy black.

Forehead and sides of face white with a prominent black band through the eye and a broad white collar on hind-neck. *Below*, chin, throat, thighs and under tail-coverts deep ferruginous. Rest of lower plumage white suffused with rust. Sexes alike; female larger.

STATUS AND HABITAT: Resident (?). Not common, but frequent in the Teesta Valley at low altitudes—up to *c.* 2000 ft. (Rangpo, Singtam). Affects the outskirts of forest and old cultivation clearings with tall dead trees to serve as foraging bases.

DISTRIBUTION OUTSIDE SIKKIM: The Himalayan foothills and terai from Kumaon to Assam. The species extends to Burma, Thailand and south Indochina.

GENERAL HABITS: Pairs or small parties. Sits upright like a shrike on the bare topmost branches of tall trees. Predatory on dragonflies, beetles, butterflies, large grasshoppers, etc. Also takes lizards and small birds. Swoops to the ground to pick them off, or captures them in its talons in mid-air, circling back to its base very like a Swallow-Shrike, and with a steep upward glide before alighting. Insect held under foot, wings pulled off and dropped to the ground, and body torn to pieces before swallowing. Like *Artamus*, it is one of the few birds that habitually take butterflies. When perched, swings tail slowly up and down like the Blackwinged Kite (*Elanus*).

NESTING: Not recorded in Sikkim and very little known except that it lays in disused barbet-holes etc. in trees.

RACIAL CHARACTERISTICS, MEASUREMENTS, ETC: A specimen (♀) collected by the Sikkim Survey measures: Wing 110; bill (from cere) 11; tarsus 25; tail 63 mm. Two specimens taken recently by Dr Ripley in E. Nepal give Wing ♂ 101; ♀ 110 mm.

Iris brown; cere dark brown; bill basally yellowish green, distally black; legs and feet blackish slate.

The English name 'Redlegged Falconet' commonly used for this bird is incorrect and misleading.

## THE SHAHIN FALCON

### *Falco peregrinus peregrinator* Sundevall

*Falco peregrinator* Sundevall, 1837, Physiogr. Sällskapets Tidsskr. 1 (2): 117, pl. 4—at sea in lat. 6° 20′ N. between Ceylon and Sumatra, 70 Swedish miles (=700 English miles) off the Nicobars.

F.B.I. 5: 34

LOCAL NAME:

SIZE: House Crow+.

FIELD CHARACTERS: A powerful, broad-shouldered, streamlined hawk with long pointed wings and swift direct flight. *Above*, slaty blue with black head. *Below*, pinkish white and rusty red, boldly cross-barred with black from abdomen down. A dark moustachial stripe on either side of throat. Sexes alike, but female appreciably larger.

STATUS AND HABITAT: ? Rare, but possibly resident and breeding on suitable crags. A fine example was obtained by Colonel Meinertzhagen's shikari at *c.* 9000 ft. elevation near Lachung (21.ii.1952). A few unconfirmed sight records between November and April at 5000 to 8000 ft. Affects rugged mountainous country.

DISTRIBUTION OUTSIDE SIKKIM: Throughout the Indian Union, Pakistan and Ceylon; east to China. The Peregrine, in several other races, is a Holarctic breeding species found in the Americas, Europe, Asia, Africa and Australia.

GENERAL HABITS: Predatory on pigeons, chukor, pheasants and other birds. Stoops on them obliquely from aloft with tremendous velocity, striking in mid-air with the powerful hind claw. Flight extremely fast and direct—a few rapid wing beats followed by an arrow-like glide.

NESTING: Not recorded in Sikkim. *Season*—March to May. *Nest*—a stick-platform lined with wool and grass. Placed in a traditional site on a ledge or niche in a cliff-face. *Eggs*—3 or 4, variable, pale stone colour to brick-red, blotched and spotted with brick-red or reddish brown. Size about 52×41 mm.

RACIAL CHARACTERISTICS, MEASUREMENTS, ETC: The N. Asiatic race *calidus* which migrates to India in winter is paler above and white or almost white on the barred underparts.

The Fauna gives Wing ♂♂ 265-295; ♀♀ 312-342 mm. Col. Meinertzhagen's Sikkim skin (♂) measures: Wing 295; expanse 911 mm.

Iris brown; bill bluish slaty, base of lower mandible yellowish; cere yellow; legs and feet dull chrome yellow to orange-yellow; claws horny black.

## THE HIMALAYAN KESTREL

*Falco tinnunculus interstinctus* McClelland

*Falco interstinctus* McClelland, 1840 (1839), *Proc. Zool. Soc. London*, pt. 7: 154—Assam.

F.B.I. 5: 62

LOCAL NAME: Ting-kyi (Lepcha).

SIZE: Pigeon.

FIELD CHARACTERS: *Male: Above,* crown, nape and sides of neck ashy grey, finely streaked with blackish. A blackish cheek stripe. Back, scapulars and wing-coverts bright brick-red with pear-shaped black spots. Rump, upper tail-coverts and tail grey, the last tipped white and with a broad black subterminal bar. *Below,* vinous buff, streaked on breast and spotted on abdomen with black.

*Female: Above,* including crown and nape, pale rufous, cross-barred on back with black. *Below,* paler than in male and with the markings denser and more brown. Also slightly larger.

STATUS AND HABITAT: According to Stevens resident in the Rungbong Valley from 5000 ft. upwards. The Sikkim Survey came across it sparingly from *c.* 1000 ft. to 11,800 ft. between November and April (Rangpo, Martam, Dikchu, Gangtok, Gezing, Kewzing,

Phalut). Meinertzhagen recorded it between 4000 and 12,500 ft. (Changu) in winter, and F. N. Betts at 13,000 ft. (Thangu) in May.

Affects open scrubby hillsides with crags etc.; also fallow terraced cultivation.

DISTRIBUTION OUTSIDE SIKKIM: *Summer* (breeding), Central and E. Asia, Tibet, E. Himalayas, Assam, Burma. *Winter*, peninsular India and Ceylon. The European-West Asiatic-W. Himalayan nominate race is also a winter migrant to peninsular India. The species is widespread over Europe, Africa, Asia, east to Japan; wintering south to the Philippines.

GENERAL HABITS: Usually seen singly perched on a high cliff or dead tree whence it pounces on creeping prey. Has jealously guarded feeding territories. Also quarters the hillsides for booty stopping dead in mid-air now and again, head to wind, hovering on rapidly beating wings for many seconds at a time while intently scanning the ground below. When the quarry is sighted, the bird drops silently on it and bears it away in its talons. *Food:* lizards, mice, large insects and small birds. *Call:* a sharp *ki-ki-ki* or *tit . . . wee* uttered on the wing. In the breeding season pairs indulge in a spectacular aerobatic display, stooping and darting at each other and zooming upward in their stride, and hovering prettily on vibrating wings.

NESTING: *Season*—April to June. *Nest*—a sparse collection of twigs, roots and rubbish in a hole in a cliff. *Eggs*—3 to 6, roundish ovals, pale pinkish or yellowish stone, profusely speckled and blotched with various reds. Size about 40×32 mm.

RACIAL CHARACTERISTICS, MEASUREMENTS, ETC: Much darker above and below than the European-West Himalayan *tinnunculus*. A specimen collected by the Sikkim Survey (♀) measures Wing 260; bill (from cere) 22; tarsus 41.5; tail 179 mm. Hartert (Vög. pal. Fauna) gives for *saturatus* (=*interstinctus*) Wing ♂♂ 230-240; ♀♀ 240-260 mm.

Nine examples collected by Schäfer in Sikkim between 15 October and 3 December (Lachen, Manshitang, Lachung, Gangtok) have been determined by Stresemann as of the paler race *tinnunculus*. He measures these: Wing 2 ad. ♂♂ 241, 252; 2 ad. ♀♀ 256, 257; 1 ♀ juv. 274; 4 oo? juv. 255, 256, 260. 265 mm. The status of the two races here needs to be elucidated.

Iris dark brown; eyelids and cere chrome yellow; bill bluish grey black at top of upper mandible and commissure; legs and feet chrome yellow; claws black.

## *Family* Phasianidae: Pheasants, Partridges, Quails

### THE SNOW PARTRIDGE

*Lerwa lerwa* (Hodgson)

*Perdix lerwa* Hodgson, 1833, *Proc. Zool. Soc. London*, pt. 1: 107—Northern region of Nepal.

**Plate 10, fig. 3 (facing p. 81)**

F.B.I. 5: 433

LOCAL NAME: Lerwa (Bhutia).

SIZE: Partridge+.

FIELD CHARACTERS: A gregarious high altitude partridge with bright red legs and bill. *Above*, closely barred black and white. *Below*, largely deep chestnut, broadly streaked with whitish on abdomen and flanks. Under tail-coverts chestnut, streaked with black and tipped with whitish. Sexes alike.

STATUS AND HABITAT: Resident. Not uncommon at elevations between 10,000 and 15,000 ft. in winter (Singalila Ridge, Thangu, Yumthang, Changu); higher in summer. Affects alpine pastures, open hillsides above the tree-line covered with grass, lichen, ferns and rhododendron bushes and frequently interspersed with snow patches. Characteristic facies normally less bare and stony than of the Snowcock.

DISTRIBUTION OUTSIDE SIKKIM: The Himalayas from Afghanistan to Sikkim, S. Tibet to W. China.

GENERAL HABITS: Keeps in coveys of up to 20 birds or more which, when flushed, rise with a whirring and clapping of wings and scatter. Both Meinertzhagen and Ludlow describe them as tame and stupid birds, permitting themselves to be approached and fired at again and again till an entire covey may be wiped out. They are good eating. *Call:* a loud harsh whistle. *Food:* lichen, moss and vegetable shoots etc. with which a large amount of grit is swallowed.

NESTING: Not specifically recorded from Sikkim. Elsewhere *season*—May to July. *Nest*—a scrape on the ground, under cover of a rock or bush, well lined with moss and leaves. *Eggs*—3 to 5, smaller editions of those of the Snowcock, measuring about 55×36 mm.

RACIAL CHARACTERISTICS, MEASUREMENTS, ETC: Meinertzhagen gives for 14 Sikkim ♂♂ Wing 183-194; bill 21.5-25.5 mm. A ♀ collected by the Survey measured Wing 185; bill 24; tarsus 33; tail 108 mm.

Iris reddish brown to blood red; bill bright coral red; legs and feet orange-red to deep red, brightest in breeding season.

## THE SIKKIM SNOWCOCK

*Tetraogallus tibetanus aquilonifer* R. & A. Meinertzhagen

*Tetraogallus tibetanus aquilonifer* R. & A. Meinertzhagen, 1926, *Bull. Brit. Orn. Cl.* 46: 99—Interior of Sikkim.

F.B.I. 5: 432

LOCAL NAMES: Hrak-pa (Bhutia); Lapeha kengmo or kongmo (S. Tibet).

SIZE: Large domestic hen+.

FIELD CHARACTERS: A stout, dumpy, grey, black, white and chestnut game bird rather like a giant Grey Partridge. In overhead flight against a bright sky, edges of wings translucent white. *Male: Above,* crown, nape and hindneck grey. Back and rump grey with pale vermiculations, the rump scalloped with buff. A pale buff collar or lunar band across upper back and shoulders. Upper tail-coverts and central tail feathers rufous, with narrow wavy bands of blackish grey. A prominent white wing-patch. *Below,* chin, throat and breast white, separated by a black-edged grey band from rest of underparts which are white boldly streaked with black, broadest on flanks and lower abdomen.

*Female:* Similar, but grey breast-band with pale fulvous vermiculations and (white) neck and breast mottled with brownish.

STATUS AND HABITAT: Resident in the Tibetan plateau facies of Northern Sikkim, 15,000-17,000 ft. (Thangu, Gyagong). Affects bare rocky sparsely scrubbed hillsides and alpine pastures.

DISTRIBUTION OUTSIDE SIKKIM: Immediately adjacent S. Tibet. Overall, the species is found from the Pamirs through Tibet to western China.

GENERAL HABITS: Keeps in pairs or parties of 3 to 5; usually shy and wary. When alarmed, runs uphill with a waddling, rather goose-like gait, tail partially erected, displaying the white under tail-coverts prominently, and jerked now and again in the manner of a waterhen. Mounts a rock before taking off and coasts effortlessly on open wings in and out with the contours of the hillsides, or long distances across the valleys and from ridge to ridge. *Call:* a wild prolonged and penetrating whistle of several notes (usually 5) repeated with great persistence from a commanding rock; in cadence somewhat reminiscent of the Common Green Pigeon's call, in quality the Curlew's. The calls can be easily imitated, and serve to decoy the birds. When flushed and flying off in alarm a continuous cackle is uttered. *Food:* bulbs, tubers, roots, grass blades etc. along with which a great deal of grit is swallowed. An unpleasant peculiarity of the bird is the foul odour or 'stink' that emanates from the flesh, otherwise good eating, within a short time after it has been killed.

NESTING: Not specifically recorded from Sikkim. In adjacent Tibet *season*—chiefly May-June. *Nest*—a 'scrape' under protection of a rock or bush, usually lined with dead leaves and grass. *Eggs*—4 to 6, pale yellowish stone colour to rich reddish buff, scantily spotted with reddish brown, often more heavily at the *smaller* end. Size about 70×50 mm.

RACIAL CHARACTERISTICS, MEASUREMENTS, ETC: The Tibetan Snowcock (*T. tibetanus*) differs from the West Himalayan *T. himalayensis* in having the lower breast and abdomen white, streaked with black, as against uniform dark grey in the latter. *Aquilonifer* of Sikkim is darker than the other races (e.g. *tibetanus* and *centralis*) on head, nape and back with the white of the throat more restricted. There is no difference in size. A ♀ collected by Schäfer at Gyagong has Wing 271 mm.

Iris brown; bill horny purple, orange-red at base; orbital skin and eyelids slaty blue; legs and feet dull orange to deep red.

## THE COMMON HILL PARTRIDGE

### *Arborophila torqueola torqueola* (Valenciennes)

*Perdix torqueola* Valenciennes, 1826 (1825), Dict. Sci. Nat., (éd. Levrault), 38: 435—Bengal.

**Plate 10, fig. 2 (facing p. 81)**

F.B.I. 5: 386

LOCAL NAMES: Peura (Nepali); Kohumbut (Lepcha); Sipung-lulu (Tibetan).

SIZE: *c.* Grey Partridge or half-grown domestic fowl.

FIELD CHARACTERS: A dumpy, short-tailed, olive-brown partridge. *Male: Above,* olive-brown mottled with black and chestnut, and with a bright chestnut cap. A patch of bare crimson skin round eye. *Below,* chin and throat black, with a white moustachial streak. Breast grey, separated from black throat by a white band. Rest of underparts grey and white with some chestnut on the flanks.

*Female: Above,* similar but with crown brown, streaked with black. *Below,* chin and throat rufous, spotted with black. Breast brownish; throat-band chestnut instead of white.

STATUS AND HABITAT: Fairly common between about 6000 and 9000 ft. elevation (Chungthang, Lachen, Gangtok, Kewzing, Pemionche). A specimen was obtained by Stevens at Gnatong *c.* 12,000 ft. (now in Chicago Museum of Natural History). Affects forest broken up by ravines etc. with heavy evergreen undergrowth.

DISTRIBUTION OUTSIDE SIKKIM: The Himalayas between *c.* 4000 and 12,000 ft. from Garhwal to E. Assam, north of the Brahmaputra. The species ranges west to Chamba, east to Burma, Yunnan, Tonkin.

GENERAL HABITS: Gregarious. Keeps in coveys of 5 to 10 birds in dense undergrowth, scratching for food amongst the mulch and humus on the forest floor—seeds, shoots, berries and insects. Trusts to its legs for escape, but when suddenly flushed, as by a dog, flies strongly, manœuvring its way with ease through tree-trunks and other obstacles, often taking refuge up in a leafy branch. Roosts at night in trees, the covey sitting huddled together. *Call:* a single low mournful whistle *c.* 1½ seconds long, repeated every 2 or 3 seconds, reminiscent of the awkward intake whistle of a beginner. Also a 2- or 3-noted low whistle repeated 3 or 4 times in ascending scale, ending abruptly. Particularly vocal in the mornings and evenings.

NESTING: *Season*—April to June. *Nest*—normally a scrape in the ground lined with grass and leaves, in forest undergrowth. *Eggs*—3 to 5, white, glossy, about 45×34 mm.

RACIAL CHARACTERISTICS, MEASUREMENTS, ETC: Specimens obtained by Dr Biswas measure:

| | Wing | Bill | Tarsus | Tail |
|---|---|---|---|---|
| 1 ♂ | 157 | 22.5 | 45 | 70 mm. |
| 1 ♀ | 144 | 21 | 41 | 59 mm. |

A Sikkim series in Schäfer's collection gives Wing 7 ♂♂ 151-160 (av. 153.7); 1 ♀ 144 mm.

Iris brown to crimson-brown; bill dark brown to black; orbital skin dusky pink to crimson-red, legs and feet olive-brown to livid grey.

BLYTH'S, OR THE RUFOUSTHROATED HILL PARTRIDGE, *Arborophila rufogularis rufogularis* (Blyth), is a fairly common resident of a generally lower altitudinal zone, between *c.* 3000 and 8000 ft. The Survey collected no specimens, but I have examined several in the Chicago Museum of Natural History obtained at Lingtam (5500-6000 ft.) by the Suydam Cutting Expedition, including a breeding female of 26 February (1931).

FIELD IDENTIFICATION: *Male* differs from *torqueola* in having the crown olive-brown instead of bright chestnut, stippled with black; throat rufous instead of black, with a *black* band separating it from the grey breast, instead of white.

*Female* differs from male in having sparser black spots on chin and throat, and more white drops on breast and abdomen.

DISTRIBUTION: Kumaon east to the Mishmi Hills, between *c.* 4000 and 8000 ft. elevation.

A third species, THE REDBREASTED HILL PARTRIDGE, *Arborophila mandellii* Hume, occupies an altitudinal zone that descends still lower—to *c.* 1000 ft. Its ceiling is about the same as that of *rufogularis.* H. Stevens procured a specimen at Lingtam (*c.* 6000 ft.) on 29 February (1931), now in the Chicago Museum.

FIELD IDENTIFICATION: ♂♀ crown and nape dull chestnut-brown. Dark grey superciliary stripes from eyes continued behind to meet on upper hindneck. Lower neck (all round) and upper back reddish chestnut with black spots. Rest of upper parts olive, spotted and narrowly scalloped with black. *Below,* chin and throat pale olive-chestnut followed by white and black rings. A small white moustachial streak. Upper breast deep chestnut; lower breast to vent grey; flanks with some chestnut, and spotted with white. Under tail-coverts olive, with white spots and rufous mottling.

DISTRIBUTION: Hills north of Brahmaputra River from Sikkim to the Mishmis and SE. Tibet, 1000 to 8000 ft. or higher.

## THE BLOOD PHEASANT

### *Ithaginis cruentus affinis* Beebe

*Ithaginis cruentus affinis* Beebe, 1912, *Zoologica* 1: 91—British Sikkim.

**Plate 10, fig. 4 (facing p. 81)**

F.B.I. 5: 352

LOCAL NAMES: Chilme, Chilmili (Nepali); Samé, Semu, Soomoong-pho (Lepcha).

SIZE: Domestic fowl.

FIELD CHARACTERS: *Male* (illustrated): Overall grey above, yellowish grey below, streaked with yellowish. Forehead black; chin and throat crimson. Upper breast splashed with crimson. Crimson on wing-shoulders, under tail-coverts and in tail.

*Female:* General plumage finely vermiculated bright rufous-brown. Feathers of face and sides of head light ochre, contrasting with grey crown.

STATUS AND HABITAT: Common and abundant at elevations between *c.* 8500 and 15,000 ft., not descending much lower even in winter (Lachen, Lachung, Zemu, Dombang, Changu, Singalila Ridge, Thangu, Yumthang, Gnatong). Schäfer obtained a specimen at Chungthang, 5000 ft., in December—an exceptionally low altitude. Affects steep pine forest and stunted rhododendron and juniper scrub.

DISTRIBUTION: The high Himalayas, up to snowline, in Sikkim and W. Bhutan. The species ranges eastward through SE. Tibet to NE. Assam, N. Burma and W. China.

GENERAL HABITS: Gregarious; usually in coveys. Primarily a runner, swift of foot and loath to take wing even for escape. Feeds in open patches in dwarf rhododendron and juniper scrub, often digging into the deep snow with its short, stout grouse-like bill. Food almost exclusively moss, fern fronds and lichens. Tame to the point of stupidity, the members of a covey coming out to investigate a fluttering companion that has been shot and allowing bird after bird to be killed by the concealed hunter. The plumage has a musty repulsive odour even when the bird has been freshly killed. Stuart Baker considered it 'excellent for the table', but even with the locals its flesh passes as much inferior to other pheasants', while Meinertzhagen feelingly describes it as 'disgusting'! *Call:* likened to the squeal of a Kite.

NESTING: Very little known in the wild state. Said to nest on the ground, laying 10-12 eggs. Sherriff's observations on the allied race *tibetanus* suggest that the birds may be polyandrous as well as polygamous (*Ibis* 1944: 381).

RACIAL CHARACTERISTICS, MEASUREMENTS, ETC: As compared with nominate *cruentus* of adjoining Nepal, ♂ *affinis* lacks the crimson on forecrown; crimson on breast much reduced; flanks greener; throat crimson with black showing through. Specimens collected by the Sikkim Survey measure:

| | Wing | Bill | Tarsus | Tail | |
|---|---|---|---|---|---|
| 2 ♂♂ | 205-208 | 22-23.5 | 69-70 | 150-158 | mm. |
| 1 ♀ | 192 | 22 | 63 | 104 | mm. |

A series obtained by Dr Biswas near Dombang has Wing 5 ♂♂ 201-220 (av. 212.8); 2 ♀♀ 197, 202 mm. Schäfer's Sikkim series gives Wing 8 ♂♂ 196-212 (av. 206.0); 3 ♀♀ 187-202 (av. 195.0) mm.

Soft parts: *Male:* Iris yellowish brown, circumorbital skin bright scarlet or salmon-crimson; bill horny black, scarlet on cere, edges of base of mandibles and angle of gape; legs and feet (2 spurs on each leg) scarlet like orbital skin; claws horny black. *Female:* Iris yellowish brown; orbital skin orange-red (smaller patch and paler than in ♂); bill horny brown at base, orange-red at tip; legs and feet as in ♂ but without spurs. Soles of feet bright orange-crimson in both sexes.

In all the 10 ♂♂ dissected (winter) the testes were minute and black-pigmented.

## THE CRIMSON HORNED PHEASANT, or SATYR TRAGOPAN

### *Tragopan satyra* (Linnaeus)

*Meleagris Satyra* Linnaeus, 1758, Syst. Nat., ed. 10, 1: 157—Bengal, *ex* Edwards, pl. 116. *Errore*, the drawing on which Edwards's plate was based was probably made from a Nepal specimen.

**Plate 10, fig. 1 (facing p. 81)**

F.B.I. 5: 343

LOCAL NAMES: Monal (Hindi, Nepal); Omo Ḅap (Bhutia); Tar-rhyak (Lepcha); Chamdong (Tibetan).

SIZE: Domestic fowl.

FIELD CHARACTERS: *Male: Above,* head and crest black with crimson markings. *Below,* a bare deep blue patch or lappet on throat. Rest of underparts crimson with black-edged white spots or ocelli.

*Female: Above,* rufous-buff, vermiculated, barred and blotched with black and narrow pale ochre central streaks. Shoulder of wing tinged with crimson. *Below,* chin and throat whitish; breast like back but paler. Abdomen still paler with large white spots.

STATUS AND HABITAT: Not uncommon at elevations between *c.* 8000 and 12,000 ft. (Lachen, Lachung, Zemu, Karponang). Schäfer obtained specimens as low as 6000 ft. (Manshitang) in winter. Affects oak, deodar and rhododendron forest on *khuds* and steep hillsides with scrubby undergrowth.

DISTRIBUTION OUTSIDE SIKKIM: Eastern Garhwal, Nepal, Bhutan, Assam hills north of Brahmaputra River.

GENERAL HABITS: Not appreciably different from the pheasants described below. Keeps in pairs, but sometimes in small parties in the nonbreeding season. *Call* (of cock): an arresting loud *kya, kya, kya,* like the bleating of a goat kid.

NESTING: Little known in the wild state. *Season*—apparently May-June. *Nest*—an untidy jumble of twigs, placed up in the branches of a tree in forest. *Eggs*—2 to 4 (?) reddish buff, freckled all over with deeper brick-red. Size about 55×43 mm.

RACIAL CHARACTERISTICS, MEASUREMENTS, ETC: A good series collected by Schäfer in Sikkim measures: Wing 4 ♂♂ ad. 260, 267, 268, 271; 2 ♀♀ ad. 228, 232 mm. A Sikkim Survey ♀ has wing 216; tail 155 mm.

Soft parts: *Male:* Iris brown; bill brownish black, paler on distal half; orbital skin and lappet Prussian blue. When extended it shows a bright sage green edge with 4 or 5 brilliant scarlet triangular patches. Legs and feet dull fleshy, suffused with crimson in breeding season; spur pale grey-brown. *Female:* Iris brown; bill horny brown; legs fleshy grey-brown (Fauna).

## THE MONAL, or IMPEYAN PHEASANT

*Lophophorus impejanus* (Latham)

*Phasianus impejanus* Latham, 1790, Index Ornith. 2: 632—India (=Sikkim. Type locality fixed by Meinertzhagen, 1952, *Bull. Brit. Orn. Cl.* 72: 85).

F.B.I. 5: 335

LOCAL NAMES: Dafia (Nepali); Fo-dong (Lepcha); Chamdong (Bhutia, Sikkim).

SIZE: Domestic hen+.

FIELD CHARACTERS: A large, dumpy pheasant. *Above,* lustrous metallic bronze-green, purple and blue with a large white rump-patch and peacock-like crest on crown. Tail short, broad, square-cut, cinnamon-rufous. *Below,* velvety black.

*Female:* brown, mottled and streaked with paler and darker brown, with a short tuft on head and white throat.

STATUS AND HABITAT: Common and locally abundant above *c.* 9000 ft. elevation (Lachen, Lachung, Thangu, Karponang, Changu, Gnatong). Blanford recorded it at 14,000-15,000 ft., above the level of forest, in September (1870). Affects open deodar and rhododendron forest, and precipitous rocky and grass-covered slopes, often under heavy snow in winter.

DISTRIBUTION OUTSIDE SIKKIM: The Himalayas from E. Afghanistan to Bhutan and S. Tibet from *c.* 7000 ft. up to tree-line (14,000-15,000 ft.).

GENERAL HABITS: Single birds or parties of 3 or 4, consisting of a cock and 2 or 3 hens or of birds all of the same sex, dig assiduously with their powerful bills in the mornings and afternoons, often in deep snow, for tubers, roots and seeds. They also eat berries (e.g., *Cotoneaster*) and insects. When flushed in the open, the birds invariably plane downhill with wild ringing cries. When suddenly come upon in forest they fly up with much cackling into the branches of a deodar and sit motionless for a while, the hen in particular becoming remarkably obliterated by her coloration. The cock has no regular 'crow', but a whistling chuckle is occasionally uttered. In courtship he spreads out and erects his tail like a turkey cock, jerking it slightly. Whistler also describes a courtship flight—the cock leaping straight up into the air from a steep hillside, moving slowly with wings held high above line of back, tail partially spread and white rump very conspicuous.

NESTING: *Season*—April to June. *Nest*—a scrape in the ground under shelter of a rock or tree-trunk, in forest undergrowth. *Eggs*—4 to 6, pale yellowish or reddish buff, freckled and spotted with reddish brown. Size about 64×45 mm.

RACIAL CHARACTERISTICS, MEASUREMENTS, ETC: Schäfer's Sikkim series gives Wing 2 ♂♂ ad. 290, 295; 4 ♀♀ ad. 264, 268, 270, 274 mm. Specimens collected by the Survey measure:

| | Wing | Bill | Tarsus | Tail |
|---|---|---|---|---|
| 1 ♂ | 300 | 54 | 80 | 223 mm. |
| 1 ♀ | 280 | 48 | 76 | 189 mm. |

Iris brown; circumorbital skin ♂ deep azure (almost royal) blue, ♀ paler blue; bill horny blackish, edge of both mandibles greyish white; legs and feet olive-brown, each scale on tarsus and toes margined with black; claws and spurs horny black.

## THE BLACKBACKED KALEEJ PHEASANT

*Lophura leucomelana melanota* (Hutton)

*Euplocomus melanotus* 'Blyth'=Hutton, 1848, *Jour. Asiat. Soc. Bengal* 17 (2): 694, in text—Darjeeling.

F.B.I. 5: 323

LOCAL NAME: Kar-rhyak (Lepcha).

SIZE: Domestic fowl.

FIELD CHARACTERS: *Male: Above,* black glossed with steel blue. Lower back, rump and upper tail-coverts with narrow white edges to the feathers. A long, pointed, glossy black, recumbent crest. Tail black, comparatively long, arching and pointed. Bare scarlet-crimson facial patches around eyes. *Below,* chin, throat and fore-neck glossy blackish with white streaks. Feathers of breast and flanks lanceolate, dull brown with whitish scalloping.

*Female:* Dark rich brown with narrow whitish scalloping, shorter brown crest and scarlet eye-patches.

STATUS AND HABITAT: Fairly common, chiefly in the foothills and up to *c.* 6000 ft. elevation (Rangpo, Singtam, Singhik, Lingtam, Temi, Gangtok). Schäfer took specimens at *c.* 9000 ft. (Lachen) in June and November, at which altitude Ludlow also found it in Bhutan in summer. Affects densely scrubbed ravines etc. in forest biotope.

DISTRIBUTION OUTSIDE SIKKIM: Western Bhutan. The contiguous Western and Eastern Himalayas respectively are inhabited by allied races. The species overall ranges through Burma and the Indochinese subregion to S. China and Hainan Island.

GENERAL HABITS: Similar to the Red Junglefowl. Pairs or small parties come out to scratch for food at the edge of forest clearings, freshly sown fields and jungle tracks in the mornings and afternoons. *Food:* grain, shoots, tubers, insects, small reptiles, etc. *Call* (or 'crow') of cock: a loud whistling chuckle. A peculiar 'drumming', like a cloth fluttering in the breeze, is produced with the wings in the breeding season, presumably as a challenge to rival cocks.

NESTING: *Season*—March to May. *Nest*—a scrape in the ground lined with dry grass and bamboo leaves, amongst dense undergrowth in ravines etc. *Eggs*—6 or 7, buff, glossy, broad ovals, about 50×40 mm.

RACIAL CHARACTERISTICS, MEASUREMENTS, ETC: In the typical West Himalayan race, *leucomelana*, the upper plumage is black, edged (or scalloped) with white; rump barred white; breast whitish. In the adjoining E. Himalayan *lathami* upper plumage black; rump boldly barred white; breast black.

Delacour[1] gives for ♂♂ Wing 215-240; tail 238-300 mm. A series collected by Schäfer in Sikkim measures: Wing 6 ♂♂ ad. 233-248 (av. 238.7); 6 ♀♀ ad. 211-222 (av. 215.0) mm.

Iris hazel to orange-brown; facial skin scarlet-crimson; bill greenish horny, black at base, paler at tip; legs and feet slaty or greenish brown.

## THE RED JUNGLEFOWL

### *Gallus gallus murghi* Robinson & Kloss

*Gallus ferrugineus murghi* Robinson and Kloss, 1920, *Rec. Ind. Mus.* 19: 14, 15—Chirala, Gaya District, Bihar.

F.B.I. 5: 295

LOCAL NAMES: Natsa-pia, Nagseya (Bhutia); Paz-ok-chi, Tankling (Lepcha).

SIZE: Domestic village fowl.

FIELD CHARACTERS: Both sexes very similar to the 'Game Bantam' breed of domestic poultry. *Male: Above*, chiefly glossy deep orange-red with long yellowish neck-hackles. Long, sickle-shaped metallic black tail. *Below*, blackish brown.

*Female: Above*, crown dull rufous. Forehead and supercilia bright chestnut, continued below to meet in a loop on foreneck. Rest of upper parts reddish brown, finely vermiculated with buff. *Below*, pale-shafted light rufous brown.

STATUS AND HABITAT: Resident at the lower altitudes, ascending to *c.* 6000 ft. (Rangpo, Singtam, Martam, Pakyong, Temi, Chungthang, Gangtok). Affects forest as well as scrub jungle near cultivation.

DISTRIBUTION OUTSIDE SIKKIM: Throughout the lower Himalayas, normally to *c.* 6000 ft., from NE. West Pakistan to E. Assam. Assam, Bengal, Bihar, Orissa, E. Madhya Pradesh. The species extends through Burma and the Indochinese subregion south to China and Java.

GENERAL HABITS: Keeps in small parties of a cock and 3 or 4 hens. Usually very shy. Comes out in the early mornings and afternoons at the edge of harvested fields and cart tracks, etc., to glean

[1] The Pheasants of the World. Country Life Ltd., London (1951).

scattered grain or scratch cattle and mule droppings. Also eats vegetable shoots, worms, lizards, etc. Bamboo seeds when in flush are always a great attraction. Roosts at night high up in trees and bamboo clumps. *Call:* unmistakably like that of the domestic Bantam cock, but shriller and with a more abrupt ending. Cocks indulge in much crowing in the early mornings and before retiring for the night, answering one another over long distances.

NESTING: *Season*—mainly March to May. *Nest*—a scrape in the ground lined with dry grass and bamboo leaves, in forest undergrowth. *Eggs*—5 or 6, like those of the domestic fowl, variable, pale buff to pale reddish brown. Size about 46×35 mm.

RACIAL CHARACTERISTICS, MEASUREMENTS, ETC: The Fauna gives the Wing as: ♂ 203-244; ♀ 177-196 mm. In 2 ♀♀ collected by Schäfer in Sikkim it measures 197, 209 mm.

Iris ♂ reddish brown or orange-red, ♀ brown; comb and wattles scarlet-crimson; lappets (♂) white or pinkish; bill base reddish in ♂, yellowish or pale fleshy in ♀ upper mandible brown, lower pale horn; legs and feet slaty brown.

## *Family* CHARADRIIDAE:

### *Subfamily* CHARADRIINAE: Plovers

### THE SPURWINGED PLOVER

***Vanellus spinosus duvaucelii*** (Lesson)

*Charadrius Duvaucelii* Lesson, 1826, Dict. Sci. Nat., (éd. Levrault), 42: 38—Calcutta.

F.B.I. 6: 184

SIZE: Partridge+.

FIELD CHARACTERS: Overall aspect pied black and white. *Above*, crown, a full crest, and nape black. Back light brown; upper tail-coverts white. Tail white at base, black on terminal half. Wings black and white. *Below*, chin, throat, and cheeks black bordered with white. Upper breast white shading to brownish grey lower down. Centre of abdomen black; rest of underparts white. Sexes alike.

In flight, which is with deliberate steady flaps like the Redwattled Lapwing, the black wing-tips with a large white patch on wings, black markings on head, and black abdomen, are conspicuous.

STATUS AND HABITAT: Resident. A fluviatile low elevation plover, fairly common on the Teesta River up to *c.* 1000 ft. (Rangpo, Singtam). Affects sand and shingle banks.

DISTRIBUTION OUTSIDE SIKKIM: Kashmir and through the Garhwal,

Nepal, and Sikkim terai to Assam, E. Pakistan and the Indochinese subregion. Also Uttar Pradesh and Madhya Pradesh.

GENERAL HABITS: Keeps in pairs or small parties on sandy islets and shingle banks in rivers. Runs about with mincing steps in spurts, picking up insects, molluscs, etc. *Call:* a single-noted, insistent, rapidly repeated *did, did, did,* etc. of the same timbre as the Redwattled Lapwing's *did-he-do-it* cries. It is also reminiscent of the monosyllabic cries of the Stone Curlew (*Burhinus*), but is shriller.

NESTING: Apparently not recorded from Sikkim territory, but it doubtless breeds on the shingle banks and islets in the rivers at the lowest elevations. *Season*—March to May. *Nest*—an unlined shallow depression in the sand. *Eggs*—3 or 4, variable, pale stone to olive-stone colour, profusely blotched and speckled with brown to black. Size about 42×30 mm.

RACIAL CHARACTERISTICS, MEASUREMENTS, ETC: This plover possesses a long, sharp, curved, horny spur on the bend of the wing; a long, slender, reticulated tarsus; and no hind toe.

Specimens collected by the Sikkim Survey measure:

| | Wing | Bill | Tarsus | Tail |
|---|---|---|---|---|
| 1 ♂ | 206 | 34 | 65 | 92 mm. |
| 1 ♀ | 199 | 34 | 64 | 89 mm. |

A '♂' from Sikkim in Schäfer's collection has Wing 191 mm.

Iris brown; bill, legs, feet and claws black. Tibia bare for *c.* 20 mm. above tarsal joint, black.

## THE PAMIRS LESSER SAND PLOVER

*Charadrius mongolus atrifrons* Wagler

*Charadrius atrifrons* Wagler, 1829, Isis von Oken 22, col. 650—Bengal.

F.B.I. 6: 174

LOCAL NAME:

SIZE: Quail.

FIELD CHARACTERS: A typical little plover with thick head, bare greenish grey legs and short pigeon-like black bill. In summer (breeding plumage): *Above,* forehead and sides of head black; crown and hindneck rust coloured or pale chestnut. Rest of upper parts pale sandy brown. *Below,* upper breast and flanks pale chestnut, separated from the glistening white throat by a blackish half-collar. Sexes alike.

STATUS AND HABITAT: *Summer* (breeding) visitor to the Tibetan plateau facies of N. Sikkim (Thangu, Gyagong, Gayamtashana). Arrives in April/May; leaves September/October. Frequents boggy ground with spongy semi-floating grass-covered 'knobs' or mounds along sprawling ill-drained streams etc.

DISTRIBUTION OUTSIDE SIKKIM: *Summer* (breeding), N. Asia south to Kashmir, Ladakh, S. Tibet, W. China. *Winter,* the seaboard of India, Ceylon, Andamans.

GENERAL HABITS: Met with mostly in pairs scattered over bogs in jealously guarded breeding territories. Runs about with rapid mincing steps, stopping abruptly from time to time and dipping forward obliquely to pick up food—insects, worms and tiny molluscs. Pursuit of intruders and territorial rivalry noticeable everywhere. Chasing birds utter a hard grating *tit-tit-trr-trrweet* of the quality of the 'stone-on-ice' calls of the Common Nightjar (*Caprimulgus asiaticus*).

NESTING: *Season*—May to July. *Nest*—an unlined scrape or hollow in dry shingle and sand around the margin of a bog. *Eggs*—3, pale stone colour to khaki or reddish buff, stippled with blackish or deep red-brown. Size about 40×27 mm.

RACIAL CHARACTERISTICS, MEASUREMENTS, ETC: For a discussion of the races of *C. mongolus* see Stresemann (*Ornithologische Monatsberichte*, 1940, pp. 51-56). Schäfer's Sikkim specimens are measured by him as follows:

| | Wing | Tarsus | Bill |
|---|---|---|---|
| 4 ♂♂ ad. | 122-124 | 16-17 | 33-34 mm. |
| 2 ♀♀ ad. | 125-126 | 17 | 32 mm. |

Iris brown; bill black; legs and feet yellowish olive to olive-slate.

## *Subfamily* SCOLOPACINAE: Sandpipers, Snipe, Woodcock, etc.

### THE REDSHANK

**_Tringa totanus eurhinus_ (Oberholser)**

*Totanus totanus eurhinus* Oberholser, 1900, *Proc. U. S. Nat Mus.* 22: 207—Tso Moriri Lake, 15,000 ft., Ladakh.

F.B.I. 6: 222

LOCAL NAME:

SIZE: Partridge+.

FIELD CHARACTERS: A large-sized sandpiper. *Above*, greyish brown with white lower back and rump. Tail white, barred with brown. *Below*, white, finely streaked with brown on breast. Legs orange-red. Sexes alike.

In flight, the white rump, a broad white border to trailing edge of wing (secondaries), and long slender *red* legs projecting behind, are leading pointers to its identity.

In summer (breeding) plumage upper parts somewhat streaked and spotted with black and fulvous, and breast more heavily streaked with brown.

STATUS AND HABITAT: A breeding bird of the Tibetan facies of N. Sikkim where Schäfer procured many adults and flightless young in July-August at 16,000-17,000 ft. altitude (Gyagong, Gayamtashana Lake). I have examined a pair (♂♀) in the Chicago Museum of

Natural History collected at Thangu (*c.* 14,000 ft.) by V. S. La Personne on 22 May (1931).

Not recorded either by Stevens or Meinertzhagen, and only a solitary example noted by the Loke-Sálim Ali Survey on the Teesta River at Singtam (1000 ft.)—6 December 1952. Presumably migrates from its high breeding grounds to its winter quarters in the Indian plains without stopping in lower Sikkim.

DISTRIBUTION OUTSIDE SIKKIM: *Summer* (breeding), Central and E. Asia. *Winter*, south to India, Ceylon, Pakistan, Burma, Malaya, S. China.

The species extends from Great Britain and W. Europe over practically the entire Palaearctic Region, wintering in Africa and S. Asia.

GENERAL HABITS: Typical sandpiper. Keeps to marshes in parties or flocks (pairs in summer) probing in the soft mud and shallow water for tiny molluscs, insects, worms, etc. *Call:* a shrill, piping, *tiwee-tiwee-tiwee* or *tew-tew-tew,* chiefly uttered on the wing. In the breeding season the male has a sweet song of strung-out quick-repeated single notes delivered during his pretty display flight.

NESTING: Not specifically recorded from Sikkim. *Season* (Tibet)—May to July. *Nest*—a deepish grass-lined scrape in the ground, on grassy bog-land surrounding shallow lakes. *Eggs*—normally 4, yellowish stone, drab or khaki, blotched with purple-brown or blackish brown, with faint secondary blotches of grey. They are inordinately large for the size of the bird, measuring about 45×31 mm.

RACIAL CHARACTERISTICS, MEASUREMENTS, ETC: Stresemann measures Schäfer's fine Sikkim series as follows:

Wing/Bill (exposed culmen)

6 ♂♂ 154/45, 154/41, 159/44, 159/46, 160/46.5, 166/45 mm.

5 ♀♀ 158/41, 158/48, 159/48, 160/48, 161/42 mm.

They agree in size with birds from Ladakh (type locality of *eurhinus*) and in colour with those from N. Kansu and Kham. He therefore considers Meinertzhagen's *terrignotae* (type locality Kuku Nor) synonymous with *eurhinus*.

Iris brown; bill black, reddish on basal one-third; legs and feet orange-red; claws black.

## THE GREEN SANDPIPER

### *Tringa ochropus* Linnaeus

*Tringa Ocrophus* (*sic*) Linnaeus, 1758, Syst. Nat., ed. 10, 1: 149—Europe, restricted to Sweden.

F.B.I. 6: 215

LOCAL NAME:

SIZE: Quail or Snipe.

FIELD CHARACTERS: A medium-sized sandpiper. *Above*, dark brown with a marked greenish bronze gloss. Rump and tail white (with fine black barring visible only at close range). *Below*, white, finely streaked with brownish on throat and flanks. Sexes alike.

The dark upper plumage contrasting sharply with the white rump, tail and underparts, absence of a wing-bar, and the shrill piping *ti-tui* or *twee-twee-twee* uttered as the bird flushes and flies away, are diagnostic.

STATUS AND HABITAT: Evidently an uncommon passage migrant in spring and autumn between its Palaearctic breeding grounds and the Indian plains. Sporadic solos are seen at low elevations chiefly at puddles (Rangpo, Singtam), but rare.

Schäfer collected two adults at Gyagong (*c.* 16,000 ft., N. Sikkim) at the end of July and in August, which were probably early autumn migrants on passage. Wing ♂ 141; ♀ 141 mm.

A smaller sandpiper, occasionally seen singly on the rivers and streams at low elevations (Rangpo, Singtam) is the COMMON SANDPIPER, *Tringa hypoleucos* Linnaeus. *Above*, olive-brown including rump and tail of which only the outer feathers are white. *Below*, white with a faint diffuse dusky band across breast.

In flight, which consists of spurts of series of rapid stiffly vibrating flaps close over the water, a narrow wing-bar is prominent. A characteristic sharp piping *tee-tee-tee* is uttered as the bird flies off.

A Palaearctic breeding species as far south as Kashmir. Winter visitor to all India and S. Asia, Africa and Australia.

## THE EASTERN SOLITARY SNIPE

### *Capella solitaria solitaria* (Hodgson)

*Gallinago solitaria* Hodgson, 1831, Gleanings in Science 3: 238—Nepal.

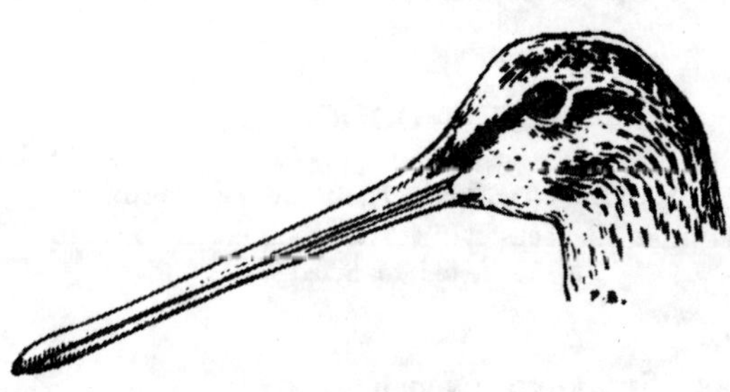

Eastern Solitary Snipe, about two-thirds

F.B.I. 6: 257

LOCAL NAME: Bharka (Nepali).

SIZE: Quail+; larger than the Common Snipe.

FIELD CHARACTERS: A typical, concealingly coloured marsh bird—mixed brown, black, rufous, fulvous and white—with a straight slender bill about 3 inches long. Difficult to tell from other snipe in the field except by its larger size, paler tone of coloration and solitary habit. Sexes alike.

STATUS AND HABITAT: Uncommon. Resident between *c.* 9000 and 15,000 ft. altitude, partially descending to a lower zone in winter. Specimens taken between October and January at Thangu, Zemu, Lachung. Affects ill-drained bogs, often semi-frozen, interspersed with spongy grassy hummocks or mounds, bordered and partly overgrown with rhododendron and other scrub.

DISTRIBUTION OUTSIDE SIKKIM: *Summer* (breeding), N. and C. Asia east to Japan, south to Sikkim. *Winter*, China, Burma, and sporadically eastern India.

GENERAL HABITS: Solitary; terrestrial; swamp-dwelling. Two or three widely separated individuals occasionally flushed on the same bog. Flight slower and heavier than the Common Snipe's. Seldom flies far before alighting, even when fired at. The characteristic *scape* or *pench*, uttered as the bird flushes, is comparatively deeper and harsher. *Food:* worms, grubs, minute snails, etc.

NESTING: The eggs recorded by Stuart Baker as obtained by Mandelli's collectors in the Darjeeling neighbourhood (at *c.* 11,000 ft.) were originally ascribed by Mandelli himself to the Wood Snipe, *G. nemoricola*! The clutches taken by Masson on the Singalila Ridge (10,000 ft.) are also of doubtful identity since the owners were not collected.

RACIAL CHARACTERISTICS, MEASUREMENTS, ETC: Wing exceeds 150 mm.; outer edges of scapulars broadly white.

A specimen (♀) obtained by the Sikkim Survey measures: Wing 171 (165 dry); bill 81; tarsus 35; tail 71 mm.

Schäfer's Sikkim examples have Wing 1 ♂ 162; 1 ♀ 159 mm.

Iris brown; bill olive-brown, blackish on terminal one-third of upper and half of lower mandible; legs and feet olive; claws horny brown.

## THE WOODCOCK

*Scolopax rusticola rusticola* Linnaeus

*Scolopax Rusticola* Linnaeus, 1758, Syst. Nat., ed. 10, 1: 146—Europe, restricted to Sweden.

F.B.I. **6**: 252

LOCAL NAME: Sim kukra (Nepali).

SIZE: Partridge.

FIELD CHARACTERS: A stout, obliteratingly-coloured brown snipe-like bird with the characteristic long, straight slender bill, soft and swollen at the tip, and comparatively short legs.

*Above*, brownish grey blotched and barred with black, rufous and buff. Nape and rump cross-barred black and rufous. *Below*, chin white; rest of underparts brownish white cross-barred with dark brown. Sexes alike.

Viewed in flight from slightly above, the wings look disproportionately short, narrow, pointed and curving scimitar-like. The bill points obliquely groundward; the tail, fanned-out in banking, gives the bird a blunt-ended appearance.

STATUS AND HABITAT: Not uncommon in suitable damp, wooded spots—ravines, glens, spinneys in cardamom cultivation, etc.—between *c.* 4000 and 9000 ft. elevation (Gangtok, Temi, Rinchinpong, Chungthang, Lachen, Laohung).

DISTRIBUTION OUTSIDE SIKKIM: The Himalayas from Kashmir to Bhutan, and perhaps farther east, normally between *c.* 7000 and 10,000 ft. Partial winter migrant to the Nilgiris and other S. Indian and Ceylon hills. Also occurs in Europe, N. Asia east to Japan.

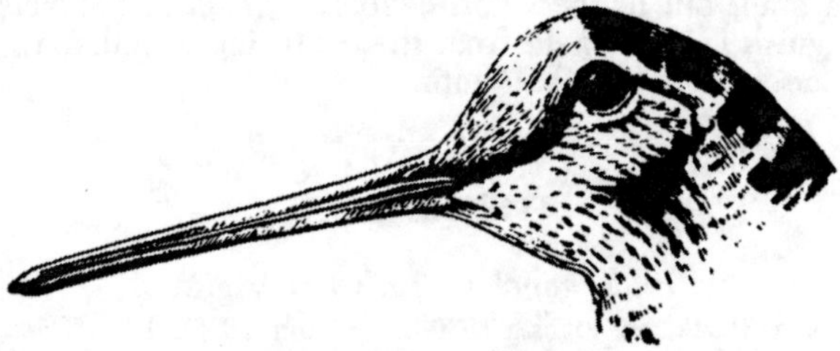

Woodcock, about two-thirds

GENERAL HABITS: Usually solitary or in separated pairs. Terrestrial and largely crepuscular and nocturnal. Probes into soft wet earth with its bill for worms and grubs, its presence in a likely locality being betrayed by the honeycomb-like holes left where the bird has been feeding. Flight rather sluggish, resembling the Painted Snipe's, but the bird is an adept at turning and twisting its way through the tree-trunks in its wooded habitat; therefore in spite of its large size, it is not easy to shoot when flushed.

In the breeding season the male (?) frequently indulges in its characteristic aerial display known as 'roding', at dusk and dawn. This consists of flapping slowly in a high arc across open glades or partially dry 'pokhries', to the accompaniment of a bat-like squeak at intervals.

NESTING: No specific record from Sikkim. Elsewhere (W. Himalayas), *season*—April to July. *Nest*—a depression in the ground lined with dry leaves, well concealed amongst bracken, rhododendron or other undergrowth, preferably near a wooded stream. *Eggs*—4, pale clay to deep buff, blotched with pale reddish brown and grey. Size about 45×35 mm. Both sexes share in incubation and tending the young.

RACIAL CHARACTERISTICS, MEASUREMENTS, ETC: A curious peculiarity of the Woodcock is its abnormally high and backwardly placed eyes—literally 'at the back of its head'.

A specimen (♂) collected by the Sikkim Survey measures: Wing 201; bill 89; tarsus 34; tail 85 mm.

Iris brown; bill pale horny brown, darker at tip, paler at base of lower mandible; legs and feet olive-brown; claws horny brown. Weight 8 to 16 oz.

A specimen of TEMMINCK'S STINT, *Calidris temminckii* (Leisler), was obtained by Schäfer in N. Sikkim at *c.* 17,000 ft. ('Kiang-Lager') on 1 October (1938). There is no previous or subsequent record of its occurrence in Sikkim, and presumably the bird was on passage from its northern Palaearctic breeding grounds to its winter quarters in peninsular India.

SIZE: Quail−.

FIELD CHARACTERS: A miniature facsimile of the Common Sandpiper. *Above,* mottled dark greyish brown or dusky. *Below,* white. The *white* outer tail feathers and *yellowish green* or *yellowish brown* legs distinguish it in the field from the confusingly similar Little Stint. Wing of the specimen (♂) 97 mm.

## THE IBISBILL

*Ibidorhyncha struthersii* Vigors

*Ibidorhyncha Struthersii* Vigors, 1830-31 (March 1832), *Proc. Comm. Zool. Soc. London:* 174—Himalayas.

**Plates 10, fig. 6,** (facing p. 81) and **26** (facing p. 337)

F.B.I. 6: 196

LOCAL NAME:

SIZE: Partridge+.

FIELD CHARACTERS: A greyish brown plover-like bird with a black facial mask and breast-band, and long, downcurved red bill. *Above,* anterior face (including throat) black. Rest of upper parts largely ashy grey-brown; rump feathers with basal brown markings. Tail ashy grey with narrow, wavy, blackish cross-bars, broad near tips of the outer feathers. A partially concealed white wing-patch. *Below,* sides of head, neck, and upper breast bluish grey. A broad black gorget, separated from upper breast by a narrow white band. Rest of lower plumage white. Sexes alike.

In flight, which resembles the Stone Curlew's, the neck and long curved bill are outstretched, and the posterior end of the bird looks rather truncated. The white wing-patches are conspicuous.

STATUS AND HABITAT: Not common. *Summer* (breeding), between *c.* 8500 and 14,000 ft. (Lachen, Lachung, Yumthang, Thangu, Yatung). Schäfer collected a pair as high as 16,500 in N. Sikkim ('Kiang-Lager') on 1 October. *Winter,* down to the lowest stream levels (Rangpo, Singtam). Affects shingle beds and rock-pebble islets in flat, sprawling stretches of rivers, e.g. the Teesta.

DISTRIBUTION OUTSIDE SIKKIM: *Summer* (breeding), Turkestan and Gilgit to W. China and southward along the Himalayas from Kashmir to Sikkim and probably farther east. *Winter,* the Himalayan foothills to almost plains level.

GENERAL HABITS: Keeps in pairs or small parties on flat shingle banks or islets in comparatively placid stretches of glacier streams. The rounded outline and grey-brown coloration of the back obliterate it astonishingly within this environment of smooth water-worn pebbles, so that the bird becomes completely invisible, even at a few feet's range, unless it moves. Feeds on insects, molluscs, etc. amongst the shingle or at the water's edge, sometimes wading in up to the belly and with the head fully submerged. Jerkily bobs head up and down and slowly wags the tail end, very like a Greenshank. *Call:* a loud ringing single note or 'whistle' quickly repeated: *tee-ti-ti-ti-ti-tee* of distinctly sandpiper quality. At the time of the male (?) relieving his mate at the nest I have recorded a very pretty trilling song, reminiscent of something between the nuptial song of the Spotted Sandpiper (*Tringa glareola*) and the Curlew (*Numenius arquata*).

NESTING: An early nester, often commencing at the end of March even before the ground in its elevated habitat is clear of snow. A nest found by the Survey at Yakthang, *c.* 13,000 ft. (near Thangu), on 19 April was typical: a slight unlined depression on a shingly islet in amongst rounded grey water-worn stones. *Eggs*—4, greenish grey, speckled all over with umber brown, sparsely at the small end. Size about 42×28 mm. The breeding biology of the Ibisbill deserves careful study as I observed certain behavioural features suggesting possible polygamy or polyandry.

RACIAL CHARACTERISTICS, MEASUREMENTS, ETC: The Fauna gives the measurements (♂ ♀) as: Wing 230-245; bill 68-80; tarsus 47-49; tail 113-120 mm. Schäfer's Sikkim skins have Wing 3 ♂♂ 237, 242, 243; 1 ♀ 244 mm.

Iris red; bill dull reddish brown to crimson; legs and feet livid and greenish grey to blood red.

## *Family* COLUMBIDAE: Pigeons, Doves

### THE PINTAILED GREEN PIGEON

*Treron apicauda apicauda* (Blyth)

*Treron apicauda* 'Hodgson'=Blyth, after May 1846 (1845), *Jour. Asiat. Soc. Bengal* 14 (2): 854—SE. Himalayas and hill ranges of Assam; common at Darjeeling.

Plate 11, fig. 6 (facing p. 96)

F.B.I. 6: 199

LOCAL NAME: Sang-pong (Lepcha).

SIZE: Pigeon.

FIELD CHARACTERS: Overall yellowish green with a long pointed tail and two conspicuous yellow bars in the black wings. *Male:* with a broad greyish olive-green collar on hindneck. *Below,* greenish yellow. Breast washed with orange-pink; under tail-coverts cinnamon, margined with whitish.

*Female:* duller, with no greyish olive hind collar or orange wash on breast.

STATUS AND HABITAT: Met with by the Survey fairly commonly in winter (November-March) in the foothills and up to *c.* 6500 ft. (Rangpo, Singtam, Temi, Kewzing, Chungthang, Gangtok), and procured by Schäfer at Lachen (*c.* 9000 ft.) in September. Moves about a great deal altitudinally and otherwise, depending on food supply. Affects forest.

DISTRIBUTION OUTSIDE SIKKIM: The lower Himalayas from Kumaon to E. Assam, normally to *c.* 6000 ft. The species extends eastward through the Indochinese subregion.

GENERAL HABITS: An arboreal fruit pigeon, only rarely descending to the ground at water or salt licks. Flocks clamber about among fruit-laden twigs with a parakeet-like hand-over-hand action, often hanging head down and lunging out to reach a drupe. Perfectly camouflaged amongst the foliage, and quite invisible when they 'freeze' on alarm. The unsuspected numbers that will dash out of a tree on the firing of a gun is quite amazing. Flight swift and direct, accompanied by a metallic whirring sound. *Call:* a number of mellow, musical whistles very like those of the Kokla Green Pigeon, transcribed as *ko-kla-oi-oi-oi-oilli-illio-kla.*

In common with other green pigeons, and also hawks, it has the habit of sitting fluffed out on the topmost bare branches of a lofty forest tree on wintry mornings to catch the first rays of the sun. Feeding commences only after the sun is well up.

NESTING: *Season*—chiefly April-May. *Nest*—the characteristic flimsy twig-platform of all pigeons, high up in a forest tree. *Eggs*—2, white, about 32×24 mm.

RACIAL CHARACTERISTICS, MEASUREMENTS, ETC: The Fauna gives the measurements (♂♀) as: Wing 160-175; tail 220-254 mm. An adult ♀ collected by Schäfer at Lachen has Wing 178 mm.

Iris lake red; ocular area blue; bill basally cobalt-blue, distal half of upper mandible green; legs and feet crimson.

## THE WEDGETAILED GREEN PIGEON

### *Treron sphenura sphenura* (Vigors)

*Vinago sphenura* Vigors, 1832 (1831), *Proc. Comm. Zool. Soc. London:* 173—Himalayas.

F.B.I. 5: 200

LOCAL NAME: Kuhu (Lepcha).

SIZE: Pigeon.

FIELD CHARACTERS: Overall yellowish green, similar to the Pintailed Green Pigeon but without the central 'pins' in the graduated tail. *Male: Above,* crown tinged with orange-rufous. A variable amount of maroon on back and scapulars. *Below,* chin and throat yellow; breast pale orange-pink.

*Female* lacks rufous on crown and maroon patch on back.

STATUS AND HABITAT: Resident in the foothills and up to *c.* 8000 ft. (Temi, Singhik, Rinchinpong, Chungthang, Gangtok). Commoner than the Pintailed species, but moves about locally and seasonally, depending on food supply—ripening of various fruits and berries. Affects forest.

DISTRIBUTION OUTSIDE SIKKIM: The lower Himalayas from Kashmir to extreme NE. Assam. Assam hills south of the Brahmaputra; Burma. The species extends to Yunnan, the Indochinese subregion, Malaya and Hainan.

GENERAL HABITS: Not appreciably different from those of the Pintailed Green Pigeon. *Call:* as described above. Like other green pigeons, a good sporting bird affording a variety of shots as it flashes through the forest trees. Also good eating.

NESTING: *Season*—April-June. *Nest* and *Eggs*—similar to the foregoing.

RACIAL CHARACTERISTICS, MEASUREMENTS, ETC: The Fauna gives the measurements (♂♀) as: Wing 173-185; tail 114-139 mm. Specimens collected by Schäfer in Sikkim have Wing 1 ♂ 173; 3 ♀♀ 165, 176, 178 mm.

Iris pinkish or reddish orange with a blue inner ring; bill basally blue, distally grey; legs and feet cherry red.

## HODGSON'S, or THE NEPAL MAROONBACKED IMPERIAL PIGEON

*Ducula badia insignis* Hodgson

*Ducula Insignis* Hodgson, 1836, *Asiat. Res.* 19 (1): 162, pl. 9—Nepal.

F.B.I. 5: 203

LOCAL NAMES: Dukul (Nepali); Fomok (Lepcha).

SIZE: Jungle Crow.

FIELD CHARACTERS: A large greyish brown forest pigeon. *Above,* crown and hindneck lilac. Back and scapulars maroon-tinged copper-brown. Rump and upper tail-coverts ashy grey. Tail black and brownish grey. *Below,* sides of head grey. Throat white; breast and lower parts vinous-grey. Under aspect of tail grey with a broad dark subterminal band. Sexes alike.

STATUS AND HABITAT: Resident in the foothills and up to *c.* 6500 ft. elevation (Martam, Singhik, Toong, Chungthang, Gangtok). Affects forest.

DISTRIBUTION OUTSIDE SIKKIM: Terai, foothills and lower Himalayas up to *c.* 7000 ft. from Nepal to NE. Assam. Assam hills; Manipur; E. Pakistan. The race *cuprea* inhabits the southern heavy rainfall section of the Western Ghats.

The species extends through Burma and the Indochinese and Malaysian subregions.

GENERAL HABITS: Arboreal and entirely frugivorous; only occasionally seen on the ground at water and salt licks. Keeps in parties or small flocks of up to 15 or 20. When shifting from one feeding ground in the forest to another, flies high above the tree-tops with seemingly leisurely but purposeful wing beats—looking rather crow-like in distant silhouette. Has the habit of perching silently on the bare tops of lofty trees in the late afternoons to catch the last rays of the sun before it sets behind the hills, flying off to its roost soon after the shadows have fallen. The male indulges in a spectacular aerobatic nuptial display, launching out from a high tree and performing a series of wave-crests and abrupt nose-dives with wings closed, somewhat like the Roller's (*Coracias*). *Call:* a loud, throaty, rather mournful, booming *ūk-ook . . . ook* or *gū-goo . . . goo.*

NESTING: *Season*—March to August, possibly two broods. *Nest*—the characteristic flimsy platform of twigs, 20 to 25 ft. up in a sapling in forest. *Eggs*—2, white, about 46×34 mm.

RACIAL CHARACTERISTICS, MEASUREMENTS, ETC: The Fauna gives the Wing (♂♀) as 228-259 mm. Schäfer collected a juvenile (Gangtok, 23 February) with Wing 232 mm.

Iris bluish grey or greyish white; eyelids magenta; bill horny grey, dull cherry red or magenta on cere and base of upper mandible; legs and feet dull cherry red.

## THE SNOW PIGEON

*Columba leuconota leuconota* Vigors

*Columba leuconota* Vigors, 1831, *Proc. Comm. Zool. Soc. London*, pt. 1: 23—Himalayas (type probably from Nepal).

**Plate 11, fig. 8** (facing p. 96)

F.B.I. **5**: 224

LOCAL NAMES: Lho-peu-rentiep (Lepcha); Bya-don (Bhutia).

SIZE: Pigeon.

FIELD CHARACTERS: A parti-coloured white and brown pigeon reminiscent of the domestic bird. In overhead flight, the white body and blackish head are pointers to its identity. Below observer's eye level, the blackish head, brown back, white rump-patch, grey wings with three dark bars, and blackish tail with a narrow white subterminal band, are diagnostic features. Sexes alike.

STATUS AND HABITAT: Resident. *Summer*, common at altitudes between 10,000 and 16,000 ft. *Winter*, down to *c.* 6000 ft. (Chungthang, Lachen, Lachung, Thangu, Manshitang, Gyagong). Affects cliffs.

DISTRIBUTION OUTSIDE SIKKIM: The high Himalayas westward through Nepal to NW. Pakistan. The East Himalayan race *gradaria* replaces it in the Chumbi Valley and eastward through Bhutan and SE. Tibet. The species overall ranges from W. Afghanistan across to W. China.

GENERAL HABITS: Similar to those of the Rock Pigeon, living and roosting on cliffs but sometimes also perching in trees. Keeps in pairs or small parties in summer, feeding on open grassy slopes or on the edge of melting snow patches. Collects in large flocks in winter, often of 150 birds or more, to feed near villages in newly sown fields of wheat and barley. When gleaning in the fields the birds run about briskly like sheep often forming a close-packed phalanx, each bird eager to be the first to investigate new ground. Its coloration is remarkably obliterative on gravelly ground even at close range, particularly amongst patches of melting snow. ***Flight:*** typical pigeon, strong and direct, with rapid wing beats. ***Call:*** described as 'a repeated croak, not unlike a hiccough'; very different from the normal *coo* of a pigeon. ***Food:*** chiefly weed seeds and grain.

NESTING: *Season*—May to July. *Nest*—the characteristic flimsy stick-platform of pigeons, on ledges and in crevices of inaccessible cliffs, often in large colonies. *Eggs*—2, white, about 40×30 mm.

RACIAL CHARACTERISTICS, MEASUREMENTS, ETC: The eastern race *gradaria* is somewhat larger and paler, with the head more slate-grey, less blackish. Sikkim birds are largely intermediate between the eastern and western populations. In freshly moulted plumage, underparts washed with pale greyish. Abdomen pale grey, darkening on under tail-coverts.

Specimens collected by the Survey measure:

| | Wing | Bill | Tarsus | Tail |
|---|---|---|---|---|
| 1 ♂ | 255 | 24.5 | 35 | 125 mm. |
| 2 ♀♀ | 246-255 | 24.5-25 | 31-34 | 122-137 mm. |

Schäfer's Sikkim series gives Wing 4 ♂♂ 239-248 (av. 243.5); 5 ♀♀ 240-256 (av. 246.4) mm.

Iris lemon yellow; bill horny brown, cere magenta-brown; legs and feet reddish pink; claws horny brown.

## THE TURKESTAN HILL PIGEON

### *Columba rupestris turkestanica* Buturlin

*Columba rupestris turkestanica* Buturlin, 1908, *Orn. Monatsb.* 16: 45—Altai.

F.B.I. 5: 222

LOCAL NAMES: Angoa, Ankhu, Oron (Tibetan).

SIZE: Pigeon.

FIELD CHARACTERS: Similar to the well-known Blue Rock Pigeon but much paler above and almost whitish below, with a pure white rump-patch and a broad white band across tail. Sexes alike.

STATUS AND HABITAT: Resident in the Tibetan facies of extreme N. Sikkim, above *c.* 15,000 ft. elevation (Gyagong, etc.). Affects open rocky country.

DISTRIBUTION OUTSIDE SIKKIM: The Tibetan Plateau facies of the high Himalayas, and northward through Tibet to Turkestan and Altai.

GENERAL HABITS: Gregarious. Lives on crags and precipices usually within easy flighting distance of villages, where it resorts to feed around the cultivation. Very tame and confiding. *Call:* a high-pitched quick-repeated *gūt-gūt-gūt-gūt* etc. reminiscent of jeering laughter!

NESTING: *Season*—chiefly April to June/July; possibly double brooded. *Nest*—the typical flimsy platform of twigs etc., placed in a hole in a bank or precipice (sometimes in the wall of a deserted dwelling); usually several nests together in a colony. *Eggs*—2, white, about 37×28 mm.

RACIAL CHARACTERISTICS, MEASUREMENTS, ETC: A good series collected by Schäfer at Gyagong gives Wing 5 ♂♂ 230-240 (av. 233.4); 6 ♀♀ 219-228 (av. 223.8) mm.

Iris deep orange; bill slaty black, tinged plumbeous or flesh-colour on cere and gape; legs and feet coral red; claws pale horny.

## THE SPECKLED WOOD PIGEON

### *Columba hodgsonii* Vigors

*Columba Hodgsonii* Vigors, 1832, *Proc. Comm. Zool. Soc. London*, pt. 2: 16—Nepal.

**Plate 11, fig. 7 (facing p. 96)**

F.B.I. 5: 234

LOCAL NAME:

SIZE: Pigeon.

FIELD CHARACTERS: *Male, Above,* head and neck, grey, the latter speckled with blackish. Upper back and wing-shoulders (coverts) claret-maroon, the latter speckled with white. Rest of upper parts dark brown and dark grey; tail blackish brown. *Below,* upper breast speckled with blackish grey and claret, changing to uniform claret on lower breast and passing into deep slaty grey on abdomen and under tail-coverts.

*Female* has grey of head brownish, and red of back and breast duller and browner.

STATUS AND HABITAT: A hill pigeon, resident and fairly common from *c.* 5000 ft. elevation to at least 13,000 (Rinchinpong, Lachen, Lachung, Yumthang, Thangu). Also obtained by Elwes at Tankra La (*c.* 13,000 ft.) in September 1870. Affects oak and other broad-leafed forest.

DISTRIBUTION OUTSIDE SIKKIM: The Himalayas from Kashmir through Nepal and Bhutan to the NE. frontier; Assam hills and Burma to W. China.

GENERAL HABITS: Keeps in parties or small flocks. Largely arboreal and frugivorous, but also gleans grain and weed seeds on the ground. Call described as 'a very deep *whock-whr-o-o . . . whrroo*'.

NESTING: *Season*—May-June. *Nest*—a rough platform of twigs, 8 to 25 ft. up in a small tree. *Eggs*—a singleton (? or two), white, about 40×30 mm.

RACIAL CHARACTERISTICS, MEASUREMENTS, ETC: A series collected by Schäfer in Sikkim gives Wing 4 ♂♂ ad. 218-232 (av. 227.7); 4 ♀♀ ad. 221-233 (av. 225.5) mm. Two ♀♀ obtained recently by Dr Ripley in central Nepal are much larger: Wing 236, 237 mm.

Iris greyish white; ocular skin grey; bill purple at base, black distally; legs and feet brownish yellow to dull green.

## THE ASHY WOOD PIGEON

### *Columba pulchricollis* Blyth

*Columba pulchricollis* 'Hodgson'=Blyth, 1846 (1845), *Jour. Asiat. Soc. Bengal* 14 (2): 866—Wooded region of E. Himalayas, i.e. Nepal.

**Plate 11, fig. 9 (facing p. 96)**

F.B.I. 5: 230
LOCAL NAME: Ka-o (Lepcha).
SIZE: Pigeon.

FIELD CHARACTERS: *Above*, dark ashy or leaden grey, with pale grey head and nape. A conspicuous buff collar, broad and spotted with black on hindneck, narrow in front. Upper back below this collar, and all round lower neck blackish with iridescent sheen of lilac and green. Tail blackish. *Below*, chin white, changing to buff on throat and passing into the glossy buff collar. Breast metallic-glossed dark slaty blue, passing to pale cinnamon or brownish buff on abdomen and vent. Sexes alike.

STATUS AND HABITAT: Rare. Resident between 4000 and 10,000 ft. elevation. Seasonal altitudinal movements not sufficiently known. Affects thick forest.

DISTRIBUTION OUTSIDE SIKKIM: From west central Nepal through Sikkim and Bhutan (?) to Assam, Burma, Thailand and Formosa.

GENERAL HABITS: Shy and keeps to the concealment of dense foliage in tall forest trees. Very silent and thus possibly often overlooked. *Call:* unrecorded. *Food:* fruits, grain and seeds.

NESTING: *Season* (Darjeeling Dist.)—May to August (?). *Nest*—a rough twig-platform 6 to 10 ft. up in a small tree. *Eggs*—2, white, about 38×28 mm.

RACIAL CHARACTERISTICS, MEASUREMENTS, ETC: The Fauna gives the measurements (♂♀) as: Wing 194-216; tail 120-130 mm. Specimens recently collected by Dr Ripley in Nepal have Wing 2 ♂♂ 211.5, 216; 1 ♀ 215 mm.

Iris white or greyish white; ocular skin grey; bill purplish at base, dull grey-green distally; legs and feet fleshy purple to a coral red.

## THE BARTAILED CUCKOO-DOVE

### *Macropygia unchall tusalia* (Blyth)

*Columba tusalia* 'Hodgson'=Blyth, 1843, *Jour. Asiat. Soc. Bengal* 12 (2): 936—Darjeeling.

**Plate 11, fig. 10 (facing p. 96)**

F.B.I. 5: 253
LOCAL NAMES: Tusal (Nepali); Ka-er (Lepcha).
SIZE: House Crow−.

FIELD CHARACTERS: *Male: Above*, forehead buff, shading to lilac-purple on crown and hindneck and into barred rufous and metallic black on rest of upper parts. Tail long, broad, graduated, largely brownish black barred with rufous. *Below*, chin and throat lilac-buff. Upper breast lilac with metallic sheen, changing to dull lilac on lower breast and into buff on lower abdomen, vent, and under tail-coverts.

*Female:* Upper parts duller. Head and breast barred with dark brown.

STATUS AND HABITAT: Resident and generally distributed from *c.* 1500 to 9000 ft. elevation (Singtam, Temi, Zemu, Gangtok, Lachen). Affects broad-leafed secondary forest interspersed with open patches and cultivation.

DISTRIBUTION OUTSIDE SIKKIM: The Himalayas, up to *c.* 9000 ft., from Kashmir through Nepal and Bhutan to east Assam. Manipur, Burma and through the Indochinese subregion to S. China and Hainan.

GENERAL HABITS: Keeps in pairs, small parties or flocks. Gleans grain and seeds on the ground in cultivation and open glades. Also eats fruits and berries, sometimes hanging upside down on a twig and lunging out for one just out of reach, like a green pigeon. Very jealous of its feeding tree, attacking and driving off bulbuls and other birds arriving on the same quest. Flight, and habit of gliding upwards into a branch when alighting, very cuckoo-like; also hind aspect of bird when perched. Silent except in the breeding season. Call described as a very deep *croo-um*, the second syllable a booming note, audible a long way off.

NESTING: *Season*—May to July. *Nest*—the typical flimsy dove structure of twigs, with a slight central depression. Placed 20-30 ft. up in a tree. *Eggs*—2, long and narrow, pale buff to *café-au-lait*. Size about 36×26 mm.

RACIAL CHARACTERISTICS, MEASUREMENTS, ETC: Schäfer's Sikkim specimens measure: Wing 1 ♂ ad. 207; 2 ♀♀ ad. 191, 200 mm. Two males recently collected by Dr Ripley in E. Nepal have Wing 196, 209 mm.

Iris outer ring pink, inner pale blue; eyelids purple; ocular skin grey; legs and feet dull cherry red or purplish brown; claws horny black.

## THE RUFOUS TURTLE DOVE

*Streptopelia orientalis agricola* (Tickell)

*Columba agricola* Tickell, 1833, *Jour. Asiat. Soc. Bengal* 2: 581—Jungles of Borabhúm and Dholbhúm.

F.B.I. 5: 238 (part)

LOCAL NAME:

SIZE: Pigeon—.

FIELD CHARACTERS: A slender rufous pigeon with dark grey terminal fringe to the rounded tail, conspicuous when bird is alighting. *Above*, rufous-brown with dark centres to the feathers producing a scaly effect. A grey-spotted black patch ('chessboard') on either side of neck. *Below*, vinous-rufous, paler and greyer on abdomen passing to slaty grey on thighs and under tail-coverts. Sexes alike.

STATUS AND HABITAT: Fairly common but not abundant, up to *c.* 13,000 ft. elevation in summer; largely migratory to the plains in winter. *Summer:* Chungthang, Gangtok, Lachen, Thangu (Schäfer); *Winter:* Martam, Dentam, Rinchinpong, etc. Affects open oak and other forest, often around cultivation.

DISTRIBUTION OUTSIDE SIKKIM: Breeding in E. Nepal, Bihar, duars of W. Bengal, Assam, E. Pakistan to Burma. The less richly coloured race *meena* breeds in the W. Himalayas to Kashmir etc. A third race, *erythrocephala,* is resident in peninsular India.

The species is widely distributed in Asia from central Siberia east to Japan, south to the Indochinese subregion, and subject to extensive winter migrations.

GENERAL HABITS: A terrestrial-feeding graminivorous dove. Keeps in pairs or small parties, forming larger flocks when migrating. Gleans scattered grain in fallow and harvested fields; also weed seeds. Flight swift and direct, typical of the pigeons. *Call:* a hoarse, rather mournful *goor . . . gūr-grūgroo.* In courtship, the male bows and bobs ludicrously in front of the female as he advances towards her in mincing hops, calling with goitred-out throat—an action very reminiscent of the *Calotes* lizard. He also displays by springing up into the air and volplaning in an arc, like other doves.

NESTING: *Season*—chiefly April-May, but males collected on 4 January had greatly enlarged testes. *Nest*—a rough flimsy platform of twigs with a slight central depression. Placed fairly low down in a bush or bamboo clump. *Eggs*—2, white, about 29×23 mm.

RACIAL CHARACTERISTICS, MEASUREMENTS, ETC: The West Himalayan race *meena,* besides being less richly coloured, has the under tail-coverts and terminal fringe to tail white as against slaty grey in *agricola.* As Stresemann points out, Sikkim birds are really intermediate between *agricola* and *orientalis* and present a good deal of individual variation. Specimens collected by the Sikkim Survey measure:

| | Wing | Bill | Tarsus | Tail |
|---|---|---|---|---|
| 2 ♂♂ | 189-198 | 22-24 | 27 | 135-140 mm. |
| 1 ♀ | 191 | 22 | 26.5 | 122 mm. |

A series from N. Sikkim in Schäfer's collection (June to September) gives Wing 10 ♂♀ 185-197 (av. 188.9) mm.

Iris orange; circumocular skin, cere and base of bill magenta; distal half of bill horny brown; legs and feet magenta; hind tarsus paler and pinkish; claws horny brown.

## THE INDIAN SPOTTED DOVE

*Streptopelia chinensis suratensis* (Gmelin)

*Columba suratensis* Gmelin, 1789, Syst. Nat. 1 (2): 778—Surat, Gulf of Cambay, India.

F.B.I. 5: 242

LOCAL NAME:

SIZE: Between Myna and Pigeon.

FIELD CHARACTERS: *Above*, pinkish brown, grey, and blackish brown, spotted with white. A white-spotted velvety black half-collar ('chessboard') on hindneck. Tail blackish brown and slate, broadly white-fringed except on the central pair of feathers. White fringe very conspicuous when tail is spread in alighting. *Below*, chin white; rest of underparts largely vinaceous-pink, whitish on abdomen. Sexes alike.

STATUS AND HABITAT: Fairly common in summer at the lower elevations, i.e. up to *c.* 5000 ft. (Rangpo, Singtam, Martam, Temi, Chungthang, Singhik, Pakyong, etc.). Migrates to the plains about October/November, returning about mid-March. Almost completely absent in winter. Affects the neighbourhood of cultivation.

DISTRIBUTION OUTSIDE SIKKIM: Practically all India excepting the desert areas. Represented in Ceylon, E. Pakistan and NE. frontier by different races. The species extends through Burma and the Indochinese subregion to S. China and Hainan.

GENERAL HABITS: A graminivorous ground-feeding dove. Gleans in stubble fields, on mule tracks etc. often in village environs, in pairs or small parties. *Call:* an oft-repeated, pleasant *krookrūk-krūkroo-kroo-kroo-kroo.*

NESTING: *Season*—chiefly April to July. *Nest*—a flimsy twig-platform placed fairly low in a bush or small tree. *Eggs*—2, white about 28×22 mm.

RACIAL CHARACTERISTICS, MEASUREMENTS, ETC: Specimens collected by Schäfer in Sikkim measure: 4 ♂♀ ad. Wing 144, 146, 153, 155 mm.

Iris outer ring pinkish red, inner hazel brown; orbital skin magenta; bill dark horny; legs and feet dull cherry or magenta; claws horny brown.

## THE EMERALD DOVE

*Chalcophaps indica indica* (Linnaeus)

*Columba indica* Linnaeus, 1758, Syst. Nat., ed. 10, 1: 164—East Indies (=Amboina).

F.B.I. 5: 215

LOCAL NAME: Ka-er (Lepcha).

SIZE: Myna+.

FIELD CHARACTERS: A brownish pink dove with metallic emerald bronze-green upper parts, and prominent white forehead and supercilia. A band of white-fringed feathers across lower back.

Rump grey. Tail brown and grey with a broad black cross-band, broken in the middle. Under side of wings chestnut, conspicuous in flight. Sexes alike.

STATUS AND HABITAT: Resident and generally distributed up to c. 6000 ft. elevation (Martam, Dikchu, Singhik, Temi, Rinchinpong, Gangtok). Affects secondary and mixed bamboo forest, chiefly in the foothills.

DISTRIBUTION OUTSIDE SIKKIM: The evergreen and moist deciduous forest biotope practically throughout India, up to *c.* 6000 ft.; East Pakistan and through the Indochinese and Malaysian subregions. The species extends to the Philippines, Australia and New Caledonia.

GENERAL HABITS: A terrestrial dove, usually seen singly or in pairs gleaning on forest tracks or flying across at top speed through shrubbery and shady glades. *Food:* mainly seeds and berries. *Call:* a soft, deep and low *hoon* with a nasal ending, repeated at intervals.

NESTING: *Season*—chiefly March to May. *Nest*—the usual flimsy twig-platform, placed 5 to 10 ft. up in a sapling or bamboo clump. *Eggs*—2, creamy yellow or *café-au-lait*, about 27×21 mm.

RACIAL CHARACTERISTICS, MEASUREMENTS, ETC: The Fauna gives the Wing (♂♀) as 148-161 mm., mentioning that females average smaller—142 mm. against 146 mm. in males. An adult ♂ collected at Dikchu by Schäfer has Wing 149 mm.

Iris brown; bill coral red (magenta on cere); legs and feet pinkish red; claws horny brown.

## *Family* PSITTACIDAE: Parrots

### THE INDIAN REDBREASTED PARAKEET

***Psittacula alexandri fasciata*** **(P. L. S. Müller)**

*Psittacus fasciatus* P. L. S. Müller, 1776, Natursyst., Suppl.: 74—Pondicherry *errore*, restricted to Arakan by Ticehurst, 1933, *JBNHS* **36**: 934.

**Plate 11, fig. 1 (facing p. 96)**

F.B.I. **4**: 210

LOCAL NAME: Imrit Bhela (Nepali).

SIZE: Myna; with long-graduated, pointed tail *c.* 9 inches.

FIELD CHARACTERS: A long-tailed grass-green parakeet with pinkish or plum-grey head (bluer in ♀) and prominent vinaceous-red throat and breast. A yellow patch on wing-shoulder where dark red in *P. himalayana.*

STATUS AND HABITAT: ? Local migrant. Obtained by G. E. Shaw up to 3800 ft. in the Teesta Valley (season?), and recorded elsewhere in the Himalayas up to *c.* 5000 ft. Affects foothills forest, often on the fringe of cultivation.

DISTRIBUTION OUTSIDE SIKKIM: The lower Himalayas and foothills from Kumaon through Nepal to Assam, E. Pakistan, Burma. The species extends through the Indochinese and Malaysian subregions to S. China and Hainan.

GENERAL HABITS: Not appreciably different from the next. *Call:* a loud, raucous screaming.

NESTING: Not recorded from Sikkim. *Season* (in the western sub-Himalayas)—March to May. *Nest*—a hole in a tree-trunk, either natural or excavated by the birds themselves, *c.* 15 to 20 ft. up. Often several pairs breed together in a colony. *Eggs*—3 or 4, white, roundish, about 31×26 mm.

RACIAL CHARACTERISTICS, MEASUREMENTS, ETC: The Fauna gives the measurements as:

| | Wing | Tail |
|---|---|---|
| ♂♂ | 162-174 | 168-189 mm. |
| ♀♀ | 157-162 | 145-171 mm. |

Iris yellow; upper mandible coral red, lower brownish black; legs and feet dusky greenish yellow or pale yellowish slate.

## THE HIMALAYAN SLATYHEADED PARAKEET

*Psittacula himalayana himalayana* (Lesson)

*Psittacus (Conurus) Himalayanus* Lesson, 1832, *in* Belanger's Voy. Ind. Orient., Zool.: 239—Valleys of the Himalayas.

**Plate 11, fig. 2** (facing p. 96)

F.B.I. 4: 206

LOCAL NAME: Suga (Nepali).

SIZE: Myna; with a long, graduated, pointed tail *c.* 10 inches.

FIELD CHARACTERS: *Male:* Overall grass-green with the entire head dark slaty; a bright verdigris-green collar on hindneck. All tail feathers broadly tipped with bright pale yellow including longest middle pair which is largely blue. A dark red patch on wing-shoulder. Chin, throat, and a broad line below cheeks black.

*Female:* Similar but with paler grey head and no red shoulder-patch.

STATUS AND HABITAT: Recorded as a local migrant up to *c.* 8000 ft. elevation. Noted as uncommon and patchy in winter (November to March) between *c.* 2000 and 4500 ft. (Martam, Dikchu, Singhik). Affects well-wooded hillsides and valleys, and the neighbourhood of terraced cultivation.

DISTRIBUTION OUTSIDE SIKKIM: The Himalayas from Kashmir to W. Assam—foothills and up to *c.* 8000 ft. Replaced by the race (or species?) *finschii* in E. Assam. The species extends through the Indochinese subregion.

GENERAL HABITS: Keeps in family parties and flocks. *Food:* chiefly wild fruits including seeds of the Chir Pine (*Pinus longifolia*); locally destructive to orchard fruit and ripening maize. Flight swift and direct, accompanied by a high-pitched double call-note *tooi? tooi?* like that of the more familiar Blossomheaded Parakeet of the plains but harsher and distinctive.

NESTING: *Season*—March to May. *Nest*—like a woodpecker's, an unlined shaft excavated in a tree-trunk, 15 to 20 ft. up or higher, with a round entrance-hole. *Eggs*—3 to 5, white, roundish, about 29×23 mm.

RACIAL CHARACTERISTICS, MEASUREMENTS, ETC: The eastern race *finschii*[1] is smaller in the wing, more yellow on the back, and with the yellow tail-tips tinged with pink. The Fauna gives the measurements of typical *himalayana* as:

| | Wing | Tail |
|---|---|---|
| ♂♂ | 162-174 | 205-246 mm. |
| ♀♀ | 154-161 | 150-161 mm. |

Iris creamy white to lemon yellow; upper mandible orange, reddish at base, yellow at tip; lower mandible yellow; legs and feet yellowish green; claws plumbeous horn.

## *Family* CUCULIDAE: Cuckoos

### THE LARGE HAWK-CUCKOO

***Cuculus sparverioïdes sparverioïdes*** **Vigors**

*Cuculus sparverioïdes* Vigors, 1832 (1831), *Proc. Comm. Zool. Soc. London* 1: 173—Himalayas.

F.B.I. 4: 146

LOCAL NAMES: Bara Bharao (Nepali); Nimbin-Piyal (Lepcha).

SIZE: Crow—; slimmer.

FIELD CHARACTERS: Overall aspect very hawk-like, including style of flight and habit of sweeping upward into a branch when alighting. *Above*, ashy grey and ashy brown. Tail banded grey and tipped white. *Below*, breast mottled rufous and ashy. Rest of lower plumage white (partially suffused with rufous) barred with blackish. Immature: brown above, rufous-buff below broadly streaked (not barred) with blackish, thus also like an immature hawk. Sexes alike.

STATUS AND HABITAT: Uncertain. Obtained at Temi and Rinchinpong in January when silent. Noisiest from mid-March between *c.* 3000 and 6500 ft. elevation (Singhik, Toong, Chungthang, Gangtok). Affects openly wooded country.

DISTRIBUTION OUTSIDE SIKKIM: *Summer* (breeding), the Himalayas up to *c.* 9000 ft. from Kashmir to E. Assam. *Winter*, south to Madhya Pradesh, Madras, Mysore, Kerala. The species extends to W. China and through the Indochinese and Malaysian subregions to the Philippines and Celebes.

[1] This may, in fact, be a full species as suggested by Husain, K. Z., 1959, *Ibis* 101 (2): 249-50.

GENERAL HABITS: Deceptively like a hawk, e.g. Shikra, particularly in flight when resemblance heightened by barred underside and lower aspect of wings. *Food:* caterpillars and other insects. *Call:* a loud, shrill, screaming whistle *brain-fever, brain-fever,* etc., reiterated with monotonous persistency in runs of 5 or 6, rising successively to a frantic pitch and breaking off abruptly. Repeated again and again throughout the day and often also during the night. The calls are exactly like those of the better-known Brainfever Bird of the plains, but much shriller.

NESTING: Brood-parasitic chiefly upon various species of laughing thrushes. *Eggs* very variable in size and coloration, but on the whole matching those of its hosts.

RACIAL CHARACTERISTICS, MEASUREMENTS, ETC: Specimens collected by the Survey measure:

| | Wing | Bill | Tarsus | Tail |
|---|---|---|---|---|
| 1 ♂ | 230 | 27.5 | 25 | 201 mm. |
| 1 ♀ | 219 | 29 | 27 | 175 mm. |
| 1 o? | 236 | 28.5 | 26 | 220 mm. |

A Schäfer skin '♀' ad. has Wing 224 mm.

Iris creamy khaki; fleshy rim round eye and angle of gape lemon yellow; upper mandible blackish brown, lower greenish horn; legs, feet and claws chrome yellow.

Schäfer obtained a specimen of HODGSON'S HAWK-CUCKOO, *Cuculus fugax nisicolor* Blyth, at Gangtok (*c.* 6300 ft.) on 14 June, '♀' Wing 178 mm. Lepcha name: Ding-pit.

FIELD IDENTIFICATION: Superficially similar to *Cuculus s. sparverioïdes* but smaller. Also differentiated from it by being unbarred on white lower abdomen and vent. Tail banded black and grey, the penultimate black band broadest, followed by a narrow band of grey-brown and another narrow black band. The call is similar to and equally as persistent as the Hawk-Cuckoo's but thinner and even more shrill. W. H. Matthews renders it as a very piercing, insistent *gee-whiz-gee-whiz-gee-whiz,* rising in pitch and tempo and ending in a slurring trill.

The race *nisicolor* occurs from Nepal eastward to Assam and E. Pakistan between *c.* 2000 and 6000 ft. elevation. Its status in Sikkim is uncertain, but Mandelli is credited with taking an oviduct egg here on 5 June.

The species *fugax* extends to S. Siberia, China and Japan, south to the Indochinese and Malaysian subregions and the Philippines.

## THE INDIAN CUCKOO

***Cuculus micropterus micropterus*** **Gould**

***Cuculus micropterus*** **Gould, 1837,** ***Proc. Zool. Soc. London:*** **137—Himalayas.**

F.B.I. 4: 144

LOCAL NAMES: Takpo (Lepcha); Kang-ka-tong (Bhutia).

SIZE: Pigeon. Slimmer.

FIELD CHARACTERS: Very similar to the Khasia Hills Cuckoo, *C. c. bakeri*—slaty grey above, black-barred white below—but readily distinguished by the broad black subterminal band on its tail (figure p. 52). *Call:* a four-noted '*orange-pekoe*' or '*crossword puzzle*'.

STATUS AND HABITAT: Uncertain. Vocal from about end of March onwards; then commonly heard between *c.* 2000 and 5500 ft. elevation (Martam, Dikchu, Toong, Chungthang). Affects fairly open wooded country.

DISTRIBUTION OUTSIDE SIKKIM: Throughout the lower Himalayas east to Assam, N. India, W. Punjab. South to Bombay State, Madhya Pradesh, W. Bengal, E. Pakistan. Also the Indochinese and Malaysian subregions.

GENERAL HABITS: As of the genus. Its four-noted call is amongst the best-known bird voices and lends itself to a wide range of local onomatopoeic renderings, e.g. *bo-kota-ko* in Bengal, *kyphal-paka* in N. India, *orange-pekoe* or *make more pekoe* among tea gardeners, *hamsota-tha* in Anglo-Indian Hindustani, *crossword puzzle* or *what's your trouble,* and so on. When in full voice the bird is obstreperous at all hours of the day and night, especially moonlit, calling almost continuously in long monotonous runs without change of cadence. One bird was timed at 23 calls a minute; another 43 calls in two minutes, without interruption. *Food:* largely caterpillars.

NESTING: Brood-parasitic on laughing thrushes, chats, shortwings, the Paradise Flycatcher and numerous other species. Gammie found a full-fledged young cuckoo being fed by a pair of Streaked Spiderhunters, *Arachnothera magna,* in Sikkim in September (*Stray Feathers* 5:386). *Eggs*—bluish, similar to those of *C. c. bakeri,* usually matching more or less the eggs of the fosterers. Size about 24×18 mm.

RACIAL CHARACTERISTICS, MEASUREMENTS, ETC: Hartert (Vög. pal. Fauna 1: 952) gives Wing ♂♀ as 192-215 mm.

Iris brown; eyelids yellow; bill: upper mandible black, lower mandible basally yellow, distally grey; legs yellow.

## THE KHASIA HILLS CUCKOO

*Cuculus canorus bakeri* Hartert

*Cuculus canorus bakeri* Hartert, 1912, Vög. pal. Fauna 2: 948—Shillong, Assam.

F.B.I. 4: 139

LOCAL NAMES: Kukku (Lepcha); Akku (Bhutia).

SIZE: Pigeon. Slimmer.

FIELD CHARACTERS: Overall aspect together with long pointed wings, speed and manner of flight very hawk-like. *Male: Above,* dark slaty. *Below,* chin, foreneck and breast pale ashy; rest of underparts white, broadly cross-barred with black.

Tails of

Khasia Hills Cuckoo Indian Cuckoo

About one-third

*Female* similar but more brownish above and on breast. Occasionally in a dimorphic 'hepatic' phase—barred chestnut and black.

STATUS AND HABITAT: Largely migratory, but very little dependable data available for Sikkim. Presence in a locality usually revealed by its well-known calls; bird apt to be overlooked when silent, as in winter. Calling only commences in spring. The Survey first heard it at Pakyong and Arita (E. Sikkim) on 10/11 April; by the last week of April (Chungthang) the birds had become plentiful and noisy, chasing one another excitedly, courting and establishing territories. Schäfer collected a specimen at Gangtok on 12 June. Affects openly wooded country, orchards near villages and outlying homesteads etc.

In adjoining Bhutan, Ludlow found it common at various elevations in summer and took specimens at 10,000 and 11,000 ft. between June and September.

DISTRIBUTION OUTSIDE SIKKIM: *Summer* (breeding), Nepal (?), Bhutan, Assam hills south of Brahmaputra River. *Winter*, Assam plains; E. Pakistan.

The species is largely migratory with a very extensive overall range in Europe, Africa, Asia, Australasia.

GENERAL HABITS: Mainly arboreal and insectivorous. Feeds commonly on hairy caterpillars taken off branches of trees; sometimes on the ground. *Call: cook-koo, cook-koo,* repeated many times, varied occasionally by *cook-cook-koo* and husky croaks and chuckles, particularly when chasing a rival. When calling the tail is partly spread and cocked, the wings drooped at the sides, and the bird oscillates lightly from side to side. The female has a rippling call likened to water bubbling, but may also utter the *cook-koo* call of the male (?).

NESTING: Brood-parasitic on pipits, chats, warblers, babblers, etc. The *season* synchronizes with that of its hosts, chiefly April to June. *Eggs*—broad, blunt ovals in shape, normally coloured like those of the fosterer, about 24×18 mm. All eggs laid by individual females are recognizable as such; she may lay 12 to 15 spread over several nests in her territory. The female is promiscuous in her sex relations.

RACIAL CHARACTERISTICS, MEASUREMENTS, ETC: Distinguished from the typical European-W. Himalayan race *canorus* by its darker, almost blackish slate upper plumage and much broader and blacker barring on the underparts.

A specimen (♂) collected by Schäfer at Gangtok has Wing 224 mm.

Iris pale to deep yellow; eyerim yellow; bill dark horny brown, paler and yellowish at base and on commissure, orange-yellow at gape; legs and feet wax yellow.

## THE HIMALAYAN CUCKOO

### *Cuculus saturatus saturatus* Blyth

*Cuculus saturatus* 'Hodgson'=Blyth, 1843, *Jour. Asiat. Soc. Bengal* 12 (2): 942—Nepal.

F.B.I. 4: 140 (=*optatus*)

LOCAL NAME: Tong-ting-vyang (Lepcha).

SIZE: Pigeon—; slimmer.

FIELD CHARACTERS: Very similar to *C. c. bakeri*—slaty grey above, barred below—but with edge of wing-shoulder pure white instead of barred brown and white. Females sometimes 'hepatic'. *Call:* a distinctive hoopoe-like *oop-oop-oop-oop.*

STATUS AND HABITAT: Partially migratory, but no definite data for Sikkim since, like the last, easily overlooked or confused with other cuckoos when silent. Commonly in voice from April between *c.* 4000 and 9000 ft. elevation (Kewzing, Pemionche, Gangtok, Singhik, Toong, Lachen). H. G. Alexander heard one at Rangpo (*c.* 1200 ft.) on 30 November. Schäfer procured specimens at Gangtok in June. Affects openly wooded country.

DISTRIBUTION OUTSIDE SIKKIM: *Summer* (breeding), E. and S. Asia including the Himalayas to E. Assam between 5000 and 10,000 ft. *Winter*, south to the Philippines, Malaya, Australasia.

GENERAL HABITS: Same as the previous species. Calls obstreperously from exposed tree-tops for considerable periods at a time: a loud *ūp . . . oop-oop-oop-oop*. The initial *ūp* is in undertone, and audible only at close range. In the distance the call may be confused with a hoopoe's except that it is almost invariably four-noted against the hoopoe's three. When calling, the grey throat swells out like a goitre. It also emits a series of harsh groans, croaks and chuckles.

NESTING: *Season*—principally April to June, corresponding with that of its usual fosterers—flycatcher- and leaf-warblers of the genera *Seicercus* and *Phylloscopus*, tiny birds less than a third its own size! *Eggs*—variable, usually matching its hosts' in coloration, and absurdly small for the size of the cuckoo, about 22×14 mm.

RACIAL CHARACTERISTICS, MEASUREMENTS, ETC: 2 ♂♂ collected by Schäfer have Wing 185, 188 mm.

Iris yellow; bill dark horny green, yellowish at gape; legs and feet wax yellow to bright yellow.

## THE SMALL CUCKOO

### *Cuculus poliocephalus poliocephalus* Latham

*Cuculus poliocephalus* Latham, 1790, Index Orn. 1: 215—India.

F.B.I. 4: 142

LOCAL NAMES: Dang-hlem (Lepcha); Pichu-giapu (Bhutia).

SIZE: Myna+; slimmer.

FIELD CHARACTERS: Smaller than, but otherwise similar to *C. c. bakeri*—slaty grey above, black-barred white below—with the underparts suffused with buff. *Call* diagnostic: a rattling 'That's your *choky* pepper'.

STATUS AND HABITAT: Uncertain. Heard from about mid-April on, between *c.* 4000 ft. (Temi) and 6500 ft. (Gangtok). Schäfer procured it at Dikchu (*c.* 2000 ft.) and Gangtok in June, and I have examined a May specimen from Chungthang in the Chicago Museum of Natural History. Affects openly wooded country.

DISTRIBUTION OUTSIDE SIKKIM: *Summer* (breeding), Gilgit and through Kashmir and the Himalayas to Assam, north and south of Brahmaputra River. *Winter*, E. Pakistan and peninsular India, Ceylon, Andamans. The species breeds from Afghanistan to Japan, between 4500 and 10,000 ft.

GENERAL HABITS: Typical cuckoo—arboreal, insectivorous. The unmistakable call is a curious rattling or chattering, rather like a bulbul's in timbre, but harsher. The first half goes up in scale, the second comes down. It is well rendered by the words *that's your choky pepper* with the accent on *choky*.

NESTING: Brood-parasitic on warblers and wrens of the genera

*Phylloscopus*, *Seicercus* and *Microura*, its laying season being synchronous with theirs—chiefly April-May. *Eggs*—broadly elliptical, usually more or less matching in coloration those of its hosts, a common type being terra cotta. Size about 21×14 mm.

RACIAL CHARACTERISTICS, MEASUREMENTS, ETC: Apart from smaller size, distinguished from both *C. c. bakeri* and *C. s. saturatus* by the edge of the wing-shoulder being ashy.

Schäfer's Sikkim skins give Wing 1 ♂ 155; 1 ♀ 157 mm.

Iris brown; eyelids yellow; bill horny black, base of both mandibles, commissure and gape yellow; legs and feet wax yellow.

## THE INDIAN PLAINTIVE CUCKOO

*Cacomantis merulinus passerinus* (Vahl)

*Cuculus passerinus* Vahl, 1797, Skriv. Naturhist.-Selsk., Kjobenhavn 4 (1): 57—Tranquebar.

F.B.I. **4: 154**

LOCAL NAME:

SIZE: Myna; slimmer.

FIELD CHARACTERS: *Above*, slaty grey. Shoulder of wing and an oblique band on the browner primaries, white; this conspicuous on the underwing in flight. Tail blackish, partly barred and with white tips. *Below*, chin and throat ashy grey; abdomen paler, fading to white on vent and under tail-coverts. Sexes alike. Immature birds, and hepatic phase of adult female: *Above*, bright chestnut barred with black. *Below*, white with narrow wavy blackish bars from breast down. Sometimes throat and breast also chestnut with obsolescent black barring.

In the chestnut phase impossible to tell apart in the field from the Baybanded Cuckoo, *Cacomantis s. sonneratii* (Latham), also recorded in Sikkim. In the hand the latter may be distinguished by the tail feathers which narrow towards their tips.

*Call: p'teer, p'teer, p'teer* and *weeti-teeti* (or *Peter-Peter*), the latter somewhat reminiscent of the *crossword-puzzle* calls of the Indian Cuckoo, but in a much higher key.

STATUS AND HABITAT: Uncertain. No specimens taken in Sikkim by the Survey or Schäfer, nor by other recent investigators. Heard from end of March between 2000 and 6500 ft. elevation (Martam, Singhik, Pemionche). Affects openly wooded country.

DISTRIBUTION OUTSIDE SIKKIM: Practically all India, locally up to *c.* 7000 ft. in the Himalayas. The species extends eastward through the Indochinese and Malaysian subregions to Hainan, the Philippines and Celebes.

GENERAL HABITS: Active. Typical cuckoo. Besides the above calls, it has a pleasant, rather plaintive whistling song *pee-pipee-pee-pipee-pee* uttered from an exposed tree-top. Particularly vocal in overcast drizzly weather.

NESTING: No specific evidence from Sikkim. Elsewhere, tailor birds and wren-warblers are its normal hosts. *Eggs* very variable, but usually resembling those of the fosterers. Size about 20×14 mm.

RACIAL CHARACTERISTICS, MEASUREMENTS, ETC: The Fauna gives for ♂♀: Wing 114-122; bill 16-17; tarsus 18-19; tail 99-119 mm.

Iris brown; bill horny brown, paler at chin and base of lower mandible; mouth orange-brick colour; legs and feet brownish yellow; claws horny brown.

## THE EMERALD CUCKOO

*Chalcites maculatus* (Gmelin)

*Trogon maculatus* Gmelin, 1788, Syst. Nat. 1 (1): 404—Ceylon.

**Plate 11, fig. 3** (facing p. 96)

F.B.I. 4: 162

LOCAL NAME: Ang-pha (Lepcha).

SIZE: Bulbul–.

FIELD CHARACTERS: A small cuckoo of resplendent plumage. *Male: Above,* head, neck and upper parts brilliant glossy green with golden bronze reflections. Some white in the wings. Tail feathers tipped white; the outermost pair with three irregular white bars. *Below,* chin, throat and upper breast glossy green like back. Rest of lower plumage white, barred with metallic bronze-green. Under tail-coverts metallic green, barred with white.

*Female: Above,* glistening emerald green with golden rufous crown and nape. *Below,* white (tinged with rufous on throat and flanks) barred with bronze-brown, narrowest on throat, broader and wider apart on abdomen. *Young:* Barred rufous and brown above, white and brown below.

STATUS AND HABITAT: Undetermined. Apparently uncommon. Stevens has records for the Sikkim Himalayas between *c.* 4250 and 4750 ft. elevation in April. The Survey came across it only at *c.* 7000 ft. (above Chungthang) in evergreen forest, also in April.

DISTRIBUTION OUTSIDE SIKKIM: *Summer* (breeding), the Himalayas from Kumaon to E. Assam, normally to *c.* 6000 ft. Extends through Burma and the Indochinese subregion. *Winter,* south to Malaya and Sumatra.

GENERAL HABITS: Unobtrusive and difficult to observe amongst the foliage canopy of tall trees which it usually affects. *Call:* 'a shrill, but not unmusical succession of three notes in an ascending scale' (Baker) in the breeding season. This is often the only indication of its presence in a locality.

NESTING: *Season*—April to July. Brood-parasitic mainly on sunbirds (*Aethopyga*) and spider-hunters (*Arachnothera*). *Eggs* white, smudged with light brown or reddish brown. Size about 17×12 mm.

RACIAL CHARACTERISTICS, MEASUREMENTS, ETC: The Fauna gives for ♂♀: Wing 105-114; bill 14-15; tarsus *c.* 15; tail 63-70 mm.

Iris ♂ reddish brown to crimson, ♀ brown; eyelids crimson; bill ♂ bright orange-yellow tipped with black, ♀ yellow only at base; legs and feet dark brownish green.

## THE INDIAN DRONGO-CUCKOO

*Surniculus lugubris dicruroïdes* (Hodgson)

*Pseudornis dicruroïdes* Hodgson, 1839, *Jour. Asiat. Soc. Bengal* 8: 136 and pl.—Mountains of Nepal.

F.B.I. 4: 165

LOCAL NAME: Kario-vyem (Lepcha).

SIZE: Myna; slimmer, with longer and forked tail.

FIELD CHARACTERS: Overall, glossy metallic black. General appearance confusingly like the Black Drongo, but under tail-coverts and outermost tail feathers usually banded with white near base.

Indian Drongo-Cuckoo (note exposed round nostril) — Indian Black Drongo (shrike-like hook-tipped bill)

About three-quarters

Sexes alike. *Call* diagnostic: 6 (sometimes 7 or 8) short musical whistling notes, *pi-pi-pi-pi-pi-pi-pi*, as if the bird were actually counting 1-2-3-4-5-6 etc., rising in scale and ending abruptly.

STATUS AND HABITAT: Undetermined. 'On the air' from about mid-April between 3500 and 5500 ft. elevation (Singhik, Toong, Chungthang). Affects open forest.

DISTRIBUTION OUTSIDE SIKKIM: The Himalayas from the Punjab (rare) to E. Assam, up to *c.* 6000 ft., and practically the entire Indian Union, E. Pakistan and Ceylon. The species extends to S. China, and south through the Indochinese and Malaysian subregions to the Philippines and Celebes.

GENERAL HABITS: Entirely arboreal and typically cuculine. Feeds on caterpillars and insects as well as fruit (*Ficus* etc.). Sometimes hawks winged insects from a tree-top like a Bronzed or Ashy Drongo. When calling, the body assumes a horizontal stance.

NESTING: Not recorded in Sikkim. Presumably, as elsewhere, lays from April to June when it is most vocal. Hosts not sufficiently known.

RACIAL CHARACTERISTICS, MEASUREMENTS, ETC: The Fauna gives for ♂♀ Wing 129-147 (av. 137.4); bill from nostril 15.5-17; tarsus *c.* 19; tail 106-133 mm.

Iris brown; bill brownish black, pale dusky orange at gape; legs and feet greyish brown; claws horny brown.

## THE LARGE HIMALAYAN GREENBILLED MALKOHA

*Rhopodytes tristis tristis* (Lesson)

*Melias tristis* Lesson, 1830, Traité d'Ornith., livr. 2, p. 132—Sumatra *errore*=Bengal.

F.B.I. 4: 178

LOCAL NAME: Sanku (Lepcha).

SIZE: Pigeon; with a long tail *c.* 15 inches.

FIELD CHARACTERS: *Above,* forehead grey with shiny bristly black shafts to the feathers. A patch of bright crimson skin round eye. Upper plumage dark ashy grey with deep green gloss. Tail darker,

Large Himalayan Greenbilled Malkoha
About one-fifth

long, broad, steeply graduated, tipped with white and cross-rayed still darker. *Below,* chin, throat and sides of head yellowish ashy grey, darkening to blackish on lower abdomen and vent. The feathers of chin, throat and breast with black bristly shafts. Sexes alike.

STATUS AND HABITAT: Presumably resident. Not common, but frequent between *c.* 1000 and 6500 ft. elevation between November and April (Rangpo, Singtam, Martam, Gangtok). Schäfer took a specimen at Gangtok, 10 February. Stevens found it in the Rungbong Valley up to 3600 ft. Affects dense secondary evergreen jungle.

DISTRIBUTION OUTSIDE SIKKIM: The Himalayas from Garhwal to the Mishmi Hills where it intergrades with the eastern race *saliens* Mayr, stretching through Burma, Yunnan and Indochina. The species is found in Malaya, Sumatra and the Kangean Islands.

GENERAL HABITS: Keeps to trees as well as low scrub, creeping through the branches, and seldom if ever descending to the ground. *Flight* laboured, with the long, white-tipped, graduated tail conspicuous. When shooting down on alarm from a tall tree down a hillside or to dive into shrubbery, looks like a tree pie. *Food:* caterpillars, large insects, lizards, etc. *Call:* a peculiar croak uttered at intervals of a few seconds.

NESTING: A non-parasitic cuckoo. *Season*—April to June. *Nest*—a sparse, shallow platform of twigs, sometimes mixed with roots and coarse grass blades, rather like a dove's nest. Placed 4 to 10 ft. up or higher in a bush, sapling or bamboo clump with no effort at concealment. *Eggs*—2 to 4, chalky white, about 34 × 26 mm.

RACIAL CHARACTERISTICS, MEASUREMENTS, ETC: Differs from *saliens* of Burma etc. in having a larger wing. 3 ♂♂ of typical *tristis* recently collected in E. Nepal by Dr Ripley measure: Wing 169-176; tail (of 2) 380, 383.5 mm. Schäfer's Sikkim ♀ has Wing/Tail 166/380 mm.

Iris brown; orbital skin crimson-magenta; a patch between base of bill and nostril same colour; bill horny green; legs and feet greenish slate.

## *Family* STRIGIDAE: Owls

### *Subfamily* TYTONINAE

### THE SIKKIM BAY OWL

*Phodilus badius saturatus* Robinson

*Phodilus badius saturatus* Robinson, 1927, *Bull. Brit. Orn. Cl.* 47: 121—Native Sikkim.

**Plate 9, fig. 1 (facing p. 80)**

F.B.I. 4: 390

LOCAL NAME:

SIZE: Pigeon—.

FIELD CHARACTERS: A small chestnut-bay owl with vinous-pink facial disc, and white ruff tipped with chestnut and black. *Above*, chestnut, spotted with black and buff. Outer webs of first two primaries barred white and black. Tail chestnut, barred with black. *Below*, vinous-pink spotted with black and white except on foreneck, and down centre of abdomen to under tail-coverts. Legs fully feathered.

STATUS AND HABITAT: Very rare. Recorded in the Teesta Valley at *c.* 2000 ft. elevation by G. E. Shaw (20 November 1915). According to Stevens, confined in the Sikkim Himalayas to heavy foothills forest.

DISTRIBUTION OUTSIDE SIKKIM: Nepal to Assam north and south of the Brahmaputra; Manipur. The species is found in Ceylon and through the Indochinese and Malaysian subregions.

GENERAL HABITS: Entirely nocturnal and almost completely blind in sunlight. *Call:* described as a soft single hoot; also much caterwauling during the breeding season. *Food:* small mammals and birds, lizards, frogs and insects.

NESTING: Not recorded in Sikkim. *Season* (in Assam)—March to May. *Nest*—a natural unlined hollow in a tree. *Eggs*—4 or 5, white, round, about 35×30 mm.

RACIAL CHARACTERISTICS, MEASUREMENTS, ETC: The Fauna gives for ♂♀: Wing 214-237; bill 30-32; tarsus 47-48; tail 92-97 mm.

'Iris deep brown or black; bill creamy yellow; legs and feet clay brown or yellowish brown, the claws paler.'

## *Subfamily* STRIGINAE

### THE HIMALAYAN COLLARED SCOPS OWL

*Otus bakkamoena lettia* (Hodgson)

*Scops lettia* Hodgson, 1833, *Asiat. Res.* 19: 176—Nepal.

**Plate 9, fig. 3 (facing p. 80)**

F.B.I. 4: 427

LOCAL NAME: Lattya kusyal (Nepali).

SIZE: Myna.

FIELD CHARACTERS: A charming little 'horned' owlet, grey-brown or rufous-brown above, vermiculated and mottled with whitish. A prominent pale half collar on upper back. *Below,* chin and throat white or buff, the latter barred and stippled with black. Rest of lower plumage white to rich buff, streaked with black and with fine wavy bars of reddish brown. Legs fully feathered or 'stockinged'. Sexes alike.

STATUS AND HABITAT: Not uncommon. Resident up to at least 6500 ft. (Singtam, Martam, Kewzing, Singhik, Gangtok). Affects open forest and groves of trees about habitations.

DISTRIBUTION OUTSIDE SIKKIM: Nepal east through Assam; Manipur, E. Pakistan. Plains and foothills and up to *c.* 8000 ft. The Western Himalayas from Murree to Garhwal are inhabited by the race *plumipes.* Several other races are found in India and the species is widely distributed in SE. Asia, including the Indochinese and Malaysian subregions.

GENERAL HABITS: Entirely nocturnal. Its presence in a locality is liable to be easily overlooked but for the diagnostic tell-tale call of the male, heard from after dark until before dawn. It is a short single musical hoot, reminiscent in the distance of the bark of a cheetal stag (but shorter), repeated every 15 or 20 seconds or so sometimes for over half an hour at a stretch. Whether the female also calls is not known. *Food:* mice, small birds, beetles, etc.

NESTING: *Season*—February to April; perhaps longer. *Nest*—a natural hollow or old woodpecker-hole in a dead tree stump, 5 to 15 ft. from the ground, unlined. *Eggs*—3 or 4, white, roundish ovals, about 33×28 mm.

RACIAL CHARACTERISTICS, MEASUREMENTS, ETC.. Differs from *plumipes* of the W. Himalayas in having only the legs feathered and the toes bare. A Sikkim Survey specimen (♂) measures: Wing 159; bill 22; tarsus 36; tail 81 mm.

Schäfer's specimen from Gangtok '♂' has Wing 169 mm.

Iris yellowish brown; bill greenish horn; feet and claws dusky olive.

THE EASTERN SPOTTED SCOPS OWL, *Otus spilocephalus spilocephalus* (Blyth), has also been recorded in the Teesta and Rungbong Valleys and is apparently not uncommon between *c.* 3000 and 6000 ft. altitude.

Size and general appearance similar to the Collared Scops, but with the collar on hindneck ill defined. Crown with numerous pale rufescent spots edged with black. Lower plumage rufous or rufescent brown, mottled and vermiculated with whitish and black, spotted and barred on breast.

Entirely nocturnal. *Call:* a metallic, plaintive, double whistle *phew . . . phew* with a half-second's pause between the two. Repeated at intervals of a few seconds for long stretches throughout the night.

## THE FOREST EAGLE-OWL

*Bubo nipalensis nipalensis* Hodgson

*Bubo nipalensis* Hodgson, 1836, *Asiat. Res.* **19**: 172—Nepal.

**Plate 9, fig. 2** (facing p. 80)

F.B.I. **4**: 418

LOCAL NAMES: Huhu (Nepali); Migdori (Bhutia).

SIZE: Kite; heavier.

FIELD CHARACTERS: A large, powerful owl with two black-and-white horn-like feather tufts above the head, fully feathered legs, and brown eyes. *Above*, dark brown scalloped with buff. *Below*, fulvous white barred with blackish on throat and breast, the bars breaking up into chevron-like spots on abdomen. Sexes alike. Young birds pale buff overall, barred with blackish above and below. Wings and tail brown barred with whitish.

STATUS AND HABITAT: Rare. Resident (?) from ? elevation up to *c.* 7000 ft. Stevens mentions two specimens procured in the Rungbong Valley 'below 5000 ft.' Affects heavy tropical forest.

DISTRIBUTION OUTSIDE SIKKIM: The lower Himalayas from Kumaon through Nepal and Bhutan (?) to Assam, East Pakistan; Shevaroy Hills, humid SW. peninsular India, Ceylon. The species extends through the Indochinese subregion.

GENERAL HABITS: Similar to those of the Tawny Fish Owl. Bold and powerful; commonly on the move in daytime. Preys largely upon kaleej pheasants and junglefowl captured at their night roosts. Also credited with killing young barking deer. *Call:* described as 'a low, deep and far-sounding moaning hoot'.

NESTING: Not recorded in Sikkim, and apparently rarely in the Himalayas. Utilizes deserted nests of eagles etc. *Egg*—normally a singleton, white, typical roundish oval, about 61×50 mm.

RACIAL CHARACTERISTICS, MEASUREMENTS, ETC: Legs fully feathered to toes. Inner claw very large. The Fauna gives the measurements (♂♀) as: Wing 425-470; tarsus 60-62; tail 229-250 mm. Stevens measured two Sikkim skins: Wing ♂ 438; ♀ 441 mm.

'Iris brown or hazel brown; bill dull wax yellow to yellow; toes dusky yellow; claws pale horny, darker at tips.'

## THE TAWNY FISH OWL

### *Bubo flavipes* (Hodgson)

*Cultrunguis Flavipes* Hodgson, 1836, *Jour. Asiat. Soc. Bengal* 5: 364, pl. 26—Nepal.

F.B.I. 4: 411

LOCAL NAME: Lak-kyo-o-mung (Lepcha)='the kyo-o-calling devil'.

SIZE: Kite.

FIELD CHARACTERS: A large powerful owl with two long ear-tufts projecting from head, partly feathered tarsus and staring golden yellow eyes. *Above,* rich orange-rufous broadly streaked with blackish brown. *Below,* rich rufous-buff streaked with reddish brown, more heavily on breast. A white patch on throat. Sexes alike.

STATUS AND HABITAT: Resident (?) up to *c.* 6000 ft. altitude where Schäfer obtained a specimen (15 June, Gangtok). I observed a pair of large owls, presumably this species, on a densely forested hillside bordering the Teesta River at Martam (*c.* 3000 ft.) in December 1952, and again at the identical spot in the same trees over two years later (March 1955)! Affects heavy tropical forest near streams.

DISTRIBUTION OUTSIDE SIKKIM: The lower Himalayas from Kashmir through Nepal and Bhutan to Assam and the hills of E. Pakistan. Extends through the Indochinese subregion to S. China.

GENERAL HABITS: Crepuscular and nocturnal, though seemingly little inconvenienced by sunlight and sometimes even hunting in daytime. *Food:* chiefly fish, frogs, crabs, etc., but frequently kills large birds such as junglefowl, and small mammals. *Call:* described by Stuart Baker as a deep *whoo-hoo;* also said to utter a curious cat-like mewing call.

NESTING: Not recorded in Sikkim. *Season* (in Assam)—December to February. *Eggs*—normally 2, white, roundish ovals, about 57×47 mm. Laid in disused nests of eagles.

RACIAL CHARACTERISTICS, MEASUREMENTS, ETC: Tarsus feathered for about one-third length behind, two-thirds in front. The Fauna gives the measurements as: ♂♀ Wing 410-455; tarsus 60-67; tail 215-227 mm. Schäfer's Sikkim skin, '♀', has Wing 430 mm.

Iris yellow; cere dingy green; bill horny black; legs yellowish grey, dingy greenish or slaty green; claws horny black.

## THE COLLARED PIGMY OWLET

*Glaucidium brodiei brodiei* (Burton)

*Noctua Brodiei* Burton, 1836 (1835), *Proc. Zool. Soc. London:* 152—Himalayas (restricted to Simla by Stuart Baker).

**Plate 9, fig. 4 (facing p. 80)**

F.B.I. 4: 450

LOCAL NAME:

SIZE: Bulbul; squatter and shorter tailed.

FIELD CHARACTERS: A passable miniature of the Barred Owlet. Overall, barred grey-brown with a prominent white supercilium, rufous half-collar on upper back, and white patch on throat. Also has a dimorphic rufous or chestnut phase. Sexes alike.

STATUS AND HABITAT: Resident. Fairly common between *c.* 2000 and at least 7000 ft. elevation (Singtam, Martam, Gangtok, Lingtam, Pemionche). In Bhutan, Ludlow obtained it up to 10,000 ft. Affects open forest.

DISTRIBUTION OUTSIDE SIKKIM: The Himalayas from the Afghan border through Kashmir, Nepal and Bhutan to Assam and E. Pakistan. The species stretches through Burma and the Indochinese and Malaysian subregions.

GENERAL HABITS: Largely diurnal. Hunts cicadas, grasshoppers, beetles, lizards, small mammals and birds. Insects are often held in one foot and brought up to the bill to be torn before swallowing, rather like a parakeet tackling a nut. Calls by day as well as night, a pleasant, tinkling, four-noted whistle *toot . . . tootoot . . . toot* repeated every few seconds. The head is turned from side to side while calling, producing a ventriloquistic effect.

NESTING: *Season*—April-May. *Nest*—an unlined natural hollow in a tree-trunk, sometimes a very large one, or an old woodpecker- or barbet-hole, 5 to 30 ft. up. *Eggs*—normally 4, white, round, about 28×24 mm.

RACIAL CHARACTERISTICS, MEASUREMENTS, ETC: Two Sikkim skins in the

Chicago Museum of Natural History examined by me, together with a male collected by the Survey, measure:

| | Wing | Bill | Tarsus | Tail |
|---|---|---|---|---|
| 1 ♂ | 87.5 | 15 | 21 | 57 mm. |
| 2 ♀♀ | 93-97 | 14-14.5 | 21 | 57-59 mm. |

Three ad. specimens (sex?) in Schäfer's Sikkim collection have Wing 91, 96, 99 mm.

Iris bright lemon yellow; bill and feet pale greenish yellow. Tarsus feathered.

## THE HIMALAYAN BARRED OWLET

### *Glaucidium cuculoides cuculoides* (Vigors)

*Noctua cuculoides* Vigors, 1831, *Proc. Comm. Zool. Soc. London:* 8—Himalayas (=Simla-Almora district).

F.B.I. 4: 444

LOCAL NAME: Tanpum (Lepcha).

SIZE: Pigeon—.

FIELD CHARACTERS: A dumpy, 'hornless', dark brown (or olive-brown) owlet, closely barred with whitish above and below. Abdomen whitish with longitudinal blackish striations. A prominent white patch on throat. Sexes alike.

STATUS AND HABITAT: Resident. Common up to *c.* 6500 ft. elevation (Singtam, Martam, Dikchu, Singhik, Temi, Kewzing, Pemionche, Gangtok). Affects thin open forest.

DISTRIBUTION OUTSIDE SIKKIM: The lower Himalayas from Murree through Nepal to W. Bhutan. The rest of Bhutan, Assam hills north of the Brahmaputra, Patkoi and Naga hills and NW. Burma are populated by the race *austerum.* The species extends through the Indochinese subregion to S. China, Hainan, Java, Bali.

GENERAL HABITS: Largely diurnal and hunting freely in the dappled sunlight of open forest. *Food:* beetles, grasshoppers, etc., as well as lizards, mice and small birds. *Flight:* obliquely dipping, as of other owlets—a series of rapid flaps followed by a pause with wings closed. *Call:* normally a rising crescendo of harsh squawks ending abruptly. Also a quavering 'whistle' *woioioioi . . . keek,* and various croaks and chuckles. Uttered mostly during daytime.

NESTING: Gammie took eggs in Sikkim at *c.* 2000 ft. elevation. *Season*—April-May. *Nest*—an unlined hollow in a tree-trunk, 20 to 40 ft. up. *Eggs*—normally 4, white, round, about 37×31 mm.

RACIAL CHARACTERISTICS, MEASUREMENTS, ETC: The adjoining eastern race *austerum* Ripley is larger, darker, and markedly rufescent.

2 ♀♀ collected by the Sikkim Survey measure: Wing 160-162; bill 20.5-22; tarsus 28-30; tail 92-98 mm. A ♀ in Schäfer's Sikkim collection has Wing 160 mm.

Iris lemon yellow; bill greenish horn; feet greyish olive-yellow; claws horny brown.

## THE HIMALAYAN BROWN WOOD OWL

*Strix leptogrammica newarensis* (Hodgson)
*Ulula newarensis* Hodgson, 1836, *Asiat. Res.* 19: 178—Nepal.

F.B.I. 4: 400
LOCAL NAMES: Bulaka (Nepali); Mik-dab-bru (Lepcha).
SIZE: Kite.

FIELD CHARACTERS: A large owl with whitish facial disc and no projecting aigrettes or 'ears'. *Above*, chocolate brown; scapulars, wings and upper tail-coverts barred with white. Tail brown, barred with fulvous and tipped with white. *Below*, chin mixed chocolate and white; a pure white patch on throat. Rest of lower plumage buffy white, suffused with brownish on breast, barred with dark brown. Sexes alike.

STATUS AND HABITAT: Recorded from the base of the hills up to 13,000 ft. in Sikkim. Schäfer obtained a specimen at Gangtok, *c.* 6300 ft., in winter (10 December). Affects forest.

DISTRIBUTION OUTSIDE SIKKIM: Throughout the Himalayas, west to east, normally between 2000-3000 and 8500 ft. elevation. The race *indranee* occurs in southern India. The species ranges through the Indochinese and Malaysian subregions to S. China, Formosa and Hainan.

GENERAL HABITS: Nocturnal. Bold and powerful, preying on pheasants and junglefowl in addition to smaller birds and mammals etc. *Call:* a deep four-noted hoot, *hoo . . . hoohoo . . . hoo.* A. E. Jones has also described what is probably a conversational note between a pair at dusk—a low, sonorous *koo-krrri* 'rather like a domestic pigeon', and querulous screams and loud snapping of the bill on detection of an intruder in the vicinity of the nest, and when apprehensive.

NESTING: *Season*—January to March. *Nest*—of a few sticks and feathers, on a shelf in a precipice or hole scraped in the ground at the foot of a steep rock in a shady ravine. *Eggs*—1 or 2, white, roundish ovals, about 57×46 mm.

RACIAL CHARACTERISTICS, MEASUREMENTS, ETC: Differs from the race *indranee* of Deccan and south India chiefly in its larger size: Wing over 380 mm. against under 370. The Fauna gives the measurements (♂ ♀) as: Wing 382-412; tail 229-335; tarsus 53-56 mm.

Iris brown; bill greenish horny, bluish near base, plumbeous on cere; toes pale leaden; claws dusky.

## THE HIMALAYAN WOOD OWL

*Strix aluco nivicola* (Blyth)

*Syrnium nivicolum* 'Hodgson'=Blyth, 1845, *Jour. Asiat. Soc. Bengal* 14 (1): 185—Himalayas (=Nepal).

F.B.I. 4: 398

LOCAL NAMES: Kashi-op tak-pum (Lepcha); Uko (Bhutia).

SIZE: Kite—.

FIELD CHARACTERS: No aigrettes or 'horns', and with a whitish facial disc. *Above,* rich rufous-brown, barred with dark brown. *Below,* rufous-fulvous, rich on breast, paler elsewhere. Close-barred on chin and throat; streaked and cross-barred with dark brown on rest of lower plumage. Sexes alike; female slightly larger.

STATUS AND HABITAT: Recorded between 6000 and 14,000 ft. elevation in the Sikkim Himalayas. Schäfer procured a specimen at Zalang near Lachen (10 September). Affects rocky forested ravines etc.

DISTRIBUTION OUTSIDE SIKKIM: The Himalayas from Murree to E. Assam north of the Brahmaputra; Lushai Hills. Normally up to *c.* 9000 ft. The race *biddulphi* replaces it in Kashmir and Gilgit to Afghanistan. The species is widespread in Europe to W. Siberia, south to N. Africa; Iran, Turkestan to China and Korea.

GENERAL HABITS: Purely nocturnal, hiding by day in a leafy tree or bush, or even on the ground in a shady ravine, sitting upright and motionless with eyes half closed. Solitary or in pairs. Seldom seen, but commonly heard during night. *Call:* unmistakable when once learnt—a deep, mellow *hoo-hoo* or *hu . . . hoo-hoo* (or *gūg . . . gū-gū-gūroo* or *twit . . . too-hoo*). *Food:* chiefly rats; also other small mammals, lizards, beetles, etc.

NESTING: *Season*—January to April. *Nest*—an unlined hollow in a tree-trunk or cliff. *Eggs*—2 or 3, white, typical round ovals about 48×42 mm.

RACIAL CHARACTERISTICS, MEASUREMENTS, ETC: The race *biddulphi* of Kashmir etc. is paler and greyer in tone of upper plumage without any rufous tinge. Also has the upper parts streaked in addition to the barring.

The Fauna gives for ♂♀ Wing 282-312; tarsus 45-48; tail 168-175 mm. Schäfer's Sikkim specimen (♂ ad.) has Wing 290 mm.

Iris brown; bill pale yellowish flesh, cere brown; tarsus woolly, toes partially feathered; ends of toes plumbeous; claws brown.

## THE SHORTEARED OWL

*Asio flammeus flammeus* (Pontoppidan)

*Strix Flammea* Pontoppidan, 1763, Dansk. Atlas 1: 617, pl. 25—Sweden.

F.B.I. 4: 394

LOCAL NAME:

SIZE: Jungle Crow.

FIELD CHARACTERS: General aspect streaked brown and buff with a darker greyish head and two short blackish 'ears' projecting from above the forwardly directed eyes. Facial disc white with bristly black feathers intermixed, surrounded by a dark brown ruff. Tail and wings barred rufous and black. In flight, the white underside of the pointed wings, blackish at tips and with a prominent blackish bar across each, diagnostic.

STATUS AND HABITAT: Irregular winter visitor and passage migrant; recorded in the Rungbong Valley and elsewhere in the foothills of the Sikkim Himalayas, up to *c.* 6000 ft.—December to end February. Affects open undulating grassy country dotted with bushes.

DISTRIBUTION OUTSIDE SIKKIM: *Summer* (breeding), the Holarctic Region. *Winter,* Africa, southern Asia including practically all India.

GENERAL HABITS: Seen singly; sometimes in loose, scattered parties. More diurnal than most owls, occasionally even hunting during daytime. Normally spends the day resting on the ground at the base of a bush or grass-tussock, often sunning itself in the mornings or afternoons spread-eagled flat on the ground. Steady, deliberate wing beats in flight reminiscent of the Houbara Bustard. *Food:* rats, mice, large grasshoppers, etc.

RACIAL CHARACTERISTICS, MEASUREMENTS, ETC: Wing ♂♀ 290-330; tail 140-160 mm. (Hartert). Tarsus (feathered) *c.* 47 mm.

Iris bright lemon yellow; bill slaty black; toes dark brown; claws horny black.

# *Family* PODARGIDAE: Frogmouths

## HODGSON'S FROGMOUTH

*Batrachostomus hodgsoni hodgsoni* (G. R. Gray)

*Otothrix hodgsoni* G. R. Gray, 1859, *Proc. Zool. Soc. London:* 101, pl. 152, Aves—Northern India = Darjeeling.

**Plate 11, fig. 5** (facing p. 96)

F.B.I. 4: 378

LOCAL NAME:

SIZE: Myna+.

FIELD CHARACTERS: An obliteratingly coloured, speckled greyish brown nightjar irregularly black-blotched on the crown, with an enormous gape and broad flattened horny bill aptly suggestive of its name.

*Female* chestnut overall with broad white patches on scapulars.

STATUS AND HABITAT: Evidently very rare. Not met with by the Sikkim Survey or by Schäfer. Has been recorded in the Great Rangeet Valley at 3000-4000 ft. by Hodgson, and at Namche by Mandelli. Affects subtropical evergreen forest.

DISTRIBUTION OUTSIDE SIKKIM: Nepal (?), Bhutan, Assam north and south of the Brahmaputra; E. Pakistan. Foothills and up to *c.* 6000 ft. elevation. The species extends eastward through the Indochinese subregion.

GENERAL HABITS: Somewhat sluggish; insectivorous, crepuscular and nocturnal. Keeps to heavy jungle. Actions and behaviour like a nightjar's, but perches on branches, lengthwise or across, and normally not on the ground. Captures beetles on the wing as well as on the ground and from branches. Said to utter a soft, rapid *croo-croo* or *cooroo-cooroo,* but voice and calls and habits very imperfectly known.

NESTING: Mandelli took a nest with eggs in Sikkim. *Season*—April to June. *Nest*—a round pad or shallow cup of soft downy feathers coated on the exterior with spider's webs, lichens, bits of bark, etc. Placed on a bare horizontal branch of a tree, 5 to 15 ft. up. *Eggs*—1 or 2, white, long, elliptical, about 27×18 mm.

RACIAL CHARACTERISTICS, MEASUREMENTS, ETC: Wings short and rounded with the fourth and fifth quills longest. Tail long and graduated. Conspicuous bristly feathers at base of bill and tufts of the same in front of the eyes. Prominent ear-tufts with bristles at end of the feathers.

The Fauna gives the measurements (♂♀) as: Wing 126-141; bill 17-18; lateral width at gape 29-32; tarsus 15-16; tail 131-143 mm.

Iris variegated grey, brown and yellow; bill fleshy pink or yellowish horn; legs and feet pinkish flesh.

## *Family* CAPRIMULGIDAE: Nightjars

### THE HIMALAYAN JUNGLE NIGHTJAR

***Caprimulgus indicus hazarae*** Whistler & Kinnear

*Caprimulgus indicus hazarae* Whistler & Kinnear, 1935, *Jour. Bombay Nat. Hist. Soc.* 38: 37—Abbotabad, Hazara Dist., NW. Himalayas.

F.B.I. 4: 367 (under *jotaka*)

LOCAL NAME: Tamor (Lepcha).

SIZE: Pigeon—; with a longer tail.

FIELD CHARACTERS: A soft-plumaged, long-winged, owl-like bird, brownish buff and grey mottled and streaked with rufous, black and white; colour remarkably obliterative when bird is squatting on the ground. Best identified by the characteristic call: *chuck-chuck* or *chucko-chucko* etc. in quick-repeated runs of 7 to 12 times.

STATUS AND HABITAT: ? Possibly an altitudinal migrant, or overlooked in winter when silent. First heard by the Survey on 17 April (Lachen, *c.* 9000 ft.), but Schäfer procured a specimen at Chungthang (*c.* 5000 ft.) on 6 December. According to Stevens occurs up to 7000 or 8000 ft. in the Sikkim Himalayas during the breeding season, and down to their base in winter. Ludlow obtained specimens in Bhutan and SE. Tibet between 6500 and 11,000 feet—April, June, July. Affects forest with ravines and glades.

DISTRIBUTION OUTSIDE SIKKIM: The Himalayas from Hazara District in NW. Pakistan east to Assam, Burma and Yunnan—from foothills up. The nominate race occupies peninsular India south of the Himalayas. The species ranges over south-east Siberia, W. China, Japan and the Palau Islands, migrating south in winter from the northern parts.

GENERAL HABITS: As of the family—insectivorous, crepuscular and nocturnal. Spends the daytime squatting on the ground at the base of a bush, or lengthwise along the branch of a tree. Has a silent, owl-like sailing flight. Captures beetles, moths, etc. on the wing, turning and twisting in their pursuit or to avoid obstacles with great dexterity. *Call: chuck* or *chucko* rapidly repeated in runs of 7 to 12, and resumed after a break of a second or so, for an hour or more at a stretch. Very vocal during the breeding season, particularly during moonlit nights and in the early hours before dawn (*c.* 2 to 4 a.m.).

NESTING: Not recorded in Sikkim. *Season*—presumably April to ?. *Eggs*—2, white, marbled with grey, about 31×23 mm. Laid on bare, often stony ground in ravines etc.

RACIAL CHARACTERISTICS, MEASUREMENTS, ETC: In the species *indicus* the tarsus is feathered. ♂: 4 outer pairs of rectrices with subterminal white spots. First four primaries with a white spot, that on the first primary very small. A white band across throat. ♀: No white tips to tail feathers; spots on the primaries small and rufous. Throat-band buff. The Himalayan race *hazarae* differs from peninsular Indian *indicus* in being warmer and browner in coloration, with the markings on back heavier and barring on tail broader. Also averages larger. A Schäfer skin (♀) from Sikkim has Wing/Tail 213/140 mm. Distance from tip of first primary to tip of fourth 22 mm. (Stresemann).

Iris reddish brown; bill blackish horn; legs brown.

Neither the Survey nor Schäfer met with the LONGTAILED NIGHTJAR, *Caprimulgus macrurus albonotatus* Tickell, in Sikkim. According to Stevens this has been obtained by G. E. Shaw in the Teesta Valley at elevations from 2500 to 3750 ft.

Size and overall appearance same as of the Himalayan Jungle Nightjar, but ♂ has only *two* outer pairs of rectrices with broad white tips. A white spot each on first four primaries, that on the second quill interrupted in the middle. ♀: spots on primaries rufous-buff; tips of the two outermost pairs of rectrices smaller and buff.

Tarsi feathered in both sexes. *Call:* a diagnostic loud, resonant *chaunk, chaunk, chaunk* likened to the distant blows of an adze on a plank. It is repeated any number of times up to 50 or so, at the rate of about 5 in four seconds. Uttered from a bough almost incessantly from dusk to dawn, especially during the breeding season.

## *Family* APODIDAE: Swifts

### *Subfamily* APODINAE

#### THE HIMALAYAN PLAINRUMPED SWIFTLET

*Collocalia brevirostris brevirostris* (McClelland)

*Hirundo brevirostris* McClelland, 1840, *Proc. Zool. Soc. London:* 155—Assam.

F.B.I. 4: 348

LOCAL NAME:

SIZE: Sparrow—.

FIELD CHARACTERS: A tiny, slender, fork-tailed, brown swift. *Above,* dark brown with a slightly paler rump. *Below,* uniformly greyish brown. Sexes alike.

STATUS AND HABITAT: Noted as uncommon but frequent at between 5000 and 6500 ft. (Chungthang, Gangtok) in April, and Schäfer obtained specimens at the latter place in June. Blanford records it from the Chola Range at 12,000 ft. in August, as well as at low elevations throughout the Teesta Valley in autumn (1870). Apparently ranges to high elevations even in winter as Stevens observed it on the Singalila Ridge near Phalut (*c.* 11,700 ft.) in February. Ludlow found it common in Bhutan and procured specimens between 5000 and 12,750 ft., August to November.

DISTRIBUTION OUTSIDE SIKKIM: The Himalayas from E. Punjab to Assam, from the foothills up to *c.* 12,000 ft. Uncommonly to the Andamans in winter. The species occurs throughout the Indochinese subregion and central and western China.

GENERAL HABITS: Gregarious like the other swifts, spending most of the day on the wing hawking insects, especially high up over river valleys and defiles. The characteristic swift flight is punctuated from time to time by interludes of pipistrelle-like fluttering. Roosts in enormous clusters in dark caves and grottoes, clinging like pipistrelle bats to the rough rock surfaces in a vertical position, head upwards. The continuous chorus of soft, twittering *chit-chit* whioh the birds utter is reminiscent of a bat roost. The ease and suddenness with which the birds are apparently able to adapt their eyesight to the pitch-dark interior of a cave, as they shoot in through a narrow entrance from the brilliant sunshine outside and find their way among its hidden recesses, is quite phenomenal.

NESTING: Breeds in dark caves in dense colonies. No record in Sikkim, but one such cave in the Chakrata District, U.P., at *c.* 9000 ft. is well described by Col. E. A. Glennie (*Jour. Bombay Nat. Hist. Soc.* 44: 549, 1944). *Season*—May-June. *Nest*—a tiny open cup of agglutinated moss with the rim sloping down from the vertical rock wall to which it is gummed with the birds' saliva. *Eggs*—2, white, long narrow blunt ovals. Size about 22×14 mm.

RACIAL CHARACTERISTICS, MEASUREMENTS, ETC: In this species the tail is forked 6-12 mm. deep, and the tarsus always feathered in front. Schäfer's Sikkim skins, 4 ad. (sex?), have Wing 123, 126, 126, 128 mm.

Iris brown; bill black; legs and feet brownish fleshy.

## THE WHITETHROATED SPINETAIL SWIFT

*Chaetura caudacuta nudipes* (Hodgson)

*Cypselus (Chaetura) nudipes* Hodgson, 1837 (1836), *Jour. Asiat. Soc. Bengal* 5: 779—Nepal.

F.B.I. 4: 340

LOCAL NAME: Silli-ang tiphi-timbo (Lepcha).

SIZE: Bulbul +.

FIELD CHARACTERS: A large blackish brown swift, normally seen hawking insects high up in the air on long, narrow, pointed, bow-shaped wings. *Above*, glossy black except back (pale brown). Wings with the secondaries largely white on the inner webs. *Below*, chin, throat and under tail-coverts pure white. Rest of underparts dark brown with a whitish patch on flanks. Sexes alike.

STATUS AND HABITAT: A bird of enormous foraging range and of sudden appearances and disappearances—here one moment, miles away the next. Therefore, local status difficult to determine unless nest colony actually found. Noted by the Survey at Pakyong, Temi and Rinchinpong in March/April. F. N. Betts observed a large flock hawking insects over the yak pastures at Thangu, *c.* 13,000 ft., on the evening of 21 May when it cleared up after a shower of rain; nowhere else during the whole of that month's trekking in northern Sikkim.

Ludlow met with large numbers on the Donga La in Bhutan, *c.* 10,000 ft., on 25 July and secured a specimen. He also collected specimens at 7000 ft. in SE. Tibet in April/May with gonads in breeding condition.

DISTRIBUTION OUTSIDE SIKKIM: The Himalayas from Hazara in the west, through Assam to Yunnan, probably breeding above *c.* 5000 ft. The species is found in N. Asia and through the Indochinese sub-region to Formosa.

GENERAL HABITS: Parties, often widely scattered, spend the day on the wing hawking beetles, bugs and other insects over the valleys, or sweeping round the contours and crags at phenomenal speed with effortless ease. It is reputed to be one of the fastest fliers among birds. The wings produce a peculiar musical sound as the birds hurtle through space. A loud, lively, shrill, 'screaming' cry is uttered, particularly when a flock is disporting itself in the air at sunset prior to retiring for the night. The birds roost in colonies, clinging to rough rock surfaces within fissures of cliffs, or inside the hollow boles of large trees.

NESTING: Unknown.

RACIAL CHARACTERISTICS, MEASUREMENTS, ETC: In the species *caudacuta* the tail feathers are rounded at the tips with the naked shafts projecting like spines a few millimetres beyond. The race *cochinchinensis* (of the Assam hills south of the Brahmaputra, etc.) differs from ours in being smaller and darker, with the chin and throat smoky grey instead of white.

The Fauna gives for *nudipes* ♂♀: Wing 196-209; tail 51-57 mm.

Iris brown; bill black; legs and feet purplish black; claws black.

THE WHITERUMPED SPINETAIL SWIFT, *Chaetura sylvatica* (Tickell) also occurs in Sikkim. Status unknown. A flock was observed by me high up in the air above Temi on 31 March (1955). Size same as of the House Swift. *Above*, black with a broad white rump-band. *Below*, chin, throat and breast greyish brown passing into white on abdomen and under tail-coverts. The white of the underparts is diagnostic.

Hawks insects over forested hillsides and river valleys.

## BLYTH'S WHITERUMPED SPINETAIL SWIFT

*Apus pacificus leuconyx* (Blyth)

*Cypselus leuconyx* Blyth, 1845, *Jour. Asiat. Soc. Bengal* 14 (1): 212—Deccan.

F.B.I. 4: 331

LOCAL NAME:

SIZE: Sparrow.

FIELD CHARACTERS: *Above*, blackish brown with a broad white band across rump. *Below*, chin and throat whitish; rest of lower plumage brown, mottled with black and white. Sexes alike.

STATUS AND HABITAT: Uncertain. Not met with in Sikkim by the Survey, nor by Stevens or Meinertzhagen, but Schäfer collected a specimen at Gangtok on 11 June. In Bhutan, Ludlow saw it frequently between 5000 and 6000 ft. in July. He took specimens at *c.* 11,500 ft. in SE. Tibet in June, and describes the bird as common in summer in the Lower Tsangpo Valley, breeding under eaves of village houses.

DISTRIBUTION OUTSIDE SIKKIM: *Summer* (breeding), the Himalayas from Murree to Bhutan; SE. Tibet; Khasia Hills. *Winter*, south in the Indian peninsula to the Deccan and Malabar. The species is found in E. Asia south to the Himalayas, the northern Indochinese subregion and S. Japan. Northern birds migrate to Australia.

GENERAL HABITS: Typical of the swifts. Gregarious; keeps in small flocks which hawk winged insects in the air.

NESTING: Not recorded in Sikkim. *Nest*—a half-cup of tiny twigs and rubbish glued together with the birds' saliva, attached to the perpendicular rock surface in clefts. In colonies, but individually and not in a clustered mass or 'village' like House Swifts' nests. *Eggs*—2 or 3, white, elongated, about 23×15 mm.

RACIAL CHARACTERISTICS, MEASUREMENTS, ETC: Schäfer's Sikkim skin (sex?) has Wing 162 mm. 3 ♂♂ collected by Ludlow in SE. Tibet give Wing 174, 175, 181 mm.[1]

Iris dark brown; bill black; legs and feet pale flesh colour; claws darker.

## THE NEPAL HOUSE SWIFT

*Apus affinis nipalensis* (Hodgson)

*Cypselus Nipalensis* Hodgson, 1836, *Jour. Asiat. Soc. Bengal* 5: 789—central region of Nepal.

F.B.I. 4: 334

LOCAL NAME: Batasi (Nepali ?).

SIZE: Sparrow—.

FIELD CHARACTERS: A smoky black swift with white throat, white rump, short square tail, and long narrow pointed wings. Sexes alike.

STATUS AND HABITAT: Not uncommon between *c.* 4500 and 6500 ft. from mid-March (Arita, Gangtok). Not noted between November and end February, so presumably spends the winter at lower altitudes (in the plains?). In Nepal it leaves the Valley in mid-October and returns in early March.

In the verandas of several of the officials' bungalows in Gangtok, mud nests of the Striated Swallow (*Hirundo daurica nipalensis*) were usurped by House Swifts. The surest indication of this, when the interlopers themselves are not present, is the untidy ruff of feathers with which the swifts invariably bedeck the entrance while lining the interior.

DISTRIBUTION OUTSIDE SIKKIM: Nepal, east through the Himalayas to W. Assam (Kamrup District). The nominate *affinis* is the race of peninsular India. The species, in many other races, is widely spread in Africa, the Middle East, India, the Indochinese and Malaysian subregions to the Philippines, S. China, Formosa.

GENERAL HABITS: Typical swift. Gregarious. Flies about at great speed throughout the day, hawking winged insects. In the evenings, before going to roost, disorderly rabbles 'ball' high up in the heavens in play, uttering shrill joyous screams as they mill around.

[1] In their larger measurements these SE. Tibet birds agree with the nominate race, but in coloration are indistinguishable from *leuconyx*. They were assigned by Lack to a new race, *Apus pacificus sálimalii* (1958, *JBNHS* 55: 160), since synonymized by Ripley with *A. p. kanoi* (Yamashina).—Synopsis Bds. India Pakistan.

NESTING: *Season*—April to July. I cannot find recorded, nor did myself come across, any 'legitimate' or self-built nest colonies or 'villages' of this swift in Sikkim. The general practice here seems to be for individual pairs to take possession of swallows' nests. One pair was observed building under the eaves of Arita dak bungalow on 11 April. *Eggs*—2 to 4, white, long and narrow, about 22×15 mm.

RACIAL CHARACTERISTICS, MEASUREMENTS, ETC: Differs from *affinis* of the plains in being darker, with the crown wholly brown without any trace of grey. The Fauna gives for ♂♀: Wing 124-134; tail 39-44 mm.

Iris brown; bill black; legs and feet pinkish brown or purplish black; claws black.

## *Family* TROGONIDAE: Trogons

### THE REDHEADED TROGON

*Harpactes erythrocephalus hodgsonii* (Gould)

*Trogon* (*Harpactes*) *Hodgsonii* Gould, 1838, Monogr. Trogonidae, pl. 34—Nepal.

**Plate 11, fig. 4 (facing p. 96)**

F.B.I. 4: 318

LOCAL NAME: Sakvor (Lepcha).

SIZE: Myna; with long tail *c.* 7 inches.

FIELD CHARACTERS: *Male:* Head, neck and breast deep crimson, sometimes with traces of a white breast-band. Back and upper parts chiefly rusty brown. Long, broad, square-ended tail chestnut, black and white. Underparts brighter and lighter crimson.

*Female:* Head, neck and breast dull orange-brown. Rest of lower plumage crimson as in male. In both sexes the white in the outer rectrices and wings is conspicuous in flight.

STATUS AND HABITAT: Resident but sparse, between *c.* 2000 and 6500 ft. (Dikchu, Singhik, Chungthang, Gangtok). Affects dense evergreen and mixed deciduous and bamboo forest.

DISTRIBUTION OUTSIDE SIKKIM: The Himalayas between 500 ft. (duars) and 5000 ft. elevation, from Kumaon through Nepal, Bhutan, central Assam hills, and Manipur. The species extends through the E. Pakistan hills, Burma, and Malaya to S. China and Hainan Island.

GENERAL HABITS: Entirely arboreal, partially crepuscular, and largely insectivorous though it also eats some berries and vegetable matter. Rather sluggish. Usually seen singly or in pairs perched upright and silent on a shady branch or stump, making occasional fluttering sorties at passing insects. These are captured on the wing, as well as picked off tree-trunks or branches. Silent on the whole; sometimes utters a single croak, and also a curious soft mewing call. In spite of its brilliant coloration, difficult to pick out from its dark shady surroundings until it flies, and particularly so if sitting with the brown back turned to observer as it has an uncanny habit of doing.

NESTING: *Season*—May to June. *Nest*—a natural hollow in a rotting tree-trunk, or a deserted woodpecker hole, 5 to 15 ft. up. *Eggs*—3 or 4, buff, spherical, highly glossed, about 29×24 mm.

RACIAL CHARACTERISTICS, MEASUREMENTS, ETC: Specimens collected by Schäfer in Sikkim measure Wing 4 ♂♂ 146, 148, 155, 155; 4 ♀♀ 144, 148, 150, 151 mm. (Stresemann). The race *hodgsonii* differs from nominate *erythrocephalus* of S. Burma in being larger, with a smaller Wing/Bill index and deeper coloration. The NE. Assam and upper Burma population (*helenae*) is intermediate between these two.

Iris dull red to crimson; orbital skin purplish blue; bill lavender blue, blackish on culmen and tips of both mandibles; legs and feet brownish flesh.

## *Family* ALCEDINIDAE: Kingfishers

### THE WEST HIMALAYAN PIED KINGFISHER

*Ceryle lugubris continentalis* Hartert

*Ceryle lugubris continentalis* Hartert, 1900, *Nov. Zool.* 7: 534—Sikkim.

F.B.I. 4: 248 (part)

LOCAL NAME: Ung-ka-zhu (Lepcha).

SIZE: House Crow—.

FIELD CHARACTERS: A large, crested, black-and-white kingfisher. *Male: Above*, including wings and tail, blackish grey, barred and spotted with white. A broad white semi-collar on hindneck. *Below*, white. Flanks and sides of abdomen barred. A prominent pectoral band of black spots mixed with rufous-brown.

*Female* similar, but with under wing-coverts and axillaries (seen only in flight) pale rufous-brown.

STATUS AND HABITAT: Not common, but frequent—solos or pairs—on the Teesta River and side streams up to *c.* 3000 ft. (Singtam, Martam), and on the Rungbong (*vide* Stevens) up to *c.* 4750 ft. Partial to well-wooded spots where rocky torrential feeder streams join the main river.

DISTRIBUTION OUTSIDE SIKKIM: The western Himalayas from Kashmir through Nepal to W. Bhutan, locally up to 7000 ft. The adjoining E. Himalayan race *guttulata* stretches from E. Bhutan to Assam, E. Pakistan and Burma. The species extends through S. China and the northern Indochinese subregion to Japan.

GENERAL HABITS: Rather parochial. Usually seen perched silently on a well-shaded rock at the edge of a stream, erecting the full crest and jerking up the tail from time to time. Dives obliquely into the water from this vantage point to capture its prey near the surface; does not normally hover in the manner of the Pied Kingfisher of the plains. *Food:* mainly fish. *Flight:* swift and powerful, with deliberate wing beats, usually low over the water.

NESTING: Not specifically recorded in Sikkim. *Season*—chiefly March-April. *Nest*—a horizontal tunnel dug into a stream bank, sometimes several feet long, ending in a widened egg-chamber. Unlined, but soon becoming strewn with smelly cast-up fish bones. *Eggs*—4 or 5, white, roundish, about 39×33 mm.

West Himalayan Pied Kingfisher
About one-fourth

RACIAL CHARACTERISTICS, MEASUREMENTS, ETC: Differs from the adjacent E. Himalayan race *guttulata* in being paler, with the back and upper wing-coverts less blackish. A ♀ collected by the Sikkim Survey measures: Wing 186; bill 74; tarsus 15; tail 112 mm.

Iris brown; bill horny black, pale plumbeous laterally at base and extreme tip of lower mandible; legs and feet greenish plumbeous; claws horny brown.

The following kingfishers have been recorded from the 'Sikkim terai' and/or are likely to be met with at the lower elevations and in the foothills.

1. BLYTH'S KINGFISHER, *Alcedo hercules* Laubmann

SIZE: Slightly larger than 2 and 3. Similar to them overall but crown and nape black, transversely barred with bluish white.

2. THE COMMON INDIAN KINGFISHER, *Alcedo atthis bengalensis* Gmelin

SIZE: Sparrow+. Blue and green above, transversely barred on head with black and blue. Rusty below. Ear-coverts ferruginous.

3. THE ASSAM BLUE-EARED KINGFISHER, *Alcedo meninting coltarti* Baker

SIZE: Sparrow+. Very similar to 2, but with ear-coverts deep blue.

4. THE THREETOED FOREST KINGFISHER, *Ceyx erithacus erithacus* Linnaeus

SIZE: Sparrow. Orange-brown, lilac and blue above; rusty orange-yellow below. A deep blue patch on either side of neck.

5. THE BROWNHEADED STORKBILLED KINGFISHER, *Pelargopsis capensis capensis* (Linnaeus)

SIZE: Pigeon−. Head brown. Upper parts pale greenish blue. Lower plumage yellowish brown or ochraceous. Enormous blood-red bill.

6. THE INDIAN RUDDY KINGFISHER, *Halcyon coromanda coromanda* (Latham)

SIZE: Myna+. Overall chestnut-rufous. Lower back and rump white mixed with pale blue.

7. THE WHITEBREASTED KINGFISHER, *Halcyon smyrnensis smyrnensis* (Linnaeus)

SIZE: Myna. Brilliant turquoise blue above, with deep chocolate brown head, neck and underparts. Breast ('shirt front') white.

## *Family* MEROPIDAE: Bee-eaters

### THE BLUEBEARDED BEE-EATER

*Nyctyornis athertoni athertoni* (Jardine & Selby)

*Merops athertoni* Jardine & Selby, 1830, Illustr. Ornith. 2: pl. 58 and text—India = near Bangalore.

F.B.I. 4: 242

LOCAL NAMES: Bukay-chara (Nepali); Saṇg-rhyok (Lepcha).

SIZE: Myna; slimmer.

FIELD CHARACTERS: A large grass-green bee-eater with slightly curved blackish bill. Forehead, throat and upper breast (including recumbent 'beard' of elongated feathers) brilliant pale blue. Rest of underparts ochre-buff, streaked with green. Tail square-cut, without projecting pin feathers. Sexes alike.

STATUS AND HABITAT: Uncommon. Resident (?) at low elevations. Recorded in the Rungbong and Teesta Valleys at 1800 ft. in September, and 3500 ft. in December. Affects secondary evergreen foothills forest.

DISTRIBUTION OUTSIDE SIKKIM: The lower Himalayas, up to c. 5000 ft., from Dehra Dun to E. Assam, and most of the hilly mixed evergreen biotopes in peninsular India. Also Burma and through the Indochinese subregion to Hainan Island.

GENERAL HABITS: Arboreal and entirely insectivorous. Hunts

bees, wasps and other winged insects in the air, sailing gracefully back after each capture to its base in the foliage canopy of some tall forest tree. *Flight:* dipping and very barbet-like, a few rapid wing beats followed by a short glide. Its presence in a forest patch is usually revealed by its harsh guttural calls, *kor-r-r, kor-r-r,* reminiscent of the noises that preface the *kutroo* calls of the Large Green Barbet. When uttering these croaks the 'beard' stands away from the breast and is clearly visible in profile.

NESTING: Not recorded in Sikkim. *Season* (elsewhere in N. India)—April-May. *Nest*—a deep horizontal tunnel bored in an earth bank or cutting. *Eggs*—4 to 6, white, roundish, about 30×28 mm.

RACIAL CHARACTERISTICS, MEASUREMENTS, ETC: Specimens of this bee-eater recently collected in Orissa measure:

| | Wing | Bill | Tarsus | Tail |
|---|---|---|---|---|
| 3 ♂♂ | 136-141 | 52-56 | 18-19 | 127-135 mm. |
| 2 ♀♀ | 135-140 | 49.5-52 | 18.5-19 | 127-130 mm. |

Iris bright golden orange; bill horny brown, grey at chin and on basal half of lower mandible; legs and feet pale sage-green; claws horny brown.

## *Family* CORACIIDAE: Rollers or Blue Jays

### THE BROADBILLED ROLLER, or DOLLAR BIRD

*Eurystomus orientalis cyanicollis* Vieillot

*Eurystomus cyanicollis* Vieillot. 1819, Nouv. Dict. d'Hist. Nat. **29**: 425—'les Indes'=Chandernagor, Bengal.

F.B.I. **4**: 228

LOCAL NAME: Tak-rel-vong (Lepcha).

SIZE: Pigeon.

FIELD CHARACTERS: A dark greenish brown and purple blue-black roller with blackish head and orange-red legs and bill. A broad pale blue roundish patch (the 'dollar') on wings, particularly conspicuous in flight. Sexes alike.

STATUS AND HABITAT: Rare. Obtained by G. E. Shaw in the Teesta Valley up to 2000 ft. elevation. Affects heavy secondary tropical jungle.

DISTRIBUTION OUTSIDE SIKKIM: The Himalayan foothills up to *c.* 3000 ft. from Kumaon through Nepal to Assam and E. Pakistan. Isolated races occur in Kerala, Ceylon and the Andamans. The species extends through the Indochinese and Malaysian subregions and China to Korea. Also the Philippines and Australasia.

GENERAL HABITS: Somewhat crepuscular. Sits with feathers fluffed out on some exposed tree-top, keeping a sharp look-out for prey on the ground and in the air. Rather lethargic, but capable of agile aerial manœuvres when in pursuit of its quarry. *Food:* large insects mostly taken on the wing, their capture facilitated by the broadened gape. Also eats lizards etc. *Call:* a harsh *chak* repeated at intervals of a second or two, varied occasionally by a rapid *chuck-chuck-chuck-chuck.*

NESTING: Not recorded in Sikkim territory. *Season*—March to May. *Nest*—a natural hollow in a lofty tree-trunk, 40 to 100 ft. up. *Eggs*—3 or 4, white, rather spherical, about 37×29 mm.

RACIAL CHARACTERISTICS, MEASUREMENTS, ETC: The Fauna gives for ♂♀ Wing 178-202; bill 23-26; tarsus 19-20; tail 93-107 mm.

Iris dark brown to crimson-brown; bill orange-red or vermilion, blackish at tip; gape orange-yellow; legs and feet orange-red or coral-red; claws blackish brown.

## *Family* UPUPIDAE: Hoopoes

### THE TIBETAN HOOPOE

*Upupa epops saturata* Lönnberg

*Upupa epops saturata* Lönnberg, 1909, Ark. Zool. 5 (9): 29—Kjachta, S. Transbaikalia.

F.B.I. 4: 310

LOCAL NAME:

SIZE: Myna.

FIELD CHARACTERS: A fawn coloured bird with prominent black-and-white zebra markings on back, wings and tail. A conspicuous black-tipped crest: full and fan-shaped when erected, falling to a point behind the head when folded. Long, slender, gently curved bill. Sexes alike.

STATUS AND HABITAT: Probably breeds in N. Sikkim, but definite data lacking. I have examined a specimen (♀) in the Chicago Museum of Natural History collected at Thangu, 13,000 ft., 21 May 1931. Schäfer procured three males at Lachen, *c.* 9000 ft., between 11 September and 12 October, and a fourth specimen, also male, at 'Kiang-Lager', N. Sikkim, *c.* 16,500 ft. (12 October) presumably while on passage to their winter quarters at lower elevations and in the Indian plains. Stevens records it as an autumn passage migrant at elevations between *c.* 3500 and 4700 ft. in September and October.

Ludlow saw it above 5000 ft. in summer throughout Bhutan, and took a specimen at 7500 ft. on 4 July.

DISTRIBUTION OUTSIDE SIKKIM: *Summer* (breeding), E. Asia in Siberia and Manchuria south to Tibet. The Tibetan facies of the high Himalayas from Nepal and Sikkim to Yunnan. *Winter*, plains in Nepal, Bihar, Orissa, Bengal, Assam, E. Pakistan. The species, in other races, often jumbled and overlapping in their winter quarters, is found in Europe and Asia, south to Africa and Madagascar, the Middle East, China, the Indochinese subregion and Malaysia.

Tibetan Hoopoe
About two-fifths

GENERAL HABITS: Affects openly wooded country. Walks and runs about on the ground with a quail-like, rather waddling gait, probing into the soil with its bill open forceps-wise for insects and larvae, worms, etc. The crest is flicked open like a fan from time to time. *Call:* a soft, musical, penetrating *hoo-po* or *hoo-po-po* repeated in interrupted runs for many minutes at a time. Also has some harsh croaks.

NESTING: Not recorded in Sikkim. *Nest*—a hole in a tree or building untidily lined with straw and rubbish, notorious for its filthiness and stench. *Eggs*—5 or 6, white. Size about 26×18 mm.

RACIAL CHARACTERISTICS, MEASUREMENTS, ETC: The race *saturata* is considered by many ornithologists to be indistinguishable from typical *epops* of Europe. It is just a trifle darker on the back and wings, and more brown less vinous on the breast than *epops*.

Stresemann measures a series collected by Schäfer in N. Sikkim and S. Tibet 13 ♂♀ Wing 141-155 (av. 148.4) mm.

Iris brown; bill brownish plumbeous, paler (pinkish) at base; legs and feet brownish plumbeous.

1. Sikkim Bay Owl (*Phodilus b. saturatus*) 2. Forest Eagle-Owl (*Bubo n. nipalensis*) 3. Himalayan Collared Scops Owl (*Otus b. lettia*) 4. Collared Pigmy Owlet (*Glaucidium b. brodiei*) 5. Bonelli's Hawk-Eagle (*Nisaëtus f. fasciatus*) 6. Black Eagle (*Ictinaëtus m. perniger*) 7. Himalayan Falconet (*Microhierax c. caerulescens*)

PLATE 9

1. Crimson Horned Pheasant, or Satyr Tragopan (*Tragopan satyra*) 2. Common Hill Partridge (*Arborophila t. torqueola*) 3. Snow Partridge (*Lerwa lerwa*) 4. Blood Pheasant (*Ithaginis c. affinis*) 5. Eastern Goosander (*Mergus m. orientalis*) 6. Ibisbill (*Ibidorhyncha struthersii*)

PLATE 10

## *Family* BUCEROTIDAE: Hornbills

### THE RUFOUSNECKED HORNBILL

*Aceros nipalensis* (Hodgson)

*Buceros nipalensis* Hodgson, 1829, *Asiat. Res.* 18 (1): 178, 2 pl.—Nepal.

F.B.I. 4: 294

LOCAL NAME: Kolep (Lepcha).

SIZE: Vulture—.

FIELD CHARACTERS: *Male:* Head (with bushy mop-like crest), neck and breast rufous, changing to maroon on abdomen, and blackish maroon further down. Rest of upper plumage black, glossed with dark green. Outer primaries tipped white. Terminal half of long, graduated tail white. Heavy horn-shaped yellow bill without casque, but grooved with blackish on sides of upper mandible. Cheeks, chin and throat unfeathered, bright scarlet. Naked patch round eye bright pale blue.

*Female:* All black, but with outer wing quills white-tipped as in male, and terminal half of tail also white.

STATUS AND HABITAT: Not met with by the Loke-Sálim Ali Survey. Present status unknown. Stevens observed one at *c.* 1800 ft. in the Sikkim Himalayas, and mentions seeing specimens collected in the Teesta Valley. Apparently fast disappearing from its former haunts and habitat following on the steady destruction of primeval forest.

DISTRIBUTION OUTSIDE SIKKIM: The Himalayan terai and foothills up to *c.* 6000 ft. elevation, from Nepal to E. Assam. Cachar, Manipur, Lushai Hills, probably E. Pakistan. Farther east through Burma and the Indochinese subregion.

NESTING: In the 1870's Gammie found a pair nesting at Poomong, *c.* 2000 ft. (Darjeeling Dist. ?) in May, in a natural hollow 80-90 ft. up in a lofty *Dysoxylon* tree. (Hume, Nests and Eggs 3: 77-79.)

MEASUREMENTS: The Fauna gives

| | Wing | Bill | Tarsus | Tail |
|---|---|---|---|---|
| ♂♂ | 445-470 | 215-240 | *c.* 74 | 395-456 mm. |
| ♀♀ | 434-440 | 188-200 | | |

### THE GREAT HORNBILL

*Buceros bicornis homrai* Hodgson

*Buceros homrai* Hodgson, 1832, *Jour. Asiat. Soc. Bengal* 1: 251—Nepal.

F.B.I. 4: 284

LOCAL NAMES: Homrai (Nepali); Kugrong, Kudong (Lepcha).

SIZE: Vulture.

FIELD CHARACTERS: A large black-and-white arboreal bird with enormous horn-shaped yellow-and-black bill surmounted by a ponderous looking, concave casque. Face, back and underparts black. Wings with double white bars conspicuous in flight. Neck, lower abdomen, upper and under tail-coverts and tail white, the last with a broad black subterminal band.

*Female:* similar but with a smaller bill.

STATUS AND HABITAT: Resident. Not common. Sparingly distributed in tropical evergreen forest biotope at the lower elevations (Martam, Toong, Dikchu). According to Stevens up to at least 4500 ft. in the Teesta Valley.

Great Hornbill
About one-seventh

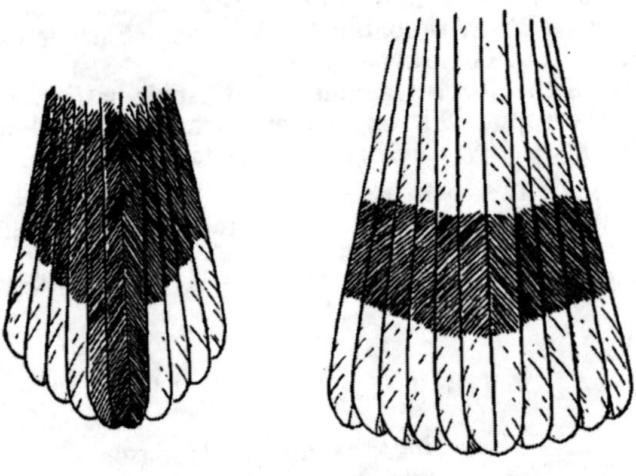

Large Indian Pied Hornbill Great Hornbill
About one-eighth

DISTRIBUTION OUTSIDE SIKKIM: The lower Himalayas from Kumaon through Nepal to Assam and E. Pakistan. The heavy rainfall section of the Western Ghats from about Khandala to S. Travancore. The species ranges through Burma and the Indochinese subregion to Malaya and Sumatra.

GENERAL HABITS: Keeps in pairs or small parties of 3 to 5. Entirely arboreal and mainly frugivorous, but also eats small mammals, young birds, lizards, etc. The birds seem to possess a very fine sense of chronometer time and travel over regular routes to and from their feeding and roosting places day after day with great punctuality. *Flight:* slow and heavy with deliberate wing beats, the rasping noise of which can be heard over long distances across the river valleys. *Call:* a deep grunt or roar, uttered with neck and bill upstretched; also a loud reverberating *tok, tok.* The white foreneck feathers and wing-bands are habitually dyed yellow with the oily exudation of the preen gland rubbed in with the bill.

NESTING: Not specifically recorded in Sikkim. *Season* (W. Himalayas)—March-April. *Nest*—an unlined natural hollow in a lofty tree-trunk, 50 to 75 ft. up or higher. The hollow is walled up by the birds using their dung as cement, leaving a narrow slit through which the male feeds his incubating spouse. The wall is broken down after the young hatch out, and rebuilt after the female has released herself in order to assist in foraging for the young until they are fledged. *Eggs*—1 or 2, white, about 66×47 mm.

RACIAL CHARACTERISTICS, MEASUREMENTS, ETC: The Fauna gives for ♂♀ Wing 500-552; bill 330-375; tarsus 73-75; tail 380-432 mm.

'Iris ♂ blood-red, ♀ pearly white; bill and casque yellow, tinged with red at the tip and with ogange in the middle. In the ♂ the front and back of the casque are black, together with the ridge of the bill just in front of the casque. In the ♀ the back of the casque is red. Bare skin round the eye fleshy pink; eyelids black; legs greenish plumbeous' (Whistler).

## *Family* CAPITONIDAE: Barbets

### THE GREAT ASSAM BARBET

*Megalaima virens magnifica* Stuart Baker

*Megalaima virens magnifica* Stuart Baker, 1926, *Bull. Brit. Orn. Cl.* 47: 43—Machi, Manipur.

**Plate 12, fig. 8 (facing p. 97)**

F.B.I. 4: 107

LOCAL NAMES: Nyahul, Neoul (Nepali); Kun-nyong (Lepcha).

SIZE: Myna+.

FIELD CHARACTERS: A gaudily coloured arboreal bird, largely green, with a violet blue-black head and bright scarlet patch under the tail. Back maroon-brown; underparts olive-brown, blue and yellow. A large ungainly yellow bill. Sexes alike.

STATUS AND HABITAT: Common between 1500 and at least 7000 ft. elevation (Singtam, Martam, Dikchu, Temi, Dentam, Rinchinpong,

Gangtok). Affects tall evergreen forest on steep hillsides flanking river valleys.

DISTRIBUTION OUTSIDE SIKKIM: The Himalayas from east central Nepal to NE. Assam including the Abor and Mishmi Hills. South to Cachar, Manipur and Mt Victoria. The adjoining W. Himalayan race *marshallorum* extends into Kashmir. The species ranges through the northern Indochinese subregion to China.

GENERAL HABITS: Entirely arboreal. Seen singly or in small parties in summer; often large gatherings of 30 to 40 in winter. Keeps to the foliage canopy of tall trees where its coloration obliterates it completely. Largely frugivorous, but also takes insects including hornets. Very obstreperous: the valleys everywhere resound with its loud monotonous wailing calls *kee-ow, kee-ow* repeated *ad nauseam*. *Flight:* noisy, strong and dipping like a woodpecker's —a few rapid flaps followed by a pause.

NESTING: *Season*—April-May. *Nest*—a hole in a tree-trunk or upright branch, 10 to 30 ft. up, usually excavated by the birds themselves. *Eggs*—3 or 4, white, longish ovals, about 35×25 mm.

RACIAL CHARACTERISTICS, MEASUREMENTS, ETC: The W. Himalayan race *marshallorum* is paler and less richly coloured generally, with the pale streaks on the hindneck more numerous, forming a collar between hindneck and upper back.

Specimens collected by the Sikkim Survey measure:

| | Wing | Bill | Tarsus | Tail |
|---|---|---|---|---|
| 1 ♂ | 145 | 46 | 30 | 98 mm. |
| 1 ♀ | 140 | 49 | 32 | 95 mm. |

Schäfer's Sikkim skins (4 ♂♀) have Wing 137, 140, 147, 147 mm. Stresemann remarks (MS. notes) that these do not differ from specimens from Mt Victoria, thus correcting his earlier verdict[1] that the Mt Victoria population is similar to that of Maymyo, Burma, i.e. typical *virens*.

Iris brownish crimson; bill yellow at base, slightly greenish anteriorly. A broad horny black band, *c.* 5 mm. wide, along ridge of terminal three-fourths of culmen; legs and feet olive-plumbeous; claws horny black.

## THE GOLDENTHROATED BARBET

*Megalaima franklinii franklinii* (Blyth)

*Bucco franklinii* Blyth, 1842, *Jour. Asiat. Soc. Bengal* **11** (1): 167—Darjeeling.

**Plate 12, fig. 7** (facing p. 97)

F.B.I. 4: 124

LOCAL NAMES: Ban-basi, Bagh-basi (Nepali).

SIZE: Myna.

FIELD CHARACTERS: A heavy-billed, 'whiskered', grass-green barbet with crimson and bright golden crown, grey ear-coverts and a broad

[1] *Mitteilungen aus dem Zoolog. Museum in Berlin* **24** (2): 232—1940.

black supercilium from bill to nape. Chin and throat golden yellow with an orange spot at base of bill. Sexes alike.

STATUS AND HABITAT: Less common than the Bluethroated Barbet. I recorded it only between *c.* 4000 and 5500 ft. elevation (Dentam, Rinchinpong, Singhik, Chungthang) in the same localities and often side by side with the next, and do not understand Stevens's statement that 'there is practically no overlapping with *M. asiatica* in any areas of its distribution'. Whether the *breeding* areas of the two are distinct, as claimed, I am unable to say.

DISTRIBUTION OUTSIDE SIKKIM: The lower Himalayas from Nepal to NE. Assam. Cachar, Naga Hills, Manipur and the Indochinese subregion. The species extends to S. Yunnan and Malaya.

GENERAL HABITS: Not appreciably different from the next species. The call, however, is definitely nearer in pattern to that of *M. virens*—*peeyu, peeyu* etc.—but in a higher key. It is repeated monotonously for considerable periods.

NESTING: *Season*—April-May. *Nest*—a hole excavated in a dead tree-trunk or partially rotten branch, *c.* 5 to 15 feet up. *Eggs*—3 or 4, white, about 28×21 mm.

RACIAL CHARACTERISTICS, MEASUREMENTS, ETC: A ♂ collected by the Survey measures: Wing 100 (dry); bill 24.5; tarsus 25; tail 62 mm. A good series of 12 ♂♀ procured by Schäfer in Sikkim gives Wing 96, 100-109 (av. 103) mm.

Iris brown; bill black, greyish at base; legs greenish slate; pads dull yellow.

## THE BLUETHROATED BARBET

*Megalaima asiatica asiatica* (Latham)

*Trogon asiaticus* Latham, 1790, Index Ornith. 1: 201—India (=Calcutta *vide* Stuart Baker).

F.B.I. 4: 116

LOCAL NAMES: Kat-tak (Lepcha); Ruturki, Basanta (Nepali).

SIZE: Myna.

FIELD CHARACTERS: A dumpy, heavy-billed, grass-green bird with verditer blue chin and throat. Base of bill surrounded by conspicuous bristly 'whiskers'. Forehead crimson, then yellowish, followed by a black band across vertex. Crown behind this crimson, with a black streak on either side running back to nape. A short supercilium and feathers round eye verditer blue. A crimson speck at base of lower mandible, and a crimson patch at base of throat on either side. Sexes alike.

STATUS AND HABITAT: Common at low elevations and up to *c.* 6500 ft. (Rangpo, Singtam, Martam, Jeluk, Chungthang, Dentam, Gangtok). Affects well-wooded country.

DISTRIBUTION OUTSIDE SIKKIM: The lower Himalayas from Kashmir to NE. Assam. Assam, Bengal. The species ranges through the Indochinese subregion to S. China.

GENERAL HABITS: Arboreal. Mainly frugivorous, but also eats

mantises and other large insects, whacking them limp against the perch before swallowing. The ringing, monotonously repeated calls, *kutroo, kutroo* etc., are almost indistinguishable from those of the more familiar Green Barbet of peninsular India, but somewhat higher in pitch. As soon as one bird commences to call, another within earshot chimes in and the duetting is kept up for a considerable time.

NESTING: *Season*—April to June. *Nest*—the typical barbet-hole excavated in a dead tree-trunk or decaying branch, 5 to 25 ft. up. When in a horizontal branch, the entrance hole is on the underside. *Eggs*—3 or 4, white, about 28×21 mm.

RACIAL CHARACTERISTICS, MEASUREMENTS, ETC: Two ♂♂ collected by the Sikkim Survey measure Wing 103-104; bill 27-28; tarsus 26.5, 26.5; tail 64-67 mm.

Schäfer's Sikkim skins (2 o?) give Wing 101, 103 mm.

Iris reddish brown; fine rim round eye brownish salmon; bill pale greenish horn. Terminal half of culmen and tip of lower mandible horny black; legs and feet sage green; claws horny plumbeous.

## *Family* INDICATORIDAE: Honeyguides

### THE YELLOWBACKED HONEYGUIDE

*Indicator xanthonotus xanthonotus* Blyth

*Indicator xanthonotus* Blyth, 1842, *Jour. Asiat. Soc. Bengal* **11** (1): 116—Darjeeling.

**Plate 12, fig. 9** (facing p. 97)

F.B.I. **4: 131**
LOCAL NAME:
SIZE: Sparrow.

FIELD CHARACTERS: A sparrow-like olive-brown bird, with a rather stout finch-like bill, and glistening orange-yellow forehead and cheeks. Middle of back pure yellow, lower back and rump orange-yellow, clearly seen when the bird sits, as is its wont, with the wings partly drooping at the sides. Upper tail-coverts and tail blackish brown. Under tail-coverts black, scalloped paler.

STATUS AND HABITAT: Exceedingly rare. Not recorded from Sikkim more recently than about 1878/9. The old Sikkim skins in the British Museum were collected in October, December, February, March and April, but bear no indication of altitudes or any other data. The species is included and illustrated here mainly in order to elicit more information from observers.

DISTRIBUTION OUTSIDE SIKKIM: The Himalayas from Nepal to Bhutan at elevations between 5000 and 9000 ft. The adjacent race *radcliffi* replaces it in the W. Himalayas, westward to Hazara in

NW. Pakistan. The species occurs also in the Naga Hills and N. Burma. Very rare and sporadic throughout its range.

GENERAL HABITS: Practically nothing recorded in India. In Africa allied species are known to feed largely on wax from the combs of wild bees, in addition to the larvae. The bird procures these by enticing a honey-eating ratel or man into following its noisy cry as it deliberately flits in front from tree to tree in the forest, finally leading them up to the comb and profiting by the remnants left after it has been taken. In India this habit has not been observed, but the frequency with which the bird is found in the vicinity of cliffs where rock-bees have their combs, suggests that its food here may also be the same.

NESTING: Unknown, but believed to be brood-parasitic upon barbets and woodpeckers, as it is in Africa, laying its white eggs within their nest-holes.

RACIAL CHARACTERISTICS, MEASUREMENTS, ETC: The Fauna gives the measurements as: Wing ♂♂ 92-96, ♀♀ 82-83; bill 8-9; tarsus 13-14; tail 56-61 mm.

'Iris brown; orbital skin pale green; bill yellow, ashy at tip; legs and feet pale greenish horny' (Stoliczka).

## *Family* PICIDAE: Woodpeckers

### THE HIMALAYAN SPECKLED PICULET

*Picumnus innominatus innominatus* Burton

*Picumnus innominatus* Burton, 1836 (1835), *Proc. Zool. Soc. London* (3): 154—Himalayas = Sikkim

F.B.I. 4: 92

LOCAL NAMES: Wi-wi (Nepali); Dang-chim (Lepcha).

SIZE: Sparrow—.

FIELD CHARACTERS: A tiny woodpecker with short, soft, rounded, black-and-white tail. *Male: Above,* forecrown black and orange. A broad white supercilium from behind the eye. Sides of head and neck whitish, with a dark moustachial streak. Upperparts yellowish olive-green. *Below,* yellowish white with bold black spots coalescing into bars on the posterior flanks.

*Female:* Similar but with the whole crown concolorous with the back.

STATUS AND HABITAT: Occurs up to *c.* 6000 ft. elevation where Schäfer obtained specimens (Gangtok) in January, February and March. Affects tropical mixed bamboo forest, e.g. at Dikchu, Singtam and Temi whence I have sight records. Also Singhik (Stevens).

DISTRIBUTION OUTSIDE SIKKIM: Central Nepal east through Bhutan to Assam north of Brahmaputra River; Khasia Hills. The adjoining W. Himalayan race *simlaensis* stretches (possibly) from W. Nepal through Kumaon to Hazara. The species is also found in SW. India, the Vizagapatam Ghats, and E. Pakistan, and ranges over the Indochinese and Malaysian subregions.

GENERAL HABITS: Keeps singly or in pairs, mostly in the large hunting bands of leaf warblers, small babblers and other insectivorous birds, amongst which it is apt to be overlooked. Runs energetically up and down or around the thin outer branches of saplings and shrubs in short jerky spurts, tapping on the bark now and again. Actions reminiscent of a nuthatch. *Call:* a sharp, squeaky *spit, spit* frequently repeated. Also a persistent little drumming on wood *br-r-r-r-r* at regular intervals.

NESTING: *Season*—April-May. *Nest*—a tiny hole drilled in a hollow bamboo or rotten branch, 3 to 15 ft. from the ground. *Eggs*—4, white, blunt ovals about 15×12 mm.

RACIAL CHARACTERISTICS, MEASUREMENTS, ETC: The W. Himalayan race *simlaensis* has a somewhat larger wing. It is paler generally and less yellow above. Four specimens collected by Schäfer in Sikkim have Wing 3 ♂♂ 56, 56, 58; 1 ♀ 57 mm.

Iris brown or reddish brown; bill dark slaty black or plumbeous, paler at tip; legs and feet dull plumbeous.

## THE RUFOUS PICULET

*Sasia ochracea ochracea* Hodgson

*Sasia ochracea* Hodgson, 1836, *Jour. Asiat. Soc. Bengal* 5: 778—Nepal.

**Plate 12, fig. 4** (facing p. 97)

F.B.I. 4: 95

LOCAL NAMES: Sasya (Nepali): Chin, Chin-pho (Lepcha).

SIZE: Sparrow—.

FIELD CHARACTERS: A diminutive, dumpy, stub-tailed bird very unlike the conventional woodpecker. Deep rufous and olive overall, with a short white supercilium. Male differs from female in having the forehead rufescent golden.

STATUS AND HABITAT: Not uncommon, though easily overlooked, up to *c.* 6500 ft. elevation (Dikchu, Singhik, Gangtok). Affects mixed secondary scrub and bamboo jungle.

DISTRIBUTION OUTSIDE SIKKIM: The Himalayas from Garhwal to NE. Assam. Replaced by the race *reichenowi* in Assam south of Brahmaputra River, Manipur, Lushai Hills and E. Pakistan. The species extends through the Indochinese subregion to S. China and Malaya.

GENERAL HABITS: Active and restless. Flits about in dense secondary growth, clinging to and spiralling jerkily up bamboo culms and stems of shrubs and looping creepers, tapping with its bill like a nuthatch. Sometimes hops amongst debris of decaying bamboo stems and mulch on the ground with its absurd little tail cocked up like a wren's. Stuart Baker describes its call as 'a querulous miniature of its larger brethren, uttered both in flight and when climbing'.

NESTING: *Season*—March-April. *Nest*—a tiny hole drilled in a decaying hollow bamboo, at fairly low heights. *Eggs*—3 or 4, white roundish ovals, about 16×13 mm.

RACIAL CHARACTERISTICS, MEASUREMENTS, ETC: *reichenowi* differs from the Sikkim population in being much paler and less olive above, with orange-rufous underparts against deep ferruginous in *ochracea*.

A specimen (♀) of *ochracea* recently collected in NE. Assam measured: Wing 54; bill 13; tarsus 13.5; tail 21 mm. Two Sikkim ♂♂ in the Schäfer collection have Wing 54, 54 mm.

Iris red; orbital skin crimson in ♂, pale magenta in ♀; bill: upper mandible blackish plumbeous, lower mandible grey, paler at tip; 'legs red, yellowish red, dull orange or greenish brown' (Baker).

## THE NORTHERN RUFOUS WOODPECKER

*Micropternus brachyurus phaioceps* Blyth

*Micropternus phaioceps* Blyth, 1845, *Jour. Asiat. Soc. Bengal* **14** (1): 195—Arrakan.

F.B.I. 4: 63

LOCAL NAME:

SIZE: Myna.

FIELD CHARACTERS: A chestnut-rufous woodpecker, narrowly cross-barred with black on upper parts, wings and tail. The pale-edged feathers of the throat produce a scaly or scalloped effect. A crescent-shaped crimson patch of feathers under the eye distinguishes the male from the female.

STATUS AND HABITAT: A bird of the lower elevations. Gammie found it breeding in the Teesta Valley at *c.* 2000 ft.; Schäfer obtained specimens at Gangtok *c.* 6000 ft. (January and February), which is probably the ceiling of its altitudinal range. Affects mixed secondary and bamboo jungle.

DISTRIBUTION OUTSIDE SIKKIM: Nepal and the E. Himalayas (chiefly foothills) to NE. Assam. E. Pakistan, W. Bengal, Orissa, Burma. The adjoining race *humei* extends westward from W. Nepal through Kumaon to about Dehra Dun and Naini Tal.

The species has a wide range over the Indian Union and Ceylon, and the Indochinese and Malaysian subregions to Hainan.

GENERAL HABITS: Typical of the woodpeckers; solitary or in widely separated pairs, and usually quiet. Feeds largely on tree-ants (*Crematogaster* spp.) and their eggs and pupae, digging into their carton-like nests with its bill. Also eats other grubs and insects, and is fond of the pulp of various wild *Fici*, and flower nectar. *Call:* a high-pitched, quick-repeated *keenk-keenk-keenk*, very like one of the more familiar 'screams' of the Common Myna.

NESTING: *Season*—April to June. *Nest*—a hole excavated in the ball-shaped carton nests of tree-ants up in the branches, strangely enough often even when occupied and swarming with the ferocious insects. That the adults and hatchlings are immune from the attacks of the owners is probably due to the smell of the ants acquired by the birds through close association and feeding on them. *Eggs*—3, white, unglossed, about 26×20 mm.

RACIAL CHARACTERISTICS, MEASUREMENTS, ETC: The western race *humei* is somewhat larger and paler, and with a longer bill.

Schäfer's Sikkim examples measure Wing 2 ♂♂ 124, 125; 1 ♀ 128 mm.

Iris brown or reddish brown; bill dark horny brown, paler and more plumbeous-green at base of lower mandible; legs and feet dull brown or greenish brown.

## THE ASSAM BLACKNAPED WOODPECKER

*Picus canus gyldenstolpei* Baker

*Picus canus gyldenstolpei* Baker, 1918, *Bull. Brit. Orn. Cl.* 39: 19—Sadiya, N. Lakhimpur, Assam.

F.B.I. 4: 15

LOCAL NAME: Mong-chok (Lepcha).

SIZE: Pigeon—.

FIELD CHARACTERS: A typical woodpecker with stiff, wedge-shaped tail and stout chisel-pointed bill. *Male:* Above, forehead and forecrown crimson. Supercilium grey, bordered above by a black line. Hindcrown, crest, and nape black. Upper parts dark green, tinged with bright yellow on rump. Tail largely black. *Below,* chin and throat greenish grey, with a black line from lower mandible down each side of throat. Rest of underparts dull yellowish olive-green.

*Female:* Entire forehead and crown black; otherwise more or less like male.

STATUS AND HABITAT: Resident. Fairly common up to *c.* 6500 ft. elevation (Rangpo, Dikchu, Rinchinpong, Gangtok). Affects mixed evergreen and bamboo forest.

DISTRIBUTION OUTSIDE SIKKIM: From central Nepal east through Assam and south to the hill tracts of E. Pakistan and the Assam-Burma border. The adjoining race *sanguiniceps* stretches westward from central Nepal to the Punjab Himalayas. The species is very widespread—from N. and C. Europe east through Transcaspia to China, Japan, SE. Asia.

GENERAL HABITS: Keeps in pairs which follow one another among the forest trees, clinging to the trunk with their specially adapted feet and supported by the stiff tail pressed against it like the third leg of a tripod. The birds tap on the bark from time to time as they work their way upward in short jerky spurts, in order to stampede insects lurking within the crevices, or to discover the hidden pupal galleries of wood-boring beetles. The long worm-like tongue of a woodpecker can be shot out far beyond the bill. It possesses a horny barbed tip by which the grubs are skewered out of their holes. This species also feeds on ants for which it often descends to the ground. Termites are dug out of ant hills, and in addition it takes various berries and flower nectar.

NESTING: *Season*—April-May. *Nest*—a hole bored more or less vertically down in a tree-trunk, 5 to 25 ft. from the ground. It may be 6 inches or more in depth, and ends in an expanded egg-chamber. *Eggs*—4 or 5, white ovals, measuring about 29×22 mm.

RACIAL CHARACTERISTICS, MEASUREMENTS, ETC: Differs from *sanguiniceps* of the western Himalayas in being more yellowish golden in colour overall, and also somewhat smaller in the wing. The Sikkim Survey specimens (2 ♀♀) measure: Wing 141-150; bill 36.5-38; tarsus 27.5-29; tail 99-102 mm.

Schäfer's Sikkim skins give Wing 1 ♂ 136; 2 ♀♀ 140, 148 mm.

Iris crimson-brown; bill horny black, plumbeous at gape; legs and feet plumbeous with slight olive tinge; claws horny brown.

## THE LARGE YELLOWNAPED WOODPECKER

*Picus flavinucha flavinucha* Gould

*Picus flavinucha* Gould, 1834 (1833), *Proc. Zool. Soc. London* (1): 120—Darjeeling.

**Plate 12, fig. 6 (facing p. 97)**

F.B.I. 4: 23

LOCAL NAME: Mong-kli-ong (Lepcha).

SIZE: Pigeon.

FIELD CHARACTERS: A large yellowish green woodpecker with rufous-banded dark brown wings and golden yellow nuchal crest. Bright yellow chin and throat; rich brown foreneck, streaked with white.

*Female* similar but with chin, throat and lower cheeks brown instead of yellow.

STATUS AND HABITAT: Resident. Fairly common up to *c.* 7000 ft. (Rangpo, Singtam, Martam, Dikchu, Lingtam, Temi, Kewzing, Gangtok). Affects tall tree forest, often surrounding old cultivation clearings on hillsides with boles of dead trees standing or strewn about.

DISTRIBUTION OUTSIDE SIKKIM: Nepal, Bhutan to Assam; Manipur, Bihar, Orissa, W. Bengal, E. Pakistan, Burma. The species extends through the Indochinese subregion to S. China and Malaysia.

GENERAL HABITS: Goes about in separated pairs or scattered family parties of 4 or 5, commonly in loose association with various species of drongos. When disturbed and flying off utters a rich 'laugh' rather like that of the Black Woodpecker (*Dryocopus*), but less loud and more musical.

NESTING: *Season*—March to May. *Nest*—the usual hole and shaft excavated between 10 and 20 ft. up in the trunk of a tree. *Eggs*—3 or 4, white broad ovals about 29×22 mm.

RACIAL CHARACTERISTICS, MEASUREMENTS, ETC: The adjoining W. Himalayan race *kumaonensis* is larger and paler.

Specimens collected by the Survey measure:

| | Wing | Bill | Tarsus | Tail |
|---|---|---|---|---|
| 1 ♂ | 175 | 43 | 32 | 116 mm. |
| 1 ♀ | 170 | 37 | 29 | 117 mm. |

Four ♀♀ in the Schäfer Sikkim collection have Wing 160, 160, 168, 171 mm.

Iris brownish crimson; bill pale bluish grey, darker at gape and base and ivory-white on tips of both mandibles; legs, feet and claws plumbeous.

## THE EAST HIMALAYAN SMALL YELLOWNAPED WOODPECKER

*Picus chlorolophus chlorolophus* Vieillot

*Picus chlorolophus* Vieillot, 1818, Dict. Nouv. d'Hist. Nat. 26: 78—Bengal.

F.B.I. 4: 17

LOCAL NAME:

SIZE: Myna+.

FIELD CHARACTERS: *Male: Above,* forehead, supercilia continued to meet at nape, and moustachial streak, crimson; crown olive-green; nuchal crest golden yellow. Upper plumage bright yellowish green. Wing-quills largely green and maroon-red. Tail brownish black with the central feathers edged bronze-green. *Below,* chin and throat brown barred with whitish. Breast olive-brown; rest of underparts barred brown and white.

*Female:* Crimson of head restricted to a short broad line from behind the eye to nape. Otherwise like the male.

STATUS AND HABITAT: Resident. Fairly common at low and moderate elevations up to *c.* 6500 ft. (Singtam, Martam, Dentam, Rinchinpong, Gangtok). According to Stevens to at least 5000 ft. in the Rungbong Valley.

DISTRIBUTION OUTSIDE SIKKIM: The lower Himalayas from E. Nepal to Assam and E. Pakistan. The adjoining W. Himalayan race *simlae* occurs from central Nepal westward to Chamba. The species is found in India, Ceylon, the Indochinese subregion to S. China and Malaysia.

GENERAL HABITS: Typical woodpecker. Often keeps amongst the mixed hunting associations in forest, of drongos, minivets, flycatchers and other insectivorous birds. Its call is described as a loud *quaa* uttered at intervals, in addition to a wide range of the characteristic woodpecker trills. It also drums on wood. *Food:* grubs and insects.

NESTING: *Season*—April-May. *Nest*—the usual woodpecker hole in a dead or decaying tree-trunk, *c.* 2 inches in diameter, first horizontally in for a couple of inches then turning down into a vertical shaft up to a foot or more, widening at the bottom. *Eggs*—3 to 5, white broad ovals, about 24×19 mm.

RACIAL CHARACTERISTICS, MEASUREMENTS, ETC: West Himalayan birds (*simlae*) are somewhat larger and more brownish on the breast.

A ♀ collected by the Sikkim Survey measures: Wing 133; bill 30; tarsus 24; tail 93 mm. A Schäfer ♂ has Wing 128 mm.

Iris brownish crimson; bare skin round eyes slaty plumbeous; bill: upper mandible and tip of lower horny brown. Upper mandible at gape and basal portion of lower mandible pale green; legs and feet greenish plumbeous; claws brown.

## THE HIMALAYAN GOLDENBACKED THREETOED WOODPECKER

*Dinopium shorii shorii* (Vigors)

*Picus shorii* Vigors, 1832 (1830-31), *Proc. Zool. Soc. London* (1): 175—Himalayas.

**Plate 12, fig. 1 (facing p. 97)**

F.B.I. 4: 74

LOCAL NAME:

SIZE: Pigeon−.

FIELD CHARACTERS: A golden-backed woodpecker with crimson crown and occipital crest, crimson rump and black tail. Hindneck black, continued forward as a black stripe to behind eye. A prominent white supercilium to nape. A broad white band down each side of neck. Black moustachial streaks continued as a double line down centre of throat, with the intervening space pale brown. *Below*, breast and underparts fulvous, boldly scalloped with black.

*Female:* Like the male but with forehead and forecrown brownish black; crown and occipital crest black with long white streaks.

STATUS AND HABITAT: Rare. Evidently confined, as in Nepal, to the terai and low foothills up to *c.* 2000 ft. Affects tall forest, deciduous as well as tropical evergreen.

DISTRIBUTION OUTSIDE SIKKIM: The Himalayas from Garhwal and Nepal to N. Assam; Manipur, E. Pakistan. The species extends to Burma.

GENERAL HABITS: Typical woodpecker. Nothing specifically recorded.

NESTING: Not recorded in Sikkim. *Nest*—the usual tree-hole.

RACIAL CHARACTERISTICS, MEASUREMENTS, ETC: In this woodpecker the hallux (first digit or inner hind toe) is absent. The Fauna gives for ♂♀ Wing 146-162; bill 32-36; tarsus 23-24; tail 95-103 mm.

Iris brown to crimson; bill dark slaty or blackish; legs and feet plumbeous or greenish brown.

## THE PALEHEADED WOODPECKER

*Gecinulus grantia grantia* (McClelland)

*Picus (Chrysonotus) grantia* McClelland, 1840 (1839), *Proc. Zool. Soc. London* (7): 165—Assam.

F.B.I. 4: 27

LOCAL NAME: Ka-ter (Lepcha).

SIZE: Myna+.

FIELD CHARACTERS: *Male: Above,* forehead and sides of head pale golden olive-brown; sides of neck, and nape, golden olive-yellow. A patch on crown crimson-pink. Rest of upper plumage dull crimson, including secondary wing-quills. Primaries brown, barred with buff. *Below,* chin and throat dull olive-yellow merging into dark brownish olive of rest of underparts.

*Female* similar, but lacking the crimson-pink patch on crown.

STATUS AND HABITAT: Not common. Met with up to *c.* 3000 ft. elevation in the Teesta Valley (Rangpo, Singtam, Martam) in secondary mixed bamboo jungle. This biotope, between *c.* 1500 and 2500 ft., is the richest in woodpeckers both as to numbers and species.

DISTRIBUTION OUTSIDE SIKKIM: E. Nepal, Bhutan to Assam; Manipur, E. Pakistan, Chin Hills. The species ranges through the Indochinese subregion to S. China.

GENERAL HABITS: A noisy woodpecker, usually seen in pairs on bamboos for preference. Its contact call is a nasal *chaik-chaik-chaik-chaik,* 5 or 6 times in succession, commencing loud and slow, increasing in tempo, becoming fainter and fading off towards the end. It also utters a loud, harsh castanet-like rattling *kerekē-kerekē-kerekē-kerekē,* reminiscent of a tree pie or Blackthroated Jay—evidently a sign of agitation or concern.

NESTING: *Season*—April-May. *Nest*—a hole in a rotten tree-trunk, 5 to 20 ft. up. *Eggs*—3, white ovals about 26×20 mm.

RACIAL CHARACTERISTICS, MEASUREMENTS, ETC: The Fauna gives the measurements (♂♀) as: Wing 128-134; bill 24-27; tarsus 23-24; tail 79-86 mm.

Iris reddish brown; bill bluish ivory, pale plumbeous at base; legs and feet olive; claws horny brown.

## THE GREAT SLATY WOODPECKER

*Mulleripicus pulverulentus mohun* Ripley

*Mulleripicus pulverulentus mohun* Ripley, 1950, *Proc. Biol. Soc. Washington* 63: 103—Jamu Ghat, Bheri River, W. Nepal.

**Plate 12, fig. 5 (facing p. 97)**

F.B.I. 4: 86 (part)

LOCAL NAME:

SIZE: House Crow.

FIELD CHARACTERS: Overall ashy slate-grey with a short broad crimson moustachial streak. Chin, throat and foreneck buffy yellow. *Female:* Similar, but without the crimson moustache.

STATUS AND HABITAT: Evidently rare and confined to the heavily forested tracts of the terai and foothills, up to *c.* 2000 ft. elevation. Little is specifically known concerning its status in Sikkim, and its inclusion and illustration here are largely in order to elicit information from observers.

DISTRIBUTION OUTSIDE SIKKIM: From the U.P. terai and foothills, east to Assam north of Brahamaputra River. The species ranges through Assam east to the Indochinese and Malaysian subregions.

GENERAL HABITS: Usually goes about in parties of 4 to 6, flying high above the tree-tops in labouring, dipping, noisy flight. Its loud intriguing calls sound like something between the bleating of a goat and the barking of a dog, and can be heard a long way off.

## THE RUFOUSBELLIED WOODPECKER

*Hypopicus hyperythrus hyperythrus* (Vigors)

*Picus hyperythrus* Vigors, 1831 (1830-31), *Proc. Zool. Soc. London* (1): 28—Himalayas (restricted to the Eastern Himalayas by Hartert, 1912).

F.B.I. 4: 30

LOCAL NAME:

SIZE: Bulbul.

FIELD CHARACTERS: Practically uncrested. *Male: Above,* forehead white; crown and nape crimson. Upper plumage to rump broadly barred black and white. Wings and tail black, largely spotted and barred with white. *Below,* chin grey; throat, sides of neck, and underparts bright chestnut. Under tail-coverts pale crimson. *Female:* Crown and nape black, spotted with white; otherwise like male.

STATUS AND HABITAT: A high-elevation woodpecker, resident between *c.* 8000 and 13,500 ft. altitude, sometimes lower (Jeluk, Lachen, Lachung, Singalila Ridge, Changu). Affects pine and rhododendron forest.

DISTRIBUTION OUTSIDE SIKKIM: E. Kumaon, Nepal, Bhutan and throughout the E. Himalayas to NE. Assam; Cachar, Naga Hills,

Manipur. The adjoining W. Himalayan race *marshalli* extends from Kumaon to Kashmir. The species ranges to Burma, N. Thailand, Indochina, China, Korea.

GENERAL HABITS: A quiet, silent woodpecker, usually single, sometimes in separated pairs, working fairly high up on large tree-trunks. Heinrich observed that often the female also drums on wood.

NESTING: *Season*—April-May. *Nest*—the typical woodpecker hole, excavated 15 ft. or so up in a tree-trunk. *Eggs*—4 or 5, white, about 23×17 mm.

RACIAL CHARACTERISTICS, MEASUREMENTS, ETC: The adjacent W. Himalayan race *marshalli* is larger, with the crimson on the head of the male more extensive.

Sikkim skins in the Chicago Museum of Natural History measure:

| | Wing | Bill | Tail |
|---|---|---|---|
| 1 ♂ | 118 | 24 | 76.5 mm. |
| 1 ♀ | 115 | 23 | 69 mm. |

Two collected by Schäfer have Wing ♂ 122; ♀ 116 mm.

Iris reddish brown; upper mandible black, lower greenish yellow; legs blackish grey (Ripley).

## THE CRIMSONBREASTED PIED WOODPECKER

*Dendrocopos cathpharius cathpharius* (Blyth)

*Picus (Dendrocopus) cathpharius* 'Hodgson'=Blyth, 1843, *Jour. Asiat. Soc. Bengal* 12 (2): 1006—Darjeeling.

F.B.I. 4: 37

LOCAL NAME:

SIZE: Bulbul—.

FIELD CHARACTERS: *Male: Above,* back and tail black (with outer rectrices barred white) as in the Darjeeling Pied Woodpecker (p. 97). Crimson of hindcrown and occipital crest extending to whole of sides of neck. *Below,* also streaked with black like *darjellensis,* but darker and more fulvous. A diffuse crimson patch on breast. Under tail-coverts edged and tipped with crimson.

*Female:* Like male, but with the entire crown black. Sides of neck whitish, faintly tinged crimson.

STATUS AND HABITAT: Has about the same altitudinal range as *darjellensis*—mainly 6000 to 10,000 ft. According to Stevens between 5000 and 6000 ft. in the Sikkim Himalayas, and unlikely as low as 3000 ft. A specimen collected by him at Lingtam, *c.* 6000 ft., is in the Chicago Museum of Natural History. However, Schäfer obtained a large series in Sikkim in practically every month of the year from *c.* 2000 ft. (June) to 13,000 ft. (10 December to 9 April): Dikchu, Manshitang, Gangtok, Lachen, Thangu. F. N. Betts observed it near Lachung at *c.* 7000 ft. in May.

DISTRIBUTION OUTSIDE SIKKIM: From Nepal through Bhutan and SE. Tibet to the Assam hills north of Brahmaputra River. The Assam hills south of this river, and Manipur, are occupied by the race

1. Indian Redbreasted Parakeet (*Psittacula a. fasciata*) 2. Himalayan Slatyheaded Parakeet (*Psittacula h. himalayana*) 3. Emerald Cuckoo (*Chalcites maculatus*) 4. Redheaded Trogon (*Harpactes e. hodgsonii*) 5. Hodgson's Frogmouth (*Batrachostomus h. hodgsoni*) 6. Pintailed Green Pigeon (*Treron a. apicauda*) 7. Speckled Wood Pigeon (*Columba hodgsonii*) 8. Snow Pigeon (*Columba l. leuconota*) 9. Ashy Wood Pigeon (*Columba pulchricollis*) 10. Bartailed Cuckoo-Dove (*Macropygia u. tusalia*)

PLATE 11

1. Himalayan Goldenbacked Threetoed Woodpecker (*Dinopium s. shorii*) 2. Darjeeling Pied Woodpecker (*Dendrocopos d. darjellensis*) 3. Redeared Bay Woodpecker (*Blythipicus p. pyrrhotis*) 4. Rufous Piculet (*Sasia o. ochracea*) 5. Great Slaty Woodpecker (*Mulleripicus p. mohun*) 6. Large Yellownaped Woodpecker (*Picus f. flavinucha*) 7. Goldenthroated Barbet (*Megalaima f. franklinii*) 8. Great Assam Barbet (*Megalaima v. magnifica*) 9. Yellowbacked Honeyguide (*Indicator x. xanthonotus*)

PLATE 12

*pyrrhothorax.* The species extends through the Indochinese sub-region to S. and W. China.

GENERAL HABITS: Not appreciably different from the Darjeeling Pied Woodpecker (below).

NESTING: *Season*—April-May. *Nest*—the typical woodpecker hole in a tree-trunk. *Eggs*—2 to 4, white, about 24×17 mm.

RACIAL CHARACTERISTICS, MEASUREMENTS, ETC: In the Assam race *pyrrhothorax* the male has the under tail-coverts, breast and a broad gorget on foreneck crimson.

A ♀ collected by the Survey measures: Wing 102; bill 18; tarsus 17; tail 60 mm. Schäfer's Sikkim series gives Wing 8 ♂♂ 97-103 (av. 99.8); 5 ♀♀ 100-103 (av. 101.0) mm. (Stresemann).

Iris brown or reddish brown; bill pale plumbeous, darker on culmen and tip; legs and feet plumbeous or greenish plumbeous (Fauna).

THE FULVOUSBREASTED WOODPECKER, *Dendrocopos macei macei* (Vieillot), was not met with in Sikkim by the Survey, and apparently neither by Schäfer. According to Stevens it occurs in the Rungbong Valley up to *c.* 3500 ft., and has been obtained in the Teesta Valley at *c.* 2400 ft.

RECOGNITION: Size, *c.* Bulbul. Distinguished from the Darjeeling and Crimsonbreasted Pied Woodpeckers by its back being transversely barred with white instead of all black, and underparts only spotted on the breast instead of boldly streaked throughout.

## THE DARJEELING PIED WOODPECKER

*Dendrocopos darjellensis darjellensis* (Blyth)

*Picus (Dendrocopos) darjellensis* Blyth, 1845, *Jour. Asiat. Soc. Bengal* 14 (1): 196—Darjeeling.

**Plate 12, fig. 2** (facing p. 97)

F.B.I. 4: 36

LOCAL NAME: Sadyer-mong-prek (Lepcha).

SIZE: Myna.

FIELD CHARACTERS: Back entirely black. Middle tail-feathers black; outer barred with white. Hindcrown red in male; black in female. Lower parts yellowish fulvous, streaked with black.

STATUS AND HABITAT: A high-elevation woodpecker. Not uncommon between *c.* 6000 and 10,000 ft. even in winter (Kewzing, Chiabhanjan, Singalila Ridge, Lachen, Lachung, Karponang). Meinertzhagen obtained it at Thangu (*c.* 13,000 ft.) in November, and Schäfer in the same locality in July. Affects pine and rhododendron forest.

DISTRIBUTION OUTSIDE SIKKIM: From central Nepal eastward through Bhutan and SE. Tibet (Himalayan facies), and N. Burma. The species extends to Tonkin and W. China.

GENERAL HABITS: Hunts high up on tree-trunks as well as on branches amongst the canopy foliage, frequently in the mixed associations of small insectivorous birds; singly or in pairs. Also searches for food on decaying storm-blown trees lying prone in forest.

NESTING: *Season*—April-May. *Nest*—the typical woodpecker hole in a tree-trunk in dense forest. *Eggs*—2 to 4, white, about 28×20 mm.

RACIAL CHARACTERISTICS, MEASUREMENTS, ETC: A specimen (♂) collected by the Sikkim Survey has Wing 127 mm.

Schäfer's Sikkim series gives Wing 2 ♂♂ 124, 127; 6 ♀♀ 124-131 (av. 126.5) mm.

Iris reddish brown to crimson, orbital skin slaty grey; bill plumbeous, blackish on upper mandible; legs and feet dull green or greenish plumbeous; claws horny.

## THE PIGMY PIED WOODPECKER

*Dendrocopos canicapillus semicoronatus* (Malherbe)

*Picus semicoronatus* Malherbe, 1849 (1848-49), *Bull. Soc. Hist. Nat. Moselle* 5: 22—Himalayas=Darjeeling.

F.B.I. 4: 49

LOCAL NAME:

SIZE: Sparrow—.

FIELD CHARACTERS: A small black-and-white woodpecker. *Male: Above,* forehead and crown ashy brown; short occipital crest scarlet, surrounded by black. A broad whitish supercilium from behind the eye continued as a wide band down sides of neck. Upper back black; wings, lower back, and rump black broadly barred with white. Upper tail-coverts and two central pairs of tail feathers black; lateral tail feathers more or less barred with white. *Below,* chin and throat whitish streaked with ashy. An ashy moustachial streak on either side. Rest of lower plumage fulvous brown streaked with black.

*Female:* Like male, but scarlet of hindcrown replaced by black.

STATUS AND HABITAT: Fairly common at altitudes under *c.* 5000 ft. (Rangpo, Singtam, Martam, Pakyong, Rinchinpong). Schäfer obtained a specimen at Penlom La, *c.* 6000 ft. (March). Affects open oak forest and secondary jungle.

DISTRIBUTION OUTSIDE SIKKIM: Bhutan to N. Assam. The adjoining W. Himalayan race *mitchellii* ranges westward from Nepal through Kumaon to Murree. The species extends through the Indochinese and Malaysian subregions to China, Korea, Formosa, Hainan.

GENERAL HABITS: A silent and unobtrusive little woodpecker, keeping in pairs, usually in association with the mixed hunting parties of small insectivorous birds. Creeps up, around and under the slender branches and end twigs in tall trees as well as low shrubs, tapping on the bark softly from time to time. Actions very like a nuthatch's. Eats small insects and grubs; also the pulp of various fruits. *Call:* a feeble, mousy *click-r-r-r.* Also drums on wood.

NESTING: *Season*—April-May. *Nest*—a shaft, a few inches in depth, bored in a thin branch, 15 to 35 feet from the ground. In horizontal branches the tiny entrance hole is on the underside. *Eggs*—4 or 5, white, about 18×14 mm.

RACIAL CHARACTERISTICS, MEASUREMENTS, ETC: The adjacent Nepal and W. Himalayan race *mitchellii* differs in having the scarlet of the hindcrown confined as a streak on either side. Specimens collected by the Sikkim Survey measure:

| | Wing | Bill | Tarsus | Tail |
|---|---|---|---|---|
| 5 ♂♂ | 84-88 | 14.5-16.5 | 15-16 | 40.5-45 mm. |
| 1 ♀ | 88 | 15.5 | 14.5 | 45 mm. |

Iris biscuit-coloured or greyish brown; bill horny brown, plumbeous on about basal two-thirds of lower mandible; legs and feet olive-plumbeous; claws horny brown.

## THE REDEARED BAY WOODPECKER

*Blythipicus pyrrhotis pyrrhotis* (Hodgson)

*Picus pyrrhotis* Hodgson, 1837, *Jour. Asiat. Soc. Bengal* 6: 108—Nepal.

**Plate 12, fig. 3 (facing p. 97)**

F.B.I. 4: 55

LOCAL NAME: Fi-ing (Lepcha).

SIZE: Pigeon—.

FIELD CHARACTERS: Overall aspect barred rufous and black. A scarlet band on nape extending to sides of neck behind the ear-coverts. Prominent greenish yellow bill.

*Female:* Like the male but without the scarlet nape band.

STATUS AND HABITAT: Not met with by the Sikkim Survey, and evidently uncommon. Schäfer obtained two specimens at Gangtok, *c.* 6300 ft. in December, and F. N. Betts observed it at Dikchu, *c.* 2000 ft. in May, in dense evergreen forest, feeding in the higher branches of some tall *Ficus elastica* trees. In the Chicago Museum of Natural History there are two specimens from Lingtam and Chungthang respectively.

DISTRIBUTION OUTSIDE SIKKIM: From central Nepal east through Assam, Manipur and the Lushai Hills to E. Pakistan and Burma. Farther, it occurs through the Indochinese subregion and Malaya to SE. China and Hainan.

GENERAL HABITS: Keeps to dense evergreen secondary jungle singly or in pairs, sometimes hunting on tree-stumps and fallen logs a few inches above ground level. *Call:* a loud, far-carrying chatter frequently repeated.

NESTING: No record for Sikkim. In Assam, *season*—May-June. *Nest*—the typical woodpecker tree-hole, 3 to 10 feet from the ground in heavily wooded ravines etc. *Eggs*—2 or 3, white, about 30×22 mm.

RACIAL CHARACTERISTICS, MEASUREMENTS, ETC: The Chicago skins measure:

| | Wing | Bill | Tail |
|---|---|---|---|
| 1 ♂ | 145 | 51 | 85 mm. |
| 1 ♀ | 147 | 51 | 85 mm. |

Stevens gives the measurements of his Sikkim birds as: ♂♂ Wing 145-148; bill (from feathers) 47-48. ♀♀ Wing 146-149; bill 45-48 mm. Stresemann found the wing range in 10 examples, ♂♀, from Mt Victoria to be 146-157 mm. Schäfer's Gangtok skins, 2 ♀♀, have Wing 137, 145 mm.

Iris (♀) reddish brown; bill yellow, greenish yellow at base of lower mandible; legs and feet blackish brown (Ripley). ♂ 'Iris dull crimson; orbital skin olive-brown . . .' (Robinson & Kloss).

## TICKELL'S GOLDENBACKED WOODPECKER

*Chrysocolaptes lucidus guttacristatus* (Tickell)

*Picus guttacristatus* Tickell, 1833, *Jour. Asiat. Soc. Bengal* 2: 578—Jungles of Borabhúm and Dholbhúm.

F.B.I. 4: 78

LOCAL NAME: Tashi-on-bau (Lepcha).

SIZE: Pigeon.

FIELD CHARACTERS: Superficially very similar to the Himalayan Threetoed Goldenback (Plate 12, fig. 1) sex for sex, and may be easily confused with it. Its chief differentiating feature is the pattern of the five narrow black throat stripes: two each from either cheek converging on sides of throat, with the fifth down centre of chin and foreneck. Cheeks, chin and throat white. In addition it has the normal four toes, all strong and well developed.

STATUS AND HABITAT: Fairly common in forested valleys and foothills country up to *c.* 5000 ft. (Rangpo, Singtam, Dikchu, Martam, Dentam, Rinchinpong).

DISTRIBUTION OUTSIDE SIKKIM: E. Nepal to Assam; N. Andhra, Bastar, Orissa, W. Bengal, E. Pakistan. The adjoining W. Himalayas to Garhwal are occupied by the race *sultaneus,* while a third, *chersonesus,* occurs throughout the W. Ghats. The species ranges through the Indochinese and Malaysian subregions to the Philippines.

GENERAL HABITS: Usually met with in noisy pairs or family parties. Food, flight, etc. typical of the woodpeckers. *Call:* a distinctive tinny 'laugh' or 'scream'.

NESTING: *Season*—March to May. *Nest*—the typical woodpecker hole in a tree-trunk, 5 to 15 feet from the ground. *Eggs*—4 or 5, white, about 30×22 mm.

RACIAL CHARACTERISTICS, MEASUREMENTS, ETC: The west Himalayan *sultaneus* is larger, with a comparatively larger bill. *Chersonesus* of the W. Ghats is smaller and more olive-crimson on the back.

A ♀ collected by the Sikkim Survey measures: Wing 173; bill 46.5; tarsus 30.5; tail 88 mm. Another ♀ in Schäfer's collection has Wing 172 mm.

Iris creamy orange or fawn; bill horny brown or black, plumbeous at gape and base of lower mandible; legs and feet greenish plumbeous; claws horny brown.

## *Family* EURYLAIMIDAE: Broadbills

### HODGSON'S, or THE NEPAL, COLLARED BROADBILL

*Serilophus lunatus rubropygius* (Hodgson)

*Raya rubropygia* Hodgson, 1839 (January), *Jour. Asiat. Soc. Bengal* 8: 36—No locality=Nepal.

**Plate 13, fig. 6** (facing p. 144)

F.B.I. 3: 470

LOCAL NAMES: Rai-suya (Nepali); Rab-kyul (Lepcha).

SIZE: Bulbul.

FIELD CHARACTERS: A sluggish, arboreal, ashy grey bird with a short recumbent crest overhanging the nape. Lower back chestnut. Wings black with contrasting chestnut, blue, and white markings. Tail black with the lateral feathers white-tipped. Prominent yellow skin round eye.

*Female* similar but with a demi-gorget of white-tipped feathers on either side of neck.

STATUS AND HABITAT: Evidently rare and confined to the lower elevations and foothills up to about 3500 ft. (Singtam, Martam). Found in mixed secondary tree and bamboo forest.

DISTRIBUTION OUTSIDE SIKKIM: Nepal eastward to E. and S. Assam; Manipur, Chittagong Hill Tracts, N. & W. Burma.

GENERAL HABITS: Arboreal and somewhat crepuscular. Small parties of 5 to 10. Active in the mornings and at dusk, but also hunting lethargically during the day. Stupidly confiding, even after being fired at. Takes insects off the branches and foliage of trees in ungainly but agile, fluttering sallies. Does not jump from branch to branch but uses its wings to make short flying hops. Its notes have been described as 'a soft, rather musical whistle and a low *chir-r-r*, uttered both when sitting and flying'.

NESTING: *Season*—May-June. *Nest*—a bulky, untidy ball of coarse grass and weeds bound together by black hair-like roots, with a round lateral entrance overhung by a porch. Lined with broad bamboo or grass leaves; draped on the exterior with spiders' egg-bags etc. and an untidy 'beard' of loose material dangling below. Nest suspended by a thin attachment from a branch or bamboo twig, normally 5 to 10 ft. up, almost invariably overhanging a trickle or pool in a ravine, and very conspicuous. *Eggs*—4 or 5, white, tinged with pale creamy pink or claret, usually speckled with minute reddish brown or purplish black dots, more densely at the broad end. Size about 24×18 mm.

RACIAL CHARACTERISTICS, MEASUREMENTS, ETC: 11 specimens of this subspecies, ♂♀, recently collected by Dr Ripley and myself in the Mishmi Hills (NE. Assam) measure: Wing 82.5-88; bill 15-16.5; tarsus (1) 20.5; tail 65.5-71 mm.

Iris brown; orbital skin bright yellow; upper mandible blue with pale edges and tip; lower mandible blue at base, yellowish green on gonys; legs and feet bright yellowish green; claws plumbeous.

## THE LONGTAILED BROADBILL

*Psarisomus dalhousiae dalhousiae* (Jameson)

*Eurylaimus dalhousiae* Jameson, 1835, *Edinburgh New Phil. Jour.* 18: 389—N. India.

**Plate 13, fig. 5** (facing p. 144)

F.B.I. 3: 472

LOCAL NAMES: Rai-i (Nepali); Dang-mo-mith, Dang-mit-pho (Lepcha).

SIZE: Myna+.

FIELD CHARACTERS: A showy grass-green arboreal bird, with a longish graduated tail largely bright blue above black below. Bright yellow chin and throat, produced in a collar broken behind. The black crown with an oblong yellow spot on either side, and a bright blue patch in the centre, make its identity unmistakable. A white patch on black underside of wings prominent in flight. Sexes alike.

STATUS AND HABITAT: Not uncommon at elevations between 1500 and 6500 ft. (Singtam, Martam, Penlom La, Gangtok). Affects evergreen forest on hillsides.

DISTRIBUTION OUTSIDE SIKKIM: The Himalayas from Kumaon (Mussooree) through Nepal and Bhutan to E. Assam; Manipur, Chittagong Hill Tracts, Burma, Thailand. The species stretches to Indochina and Malaysia.

GENERAL HABITS: Arboreal; sociable. In flocks of 15 to 30 moving about in the foliage canopy or middle storey in forest, in irregular follow-my-leader fashion from tree to tree. Flight silhouette from below, upright stance when perched, and method of fluttering in front of sprigs to take insects, all very reminiscent of the minivets (*Pericrocotus*) though actions much more sluggish. Like Hodgson's Broadbill, tame and confiding often to the point of stupidity, even after several of a flock have been shot. *Food:* orthopterous insects, ants, bugs, caterpillars, and spiders. *Call:* a distinctive sharp, thin whistle *tseeay, tseeay* repeated 5 to 8 times in quick succession. Close hunting association between this species and the Haircrested Drongo (*Dicrurus hottentottus*) was frequently observed in Sikkim, the drongos swooping upon any moths or other winged insects dislodged from the foliage by the fluttering broadbills.

NESTING: *Season*—May-June. *Nest*—a well made pear-shaped pouch of bamboo spathes, grass, roots, moss, and creeper stems etc. with a ragged 'beard' hanging from the bottom, and decorated on the outside with spiders' egg-bags, scraps of green moss etc. Suspended by a thin pliant attachment 6 to 30 ft. up from trees usually overhanging streams in wooded ravines. *Eggs*—5 or 6, variable, white to salmon-pink blotched with pale brick-red, brick-pink or deep rich red-brown, and secondary lilac-grey markings. Size about 28×20 mm.

RACIAL CHARACTERISTICS, MEASUREMENTS, ETC: The Sikkim Survey specimens measure:

| | Wing | Bill | Tarsus | Tail | |
|---|---|---|---|---|---|
| 1 ♂ | 103 | 21 | 28 | 124 | mm. |
| 3 ♀♀ | 103-105 | 21.5-23.5 | 27.5-30 | 123-130 | mm. |

Width of bill at forehead (nostrils) *c.* 15 mm.

Two adults (sex?) collected by Schäfer have Wing 104, 106 mm.

Iris khaki; bill sage green; upper mandible bluish at gape; underside of lower mandible pinkish orange at chin and basal two-thirds, bluish green at tip; fine rim round eye greenish yellow; legs and feet sage green; claws horny black.

## *Family* PITTIDAE: Pittas

### THE BLUENAPED PITTA

*Pitta nipalensis* (Hodgson)

*Paludicola nipalensis* Hodgson, 1837, *Jour. Asiat. Soc. Bengal* 6: 103—Nepal.

**Plate 13, fig. 7 (facing p. 144)**

F.B.I. 3: 444

LOCAL NAME:

SIZE: Myna+.

FIELD CHARACTERS: A dumpy, stub-tailed bird, largely blue and greenish brown above; plain fulvous below. Tail brown, tinged with green. Nape and hindneck blue.

*Female:* General colour of head duller rufous; throat whitish.

STATUS AND HABITAT: Occurs sparingly in the foothills and up to *c.* 6500 ft. (Gangtok) where Schäfer collected specimens in January, February and March. Gammie found it breeding at *c.* 5000 ft. in June. Affects dense secondary tropical jungle.

DISTRIBUTION OUTSIDE SIKKIM: The lower Himalayas from E. Nepal to extreme E. Assam, Assam, Manipur, Chittagong Hill Tracts, N. Burma. The species extends to Tonkin.

GENERAL HABITS: Almost entirely terrestrial. Keeps singly under shrubbery, digging into the soft earth or mulch with its stout bill for insects, worms, lizards and other small animals. Progresses in very long hops, like a rat in a hurry, and at a fleeting glimpse may be mistaken for one. Ventures on to the edge of paths through forest in the early mornings and at dusk, when also may be heard its loud, ringing, double-noted whistling calls. In low flight from one thicket to another, silhouette very like a waterhen's (*Amaurornis*).

NESTING: *Season*—May-June. *Nest*—a large oblong domed structure like a Rugby football, of bamboo leaves, coarse roots and grass, with the entrance at one end. Placed on the ground in the base of a bamboo clump or other bush, or a few feet up in the forking branch of a tree. *Eggs*—4 or 5, glossy china white sparsely spotted with reddish brown and lavender grey. Size about 30×23 mm.

RACIAL CHARACTERISTICS, MEASUREMENTS, ETC: The Fauna gives for ♂♀: Wing 116-129; bill 22-26; tarsus 51-59; tail 61-68 mm. Three ♀♀ collected by Schäfer in Sikkim have Wing 122, 126, 127 mm.

Iris brown; eyerim pale salmon; bill horny brown, paler at tip; legs and feet brownish flesh; claws paler.

## *Family* ALAUDIDAE: Larks

Larks are plain-coloured brown birds with streaked or scalloped upper parts. They resemble the pipits but are squatter in build and have shorter tails which are not wagged up and down. They live in scattered flocks in open country gleaning their food—seeds and insects—on the ground.

### THE TIBETAN SHORT-TOED LARK

*Calandrella acutirostris tibetana* Brooks

*Calandrella tibetana* Brooks, 1880, *Stray Feathers* 8: 488—Tibet.

F.B.I. 3: 328

LOCAL NAME:

SIZE: Sparrow.

FIELD CHARACTERS: *Above*, greyish sandy, streaked with blackish. Tail black with central feathers pale and the two outer pairs largely white. *Below*, white suffused with brown, with a few blackish streaks on breast and a dusky patch on either side of lower neck. Sexes alike.

In the non-breeding season the chief characteristic of short-toed larks is the enormous flocks in which they live.

STATUS AND HABITAT: The Tibetan Plateau facies of N. Sikkim, 15,000 to 16,500 ft. altitude, where Schäfer obtained a good series, including juveniles, in July and August (Gyagong, 'Kiang-Lager').

DISTRIBUTION OUTSIDE SIKKIM: *Summer*, the Tibetan Plateau from about the longitude of Mt Everest eastward to Kuku Nor. The western (nominate) race stretches over Kashmir, (Ladakh ?)[1], Afghanistan to Iran. *Winter*, the Indo-Gangetic Plain and East Pakistan.

GENERAL HABITS: Terrestrial. Highly gregarious in the non-breeding season, keeping in large flocks on migration and in its winter quarters. Affects bleak shingly and stony wastes, sharing its abundance here with Horned Larks. Feeds on the ground on seeds and insects, and is especially partial to the damp margins of bogs. In courtship display the male struts around the female with tail cocked up between drooping wings, like a cock sparrow. Occasionally he also soars wanderingly a few feet up in the air, singing a feeble disjointed 'song'—mostly strung-out repetitions of the normal call note *trree*.

NESTING: *Season*—June-July. *Nest*—a cup-like depression in the ground under a diminutive stone or bush, neatly lined with grass and wool; often entirely felted with the latter. *Eggs*—normally 3, greyish white faintly stippled with pale brown, more densely at the broad end. Size about 22×16 mm.

RACIAL CHARACTERISTICS, MEASUREMENTS, ETC: Differs from the western race *acutirostris* in the greater extent and purer white in the tail feathers.

A large series collected by Schäfer in N. Sikkim, including juveniles, in July-August and October. Adults measure: Wing 7 ♂♂ 91-95 (av. 93.4); 3 ♀♀ 87, 87, 93 mm.

Iris brown; bill yellowish horn, blackish on culmen and tip; legs and feet brownish flesh; claws darker.

THE RUFOUS SHORT-TOED LARK, *Calandrella cinerea dukhunensis* (Sykes), was not met with by the Survey between November and April, when it was presumably away in its winter quarters in the Indian plains. Its status in Sikkim is indeterminate. In September and October (1870), Blanford recorded it 'in large flocks of several hundreds' in N. Sikkim—at Yumthang (12,000 ft.), Mome Samdong (15,000 ft.) and Phalung (16,000 ft.).

In the hand this species may be readily differentiated from *acutirostris* by the fourth wing primary (from outside) being appreciably shorter than the first three. In *acutirostris* all the first four primaries are of about equal length.

THE SKYLARK, *Alauda arvensis* Linn. Tibetan: Cho-mo; Nam-che. Col. R. Meinertzhagen obtained a male from a small flock at Thangu (13,100 ft.) on 19 November (1925) belonging to the grey, round-winged form *inopinata* Bianchi. Wing 109 mm. Also a specimen

[1] Meinertzhagen considers Ladakh birds to be *tibetana*.

of the rather similar but smaller *gulgula* at Dentam (4500 ft.) on 9 January (1926). Wing 98 mm. The status of this species in Sikkim is uncertain. The skylarks have a peculiar fluttering flight by which they rise high up in the air remaining practically stationary on rapidly vibrating wings and singing spiritedly for long unbroken periods.

## THE TIBETAN, or ELWES'S, HORNED LARK

*Eremophila alpestris elwesi* (Blanford)

*Otocoris elwesi* Blanford, 1872, *Jour. Asiat. Soc. Bengal* 41 (2): 62—Sikkim.

F.B.I. 3: 310

LOCAL NAME:

SIZE: Bulbul.

FIELD CHARACTERS: *Male: Above,* forehead white. Face boldly marked black and white. A pointed black horn-like tuft on either side of crown. Upper plumage dark-streaked vinous or pinkish grey-brown. Tail black, margined with white. *Below,* white, washed with vinous on flanks and breast. A broad black gorget or breast-band.

*Female* only differing in details.

Tibetan, or Elwes's, Horned Lark
About one-half

STATUS AND HABITAT: A hardy high elevation lark, resident at 15,000 to 16,000 ft. in the Tibetan facies of N. Sikkim (Gyagong, 'Kiang-Lager'). Blanford obtained it at 18,000 ft. (Dongkia La) in September. Seldom descends as low as 10,000 ft. even in severe winters. A sudden spell of freakish weather will, however, force some individuals down to unusually low elevations temporarily, (e.g. Chungthang *c.* 5000 ft., 18.i.1953).

DISTRIBUTION OUTSIDE SIKKIM: The Tibetan plateau eastward to at least the upper reaches of the Yangtse River. The larger, longer-billed western race *longirostris* adjoins it, stretching to Kashmir north to the Karakorams; Afghanistan, Baluchistan. In many other races the species is spread practically over the entire Holarctic Region.

GENERAL HABITS: Keeps in pairs or scattered flocks, often large ones in the non-breeding season, to bleak stony hillsides and barren windswept plains dotted with scanty tufts of grass and furze 'hedgehogs'. Runs about on the ground in short spurts picking up seeds and insects. In the breeding season the male has a feeble squeaky song of several disjointed strophes, of rather the volume and quality of a leaf warbler's song. It is delivered from a perch, generally on top of a rock. A single occasional note *peo*, uttered in flight, is reminiscent of the Crested Lark's.

NESTING: *Season*—May to July. *Nest*—a cup-like depression in the ground lined with grass, roots, wool, etc. under shelter of a tiny bush or stone; sometimes quite unprotected. *Eggs*—2 or 3, yellowish stone or yellowish grey, minutely speckled with brown, more densely at the broad end. Size about 24×16 mm.

RACIAL CHARACTERISTICS, MEASUREMENTS, ETC: In fresh plumage *elwesi* has the upper parts darker and warmer-coloured than the western race *longirostris*. The nape and back are a deeper pink, and the bill smaller—13-15 mm. against 15-19.

Specimens collected by the Sikkim Survey and Dr Biswas at Chungthang from a flock which suddenly appeared following heavy snowstorms at the higher altitudes (18-26 January 1953) measure:

| | Wing | Bill | Tarsus | Tail |
|---|---|---|---|---|
| 6 ♂♂ | 117-123 (av. 120.3) | 12.5-15 | 22-23 | 78.5-87 mm. |
| 1 ♀ | 110 | 13.5 | 22 | 73 mm. |

All of Schäfer's skins collected in July have the wing tips too frayed for accurate measurement, while his October specimens are moulting the outer primaries.

Iris brown; upper mandible horny black, lower plumbeous, brownish at tip; legs, feet and soles of feet and swollen pads under each joint of toes greyish white, claws dark horny brown.

Col. R. Meinertzhagen obtained 2 specimens (♂) of the LONGBILLED CALANDRA LARK, *Melanocorypha maxima maxima* Gould, at Yumthang, 11,650 ft., on 7 December (1925). They were feeding on some flat ground near the Lachung River. This is typically a bird of ill-drained bogland in the high Tibetan Plateau facies.

RECOGNITION: Size Bulbul but heavily built; with a thick bill and relatively short tail. *Above*, greyish- and rufous-brown, the feathers dark-centred. Conspicuous white and rufous supercilium and cheeks. Wing quills brown; secondaries broadly white-tipped, showing as a white band on trailing edge of wing. Tail brown, broadly edged and tipped with white. *Below*, dull white, sometimes with a few brown spots on sides of upper breast (broken collar).

## *Family* HIRUNDINIDAE: Swallows, Martins

### THE EASTERN SWALLOW

*Hirundo rustica gutturalis* Scopoli

*Hirundo gutturalis* Scopoli, 1786, Del Flor. et Faun. Insub. 2: 96—New Guinea, *errore*=Panay, Philippines.

F.B.I. 3: 241

LOCAL NAME:

SIZE: Sparrow+.

FIELD CHARACTERS: *Above*, glossy steel blue with chestnut forehead. *Below*, throat chestnut bordered by a broad blue-black breast band. Rest of lower plumage creamy- or pinkish-white. Typical deeply forked black 'swallow' tail, all but the central pair of feathers with a white patch clearly visible when the bird banks in flight. Sexes alike.

STATUS AND HABITAT: In summer (breeding) up to *c.* 6500 ft. elevation (Gangtok, Arita); in winter mostly down in the warm valleys and plains.

DISTRIBUTION OUTSIDE SIKKIM: *Summer:* Throughout the Himalayas east of Kashmir, and on into NE. Asia. *Winter:* Eastern India; Indochinese and Indomalayan subregions.

GENERAL HABITS: Gregarious. Keeps to the neighbourhood of human habitations and cultivation. Hawks dipterous insects on the wing, both high up in the air and whilst skimming over the surface of land or water. In Gangtok town and bazaar it is a familiar sight to see numbers of swallows shooting up and down at high speed close over the road surface in pursuit of midges and flies, twisting and dodging their way in amongst mules, loiterers and other obstacles with the utmost dexterity and confidence of safety. Breeding preliminaries commence in March when birds take possession of traditional sites within bazaar shops and dwellings, perching on brackets, wall clocks and the like, and twittering spiritedly an arm's length above the heads of noisily haggling customers!

NESTING: *Season*—May to June/July. *Nest*—a deepish saucer of mud-pellets reinforced with grass and straw. Fixed near the ceiling against a rafter or under the eaves. *Eggs*—4 to 6, white, dotted and speckled with reddish- or purplish-brown, more densely at the broad end. Size about 19×14 mm.

RACIAL CHARACTERISTICS, MEASUREMENTS, ETC: The majority of Sikkim birds appear to have the blue-black pectoral band unbroken in the middle, a character on which Stresemann separated this population from *gutturalis* with which it is otherwise identical in size of wing and relative length of outermost tail feathers. Some examples of *gutturalis* also have the pectoral band unbroken, and recent reviewers have synonymised his *ambigua* with that race, an action with which I agree.

Four adult ♂♂ collected by Schäfer at Gangtok in June (breeding season) measure Wing/Outer tail 115/91, 120/82, 120/93, 120/95 mm.

Iris dark brown; bill black; legs and feet black.

## THE HIMALAYAN STRIATED SWALLOW

*Hirundo daurica nipalensis* Hodgson

*Hirundo nipalensis* Hodgson, 1836, *Jour. Asiat. Soc. Bengal* 5: 780—Nepal.

F.B.I. 3: 250

LOCAL NAME:

SIZE: Sparrow.

FIELD CHARACTERS: *Above*, glossy deep blue, including wings and deeply forked tail. A chestnut half-collar on nape (usually broken in the middle), and pale rufous rump. *Below*, fulvous white, coarsely streaked with blackish. Sexes alike.

STATUS AND HABITAT: Fairly common and widespread, breeding at least to elevations between 5000 and 7000 ft. (Arita, Gangtok, Pemionche); perhaps higher. Largely migratory in winter (to the peninsular Indian plains), returning again to the old nests, March/April.

DISTRIBUTION OUTSIDE SIKKIM: *Summer* (breeding): The Himalayas from Kulu to Sikkim and SE. Tibet. The species is very widely distributed in S. and E. Europe, N. Africa and Asia.

GENERAL HABITS: Similar to those of the Eastern Swallow. In enormous flocks on migration and in its winter quarters. Not gregarious when nesting, then usually seen in pairs or family parties based on verandas and living rooms of rest houses and residential bungalows. In April 1955 there was an occupied nest in the Dewan's office in Gangtok. The pair of owners flew in and out freely all day long regardless of the noise of the telephone and typewriters and the bustle of chattering clerks and visitors in the low-ceilinged little room. The building was shut up every evening after office hours and not opened again next morning till well after sun-up, so that the birds had to co-ordinate their daily chores closely with the working hours of the Government Secretariat!

NESTING: *Season*—April to July. *Nest*—a retort-shaped structure of mud-pellets with a tubular entrance, and with the bulbous egg-chamber lined with feathers. Stuck flat against the ceiling in the corner of a room or veranda; sometimes on cliff overhangs. In the latter situations occasionally in small colonies. Eggs—3 or 4; pure white, measuring about 21×14 mm. Often two successive broods are raised, and both sexes share all the domestic chores.

RACIAL CHARACTERISTICS, MEASUREMENTS, ETC: This Himalayan race differs from the more familiar *erythropygia* of peninsular India in having the striations on the lower plumage much broader and coarser, and not merely fine shaft-streaks.

Five adult ♂♀ collected by Schäfer in Gangtok (June) give Wing 111, 112, 114, 117, 118 (av. 114.4) mm.

Iris dark brown; bill, legs, feet and claws blackish brown.

## THE KASHMIR HOUSE MARTIN

*Delichon urbica cashmeriensis* (Gould)

*Chelidon cashmeriensis* Gould, 1858, *Proc. Zool. Soc. London:* 536—Kashmir.

F.B.I. 3: 228

LOCAL NAME:

SIZE: Sparrow.

FIELD CHARACTERS: Differs from the next (*Delichon nipalensis*) in the tail being deeply forked instead of square-cut, and the under tail-coverts white instead of black. Sexes alike.

STATUS AND HABITAT: A bird of higher elevations than the Nepal House Martin, recorded in Sikkim between 9000 and 16,000 ft. (Lachen, Thangu, Yumthang, Gnatong, Gyagong).

DISTRIBUTION OUTSIDE SIKKIM: The Himalayas from Chitral and Kashmir through Nepal, Bhutan and Tibet to W. China. In winter at lower levels and sporadically also in peninsular India.

GENERAL HABITS AND NESTING: Similar to those of the Nepal House Martin.

MEASUREMENTS: Sikkim specimens in the Chicago Museum of Natural History measured by me have Wing 2 ♂♂ 100-102; 2 ♀♀ 99-101 mm.

Eight adult ♂♀ obtained by Schäfer at Thangu have Wing 96-107 (av. 100.2) mm.

## THE NEPAL HOUSE MARTIN

*Delichon nipalensis nipalensis* Horsfield & Moore

*Delichon nipalensis* Horsfield & Moore, 1854, Cat. Birds Mus. E. I. Co. 1: 384—Nepal.

Nepal House Martin
About two-thirds

F.B.I. 3: 230

LOCAL NAME:

SIZE: Sparrow—.

FIELD CHARACTERS: *Above*, including ear-coverts, wings and the short square-cut tail steely black. A broken white collar on hind-neck. Rump conspicuously white. *Below*, chin and throat dull black; under tail-coverts glistening black. Rest of lower plumage white, including the feathered legs and feet ('stockings'). Sexes alike.

STATUS AND HABITAT: Resident at moderate elevations. Recorded between *c.* 1000 and 6500 ft. at all seasons (Rangpo, Martam, Dikchu, Shamdong, Singhik, Rangeet Valley, Dentam, Rinchinpong, Chungthang, Gangtok). Loose flocks hawking above forested river valleys.

DISTRIBUTION OUTSIDE SIKKIM: The Himalayas from Kumaon (Naini Tal) to E. Assam; Cachar, Manipur, NE. Burma.

GENERAL HABITS: Typical swallow. Highly sociable, especially when nesting. Small loose parties—sometimes large gatherings of a hundred or more—fly about 100 to 150 ft. up, hawking tiny winged insects above stream valleys and the flanking hillsides and cultivation terraces. Flight swift and graceful—a few rapid wing strokes followed by an effortless glide with agile turning, twisting, and banking movements.

NESTING: Not recorded in Sikkim. *Season*—probably as elsewhere, April to June. *Nest*—an inverted bowl of mud pellets, reinforced with grass etc. and lined with feathers, with a narrow slit near the top for entrance. Stuck under a rock overhang on an inaccessible cliff, often from fifty to several hundred nests close together in a colony. *Eggs*—4 or 5, white, measuring about 18×13 mm.

RACIAL CHARACTERISTICS, MEASUREMENTS, ETC: Specimens collected by the Sikkim Survey measure:

| | Wing | Bill | Tarsus | Tail |
|---|---|---|---|---|
| 1 ♂ | 92 | 7.5 | 11 | 38.5 mm. |
| 1 ♀ | 92 | 8 | 11 | 37 mm. |
| 1 o? | 96 | 7-8 | 11 | 39-41.5 mm. |

Iris brown; bill horny black; legs and feet (showing through 'stockings') brownish flesh; claws pale horny brown.

## *Family* CAMPEPHAGIDAE: Cuckoo-Shrikes, Minivets

### THE BROWNBACKED PIED FLYCATCHER-SHRIKE

*Hemipus picatus capitalis* (McClelland)

*Muscicapa capitalis* McClelland, 1840, *Proc. Zool. London:* 157—(Assam).

F.B.I. 2: 307

LOCAL NAME:

SIZE: Sparrow+.

FIELD CHARACTERS: A small black-and-white flycatcher-like bird. *Male: Above,* head glossy black; rest of upper plumage dark brown with a broad white band across rump. Tail black, tipped and edged with white. Wings black, with a white patch, or band (median coverts), at shoulder, and broadly white-edged inner secondaries.

*Below*, chin, cheeks, and sides of neck (semi-collar) white; rest of lower plumage pinkish or vinaceous.

*Female:* like male, but with head brown like the back.

Brownbacked Pied Flycatcher-Shrike
About one-half

Its characteristic posture when perched is rather hunchbacked—neck pulled in and tail depressed.

On a superficial glance confusable with the Little Pied Flycatcher (q.v.), but the broad white supercilium of the latter is sufficiently diagnostic.

STATUS AND HABITAT: Resident. Fairly common at low and moderate altitudes, up to *c.* 5000 ft. (Rangpo, Singtam, Martam, Temi, Dentam, Rinchinpong). Affects secondary forest.

DISTRIBUTION OUTSIDE SIKKIM: Kumaon and eastward through Nepal and Bhutan to Assam; Manipur, N. Burma, N. Thailand, Yunnan, Cochinchina. The blackbacked nominate race occupies peninsular India and Burma.

GENERAL HABITS: Entirely arboreal. More like the minivets and flycatchers than the true shrikes. Keeps in pairs or family parties, frequently amongst the mixed hunting flocks of small insect-eating birds. The individuals follow one another from tree to tree, searching among the leaf-sprigs or making short agile aerial sallies after winged insects. Utters a feeble, wheezy *whi-riri, whi-riri* etc. as of a cheap Christmas-cracker whistle. Entirely insectivorous.

NESTING: *Season*—May-June. *Nest*—a neat, diminutive, shallow cup of roots, lined with fine grass stalks. Draped on the outside with lichens and secured with cobwebs to the upper surface of a horizontal branch between 15 and 25 ft. up. *Eggs*—2 or 3, variable, white either blotched with chocolate with underlying spots of grey, more densely and forming a ring at the broad end, or lightly speckled and spotted with blackish brown or reddish brown overlying inky spots. Size about 16×13 mm. Both sexes share all the domestic chores.

RACIAL CHARACTERISTICS, MEASUREMENTS, ETC: A specimen collected by the Sikkim Survey (o?) measures Wing 65; bill 15.5; tarsus 13.5; tail 62.5 mm. The Fauna gives the range for ♂ ♀ Wing 60-67; tail 52-60 mm.

Iris yellowish brown; bill black; legs, feet and claws blackish brown.

## THE NEPAL WOOD SHRIKE

*Tephrodornis virgatus pelvica* (Hodgson)

*Tenthaca pelvica* Hodgson, 1837, *Indian Review* 1: 447—Nepal.

F.B.I. 2: 309

LOCAL NAMES: Ramnun-pho or Rabnun-pho (Lepcha).

SIZE: Myna.

FIELD CHARACTERS: A short and square-tailed grey-brown shrike. *Male: Above,* crown and nape ashy grey changing to ashy brown on back, wings and tail, the last tipped blackish and rufous. A broad black band from lores through eye to ear-coverts, which are whitish. Rump and upper tail-coverts fluffy, whitish and ashy brown, barred with black and with a pure white band across. *Below,* chin, throat and breast pale ashy fawn, fading to white on centre of abdomen.

*Female:* like male, but with crown same colour as back, and eye-band brown.

STATUS AND HABITAT: Normally a bird of the low foothills. Uncommon. Met with by the Sikkim Survey between 1000 and 5000 ft. during November to January (Singtam, Martam, Dentam, Rinchinpong). Previously recorded only up to *c.* 3300 ft. in the Teesta Valley. Affects mixed forest.

DISTRIBUTION OUTSIDE SIKKIM: Nepal, Bhutan, Assam, W. Bengal, E. Pakistan, Orissa, N. Andhra. Also Burma, Thailand, Yunnan. An allied race inhabits the Western Ghats. The species extends through the Indochinese and Malaysian subregions.

GENERAL HABITS: Arboreal. Keeps in small parties, often associated with minivets and other insectivorous birds in forest. The individuals follow one another among the trees, gracefully volplaning from branch to branch, searching the foliage. Also launches short, looping, flycatcher-like sallies after moths and other winged insects. Has harsh chuckling notes, and a rather musical *kew-kew-kew-kew* quickly repeated 4 to 6 times. These calls sound appreciably different from those of the Western Ghats race.

NESTING: Mandelli's record at 3000 ft., below Darjeeling, has been discredited. No other record from this neighbourhood, and strangely enough very few elsewhere.

RACIAL CHARACTERISTICS, MEASUREMENTS, ETC: The Western Ghats race *sylvicola* differs in having the upper plumage dark bluish ashy, and concolorous with the crown and nape.

Specimens of *pelvica* recently collected in Orissa measure:

| | Wing | Bill | Tarsus | Tail |
|---|---|---|---|---|
| 2 ♂♂ | 120-122.5 | 26 | 21-22 | 86-87 mm. |
| 1 ♀ | 124 | 26.5 | 22.5 | 91.5 mm. |

Iris yellowish brown; bill brown, pale yellowish horny at base and gonys; legs and feet plumbeous; claws brown.

## THE DARK GREY CUCKOO-SHRIKE

*Coracina melaschista melaschista* (Hodgson)

*Volvocivora melaschistos* Hodgson, 1836, *Indian Review* 1: 328—Nepal.

F.B.I. 2: 337

LOCAL NAME:

SIZE: Between Bulbul and Myna.

FIELD CHARACTERS: *Male:* Overall dark bluish grey. Lores and feathers round eye black. Wings black. Tail black, the central rectrices narrowly, the lateral ones broadly tipped with white.

*Female:* Similar, but paler grey and often with barred underparts as in the young.

A roundish white patch under each wing, and white terminal margin to the tail conspicuous in flight, the latter particularly while the bird is alighting.

STATUS AND HABITAT: Resident up to *c.* 6000 ft. elevation (Rangpo, Singtam, Martam, Singhik, Dentam, Gangtok). Affects open forest.

DISTRIBUTION OUTSIDE SIKKIM: The Himalayas from Murree eastward through Nepal and Bhutan to Assam; E. Pakistan, N. Burma, NW. Yunnan. The species extends to the Indochinese subregion.

GENERAL HABITS: Arboreal, insectivorous, and in many ways resembling the minivets. Unlike them, however, it normally keeps singly or in pairs. Often associates with drongos and minivets in itinerant hunting bands. Its general actions and behaviour—hopping and volplaning from branch to branch, upright stance when perched, and fluttering or hovering in front of leaf-sprigs to take insects—are all strongly reminiscent of the minivets. *Call:* of four whistling notes (sometimes only three) in descending scale; fairly loud but rather monotonous and plaintive.

NESTING: Not specifically recorded in Sikkim. In Nepal and neighbouring areas *season* April to June. *Nest*—a shallow cup of pliant twigs, roots and fibres matted together with cobwebs, and draped on the outside with lichen, bits of bark, caterpillar droppings, etc. Fixed on the upper surface or in the fork of a branch, 15 to 25 ft. up; very inconspicuous. *Eggs*—normally 3, pale grey-green or sea-green with longitudinal blotches of umber brown and secondary markings of inky grey. Size about 24×17 mm. Both sexes share the domestic chores.

RACIAL CHARACTERISTICS, MEASUREMENTS, ETC: A Sikkim Survey ♂ measures: Wing 122.5; bill 21; tarsus 23; tail 111 mm.

Schäfer's Sikkim skins give Wing 4 ♂♂ 119, 121, 121, 124; 3 ♀♀ 113, 119, 123 mm.

Iris orange-brown; bill black; legs, feet and claws brownish black.

## THE SCARLET MINIVET

*Pericrocotus flammeus speciosus* (Latham)

*Turdus speciosus* Latham, 1790, Index Orn. 1: 363—India (restricted by Stuart Baker to Darjeeling).

F.B.I. 2: 319

LOCAL NAME:

SIZE: Between Bulbul and Myna.

FIELD CHARACTERS: *Male:* A gorgeous slim glossy black and deep scarlet bird. *Above,* head, neck and upper back glossy blue-black. Lower back and rump deep scarlet. Wings and graduated tail particoloured black and scarlet. *Below,* throat black; rest of underparts bright scarlet.

*Female: Above,* forehead and short supercilium bright yellow; rest of upper parts yellowish grey. Tail and wings particoloured, as in male, with scarlet replaced by yellow. *Below,* bright yellow.

STATUS AND HABITAT: Resident. Fairly common at low elevations and up to *c.* 6000 ft. (Rangpo, Singtam, Rinchinpong, Dentam, Dikchu, Singhik, Gangtok). Affects foliage canopy of tall trees, as well as the middle storey in forest.

DISTRIBUTION OUTSIDE SIKKIM: The Himalayas from Kulu through Nepal and Bhutan to eastern Assam north of the Brahmaputra. Assam south of this river is inhabited by the race *fraterculus.*

The species ranges from India and Ceylon east to Malaysia, the Indochinese subregion and the Philippines.

GENERAL HABITS: Gregarious, arboreal and insectivorous. Normally met with in family parties; in larger flocks in winter. Flits amongst the foliage hovering in front of a sprig or flower to capture an insect or spider. Sometimes volplanes from branch to branch. *Call:* a musical double whistle *wee-twee* or *wi-weet* with a rather interrogative intonation.

NESTING: *Season*—April to June. *Nest*—typical of the minivets: a loose, shallow cup of twigs, roots, grass, etc. densely coated with cobweb and draped with lichens. Attached on the upper surface of a horizontal branch 15 to 25 ft. or more from the ground. *Eggs*—2 or 3, variable, commonly greenish white covered with longitudinal blotches of grey-brown or reddish brown, more densely at the broad end. Size about 22×17 mm.

RACIAL CHARACTERISTICS, MEASUREMENTS, ETC: The adjoining race of Assam south of the Brahmaputra River, *fraterculus,* is somewhat smaller and deeper-coloured in both sexes.

Specimens collected by the Sikkim Survey measure:

| | Wing | Bill | Tarsus | Tail |
|---|---|---|---|---|
| 1 ♂ | 105 | 19 | 19 | 102 mm. |
| 1 ♀ | 100 | 19.5 | 19 | 100.5 mm. |

A good series in the Schäfer Sikkim collection gives: Wing 7 ♂♂ 98-104 (av. 102.3) mm.; 2 ♀♀ 97, 98 mm. Regarding these males Stresemann remarks as follows:

'*Tail:* The outer web of the central pair of rectrices is entirely black in 3 specimens; black with red edges in 4.

'*Wing:* In all the ♂♂ only the 2 outermost primaries are entirely black; the outer web of the third primary bears a red (oval) drop.'

Iris brown; bill black; legs, feet and claws dark brown.

## THE SHORTBILLED MINIVET

*Pericrocotus brevirostris brevirostris* (Vigors)

*Muscipeta brevirostris* Vigors, 1830, *Proc. Zool. Soc. London:* 43—Himalayas=Sikkim foothills *vide* Mayr, 1940.

**Plate 14, fig. 2** (facing p. 145)

## THE SIKKIM LONGTAILED MINIVET

*Pericrocotus ethologus laetus* Mayr

*Pericrocotus ethologus laetus* Mayr, 1940, *Ibis:* 717—Jeyluk, Sikkim.

F.B.I. 2: 324 (=*affinis*)

LOCAL NAME:

SIZE: Bulbul.

FIELD CHARACTERS: A slim, brilliant glossy black and deep scarlet bird with a broad scarlet band running through the black wing, and a black and scarlet steeply graduated tail.

*Female:* grey above, yellow below, with yellow replacing scarlet in wings and tail.

The two species are superficially almost identical (sibling) and have been confused in the past under the name of *Pericrocotus brevirostris affinis.* They cannot be told apart in the field with certainty except with much practice. (For diagnosis see below).

STATUS AND HABITAT: Resident, but with a certain amount of seasonal altitudinal movement. A careful analysis by Stresemann of Schäfer's excellent material of both forms, collected in Sikkim practically throughout the year, suggests that they are ecologically differentiated, *ethologus* breeding in a higher zone (Lachen *c.* 9000 ft.) than *brevirostris* (Gangtok *c.* 6000 ft.). It also suggests that *ethologus* descends in winter to occupy the summer range of *brevirostris* while the latter has vacated it for lower elevations in the tropical zone. Between November and February the Sikkim Survey found *brevirostris* common and abundant between *c.* 1000 and 3000 ft. (Rangpo, Singtam, Martam). At the end of March it was back again in its breeding zone of *c.* 6000-7000 ft. elevation (Gangtok, Pemionche). Stevens records parties of '*affinis*' at 11,000 ft. on the Sikkim-Nepal frontier in February, when the bare branches of the trees were wreathed in snow!

Affects foliage canopy and middle storey in open forest.

DISTRIBUTION OUTSIDE SIKKIM: *P. b. brevirostris.* The Himalayas from Nepal eastward through Assam and E. Bengal to Burma and the Indochinese subregion.

*P. e. laetus.* E. Nepal to E. Assam north of Brahmaputra River; Khasia Hills. The species ranges overall from Afghanistan to Annam and NE. China.

GENERAL HABITS: Not appreciably different from those of the Scarlet Minivet. Seen in large flocks in winter—often with female-plumaged birds in preponderance—flying among the tops of the lofty trees on the mountain-sides, or high across a stream valley. The birds make a pretty sight as they flutter or hover against the leaf clusters in search of insects.

NESTING: No records exist for *P. b. affinis* hitherto considered as the race occurring in Sikkim, but which in reality now proves to have been a jumble of *brevirostris* and *ethologus*. The nests and eggs of both forms are typical of the minivets.

RACIAL CHARACTERISTICS, MEASUREMENTS, ETC: Male *ethologus* can be diagnosed from its 'double', among other points, by the central pair of rectrices being entirely black. The next pair is red only on the outer webs excepting at the base and for about 10 mm. at the tip. In ♂ *brevirostris* the central rectrices are narrowly margined with red on the outer webs. In the next pair the red stretches not only on the outer web right up to the tip, but also over much of the inner web, so that the tip is wholly red with a black wedge-shaped zone from the base towards the edge ending *c.* 25 mm. before the tip.

In the females of the two forms the respective tail patterns are the same as in their males, but with yellow replacing the red. Moreover, in Sikkim the throat of female *ethologus* is yellowish white, contrasting with the purer yellow of the lower plumage; in ♀ *brevirostris* the throat is yellow concolorous with the underparts.

In female *ethologus* the forehead is narrow and dirty yellow, sharply cut off from the dark grey crown. In *brevirostris* it is broader and golden yellow, changing gradually to greenish on the forecrown and into dark grey on the hindcrown.

In male *brevirostris* the scarlet of the underside, rump and wings is deeper and brighter (not so yellowish) as in *ethologus*. The latter species is, in addition, somewhat larger and with a relatively longer tail on the average.

Schäfer's Sikkim series measure:

| | Wing | Tail | Tail/Wing Index[1] |
|---|---|---|---|
| *P. b. brevirostris* | | | |
| 17 ♂♂ | 85-90 (av. 87.1) | 90-100 | 103.4-112.3 mm. |
| 10 ♀♀ | 85-89 (av. 87.0) | 90-100 | 105.9-113.6 mm. |
| *P. e. laetus* | | | |
| 4 ♂♂ | 91, 91, 91, 95 | 104, —, 106, 104 | 109.6-116.5 mm. |
| 3 ♀♀ | 89, 89, 90 | 107, 100, — | 112.3-120.2 mm. |

Iris brown; bill, legs, feet and claws black.

[1] $\frac{\text{Tail} \times 100}{\text{Wing}}$

## THE YELLOWTHROATED MINIVET

*Pericrocotus solaris solaris* Blyth

*Pericrocotus solaris* Blyth, 1846, *Jour. Asiat. Soc. Bengal* **15**: 310—Darjeeling.

**Plate 14, fig. 3** (facing p. 145)

F.B.I. **2**: 326

LOCAL NAME:

SIZE: Bulbul.

FIELD CHARACTERS: *Male: Above,* crown and back dark slaty, not black; rump and upper tail-coverts deep scarlet crimson; wings and tail black and red. *Below,* chin greyish white; throat orange-yellow; rest of lower plumage bright scarlet.

*Female: Above,* crown, neck and upper back ashy grey, changing to olive-green on lower back and to dark yellow on upper tail-coverts. Wing and tail as in male, but red replaced by yellow. *Below,* chin grey; rest of lower plumage bright yellow.

STATUS AND HABITAT: Not common. Stevens records it at Dikchu, 2300 ft., in February. The Loke-Sálim Ali Survey came across this minivet only between 3500 and 5000 ft. elevation (Temi, Chungthang)—November to April—but Schäfer collected specimens also at Gangtok (*c.* 6000 ft.) in December, February and March. Blanford obtained a female from a flock at *c.* 10,000 ft. (Lachung) in September. This seems exceptionally high for the species, though Ludlow also found it at that elevation in Bhutan in June. Like other minivets, affects open tree forest.

DISTRIBUTION OUTSIDE SIKKIM: Nepal eastward to Assam; East Pakistan, Burma. The species extends to the Indochinese subregion and S. China.

GENERAL HABITS: In my experience, keeps in smaller parties or flocks than other minivets, but otherwise not markedly different.

NESTING: *Season*—April-May. *Nest*—typical of the minivets, a shallow cup fixed on the upper surface of a horizontal branch, well plastered on the outside with cobweb and draped with lichen, looking from below like a natural excrescence. *Eggs*—normally 3, variable, pale sea-green flecked with pale reddish or brownish, resembling the eggs of the House Sparrow. Size about 19×14 mm.

RACIAL CHARACTERISTICS, MEASUREMENTS, ETC: The Survey specimens (2 ♂♂) measure: Wing 84-90; bill 13.5-14; tarsus 17 (1); tail 94-95 mm.

Schäfer's Sikkim skins have Wing 3 ♂♂ 85, 86, 87; 1 ♀ 85 mm.

Iris brown; bill brownish black; legs, feet and claws blackish brown.

Males also breed in the sub-adult female plumage.

## *Family* IRENIDAE: Fairy Bluebird, Chloropses, Ioras

### THE GOLDFRONTED CHLOROPSIS

*Chloropsis aurifrons aurifrons* (Temminck & Laugier)

*Phyllornis aurifrons* Temminck & Laugier, 1829, Planch. Color. d'Ois., livr. 81, pl. 484, fig. 1—'Sumatra, India'=Cachar.

F.B.I. 1: 346

LOCAL NAMES: Subz-harewa (Nepali); Skalem-pho (Lepcha).

SIZE: Bulbul.

FIELD CHARACTERS: An active leaf-green bulbul with bright golden forehead, bright verdigris-blue shoulder patches, and slender slightly curved black bill. Lores, round eye, ear-coverts and lower throat black; chin, cheeks and upper throat purple-blue.

*Female* with the forehead paler orange-yellow and less extensive, and less yellow surrounding the black lower throat.

STATUS AND HABITAT: Resident at fairly low elevations, up to *c.* 2500 ft. (Rangpo, Singtam, and elsewhere in the Teesta Valley). Affects open wooded country in evergreen and moist deciduous forest.

DISTRIBUTION OUTSIDE SIKKIM: Throughout the Indian Union, East Pakistan, Ceylon, Burma, Thailand to Annam, Sumatra. Several races.

GENERAL HABITS: Entirely arboreal. Keeps in pairs or small parties to thick foliage of trees where its plumage blends perfectly with the green leaves, making it difficult to spot. Eats berries, insects, spiders, and to a large extent the nectar of numerous species of wild flowers, which it helps to pollinate. The normal call notes are a musical drongo-like *swich-chich-chich-wee* (accent on first syllable, and last much prolonged). But it is an accomplished mimic and loves to imitate many other birds' calls in quick succession, and seemingly to enjoy the discomfiture of its hearers!

NESTING: *Season*—Not recorded for Sikkim. Elsewhere May to August. *Nest*—a loose cup of tendrils, rootlets, etc. high up in the fork of an outhanging branch of a forest tree, well concealed among foliage. *Eggs*—2 or 3, cream or reddish cream, speckled with claret. Size about 24×16 mm.

RACIAL CHARACTERISTICS, MEASUREMENTS, ETC: ♂♀ Wing 94-98; bill 17-18; tarsus *c.* 18; tail 70-75 mm. (F.B.I.).

Iris brown; bill black, gape and base of lower mandible horny; legs and feet plumbeous.

## THE ORANGEBELLIED CHLOROPSIS

*Chloropsis hardwickii hardwickii* Jardine & Selby
*Chloropsis hardwickii* Jardine & Selby, 1830, Illustr. Orn. 2: Add. pl. 1—Nepal.

**Plate 15, fig. 1** (facing p. 160)

F.B.I. 1: 349
LOCAL NAME:
SIZE: Bulbul.

FIELD CHARACTERS: *Male: Above,* bright leaf-green with verdigris-blue shoulder patches, and deep purplish blue wings and tail. *Below,* bright brownish orange, with breast, throat, chin, and sides of head deep bluish black. A bright cobalt blue moustachial streak.

*Female* has breast, throat, etc. leaf-green like upper parts. Orange underparts paler and less extensive; wings largely brown; tail green, and moustachial streak a paler blue.

STATUS AND HABITAT: Resident in a higher zone than occupied by the Goldfronted species. Fairly common in forested country between about 2000 and 6000 ft. elevation (Martam, Dikchu, Gangtok, Penlom, Kewzing, etc.).

DISTRIBUTION OUTSIDE SIKKIM: The appropriate altitudinal zone of the Himalayas from Simla and Mussooree to E. Assam. Manipur, Burma, Thailand, Malaya. Several races.

GENERAL HABITS: Arboreal. Keeps in pairs or small parties in the foliage canopy. On one occasion a gathering of over 50 observed feeding from a flush of *Bassia* flowers in company with sibias, spiderhunters, yellowbacked sunbirds and white-eyes. Inseparable from *Loranthus* tree-parasites infesting the lofty forest trees, hopping about and clinging amongst the clumps in all manner of acrobatic positions to probe into the flower tubes. Nectar is its principal food, and it thus helps to pollinate numerous species of wild flowers. Insects and berries are also eaten. Individuals have their own feeding territories and circuits, encroachment of which by others of their kind is actively resented. It is a remarkably versatile songster and an excellent mimic.

NESTING: *Season*—chiefly May-June. *Nest*—similar to that of the Goldfronted Chloropsis: a cradle of roots and fibres suspended near the end of an outhanging branch 20 to 30 ft. up. *Eggs*—also similar. Size about 23×16 mm.

RACIAL CHARACTERISTICS, MEASUREMENTS, ETC: Specimens collected in Sikkim measure:

| | Wing | Bill | Tarsus | Tail |
|---|---|---|---|---|
| 2 ♂♂ | 94-94.5 | 24.5-25 | 19-19.5 | 70-73.5 mm. |
| 1 ♀ | 90 | 22.5 | 18.5 | 68.5 mm. |

Seven adult specimens in the Schäfer Sikkim collection have Wings: ♂♂ 95, 95, 100; ♀♀ 92, 92, 94, 94 mm.

Iris brown; bill black; legs and feet bluish plumbeous; claws slaty brown.

## THE SIKKIM FAIRY BLUEBIRD

*Irena puella sikkimensis* Whistler & Kinnear

*Irena puella sikkimensis* Whistler & Kinnear, 1933, *Jour. Bombay Nat. Hist. Soc.* 36: 582—Sukna, Darjeeling.

F.B.I. 3: 1 (part)

LOCAL NAME:

SIZE: Myna+.

FIELD CHARACTERS: *Male: Above,* brilliant ultramarine blue. *Below,* deep velvety black.

*Female:* dull blue-green, with blackish lores and round the eyes.

STATUS AND HABITAT: Resident (?); evidently rare. An inhabitant of tropical forested valleys and foothills; recorded in the Sikkim Himalayas up to 4000 ft. elevation. Not met with by the Sikkim Survey nor by other recent investigators. Ludlow does not record it from Bhutan, but he obtained it in the tropical Himalayan facies of SE. Tibet at *c.* 1000 ft.

DISTRIBUTION OUTSIDE SIKKIM: The eastern Himalayas from Sikkim to E. Assam; Burma, Thailand, Indochina. The typical race occurs in the heavy rainfall areas of SW. India. The species extends to Malaya and Indonesia.

GENERAL HABITS: Keeps to the tree-tops in pairs or small parties. *Food:* fruits, berries and flower nectar. *Flight:* swift, direct and thrush-like. *Call:* a rich, mellow, percussive *peepit* or *chichichichik* uttered every few seconds, the latter in flight.

NESTING: Not recorded in Sikkim. *Nest*—a fragile saucer of roots, twigs, moss, etc. 5 to 20 feet up in a bush or sapling in dense moist forest. *Eggs*—2, olive-grey or greenish white, irregularly blotched with brown, more densely at the broad end. Size about 28×20 mm.

RACIAL CHARACTERISTICS, MEASUREMENTS, ETC: This northern race *sikkimensis* differs from the SW. Indian *puella* only in having a longer Wing: 133-144 mm. against 123-131 mm.

Iris claret colour or scarlet; bill brownish black (♀) or black (♂); legs, feet and claws black.

## *Family* Pycnonotidae: Bulbuls

### THE BLACKCRESTED YELLOW BULBUL

*Pycnonotus melanicterus flaviventris* (Tickell)

*Vanga flaviventris* Tickell, 1833 (Nov.), *Jour. Asiat. Soc. Bengal* 2: 573—Dhulbhúm.

F.B.I. 1: 397

LOCAL NAME: Mandiph-hur (Lepcha).

SIZE: Bulbul.

FIELD CHARACTERS: Head, erect crest, face and throat glossy black. Rest of upper parts olive; tail largely brown. Underparts bright oil yellow, darker on breast. Pale yellow eyes conspicuous at short range. Sexes alike.

STATUS AND HABITAT: Fairly common, and locally abundant, at low elevations and up to 5000 ft. (Kewzing). Affects dense secondary jungle. Also scrub and bush country about terraced cultivation and villages.

DISTRIBUTION OUTSIDE SIKKIM: The lower Himalayas, eastward from about Mussooree. Nepal, Bhutan, Assam south of the Brahmaputra, central India, Orissa; Burma, Thailand, Malaya, Borneo, Yunnan, Indochina. A smaller race (*minor*) in Ceylon.

GENERAL HABITS: Similar to the bulbuls described further. Its voice, notes, and superficial appearance are very reminiscent of the Rubythroated Bulbul (*P. gularis*) of SW. India. Some of the calls also resemble those of the Black Bulbul. Keeps in pairs or small parties. Mainly frugivorous, but also eats insects.

NESTING: *Season*—principally May-June. *Nest*—a cup of coarse grass and twigs, similar to that of the Redvented Bulbul but somewhat smaller. Placed 2 to 6 or 8 ft. up in a raspberry bush or sapling. *Eggs*—3 or 4, pinkish white, densely covered with numerous freckles of pinky red, or specks of deep red. Size about 23×17 mm.

RACIAL CHARACTERISTICS, MEASUREMENTS, ETC: A Sikkim Survey specimen (♀) measures: Wing 89, bill 15.5, tarsus 17, tail 82 mm.

Iris yellowish white; bill black; legs, feet and claws horny brown.

### THE WHITECHEEKED BULBUL

*Pycnonotus leucogenys leucogenys* (Gray)

*Brachypus leucogenys* Gray, 1835, *in* Hardwicke's Illustr. Zool. 2, pl. 35, fig. 3—Darjeeling.

F.B.I. 1: 389

LOCAL NAMES: Manglio-kur or Mankliph-kur (Lepcha).

SIZE: Bulbul.

FIELD CHARACTERS: A sprightly earth-brown bulbul, with a jaunty forwardly curving pointed crest, glistening white cheek patches, black chin and throat, and bright sulphur yellow under base of tail (coverts). Sexes alike.

STATUS AND HABITAT: Common and locally abundant up to altitudes of *c.* 6000 ft. in the Teesta and Great Rangeet valleys (Rangpo, Singtam, Martam, Temi, Dentam, Rinchinpong, Gangtok, etc.). In northern Sikkim beyond Gangtok, only noted at Chungthang. Affects open scrub-and-bush country about homesteads and terraced cultivation.

DISTRIBUTION OUTSIDE SIKKIM: Throughout the lower Himalayas west to east. The crestless race *leucotis* occurs in north-western and central India.

GENERAL HABITS: Similar to those of the Redvented Bulbul. Goes about in pairs or small parties. In winter, large assemblages collect where food is plentiful, consorting on fruit-laden trees and bushes with many frugivorous species. Along with other bulbuls it will also take insects (winged termites etc.) on the ground, or on the wing by springing vertically up into the air from its perch. Has a number of cheery tinkling notes, some of which may be easily confused in the distance with those of the European or Bluecheeked Bee-eaters.

NESTING: *Season*—overall April to July. *Nest*—the typical bulbul structure: a shallow, flimsy cup of fine plant stems and grass blades, lined with finer grass. Placed in a low bush or small tree. *Eggs*—normally 3, like those of the Redvented Bulbul, pinkish white, profusely blotched with purplish brown or claret. Size about 22×16 mm.

RACIAL CHARACTERISTICS, MEASUREMENTS, ETC: A Survey specimen (♂) measures: Wing 94.5, bill 19.5, tarsus 22, tail 85. Ten Sikkim skins in the Schäfer collection give Wing 84 (♀) to 93 (♂) mm.—av. 87.5.

Iris brown; bill brownish black; legs, feet and claws blackish brown.

## THE REDVENTED BULBUL

*Pycnonotus cafer bengalensis* Blyth

*Pycnonotus bengalensis* Blyth, 1845, *Jour. Asiat. Soc. Bengal* **14**: 566—Bengal.

F.B.I. **1**: 387

LOCAL NAMES: Paklom (Bhutia); Mancleph-pho (Lepcha).

SIZE: Myna— (8 inches).

FIELD CHARACTERS: A perky smoke-brown bird with partially crested black head, whitish scale-like markings on breast and back, a conspicuous crimson patch below root of tail, and a white rump; the last particularly conspicuous in flight. Tail brown, all the feathers tipped with white. Sexes alike.

STATUS AND HABITAT: Found at all elevations up to about 6000 ft. (Gangtok—scarce). Very common in southern and western Sikkim (Rangpo, Singtam, Martam, Dentam (4500 ft., Great Rangeet Valley) and Rinchinpong, *c.* 5000 ft.). Not observed northward of Dikchu.

Affects open secondary bush and scrub country about homesteads and terraced cultivation.

DISTRIBUTION OUTSIDE SIKKIM: Nepal, Bhutan. Other races over practically all India, Burma, Thailand to Indochina and Java.

GENERAL HABITS: A tame and familiar species. Sometimes congregates in large loose gatherings where food is plentiful, but not in regular flocks like the Black Bulbul. Eats berries, wild figs, flower nectar and insects. Has a variety of pleasant, joyous calls, but no song as such.

NESTING: *Season*—chiefly April to June. *Nest*—a cup of rootlets and moss etc., sometimes plastered on the outside with a little cobweb. Placed in a bush or small tree, 3 to 30 ft. from the ground, usually fairly low. *Eggs*—3 or 4, pinkish white, profusely blotched with purplish brown or claret; variable. Size about 23×17 mm.

RACIAL CHARACTERISTICS, MEASUREMENTS, ETC: Sikkim birds are very black on the head, neck, upper back and breast, with sharply contrasting brown ear-coverts.

Specimens measure:

| | Wing | Bill | Tarsus | Tail |
|---|---|---|---|---|
| 2 ♂♂ | 105-106 | 20-21 | 24-25 | 102 mm. |
| 1 ♀ | 100 | 21 | 25 | 96 mm. |

For Schäfer's birds, Stresemann gives Wing 10 ♂♂ 98-106 (av. 102.2); 3 ♀♀ 93, 96, 96 mm.

Iris brown; bill black; legs, feet and claws blackish brown.

## THE STRIATED GREEN BULBUL

*Pycnonotus striatus striatus* (Blyth)

*Trichophorus striatus* Blyth, 1842, *Jour. Asiat. Soc. Bengal* **11**: 184—no locality = Nepal.

**Plate 15, fig. 5** (facing p. 160)

F.B.I. **1**: 379

LOCAL NAMES: Senim-plek-pho (Lepcha); Chichiam (Bhutia).

SIZE: Bulbul.

FIELD CHARACTERS: Crested. *Above*, olive-green with fine white streaks; darker (brownish) on crown and crest. Tail and wings largely brown and olive, the former yellowish on underside and tipped whitish on outer rectrices. *Below*, yellow, stippled on throat, heavily streaked on breast with greyish or sooty brown, and on abdomen with olive-brown. Lores, chin, and under tail-coverts unmarked bright yellow. A fine yellow rim round eye. Sexes alike.

In life, the full upstanding crest looks greyish brown and the breast black. The rest of the yellow underparts—boldly brown-streaked—are reminiscent of an immature Golden Oriole.

STATUS AND HABITAT: Fairly common, but locally distributed, at moderate elevations *c.* 3500 to 6000 ft.; occasionally higher (Temi, Chungthang, Gangtok). Affects heavy secondary evergreen jungle.

DISTRIBUTION OUTSIDE SIKKIM: Nepal, Bhutan, Assam hills north and south of the Brahmaputra; Manipur, Burma, Thailand, Yunnan, Tonkin.

GENERAL HABITS: Usually seen in flocks of 6 to 15 birds which fly from tree to tree in 'follow-my-leader' style. Has pleasant calls and song of the characteristic bulbul pattern, but easily distinguishable from those of the Redvented and other familiar species. *Food:* chiefly berries; also insects.

NESTING: *Season*—May-June. *Nest*—a fairly compact cup of twigs, fern-roots, weed stems, etc., lined with fine shreds of grass. Placed rather low down in a thick bush or bamboo clump. *Eggs*—2 or 3, variable, but in a general way very similar to those of the Redvented Bulbul—pale cream, blotched with reddish brown or purplish brown. Size about 22×17 mm.

RACIAL CHARACTERISTICS, MEASUREMENTS, ETC: The Fauna gives the measurements as: ♂♀ Wing 102-112, bill 15-16, tarsus *c.* 20, tail 96-108 mm. Stresemann measures Wing of 5 Schäfer skins (sex ?) 103, 106, 108, 109, 112 mm., and remarks that Sikkim birds are somewhat larger than those from Burma and Yunnan.

Iris reddish brown; bill black; legs and feet plumbeous brown.

## THE WHITETHROATED BULBUL

*Criniger flaveolus flaveolus* (Gould)

*Trichophorus flaveolus* Gould, 1836, *Proc. Zool. Soc. London:* 6—Himalayas, Cachar.

**Plate 15, fig. 4 (facing p. 160)**

F.B.I. 1: 363

LOCAL NAME: Kussap-eechiop-pho (Lepcha).

SIZE: Myna.

FIELD CHARACTERS: A large, crested bulbul. Perches with the tail well fanned out. *Above,* rufescent olive-yellow, with rufous-brown wings and tail. Lores and sides of head grey, with a whitish supercilium. *Below,* bright yellow with white chin and throat. Sexes alike.

STATUS AND HABITAT: A low-elevation bulbul, normally up to *c.* 2000 ft. (Dikchu, Singtam, Martam and elsewhere in the Teesta Valley) though Mandelli even found it nesting at 4000 ft. in Sikkim. Affects well-wooded secondary evergreen jungle.

DISTRIBUTION OUTSIDE SIKKIM: Nepal, Bhutan, Assam hills N. and S. of the Brahmaputra; Manipur. The species extends through Burma, Malaysia, Yunnan.

GENERAL HABITS: A noisy, sociable bulbul, usually seen in parties of 5 or 6 or larger flocks in the non-breeding season, chasing one another or 'flowing' from one patch of jungle to the next. Feeds on various berries and wild figs, but also on insects which it will sometimes take on the wing. The loud, harsh chattering notes, *kek-*

*kek* etc., are somewhat between the calls of a Jungle Babbler (*Turdoides somervillei*) and the cries of a frog caught by a snake. It also has a loud, sweet note.

NESTING: *Season*—principally May-June. *Nest*—a deep, heavily-built hemispherical cup of bamboo leaves, grass and weed stems, lined with fern- and bracken-roots. Placed in thick tangles of cane and bushes; occasionally up in small trees. *Eggs*—3 or 4, beautiful glossy deep salmon with profuse irregular lines, speckles and blotches of blood red or maroon, sometimes more dense at the larger end. Size about 27×19 mm.

RACIAL CHARACTERISTICS, MEASUREMENTS, ETC: The long pointed crest, strong bill, rufous tail, and the presence of numerous long hairs springing from the nape are diagnostic of this bulbul.

A specimen collected by Schäfer in Sikkim (♂) has Wing 104 mm. Examples of this race recently procured by Dr Ripley and myself in the Lohit Valley (NE. Assam) measure:

| | Wing | Bill | Tarsus | Tail |
|---|---|---|---|---|
| 4 ♂♂ | 101-106 | 20-25.5 | c. 23 | c. 90 mm. |
| 2 ♀♀ | 100-101 | 21-23 | | |

Therefore, Wing as given in F.B.I. '88-96 mm.' certainly seems erroneous. Iris brown; bill bluish plumbeous; legs and feet greyish brown.

## THE RUFOUSBELLIED BULBUL

*Hypsipetes virescens mcclellandi* Horsfield

*Hypsipetes mcclellandi* Horsfield, March 1840 (1839), *Proc. Zool. Soc. London:* 159—Assam.

**Plate 15, fig. 3** (facing p. 160)

F.B.I. 1: 377

LOCAL NAMES: Chinchiok-pho, Chichiam (Lepcha).

SIZE: Myna+.

FIELD CHARACTERS: A stout, slightly crested bulbul. *Above*, olive-green including tail. Crown and crest dark rufous-brown with fine whitish streaks. Wings olive-green and brown. *Below*, chestnut; darker and streaked with white on breast, paler on abdomen. Throat dark grey, heavily streaked with white, the feathers pointed and tousled. Under tail-coverts yellowish, tinged with rufous. Sexes alike.

STATUS AND HABITAT: Common at moderate elevations, *c.* 3000 to 6000 ft. (Rinchinpong, Teesta Valley, Gangtok). Affects well-wooded secondary jungle.

DISTRIBUTION OUTSIDE SIKKIM: The Himalayas from about Naini Tal eastwards—Nepal, Bhutan, Assam hills north and south of the Brahmaputra; Manipur, Arakan, Chin Hills. The species extends to Burma, Thailand, Malaya, Yunnan, Indochina.

GENERAL HABITS: Less sociable than the Black or Browneared Bulbuls. Usually in pairs or small parties in tall trees or fruiting bushes. *Food:* mainly berries. *Calls:* pleasant and varied; also a full sweet song of three bars, constantly repeated in the breeding season. While singing, erects crest and puffs out lanceolate throat feathers.

NESTING: *Season*—chiefly May and June. *Nest*—rather like an oriole's, of coarse grasses, bamboo leaves and soft fibres. Suspended in the fork of a small branch 20 feet or more up. *Eggs*—2 or 3, very like those of the Black Bulbul; variable. Size about 26×18 mm.

RACIAL CHARACTERISTICS, MEASUREMENTS, ETC: A specimen (♀) collected in Sikkim has Wing 100.5, bill 25, tarsus 17, tail 93 mm. Stresemann measures the wings of 5 Schäfer skins (sex ?) as 108, 109, 111, 111, 111 mm.

Iris brown; upper mandible horny brown, lower brownish flesh colour; legs, feet and claws brownish flesh colour.

## THE BROWNEARED BULBUL

*Hypsipetes flavalus flavalus* (Blyth)

*Hemixos flavala* Blyth, 1845, *Jour. Asiat. Soc. Bengal* **14**: 527—sub-Himalayan Ranges.

F.B.I. **1**: 374

LOCAL NAME: Nalli-pindi (Lepcha).

SIZE: Bulbul.

FIELD CHARACTERS: *Above*, dark ashy with short tuft-like crest. Wings and tail brownish, the former with a large prominent olive-yellow patch. Cheeks black; ear-coverts bronze-grey with a silky sheen. *Below*, pale grey, with white throat and abdomen. Sexes alike.

STATUS AND HABITAT: Resident. Common in the foothills and up to *c.* 4000 ft. elevation (Rangpo, Singtam, Martam, and elsewhere). Keeps to climax as well as secondary forest.

DISTRIBUTION OUTSIDE SIKKIM: The Himalayas from about Mussooree to the NE. Frontier; Assam; Manipur. The species is found in Burma, Yunnan, Malaysia, Indochina.

GENERAL HABITS: Arboreal and sociable. A forest bulbul, found also in secondary scrub-and-bush growth at the edge of or in overgrown clearings. Keeps in noisy flocks in winter, which break up into small parties or pairs in the nesting season. Has a pleasant jerky song, and a flute-like note. *Food:* berries, flower nectar, and insects. A bird will sometimes flutter against a sprig to pluck a berry, or launch a short aerial sally after a winged insect disturbed amongst the foliage. In its general actions and behaviour, and also partly in its voice and calls, close relationship with the Black Bulbul is clearly evident.

NESTING: *Season*—May and June. *Nest*—a deepish cup of grass, dead leaves and fine twigs etc. in a small tree or bush—sometimes slung like an oriole's nest—usually under 8 ft. up. *Eggs*—2 or 3. variable. The commonest type is pale cream colour, speckled all over with bright light brick-red. Size about 25×18 mm.

RACIAL CHARACTERISTICS, MEASUREMENTS, ETC: The Sikkim Survey specimens measure:

| | Wing | Bill | Tarsus | Tail |
|---|---|---|---|---|
| 1 ♂ | 99 | 19.5 | 18.5 | 87 mm. |
| 1 ♀. | 98 | 19.5 | 18 | 88 mm. |

Iris brownish crimson; bill black; legs, feet and claws horny brown.

## THE HIMALAYAN BLACK BULBUL

*Hypsipetes madagascariensis psaroïdes* Vigors

*Hypsipetes psaroïdes* Vigors, 1831, *Proc. Zool. Soc. London:* 43—Himalayas (=Simla).

F.B.I. 1: 369

LOCAL NAME: Phaki-pho (Lepcha).

SIZE: Myna+. Slimmer.

FIELD CHARACTERS: A dark grey bulbul with black crest, slightly but distinctly forked tail, and bright red bill, legs and feet.

STATUS AND HABITAT: Resident. Common between 4000 and 10,000 ft. elevation (Temi, Kewzing, Rinchinpong, Pemionche, Gangtok, Singhik, Chungthang, Lachen, etc.). Occasionally lower. Partial to tall forest, especially oak and rhododendron.

DISTRIBUTION OUTSIDE SIKKIM: Throughout the Himalayas from Chitral and Kashmir to Nepal, Bhutan, S.E. Tibet. Other races occur in the Assam hills, and E. and W. Ghats. The species ranges to Burma and Thailand.

GENERAL HABITS: Arboreal, gregarious, and very noisy. Flocks of 6 to 10 birds—up to a hundred or more in autumn and winter—keep to the lofty tree-tops and fly noisily up or down the hillsides or across the stream valleys. *Food:* berries, flower nectar and insects. Agile twisting sallies are sometimes launched in the air to capture winged prey. Rhododendron and *Erythrina* blossoms are unfailingly visited for the nectar, and the birds display much aggressiveness towards Blackheaded Sibias and Haircrested Drongos visiting the trees in the same quest. Has a large variety of loud squeaky notes. One of the commoner ones—a long-drawn *wheenh*—has been aptly likened to the musical creaking of a gate hinge!

NESTING: *Season*—chiefly May and June. *Nest*—a neat but flimsy-bottomed cup of dead leaves, grass, and woody stalks, plastered on the outside with cobwebs and lined with finer fibres. Placed 25 to 40 ft. up in a high tree. *Eggs*—3 or 4, very variable in colour and markings. Perhaps the commonest type is white or whitish, sparsely to very densely speckled with fine reddish brown or purplish brown. Size about 26×19 mm.

RACIAL CHARACTERISTICS, MEASUREMENTS, ETC: Differs from the S. Indian race *ganeesa* in being a paler grey overall, and in the presence of a black streak behind and under the ear-coverts. The Sikkim Survey specimens measure:

| | Wing | Bill | Tarsus | Tail |
|---|---|---|---|---|
| 1 ♂ | 126 | 27.5 | 19.5 | 114 mm. |
| 1 ♀ | 118 | 28 | 20 | 106 mm. |

A large series from Sikkim in the Schäfer collection gives Wing 16 ♂♂ 120-130 mm. (av. 124.7); 2 ♀♀ 115, 116 mm.

Iris reddish brown; bill, legs and feet scarlet-red; claws horny brown.

## *Family* MUSCICAPIDAE:

### *Subfamily* MUSCICAPINAE: Flycatchers

### THE NEPAL SOOTY FLYCATCHER

*Muscicapa sibirica cacabata* Penard

*Muscicapa sibirica cacabata* Penard, 1919, *Proc. New England Zool. Club* 7: 21 (New name for *Hemichelidon fuliginosa* Hodgson, preoccupied)—Nepal.

F.B.I. 2: 204

LOCAL NAME: Dang-chim-pa-pho (Lepcha).

SIZE: Sparrow—.

FIELD CHARACTERS: *Above*, sooty brown, feathers of head with faint dark centres. A whitish ring round eye. *Below*, centre of chin, a patch on lower throat, abdomen, and vent white. Rest of underparts smoky brown, marked with white on breast and flanks. Tips of closed wings reaching almost to end of tail. Sexes alike.

STATUS AND HABITAT: Not common. According to Stevens breeds at and above elevations of 6000 or 7000 ft. Descends lower in winter, rarely straggling to 2000 ft. or even less. The Chicago Museum has two specimens collected at Chungthang, *c.* 5500 ft., in May (1931). Schäfer obtained it at Thangu, 13,000 ft., on 1 July, and at *c.* 9000 ft. (Lachen) on 27 August. Blanford recorded it at 9000 ft. in the Lachung Valley in September. Affects glades in tall forest.

DISTRIBUTION OUTSIDE SIKKIM: Nepal, Bhutan to eastern Assam, Burma, Thailand, Malaya. The adjoining race *gulmergi* stretches westward from Garhwal through Kashmir to Afghanistan. The species ranges through E. Siberia, Manchuria, Kamschatka, Japan.

GENERAL HABITS: Entirely arboreal. Usually solitary; occasionally 3 or 4 individuals hunting in loose association in the same forest glade. Perches bolt upright, wings slightly drooping, on the tip of a tall conifer, preferably a dead trunk, or at the end of an outhanging branch lower down, or on the upturned roots of a fallen tree. From here it launches agile sorties to capture midges and other tiny winged insects in the air, gliding back to the same perch or to a nearby one. It is a silent bird, except for a feeble little twitter uttered in the breeding season.

NESTING: *Season*—May-June. *Nest*—a shallow cup of moss and lichens bound with cobwebs, and lined with hair etc. Usually placed on a horizontal spruce or fir branch 30 or 40 ft. up. *Eggs*—3 or 4, pale olive-grey or olive-stone colour, sparsely freckled with pale reddish, sometimes more densely at the broad end. Size about 17×12 mm.

RACIAL CHARACTERISTICS, MEASUREMENTS, ETC: The adjoining west Himalayan race, *gulmergi*, is paler and more grey both above and below.

The Fauna gives for ♂♀ Wing 70-75; bill 8-9; tarsus *c.* 13; tail 50-55 mm. Schäfer's Sikkim specimens have Wing 2 ♂♂ 75, 75; 1 ♀ 69 (moulting).

Iris brown; bill: upper mandible dark brown, lower yellowish; legs and feet brownish black or black.

## THE FERRUGINOUS FLYCATCHER

*Muscicapa ferruginea* (Hodgson)

*Hemichelidon ferruginea* Hodgson, 1845, *Proc. Zool. Soc. London:* 32, ex *Zool. Miscell.*, 1844, p. 84, *nom. nud.*—Nepal.

F.B.I. 2: 206

LOCAL NAME: Dang-chim-pa-pho (Lepcha).

SIZE: Sparrow—.

FIELD CHARACTERS: Differs from the Sooty Flycatcher in the general tone of the plumage being ferruginous. *Above*, forehead, crown and nape brownish slate. A whitish ring round eye. Rump and upper tail-coverts chestnut. Tail reddish brown with darker tips. Secondary wing quills broadly edged chestnut. *Below*, a patch of white on throat and foreneck. Breast rufous, with brown centres to the feathers. Rest of underparts chestnut except centre of abdomen and vent, which are white. Sexes alike.

STATUS AND HABITAT: Uncommon. Inglis obtained it at Rinchinpong, *c.* 6000 ft., (season?) and Schäfer at Gangtok, *c.* 6300 ft., in June. The Survey failed to meet with it in Sikkim between November and April, though Meinertzhagen collected a pair at Dentam, *c.* 4500 ft., in the Great Rangeet Valley on 9 January (1926).

DISTRIBUTION OUTSIDE SIKKIM: *Summer*, Garhwal, Nepal, Bhutan to eastern Assam; Manipur, N. Burma, Thailand to W. China. *Winter*, Burma, Malaya, Indonesia, Hainan, Formosa.

GENERAL HABITS: Similar to the Sooty Flycatcher, but less restless and also somewhat crepuscular.

NESTING: Osmaston found it common and breeding about Darjeeling in June and July. *Nest*—a cup of green moss and lichen, lined with root-hairs etc. Placed on a dead tree-trunk in a natural swelling, on a snag where a large branch has broken off, and in similar situations. *Eggs*—2 or 3, very like those of the Sooty species. Size about 18×14 mm.

RACIAL CHARACTERISTICS, MEASUREMENTS, ETC: The Fauna gives the measurements ♂♀ as Wing 68-75; bill 8-9; tarsus 12-13; tail 43-50 mm. An adult ♂ in Schäfer's Sikkim collection has Wing 72 mm.

Iris brown; bill black, commissure and base of lower mandible yellowish; legs and feet fleshy brown.

## THE ORANGEGORGETTED FLYCATCHER

*Muscicapa strophiata strophiata* (Hodgson)

*Siphia strophiata* Hodgson, 1837, *Ind. Review* 1: 651—Nepal.

**Plate 16, fig. 1** (facing p. 161)

F.B.I. 2: 208

LOCAL NAMES: Siphia (Nepali); Phatt-tagrak-pho (Lepcha).

SIZE: Sparrow—.

FIELD CHARACTERS: *Male: Above,* forehead narrowly black with a conspicuous white band above this stretching backward to eyes. Upper parts olive-brown. Tail black with white bases. *Below,* sides of face deep slaty, changing to black on chin and throat; breast and flanks slaty grey. An oval spot on upper breast bright orange-chestnut—sometimes very indistinct. Abdomen white.

*Female,* similar but without the black and with very little white on forehead. Orange throat-patch smaller. Black parts of chin, throat, etc. replaced by ashy.

STATUS AND HABITAT: Common at all elevations between 1000 and 12,000 ft., with a lower ceiling in winter of *c.* 6000-7000 ft. (Rangpo, Martam, Pakyong, Kewzing, Rinchinpong, Gangtok, Pemionche, Manshitang, Lachen, Yumthang). Affects glades in shady forest, 'jhoomed' hillsides, edge of mule paths through jungle, etc.

DISTRIBUTION OUTSIDE SIKKIM: Throughout the Himalayas from Kashmir (?) to E. Assam. N. Burma, Thailand to W. China. In winter at lower elevations than in summer.

GENERAL HABITS: Usually seen singly, perched upright on a bare twig of a bush, a fallen log or a stump on the edge or in the middle of a forest clearing. From here it launches short aerial sallies after midges and other tiny winged insects, returning to its base after each capture. Sometimes descends to the ground to pick up a crawling insect. From time to time jerks open and cocks tail, displaying the white patch at its base, and utters the characteristic *tick* or *tick-tick.* Also has a short, spirited, typically flycatcher song in the breeding season.

NESTING: *Season*—April to June. *Nest*—a loose cup of moss, fern stems, etc. lined with fern roots, papery bark and feathers. Placed in a hole or rift in a tree-trunk fairly low down. *Eggs*—3, white, slightly glossy. Size about 18×13 mm.

RACIAL CHARACTERISTICS, MEASUREMENTS, ETC: Tail feathers pointed as in *Erithacus hyperythrus.* The Survey specimens (3 ♂♂) measure: Wing 75-76; bill 12-13; tarsus 19.5-20; tail 56-59 mm.

A series of 15 adults collected by Schäfer in Sikkim give Wing 70 (♀), 78 (♂) mm.

Iris brown; bill black; legs, feet and claws horny brown.

## THE SIKKIM WHITEGORGETTED FLYCATCHER

*Muscicapa monileger monileger* (Hodgson)

*Dimorpha monileger* Hodgson, 1845, *Proc. Zool. Soc. London:* 26—Nepal.

F.B.I. 2: 244 (=*Anthipes m. moniliger*)

LOCAL NAME: Phatt-tagrak-pho (Lepcha).

SIZE: Sparrow—.

FIELD CHARACTERS: *Above,* including crown and sides of head olive-brown changing to ferruginous on upper tail-coverts and tail. Wing feathers brown edged with rufous. Short, broad, bright fulvous supercilia almost meeting on forehead. Lores, ear-coverts and under the eye grey-brown. *Below,* chin and throat white surrounded with black. Rest of lower plumage fulvous olive, whitish on abdomen. Sexes alike.

STATUS AND HABITAT: Rare. Presumably resident and breeding (also wintering) up to *c.* 6000 ft. elevation. Meinertzhagen procured specimens on 13 January (1926) at Rinchinpong, *c.* 5000 ft., and Schäfer at Gangtok, *c.* 6300 ft., on 12 June as well as 15 December (1938). Affects bush jungle.

DISTRIBUTION OUTSIDE SIKKIM: E. Nepal; Bhutan to Assam hills north and south of Brahmaputra River. Replaced by allied races in Assam, Manipur, Burma, Thailand, Malaysia.

GENERAL HABITS: Very little recorded. Keeps singly to bush jungle close to the ground where it draws attention to itself by its chattering notes. Often hops about on the ground like a shortwing. Stevens refers to one (♂?—24 May) 'giving forth to the best of its vocal efforts with a rapid quivering of the wings, from its stance amongst brushwood in the close forest'. No description of the song is available.

NESTING: Mandelli, in the 1870's, sent supposed nests of this flycatcher taken at Lebong, 5800 ft., to Hume, but Stuart Baker doubts their authenticity. Nothing further as regards its nesting is known since.

RACIAL CHARACTERISTICS, MEASUREMENTS, ETC: The Fauna gives for ♂♀. Wing 60-65; bill *c.* 10; tarsus *c.* 23; tail 45-50 mm.

Schäfer's Sikkim skins have Wing 1 '♂' 60; 1 ♀ 62 mm.

Iris brown; bill dark horny brown, paler at base (all black in breeding season); legs and feet fleshy white.

## THE RUFOUSBREASTED BLUE FLYCATCHER

*Muscicapa hyperythra hyperythra* Blyth

*Muscicapa hyperythra* Blyth, 1842, *Jour. Asiat. Soc. Bengal* **11**: 885—India.
*Dimorpha superciliaris* Blyth, 1842—Nepal, Darjeeling; not *M. superciliaris* Jerdon 1840.

F.B.I. 2: 217

LOCAL NAME:

SIZE: Sparrow—.

FIELD CHARACTERS: *Male: Above,* slaty blue with black forehead and narrow white supercilium. Tail brown suffused with blue, and with the base largely white. *Below,* orange-chestnut, paler on abdomen and under tail-coverts. Chin and cheeks black.

*Female: Above,* olive-brown; fulvous-tinged on rump. *Below,* ochraceous; darkest on breast and flanks, palest on chin and abdomen.

The male can be told from *hodgsonii* (p. 134) by its smaller size, and the more prominent white supercilium. Female smaller than female *hodgsonii* but otherwise undistinguishable in the field with certainty.

STATUS AND HABITAT: Uncommon between November and April. The Survey met with it only at Chungthang, *c.* 5500 ft., in February. According to Stevens 'a summer migrant to elevations probably not exceeding 7000 ft. on the Outer Ranges' (Sikkim Himalayas) though in neighbouring Bhutan Ludlow obtained most of his specimens, July-October, between 9500 and 8000 ft. Col. Meinertzhagen procured a ♂ at Singhik, 4500 ft., on 30.x.1925 and Dr Schäfer a ♀ at Gangtok, *c.* 6300 ft., on 12.vi.1938. Affects dense forest.

DISTRIBUTION OUTSIDE SIKKIM: Garhwal, Nepal, Bhutan, SE. Tibet, Assam hills. The species extends through Burma and Thailand to Malaya and Indonesia.

GENERAL HABITS: Typical flycatcher. Silent. Usually hunts from low perches in the forest understorey, and often descends to the ground like a chat to capture insects.

NESTING: Unrecorded in Sikkim. Elsewhere, *season*—April and May. *Nest*—a tiny cup of moss, lined with fine moss-roots etc. Placed in a hole in a steep mossy bank. *Eggs*—4, variable, pale yellowish grey or stone colour to pinkish red, faintly stippled or with well-defined blotches and mottlings of reddish brown. Size about 18×14 mm. Evidently both sexes incubate.

RACIAL CHARACTERISTICS, MEASUREMENTS, ETC: The Fauna gives for ♂♀ Wing 55-63; bill *c.* 9; tarsus *c.* 19; tail 38-40 mm. Schäfer's Sikkim ♀ has Wing 58 mm.

'Iris dark brown; bill black; legs and feet silvery white to pale fleshy brown or fleshy pink, the claws a little darker and browner.' In the ♀ the base of the bill is sometimes paler and horn coloured.

## THE REDBREASTED BLUE, or SLATYBACKED, FLYCATCHER

*Muscicapa hodgsonii* (Verreaux)

*Siphia hodgsonii* Verreaux, 1871, *Nouv. Arch. Mus. Bull.* 6: 34—Chinese. Tibet=Chwanben.

F.B.I. 2: 216

LOCAL NAME: Paon-pali (Tibetan).

SIZE: Sparrow—.

FIELD CHARACTERS: *Male: Above,* slaty blue with the upper tail-coverts almost black. Tail black, narrowly edged outside with blue, with the bases largely white. Lores and cheeks velvety black. *Below,* chin, throat, breast, and flanks orange-chestnut paling to rusty olive on vent and under tail-coverts.

*Female: Above,* olive-brown with the upper tail-coverts tinged fulvous. Lores and a ring round eye whitish. *Below,* ashy brown fading to whitish on abdomen and vent.

STATUS AND HABITAT: Apparently rare. The only four records I can trace for Sikkim territory proper are Stevens's specimen (♂) from Mangan, *c.* 4300 ft. near Ringim Gompa, 21.iii.1916; a ♂ collected by Col. Meinertzhagen, Dentam, *c.* 4500 ft. (in the Great Rangeet Valley), 9.i.1926; and my own sight records of a ♂ at Kewzing, *c.* 5400 ft., 27.iii.1955 and another at Gangtok, *c.* 6000 ft., 18.iv.1955.

DISTRIBUTION OUTSIDE SIKKIM: Bhutan; Assam hills north and south of Brahmaputra River; Manipur, Burma, Thailand, Yunnan, Kansu. Ludlow did not obtain it in Bhutan, though he found it common in summer in the pine forests of adjacent SE. Tibet.

GENERAL HABITS: Very similar to those of the Orangegorgetted Flycatcher. According to Ludlow it keeps to the tops of trees, uttering a constant ripple of whistling notes.

NESTING: Not recorded in Sikkim.

RACIAL CHARACTERISTICS, MEASUREMENTS, ETC: Slaty blue upper plumage, orange-chestnut below, white base of tail and absence of white supercilium usually diagnostic of the male. Olive-brown upper plumage; ashy brown underparts paling to white on abdomen, with no white in the tail, are suggestive clues to the female.

The Fauna gives the measurements as: ♂♀ Wing 69-74; bill *c.* 9; tarsus *c.* 17; tail 50-53 mm.

'Iris deep brown; bill all black in the breeding season, the base horny brown in the non-breeding season; legs and feet dark reddish brown.' In the female the bill apparently never turns wholly black.

## THE LITTLE PIED FLYCATCHER

*Muscicapa westermanni collini* Rothschild

*Muscicapa collini* Rothschild, 1925, *Bull. Br. Orn. Cl.* **45**: 90 (New name for *Muscicapula melanoleuca* Blyth, 1843, *Jour. Asiat. Soc. Bengal* **12**: 940)—Nepal, Darjeeling.

F.B.I. **2**: 224 (= *melanoleuca*)
LOCAL NAME: Tuni-ti-ti (Lepcha).
SIZE: Sparrow −.

FIELD CHARACTERS: *Male: Above*, velvety black with a broad white supercilium, and some white on the wings. Tail black, with basal half mostly white. *Below*, white.

*Female: Above*, olive-brown. Upper tail-coverts bright ferruginous. Tail brown, edged with ferruginous. Some fulvous white on wings. *Below*, smoky white, superficially a good replica of the Rufoustailed Flycatcher, *Muscicapa ruficauda*.

STATUS AND HABITAT: Met with by the Survey only at Gangtok, *c.* 6000 ft., 24 March, and Kewzing, 5400 ft., 27 March. Meinertzhagen collected specimens between Gangtok and Dikchu on 13 February, and Schäfer at Dikchu and Gangtok in February, March and June. The records from other parts of the Sikkim Himalayas also suggest that the bird descends to lower (plains?) levels between October/November and February. According to Stevens, its upper limit (breeding) in the Sikkim Himalayas is *c.* 7000 ft. Affects the middle storey of forest.

DISTRIBUTION OUTSIDE SIKKIM: Garhwal, Nepal, Bhutan, to extreme NE. Assam. Another race in Assam, Burma, Thailand. The species extends to Malaya, Indonesia, Celebes.

GENERAL HABITS: Usually hunts within the foliage canopy of trees, making little fluttering flights from branch to branch, rather than aerial sallies into space from the outside branches. On the whole very silent, but a soft warbling has been recorded, interspersed with low grating notes.

NESTING: No record for Sikkim. Elsewhere, *season*—April to June. *Nest*—a tiny cup of moss, maidenhair fern stems, etc., lined with fine hairlike roots. Placed at low heights in a crevice in a rock, a hole in a bank or among the exposed roots of a tree. *Eggs*—3 or 4, warm buff, the whole surface densely covered with minute dark reddish brown specks. Size about 15 × 12 mm. Both sexes incubate.

RACIAL CHARACTERISTICS, MEASUREMENTS, ETC: Female *collini* may be differentiated from female *leucomelanura* (p. 137) in having the chin, throat and breast buff. In the latter the chin and abdomen are pure white. But field identification of females (when unaccompanied by males) is difficult and unsatisfactory, since apart from their close superficial similarity with each other, both of them can be readily confused with the slightly larger Rufoustailed Flycatcher, *Muscicapa ruficauda*, of the western Himalayas.

The Fauna gives for ♂♀ Wing 50-59: bill *c.* 9; tarsus 15-16: tail

40-43 mm. Schäfer's Sikkim specimens have Wing 5 ♂♂ 57, 59, 59, 60, 61; 1 ♀ 56 mm. (Stresemann).

Iris dark brown; bill, legs, feet black.

## THE LITTLE BLUE-AND-WHITE FLYCATCHER

*Muscicapa superciliaris aestigma* Gray

*Muscicapa aestigma* Gray, 1846, Cat. Mamms. Birds Nepal, Thibet; 90, 155, *ex* Hodgson's *Zool. Miscell.*, 1844, p. 84, *nom. nud.*—Nepal.

F.B.I. 2: 223

LOCAL NAME: Tuni-ti-ti (Lepcha).

SIZE: Sparrow—.

FIELD CHARACTERS: *Male: Above*, deep blue, with a white patch at base of tail. *Below*, white, with a blue-black band across breast broken in the middle.

*Female: Above*, greyish brown with blue upper tail-coverts. Tail blackish, edged with blue. *Below*, sullied whitish, with glistening white throat and upper breast.

STATUS AND HABITAT: Not common. The Survey came across it only once at Rangpo, *c.* 1000 ft., in November. Stevens records it from the Sikkim Himalayas, but outside the State territory, at *c.* 4700 ft. in March, April, September, October. In Bhutan, Ludlow found it breeding at 9000 ft. in June. Partial to fairly open oak and mixed broad-leafed forest.

DISTRIBUTION OUTSIDE SIKKIM: E. Nepal, Bhutan to NE. Assam, Assam hills, Manipur, N. Burma, N. Thailand. The better known west Himalayan race is found from western Nepal to the Afghan frontier.

GENERAL HABITS: Typical. Keeps largely to the middle storey of the forest, often in the mixed hunting parties of small insectivorous birds. Constantly jerks up tail with a *chr-r-r* or *tr-r-r* at each jerk. In summer the male utters a short feeble song *chiri-ri-ri*.

NESTING: Not recorded in Sikkim. Elsewhere, *season*—May to July. *Nest*—a well made cup of dry moss lined with fibres, roots or hair. Placed in a hole or rift in a tree-trunk, 5 to 25 ft. up. *Eggs*—3 or 4, pale olive-greenish to dull stone-buff colour with minute freckles of reddish brown, sometimes dense and forming a cap at the broad end. Size about 15×12 mm. Both sexes build the nest and feed the young.

RACIAL CHARACTERISTICS, MEASUREMENTS, ETC: The nominate west Himalayan race is readily distinguished by the presence of a prominent white eyebrow. In the British Museum there are two specimens of that race collected near Darjeeling by J. Gammie in March 1874.

The Fauna gives the measurements as: ♂♀ Wing 62-68; bill *c.* 9; tarsus 16-17; tail 43-45 mm.

Iris dark brown; bill black; legs and feet deep brown or 'purplish black'.

## THE SLATY BLUE FLYCATCHER

*Muscicapa leucomelanura leucomelanura* (Hodgson)

*Digenea leucomelanura* Hodgson, 1845, *Proc. Zool. Soc. London:* 28—Nepal. (Restricted to eastern Nepal by Vaurie, 1953, *Am. Mus. Novit.*, No. 1641 : 4).

**Plate 16, fig. 3** (facing p. 161)

F.B.I. **2**: 219

LOCAL NAME:

SIZE: Sparrow—.

FIELD CHARACTERS: *Male: Above,* slaty blue with forehead and sides of crown a paler brighter grey-blue. Lores and sides of head black. Upper tail-coverts black. Tail black with white base. *Below,* greyish white tinged with fulvous on breast and flanks.

*Female: Above,* olive-brown tinged on rump with rufous. Upper tail-coverts and tail ferruginous. A fulvous ring round eye. *Below,* fulvous white paling to pure white on chin and abdomen.

The male can be told from male *hyperythra* by absence of white supercilium and greyish fulvous underparts. *M. hodgsonii,* which also lacks the supercilium, has orange-chestnut underparts. The female is a very good replica of the slightly larger Rufoustailed Flycatcher (*Muscicapa ruficauda*) and can be readily confused with it in the field.

STATUS AND HABITAT: Stevens describes it as occurring in the outer ranges of the Sikkim Himalayas at all elevations from 3500 to 10,000 ft., according to season, and as probably descending to the foothills in winter. Noted by the Sikkim Survey, November to April, between *c.* 1000 ft. (Rangpo) and 6000 ft. (Gangtok), but as far from common. Schäfer collected specimens at 13,000 ft. (Thangu) in July, and at 9000 ft. (Lachen) in September. Affects forest with dense undergrowth.

DISTRIBUTION OUTSIDE SIKKIM: The Himalayas from Kashmir to Assam. The species extends into Manipur, Burma and Thailand.

GENERAL HABITS: Typical. Keeps singly to the forest understorey, hunting from bushes. Its alarm notes are well described by Heinrich as a quick-repeated *zieh-ticktickticktick.* As in other flycatchers, the tail is jerked up from time to time to the cocked position with the wings partly drooping at the sides.

NESTING: *Season*—May-June. *Nest*—a massive little cup of moss, mixed with leaves, wool, fur, etc. Placed in a hollow or crevice in a tree-trunk. *Eggs*—3 or 4, whitish pink to creamy pink, minutely speckled all over with pinkish red, sometimes thickly at the broad end to form a cap. Size about 16×12 mm.

RACIAL CHARACTERISTICS, MEASUREMENTS, ETC: The Fauna gives for ♂♀ Wing 57-72 (*sic*): bill *c.* 9; tarsus 19-20; tail 48-50 mm.

Schäfer's Sikkim specimens (4 ♂♂) have Wing 60, 61, 61, 63 mm.

Iris dark brown; bill black; legs and feet pale horny brown to dark brown.

## THE SAPPHIREHEADED FLYCATCHER

*Muscicapa sapphira* (Blyth)

*Muscicapula sapphira* Blyth, 1843, *Jour. Asiat. Soc. Bengal* 12: 939—Darjeeling.

**Plate 16, fig. 2** (facing p. 161)

F.B.I. 2: 225

LOCAL NAME:

SIZE: Sparrow—.

FIELD CHARACTERS: Adult *Male: Above,* forehead, crown and nape brilliant ultramarine blue. A line through the eye black. Sides of head and upper parts deep purplish blue. Upper tail-coverts bright blue. Tail and wings black, edged with blue. *Below,* chin, throat and upper breast light chestnut. A broken breast-band deep blue. Rest of underparts pale blue-grey.

Winter (and/or first year ?) plumage like the female, but with wings, rump, upper tail-coverts and tail as above. Males also breed in this plumage.

*Female: Above,* rufous-olive. Upper tail-coverts bright ferruginous. Tail dark brown, tinged ferruginous. A bright fulvous ring round eye. *Below,* chin, throat and breast pale orange-chestnut. Rest of underparts dull white, brownish on flanks and under tail-coverts.

STATUS AND HABITAT: Fairly common between November and April from 1000 to 5500 ft. altitude, chiefly under 2500 ft. (Rangpo, Singtam, Martam, Kewzing). Recorded as a permanent resident in Sikkim. Affects the middle storey of forest.

DISTRIBUTION OUTSIDE SIKKIM: E. Nepal, Bhutan to E. Assam, E. Bengal; Naga, Chin and Kachin Hills.

GENERAL HABITS: Typical flycatcher. Droops wings at sides and jerks up tail from time to time, uttering *tick-tick* at each jerk. Hunts chiefly within the foliage canopy of a tree, but also from bushes and end branches of large trees.

NESTING: Not recorded in Sikkim. Elsewhere, *season*—May-June. *Nest*—a small cup of moss, moss-roots, maidenhair fern stems, etc. neatly rounded off inside. Placed in a hollow in a vertical bank or hole in a tree-stump. *Eggs*—4, pale yellowish grey to warm buff-stone, varyingly stippled with pale reddish to reddish brown. Size about 15×12 mm. Both sexes incubate.

RACIAL CHARACTERISTICS, MEASUREMENTS, ETC: The Sikkim Survey specimens measure:

| | Wing | Bill | Tarsus | Tail |
|---|---|---|---|---|
| 3 ♂♂ | 60-65 | 12-13 | 16.5 | 44-51 mm. |
| 2 ♀♀ | 57.5-61 | 12-12.5 | 17 | 40-43.5 mm. |

Iris brown; bill black, legs, feet and claws horny brown or brownish black.

## THE LARGE NILTAVA

*Muscicapa grandis grandis* (Blyth)

*Chaitaris grandis* Blyth, 1842, *Jour. Asiat. Soc. Bengal* 11: 189—Darjeeling.

**Plate 16, fig. 5** (facing p. 161)

F.B.I. 2: 257

LOCAL NAME: Margong (Lepcha).

SIZE: Between Bulbul and Myna.

FIELD CHARACTERS: A large, rather sluggish flycatcher. *Male: Above,* dark purplish blue. Lores, forehead and sides of head black. Crown, rump, upper tail-coverts, a shoulder-patch and a patch on either side of the neck brilliant cobalt blue. Tail- and wing feathers black, edged with blue. *Below,* chin, throat and upper breast black, changing lower to blue-black, and to bluish ashy on abdomen and under tail-coverts; the last scalloped with white.

*Female: Above,* fulvous brown. Tail- and wing feathers edged with deep rufous. *Below,* olive-brown with pale buff chin, throat and upper breast; a diagnostic patch of bright blue on either side of neck.

STATUS AND HABITAT: Fairly common. The Survey came across it between 4000 and 7000 ft. elevation in winter—November to April (Temi, Kewzing, Rinchinpong, Pemionche, Gangtok). Apparently resident at all seasons. Schäfer collected specimens around Gangtok, *c.* 6000 ft., December to March, and also in June. Affects dense secondary jungle.

DISTRIBUTION OUTSIDE SIKKIM: Central Nepal, Bhutan, Assam hills north and south of Brahmaputra River; Manipur, Burma, Thailand. The species extends to Yunnan and the Indochinese and Malaysian subregions.

GENERAL HABITS: Comparatively sluggish for a flycatcher. Seen singly or in separated pairs, often in low bushes or even on the ground. *Food:* insects and berries; the latter picked from trees and also off the ground (?). *Call* (or song ?): a thin, rather mournful, rising three-noted whistle *whee-whee-wip,* repeated monotonously from a tree-top for several minutes at a stretch.

NESTING: *Season*—May-June. *Nest*—a cup of green moss lined with fine moss-roots. Placed in a crevice of a rock, a hollow in a bank, amongst the exposed roots of a tree, and in similar situations. *Eggs*—normally 4, creamy white or pinkish white to warm buff, variously freckled with light reddish or buffy brown. Size about 25×18 mm.

RACIAL CHARACTERISTICS, MEASUREMENTS, ETC: The Sikkim Survey specimens (3 ♂♂) measure Wing 108-112; bill 18-20: tarsus 23-25; tail 92-99 mm.

A large series collected by Schäfer gives Wing 13 ♂♂ 102-108 (av. 105.5); 3 ♀♀ 102, 103, 104 mm. (Stresemann).

Iris brown; bill, legs, feet and claws black; soles greyish flesh colour.

## THE RUFOUSBELLIED NILTAVA

*Muscicapa sundara sundara* (Hodgson)

*Niltava sundara* Hodgson, 1837, *Ind. Review* 1: 650—Nepal.

F.B.I. 2: 259

LOCAL NAMES: Niltava (Nepali); Marong (Lepcha).

SIZE: Sparrow.

FIELD CHARACTERS: *Male: Above*, dark blue and cobalt blue, with glistening black forehead and sides of neck. *Below*, bright chestnut, with black throat and a distinctive patch of bright blue on either side of neck.

*Female:* fulvous olive-brown with chestnut tail, a patch of lustrous blue on either side of neck, and a large round white patch below the throat.

STATUS AND HABITAT: Fairly common. Resident. The Survey recorded it between 1000 and 7000 ft. elevation from November to April (Rangpo, Singtam, Martam, Kewzing, Dentam, Gangtok). Schäfer obtained specimens at Lachen, *c.* 9000 ft., in September including some just moulting out of juvenile plumage, indicating that they were bred in that neighbourhood. Affects secondary and bush jungle.

DISTRIBUTION OUTSIDE SIKKIM: Nepal, Bhutan, Assam hills; Manipur, Burma. The contiguous western Himalayas, to Murree, are occupied by the paler race *fastuosa*. The species extends to the Indochinese and Malaysian subregions.

GENERAL HABITS: Hunts from low bushes in the typical flycatcher manner, and also freely descends to the ground like a bushchat. Often associates with the mixed hunting flocks of small birds in forest. Eats insects as well as berries. Silent except for a harsh *tr-r-r-tchik* or *tzi, tzi, tzi* sometimes heard. Stuart Baker mentions that 'it is a beautiful singer as are all the Niltavas'. Personally I have never heard its song, and cannot trace where it has been described. Neither have I heard or seen described the song of the Small Niltava; and the vocal performance of the Large Niltava (above) can hardly be called a beautiful song!

NESTING: *Season*—May-June, from *c.* 3500 ft. elevation up. *Nest*—a neat and compact cup of green moss, lined with fine moss-roots. Placed in a hollow amongst the exposed roots of a tree or a moss-covered bank; well concealed. *Eggs*—4, very similar to those of the Large Niltava, creamy white or pinkish white to warm buff, freckled with light reddish or brownish. Size about 21×16 mm. Both sexes partake in the domestic chores.

RACIAL CHARACTERISTICS, MEASUREMENTS, ETC: At a superficial glance, particularly when seen from below, ♂ liable to be confused with the Blue-fronted Redstart in its winter quarters. The redstart is, however, readily distinguished by its blue-black throat extending down to upper breast, and by its chestnut rump and tail.

The Sikkim Survey specimens measure:

| | Wing | Bill | Tarsus | Tail |
|---|---|---|---|---|
| 2 ♂♂ | 85 | 15.5-17.5 | 22 | 69-71.5 mm. |
| 3 ♀♀ | 80-83 | 16-17 | 21.5-22.5 | 62-66 mm. |

Schäfer's Sikkim skins give Wing 4 ad. ♂♂ 84-87 (av. 85.7); 4 ♀♀ 78-82 (av. 85.7) mm.

Iris brown; bill ♂ black, ♀ blackish brown; legs and feet plumbeous brown; claws horny brown.

## THE SMALL NILTAVA

*Muscicapa macgrigoriae* (Burton)

*Phoenicura macgrigoriae* Burton, 1835, *Proc. Zool. Soc. London*: 152—Himalayas.

F.B.I. 2: 260

LOCAL NAME: Phat-tagrak-pho (Lepcha).

SIZE: Sparrow—.

FIELD CHARACTERS: *Male: Above*, including exposed parts of wings and tail purple-blue. Forecrown, sides of crown, rump, upper tail-coverts, and a patch on either side of neck brilliant cobalt blue. Forehead, lores, and around eyes black. *Below*, chin, throat, sides of neck and upper breast deep purple-blue, shading to ashy grey on lower breast and to pale ashy on abdomen, flanks and under tail-coverts.

*Female: Above*, fulvous olive-brown, strongly tinged with rufous on rump and upper tail-coverts. Wing- and tail feathers edged with rufous excepting the middle pair of rectrices which are wholly rufous. *Below*, chin pale rufous; rest yellowish ashy, paling on abdomen and vent. A spot of brilliant blue on either side of neck.

STATUS AND HABITAT: Fairly common. Resident between 3000 and 6000 ft. elevation; down to *c.* 1000 ft. in winter (Rangpo, Singtam, Dikchu, Singhik, Temi, Kewzing, Gangtok). Affects dense bush jungle and edges of forest glades.

DISTRIBUTION OUTSIDE SIKKIM: The Himalayas from about Mussooree eastward through Nepal and Bhutan to eastern Assam; Manipur, Burma, Thailand and the Indochinese subregion.

GENERAL HABITS: Keeps singly or in pairs, hunting winged insects in the air in the typical flycatcher style, from bushes. Seldom on ground like the two other niltavas. Prefers deep shady glades, and is more active in the early mornings and about dusk. Said to have a curious low grating subsong.

NESTING: *Season*—May-June. *Nest*—a cup of green moss etc. similar to that of the other niltavas, somewhat deeper. Placed in a hollow in a vertical bank. *Eggs*—normally 4, variable, creamy white to greyish yellow, profusely or sparsely covered with pale dull reddish markings, more numerous and forming a ring or cap at the broad end. Size about 18×13 mm.

RACIAL CHARACTERISTICS, MEASUREMENTS, ETC: The Sikkim Survey specimens measure:

| | Wing | Bill | Tarsus | Tail |
|---|---|---|---|---|
| 1 ♂ | 65 | 11.5 | 18 | 54 mm. |
| 2 ♀♀ | 64 | 12-12.5 | 18-18.5 | 48-50 mm. |

Schäfer's Sikkim skins have Wing 4 ♂♂ 65-67; 2 ♀♀ 65-66 mm.

Iris brown; bill horny black; legs, feet and claws horny brown.

## THE PALE BLUE FLYCATCHER

*Muscicapa unicolor unicolor* (Blyth)

*Cyornis unicolor* Blyth, 1843, *Jour. Asiat. Soc. Bengal* 12: 1007—Darjeeling.

F.B.I. 2: 230

LOCAL NAME:

SIZE: Sparrow.

FIELD CHARACTERS: Adult *Male: Above*, including exposed portions of wings and tail light blue, deeper on upper tail-coverts and edges of tail feathers. Forehead, front and sides of crown, a narrow ring round eye, and a shoulder-patch (lesser wing-coverts) ultramarine or lapis blue. Lores black. *Below*, pale dull blue, changing to greyish white on abdomen, flanks and under tail-coverts—the last broadly scalloped with white.

Differs from male Verditer Flycatcher, *Muscicapa thalassina* (p. 144), in being more blue, less blue-green, and lacking the prominent black eye-stripe.

*Female: Above*, fulvous olive-brown. Tail, and edges of wing feathers ferruginous. Lores, and a ring round eye whitish. *Below*, pale earthy brown.

STATUS AND HABITAT: Resident, but possibly with some seasonal altitudinal movement. The British Museum has Sikkim skins collected in all months of the year (elevations unrecorded). Meinertzhagen obtained specimens between *c.* 2000 and 6000 ft. in September/October 1925 (Dikchu, Singhik, Gangtok). The recent Survey met with the species between 5000 and 5500 ft. in the last week of March (Temi, Kewzing). A pair at Temi was obviously nesting on 31 March. Affects oak and mixed broad-leafed forest on hillsides.

DISTRIBUTION OUTSIDE SIKKIM: Nepal, Bhutan to eastern Assam; Burma, Thailand, Malaya.

GENERAL HABITS: Typical flycatcher. Utters the characteristic *tr-r-r* as it twitches up its tail half-cocked between the drooping wings. The song is described as being richer than that of any other member of the *Muscicapa* group.

NESTING: *Season*—April-May. *Nest*—a massive cup of moss and fern-stems etc. felted together; lined with fern-roots. Placed in a hole in a bank, or at the junction of a large branch with the trunk of a tree, fairly low down. *Eggs*—3 or 4, pale yellowish or buff, with numerous dark reddish brown blotches, dense at the broad end often forming a cap. Size about 23×18 mm.

RACIAL CHARACTERISTICS, MEASUREMENTS, ETC: The Fauna gives for ♂♀ Wing 78-85; bill 14-15; tarsus 17-18; tail 68-75 mm.

Iris dark brown; bill black, base of lower mandible grey; legs and feet dark brown.

## THE BLUETHROATED FLYCATCHER

*Muscicapa rubeculoides rubeculoides* (Vigors)

*Phoenicura rubeculoides* Vigors, 1831, *Proc. Zool. Soc. London*: 35—Darjeeling.

F.B.I. 2: 231

LOCAL NAME: Manzil-pho (Lepcha).

SIZE: Sparrow.

FIELD CHARACTERS: *Male: Above*, dark blue including exposed portions of wings and tail. Forehead, and a streak over eye, glistening azure blue. A bright blue shoulder patch (lesser wing-coverts). *Below*, chin, throat, sides of neck and breast, deep blue. Breast bright ferruginous, paling on flanks and whitening on abdomen and under tail-coverts.

*Female: Above*, olive-brown, tinged with rufous on forehead and rump. A fulvous ring round eye. Wings and tail brown edged with ferruginous. *Below*, ferruginous, paler on chin and throat, white on abdomen and vent.

STATUS AND HABITAT: Undetermined. Stevens had the impression that it does not go higher than the foothills. The Survey came across it only at Singtam, *c.* 1000 ft., in April, but Meinertzhagen collected specimens at Rangpo, *c.* 1000 ft., and also Gangtok, *c.* 6000 ft., in the second half of October (1925). Elsewhere in the Sikkim Himalayas it has been taken at 3750 ft. in January. Affects secondary and bamboo jungle.

DISTRIBUTION OUTSIDE SIKKIM: *Summer*, lower Himalayas from Kashmir to eastern Assam, north and south of Brahmaputra River; N. Burma, Thailand, Yunnan. *Winter*, peninsular India; Ceylon. The species extends through the Indochinese subregion.

GENERAL HABITS: Typical. In summer the male has a pleasant little metallic trill, similar in pattern to the song of the more familiar Tickell's Redbreasted Blue Flycatcher (*Muscicapa tickelliae*) of peninsular India, but somewhat richer.

NESTING: No record for Sikkim. In Nepal, *season*—April-May. *Nest*—a collection of moss, dead leaves and lichen, with a cup-shaped lining of fine moss-, fern- or grass-roots, fitted within a hollow in a mossy bank, a hole in a tree-stump, etc. *Eggs*—mostly 4, pale olive-brown, sometimes with an ill-defined darker cap or ring at the broad end. Size about 19×14 mm. Both sexes incubate.

RACIAL CHARACTERISTICS, MEASUREMENTS, ETC: The Fauna gives for

| | Wing | Bill | Tarsus | Tail |
|---|---|---|---|---|
| ♂♂ | 65-75 | 11.5-12.5 | *c.* 20 | 53-60 mm. |
| ♀♀ | 69-74 | 11-12 | *c.* 19 | 49-52 mm. |

Iris brown; bill brownish black; legs and feet greyish brown, sometimes with a pinkish tinge.

## THE VERDITER FLYCATCHER

*Muscicapa thalassina thalassina* Swainson

*Muscicapa thalassina* Swainson, 1838, Nat. Library, Flycatchers: 252—India.

F.B.I. 2: 239

LOCAL NAME: Sibyell-pho (Lepcha).

SIZE: Sparrow.

FIELD CHARACTERS: A conspicuous bright blue-green flycatcher with black forehead and lores produced backward as a streak under the eye.

*Female:* duller and greyer.

STATUS AND HABITAT: Common summer (breeding) visitor, from *c.* 2000 to 10,500 ft. elevation (Singhik, Chungthang, Kewzing, Pemionche, Gangtok, Karponang). Absent between November and March. Affects openly forested hillsides. Commonly breeding in and about Gangtok town.

DISTRIBUTION OUTSIDE SIKKIM: *Summer,* throughout the Himalayas, east to west, between *c.* 4000 and 10,000 ft. elevation; Assam, Burma. *Winter,* more or less the entire Indian Union and E. Pakistan. The species extends through Malaysia.

GENERAL HABITS: Typical flycatcher. Hunts from tops of tall trees, dead stumps or overhead electric wires (Gangtok). In summer the males constantly sing from tree-tops and other exposed stances, a pleasant jingling warble reminiscent of the White-eye's (*Zosterops*), but louder.

NESTING: *Season*—April-May. *Nest*—a thick-sided cup of green moss, roots and fibres, lined with fine moss-roots etc. Placed in a pocket in an earth-bank, or a hollow in a decaying tree-stump. Sometimes on a ledge or hole in the wall of a building. *Eggs*—4 or 5, mostly creamy pink, sparsely freckled with reddish. more densely in a ring at the broad end. Size about 19×14 mm. Both sexes share all the domestic chores.

RACIAL CHARACTERISTICS, MEASUREMENTS, ETC: ♂ differs from ♂ of *M. unicolor* in being more blue-green or verditer blue, and in its black forehead and eyestripe.

The Fauna gives the measurements as ♂♀ Wing 79-89; bill *c.* 11; tarsus *c.* 18; tail 60-74 mm.

Schäfer's Sikkim skins have Wing 6 ♂♂ 83-90 (av. 85.5); 3 ♀♀ 78-81 (av. 79.3) mm.

Iris brown; bill black, angle of gape flesh colour; legs, feet and claws brownish black or black.

1. Mrs Gould's Yellowbacked Sunbird (*Aethopyga g. gouldiae*) 2. Blackbreasted Sunbird (*Aethopyga s. saturata*) 3. Firetailed Yellowbacked Sunbird (*Aethopyga i. ignicauda*) 4. Firebreasted Flowerpecker (*Dicaeum i. ignipectus*) 5. Longtailed Broadbill (*Psarisomus d. dalhousiae*) 6. Hodgson's, or the Nepal, Collared Broadbill (*Serilophus l. rubropygius*) 7. Bluenaped Pitta (*Pitta nipalensis*)

PLATE 13

1. Greybacked Shrike (*Lanius t. tephronotus*) 2. Shortbilled Minivet (*Pericrocotus b. brevirostris*) 3. Yellowthroated Minivet (*Pericrocotus s. solaris*) 4. Maroon Oriole (*Oriolus t. traillii*) 5. Spottedwinged Stare (*Saroglossa spiloptera*) 6. Common Rubythroat (*Erithacus calliope*) 7. Golden Bush Robin (*Erithacus c. chrysaeus*) 8. Whitebrowed Bush Robin (*Erithacus i. indicus*)

PLATE 14

## THE PIGMY BLUE FLYCATCHER

*Muscicapella hodgsoni hodgsoni* (Moore)

*Nemura hodgsoni* Moore, *in* Horsfield & Moore, 1854, Cat. Birds, Mus. E. I. Co., 1: 300—Nepal.

**Plate 16, fig. 4 (facing p. 161)**

F.B.I. 2: 237 (=*Nitidula hodgsoni*)

LOCAL NAME:

SIZE: Sparrow−.

FIELD CHARACTERS: A diminutive flycatcher with a slender warbler-like bill. *Male: Above*, bright dark blue, brightest and more ultramarine on crown. Wings and tail black, edged with deep blue. Forehead, lores and sides of head blue-black. *Below*, pale orange-yellow, paling to whitish on central abdomen.

*Female: Above*, olive-brown, more rufous on rump and upper tail-coverts. Wing- and tail feathers brown, edged with rufous. *Below*, pale yellow; whitish on central abdomen, vent and under tail-coverts.

STATUS AND HABITAT: Rare. Recorded as resident 'up to 7000 ft. or higher'. Seasonal movements undetermined. The Survey came across it only between 1500 and 2000 ft. elevation (near Rangpo and Singtam) in December. Affects shrubs and large trees on the edge of glades and clearings in forest, or lining hill streams.

DISTRIBUTION OUTSIDE SIKKIM: Nepal, Bhutan, Assam hills north and south of the Brahmaputra; Naga Hills, Burma, Thailand, south to the Malaysian subregion.

GENERAL HABITS: Keeps singly. Very lively and restless. Actions reminiscent of both flycatcher and leaf warbler. Descends to ground to pick up an insect, twitching up and cocking tail from time to time between half-drooping wings in typical flycatcher style. When on ground looks rather like a shortwing. Also makes short aerial sorties after midges etc. within the spreading foliage canopy of large trees. Sometimes flutters at leaf-sprigs like a *Phylloscopus*. The song, if any, is unrecorded.

NESTING: Unknown.

RACIAL CHARACTERISTICS, MEASUREMENTS, ETC: The Survey specimens (2 ♂♂) measure: Wing 50-51; bill 11; tarsus 16-17; tail 35 mm.

Iris brown; bill black, horny at base of lower mandible; legs and feet greyish flesh colour.

## THE GREYHEADED FLYCATCHER

*Culicicapa ceylonensis calochrysea* Oberholser

*Culicicapa ceylonensis calochrysea* Oberholser, 1923, *Smith. Misc. Coll.* 76: 8—Quaymoo Choung=left bank of Thaungyin River, lat. 17° 15′ N., Amherst District, Burma.

F.B.I. 2: 255

LOCAL NAME:

SIZE: Sparrow—.

FIELD CHARACTERS: Head, neck, throat and breast ashy grey, darker on crown. Bright yellowish green above, with yellow rump; bright yellow on underparts. Wing- and tail feathers brown, edged with greenish yellow. Sexes alike.

STATUS AND HABITAT: Common. Resident up to *c.* 7,000 ft. elevation, with little seasonal altitudinal movement (Rangpo, Singtam, Kewzing, Rinchinpong, Gangtok, Pemionche). Affects openly wooded country and forest glades.

DISTRIBUTION OUTSIDE SIKKIM: *Summer*, throughout the Himalayas from the Afghan border to Assam; Burma, Thailand and the Indochinese subregion. *Winter*, peninsular India south to about Hyderabad. The nominate race occupies Ceylon and southern India.

GENERAL HABITS: Active and restless. Makes agile acrobatic swoops after gnats, moths, etc. from a bare twig or liana stem, turning, twisting and looping in the air and returning to its base. One or two commonly present amongst the mixed hunting parties of small insectivorous birds in forest. Utters a distinctive sharp twittering note as it hunts. *Song:* a lively little interrogative *chik . . . whichee-whichee,* amazingly loud, constantly repeated.

NESTING: *Season*—May-June, at *c.* 5000 ft. elevation. *Nest*—a tiny cup of moss and lichens, placed 5 to 20 ft. up, amongst thick moss against a tree-trunk or in the angle of outflaking bark, well obliterated in its surroundings. *Eggs*—3 or 4, greyish- or creamy white, blotched with pale yellowish grey, more densely at the broad end. Size about 15×12 mm.

RACIAL CHARACTERISTICS, MEASUREMENTS, ETC: The Ceylonese-south Indian race *ceylonensis* is more richly coloured.

The Sikkim Survey specimens measure:

| | Wing | Bill | Tarsus | Tail |
|---|---|---|---|---|
| 2 ♂♂ | 63-65 | 12.5 | 13.5-14 | 51-53 mm. |
| 1 o? | 61 | 12.5 | 12.5 | 50 mm. |

Six specimens (sex ?) collected by Schäfer in Sikkim have Wing 60-65 (av. 62.6) mm.

Iris brown; bill brown, lower mandible paler or pinkish flesh; legs and feet yellow or yellowish brown; claws horny brown.

## THE YELLOWBELLIED FANTAIL FLYCATCHER

*Rhipidura hypoxantha* Blyth

*Rhipidura hypoxantha* Blyth, 1843, *Jour. Asiat. Soc. Bengal* **12**: 935—Darjeeling.

**Plate 16, fig. 6 (facing p. 161)**[1]

F.B.I. 2: 275 (=*Chelidorhynx*)

LOCAL NAME: Sitte kloom (Lepcha).

SIZE: Sparrow—.

FIELD CHARACTERS: A restless diminutive fantail flycatcher. *Male: Above,* dark olive-brown with forehead and broad supercilium bright yellow. Ear-coverts and a line through eye black. Tail feathers brown, conspicuously white-shafted; all except central pair broadly tipped with white.

*Female* differs only in having the eye-stripe blackish olive-brown.

STATUS AND HABITAT: Common. Resident. Recorded between November and April at all elevations from 1000 to 12,000 ft. (Rangpo, Singtam, Martam, Singhik, Dentam, Rinchinpong, Chungthang, Manshitang, Gangtok, Penlom La, Karponang, Sandakphu). Schäfer also collected specimens at Lachen, *c.* 9000 ft., in August and September. Affects glades in tall forest as well as secondary jungle.

DISTRIBUTION OUTSIDE SIKKIM: The Himalayas from about Sialkot (Punjab) eastward through Nepal and Bhutan to extreme eastern Assam; Manipur, Burma, Thailand, Yunnan and the Indochinese subregion.

GENERAL HABITS: Entirely arboreal. Extremely lively and restless. Usually met with singly or in pairs, and almost invariably as an outrider of active hunting flocks of 'tinies' in forest. Flits amongst the branches and foliage, pirouettes with fanned-out tail and partly drooping wings, and launches agile turning and twisting aerial sallies after midges etc. Constantly utters a feeble sharp *sip, sip.* Its song is described as 'a feeble little goldfinch-like trill'—a rapid repetition of the same high-pitched note.

NESTING: *Season*—May-June, up to the highest elevations. *Nest*—a deep, straight-sided little cup of moss, mixed with lichen, hair, wool, etc., built on a horizontal branch, *c.* 6 to 15 ft. from the ground. *Eggs*—2 or 3, pink, deeper coloured at the broad end. Size about 14×11 mm.

RACIAL CHARACTERISTICS, MEASUREMENTS, ETC: The Survey specimens measure:

| | Wing | Bill | Tarsus | Tail |
|---|---|---|---|---|
| 2 ♂♂ | 58 | 10-10.5 | 14-15 | 57 mm. |
| 1 o? | 57 | 9.5 | 15 | 55 mm. |

[1] In the illustration the tail position is inaccurate. Characteristically it is carried half erect and fanned out.

A large series collected in Sikkim by Schäfer gives Wing 15 ad. ♂♀ 53-57 (av. 55.5) mm.

Iris brown; bill: upper mandible horny brown, lower orange-yellow or yellowish flesh; legs and feet brown with yellowish tinge; claws horny brown with slight olive tinge.

## THE WHITETHROATED FANTAIL FLYCATCHER

*Rhipidura albicollis albicollis* (Vieillot)

*Platyrhynchus albicollis* Vieillot, 1818, Nouv. Dict. d'Hist. Nat. 72: 13—Bengal.

F.B.I. 2: 279

LOCAL NAME: Nam-dit-nom (Lepcha).

SIZE: Between Sparrow and Bulbul.

FIELD CHARACTERS: A restless, dark sooty brown fantail flycatcher with a prominent white band or semi-collar across the throat, short

Whitethroated Fantail Flycatcher
About one-half

white supercilia, and broadly white-tipped tail. Forehead, forecrown, lores, over and under eye, and ear-coverts, black. Sexes alike.

STATUS AND HABITAT: Fairly common. Resident up to *c.* 6000 ft. elevation (Rangpo, Singtam, Martam, Kewzing, Manshitang, Gangtok). Affects secondary jungle.

DISTRIBUTION OUTSIDE SIKKIM: The Himalayas from Kashmir through Nepal and Bhutan to eastern Assam; Burma, Thailand, Yunnan. The species extends through the Indochinese and Malaysian subregions.

GENERAL HABITS: Seen singly or in pairs, often in association with the mixed hunting flocks in forest. Flits tirelessly amongst branches and foliage in the middle storey, waltzing and pirouetting with fanned-out erect tail, and wings drooping at the sides. Makes short looping aerial sallies after gnats and other tiny winged insects which comprise its diet. Utters a harsh *chuck* or *chuck-r*. Has a lively but rather feeble jerky whistling song *tri-riri-riri*, reminiscent of the Largebilled Leaf Warbler's (*Phylloscopus magnirostris*).

NESTING: *Season*—May-June. *Nest*—a beautiful little cup of fine grass and fibres, neatly plastered on the outside with cobwebs, and with a bunch of strips of the nest material dangling below. Built in a horizontal fork or elbow of a twig, seldom more than 8 ft. up. *Eggs*—3 or 4, pale sandy white with tiny brown specks, forming a ring round the broad end. Size about 17×13 mm.

RACIAL CHARACTERISTICS, MEASUREMENTS, ETC: Birds from the western Himalayas, westward to Kashmir, are slightly paler, but hardly worth recognition as the separate race *canescens* proposed by Koelz. The same applies to the slightly darker birds of Bhutan and eastward, separated as the race *stanleyi* by Baker.

A specimen collected by the Sikkim Survey (♀) measures: Wing 80; bill 15.5; tarsus 19.5; tail 101 mm.

Seven adult ♂♀ in Schäfer's Sikkim collection give Wing 73-79 (av. 76.3) mm.

Iris brown; bill brownish black; legs, feet and claws horny brown.

## *Subfamily* TIMALIINAE: Babblers

### THE SIKKIM SPOTTED BABBLER

***Pellorneum ruficeps mandellii*** **Blanford**

*Pellorneum mandelii* Blanford, 1871, *Proc. Asiat. Soc. Bengal* 9: 216—Sikkim.

**Plate 17, fig. 3 (facing p. 208)**

F.B.I. 1: 240

LOCAL NAME:

SIZE: Between Sparrow and Bulbul.

FIELD CHARACTERS: Olive-brown above with reddish brown cap. Whitish below, boldly streaked and spotted on breast with dark brown. Sexes alike.

STATUS AND HABITAT: Resident. Confined to the foothills, up to about 3500 ft. elevation (Rangpo, Singtam, Martam). Affects thickets in secondary scrub and bamboo jungle.

DISTRIBUTION OUTSIDE SIKKIM: Nepal; Bhutan; Assam north and south of Brahmaputra River. The species, in several races, is widely distributed in India, Burma, Malaya, Annam, Cochin-China.

GENERAL HABITS: Pairs or small parties skulk in the undergrowth, rummaging on the ground among fallen leaves for food. The birds walk about like quail or proceed in long thrush-like hops. *Food:* chiefly insects and their larvae. *Calls:* normally, a plaintive whistle *beat-you* or *he'll beat you* (or *pretty-sweet*) repeated monotonously every five seconds or so with great persistency, sometimes for over 10 minutes at a stretch. It also has a charming, lively song heard chiefly in the breeding season but also sporadically otherwise. It is a percussive, loud, clear whistling of several notes rambling up and down the scale, sometimes lasting 3 minutes or more with practically no break. A subdued *chr-r, chr-r* or *kraa, kraa* is uttered on alarm.

NESTING: *Season*—chiefly April to June. *Nest*—a large untidy ball of dry bamboo and other leaves with a lateral entrance hole. Placed among dead leaves on the ground on steep earth banks etc. in forest. *Eggs*—2 or 3, white or faint dull cream with numerous small brown specks, spots and blotches. Size about 23×17 mm.

RACIAL CHARACTERISTICS, MEASUREMENTS, ETC: The race *mandellii* differs from nominate *ruficeps* of the greater part of India in being a more rufous-olive above, with the upper back streaked with dark brown; crown more chestnut than rufous; forehead and eyebrows with black shaft-streaks. Breast and belly suffused with ochraceous.

The Fauna gives the measurements as: ♂♀ Wing 66-73 (av. 70); bill 16-17; tarsus 25-26; tail 66-68 mm.

Iris hazel to crimson-brown; upper mandible dark horny brown, lower pale yellowish; legs and feet pale brownish flesh colour.

## THE SLATYHEADED SCIMITAR BABBLER

*Pomatorhinus schisticeps schisticeps* Hodgson

*Pomatorhinus schisticeps* Hodgson, 1836, *Asiat. Res.* 19: 181—Nepal.

F.B.I. 1: 206

LOCAL NAMES: Phoyeum-pho or Phurreeam-pho (Lepcha).

SIZE: Myna−.

FIELD CHARACTERS: Olive-brown above, maroon-chestnut and white below, with dark slaty head and prominent white eyebrow. Curved, pointed black-and-yellow bill. Sexes alike.

STATUS AND HABITAT: Uncommon. At low elevations in the Teesta Valley, normally to about 2000 ft. (?)—Rangpo, Singtam. Meinertzhagen obtained a specimen at Gangtok, 6400 ft., on 18 December. Affects thickets, particularly on the site of abandoned cultivation, and in secondary and mixed bamboo forest.

DISTRIBUTION OUTSIDE SIKKIM: Nepal; Bhutan. The species, in several races, occurs from the NW. Himalayas right across to our extreme NE. frontier. Hills of Assam, N. Burma, Thailand, Malaya, Indonesia.

GENERAL HABITS: Shy and secretive, and a great skulker. Pairs or family parties, sometimes associated with various laughing thrushes, keep to dense shrubbery rummaging for food among the mulch on the ground, or hopping amongst the undergrowth or bamboo culms. When undisturbed and moving about in quest of food the birds keep in touch with one another by constant mellow gurgling flute-like calls uttered by the male and promptly acknowledged by the female with a shorter unmusical note. These notes are very similar to those of the Deccan Scimitar Babbler, and the birds can be easily decoyed by an imitation of their calls. A harsh *kr-r-r-r* is uttered on the slightest alarm. *Food:* insects, berries and seeds.

NESTING: *Season*—April to June. *Nest*—a deep saucer (apparently not domed as in most other scimitar babblers) of grass, leaves and fern fronds, lined with finer grass. Placed on or near the ground in brushwood or grass. *Eggs*—3 or 4, pure white. Size about 25×19 mm.

RACIAL CHARACTERISTICS, MEASUREMENTS, ETC: A specimen (♂) collected in Sikkim measures: Wing 99; bill 30; tarsus 37; tail 103 mm.

The Fauna gives for ♂♀ Wing 98-106; bill *c.* 27; tarsus *c.* 32; tail 115-120 mm.

Iris yellowish biscuit, or cream colour; bill yellow, horny brown on basal two-thirds of culmen; legs and feet bluish plumbeous; claws horny brown.

## THE SIKKIM RUFOUSNECKED SCIMITAR BABBLER

*Pomatorhinus ruficollis godwini* Kinnear

*Pomatorhinus ruficollis godwini* Kinnear, 1944, *Ibis* 86: 79—Chungkar, SE. Bhutan, 6000 ft.

**Plate 20, fig. 5 (facing p. 225)**

F.B.I. 1: 216 (part)

LOCAL NAME:

SIZE: Bulbul.

FIELD CHARACTERS: Ruddy brown above; sides of neck and collar on hindneck bright ferruginous. Chin, cheeks and throat white. Upper breast and centre of abdomen white, streaked with olive brown. Sides of breast and abdomen, and rest of underparts, olive-brown. A broad white supercilium from bill to nape. Sides of face, including ear-coverts, black. Sexes alike.

STATUS AND HABITAT: Uncommon and sporadic. Occupies a broad altitudinal zone, between about 2500 and 10,000 ft., even in winter (Gangtok, Singhik, Dentam, Rinchinpong, Kewzing, Singalila Ridge). Affects thick forest or more open country with dense undergrowth on hillsides and in ravines. Also moss-draped forest of small trees, rhododendron shrubs and bracken at the higher elevations.

DISTRIBUTION OUTSIDE SIKKIM: Eastern Nepal (east of Arun-Kosi River), Bhutan, SE. Tibet, Dafla and (presumably) other Assam hills north of Brahmaputra River. Other races replace it in the W. Himalayas, Assam, Burma, Yunnan, Indochina, S. China.

GENERAL HABITS: Not noticeably different from those of other scimitar babblers. Shy, and keeps to dense undergrowth in pairs oftener than parties. Has the same range of harsh churring notes and pleasant mellow flute-like calls. When questing for mate which has become separated, utters a double-noted call very reminiscent of the Redvented Bulbul, but louder and with a thrush-like clearness, repeated persistently every few seconds while hopping around, in obvious expectancy of an answer.

NESTING: *Season*—April to June. *Nest*—a domed structure of dry grass, bracken and bamboo leaves, loosely put together and lined with fibres. Placed on the ground under weeds and grass. *Eggs*—3 to 5, white, measuring about 24×18 mm.

RACIAL CHARACTERISTICS, MEASUREMENTS, ETC: *Godwini* differs from the adjoining nominate race of the W. Himalayas and W. and central Nepal in being darker overall—more chestnut above, more olive below.

Two ♂♂ collected by the Sikkim Survey measure: Wing 79; bill 22.5-24; tarsus 30-31.5; tail 81-85 mm. Three adults in the Schäfer Sikkim collection have Wing 79, 81, 82 mm.

Iris crimson-brown; bill pale yellow, horny black on two-thirds basal portion of upper mandible; legs and feet brownish plumbeous; claws horny brown.

## THE SIKKIM RUSTYCHEEKED SCIMITAR BABBLER

*Pomatorhinus erythrogenys haringtoni* Stuart Baker

*Pomatorhinus erythrogenys haringtoni* Stuart Baker, 1914, *Bull. Brit. Orn. Cl.* 33: 123—Darjeeling.

F.B.I. 1: 220

LOCAL NAME: Yongo-hut-pho (Lepcha).

SIZE: Myna.

FIELD CHARACTERS: Olive-brown above. Chin, throat and upper breast dark ashy, finely stippled and streaked with white. Centre of abdomen white. Sides of breast and body olive-chestnut. Forehead, ear-coverts, sides of neck, thighs and under tail-coverts chestnut. A dark moustachial streak. No supercilium. Rather heavy yellowish curved pointed bill. White iris. Sexes alike.

STATUS AND HABITAT: The commonest scimitar babbler in Sikkim, found between about 1000 and 7000 ft. elevation (Rangpo, Gangtok, Penlom La, Kewzing, Rinchinpong). Inhabits dense scrub on the edge of forest, and about abandoned cultivation and in ravines.

DISTRIBUTION OUTSIDE SIKKIM: Eastern Nepal; Bhutan. Other races replace it in the western Himalayas, Assam hills north and south of Brahmaputra River, Burma, Yunnan.

GENERAL HABITS: Those of the genus. Pairs in summer; small parties in winter. A pair keep in touch with each other by the male constantly calling a melodious *Q . . . P* (*cue pee*, accent on *Q*) or *cue-ook* to which the female responds promptly with *quip*. These three notes follow one another so quickly that they sound as coming from the same bird. The alarm note, a gurgling *quoik*, is similarly answered by the female's *tchur*.

NESTING: *Season*—April to June. *Nest*—a cup of rootlets domed with a loose canopy of dry bamboo leaves. Placed in an earth pocket or under a bush on the side of a moist scrub-covered ravine. *Eggs*—normally 3, white, with a pinkish tinge when fresh. Size about 28×21 mm.

RACIAL CHARACTERISTICS, MEASUREMENTS, ETC. The adjoining race of the W. Himalayas, *erythrogenys*, is paler above and below and has the chin, throat and breast white instead of dusky grey. An intermediate race, *ferrugilatus*, has recently been named by Ripley from western and central Nepal. It is clinally darker than *erythrogenys* and paler than *haringtoni*. *Mcclellandi* of Assam has the flanks more olivaceous, less chestnut; chin, throat, breast and belly white with a band of triangular brown spots on lower throat and rounder ones on sides of breast.

Two ♂♂ collected by the Sikkim Survey measure: Wing 95-96.5; bill 38-39; tarsus 36.5-38; tail 101-103 mm.

Nine adults ♂♀ from Sikkim in Schäfer's collection give Wing 92-99 (av. 95.9) mm.

Iris creamy or greyish white; bill brownish flesh colour, dark brown for about half basal portion; legs and feet brownish flesh colour; claws pale horny.

## THE CORALBILLED SCIMITAR BABBLER

*Pomatorhinus ferruginosus ferruginosus* Blyth

*Pomatorhinus ferruginosus* Blyth, 1845, *Jour. Asiat. Soc. Bengal* **14**: 597—Darjeeling.

**Plate 20, fig. 3 (facing p. 225)**

F.B.I. 1: 213

LOCAL NAMES: Piong-kohut or Poniong-hut (Lepcha).

SIZE: Myna.

FIELD CHARACTERS: Upper parts rufous olive-brown. Breast and centre of abdomen bright ferruginous; rest of underparts olive-brown. Forehead rufous. Long white supercilium to nape. Chin, cheeks, throat and moustachial streaks white; rest of head including ear-coverts black. The deep coral red bill distinguishes it immediately from any other scimitar babbler in Sikkim. Sexes alike.

STATUS AND HABITAT: Sparse and local. Gammie found it breeding at 5000 ft. elevation in the Teesta Valley; Meinertzhagen collected specimens above Lachen at 11,700 ft. and Thangu 12,600 ft. in winter (26 December and 16 November 1925), therefore it is evidently a high-altitude species. Affects dense shrubbery and ringal bamboo jungle.

DISTRIBUTION OUTSIDE SIKKIM: Nepal; Assam hills north of Brahmaputra River. Other races in Assam hills south of the Brahmaputra; Burma, Tenasserim, N. Thailand, Tonkin.

GENERAL HABITS: Like the other scimitar babblers, shy and elusive, seldom giving a glimpse of itself among the thickets where pairs or small parties rummage on the ground, turning over fallen leaves and digging in the earth for insects and their larvae. In addition to the low grating *churr* uttered on alarm, it has a number of musical hooting calls.

NESTING: *Season*—late April to end June. *Nest*—a horizontal oval ball made of bamboo leaves and grass, lined with soft fibres, with entrance hole at one end. Placed a foot or two from the ground in a bamboo clump or some thick bush. *Eggs*—3 to 5, pure white. Size about 24×18 mm.

RACIAL CHARACTERISTICS, MEASUREMENTS, ETC: Stuart Baker gives the measurements of this race as: ♂♀ Wing 90-95; bill 27-28; tarsus *c.* 30; tail *c.* 110 mm.

Iris yellow or golden yellow; bill deep coral red; legs and feet light yellowish brown, sometimes with a greenish or leaden tinge.

## THE SLENDERBILLED SCIMITAR BABBLER

*Xiphirhynchus superciliaris superciliaris* Blyth

*Xiphirhynchus superciliaris* Blyth, 1842, *Jour. Asiat. Soc. Bengal* **11**: 176—Darjeeling.

**Plate 20, fig. 10** (facing p. 225)

F.B.I. **1: 224**

LOCAL NAME: Karriok-tamveep (Lepcha).

SIZE: Between Bulbul and Myna.

FIELD CHARACTERS: The long, slender, curved bill is the most distinctive feature of this scimitar babbler. Head dark slate, with long white supercilium from base of bill. Rest of upper parts bright rufous-brown; wings and tail dark brown. Chin and throat white; rest of underparts paler rufous-brown. Sexes alike.

STATUS AND HABITAT: Uncommon. Occurs at elevations between about 5000 and 10,000 ft. in summer (Chungthang, Gangtok, Singalila Ridge); perhaps lower in winter (Badamtan, Darjeeling District, *c.* 2000 ft.—January). Affects dense ringal bamboo thickets on mountain-sides.

DISTRIBUTION OUTSIDE SIKKIM: Eastern Nepal; Bhutan; Assam hills north of Brahmaputra River (?); Manipur. The species extends to Burma, Yunnan and Tonkin.

GENERAL HABITS: Goes about in pairs or small noisy parties; on the whole very like other scimitar babblers. Shy and restless. Hunts on the ground and in undergrowth for food—insects and larvae, fruits like raspberries etc. Is very fond of the nectar of the red silk-cotton flowers (*Salmalia*) for which it mounts up into the leafless trees. The call is a pleasing ripple of whistling notes.

NESTING: *Season*—chiefly May and June. *Nest*—a large globular structure of dry bamboo leaves and green grass, intermingled and lined with fine roots and fibres. Placed in the top of an old tree-stump or among grass tufts and bushes 2 to 3 ft. above the ground, and sometimes on the ground itself. *Eggs*—3 to 5, white, glossy, unmarked, measuring about 24×18 mm.

RACIAL CHARACTERISTICS, MEASUREMENTS, ETC: An intermediate race, *intextus*, has recently been described by Ripley from the Mishmi Hills. It is paler than *superciliaris* and darker and more richly coloured than *forresti* of Indochina etc.

The F.B.I. gives the measurements of *superciliaris* as: ♂♀ Wing 72-77; bill 55-60; tarsus *c.* 30; tail *c.* 90 mm.

For 6 Schäfer skins from Sikkim (♂♀) Stresemann gives Wing 74, 75, 76, 76, 77, 78 mm.

Iris reddish brown to almost vermilion; bill black, paler at tip; legs and feet dull grey or plumbeous brown.

## THE LONGBILLED WREN-BABBLER

*Rimator malacoptilus malacoptilus* Blyth

*Rimator malacoptilus* Blyth, 1847, *Jour. Asiat. Soc. Bengal* 16: 154—Darjeeling.

**Plate 17, fig. 5 (facing p. 208)**

F.B.I. 1: 255

LOCAL NAME: Karriak-tungbrek-pho (Lepcha).

SIZE: Sparrow.

FIELD CHARACTERS: A brown, stub-tailed, fluffy-plumaged babbler with a longish, slightly curved bill. Dark rufescent brown above with buff shaft-streaks. Chin white. Throat, breast and abdomen pale rufescent brown with whitish shaft-streaks. Sides of body plain rufescent brown. Under tail-coverts ferruginous. Sexes alike.

STATUS AND HABITAT: Rare. Apparently resident at moderate elevations, i.e. about 5000 ft. Affects dense scrub in broken country in forest and abandoned clearings.

DISTRIBUTION OUTSIDE SIKKIM: Bhutan to E. Assam north and south of Brahmaputra River; Manipur; Lushai. Another race in Tonkin and Sumatra.

GENERAL HABITS: Very little known. A great skulker; usually in pairs. Chiefly terrestrial, rummaging among fallen leaves and mulch for insect food like scimitar babblers. Said to possess a 'sweet chirping whistle'.

NESTING: Not recorded in Sikkim. *Season* (in Assam): April to July. *Nest*—large, domed, of dead leaves, bracken fronds, etc. Placed on the ground amongst roots of bushes or at the foot of a tree. *Eggs*—3 or 4, white with a faint lilac tinge, spotted and blotched with reddish or purplish brown with paler smears of lilac grey and darker reddish brown squiggles. Size about 22×16 mm.

RACIAL CHARACTERISTICS, MEASUREMENTS, ETC: The Fauna gives the measurements as: ♂♀ Wing 57-60; bill 21-24; tarsus *c.* 23; tail *c.* 25 mm.

Iris light red-brown; upper mandible dark horny, blackish at base paler at tip; gape and edge of lower mandible blackish, remainder pale horny; legs and feet pale livid fleshy, brownish on tarsi. Soles, claws and joints very pale.

## THE SCALYBREASTED WREN

*Microura albiventer albiventer* (Hodgson)

*Tesia albiventer* Hodgson, February 1837, *Jour. Asiat. Soc. Bengal* 6: 102—Nepal.

F.B.I. 1: 458

LOCAL NAME: Marchok-bong (Lepcha).

SIZE: Sparrow—.

FIELD CHARACTERS: A plump, tailless, squamated little ground-skulker. *Above,* rich brown, streaked, spotted and barred with fulvous. Wings largely chestnut-brown. *Below,* chin and throat white, the feathers margined with brown. Breast and abdomen white, flanks fulvous, all spangled with black producing a scaly effect. The species is dimorphic; in the other form golden brown replaces white on the underparts in either sex. Sexes alike.

STATUS AND HABITAT: Not uncommon between about 5000 and 10,000 ft. elevation (Chungthang, Gangtok, Zemu, Manshitang, Lachen, Lachung, etc.). Down to 2000 ft. in winter; up to 12,000 ft. in summer. Affects dense undergrowth of ferns and nettles etc. on damp shady hillsides, and in ravines, in evergreen forest. Also cardamom plantations.

DISTRIBUTION OUTSIDE SIKKIM: E. Nepal; Bhutan; Assam hills N. and S. of Brahmaputra River; Burma. The Himalayas west of Nepal, and up to Kangra Valley, are occupied by the race *pallidior.* The species extends to Yunnan, Szechwan, Formosa.

GENERAL HABITS: Terrestrial. Solitary. Bounces like a spring toy and creeps about in dense tangled undergrowth, nervously flicking its wings like a *Phylloscopus,* searching amongst the mulch and fern stems and roots, over and under decaying, moss-covered, fallen tree-trunks for insect food. A great skulker and very difficult to observe. Its presence in the dense scrub is given away only by its loud, squeaky, double-noted call *seek . . . sik,* exactly like an unoiled 'patla' swinging back and forth. Calls markedly ventriloquial, the *seek* seeming to come from an entirely different direction to the *sik* which follows a half second later! Very inquisitive, and when agitated by the observer's proximity explodes into a scolding, chittering *tsik, tsik,* quite indistinguishable from that of the Brown Wren and reminiscent also of the Nepal Wren. It is said to have a song (not heard by me), but this has been unsatisfactorily described.

NESTING: *Season*—April to June. *Nest*—either a round ball of moss like the Brown Wren's, or built about 3 ft. up in moss growing on the trunk of a large tree in the shape of an egg bisected lengthwise and stuck upright against the trunk by its flat side, leaving an entrance at the top. *Eggs*—3 to 5, white, unmarked, longish ovals. Size about 19×14 mm.

RACIAL CHARACTERISTICS, MEASUREMENTS, ETC: In the adjoining west Himalayan race, *pallidior*, the upper parts are more olive and the underparts of the fulvous form paler.

Two specimens (♂♀) collected by the Sikkim Survey measure: Wing 63-64; bill 12.5-13; tarsus 24-25; tail 22-23 mm.

Two adult Schäfer skins (sex ?) have Wing 60, 62 mm.

Iris brown; upper mandible horny brown, lower brownish flesh colour excepting tip which is horny brown; legs, feet and claws horny brown or brownish flesh colour.

## THE BROWN WREN

*Microura pusilla pusilla* (Hodgson)

*Pnoepyga pusilla* Hodgson, 1845, *Proc. Zool. Soc. London* 13: 25—Nepal.

Plate 18, fig. 4 (facing p. 209)

F.B.I. 1: 459

LOCAL NAME:

SIZE: Sparrow—.

FIELD CHARACTERS: An exact miniature of the Scalybreasted Wren, with the same dimorphism in the underparts of either sex—white and golden brown. Sexes alike.

STATUS AND HABITAT: Fairly common. Normally, and on the whole, a lower-elevation representative of the Scalybreasted Wren, from *c.* 1000 to 6000 ft. (Rangpo, Singtam, Dikchu, Singhik, Dentam, Gangtok), with a wide margin of overlap in their altitudinal ranges. Less commonly it overlaps the larger species at the higher elevations also: Meinertzhagen obtained specimens at Karponang (9000 ft.) and Changu (11,700 ft.) in December, and Sandakphu (11,400 ft., Darjeeling District) in January. Affects heavy humid brushwood, and tangled undergrowth of ferns, nettles, brambles, etc., and cardamom plantations—identical facies with that of the previous bird.

DISTRIBUTION OUTSIDE SIKKIM: Nepal, Bhutan; Assam hills north and south of the Brahmaputra; Burma, Thailand, Yunnan, S. China. The species extends to Malaya, Indonesia, Indochina.

GENERAL HABITS: Terrestrial, solitary, skulking, restless; very similar to those of its larger counterpart, the Scalybreasted Wren, and also *Tesia cyaniventer* (p. 215). The ecology of these damp undergrowth-haunting species appears to be identical.

When pressed or disturbed, it flushes readily but flies only a couple of yards, skimming the herbage in a short hop, diving into the weeds again and creeping away like a mouse through the moss and rootstocks. So lightly and quietly does it move that hardly a fern-stalk stirs to mark its progress. Thus when further pressed it will flush from quite a different spot to where expected, and as quickly disappear again. Utters a sharp single *tsik* every half second or so when at ease (as of clicking the tongue against closed teeth), and an agitated 'scolding' *chiruk, chiruk* when alarmed. Whether it also produces the double noted *seek*... *sik* of the Scalybreasted Wren, or any song, is not reliably recorded.

NESTING: *Season*—April to June. *Nest*—of two types: (1) a pad of moss-roots etc. fastened inside living green moss on a tree-trunk in wet shady forest, 4 to 6 ft. from the ground or higher, and (2) a globular structure of bright green moss lined with moss-roots, built in the moss hanging down the face of a vertical rock. *Eggs*—3, white, unmarked. Size about 18×14 mm.

RACIAL CHARACTERISTICS, MEASUREMENTS, ETC: The Sikkim Survey specimens measure:

| | Wing | Bill | Tarsus |
|---|---|---|---|
| 2 ♂♂ | 50-51 | 12.5-13 | 19-20 mm. |
| 1 ♀ | 50 | 12.5 | 19 mm. |
| 2 o? | 51-53 | 13 | 20 mm. |

Iris brown; bill dark horny brown, paler on lower mandible; legs, feet and claws pale horny brown.

## THE TAILED WREN

*Spelaeornis caudatus* (Blyth)

*Tesia caudata* Blyth, 1845, *Jour. Asiat. Soc. Bengal* 14: 588—Darjeeling.

**Plate 18, fig. 2** (facing p. 209)

F.B.I. 1: 456

LOCAL NAME:

SIZE: Sparrow−. Slightly larger than the Nepal Wren.

FIELD CHARACTERS: *Above,* olive-brown scalloped with black. Lores and sides of head grey. Closed wings and tail chestnut-brown. *Below,* chin and throat chestnut; breast and sides of body paler and black spotted. Abdomen black with white streaks and square spots. Sexes alike.

STATUS AND HABITAT: Rare, and very little known. The Survey did not come across it. Recorded for Sikkim 'at considerable heights'. Meinertzhagen procured a specimen at Phalut (10,400 ft., Darjeeling District) in January, in damp undergrowth in thick forest.

DISTRIBUTION OUTSIDE SIKKIM: Bhutan. Possibly also Assam hills N. of the Brahmaputra.

GENERAL HABITS: Terrestrial, restlessly active, inquisitive, and typically wren-like. Call unrecorded.

NESTING: Published records not completely reliable. *Season*—April to June. *Nest*—described as egg-shaped, of leaves, fine twigs, bracken and grass, with entrance hole near the top. On ground, in heavy wet evergreen forest over 8000 ft. elevation.

RACIAL CHARACTERISTICS, MEASUREMENTS, ETC: The Fauna gives for ♂♀ Wing 47-51; bill 11-12; tarsus *c.* 20; tail 31-35 mm.

Iris brown; bill blackish; legs and feet brown.

## THE SPOTTED WREN

*Spelaeornis formosus* (Walden)

*Troglodytes formosus* Walden, January 1874, *Ibis:* 91—Darjeeling.

**Plate 18, fig. 1 (facing p. 209)**

F.B.I. 1: 449

LOCAL NAME: Marchek-pho (Lepcha).

SIZE: Sparrow—. Slightly larger than the Nepal Wren.

FIELD CHARACTERS: *Above,* dark brown. Rump and upper tail-coverts tinged with rufous and finely white-and-black spotted. Exposed portions of flight feathers barred chestnut and white. *Below,* pale fulvous tinged with rufous, marked with fine white lines and triangular spots. Sexes alike.

STATUS AND HABITAT: Rare. Very little known. I have a sight record from Kewzing, *c.* 7700 ft. (31 March), in dank rhododendron forest with thick fern ground cover and mossy rocks and decaying trunks of fallen trees, and brushwood. In Bhutan, Ludlow obtained it at 4000 ft. elevation (November) in long grass and scrub.

DISTRIBUTION OUTSIDE SIKKIM: Recorded only from Bhutan, Assam hills north of Brahmaputra River; South China (Fukien).

GENERAL HABITS: Evidently similar to those of the Scalybreasted Wren. Also, according to Ludlow, 'its note resembles that of *Microura p. pusilla* (the Brown Wren) but is sharper'. The bird glassed at Kewzing was decoyed out of dense fern undergrowth by Mr Loke imitating its squeaky calls—*seek . . . sick*—which sounded almost identical with those of the commoner scaly-bellied species.

NESTING: Not authentically recorded.

RACIAL CHARACTERISTICS, MEASUREMENTS, ETC: Differs from the Nepal Wren (p. 294) in its shrubby habitat, larger size, stouter bill, more graduated tail, and its spotted (not barred) plumage. The Fauna gives the measurements as: ♂♀ Wing 49-60; bill 11-12; tarsus 18-19; tail 30 mm. A Stevens specimen from Mangpu (4300 ft., N. Bengal)—♀ (?), 2.xi.1930—in the Chicago Museum of Natural History measures: Wing 46.5; bill 14; tarsus 17.5; tail 25 mm.

Iris brown; bill, legs and feet horny brown.

## HUME'S WEDGEBILLED WREN

*Sphenocichla humei humei* (Mandelli)

*Heterorhynchus humei* Mandelli, 1873, *Stray Feathers* 1: 415—Sikkim.

F.B.I. 1: 461

LOCAL NAME:

SIZE: Sparrow+.

FIELD CHARACTERS: A stout, squat, heavy looking wren with powerful legs and feet (as in the laughing thrushes, *Garrulax* spp.), and conical sharp-pointed blackish bill. *Above*, rich golden brown with a black scaly pattern, the feathers narrowly barred with blackish except on crown and nape. Finely white-streaked on forehead, crown, neck and mantle. A broad white supercilium from back of eye to nape. Closed wings blackish edged with golden brown. Tail golden brown narrowly cross-barred with black. *Below*, dark brown narrowly scalloped and streaked with white. Abdomen ashy grey. Under tail-coverts golden brown. Sexes alike.

STATUS AND HABITAT: Very rare. No investigator seems to have come across it in Sikkim since first obtained there by Mandelli's collectors over 80 years ago.

DISTRIBUTION OUTSIDE SIKKIM: Only known from the Aka Hills (Balipara Frontier Tract, Assam), where a single specimen (♀) was collected by G. S. Lightfoot at 4000 ft. elevation, in December 1938 (*JBNHS* 41: 419).

GENERAL HABITS AND NESTING: Unknown.

MEASUREMENTS: Mandelli's specimens in the British Museum, according to the Fauna, measure: Wing 70-74; bill 22-24; tarsus 26-27; tail 64-71 mm.

## THE ASSAM REDFRONTED BABBLER

*Stachyris rufifrons ambigua* (Harington)

*Stachyridopsis rufifrons ambigua* Harington, 1915, *Jour. Bombay Nat. Hist. Soc.* 23: 631—Gunjong, N. Cachar.

**Plate 21, fig. 7** (facing p. 272)

F.B.I. 1: 269

LOCAL NAME:

SIZE: Sparrow−.

FIELD CHARACTERS: Confusingly like *S. ruficeps* (next species) superficially. Distinguished from it by white (instead of yellow) chin and throat with black shaft-streaks. Sides of head more ashy; lores and ring round eye paler. Rufous crown duller, not extending to nape, and with the black shaft-lines more distinct. Sexes alike.

STATUS AND HABITAT: Occupies a lower altitudinal zone in Sikkim than the Redheaded Babbler (next), i.e. up to between 2000 and 3000 ft.

1. Orangebellied Chloropsis (*Chloropsis h. hardwickii*) 2. Redtailed Minla (*Minla i. ignotincta*) 3. Rufousbellied Bulbul (*Hypsipetes v. mcclellandi*) 4. Whitethroated Bulbul (*Criniger f. flaveolus*) 5. Striated Green Bulbul (*Pycnonotus s. striatus*) 6. Beautiful Nuthatch (*Sitta formosa*) 7. Nepal Tree Creeper (*Certhia f. mandellii*) 8. Wall Creeper (*Tichodroma muraria*)

PLATE 15

1. Orangegorgetted Flycatcher (*Muscicapa s. strophiata*) 2. Sapphireheaded Flycatcher (*Muscicapa sapphira*) 3. Slaty Blue Flycatcher (*Muscicapa l. leucomelanura*) 4. Pigmy Blue Flycatcher (*Muscicapella h. hodgsoni*) 5. Large Niltava (*Muscicapa g. grandis*) 6. Yellowbellied Fantail Flycatcher (*Rhipidura hypoxantha*) 7. Collared Bushchat (*Saxicola t. indica*) 8. Whitethroated Redstart (*Phoenicurus s. schisticeps*) 9. Güldenstädt's Redstart (*Phoenicurus e. grandis*)

PLATE 16

DISTRIBUTION OUTSIDE SIKKIM: Bhutan (duars) to head of Assam Valley; Assam, Manipur. Other races in Burma, Yunnan, Thailand, Malaya, Indochina, Indonesia.

GENERAL HABITS: Similar to the next. Has been reported sometimes taking insects on the wing like a flycatcher.

NESTING: Not recorded in Sikkim. *Nest* and *eggs* not different from those of the Redheaded Babbler. The breeding areas of the two often overlap, so that unless the owners are actually taken on the nest their identity remains in doubt.

RACIAL CHARACTERISTICS, MEASUREMENTS, ETC: For diagnosis see under *S. r. ruficeps* and also *Macronous g. rubricapilla* (p. 164).

The Fauna gives the measurements as: ♂♀ Wing 48-53; bill 9-10; tarsus 17-18; tail 46-48 mm.

Iris brown or reddish brown; bill dark grey or bluish horn; legs and feet greenish yellow or olive.

## THE REDHEADED BABBLER

*Stachyris ruficeps ruficeps* Blyth

*Stachyris ruficeps* Blyth, 1847, *Jour. Asiat. Soc. Bengal* **16**: 452—Darjeeling.

F.B.I. 1: 268

LOCAL NAME: Syak-birang-pho (Lepcha).

SIZE: Sparrow—.

FIELD CHARACTERS: Olive-brown above with rufous tinge; fulvous yellow below with sides of body, thighs and under tail-coverts tinged with olive. Forehead, crown and nape bright chestnut, the frontal feathers with faint black shaft-streaks. Chin and throat yellow with conspicuous black shafts. Sexes alike.

STATUS AND HABITAT: Resident at moderate elevations, seasonally between about 2000 and 7000 ft. (Chungthang, Gangtok); occasionally higher. Affects thick undergrowth, scrub and bamboo jungle.

DISTRIBUTION OUTSIDE SIKKIM: Nepal, Bhutan, Assam hills north and south of the Brahmaputra River; Naga Hills; Manipur. The species occurs in N. Burma, Thailand, Yunnan, Annam, Indochina, Hainan, Formosa.

GENERAL HABITS: Social and arboreal. Very similar to the next and to the numerous other small babblers, the restless, active, mixed hunting parties of which are such a feature of the bird life at moderate elevations in the eastern Himalayas. The low conversational chittering as the birds move about in the undergrowth is reminiscent of *Dumetia hyperythra*. A low soft whistle is also uttered.

NESTING: *Season*—April to June. *Nest*—of two types, (1) a deep cup, (2) domed, oval-shaped, with lateral entrance hole. Built fairly compactly of dry bamboo leaves etc. lined with fine grasses, in low shrubs. *Eggs*—white, finely spotted and blotched with brown or reddish brown, more densely at the broad end. Size about 16×13 mm.

RACIAL CHARACTERISTICS, MEASUREMENTS, ETC: Distinguishable from *S. r. rufifrons* by its fulvous yellow underparts and yellow throat, as against tawny buff underparts and white throat in that species. Either of them may easily be confused in the field with the Yellowbreasted Babbler, *Macronous g. rubricapilla* (p. 164), found in the foothills at practically plains level.

The Fauna gives the measurements as: ♂♀ Wing 54-58; bill *c.* 10; tarsus 17-18; tail 50-52 mm. Ten specimens collected in Sikkim by Schäfer have Wing 52 (♀) to 57 (♂)—average 54.6 mm.

Iris light brown to red; upper mandible plumbeous, lower pale flesh; legs and feet brownish yellow, greenish brown, or yellowish grey.

## THE NEPAL GOLDENHEADED BABBLER

### *Stachyris chrysaea chrysaea* Blyth

*Stachyris chrysaea* Blyth, 1844, *Jour. Asiat. Soc. Bengal* 13: 379—Nepal, Arakan.

**Plate 21, fig. 1 (facing p. 272)**

F.B.I. 1: 265

LOCAL NAME: Syak-birang-pho (Lepcha).

SIZE: Sparrow —.

FIELD CHARACTERS: Bright olive-yellow above; bright yellow below. Forehead, crown and nape bright golden yellow, the last two streaked with black. Lores and a short moustachial streak black. Ear-coverts oil-yellow. Sexes alike.

STATUS AND HABITAT: Resident at moderate elevations up to about 6000 ft. (Toong, Gangtok). Affects dense bushes and undergrowth in humid secondary jungle and abandoned forest clearings.

DISTRIBUTION OUTSIDE SIKKIM: Nepal, Bhutan, Assam, Manipur. Other races extend the species to Malaya, Indochina and Indonesia.

GENERAL HABITS: Similar to those of the blackthroated species (*S. nigriceps*) with which, together with other small babblers, flycatchers, etc., it habitually associates in hunting parties. Feeds among low cover and bamboo clumps, as well as up in the foliage canopy of trees, clinging to sprigs and peering under leaves in search of insects like a tit. The mixed flocks work feverishly, and sweep on rapidly from tree to tree. A low twittering cheep is constantly uttered.

NESTING: *Season*—May to July. *Nest*—loosely domed, of bamboo leaves, more or less like that of the Blackthroated Babbler but smaller. Also in similar situations. *Eggs*—4, pure white, measuring about 16×12 mm.

RACIAL CHARACTERISTICS, MEASUREMENTS, ETC: Stuart Baker gives the measurements as: ♂♀ Wing 48-51; bill *c.* 12; tarsus 18-19; tail *c.* 50 mm. As against the above, Stresemann measures 3 specimens (sex ?) collected by Schäfer in Sikkim: Wing 53, 53, 56 mm.

Iris golden brown or light brown; upper mandible dark slaty horn; lower mandible paler; legs and feet pale yellowish brown to greenish brown.

## THE SIKKIM BLACKTHROATED BABBLER

*Stachyris nigriceps nigriceps* Blyth

*Stachyris nigriceps* Blyth, 1844, *Jour. Asiat. Soc. Bengal* **13**: 378—Nepal.

**Plate 21, fig. 6 (facing p. 272)**

F.B.I. 1: 264

LOCAL NAME: Sangriam-pho (Lepcha).

SIZE: Sparrow.

FIELD CHARACTERS: Rich olive-brown above; bright fulvous below. Flanks, abdomen and under tail-coverts tinged with olivaceous. Forehead, crown and nape black streaked with white. Chin grey; throat deep blackish grey. Cheeks white. Ear-coverts golden brown. A conspicuous blackish supercilium. Sexes alike.

STATUS AND HABITAT: Resident at low and moderate elevations (Dikchu, Gangtok), up to at least 6000 ft., according to Stevens. Affects secondary scrub and bamboo jungle.

DISTRIBUTION OUTSIDE SIKKIM: Nepal; Bhutan; Assam hills north of Brahmaputra River. Other races occur in Assam (south of the Brahmaputra), Burma, Yunnan, Malaya, Indochina, Indonesia, etc.

GENERAL HABITS: Keeps in flocks of 6 to 8 or more, commonly associated with other small babblers in the itinerant hunting parties. A great skulker in thickets and shrubbery, and difficult to observe. Very active and restless and incessantly on the move. When one bird flies across to another thicket, the rest promptly follow in disorderly twos and threes, and the flock thus rapidly flows on in its quest for food. This behaviour is typical of many of the smaller babblers found in Sikkim. *Food:* almost entirely insects. These are obtained among the lower growth and not on the ground as with scimitar babblers. Flower nectar is also eaten. It has an occasional low, sweet, rather mournful whistle.

NESTING: *Season*—April to June. *Nest*—a cup of roots, fibres, fern fronds, etc., loosely covered on the outside and domed (or partially domed) with dry bamboo leaves. Placed either on sloping ground, concealed in bushes, or low down in a bamboo clump or thicket, well camouflaged. *Eggs*—normally 4, pure white, measuring about 19×15 mm.

RACIAL CHARACTERISTICS, MEASUREMENTS, ETC: In this race the throat is blackish grey conspicuously mottled with white.

A specimen (♂?) collected by the recent Survey measures: Wing 60; bill 17; tarsus 22; tail 51.5 mm. Stresemann gives the Wing of 3 skins (sex ?) in the Schäfer Sikkim collection as 58, 59, 62 mm.

Iris pinkish biscuit colour, orange-brown or reddish brown; upper mandible horny brown, lower mandible pale flesh colour, darker in summer; legs and feet olive-yellow.

## THE YELLOWBREASTED BABBLER

*Macronous gularis rubricapilla* (Tickell)

*Motacilla rubricapilla* Tickell, Nov. 1833, *Jour. Asiat. Soc. Bengal* **2**: 576—Borabhúm.

F.B.I. 1: 273

LOCAL NAME:

SIZE: Sparrow.

FIELD CHARACTERS: Upper plumage olive-green. Crown pale ferruginous; supercilium, lores and forehead yellow, the latter two with black shafts. Cheeks, chin, throat and upper abdomen yellow; rest of lower plumage dull ashy yellow. Sexes alike.

STATUS AND HABITAT: A low-elevation species, only observed by the Survey at Rangpo (Teesta Valley), *c.* 1200 ft. According to Stevens 'probably does not occur beyond the base of the foothills'. Frequents secondary and bamboo jungle.

DISTRIBUTION OUTSIDE SIKKIM: Eastern Nepal, Bhutan duars (?), Bengal, Assam, eastern Madhya Pradesh, Orissa, Visakhapatnam Ghats, Arakan. Other races extend the species to Thailand, Malaya, etc.

GENERAL HABITS: Very similar to the *Stachyris* group of babblers. While feeding, a flock keeps up a soft conversational *pick, pick* etc. *Call: kew-kew-kew-kew* etc. repeated for several minutes at a stretch, occasionally varied by a harsh *chrr-chi-choo*; the former somewhat reminiscent of the tailor bird (*Orthotomus*), but louder and richer.

NESTING: Not recorded in Sikkim. *Nest*—roughly domed, of grass and bamboo leaves, 4 or 5 ft. up in a bamboo clump. *Eggs*—normally 3, white with numerous small specks and blotches of red or reddish brown. Size about 17×13 mm.

RACIAL CHARACTERISTICS, MEASUREMENTS, ETC: ♂♀ Wing 53-58; bill 10-11; tarsus *c.* 18; tail 52-54 mm. (Fauna).

Iris whitish yellow; bill slate, darker on upper mandible; legs and feet pale brown.

## THE BENGAL REDCAPPED BABBLER

*Timalia pileata bengalensis* Godwin-Austen

*Timalia bengalensis* Godwin-Austen, 1872, *Jour. Asiat. Soc. Bengal* **41**: 143—Khasia Hills.

**Plate 17, fig. 1** (facing p. 208)

F.B.I. 1: 226

LOCAL NAME:

SIZE: Sparrow+.

FIELD CHARACTERS: A small, restless, gregarious babbler. *Above*, forehead white, continued backward as a prominent streak on either side above the eyes. Crown deep rufous. Upper plumage fulvous olive-brown; ashy on mantle with blackish shaft-streaks. *Below*, cheeks, chin, throat and breast white, the last with narrow black shaft-lines. Sides of neck and sides of breast deep grey. Rest of underparts ferruginous, tinged with olivaceous on sides of abdomen. Sexes alike.

STATUS AND HABITAT: Mainly a plains dweller and up to *c.* 3000 ft. elevation, affecting low-lying swampy areas with tall grass and scrub. According to Stevens, recorded for the lower hills along the (southern) border of Sikkim.

A skulker in tall grass and bushes, seldom exposing itself to view. Its presence is usually announced by its sharp conversational calls—a rolling *prrew*, reminiscent of the note of the Black-and-Yellow Grosbeak.

## THE GREAT PARROTBILL

*Conostoma aemodium* Hodgson

*Conostoma aemodius* Hodgson, 1841, *Jour. Asiat. Soc. Bengal* **10**: 857—Northern regions of Nepal.

**Plate 25, fig. 5** (facing p. 336)

F.B.I. 1: 104

LOCAL NAME: Lho-rannio-pho (Lepcha).

SIZE: Myna+.

FIELD CHARACTERS: A mouse-brown bird resembling a large laughing thrush, with an upright carriage and prominent whitish forehead, dark lores and stout orange-yellow bill.

*Above*, rufous olive-brown including wings and tail. A dark brown patch round eye extending to bill. *Below*, chin, throat and sides of head vinous brown; rest of underparts paler. Sexes alike.

STATUS AND HABITAT: Resident in a high zone from 10,000 to 12,000 ft. (Singalila Ridge, Gnatong, Karponang, etc.), descending to some 6000 ft. in winter. Affects dense thickets of 'maling' bamboo, and rhododendron scrub.

DISTRIBUTION OUTSIDE SIKKIM: Nepal, Bhutan, N. Assam, N. Burmese hills, N. Yunnan, Szechwan.

GENERAL HABITS: Pairs or small parties, often associated with laughing thrushes, which the bird superficially resembles in appearance and habits. Like them it hops about among the bamboo stems or on the ground, even in snow, and rummages for beetles and other insects. Bamboo shoots, crab-apple seeds and wild raspberries are also eaten. Stanford found it unafraid and intensely curious, being readily decoyed by an imitation of its calls. These are described as a fourfold grating croak, a clear musical *wheou, wheou*, and a *churr*.

NESTING: *Season*—May-June. A ♀ collected by Stevens on 15 March had a coarsely granular ovary, as sketched on the label. *Nest*—a deep compact cup of coarse grass and bamboo leaves, lined thickly with fine grass stems; built in a clump of 'maling' bamboos. *Eggs*—2 or 3, white, sparsely blotched, streaked and smudged with yellowish brown or reddish, more densely at the broad end where there may also be some inky purple spots and clouds. Size about 28×21 mm.

RACIAL CHARACTERISTICS, MEASUREMENTS, ETC: *Conostoma* is characterized by a tail longer than the wing, with the rectrices considerably less graduated than in the genus *Paradoxornis*. Its bill also is proportionately less deep and parrot-like than in *Paradoxornis*.

Stevens gives the Wing of 2 ♂♂ as 125-128 mm. A ♀ from Gnatong in the Stevens Sikkim collection, Chicago Mus. of Nat. Hist. (No. 84770), measures: Wing damaged; bill 23; tarsus 40; tail 130 mm.

According to the Fauna, ♂♀ Wing 130-133; bill *c.* 20; tarsus *c.* 37; tail *c.* 140 mm.

Iris pale orange-yellow; bill ochraceous yellow, lighter at tip; legs and feet ochraceous or plumbeous horn. (Whistler MS.)

## THE BROWN PARROTBILL

*Paradoxornis unicolor unicolor* (Hodgson)

*Heteromorpha unicolor* Hodgson, 1843, *Jour. Asiat. Soc. Bengal* **12**: 448 (pl. facing p. 450)—Cachar, Nepal.

F.B.I. **1**: 208

LOCAL NAME: Lho-rannio-pho (Lepcha).

SIZE: Bulbul.

FIELD CHARACTERS: A brown babbler-like bird with conspicuous black eyebrow and short thick yellow bill. *Above*, olive-brown tinged with rufous on tail and wings. Forehead and short thick crest rufous-brown; sides of head vinous brown. Black lores and supercilia well defined, reaching to the nape. *Below*, chin vinous brown; throat and sides of neck greyish brown; rest of underparts dull fulvous. Sexes alike.

STATUS AND HABITAT: Uncommon and local. Resident, according to Stevens, in the interior of Sikkim between 6500 and 10,000 ft. (Kedom, Lachung Valley, Lachen, Singalila Ridge). Meinertzhagen obtained a specimen near Changu at 11,200 ft. in December. Affects dense 'maling' bamboo and dwarf rhododendron growth.

DISTRIBUTION OUTSIDE SIKKIM: Nepal, Bhutan, SE. Tibet (Himalayan facies).

GENERAL HABITS: A high-elevation bird regarding which little is known. Small parties of half a dozen or so skulk about in bamboo jungle, seldom flying far even when fired at, merely fluttering into denser cover. Meinertzhagen records 'chirrups and a sort of bleating sound for many minutes' when a party was alarmed.

NESTING: Unknown. A male collected by Mr C. M. Inglis at Tonglu (*c.* 10,000 ft.—Darjeeling District) at the end of June had greatly enlarged testes.

RACIAL CHARACTERISTICS, MEASUREMENTS, ETC: For 5 Sikkim specimens, Stevens gives the following measurements:

| | Wing | Bill |
|---|---|---|
| 4 ♂♂ | 85-92 (av. 88.8) | 14-15 (av. 14.6) mm. |
| 1 ♀ | 88 | 14 mm. |

Dr Dillon Ripley measures a male collected by him in eastern Nepal: Wing 92; bill 15; tail 99+(worn). A Schäfer specimen from Lachen (♂, 27 August) has Wing 86 mm. (Stresemann).

'Iris stone-grey of a beautiful tint; bill fleshy yellow for two-thirds, remaining portion at tip of both mandibles lighter yellow; tarsus greenish grey' (Stevens).

## THE FULVOUSFRONTED PARROTBILL

*Paradoxornis fulvifrons fulvifrons* (Hodgson)

*Temnoris fulvifrons* Hodgson, Aug. 1845, *Proc. Zool. Soc. London:* 31—Nepal.

**Plate 24, fig. 2 (facing p. 289)**

F.B.I. 1: 113

LOCAL NAME:

SIZE: Sparrow—. About that of a munia.

FIELD CHARACTERS: *Above*, forehead, short supercilium, and centre of crown bright orange-fulvous. Back yellowish olive. Wings orange-brown and dark brown, with some white. *Below*, chin, cheeks, sides of neck, and breast bright orange merging into deep grey and white on flanks and abdomen. Under tail-coverts fulvous. Sexes alike.

STATUS AND HABITAT: Resident. Sparingly distributed at about 8500 to 12,000 ft. (Singalila Ridge, Karponang). Range coincident, according to Stevens, with that of the high-elevation bamboos 'prong' (*Arundinaria aristata*) and 'maling' (*A. racemosa*), the dense thickets of which it frequents.

DISTRIBUTION OUTSIDE SIKKIM: Nepal and Bhutan. Other races in S. Tibet, NW. Yunnan, Szechwan and Shensi.

GENERAL HABITS: Apparently not differing from those of *P. n. humii* (below). The same feverish haste characterizes their foraging, while a continuous twitter of faint mousy cheeps is uttered by the members of a flock as they work restlessly up and down bamboo culms and leaves. The recorded food is insects and bamboo shoots.

NESTING: Nothing recorded.

RACIAL CHARACTERISTICS, MEASUREMENTS, ETC: Stevens gives the measurements of specimens collected in eastern Nepal and Sikkim as:

| | Wing | Bill |
|---|---|---|
| ♂♂ | 56-57, | 7 mm. |
| ♀♀ | 55-56 | 6.5-7 mm. |

Tarsus 20-22; tail *c.* 66 mm. (Stuart Baker).

'Iris red-brown; bill horny pink; culmen with a broad band dark horny; tarsus brownish plumbeous' (Stevens).

## THE BLACKFRONTED PARROTBILL

*Paradoxornis nipalensis humii* (Sharpe)

*Suthora humii* Sharpe, 1883, Cat. Birds Brit. Mus. 7: 487—Nepal.

**Plate 24, fig. 1** (facing p. 289)

F.B.I. 1: 110

LOCAL NAME:

SIZE: Sparrow—. About that of the Redheaded Tit.

FIELD CHARACTERS: A tiny bird, bright orange-brown above including crown and nape; bluish grey below, with the flanks, vent and under tail-coverts fulvous. Forehead and broad supercilium from bill to nape black. Chin and throat black, the latter looking like a bib. Lores, cheeks, and a short line above eye white. Ear-coverts and sides of neck orange-chestnut. A good deal of black and white in the wings. Sexes alike.

STATUS AND HABITAT: Resident, normally between 4000 and 8000 ft. (Singhik, Gangtok, Manshitang, etc.). Meinertzhagen collected a specimen near Changu at 11,200 ft. Generally distributed but not common. Affects mixed secondary and bamboo jungle.

DISTRIBUTION OUTSIDE SIKKIM: E. Nepal through to E. Bhutan. The nominate race (*nipalensis*) is restricted by Ripley to the Kathmandu Valley, central Nepal. The species, in other races, extends eastward to the hills of Assam, including the Mishmis. Also hills of Burma, Thailand and on into Yunnan.

GENERAL HABITS: Sociable and confiding little birds, rather reminiscent of the Redheaded Tit. Large flocks of 30 or more, often in association with parties of other small babblers and tits, hunt with feverish activity among bamboo clumps and low bushes, clinging to sprigs and leaves in acrobatic positions in search of insect food. The flock keeps up a continuous twittering chirrup. A feature of these gatherings is the speed and energy with which the birds work their way from one tree or bamboo clump to another. Suddenly one bird flies off to the next tree and the entire flock flows after him in a disorderly stream; and anon they are off to the next tree. Interspersed in this round of feverish activity are short pauses of rest when some members of the flock will huddle together along a branch like munias to preen and relax. But this is only momentary, for soon the birds stream on with the rest of the flock.

NESTING: *Season*—May-June. *Nest*—a tiny, neat and compact cup of bamboo leaves and fine grasses, coated on the outside with cobwebs, lined with finer grasses and root hairs. Fixed in a cluster of twigs springing from a bamboo node, or in a bush, less than two feet from the ground. *Eggs*—2 to 4, a beautiful pale blue. Size about 16×12 mm.

RACIAL CHARACTERISTICS, MEASUREMENTS, ETC: The western or central Nepal (typical) race, with which *humii* intergrades in E. Nepal, has the crown ashy brown, upper plumage orange-brown, ear-coverts slaty blue. *Humii* has both crown and upper plumage orange-brown, ear-coverts orange-chestnut.

Wing ♂♀ 45-48; bill *c.* 7; tarsus *c.* 19; tail *c.* 52 mm.

Five specimens (sex ?) collected by Schäfer have Wing 48-51 mm. (Stresemann).

Iris brown; bill black (Stevens), horn yellow (Meinertzhagen); legs and feet slaty blue or pale plumbeous.

## THE LESSER REDHEADED PARROTBILL

### *Paradoxornis atrosuperciliaris oatesi* (Sharpe)

*Suthora oatesi* Sharpe, 1908, Handl. Gen. Bds. 4: 70. New name for *Chleuasicus ruficeps* Blyth, 1845, *Jour. Asiat. Soc. Bengal* 14: 578—Darjeeling.

**Plate 24, fig. 4 (facing p. 289)**

F.B.I. 1: 114

LOCAL NAME: Chongto-phep-pho (Lepcha).

SIZE: Sparrow.

FIELD CHARACTERS: *Above*, forehead, rounded tuft-like crest, nape, and hindneck bright chestnut; sides of head and neck paler. Rest of upper parts rufous-brown, deeper on wings and tail. *Below*, white, tinged with pink on breast and finely black-streaked on chin. Sexes alike.

Differs from the better known Blackbrowed Parrotbill (*P. a. atrosuperciliaris*) of the Assam hills, N. Burma, etc. in being less richly coloured and in lacking the short black line over and behind the eye.

Easily confused with *Paradoxornis ruficeps* (below), but is smaller and has a blunter bill and more graduated tail.

STATUS AND HABITAT: Has been obtained in Sikkim, but no details recorded. Believed to be resident at about 7000 ft. elevation. Not met with by any recent investigator, and evidently very rare.

## THE REDHEADED PARROTBILL

### *Paradoxornis ruficeps ruficeps* Blyth

*Paradoxornis ruficeps* Blyth, 1842, *Jour. Asiat. Soc. Bengal* 11: 177—Bhutan

F.B.I. 1: 116

LOCAL NAME: Chongto-phep-pho (Lepcha).

SIZE: Bulbul.

FIELD CHARACTERS: Slightly larger than the last but otherwise very similar to it and difficult to distinguish in the field. The bill is less blunt and the tail less graduated. Also, lower parts white, washed with rust colour on the flanks and under tail-coverts. Sexes alike.

STATUS AND HABITAT: Locally distributed at moderate elevations, between 2000 and 5000 ft., with some up-and-down seasonal movement. Affects scrub and bamboo jungle.

DISTRIBUTION OUTSIDE SIKKIM: Bhutan and eastward to the Miri and Abor hills, north of Brahmaputra River. The species extends through Assam and Burma to Tenasserim; N. Yunnan; Tonkin.

GENERAL HABITS: Social. Usually in pairs or small parties in association with hunting flocks of minlas, barwings and other insectivorous birds. Actions and behaviour like tits and the smaller parrotbills, but slower. Also reminiscent of the Yelloweyed Babbler (*Chrysomma*). *Flight:* weak like a babbler's—a few wing flaps followed by a short glide. A great skulker, and when disturbed makes its way from reed to reed without showing itself and disappears in dense cover. *Call:* described as 'a squirrel-like chitter interrupted with a series of rather slowly pronounced double notes *tee-ur*'. Another cry is said to be exactly like the bleating of a young goat kid. A peculiar snapping of the bills may be heard from a party feeding amongst reeds. Mainly insectivorous, but also eats seeds.

NESTING: *Season*—late April to June. *Nest*—a deep compact cup of coarse grass with some cobwebs, lined with fibrous threads from bamboo stems. Placed in a small sapling in evergreen forest, or in a bamboo clump in bamboo jungle. *Eggs*—2 to 4, of two types: (1) white to dull creamy, marked with light to dark brown smudges and blotches, more numerous at the larger end, and (2) blue-grey or greenish grey with the markings darker brown (or blackish) and paler reddish brown. Size about 23×17 mm.

RACIAL CHARACTERISTICS, MEASUREMENTS, ETC: The better known race *bakeri* of Assam has the underparts more buffish white.

Wing ♂♀ 84-86; bill *c.* 14; tarsus *c.* 28; tail *c.* 85 mm.

Iris deep red-brown; eye-rim (circumorbital skin) slaty blue; bill horny brown above, fleshy horn below; mouth slaty blue; legs and feet plumbeous blue; claws brown.

## THE GREYHEADED PARROTBILL

*Paradoxornis gularis gularis* Gray

*Paradoxornis gularis* Gray, 1845, Gen. Birds 2: 389 (pl. 94, fig. 2) *ex* Horsfield MS.—Sikkim (Bhutan).

F.B.I. 1: 118

LOCAL NAME: Chongto-phep-pho (Lepcha).

SIZE: Sparrow.

FIELD CHARACTERS: *Above,* rufous-brown, with darker wings and tail. Forehead black continued behind in two lines to the nape on either side of crown. Crown and nape dark grey. Lores, face and cheeks greyish. *Below,* chin grey; upper throat black. Rest of lower plumage white, faintly washed with fulvous on sides of breast and abdomen. Sexes alike.

STATUS AND HABITAT: Evidently scarce and local. Recorded in Sikkim between 3600 and 8000 ft. elevation. Affects bamboo and scrub jungle.

DISTRIBUTION OUTSIDE SIKKIM: Bhutan; Miri Hills (north of Brahmaputra River). The hills of Assam south of the Brahmaputra, N. Burma, S. Shan States and Karenni are occupied by the race *transfluvialis*. The species extends to Thailand, Szechwan and S. China.

GENERAL HABITS: Similar to other parrotbills. Small parties of 6 or 8 birds in bushes and low trees in scattered bamboo jungle, apparently not often consorting with the mixed hunting parties. A loud call of 4 notes is used when one bird of a pair is calling to the other (Smythies).

NESTING: The only specific record for Sikkim is Mandelli's, who found a nest at 8000 ft. on 17 May: a massive compact cup of coarse grass thinly bound with 'wild silk' on the exterior and lined with 'extremely fine grass stems'. Placed in a fork amongst the branches of a medium sized tree, 30 feet from the ground. *Eggs*—2 or 3, similar in colour and markings to those of *Paradoxornis ruficeps*. Size about 21×15 mm. Schäfer obtained a nestling at Gangtok on 14 June.

RACIAL CHARACTERISTICS, MEASUREMENTS, ETC: The race *transfluvialis* is somewhat smaller ('Wing 86-89.5') and has the whole of the underside suffused with fulvous.

Stuart Baker gives the following measurements for typical *gularis*: ♂♀ Wing 90-95; bill 10-13 long and 10-11 deep; tarsus *c.* 27; tail *c.* 80 mm.

Four Schäfer skins from Gangtok, 11-25 January (sex ?), have Wing 89-90 mm. Iris red-brown; bill chrome yellow; legs and feet greenish horn. (Whistler MS.)

## GOULD'S PARROTBILL

### *Paradoxornis flavirostris flavirostris* Gould

*Paradoxornis flavirostris* Gould, 1936, *Proc. Zool. Soc. London:* 17—Nepal.

F.B.I. 1: 105

LOCAL NAME:

SIZE: Bulbul.

FIELD CHARACTERS: A fulvous brown bird like a babbler with chestnut head, black-and-white face and throat, and short, deep, yellow, parrot-like bill.

Head and sides of neck dull pale chestnut; throat, lores, and ear-coverts black; a broad white patch below the eye extending to sides of throat, mottled with black. Chin white, barred with black. Sexes alike.

STATUS AND HABITAT: Resident from the foothills up to about

7000 ft. elevation (Rangiroon, Darjeeling District, 6300 ft.—Meinertzhagen). Affects bamboo jungle and thickets of reeds and coarse grass in wet or boggy patches in jungle.

DISTRIBUTION OUTSIDE SIKKIM: Eastern Himalayas from Nepal to the Mishmi Hills. Also Assam hills south of the Brahmaputra River, Chin Hills, etc.

GENERAL HABITS: A skulker; shy and difficult to observe. Small parties of 5 to 7 move about amongst reeds and bamboos, the birds seldom showing themselves except in the early mornings and before sunset when they clamber up to the tops of the reeds and make short flights across. Their presence within a reed patch is revealed by the curious sound of their mandibles nibbling at the grasses; also by a striking whistle *phew-phew-phew-phuit*, commencing in a low tone and ascending rapidly in scale and volume. *Food:* bamboo shoots and vegetable matter, and insects.

NESTING: *Season*—April to June. *Nest*—a deep compact cup of coarse grass and bamboo leaves and bark, bound with cobweb and lined with finer grasses. Suspended between stems of reeds 3 to 5 ft. up, or placed among the clusters of twigs sprouting from a bamboo node. *Eggs*—normally 2 or 3, white, sparsely speckled at the broad end with pale reddish or deep reddish brown. Size about 22×16 mm.

RACIAL CHARACTERISTICS, MEASUREMENTS, ETC: The race *guttaticollis*, of Assam (exact distribution undetermined) and N. Burma to W. China, differs in having the throat pale fulvous with black arrow-head markings and no black band bordering it below.

Stuart Baker gives the measurements of *flavirostris* as: ♂♀ Wing 85-90; bill *c.* 12; tarsus *c.* 30; tail 100-110 mm.

Iris olive-brown or red-brown; bill bright yellow, horny white at tip; legs and feet plumbeous.

## THE WHITETHROATED LAUGHING THRUSH

*Garrulax albogularis albogularis* (Gould)

*Ianthocincla albogularis* Gould, 1836, *Proc. Zool. Soc. London:* 187—Nepal.

F.B.I. 1: 153

LOCAL NAME: Karriam-pho (Lepcha).

SIZE: Pigeon—.

FIELD CHARACTERS: A large uncrested laughing thrush, olive-brown above, bright ferruginous below. Glistening white cheeks, throat and breast bordered by a broad olive-brown pectoral band. White tips of tail feathers show up strikingly as a broad white terminal band, especially in flight and whilst alighting. Sexes alike.

STATUS AND HABITAT: Not uncommon, but very local and patchy, between about 5500 and 9000 ft. elevation (Toong, Manshitang, Pemionche, Gangtok, Lachen, Lachung). Affects forest, preferably thin and open, and scrubby hillsides.

DISTRIBUTION OUTSIDE SIKKIM: Nepal; Bhutan. The west Himalayan race *whistleri* ranges from the Murree hills to Garhwal and Kumaon.

GENERAL HABITS: Sociable and gregarious; in every way typical of the laughing thrushes. Commonly associates with tree pies, Blue Magpies, jays and other laughing thrushes. Flocks of 30 or more sometimes seen in harvested fields, hopping about on the ground like Jungle Babblers and digging with their bills for food (insects ?). They have peculiar hissing, squealing notes and are very noisy, bursting into choruses of squeaky 'laughter' on any disturbance or excitement.

NESTING: *Season*—April to June. *Nest*—a cup of coarse grass, creepers, moss, etc., usually lined with fine roots and such-like material; placed in a small tree or shrub 3 to 10 feet up. *Eggs*—3 or 4, deep blue, unmarked, glossy. Size about 29×21 mm.

RACIAL CHARACTERISTICS, MEASUREMENTS, ETC: The better known race of the western Himalayas, *whistleri*, has the upper parts paler and more greyish. The red of the underparts is paler. It is also somewhat larger in size.

Thirteen adult specimens (♂♀) collected by Schäfer in Sikkim have Wing 128-138 mm. (av. 131.4 mm.).

Iris bluish white; bill black, brownish at tip; legs and feet pale lead grey.

## THE NECKLACED LAUGHING THRUSH

*Garrulax moniligerus moniligerus* (Hodgson)

*Cinclosoma moniligera* Hodgson, 1836, *Asiat. Res.* 19: 147—Nepal.

F.B.I. 1: 151

LOCAL NAMES: Ol-pho (Lepcha); Piang-kam (Bhutia).

SIZE: Pigeon—.

FIELD CHARACTERS: Very similar to the Blackgorgetted Laughing Thrush (below), but somewhat smaller and lacks the black patch on wing-shoulder. A white line from base of bill bordering the black cheeks. Sexes alike.

STATUS AND HABITAT: More or less coincident with the next species. A low-level and foothills laughing thrush, not usually met with above 3500 ft. in Sikkim (Singhik).

DISTRIBUTION OUTSIDE SIKKIM: Nepal; Bhutan; Assam hills north and south of Brahmaputra River. Overall species distribution about the same as *pectoralis* with a parallel breaking-up into races.

GENERAL HABITS: Similar to the Blackgorgetted Laughing Thrush.

NESTING: Season, site, nest and eggs differ in no way from the above, only the eggs average smaller, about 28.5×21.5 mm.

RACIAL CHARACTERISTICS, MEASUREMENTS, ETC: No specimens collected in Sikkim, but for comparison of size with *pectoralis*, the measurements of two males from the Lohit Valley (NE. Assam) are as follows:

Wing 120; bill 29-30; tarsus 40.5-43; tail 126-132 mm.

Iris yellow, orange-yellow, or reddish yellow; bill black; legs and feet yellowish brown or brownish flesh.

# THE BLACKGORGETTED LAUGHING THRUSH

*Garrulax pectoralis melanotis* Blyth

*Garrulax melanotis* Blyth, 1843, *Jour. Asiat. Soc. Bengal* **12**: 949—Arakan.

F.B.I. 1: 150

LOCAL NAME: Ol-pho (Lepcha).

SIZE: Pigeon—.

FIELD CHARACTERS: A large uncrested laughing thrush, olive-brown above with a fulvous collar on hindneck; fulvous white below with a prominent black collar across breast commencing at gape and continuing down side of neck. A narrow white supercilium. Ear-coverts variable: all black, black-and-white, or all white. A black patch on wing-shoulder (primary coverts). Tail broadly tipped with black and white. Sexes alike.

STATUS AND HABITAT: Erratic and local. At low and moderate elevations along the Teesta, Rangeet, and other deep river valleys, and up to about 5500 feet (Rangpo, Shamdong, Rinchinpong, etc.). Affects dense scrub and bamboo jungle, and overgrown cultivation clearings.

DISTRIBUTION OUTSIDE SIKKIM: Bhutan; Assam hills north and south of Brahmaputra River; Burma. Other races in Nepal, Thailand, Yunnan, Indochina, S. China.

GENERAL HABITS: Typical. Gregarious and noisy. Flocks of considerable size, often in company with other laughing thrushes. The birds keep up an incessant querulous conversational squeaking—a nasal *week, week, week*. On alarm they mount into trees, hopping from branch to branch, and flow from one thicket to another in straggling follow-my-leader fashion.

NESTING: *Season*—May to July. *Nest*—a broad and shallow, rather untidily built cup of bamboo leaves mixed with roots, moss, etc., lined with finer roots and grass stems. Placed in bushes or small trees, 2 to 20 ft. up. *Eggs*—4 or 5, deep blue, unmarked. Size about 32×23 mm.

RACIAL CHARACTERISTICS, MEASUREMENTS, ETC: Confusingly like the previous species, *G. moniligerus*, with which it often consorts. Distinguished from it by (1) slightly larger size, (2) the large black patch on shoulder of closed wing (primary-coverts), and (3) colour of legs and feet which is greyish as against yellowish in *moniligerus*.

Three specimens collected by the Sikkim Survey measure:

| | Wing | Bill | Tarsus | Tail |
|---|---|---|---|---|
| 1 ♂ | 140 | 33.5 | 48 | 132 mm. |
| 2 ♀♀ | 133-144 | 32-33.5 | 49 | 118-135 mm. |

Iris orange-brown; fleshy circumorbital ring chrome yellow; bill horny brown, pale plumbeous at base of lower mandible, white at extreme tip; legs and feet pale bluish plumbeous; claws horny white.

## THE SIKKIM STRIATED LAUGHING THRUSH

*Garrulax striatus sikkimensis* (Ticehurst)

*Grammatoptila striata sikkimensis* Ticehurst, 1924, *Bull. Brit. Orn. Cl.* 44: 104—Sikkim.

**Plate 20, fig. 4 (facing p. 225)**

F.B.I. 1: 184

LOCAL NAMES: Nampiok-pho (Lepcha); Kopiam (Bhutia).

SIZE: Pigeon −.

FIELD CHARACTERS: A large, conspicuously white-streaked umber brown laughing thrush with a full mop-like crest, and partially white-tipped chestnut tail. Sexes alike.

STATUS AND HABITAT: Not uncommon, but local, between about 2500 and 7500 ft. elevation (Dikchu, Singhik, Gangtok, Manshitang, Chungthang). Inhabits forest with dense shrubby undergrowth, and wooded nullahs.

DISTRIBUTION OUTSIDE SIKKIM: Eastern Nepal to western and central Bhutan. Other races in western and eastern Himalayas; Assam hills; N. Burma.

GENERAL HABITS: More arboreal than most other laughing thrushes, feeding chiefly in shrubs and also up in the foliage canopy of tall trees. Keeps in pairs or small noisy parties of 4 or 5 birds, frequently in association with tree pies, Whitethroated and other laughing thrushes. Tickell remarks on its habit of suddenly throwing the bill downwards and jerking up its mop-like crest as if about to pitch it at the observer! Utters a variety of loud discordant cackling notes and sometimes a harsh unmusical chorus of chattering 'laughter'. A lively, rich whistling call usually betrays the presence of the birds a long way off. One observer has well rendered it as *o see saw whitey—oh white*. *Food:* insects and berries.

NESTING: *Season*—May to July. *Nest*—a large shallow cup of moss, tendrils, roots, etc., lined with finer roots and fibres. Placed in bushes or small trees, 3 to 20 ft. up. *Eggs*—2, pale blue, unmarked. Size about 33×23 mm. They are reported to be more pointed than those of the neighbouring W. Himalayan race, a peculiarity worthy of investigation.

RACIAL CHARACTERISTICS, MEASUREMENTS, ETC: *Sikkimensis* differs from the typical W. Himalayan *striatus* in being less olive in general tone; browner on flanks and underparts, and darker overall. It is also slightly smaller: Wing 130-141 mm. as against 145-165 (Ticehurst). An intermediate race *vibex* has recently been described from Nepal by Ripley.

Two ♀♀ collected by the Sikkim Survey measure: Wing 135-136; bill 26.5-30; tarsus 44; tail 123-127 mm.

Fourteen Schäfer skins from Sikkim (♂♀) give Wing 131-143 (av. 137.2) mm.

Iris reddish brown; bill blackish brown; legs and feet plumbeous; claws horny brown. (In one of the above specimens, iris, examined immediately after death, pinkish biscuit colour; two hours later brownish scarlet!)

## THE HIMALAYAN WHITECRESTED LAUGHING THRUSH

*Garrulax leucolophus leucolophus* (Hardwicke)

*Corvus leucolophus* Hardwicke, 1815, *Trans. Linn. Soc.* 11: 208 (pl. 15)—Mountains above Hardwar.

F.B.I. 1: 146

LOCAL NAMES: Karrio-pho (Lepcha); Karria-goka (Bhutia).

SIZE: Myna+.

FIELD CHARACTERS: Head, crest, nape, and throat to lower breast white; crest feathers tipped with ashy grey. A broad black streak from bill to ear-coverts, enclosing eye. Upper parts olive-brown with a ferruginous hind-collar. Underparts ferruginous. Sexes alike.

STATUS AND HABITAT: The commonest laughing thrush in Sikkim with an altitudinal range from about 1000 ft. (Rangpo, November) to at least 7000 ft. (Pemionche, March). Schäfer collected specimens at Gangtok, *c.* 5800 ft., in December. Most abundant between 2000 and 4500 ft. Partial to secondary scrub-and-bush jungle on the overgrown sites of shifting cultivation clearings and bordering terraced fields.

DISTRIBUTION OUTSIDE SIKKIM: NW. Himalayas from Chamba to Almora; Nepal. The species in other races extends to NE. Assam and down through to Tenasserim; Thailand, Yunnan, Cambodia, etc.

GENERAL HABITS: Sociable and highly gregarious among themselves (a flock of over 40!) and also associating freely with parties of Himalayan Tree Pies, Green Magpies, and other species of laughing thrushes. Their noisy 'laughter' is a feature of the countryside. One bird leads with a loud, pleasant *pick* or *pick-wo* and the whole flock follows with a tumult of discordant cackling which resounds through the forest. Through all this boisterous performance the leader maintains his refrain *pick-wo* at regular intervals. The birds dance and posture around, and flap their wings in accompaniment.

NESTING: *Season*—April to June. *Nest*—a large shallow cup of coarse grasses and bamboo spathes wound round with pliant creeper stems etc. and lined with fine roots; placed low down in shrubs and small trees. *Eggs*—normally 4, pure china white, unmarked, finely pitted on the surface. Size about 30×24 mm.

RACIAL CHARACTERISTICS, MEASUREMENTS, ETC: The adjoining race *patkaicus*, which gradually replaces it in Bhutan and further east, is darker on the belly, more olive, less rufous. Two specimens collected by the Sikkim Survey measure:

| | Wing | Bill | Tarsus | Tail |
|---|---|---|---|---|
| 1 ♂ | 135 | 28.5 | 48 | 131 mm. |
| 1 ♀ | 138 | 30 | 45 | 131 mm. |

Nine examples (♂♀) in the Schäfer collection have Wing 126-136 mm. (av. 133.1 mm.).

Iris brownish crimson; bill black; legs and feet greyish brown; claws horny brown.

## THE RUFOUSCHINNED LAUGHING THRUSH

*Garrulax rufogularis rufogularis* (Gould)

*Ianthocincla rufogularis* Gould, 1835, *Proc. Zool. Soc. London:* 48—Himalayas (=Sikkim).

**Plate 20, fig. 6 (facing p. 225)**

F.B.I. 1: 158

LOCAL NAME: Narbigivan-pho (Lepcha).

SIZE: Myna.

FIELD CHARACTERS: Crown, nape and ear-coverts black. Lores white. A greyish ring round eye. Cheeks and sides of face mingled black and white. Broad supercilium reaching to nape, and sides of neck, olive-brown. Upper parts olive-brown tinged with fulvous; barred on back with black, and spotted on closed wings with black and white. Point of chin rufous; throat white; under tail-coverts bright rufous; rest of lower plumage ashy brown, spotted with black except on abdomen, which is whitish. Tail feathers rufescent, with rufous tips and subterminal black bands. Sexes alike.

STATUS AND HABITAT: Local and patchy. The Survey recorded it from between 2000 and 4500 ft. in W. Sikkim (November to February). Meinertzhagen obtained specimens at 11,600 ft. (Yumthang) in December, so it evidently occupies a wide altitudinal range. Affects dense shrubby undergrowth in and about oak and rhododendron forests, and bordering cultivation.

DISTRIBUTION OUTSIDE SIKKIM: Nepal; Bhutan; Assam hills north of Brahmaputra River. Other races occur in W. Himalayas from Kashmir to Kumaon; W. Nepal; Assam hills south of the Brahmaputra.

GENERAL HABITS: Usually keeps in pairs or small parties. A great skulker, seldom showing itself above the thickets. Has the usual assortment of squeaks and chuckles, but is not noisy and thus doubtless often overlooked.

NESTING: *Season*—May to July (and on to September). *Nest*—a moderately deep cup of creeper tendrils lined with fine black roots. Placed in the fork of a bush or small tree, 5 to 15 feet from the ground. *Eggs*—white, unspotted, glossy, measuring about 26×20 mm.

RACIAL CHARACTERISTICS, MEASUREMENTS, ETC: The adjoining race of W. Nepal, *grosvenori*, differs in being much paler and less heavily barred above.

Two specimens collected by the recent Sikkim Survey measure:

| | Wing | Bill | Tarsus | Tail |
|---|---|---|---|---|
| 1 ♂ | 88 | 24 | 35 | 98 mm. |
| 1 ♀ | 92 | 24 | 37 | 97 mm. |

Iris crimson-brown; upper mandible horny brown; lower mandible pale whitish horn, darker at gape; legs and feet greyish horny brown; claws pale horny brown.

## THE WHITESPOTTED LAUGHING THRUSH

*Garrulax ocellatus ocellatus* (Vigors)

*Cinclosoma ocellatum* Vigors, 1831, *Proc. Zool. Soc. London:* 55--Himalayas (=Simla-Almora Dist. Ticehurst & Whistler).

**Plate 20, fig. 8 (facing p. 225)**

F.B.I. 1: 155

LOCAL NAME: Lho-karreum-pho (Lepcha).

SIZE: Pigeon.

FIELD CHARACTERS: A large uncrested laughing thrush, chiefly reddish brown above, spotted with white on back and wings. Fulvous buff below, barred on the breast with black. Head brownish black with fulvous face and supercilium. Centre of throat black with narrow rufous ripple marks. Tail chestnut and ashy brown with white tips and black terminal band, conspicuous when spread in flight. Sexes alike.

STATUS AND HABITAT: A high-elevation bird inhabiting the zone between 9000 and 12,000 ft. altitude (Lachung, Karponang, Changu, Singalila Ridge). Seldom below 9000 ft., even in winter. Not common. Affects oak and rhododendron forest with *Rubus* and dwarf rhododendron scrub.

DISTRIBUTION OUTSIDE SIKKIM: Kumaon Himalayas, Nepal, Bhutan, SE. Tibet (Himalayan facies). Other races in N. Yunnan and Szechwan.

GENERAL HABITS: Usually keeps in small flocks of 6 to 10 birds. A great skulker, keeping to dense thickets and seldom showing itself. Also less noisy, and therefore perhaps easily overlooked. Has 'a piercing eight-syllabled call' (Ludlow).

NESTING: No record for Sikkim. Very little known, and that apparently only from two nests taken in May and ? near Darjeeling. B. B. Osmaston described one he found at about 8500 ft. as 'of moss, dry grass and bamboo leaves, built in a small tree in scrub forest, about 6 ft. from the ground'. It contained one egg, spotless blue, measuring about 31×21 mm.

RACIAL CHARACTERISTICS, MEASUREMENTS, ETC: A specimen (♀) collected by the Loke-Sálim Ali Survey measures: Wing 122; bill damaged; tarsus 45; tail 149 mm.

Three ♂♂ in the Schäfer collection have Wing 126, 130, 133 mm.; 1 ♀ 117 mm.

Iris greyish khaki; legs, feet and claws pale flesh colour.

## THE SIKKIM GREYSIDED LAUGHING THRUSH

*Garrulax caerulatus caerulatus* (Hodgson)

*Cinclosoma caerulatus* Hodgson, 1836, *Asiat. Res.* 19: 147—Nepal.

**Plate 20, fig. 7 (facing p. 225)**

F.B.I. 1: 141

LOCAL NAMES: Tarma--pho (Lepcha); Piang-kam (Bhutia).

SIZE: Myna+.

FIELD CHARACTERS: Forehead and face black; ear-coverts black and rufous-tipped whitish; cheeks reddish brown. Upper parts, sides of neck, and crown rufous-brown—the last with fine black scale-like markings. Underparts and chin white, excepting sides of breast and belly which are ashy grey, and extreme point of chin which is black. Sexes alike.

STATUS AND HABITAT: Occupies a zone between about 3500 and 6000 ft. elevation (Toong, Chungthang, Singhik, Gangtok, Rinchinpong, Lingtam) and perhaps higher as in Nepal. Stevens is reported to have obtained it breeding at 9000 ft. in Sikkim. Affects scrub and 'maling' bamboo-covered hillsides.

DISTRIBUTION OUTSIDE SIKKIM: Nepal, Bhutan, Assam hills north of Brahmaputra River; hills of NE. Burma. The species extends to northern Yunnan.

GENERAL HABITS: Social. Typical of the laughing thrushes as described. 'Sisterhoods' of 7 to 12 birds or more feed on the ground as well as in low bushes. Said to be more silent than the Rufous-necked species (next). Has a sweet, human-like, chuckling whistle of three or four notes in addition to some harsh calls. Flight weak and ill-sustained. Usually escapes by hopping from branch to branch in the undergrowth.

NESTING: *Season*—May and June. *Nest*—a rather shallow cup of dry bamboo leaves and twigs lined with root fibres, 6 to 12 ft. up in a tree. *Eggs*—2 or 3, glossy pale blue, unmarked. Size about 30×22 mm.

RACIAL CHARACTERISTICS, MEASUREMENTS, ETC: The chestnut-brown tail without pale tips is a conspicuous feature of this race. The adjoining races of the Assam hills have the three outermost pairs of rectrices broadly white-tipped. Two Sikkim specimens in the Chicago Museum of Natural History measure:

| | Wing | Bill | Tarsus | Tail |
|---|---|---|---|---|
| ♂ | 109 | 24 | 42 | 124 mm. |
| ♀ | 105 | 25 | 40 | 114 mm. |

Three unsexed skins in the Schäfer collection (Gangtok, February and June) have Wing 103, 108, 110 mm. (Stresemann).

Iris red or reddish brown; eye-rim (circumorbital) livid; bill horny black, paler at base; legs and feet pale flesh. (Whistler MS.)

## THE RUFOUSNECKED LAUGHING THRUSH

*Garrulax ruficollis* (Jardine & Selby)

*Ianthocincla ruficollis* Jardine & Selby, 1838, Ill. Orn. 2: pl. 21—Himalayas (=Sikkim, restricted by Meinertzhagen, 1928, *Ibis:* 515).

F.B.I. 1: 139

LOCAL NAME: Rapchen-pho (Lepcha).

SIZE: Myna+.

FIELD CHARACTERS: A dark babbler with black head and throat and conspicuous chestnut sides to the neck.

Crown and nape slaty grey; rest of head (including ear-coverts), throat, and centre of upper breast black. Sides of neck bright chestnut. Upper plumage and underparts olive-brown excepting centre of lower abdomen and under tail-coverts, which are bright chestnut. Sexes alike.

STATUS AND HABITAT: Resident; normally at low elevations—between 2000 (Martam) and 4500 ft. Occasionally to about 5500 ft. (Gangtok, Rinchinpong). Affects bushes and bramble thickets on scrubby hillsides and on the edge of terrace cultivation.

DISTRIBUTION OUTSIDE SIKKIM: Eastern Nepal; Bhutan to NE. frontier. Assam; Manipur; Chittagong hill tracts (E. Pakistan).

GENERAL HABITS: Social. Invariably in noisy flocks or 'sisterhoods' of 7 to 12 or more, hopping about on the ground or in low shrubs. The birds rummage amongst the mulch, flicking aside or turning over the dry leaves in search of insects, and also feed on wild raspberries and other fruit. Constant churring calls as they work through the thickets keep a sisterhood together. They have a three-noted mellow whistle, the first note of which sounds as if produced by a broken reed; and from time to time the birds burst into loud squeaky choruses.

NESTING: *Season*—mainly May. *Nest*—a deep cup of grass, bamboo leaves, weed stems, etc. bound together with tendrils, usually well concealed, 3 to 5 ft. up in a bamboo clump or bramble thicket. *Eggs*—3 or 4, very pale bluish white, unmarked, glossy. Size about 25×20 mm.

RACIAL CHARACTERISTICS, MEASUREMENTS, ETC: A ♂ collected by the Sikkim Survey measures: Wing 98; bill 23; tarsus 37; tail 111 mm. Another ♂ in the Schäfer collection has Wing 100 mm.

Three specimens from Sadiya (NE. Assam) measure:

| | Wing | Bill | Tarsus | Tail |
|---|---|---|---|---|
| 1 ♂ | 99 | 24 | 37 | 108 mm. |
| 2 ♀♀ | 98-100 | 24 | 36-37 | 109 mm. |

Iris brownish crimson; eye-rim (circumorbital) yellow; bill, legs, feet and claws dark horny brown.

## THE STREAKED LAUGHING THRUSH

*Garrulax lineatus setafer* (Hodgson)

*Cinclosoma setafer* Hodgson, 1836, *Asiat. Res.* **19**: 148—Nepal.

F.B.I. **1**: 180

LOCAL NAME:

SIZE: Myna—.

FIELD CHARACTERS: A small, finely white-streaked olive-rufous laughing thrush with ashy brownish head and rusty ear-coverts. Longish, loose tail cross-rayed rufous, ending in a black band with terminal grey tips. No distinct eyebrow. Sexes alike.

STATUS AND HABITAT: Rare. Not recorded by Stevens, nor met with by Schäfer or the recent Sikkim Survey. Meinertzhagen only once came upon a small party feeding on a forest path at 4700 ft. near Dentam (W. Sikkim). Frequents open scrub country; avoids forest.

DISTRIBUTION OUTSIDE SIKKIM: Central Nepal. The species, in several races, extends throughout the Himalayas (between about 5000 and 9000 ft.) from Baluchistan to Bhutan.

GENERAL HABITS: Skulking, sociable birds, met with in parties of 4 or 5, hopping on the ground under bushes, scuttling like rats from cover to cover on alarm, seldom flying. They keep up a churring and squeaky conversation among themselves. In the breeding season the males sing from exposed bush-tops etc. a clear, squeaky, whistling song well syllabified by Whistler as *titty-titty-we-are*, rapidly repeated. Insects as well as berries are eaten.

NESTING: No record from Sikkim. Elsewhere *season*—April to August. *Nest*—a deep cup of grass, rootlets, etc. placed in a wild raspberry or similar bush, 3 to 7 ft. up, well concealed. *Eggs*—3, turquoise or greenish blue, unmarked. Size about 25×18 mm.

RACIAL CHARACTERISTICS, MEASUREMENTS, ETC: Differs from the better known W. Himalayan race *lineatus* in having the head browner (less ashy), the rump darker, the ear-coverts and streaks of the underparts darker, the streaks more extensive on each individual feather. The black subterminal bands on the tail are well marked. ♂♀ Wing 74-77; bill 18.5-20.5; tarsus *c.* 27; tail *c.* 90 mm. (Fauna).

Iris brown; bill horny brown, paler on commissure and lower mandible: mouth pale yellowish flesh; legs and feet pale horny brown.

## THE BLUEWINGED LAUGHING THRUSH

*Garrulax squamatus* (Gould)

*Ianthocincla squamata* Gould, 1835, *Proc. Zool. Soc. London*: 48—Himalayas (=Sikkim).

**Plate 20, fig. 9 (facing p. 225)**

F.B.I. 1: 174

LOCAL NAMES: Tarmal-pho (Lepcha); Nabom (Bhutia).

SIZE: Myna.

FIELD CHARACTERS: Upper plumage rufescent olive-brown; lower plumage fulvous. Scalloped with brown scale-like markings above; more finely below. A black eyebrow from forehead to nape. Upper and under tail-coverts bright chestnut. Flight feathers in the closed wing pale blue and chestnut. Tail bronzy brown with bright cinnamon tip. Sexes alike. Individually somewhat variable in coloration.

The blue and chestnut wings and bright cinnamon tail-tip are conspicuous in flight, and leading pointers to its identity.

STATUS AND HABITAT: Occurs normally between about 4000 and 8000 feet. Meinertzhagen obtained specimens at 11,900 feet (Sandakphu) in January. Affects ringal bamboo jungle and rhododendron forest with dense scrubby undergrowth.

DISTRIBUTION OUTSIDE SIKKIM: Nepal, Bhutan, Assam hills north and south of the Brahmaputra. Manipur, N. Burma, Shan States, N. Yunnan, Tonkin.

GENERAL HABITS: Keeps in pairs or small family parties. Shy and an inveterate skulker in undergrowth, seldom taking wing when alarmed, diving into thicker cover and working its way to safety silently and unseen. Its notes, not often heard, are described as 'rich and full'.

NESTING: *Season*—April to June. *Nest*—a deep compact cup of leaves, fine twigs, grass, etc., scrappily draped with green moss on the outside and lined with fine roots and rhizomorphs. Placed 2 to 7 ft. up in a bush or sapling. *Eggs*—2 to 4, deep greenish blue, unspotted, with a fine satiny surface. Sikkim eggs average about 30×22 mm.

RACIAL CHARACTERISTICS, MEASUREMENTS, ETC: ♂♀ Wing 93-99; bill *c.* 20; tarsus *c.* 37; tail *c.* 100 mm. (Stuart Baker).

Iris bluish white (brown in juvenile); bill black, paler and greyer at tip and on base of lower mandible; legs and feet pale flesh to fleshy brown.

## THE PLAINCOLOURED LAUGHING THRUSH

*Garrulax subunicolor subunicolor* (Blyth)

*Trochalopteron subunicolor* Blyth, 1843, *Jour. Asiat. Soc. Bengal* 12: 952—Nepal.

F.B.I. 1: 171

LOCAL NAME:

SIZE: Myna.

FIELD CHARACTERS: Forehead, crown and nape dark ashy brown with black scaly markings. Plumage above and below olive-brown, fulvescent on abdomen. Scaly black markings on upper back, throat, breast and upper abdomen conspicuous. Tail olive-brown and black, unmarked; tipped with white. A golden olive-yellow patch on flight feathers. Sexes alike.

The brownish plumage with bright olive-yellow wings and white-tipped tail simplify identification in flight.

STATUS AND HABITAT: Local and patchy, normally at high elevations between about 5000 and 12,000 ft. (Chungthang, Lachen, Lachung, Changu, Sandakphu). Not uncommon where occurring. Affects thickets of *Rubus* and dwarf rhododendron etc.

DISTRIBUTION OUTSIDE SIKKIM: Nepal; Bhutan to NE. Assam, north of Brahmaputra River. The species, in other races, extends to N. Burma, N. Yunnan, Tonkin.

GENERAL HABITS: Often seen in flocks of 20 birds or more. Besides the usual squeaky conversational chuckles, has a clear whistle of four notes.

NESTING: *Season*—chiefly May and June. *Nest*—a large cup of grass and mosses, lined with soft bamboo leaves; placed in a low shrub, about 3 ft. up. *Eggs*—3 or 4, spotless blue. Size about 30×23 mm.

RACIAL CHARACTERISTICS, MEASUREMENTS, ETC: Stuart Baker gives the measurements (♂♀) as: Wing 90-95; bill *c.* 18; tarsus *c.* 35; tail 100-105 mm.

Seven adult examples (♂♀) in Schäfer's Sikkim collection have Wing 89-96 mm. (av. 93.0 mm.).

Iris reddish brown or straw colour; bill blackish brown; legs and feet horny brown.

## THE BLACKFACED LAUGHING THRUSH

***Garrulax affinis bethelae* Rand & Fleming**

*Garrulax affinis bethelae* Rand & Fleming, 1956, *Fieldiana* 39 (1): 2—Thangu, Sikkim.

F.B.I. 1: 172

LOCAL NAME:

SIZE: Myna+.

FIELD CHARACTERS: Head and chin black. Cheeks glistening white. Ear-coverts black with a diffuse greyish white patch on sides of nape. Upper parts rufous-brown scalloped with fine brownish scale-like markings. Upper tail-coverts ferruginous. Lower parts rufous-brown with diffuse grey spots on breast, and grey scaly marking on upper abdomen. Bright yellowish olive in wings and tail, both of which are broadly tipped slaty blue. Sexes alike.

The scalloped back, black face, white cheek-patches and greyish sides of head, combined with yellow-and-bluish wings and tail, are diagnostic in the field.

STATUS AND HABITAT: A high-elevation species normally ranging between about 9000 and 13,000 ft. (Lachen, Lachung, Yumthang, Thangu, Karponang, Changu). Recorded at about 5500 ft. in February (Gangtok, Chungthang). Frequents juniper and bramble thickets around alpine pastures in rhododendron and fir biotope, and ringal bamboo jungle.

DISTRIBUTION OUTSIDE SIKKIM: E. Nepal, Bhutan, SE. Tibet (Himalayan facies). The species is found in N. Burma, N. Yunnan, Szechwan, Tonkin.

GENERAL HABITS: Has perhaps the highest altitudinal range of all the laughing thrushes. Small parties sometimes met with among snow-covered shrubs with the temperature below freezing point. Has the usual low conversational chuckles, and also a melodious whistling 'song' *to-we* or *to-we-you*.

NESTING: *Season*—May and June. *Nest*—a deep, well built cup of moss, grass, roots, etc., lined with finer roots and rhizomorphs. Placed 5 to 8 feet up in a *Viburnum*, rhododendron or similar bush. *Eggs*—2 or 3, blue with a greenish tinge, sparsely spotted and blotched with brownish- or reddish black, and with one or two short twisted lines. Size about 29×21 mm.

RACIAL CHARACTERISTICS, MEASUREMENTS, ETC: Two specimens collected by the Sikkim Survey measure:

| | Wing | Bill | Tarsus | Tail |
|---|---|---|---|---|
| 1 ♂ | 115 | 24 | 40 | 135 mm. |
| 1 o? | 103 | 23.5 | 40 | 121 mm. |

A large series (28 adult ♂♀) in the Schäfer Sikkim collection gives Wing 99 (♀)-109 (♂) mm.

Iris olive-brown; bill black; legs and feet pinkish brown or brownish flesh colour; claws horny brown.

## THE SIKKIM REDHEADED LAUGHING THRUSH

*Garrulax erythrocephalus nigrimentum* (Oates)

*Trochalopteron nigrimentum* Oates, 1889, Fauna Brit. India, Birds, ed. 1, 1: 91—Himalayas, Nepal to Assam (inferentially restricted to Sikkim by Kinnear, 1937, *Ibis:* 32).

**Plate 20, fig. 2 (facing p. 225)**

F.B.I. 1: 163

LOCAL NAME:

SIZE: Myna+.

FIELD CHARACTERS: An uncrested olive-brown and fulvous laughing thrush with chestnut-red crown, blackish chin and face, and a bright ferruginous nape patch and wing-shoulder. Upper back olive-brown with bold black oval spots and paler scalloping. Finer crescentic black spots on sides of neck and ferruginous breast. Some golden olive-yellow and slaty grey in wings and tail. Lower parts ferruginous. Sexes alike.

STATUS AND HABITAT: Occupies an altitudinal zone between 5000 and 12,000 ft. (Gangtok, Lachen, Lachung, Manshitang, Chiabhanjan, Phalut), even in winter. Affects dense shrubby growth of dwarf rhododendron, *Berberis*, brambles, etc. on hillsides, along stream valleys, and at the edge of cultivation and pastures. It was noted as the commonest laughing thrush at *c.* 9000 ft. in the Lachung area in February and March.

DISTRIBUTION OUTSIDE SIKKIM: E. Nepal, Bhutan, SE. Tibet (Himalayan facies), Assam hills north of Brahmaputra River. The species, in numerous other races, extends across from SE. Kashmir down through Assam, Burma, Thailand to Tenasserim, Malaya, etc.

GENERAL HABITS: Perhaps less gregarious than most other laughing thrushes. A great skulker, and not noisy. A low conversational chuckling murmur usually betrays a party moving amongst the thickets. Has a loud, musical, double-noted whistle *pheeou* or *piweep*, constantly repeated, by an imitation of which the birds can be decoyed. Food and feeding habits do not differ from those described.

NESTING: *Season*—May to July. *Nest*—a deep cup of grass and dead leaves secured with creeper stems and tendrils, scantily lined with fine grass and roots. Occasionally covered with green moss. Built in a small tree or dense bush normally between 3 and 8 feet up. *Eggs*—2, rarely 3, blue-green, boldly blotched and streaked with deep reddish brown to black. Size about 29×21 mm.

RACIAL CHARACTERISTICS, MEASUREMENTS, ETC: The Sikkim race *nigrimentum* differs from the W. Himalayan *erythrocephalus* in having the ear-coverts black (finely edged pinkish white—scaly patterned) instead of chestnut (tipped black and white).

Five specimens collected by the Sikkim Survey measure:

| | Wing | Bill | Tarsus | Tail |
|---|---|---|---|---|
| 1 ♂ | 104 | 24 | 38 | 114 mm. |
| 4 ♀♀ | 100-103 | 22.5-24 | 39-40 | 111-125 mm. |

Twelve adult ♂♀ in Schäfer's Sikkim collection have Wing 98-107 mm.

Iris olive-brown or hazel-brown; bill horny black; legs and feet brownish flesh colour; claws horny brown.

## THE NEPAL CRIMSONWINGED LAUGHING THRUSH

*Garrulax phoeniceus phoeniceus* (Gould)

*Ianthocincla phoenicea* Gould, 1837, Icones Avium, pl. 3—Nepal.

**Plate 20, fig. 1** (facing p. 225)

F.B.I. 1: 168

LOCAL NAMES: Tilji-pho (Lepcha); Repcha (Bhutia).

SIZE: Myna.

FIELD CHARACTERS: A crestless olive-brown laughing thrush with bright crimson sides of head and neck, wings and under tail-coverts. A black supercilium. Tail black, broadly tipped and margined outwardly with orange. Sexes alike.

The brownish coloration and dazzling crimson wings make the bird quite unmistakable in flight.

STATUS AND HABITAT: Apparently not uncommon at low and moderate elevations—foothills to about 6000 ft.—with no perceptible up-and-down seasonal movement. Affects heavy scrub in overgrown jungle clearings, on the edge of cultivation and along stream valleys.

DISTRIBUTION OUTSIDE SIKKIM: Nepal; Bhutan to extreme NE. Assam, north of Brahmaputra River. Other races in Assam south of the Brahmaputra, Manipur, N. Burma, N. Thailand, SE. Yunnan.

GENERAL HABITS: Typical. Normally seen in pairs and small parties. Has a variety of squeaky conversational notes in addition to some musical calls.

NESTING: *Season*—May and June. *Nest*—the usual cup of grasses etc. covered on the outside with green moss. Placed in a bramble thicket or shrub, 4 to 10 ft. from the ground. *Eggs*—2 to 4, blue, normally with numerous short dark brown lines and some spots. Size about 26×19 mm.

RACIAL CHARACTERISTICS, MEASUREMENTS, ETC: The adjoining race of Assam, *bakeri*, is paler above and below, and has the ashy grey wash on centre of abdomen more pronounced.

Stuart Baker gives the measurements (♂♀) as: Wing 81-93; bill *c.* 18; tarsus *c.* 32; tail *c.* 100 mm.

Iris brown (juv.) to deep crimson or lac-red; orbital skin dull leaden brown; bill blackish brown; legs and feet brown with a purplish tinge.

## THE SILVEREARED MESIA

*Leiothrix argentauris argentauris* (Hodgson)

*Mesia argentauris* Hodgson, 1838, *Ind. Review* **2**: 88—Nepal.

F.B.I. 1: 354

LOCAL NAME: Dang-rapchil-pho (Lepcha).

SIZE: Bulbul.

FIELD CHARACTERS: A bright-coloured babbler, chiefly olive-yellow, fulvous yellow, slaty green, crimson, and black. *Male: Above*, forehead golden yellow; crown and nape black, set off by glistening silvery white ear-coverts. Rest of upper parts fulvous yellow, slaty and slaty green, with crimson upper tail-coverts. Tail blackish, edged with yellowish. Wings edged yellow and crimson. *Below*, chin and throat deep orange-yellow, changing to olive-yellow on rest of underparts. Under tail-coverts crimson.

*Female:* Upper and lower tail-coverts orange-buff instead of crimson. Immature bird like female, but with the crown yellowish.

STATUS AND HABITAT: Resident. Less common than the Pekin Robin (next), with more or less the same altitudinal range (3000 to 7000 ft.) though both may also occur lower down (Dikchu, *c.* 2000 ft.). Affects identical facies—secondary jungle, scrub-covered ravines, etc.

DISTRIBUTION OUTSIDE SIKKIM: Garhwal, Nepal, Bhutan, Assam hills north and south of the Brahmaputra; Manipur. The species extends through Burma, Thailand, Malaya, Yunnan, Indonesia, Indochina.

GENERAL HABITS: Very similar to the Pekin Robin, though perhaps more strictly arboreal. In large mixed hunting flocks in winter, rapidly flowing from tree to tree. Makes occasional short flycatcher-like sallies after winged insects disturbed in the foliage, in addition to the tit-like acrobatics while searching under leaves. Silent except for a low, subdued conversational cheeping. The clear, sweet, whistling summer song of the male has been rendered as *cheroi-cherit*.

NESTING: *Season*—mainly May and June. *Nest, eggs* and site indistinguishable from those of the Pekin Robin, so that unless the owner of a nest is actually seen or collected it is not safe to give it a name.

RACIAL CHARACTERISTICS, MEASUREMENTS, ETC: Tail square-ended (not slightly forked) and with the outermost feathers curving outwards. In all other respects obviously a close relation of the Pekin Robin. The Fauna gives the measurements as: ♂♀ Wing 74-78; bill 12-13; tarsus *c.* 25; tail *c.* 45 mm.

Three ♂♂ collected in Sikkim by Schäfer have Wing 74, 75, 76 mm.

Iris brown to red-brown; bill orange, tinged with brown at base; legs and feet yellowish flesh.

## THE REDBILLED LEIOTHRIX, or 'PEKIN ROBIN'

*Leiothrix lutea calipyga* (Hodgson)
*Bahila calipyga* Hodgson, 1837, *Ind. Review* 2: 88—Nepal.

**Plate 17, fig. 11** (facing p. 208)

F.B.I. 1: 328

LOCAL NAME: Rapchil-pho (Lepcha).

SIZE: Sparrow.

FIELD CHARACTERS: A sprightly, handsome, crestless, olive-green bird with bright yellow throat and breast, a yellow ring round the eye, a narrow dusky-green moustachial streak, and conspicuous coral red bill. Closed wings edged with yellow and crimson. Tail glistening black, slightly forked as in the rosefinch, narrowly tipped white. Ear-coverts silvery grey. The *female* differs in having the crimson of the wings replaced by yellow.

STATUS AND HABITAT: Fairly common between about 3000 and 7000 ft. elevation, in the Great Rangeet and Teesta valleys (Singhik, Dentam, Kewzing, Gangtok). Affects secondary jungle. Partial to overgrown ravines and tangled scrub of wild raspberry (*Rubus*) etc.

DISTRIBUTION OUTSIDE SIKKIM: Throughout the Himalayas from about Simla to the NE. frontier; Assam hills; Manipur. Other races in Burma, Yunnan, Szechwan.

GENERAL HABITS: Sociable. Parties, often in the usual mixed bird associations. Chiefly arboreal, but keeps more to thickets and shrubbery than to tree-tops. Also feeds on the ground, under bushes, hopping about like a laughing thrush and flicking aside the dry leaves. *Food:* insects as well as berries and seeds. *Calls:* a pleasant conversational *tee-tee-tee* kept up whilst a party is feeding. The loud, cheerful song of the male is commonly heard on the approach of the breeding season. In timbre, quality and pattern it is reminiscent of the Redwhiskered Bulbul's—rather more prolonged and more musical.

NESTING: *Season*—mainly May and June. *Nest*—a substantially made cup of dead leaves, moss, lichens and pliant twigs, lined with roots and finer material. Placed 2 to 8 ft. up in a tangled bush or sapling, in an overgrown ravine. *Eggs*—white to pale blue, boldly blotched with dark brown or umber brown. Size about 22×16 mm.

RACIAL CHARACTERISTICS, MEASUREMENTS, ETC: The Fauna gives the measurements as: Wing ♂♂ 65-71, ♀♀ 61-65; bill 10-11; tarsus *c.* 25; tail 55-60 mm.

A Sikkim Survey specimen (♀) measures: Wing 69; bill 14.5; tarsus 24; tail 58 mm.

Iris brown or reddish brown; bill coral red, blackish at base of both mandibles; legs, feet and claws pale horny brown.

## THE FIRETAILED MYZORNIS

*Myzornis pyrrhoura* Blyth

*Myzornis pyrrhoura* Blyth, 1843, *Jour. Asiat. Soc. Bengal* 12 (2): 984, *ex* Hodgson MS.—Nepal.

**Plate 21, fig. 2** (facing p. 272)

F.B.I. 1: 345

LOCAL NAME: Lho-sagvit-pho (Lepcha).

SIZE: Sparrow –.

FIELD CHARACTERS: *Male: Above,* bright dark green; forehead and crown scaled (or scalloped) with black. A black band from bill through eye, bordered above and below with brighter green streaks. *Below,* breast and abdomen largely suffused with rusty red; vent and under tail-coverts fulvous yellow or chestnut. Flight feathers black, largely tipped with white and pinkish, and margined with red. Tail largely red and green.

*Female: Above,* head less marked with black and therefore a lighter green; below duller and more orange.

STATUS AND HABITAT: Uncommon and locally distributed at elevations between 6000 and 12,000 ft. (Gangtok, Singalila Ridge, Cho La Range). Affects rhododendron forest.

DISTRIBUTION OUTSIDE SIKKIM: Nepal, Bhutan, N. Assam hills (?). NE. Burma to NW. Yunnan.

GENERAL HABITS: Imperfectly known. Arboreal. Keeps in pairs or small parties searching for insect (?) food in bushes and low trees. It habitually feeds at rhododendron flowers, hovering in front of them with rapidly beating wings in the manner of a flowerpecker, and is said also to make short sallies like a flycatcher. Wild raspberries have been taken from the stomach of a specimen. Its note is described as 'a feeble but distinct call'.

NESTING: Unknown authentically.

RACIAL CHARACTERISTICS, MEASUREMENTS, ETC: The Fauna gives for ♂ ♀ Wing 59-63; bill *c.* 13; tarsus *c.* 22-23; tail *c.* 70-75 mm.

Two ♂ ♂ collected by Schäfer at Gangtok have Wing 62, 63; 3 ♀ ♀ 58, 60, 60 mm.

Iris dark brown; bill black; legs and feet yellowish or greenish brown.

## THE NEPAL CUTIA

*Cutia nipalensis nipalensis* Hodgson

*Cutia nipalensis* Hodgson, 1836, *Jour. Asiat. Soc. Bengal* 5: 774—Nepal.

**Plate 17, fig. 10** (facing p. 208)

F.B.I. 1: 329

LOCAL NAMES: Rapnoon or Rapnun-pho; Motum-pho (Lepcha).

SIZE: Between Sparrow and Bulbul.

FIELD CHARACTERS: A handsome, rather dumpy, arboreal bird,

chestnut and grey-blue with bold black rib-like markings on the white underside.

*Male: Above,* crown slaty blue; lores and a broad band through eye and ear-coverts to nape glossy black; tail black; rest of upper parts bright chestnut. *Below,* pale buffy white; sides of body with bold black rib-like bars.

*Female:* Crown paler; band round head chocolate-brown instead of black; back and scapulars reddish brown with large oval black spots. Rest as in male.

STATUS AND HABITAT: Locally distributed between *c.* 5000 and 7000 ft. elevation. Met with by the Sikkim Survey only near Singhik, *c.* 4500 ft. Schäfer collected specimens at Gangtok, 6000-7000 ft., January to March. Affects oak and evergreen forest.

DISTRIBUTION OUTSIDE SIKKIM: E. Nepal, Bhutan, Assam hills north of Brahmaputra River; Naga Hills, Manipur. The species extends to N. Burma, NW. Thailand, Yunnan, Tonkin, Malaya, Indochina.

GENERAL HABITS: Arboreal. Keeps in small parties, commonly in the mixed roving bands of small babblers and other birds, usually high up in the canopy foliage. Runs swiftly along the branches. Feeds on insects as well as berries and seeds. Very silent. Its call or song is unrecorded.

NESTING: Unknown.

RACIAL CHARACTERISTICS, MEASUREMENTS, ETC: ♂♀ Wing 90-96; bill *c.* 17; tarsus *c.* 30; tail *c.* 55 mm. (Fauna). A Survey ♂ has Wing 89 mm. Seven examples collected by Schäfer give Wing 3 ♂♂ 90, 91, 92; 4 ♀♀ 87, 88, 89, 89, mm. (Stresemann).

Iris crimson-brown; bill: upper mandible black, lower bluish horn, blackish at base and tip; legs, feet and claws bright chrome yellow.

## THE RUFOUSBELLIED SHRIKE-BABBLER

*Pteruthius rufiventer rufiventer* Blyth

*Pteruthius rufiventer* Blyth, 1842, *Jour. Asiat. Soc. Bengal* **11**: 183, No locality=Darjeeling.

**Plate 17, fig. 7** (facing p. 208)

F.B.I. **1**: 337

LOCAL NAME:

SIZE: Bulbul.

FIELD CHARACTERS: A long-tailed shrike-babbler. *Male: Above,* chestnut. Forehead, crown, nape, sides of head, wings and tail glossy black, the last tipped chestnut. *Below,* chin, throat and upper breast ashy, divided from black of head by a white line. Rest of underparts pinkish brown, paler on abdomen. A patch of golden yellow on either side of breast.

*Female: Above,* bright greenish yellow, irregularly barred with black; rump and upper tail-coverts chestnut. Crown and nape black;

forehead largely grey. Wings black and yellowish green. *Below*, dark vinous brown with a yellowish patch on either side of breast. Sides of head, chin, throat, and breast grey. A black patch on ear-coverts.

STATUS AND HABITAT: Resident. Sparse. Affects canopy foliage of lofty trees in forest, between *c.* 6000 and 8000 ft. elevation.

DISTRIBUTION OUTSIDE SIKKIM: E. Nepal, Bhutan (?), Assam hills north and south of Brahmaputra River; Manipur hills, NE. Burma to N. Yunnan and N. Tonkin.

GENERAL HABITS: Little recorded beyond that it goes about in small flocks and may sometimes present a striking resemblance to Hodgson's Broadbill (*Serilophus rubropygius*), both in its superficial appearance and lethargic behaviour.

NESTING: Unknown.

RACIAL CHARACTERISTICS, MEASUREMENTS, ETC: Differs from other shrike-babblers in its much longer, greatly graduated tail. Stuart Baker gives the measurements as: ♂♀ Wing 85-88; bill 15-16; tarsus *c.* 30; tail *c.* 85 mm. Two specimens secured by Schäfer at Gangtok have Wing 88 (♂) and 89 (♀) mm.

'Iris bluish grey; bill upper mandible black, lower pearl grey; feet brown to brownish whitish' (Ripley).

## THE REDWINGED SHRIKE-BABBLER

*Pteruthius flaviscapis validirostris* Koelz

*Pteruthius erythropterus validirostris* Koelz, 1951, *Jour. Zool. Soc. India* 3: 28—Kohima, Naga Hills, Assam.

**Plate 17, fig. 6** (facing p. 208) [1]

F.B.I. 1: 331

LOCAL NAME:

SIZE: Between Bulbul and Myna.

FIELD CHARACTERS: A stocky, short-tailed, black-and-white shrike-like bird with chestnut wings. *Male: Above*, upper part of head black with a broad white band from above eye to nape. Back grey; closed wings bright chestnut; tail black. *Below*, pale greyish white; posterior flanks vinaceous. In flight the black head and tail, the white inner edges to the primaries, and the white underwing, give a very white and black overall effect to the bird.

*Female: Above*, upper part of head bluish grey with a faint broken white supercilium. Upper plumage chiefly olive-grey; closed wings chestnut and yellowish green. Tail largely black and green, tipped yellow. *Below*, pale buff.

STATUS AND HABITAT: Fairly common. Resident between 1000 ft. and 6000 ft. elevation (Rangpo, Martam, Kewzing, Rinchinpong, Gangtok and elsewhere in the Rangeet and Teesta valleys). Stevens apparently found it as high as 9500 ft. in winter. Affects *Schima*, oak, rhododendron and mixed evergreen forest on hillsides.

[1] Captioned as *Pteruthius e. erythropterus*, the old name since revised (Ripley, 1960, Synopsis Bds. Ind. Pakistan: 400).

DISTRIBUTION OUTSIDE SIKKIM: The Himalayas from Murree to the NE. frontier; Assam hills south of the Brahmaputra; Manipur. The species extends through Burma, Thailand, Malaya, Indonesia, Indochina.

GENERAL HABITS: Strictly arboreal. Parties, commonly in the mixed hunting bands which include drongos, minivets, nuthatches and many other species. The birds keep high up in the foliage and branches of forest trees, and hop from branch to branch in search of insects. Occasionally one will run briskly up and along a bough, or cling on the trunk sideways like a nuthatch, to peer into crevices of the bark or under moss. A harsh, quick-repeated grating call, like the 'churring' of a shrike, is sometimes uttered while the birds are foraging, occasionally varied by a loud *ke-kew* or *kew-kew* repeated 3 or 4 times (by the male ?). This has rather the tone-quality of a tailor bird's call (*Orthotomus*), but is much louder; it is usually prefaced by a subdued *kik* audible only at short range. This call is also reminiscent of the 'wailing' of a month-old domestic chicken that has got separated from its mother.

NESTING: *Season*—April (?), May, June. *Nest*—a loosely made cup of green moss, with a good deal of wool and cobwebs intermixed, lined with fine roots. Suspended like a hammock between horizontal twigs up near the tops of trees. Difficult to find and to get at. *Eggs*—2 or 3, white, with a faint tinge of lilac or pink, flecked with reddish- or purplish brown, more densely and forming a cap at the larger end. They resemble the eggs of the Himalayan Black Bulbul, and measure about 23×17 mm.

RACIAL CHARACTERISTICS, MEASUREMENTS, ETC: A Sikkim Survey specimen (♀) measures Wing 82.5; bill 19.5; tarsus 28.5; tail 60 mm.

Five ♂♂ in the Schäfer Sikkim collection have Wing 82-86 mm. (av. 84.4); 1 ♀ 85 mm.

Iris deep 'Nordic' blue (♂), or slaty grey (♀); bill: upper mandible black, lower mandible and commissure at gape of upper bluish grey; legs and feet brownish flesh; claws horny brown.

## THE GREEN SHRIKE-BABBLER

*Pteruthius xanthochloris xanthochloris* Gray

*Pteruthius xanthochlorus* [*sic*] Gray, 1846, Cat. Mamms. Birds Nepal: 95—Nepal.

F.B.I. 1: 335

LOCAL NAME:

SIZE: Sparrow−.

FIELD CHARACTERS: *Male: Above,* olive-green. Crown and nape blackish grey. Forehead, sides of crown, and around eye dark grey. Flight feathers and tail largely dark brown. Outer web of outermost rectrices and tips of the others whitish. A black patch on closed wing (primary coverts). *Below,* bright yellow, with pale ashy chin, throat and breast.

*Female* similar, but crown and nape dark grey, paler at the sides and round eye.

STATUS AND HABITAT: According to Stevens, found up to higher elevations than the Redwinged and Chestnut-throated Shrike-Babblers —in winter between 7000 and 9500 ft. (Lachung, Karponang). Schäfer procured specimens at Gangtok, Lachen, Lachung and Manshitang.

DISTRIBUTION OUTSIDE SIKKIM: Nepal, Bhutan, Chin Hills (Burma). The race *occidentalis* occurs from W. Nepal westward to the Sutlej valley (NW. Himalayas). The species extends to Yunnan, Szechwan and N. Tonkin.

GENERAL HABITS: Strictly arboreal. In pairs or small (family?) parties. Possibly commoner than it seems, since it is apt to be easily overlooked or mistaken in the mixed hunting flocks of leaf warblers, small babblers, etc., with which it habitually associates in tall trees. But if carefully scrutinized, its quiet, unobtrusive demeanour and stiff upright carriage, and its habit of sometimes running along a horizontal branch like a nuthatch, usually give it away. The call is a quick-repeated single note *whit*.

NESTING: *Season*—May and June. Nests have been taken in wet tree forest on the Singalila Ridge (W. Sikkim). *Nest*—a fragile structure of fine fibres bound together with cobwebs, and plastered on the outside with lichens etc. Suspended hammockwise in a forked twig 2 to 12 ft. from the ground, sometimes higher. *Eggs*—3 or 4, pale pinkish- or greyish white, with grey-brown or reddish brown freckles, mostly at the larger end. Size about 19×15 mm.

RACIAL CHARACTERISTICS, MEASUREMENTS, ETC: ♂♀ Wing 62-65; bill *c.* 8; tarsus *c.* 20; tail 48-50 mm. (Fauna). Schäfer's Sikkim specimens measure: Wing 5 ♂♂ 60-63 (av. 61.8); 8 ♀♀ 58-64 (av. 61.0) mm.

Iris grey or grey-brown; bill black, blue-grey on lower mandible and tip; legs and feet greyish flesh.

First-year birds are distinguishable by pale tips to unmoulted great coverts.

The adjoining western race *occidentalis* is paler, with the whole crown and nape ashy in male; washed with greenish in female.

## THE CHESTNUT-THROATED SHRIKE-BABBLER

***Pteruthius melanotis melanotis*** **Hodgson**

*Pteruthius melanotis* Hodgson, 1847, *Jour. Asiat. Soc. Bengal* **16**: 448—Terai, SE. Himalayas.

**Plate 21, fig. 3 (facing p. 272)**

F.B.I. 1: 333

LOCAL NAME: Ku-er-pho (Lepcha).

SIZE: Sparrow—.

FIELD CHARACTERS: *Male: Above,* greenish yellow; closed wing bluish grey and brown, the feathers mostly white-tipped. A whit ring round eye, and a broad bluish white supercilium. Lores black continued in a line above eye and another below, meeting behind eye. A black spot behind yellow ear-coverts. Tail green and black, increasingly white-tipped on the outer feathers, the outermost almost wholly white. *Below*, chin, throat and upper breast deep chestnut; rest of underparts bright yellow.

*Female:* Like male but with tips of greater wing-coverts salmon colour instead of white. Chestnut restricted to throat only. Lines above and below eye pale brown instead of black.

STATUS AND HABITAT: Widely distributed and not uncommon at elevations up to *c.* 9000 ft. (Karponang), chiefly between *c.* 2000 and 6000 ft. (Martam, Singhik, Chungthang, Gangtok). Affects tall open forest.

DISTRIBUTION OUTSIDE SIKKIM: Nepal, Bhutan, Assam hills north and south of the Brahmaputra; Manipur. Burma, N. Thailand, Yunnan, N. Tonkin, N. Annam.

GENERAL HABITS: Pairs or small family parties almost invariably associated with large mixed hunting flocks of minlas, sivas, leaf warblers, and flycatchers (particularly *Rhipidura hypoxantha* and *Culicicapa*) in the foliage canopy of trees. Easily overlooked amongst them, but its slower actions usually give it away. *Food:* insects. Call recorded as a pleasant double note *too-weet, too-weet,* uttered when the birds get separated from one another.

NESTING: *Season*—April to June. *Nest*—a shallow cup of fern- and bracken-roots etc., covered on the outside with moss, lichens, and spiders' webs. Suspended hammockwise from forking horizontal twigs of small trees, between 5 and 15 ft. from the ground. *Eggs*—4 or 5, variable, normally pale lilac white, stippled with purplish brown, the marks coalescing to form a ring at the broad end. Size about 18×13 mm.

RACIAL CHARACTERISTICS, MEASUREMENTS, ETC: Specimens collected in Sikkim measure:

| | Wing | Bill | Tarsus | Tail |
|---|---|---|---|---|
| 2 ♂♂ | 61 | 11 | 20-20.5 | 39.5-42 mm. |
| 1 ♀ | 58 | 11.5 | 20 | 38 mm. |

Iris hazel-brown or brown; upper mandible slaty brown, lower dark plumbeous; legs and feet pale brownish flesh colour; claws horny brown.

## THE WHITEHEADED SHRIKE-BABBLER

### *Gampsorhynchus rufulus rufulus* Blyth

*Gampsorhynchus rufulus* Blyth, 1844, *Jour. Asiat. Soc. Bengal* 13, pl. i: 371—Darjeeling.

**Plate 17, fig. 2 (facing p. 208)**

F.B.I. 1: 231

LOCAL NAME: Chongto-phep-pho (Lepcha).

SIZE: About Myna.

FIELD CHARACTERS: General appearance and flight reminiscent of a bulbul. Whole head, neck and breast white. Upper plumage golden brown; lower plumage pale fulvous. Edge of wing, and upper wing-coverts (lesser and median) white. Sexes alike.

STATUS AND HABITAT: Not common. A fairly low-elevation species (Teesta Valley). Affects bamboo jungle with dense tangled undergrowth.

DISTRIBUTION OUTSIDE SIKKIM: Foothills, from Sikkim to NE. frontier; Assam. The species extends to Burma, Thailand, Malaya and Indochina.

GENERAL HABITS: Pairs or small noisy parties, often in association with scimitar babblers. Very like them in behaviour, but more arboreal. Inquisitive and normally not shy. According to Smythies (1953) has 'a weird grating call note *kaw-ka-yawk*'. *Food:* beetles and other insects; probably also berries.

NESTING: *Season*—end April to June. *Nest*—a shallow flimsy cup of dead leaves etc. untidily bound with cobwebs and lined with tendrils and fine roots. Built fairly low down (5 to 8 ft.) in a bush or bamboo clump. *Eggs*—2 to 4, variable, usually pale yellowish, freckled and blotched with reddish brown. Size about 24×18 mm.

RACIAL CHARACTERISTICS, MEASUREMENTS, ETC: Stuart Baker gives the measurements of this race as: ♂♀ Wing 90-100; bill 20-21; tarsus 26-28; tail 110-120 mm.

Iris yellow; bill dark horn; legs and feet brownish white.

## THE NEPAL BARWING

*Actinodura egertoni egertoni* Gould

*Actinodura egertoni* Gould, 1836, *Proc. Zool. Soc. London:* 18—Sikkim.

F.B.I. 1: 303

LOCAL NAME: Ramnio-pho (Lepcha).

SIZE: Bulbul+.

FIELD CHARACTERS: *Above*, forehead rufous; loose rounded crest rich ashy brown; back, rump and upper tail-coverts rufous-brown. Closed wings finely barred with blackish. Tail rufous-brown, graduated, cross-rayed; the rectrices broadly tipped with white. *Below*, chin rufous; rest of underparts fulvous excepting centre of abdomen, which is white. Sexes alike.

STATUS AND HABITAT: Fairly common at elevations between about 3500 and 6000 ft. (Rungbong and Teesta valleys, Gangtok, Penlom La). Affects evergreen forest; partial to dense secondary growth.

DISTRIBUTION OUTSIDE SIKKIM: Eastern Nepal, Bhutan, Dafla Hills. Other races in the Mishmi Hills, Assam hills south of the Brahmaputra, Burma, Thailand.

GENERAL HABITS: Arboreal. Keeps in flocks of 6 to 10 birds up in the canopy foliage of tall trees as well as in low shrubbery. Flocks 'follow-my-leader' from tree to tree, diving into undergrowth on alarm. Actions and general behaviour very like laughing thrushes and sibias, with which it often associates. *Food:* mainly insects; also berries. Occasionally flutters in front of a sprig for an insect, or clings upside down on a branch or mossy tree-trunk like a tit or nuthatch. A feeble conversational *cheep* is constantly uttered whilst hunting.

NESTING: *Season*—April to end June. *Nest*—a compact cup of grass, dry leaves, etc. mixed with tendrils and weed-stems, and lined with fine roots and rhizomorphs; usually draped on the outside with some moss. Placed 4 to 20 ft. up in a small tree or bush. *Eggs*—3 or 4, pale greyish blue with blotches, specks, loops and irregular lines of dark brown. Size about 30×18 mm. Both nest and eggs can easily be mistaken for those of some laughing thrush.

RACIAL CHARACTERISTICS, MEASUREMENTS, ETC: The Fauna gives the measurements as: ♂♀ Wing 80-85; bill *c.* 15; tarsus *c.* 28; tail 105-115 mm.

Seven specimens collected by Schäfer in Sikkim have Wing 82 (♀) to 90 (♂) mm. (av. 86.4)—Stresemann.

Iris bluish brown; bill dull horny yellow, darker on culmen and tip; legs and feet brownish flesh.

## THE SIKKIM HOARY BARWING

*Actinodura nipalensis vinctura* Ripley

*Actinodura nipalensis vinctura* Ripley, 1950, *Proc. Biol. Soc. Washington* 63: 104—Mangalbare, Dhankuta District, E. Nepal.

**Plate 17, fig. 9 (facing p. 208)**

F.B.I. 1: 307

LOCAL NAME: Ramnio-pho (Lepcha).

SIZE: Bulbul.

FIELD CHARACTERS: *Above,* forehead and loose mop-like crest, coffee brown with pale (hoary) shaft-streaks. Back rufescent brown; rump and upper tail-coverts more rufous. Tail graduated, browner than back, the feathers tipped with white. Exposed parts of closed wings and tail finely but conspicuously barred with blackish. Cheeks and moustachial streak blackish. *Below,* chin, throat and breast fulvous ashy; flanks, lower abdomen and under tail-coverts ferruginous. Sexes alike.

STATUS AND HABITAT: Fairly common at high elevations, *c.* 6000 to 10,500 ft., even in winter (Chungthang, Manshitang, Gangtok, Lachung, Lachen, Singalila Ridge). Affects mixed deciduous and conifer forest, and dense undergrowth of rhododendron, *Rubus,* etc.

DISTRIBUTION OUTSIDE SIKKIM: Eastern Nepal, Bhutan. The species in several races is found from central Nepal across to Assam, Manipur, Burma, N. Yunnan.

GENERAL HABITS: Very similar to the Nepal Barwing and to some of the smaller laughing thrushes. Keeps in small parties to tree-tops and moss- and lichen-covered trunks and branches. Also thickets. Some of its low churring notes resemble those of the Streaked Laughing Thrush. *Food:* insects and berries.

NESTING: *Season*—April to June. *Nest*—a neat compact cup of fine grass and lichen, lined with roots. *Eggs*—2 (or 3?), pale pinky white with bold primary blotches of reddish brown and secondary ones of inky grey, especially round the broad end. *Size* about 27×19 mm. Very few authentic nests and eggs have been taken, and there are some discrepancies in the descriptions.

RACIAL CHARACTERISTICS, MEASUREMENTS, ETC: The race *vinctura* differs from typical *nipalensis* (central Nepal) in having a much wider black terminal bar on the upper surface of the tail. Also in having the barring on the wings and tail heavier. The adjoining eastern race *daflaensis* (Dafla, Miri and Mishmi Hills) has the chin, throat and breast grey with brown centres to the feathers.

The Fauna gives the measurements as: ♂♀ Wing 84-91; bill 17-18; tarsus *c.* 30; tail 80-85 mm.

Eighteen specimens collected by Schäfer in Sikkim give Wing ♂♀ 86-94 mm.

Iris brown; bill black; legs and feet light greyish brown.

## THE REDTAILED MINLA

### *Minla ignotincta ignotincta* Hodgson

*Minla ignotincta* Hodgson, 1837, *Ind. Review* 2: 32. 44—Nepal.

**Plate 15, fig. 2** (facing p. 160)

F.B.I. 1: 355

LOCAL NAMES: Minla (Nepali); Megblim-ayene (Lepcha).

SIZE: Sparrow+.

FIELD CHARACTERS: *Male: Above,* chocolate brown with glossy black forehead, crown and nape. A broad white eyebrow from bill to nape. Ear-coverts and a band below the white supercilium, black. Tail black, tipped and edged with crimson, and with some white and pinkish near the base. Wings black, with white tips and crimson and orange margins. *Below,* pale yellow with whitish chin and throat.

*Female* like male but with the mantle olive-brown instead of chocolate; margins to wings and tail, and yellow of underparts paler.

When flitting high up in tall trees, the tail looks comparatively long and narrow, making the birds reminiscent of Redheaded Tits (*Æ. concinnus*).

STATUS AND HABITAT: Resident. Quite common in well-wooded country between *c.* 2000 and 9000 ft. (Martam, Singhik, Kewzing, Rinchinpong, Gangtok, Lachen, Lachung) with a marked seasonal altitudinal movement. Rare above 6000 ft. in winter.

DISTRIBUTION OUTSIDE SIKKIM: Nepal, Bhutan, Assam hills N. and S. of Brahmaputra River; Manipur. NE. Burma to Yunnan, Szechwan, Indochina.

GENERAL HABITS: Arboreal, sociable, and very similar to those of other sivas and leiothrix. The flocks keep up a continuous twittering cheep. The birds sometimes make short hopping or sidling spurts along a sloping branch, like a nuthatch, searching diligently for insects under the moss and lichens.

NESTING: *Season*—May and June. *Nest*—a rather deep cup of mosses, rootlets and hair, in a bushy tree at moderate heights. *Eggs*—normally 2, sometimes 3, pale blue sparsely and finely specked and spotted with black or reddish brown, coalescing in a ring about the larger end. Size about 20×14 mm.

RACIAL CHARACTERISTICS, MEASUREMENTS, ETC: The Sikkim Survey specimens measure:

| | Wing | Bill | Tarsus | Tail | |
|---|---|---|---|---|---|
| 1 (♂) | 67 | 13 | 20 | 55.5 | mm. |
| 3 ♀♀ | 63-66 | 12.5-14 | 19.5-20 | 56-57.5 | mm. |

Iris fawn colour to brown; bill: upper mandible horny brown, lower plumbeous, brownish at tip; legs, feet and claws olive-brown.

## THE BARTHROATED SIVA

### *Minla strigula strigula* (Hodgson)

*Siva strigula* Hodgson, 1837, *Ind. Review* 2: 89—Nepal.

**Plate 17, fig. 4** (facing p. 208)

F.B.I. 1: 313

LOCAL NAME: Megblim (Lepcha).

SIZE: Sparrow+.

FIELD CHARACTERS: *Above,* forehead, crown, and nape bright orange-brown; a yellow ring round the eye; sides of head grey, mottled with whitish and dusky. Rest of upper plumage slaty green. Tail chestnut-red and black, tipped with white. Wing-quills black and slaty grey, edged with orange and yellow and tipped with white. *Below,* bright yellow; throat paler and narrowly barred with black. A narrow black moustachial streak, and black patch on side of neck. Sexes alike.

The slightly tufted orange-brown head, black moustachial streak, barred throat, white-tipped chestnut-and-black tail, white-tipped black wings, and yellow underparts help diagnosis.

STATUS AND HABITAT: Fairly common between about 2500 and 9000 ft. with perhaps a slight downward movement from the highest levels in winter (Dikchu, Singhik, Rinchinpong, Kewzing, Gangtok, Chungthang, Lachung). Schäfer collected it at Changu, *c.* 12,500 ft. (Cho La Range) on 11 February. Affects oak and rhododendron forest.

DISTRIBUTION OUTSIDE SIKKIM: Nepal, Bhutan. The species, in several races, extends from NW. Himalayas to Yunnan; Assam, Burma, Thailand, Malaya, Indochina.

GENERAL HABITS: Arboreal. Sociable. Small flocks in the mixed itinerant bird associations, hunting energetically for insects among the canopy foliage of tall trees and shrubs in the manner of tits, and flowing from tree to tree. Berries are also eaten. Its most regular and almost inseparable feeding companions in these mixed parties are Redtailed Minlas and Bluewinged Sivas. The flocks keep up a constant cheeping. In summer a distinctive three-noted call *pweei-pweei-pweei* is heard, the middle note higher pitched. It has also been rendered as *too-sweet-sweet*.

NESTING: *Season*—May-June. *Nest*—a small, deep, compact cup of moss and dead leaves, thickly lined with hair. Placed in a bush or sapling in evergreen forest. *Eggs*—2 or 3, deep blue or blue-green, lightly spotted and freckled with black or light red at the larger end. Size about 21×16 mm.

RACIAL CHARACTERISTICS, MEASUREMENTS, ETC: The adjacent west Himalayan race *simlaensis* (Kangra to Naini Tal) is paler, with the crown more lemon-rufous. The adjacent east Himalayan *yunnanensis* (Dafla, Miri, Mishmi Hills, etc.) is darker than *strigula*.

Specimens collected by the Sikkim Survey measure:

| | Wing | Bill | Tarsus | Tail | |
|---|---|---|---|---|---|
| 1 ♂ | 70 | 14 | 25 | 70 | mm. |
| 1 ♀ | 68 | 13.5 | 26 | 67 | mm. |
| 2 o? | 66-69 | 13-14 | 25.5-26 | 65-66 | mm. |

Twenty adult examples in the Schäfer Sikkim collection give Wing 64 (♀) to 70 (♂) mm.

Iris brown; bill horny brown, paler on lower mandible and tips of both mandibles; legs and feet greyish brown; claws horny brown.

## THE NEPAL BLUEWINGED SIVA

*Minla cyanouroptera cyanouroptera* (Hodgson)

*Siva cyanouroptera* Hodgson, 1837, *Ind. Review* 2: 88—Nepal.

F.B.I. 1: 314

LOCAL NAME: Megblim adum (Lepcha).

SIZE: Sparrow.

FIELD CHARACTERS: A slim, slightly tufted, greyish-looking bird with rufous back and white-tipped dark wings. The blue of head, wings and tail (very clear-cut, square-ended) is not noticeable except at close quarters or through binoculars.

*Above*, top of head blue, streaked with whitish on forecrown; lores, round the eye and a broad streak behind eye white; ear-coverts and sides of neck vinous grey. Rest of upper parts bright yellowish brown (ochraceous). Tail blue and black, tipped with white. Closed wings cobalt blue and bluish grey, tipped with white. *Below*, pale greyish buff with a vinous tinge. Sexes alike.

STATUS AND HABITAT: Generally distributed and quite common between about 1000 ft. (Rangpo) and 7000 ft. elevation (above

Residency, Gangtok). Affects secondary growth and mixed deciduous and evergreen forest—of oak, *Schima*, etc.

DISTRIBUTION OUTSIDE SIKKIM: Nepal, Bhutan, Dafla, Miri and Mishmi Hills. The species is found in the Assam hills south of the Brahmaputra, Manipur, Burma, Thailand, Malaya, Indochina.

GENERAL HABITS: Very similar to those of the foregoing species with which it commonly consorts in the large mixed hunting flocks of 'tinies'. It is one of the most regular and abundant constituents of such flocks.

NESTING: *Season*—May, June, July? *Nest*—a well made cup of dead leaves, moss, lichens, pliant twigs and tendrils, lined with hair or fine roots. Placed in a bush or sapling 4 or 5 ft. up, well concealed by the undergrowth. *Eggs*—2 to 4, deep blue with a few black spots and specks at the larger end. Size about 19×14 mm.

RACIAL CHARACTERISTICS, MEASUREMENTS, ETC: Six specimens collected by the Sikkim Survey measure:

| | Wing | Bill | Tarsus | Tail | |
|---|---|---|---|---|---|
| 4 ♀♀ | 60-65 | 14.5-16 | 21.5-23 | 60-65 | mm. |
| 2 o? | 63-65 | 14-15 | 22.5-23 | 65 | mm. |

Seven examples in the Schäfer Sikkim collection have Wing ♂ 63, 63, 64, 67; ♀ 60, 61, 61 mm.

Iris greyish brown; bill yellowish flesh colour, brownish on culmen for about one-quarter length at tip; legs and feet brownish flesh colour; claws horny brown.

## THE WHITEBROWED, or HUME'S, STAPHIDA

*Yuhina castaniceps rufigenis* (Hume)

*Ixulus rufigenis* Hume, 1877, *Stray Feathers* 5: 108—Sikkim (Darjeeling).

**Plate 21, fig. 10 (facing p. 272)**

F.B.I. 1: 311

LOCAL NAME:

SIZE: Sparrow.

FIELD CHARACTERS: *Above*, head (slightly crested) greyish brown or sooty brown with a narrow white supercilium from eye to ear-coverts and a rufous band above this. Rest of upper plumage olive-brown; head, mantle and back with grey striations (shaft-stripes). Ear-coverts and sides of neck dull chestnut. Closed wings and tail dark olive-brown, the outer three or four pairs of tail feathers broadly tipped with white. *Below*, dull greyish white. Sexes alike.

STATUS AND HABITAT: Apparently not uncommon at moderate elevations—*c.* 2000 to 5000 (?) ft. (Martam and elsewhere in the Teesta Valley). Affects secondary forest with shrubby undergrowth.

DISTRIBUTION OUTSIDE SIKKIM: Bhutan, Assam hills north and north-east of the Brahmaputra. Other races in the Naga Hills, Burma, Thailand, W. Yunnan. The species extends to Borneo.

GENERAL HABITS: Arboreal. Keeps in flocks of as many as 20 or 30 birds, often in the mixed hunting parties of 'tinies'. The birds hunt feverishly among the foliage of lofty trees and shrubbery alike, and rapidly sweep on to the next tree in disorderly 'follow-my-leader' fashion. Their movements as they cling to the leaves and branches are reminiscent of the tits, and the flocks keep up a comparatively loud cheeping or twittering, like *Yuhina nigrimenta,* all the while. *Food:* chiefly insects, but also seeds.

NESTING: *Season*—April to June. *Nest*—of soft shreds of grass and fibrous material stuffed into a natural hollow high up in a roadside cutting or steep earth bank, with a cup-like depression for the eggs. It is often concealed by overhanging grass or weeds. *Eggs*—3 or 4, white with a very faint greenish or pinkish tinge, finely blotched all over with vandyke brown or reddish brown, more densely at the broad end. Size about 17×14 mm.

RACIAL CHARACTERISTICS, MEASUREMENTS, ETC: A specimen (♀) collected by the Sikkim Survey measures: Wing 60; bill 10.5; tarsus 16.5; tail 53.5 mm.

The Fauna gives the Wing ♂♀ as 60-63 mm.

Iris reddish brown; bill horny brown with a pinkish tinge; legs and feet brownish yellow; claws horny brown.

## THE CHESTNUT-HEADED, or WHITENAPED, IXULUS

*Yuhina bakeri* Rothschild

*Yuhina bakeri* Rothschild, 1926, *Novit. Zool.* 33: 276—Darjeeling. New name for *Siva occipitalis* Blyth, 1844, preoccupied.

F.B.I. 1: 321

LOCAL NAMES: Temgyeng-pho or Turinging-pho (Lepcha).

SIZE: Sparrow—.

FIELD CHARACTERS: A perky hair-brown tit-like little bird with chestnut head and upstanding crest, conspicuous blackish lores and a white nuchal patch.

*Above,* forehead and crest rusty brown (ferruginous); a large white patch on nape; lores and round the eye dusky. Back olive-green, streaked with whitish on mantle; upper tail-coverts and tail fulvous brown. *Below,* chin and throat white; breast vinaceous, streaked with brown. Abdomen olivaceous; under tail-coverts ferruginous. Sexes alike.

STATUS AND HABITAT: Apparently only at moderate elevations—about 2000 to 6000 ft. (Dikchu, Singhik, Chungthang, Gangtok). Affects secondary jungle by the side of mule tracks and along the edge of abandoned overgrown forest clearings etc.

DISTRIBUTION OUTSIDE SIKKIM: Nepal, Bhutan, Assam hills north and south of Brahmaputra River; Manipur, N. Burma.

GENERAL HABITS: Arboreal, sociable, tit-like and similar to the other yuhinas. Moves about in mixed flocks amongst tree-tops and bushes, feeding on insects and berries.

NESTING: *Season*—May-June. *Nest*—either domed or cup-shaped; of moss, leaves, bracken roots and tendrils, lined with fine fern- and moss-roots. Placed a few feet up in forest trees, overhung with green moss, or in thickets of wild raspberries etc. *Eggs*—3 or 4, white, heavily blotched with reddish brown to deep umber brown. They are reminiscent of swallows' eggs. Size about 19×14 mm.

RACIAL CHARACTERISTICS, MEASUREMENTS, ETC: The prominent white nuchal patch at once distinguishes this ixulus from all its near relations.

Four specimens collected by the Sikkim Survey measure:

| | Wing | Bill | Tarsus | Tail |
|---|---|---|---|---|
| 2 ♂♂ | 70 | 12-12.5 | 21.5-22 | 51-53 mm. |
| 2 ♀♀ | 66-68 | 11-13.5 | 20-23.5 | 46.5-48 mm. |

A Schäfer skin from Sikkim (o?) has Wing 64 mm.

Iris yellowish brown; bill horny brown; legs, feet and claws horny brown.

## THE YELLOWNAPED IXULUS

### *Yuhina flavicollis flavicollis* Hodgson

*Yuhina flavicollis* Hodgson, 1836, *Asiat. Res.* 19: 167—Nepal (restricted to central Nepal, Ripley 1959, Synopsis).

**Plate 21, fig. 9 (facing p. 272)**

F.B.I. 1: 322

LOCAL NAME:

SIZE: Sparrow—.

FIELD CHARACTERS: Brown-crested, tit-like, rather similar to the Chestnut-headed Ixulus but with no white patch on nape. A broad rusty yellow collar round hindneck; black lores and moustachial streak. Underside with a strong wash of yellow. The crest is frequently erected, highlighting the mousy grey nape and yellow hind-collar. Sexes alike.

STATUS AND HABITAT: Resident between about 1000 and 9000 ft. elevation, even in winter; commonest between 2000 and 3000 ft. (Rangpo, Singtam, Temi, Gangtok, Chungthang, Lachen). Affects the same facies as the last.

DISTRIBUTION OUTSIDE SIKKIM: Central and eastern Nepal, Bhutan. Other races replace it in the western Himalayas, and in the Assam hills east of Bhutan. The species extends through Assam, Manipur, N. Burma, N. Thailand to Yunnan and Indochina.

GENERAL HABITS: Not appreciably different from other yuhinas and ixulus. The flocks keep up a continuous murmuring twitter, punctuated by a harsh *chi-chi-chiu* like similar notes of the Quaker Babbler (*Alcippe poioicephala*) of peninsular India. Another call has been described as a querulous *screech-screech* followed by a pleasant warble. Feeds in tit-like manner largely on wild raspberries (*Rubus*) and other small berries, particularly of a species of shrub like *Trema* (?) which are a favourite food also of many laughing thrushes.

NESTING: *Season*—May-June. *Nest* and site similar to those of the Chestnut-headed Ixulus. *Eggs* also indistinguishable. Very slightly larger, about 20×15 mm.

RACIAL CHARACTERISTICS, MEASUREMENTS, ETC: The west Himalayan race *albicollis* (Kangra to W. Nepal) is paler and greyer with a white posterior border to the hind collar. The adjoining eastern race *baileyi* is darker than *flavicollis*, not paler as stated in the original description (Stuart Baker, *Bull. Brit. Orn. Cl.* 1914, 35: 17).

Specimens collected by the Sikkim Survey measure:

| | Wing | Bill | Tarsus | Tail |
|---|---|---|---|---|
| 1 ♂ | 66 | 13 | 19.5 | 48.5 mm. |
| 3 ♀♀ | 60-65 | 12-13 | 18.5-20.5 | 46-49 mm. |

A fine series of 19 adults in the Schäfer Sikkim collection gives Wing 60 (♀) to 66 (♂) mm. (av. 62.8.) (Stresemann).

Iris brown or hazel-brown; a fine ring of minute white feathers round eye; bill horny brown, paler on lower mandible; legs and feet yellowish flesh colour; claws brownish flesh.

## THE STRIPEDTHROATED YUHINA

### *Yuhina gularis gularis* Hodgson

*Yuhina gularis* Hodgson, 1836, *Asiat. Res.* 19: 166—Nepal.

**Plate 21, fig. 4 (facing p. 272)**

F.B.I. 1: 317

LOCAL NAME: Fugi-pho (Lepcha).

SIZE: Sparrow.

FIELD CHARACTERS: A small, active, brown-crested, tit-like bird, reminiscent also of a miniature bulbul, with soft buffy pink coloured breast, working through tree-tops in parties.

*Above*, forehead and crest rich hair brown. Rest of upper plumage olive-brown, fulvous on rump and upper tail-coverts. Closed wings edged with orange-brown. Lores, cheeks and ear-coverts grey. *Below*, chin and throat pale vinous, streaked black; breast rufescent; rest of underparts dull orange-brown. Sexes alike.

STATUS AND HABITAT: Fairly common between about 6000 and 13,000 ft. elevation (Kewzing, Gangtok, Manshitang, Lachung, Lachen, Thangu). Affects oak, rhododendron and mixed conifer forest, and shrubbery.

DISTRIBUTION OUTSIDE SIKKIM: Garhwal, Kumaon, Nepal, Bhutan, Assam hills north of Brahmaputra River. Another race in Assam hills south of the Brahmaputra, Manipur, Upper Burma.

GENERAL HABITS: Arboreal. Parties, commonly in association with *Yuhina flavicollis* and *Y. occipitalis* and other small babblers and 'tinies', hunt energetically in the foliage canopy of tall trees and shrubs. *Food:* insects and berries. A constant conversational twitter is kept up whilst feeding, and it has also a curious long drawn-out call *kweeee*.

NESTING: *Season*—April to July. *Nest*—not well authenticated.

Described variously as a massive globular structure of moss, and as a fragile-looking cradle of roots etc., placed in the fork of a tree or between rocks. *Eggs*—4, dingy grey-green, speckled freely with dark reddish brown, the markings coalescing at the larger end into a ring or cap. Size about 17×13 mm.

RACIAL CHARACTERISTICS, MEASUREMENTS, ETC: Differs from *Yuhina occipitalis* in having the throat black-streaked, and no orange-rufous ring round the occiput (=back of the head).

Three specimens collected by the Sikkim Survey measure:

| | Wing | Bill | Tarsus | Tail |
|---|---|---|---|---|
| 1 ♂ | 75 | 16.5 | 22.5 | 61 mm. |
| 2 o? | 72-75 | 16-17.5 | 21-23 | 55-58 mm. |

Twelve examples in the Schäfer Sikkim collection, measured by Stresemann, give Wing 71 (♀) to 78 (♂) mm. (av. 14.5). Against this the Fauna gives for ♂♀ '68-72' mm.

Iris reddish brown; bill: upper mandible horny brown, lower paler with orange tinge; legs and feet orange-brown; claws horny brown.

## THE SLATYHEADED, or RUFOUSVENTED, YUHINA

*Yuhina occipitalis occipitalis* Hodgson

*Yuhina occipitalis* Hodgson, 1836, *Asiat. Res.* 19: 166—Nepal.

F.B.I. 1: 319

LOCAL NAME: Turinging-pho (Lepcha).

SIZE: Sparrow—.

FIELD CHARACTERS: An active, brown, tit-like bird with slaty crest, a white ring round eye, a black moustachial streak, pale chestnut nape and bright chestnut under tail-coverts. Parties in tree-tops.

*Above*, forehead, crest and ear-coverts slate-grey with whitish streaks. Hind part of crest, and nape pale chestnut. Rest of upper parts rufous-brown. *Below*, chin, throat, breast and sides of neck vinous; rest of underparts pale rusty, deepening to bright chestnut on vent and under tail-coverts. Sexes alike.

STATUS AND HABITAT: More or less coincident with that of the Stripedthroated Yuhina, between about 6000 and 13,000 ft. elevation (Gangtok, Chungthang, Lachen, Thangu). Affecting identical facies.

DISTRIBUTION OUTSIDE SIKKIM: Nepal, Bhutan, Chumbi Valley (S. Tibet). The species extends to NW. Yunnan.

GENERAL HABITS: Very similar to the Stripedthroated Yuhina with which, and with other small timaliids, it commonly associates in mixed flocks. Hunts insects in canopy foliage as well as on moss-covered tree-trunks and branches, and in bushes. Also feeds largely from rhododendron blossoms (nectar ?). The members maintain contact with one another by churring conversational notes. It has a distinctive pleasing 'song' besides.

NESTING: Not recorded in Sikkim or elsewhere.

RACIAL CHARACTERISTICS, MEASUREMENTS, ETC: The *Fauna* gives the measurements as: ♂♀ Wing 59-62; bill 11-12; tarsus *c.* 18; tail *c.* 50 mm.

Three adult specimens collected by Schäfer in Sikkim (sex ?) have Wing 65, 66, 66 mm.

Iris red-brown; bill reddish brown; legs and feet orange-buff; claws horny brown.

## THE BLACKCHINNED YUHINA

### *Yuhina nigrimenta nigrimenta* Hodgson

*Yuhina nigrimenta* Hodgson 1845, *in* Blyth, *Jour. Asiat. Soc. Bengal* 14: 562—Nepal.

F.B.I. 1: 320

LOCAL NAME: Turinging-pho (Lepcha).

SIZE: Sparrow— (about Munia).

FIELD CHARACTERS: A restless, dainty little greyish brown bird with black and grey crest and face, and black-and-red bill. Flocks in trees and bushes.

*Above,* forehead and crest black with scale-like grey edging to the feathers; nape and sides of head grey; lores black. Back and rest of upper plumage greyish olive-brown. *Below,* chin black; throat white; rest of underparts pale fulvous. Sexes alike.

STATUS AND HABITAT: Found at fairly low elevations, between about 1200 and 3000 ft. (Rangpo, Singtam, Dikchu and elsewhere in the Teesta Valley). Affects secondary jungle, and is partial to overgrown cultivation clearings.

DISTRIBUTION OUTSIDE SIKKIM: From Garhwal and Naini Tal eastward: Nepal, Bhutan, Assam hills north and south of the Brahmaputra; Manipur. The species extends through N. Burma to Yunnan, Indochina and S. China.

GENERAL HABITS: Arboreal and sociable. In restless flocks, by themselves or mixed with other 'tinies', hunting tit-like for insects in the foliage canopy of tall trees or low shrubs with feverish energy, and rapidly 'flowing' or sweeping on from tree to tree. The birds keep up a lively chorus of low cheeping twitters the while.

NESTING: *Season*—April to June (July?). *Nest*—a comparatively massive, compact little cradle or hammock of scraps of dead moss and moss-roots bound with cobwebs, slung between lichens growing on a low branch. It is lined with fine soft grass. *Eggs*—3 or 4, normally pale sea-green, profusely spotted all over with pale brown blotches and finer speckles. The markings are dense at the larger end where they tend to form a broad ring. Size about 17×13 mm.

RACIAL CHARACTERISTICS, MEASUREMENTS, ETC: The unstreaked white throat, and black chin and lores, distinguish this species from the other small crested babblers of the genus.

Three specimens collected in Sikkim measure:

| | Wing | Bill | Tarsus | Tail | |
|---|---|---|---|---|---|
| 1 ♂ | 58 | 13 | 16.5 | 38 | mm. |
| 3 ♀♀ | 54.5-55.5 | 13-14 | 16 | 36-36.5 | mm. |

Iris brown; bill: upper mandible horny brown, lower coral red with brownish tip; mouth bright orange-red; legs and feet yellowish brown; claws pale horny brown.

## THE WHITEBELLIED ERPORNIS

*Yuhina zantholeuca zantholeuca* (Hodgson)

*Erpornis zantholeuca* Hodgson, 1844, *Jour. Asiat. Soc. Bengal* 13: 380—central region of Nepal.

F.B.I. 1: 325

LOCAL NAME: Dung-pu-pho (Lepcha).

SIZE: Sparrow—.

FIELD CHARACTERS: A partially tufted, plain-looking babbler, greenish yellow above, greyish white below, with ashy white ear-coverts and bright yellow under tail-coverts. Sexes alike.

STATUS AND HABITAT: Met with by me only at Rangpo (*c.* 1200 ft.), Singtam (*c.* 1800 ft.), Kewzing (*c.* 5000 ft.) and below Lachen (*c.* 7500 ft.). According to Stevens 'it occurs up to an elevation of 3300 ft. in the Teesta Valley'! In Nepal, both Dr Dillon Ripley and Mrs Desirée Proud found it between 6000 and 7000 ft. in autumn and spring, as well as in winter. Affects secondary evergreen jungle.

DISTRIBUTION OUTSIDE SIKKIM: Nepal, Bhutan, Assam hills north and south of the Brahmaputra; Manipur, Burma, Tenasserim. The species extends to Malaya, Indonesia, Indochina, Formosa, Hainan.

GENERAL HABITS: Not markedly different from the other members of the genus described. Keeps in pairs or small parties usually mixed up in the restless assemblages of small babblers, nuthatches, fly-catchers and warblers, feeding in a tit-like manner amongst leafy treetops or in shrubbery, and 'flowing' on with them rapidly from tree to tree. Unobtrusive and silent. Its call is unrecorded.

NESTING: *Season*—April, May, June (?). *Nest*—a little cradle or hammock of fine fibres, moss, fern-roots, etc., lined with black root-hairs. Slung between small horizontal twigs in a bush or sapling, 2 to 4 ft. up. *Eggs*—2 or 3, china-white, scantily freckled and finely blotched with pale pinkish red. Size about 17×13 mm.

RACIAL CHARACTERISTICS, MEASUREMENTS, ETC: The Fauna gives the measurements as: ♂♀ Wing 63-70; bill 10-10.5; tarsus *c.* 16; tail *c.* 45 mm. In two recently collected specimens of this race the bill from forehead measures *c.* 15 mm.; tarsus *c.* 19 mm.; these figures seem more accurate.

Iris brown; bill: upper mandible brown, lower mandible whitish grey; legs and feet whitish grey. (Ripley.)

## THE GOLDENBREASTED BABBLER

*Alcippe chrysotis chrysotis* (Blyth)

*Proparus chrysotis* Blyth, 1844, *Jour. Asiat. Soc. Bengal* 13: 938—Himalayas (=Nepal).

**Plate 21, fig. 5** (facing p. 272)

F.B.I. 1: 293

LOCAL NAME: Prong-samyer-pho (Lepcha).

SIZE: Sparrow−.

FIELD CHARACTERS: A small tit-like babbler: ashy olive and olive-green above; bright orange-yellow below, with chin and throat silvery ash-brown. Forehead, crown, and nape blackish ashy. Ear-coverts, cheeks and a ring round the eye silvery white. A whitish bar in the dark wings. Sexes alike.

STATUS AND HABITAT: According to Stevens, widely distributed between about 6500 and 10,000 ft., but not common. Schäfer obtained specimens at between 6000 and 7000 ft. (Gangtok, Penlom La, Manshitang). Affects dense growth on steep hillsides; partial to thick bamboo patches.

DISTRIBUTION OUTSIDE SIKKIM: Nepal, Bhutan, Assam hills north and south of Brahmaputra River; Manipur. Other races in Burma, Tonkin.

GENERAL HABITS: Flocks of 20 to 30 or more, sometimes intermixed with other small babblers, forage through low bushes and bamboo scrub, and quickly 'flow' on. The actions and behaviour when feeding are rather tit-like, and also do not differ appreciably from those of the Sikkim Fulvetta (p. 209). The call notes and song are undescribed. *Food:* insects and small seeds.

NESTING: Not recorded in Sikkim, and apparently seldom elsewhere. Near Darjeeling, May and June are said to be the breeding months. *Nest*—an upright egg-shaped structure of dry bamboo leaves and coarse grass, lined with finer grass and moss roots, with a lateral entrance hole. Built in a bamboo clump a few feet above the ground. *Eggs*—3 or 4, pinky white, speckled and spotted with brownish red, more densely at the broad end. Size about 16×13 mm.

RACIAL CHARACTERISTICS, MEASUREMENTS, ETC: ♂♀ Wing 50-54; bill *c.* 8; tarsus *c.* 23; tail *c.* 50 mm. (Fauna).

Seven specimens collected in Sikkim by Schäfer (♂♀) have Wing 51-54 mm (av. 52.6).

Iris brown; bill plumbeous, paler below; legs and feet fleshy.

## THE DUSKY GREEN, or YELLOWTHROATED, BABBLER

*Alcippe cinerea* (Blyth)

*Minla cinerea* Blyth, 1847, *Jour. Asiat. Soc. Bengal* 16: 449—Darjeeling.

F.B.I. 1: 287

LOCAL NAME:

SIZE: Sparrow—.

FIELD CHARACTERS: *Above*, yellowish green (fading to 'dusky' green in museum specimens, whence the name); feathers of crown and nape margined with black. *Below*, yellow; olivaceous on sides of neck, breast and abdomen.

A black streak through the eye, a conspicuous yellow supercilium above it from bill to nape, and a broad black band from forehead to nape above the supercilium, are diagnostic points. Sexes alike.

STATUS AND HABITAT: Locally distributed 'at elevations probably not exceeding 4000 ft. in the hot, moist valleys' (Stevens). Schäfer obtained a specimen at Manshitang, *c.* 5850 ft.

DISTRIBUTION OUTSIDE SIKKIM: Nepal, Bhutan, Assam north and south of the Brahmaputra.

GENERAL HABITS: Very similar to *Alcippe n. nipalensis* and the other small babblers with which it habitually associates in restless hunting parties.

NESTING: *Season*—May and June. *Nest*—a deep cup, sometimes domed, of bamboo leaves and fern fronds, usually lined with moss- or fern-roots etc. *Eggs*—4, variable. The commonest type is buff stippled with reddish brown, densely at the broad end where the spots often coalesce to form a ring. Size about 19×15 mm.

RACIAL CHARACTERISTICS, MEASUREMENTS, ETC: ♂♀ Wing 53-58; bill *c.* 10, tarsus *c.* 23; tail 42-44 mm. (Fauna). Schäfer's specimen (♀) has Wing 56 mm.

Iris brown or reddish brown. bill dark horny brown, paler (bluish white) on lower mandible; legs and feet pale yellowish horn.

## THE CHESTNUT-HEADED BABBLER

*Alcippe castaneceps castaneceps* (Hodgson)

*Minla castaneceps* Hodgson 1837, *Ind. Review* 2: 33—Nepal (restricted to Chandragiri Pass, central Nepal, by Ripley 1950, *Jour. Bombay Nat. Hist. Soc.* 49: 397).

**Plate 21, fig. 11 (facing p. 272)**

F.B.I. 1: 288

LOCAL NAME:

SIZE: Sparrow—.

FIELD CHARACTERS: *Above*, olive-green tinged with fulvous. Forehead, crown and nape chestnut-brown; forehead streaked with white, crown and nape with pale rufous. A broad white supercilium. A

1. Bengal Redcapped Babbler (*Timalia p. bengalensis*) 2. Whiteheaded Shrike-Babbler (*Gampsorhynchus r. rufulus*) 3. Sikkim Spotted Babbler (*Pellorneum r. mandellii*) 4. Barthroated Siva (*Minla s. strigula*) 5. Longbilled Wren-Babbler (*Rimator m. malacoptilus*) 6. Redwinged Shrike-Babbler (*Pteruthius e. erythropterus*) 7. Rufousbellied Shrike-Babbler (*Pteruthius r. rufiventer*) 8. Sikkim Chestnutrumped Sibia (*Heterophasia a. annectens*) 9. Sikkim Hoary Barwing (*Actinodura n. vinctura*) 10. Nepal Cutia (*Cutia n. nipalensis*) 11. Redbilled Leiothrix, or 'Pekin Robin' (*Leiothrix l. calipyga*)

PLATE 17 [*c.* × $\frac{1}{3}$]

1. Spotted Wren (*Spelaecornis formosus*) 2. Tailed Wren (*Spelaecornis caudatus*) 3. Chestnut-headed Wren (*Tesia c. castaneocoronata*) 4. Brown Wren (*Microura p. pusilla*) 5. Sikkim Goldcrest (*Regulus r. sikkimensis*) 6. Sikkim Firecapped Tit-Warbler (*Cephalopyrus f. saturatus*) 7. Spotted Bush Warbler (*Bradypterus t. thoracicus*) 8. Dusky Leaf Warbler (*Phylloscopus f. fuscatus*) 9. Orangebarred Leaf Warbler (*Phylloscopus p. pulcher*) 10. Dull Green Leaf Warbler (*Phylloscopus t. trochiloides*)

PLATE 18

broad line through eye, and moustachial streak, black. Rest of head white. *Below*, pale fulvous white; sides of breast and body ochraceous. Sexes alike.

STATUS AND HABITAT: A moderate to high elevation species. Generally distributed; according to Stevens from about 3500 ft. (Rungbong Valley) to 10,000 ft. (Singalila Ridge), seasonally. Schäfer collected specimens at Gangtok, Chungthang, Lachung and Karponang (*c.* 5000 to 9000 ft.). The recent Loke-Sálim Ali Survey observed it near Singhik, Temi and Kewzing between 2500 and 7700 ft. Affects heavy evergreen undergrowth at the edge of forest and in abandoned clearings.

DISTRIBUTION OUTSIDE SIKKIM: Nepal, Bhutan, Assam hills north of the Brahmaputra; parts of Burma. Other races in Assam south of the Brahmaputra, Burma, Thailand, Malaya, Indochina, etc.

GENERAL HABITS: Not different from those of *Alcippe nipalensis*, but often also seen in more or less pure flocks (unmixed with other species) of up to 30 or more birds. The flock (whether pure or mixed) hunts with feverish energy through the foliage of bushes and trees and 'flows' on rapidly from tree to tree.

NESTING: *Season*—May-June. *Nest*—a compact cup of green moss, usually domed; sometimes built against a moss-covered tree-trunk, at others placed in a tangle of creepers, 5 to 10 ft. from the ground. *Eggs*—4, white, blotched with inky black and with secondary markings of pale inky lavender. Size about 18×14 mm.

RACIAL CHARACTERISTICS, MEASUREMENTS, ETC: A female obtained by the Survey measures: Wing 56; bill 11; tarsus 20.5; tail 41 mm.

Eighteen adults in Schäfer's Sikkim collection give Wing 53 (♀) to 59 (♂) mm.

Iris brown; bill horny brown, paler (yellowish) at base of lower mandible; legs, feet and claws olive-brown; soles bright yellow.

The juvenile plumage is exactly like the adult in coloration, but the feathers are softer and fluffier (Stresemann.)

## THE SIKKIM FULVETTA

*Alcippe vinipectus chumbiensis* (Kinnear)

*Fulvetta vinipectus chumbiensis* Kinnear, 1939, *Ibis:* 751—Yatung, Chumbi Valley.

**Plate 21, fig. 12 (facing p. 272)**

F.B.I. 1: 290

LOCAL NAME:

SIZE: Sparrow−.

FIELD CHARACTERS: A tiny, fluffy-plumaged, pinkish brown babbler with white throat and breast and conspicuous long white and black eyebrow.

*Above*, vinous brown, with ferruginous rump and upper tail-coverts. *Below*, chin, throat and upper breast white; breast pale vinous brown; abdomen, flanks and under tail-coverts pale fulvous. A very broad white supercilium to the nape, bordered above by a dull black band reaching beyond the nape. Cheeks and ear-coverts vinaceous brown. Sexes alike.

STATUS AND HABITAT: Common to very common at high elevations, between about 7000 and 12,000 ft., even in winter (Kewzing, Lachen, Lachung, Zemu, Phalut, Singalila Ridge). Affects low scrub growth of rhododendron, *Berberis*, juniper, etc.

DISTRIBUTION OUTSIDE SIKKIM: Nepal; Chumbi Valley, S. Tibet; Bhutan and Assam hills north of Brahmaputra River. Other races in the western Himalayas, Assam hills south of the Brahmaputra, Manipur, N. Burma, Indochina.

GENERAL HABITS: Keeps in active parties and flocks; usually tame and confiding. Prefers low bushes to trees. The birds incessantly utter a soft, high-pitched, merry, chittering *chip, chip,* which first betrays their presence. Said to have 'a sweet, gentle, little song' in the breeding season. Actions when feeding rather tit-like, often hanging upside down on twigs and peering and pecking under leaves, the flocks 'flowing' on from bush to bush. *Food:* small seeds and insects.

Was observed as one of the commonest birds at Lachung in winter, hunting complacently even among bushes partially buried under heavy snow.

NESTING: *Season*—May-June. *Nest*—a deep compact cup of grass, moss and roots, lined with hair. Built between stems of ringal bamboo or in a bush, about 2 ft. from the ground. *Eggs*—3, deep soft grey-blue, sparsely blotched with black or rarely with freckles of reddish brown, at the larger end. Size about 19×14 mm.

RACIAL CHARACTERISTICS, MEASUREMENTS, ETC: *Chumbiensis* differs from the adjoining nominate race (*vinipectus*) of the western Himalayas in being much darker, with pronounced dusky streaking on the throat.

Six specimens collected by the Sikkim Survey measure:

| | Wing | Bill | Tarsus | Tail |
|---|---|---|---|---|
| 2 ♂♂ | 62 | 10-11 | 23.5-24 | 55 mm. |
| 4 ♀♀ | 58-60 | 9.5-10.5 | 23-24.5 | 51.5-54 mm. |

Twenty specimens in the Schäfer Sikkim collection (♂♀) have Wing 56-62 mm. (av. 58.1). One other has an exceptionally large wing, 64 mm. (Stresemann).

Iris creamy white, biscuit colour, or brown; bill horny brown, flesh colour at base of lower mandible; legs, feet and claws horny brown.

# THE NEPAL WHITE-EYED QUAKER BABBLER

*Alcippe nipalensis nipalensis* (Hodgson)

*Siva nipalensis* Hodgson, 1837, *Ind. Review* 2: 89—Nepal.

**Plate 21, fig. 8 (facing p. 272)**

F.B.I. 1: 275

LOCAL NAME:

SIZE: Sparrow.

FIELD CHARACTERS: Fulvous brown above; pale buff below, whitish on chin and belly. Head and neck pale brownish ashy. The conspicuous ring of white feathers round eye, and blackish supercilium from eye to nape, are diagnostic. Sexes alike.

STATUS AND HABITAT: Fairly common between about 2000 and 7000 ft. (Martam, Singhik, Penlom La, Gangtok). Affects moist forest with thick scrub undergrowth.

DISTRIBUTION OUTSIDE SIKKIM: Eastern Nepal, Bhutan, Assam north and south of Brahmaputra River; Chittagong Hill Tracts; Burma. The species extends through Thailand, Malaya, Yunnan, Indochina. Also Hainan, Formosa, etc.

GENERAL HABITS: Keeps in active, restless flocks working feverishly through undergrowth and foliage canopy of trees, clinging sideways and upside down on twigs, and fluttering momentarily in the air in front of sprigs like a flycatcher or leaf warbler. The next instant the flock has swept on in disorderly follow-my-leader fashion to the next tree! These itinerant flocks are often mixed with other small babblers. Whilst foraging the birds keep up a constant twittering—'a shrill whinnying note' according to Stanford. *Food:* mainly tiny insects.

NESTING: *Season*—April to June. *Nest*—cup-shaped, fairly compact, of bamboo leaves and coarse grass, bound with cobwebs and lined with fine roots, moss, etc. *Eggs*—3 or 4, very variable: white, cream or pale pink, speckled, blotched and smeared with lilac-purple, brick-red or purple-red, and sometimes with a few twisted lines. Size about 19×14 mm.

RACIAL CHARACTERISTICS, MEASUREMENTS, ETC: Two specimens collected by the Sikkim Survey measure:

| | Wing | Bill | Tarsus | Tail |
|---|---|---|---|---|
| 1 ♂ | 61 | 13.5 | 22 | 59 mm. |
| 1 ♀ | 60 | 12 | 22 | 57 mm. |

Three examples (sex ?) in the Schäfer collection have Wing 58, 59, 60 mm. (Stresemann).

Iris brown; bill greyish horn, brown on basal two-thirds of upper mandible; legs, feet and claws plumbeous horny brown.

## THE SIKKIM CHESTNUTRUMPED SIBIA

*Heterophasia annectens annectens* (Blyth)

*Leioptila annectans* [*sic*] Blyth, 1847, *Jour. Asiat. Soc. Bengal* 16: 450—Darjeeling.

**Plate 17, fig. 8** (facing p. 208)

F.B.I. 1: 300

LOCAL NAME: Rubnun-pho (Lepcha).

SIZE: Bulbul—.

FIELD CHARACTERS: *Above,* including top and sides of head and ear-coverts, black. Hindneck boldly white-streaked. Middle of back, rump and upper tail-coverts chestnut-red. Scapulars pale rufous. Some bluish white and chestnut on the black wing quills. Tail black, graduated, with the feathers broadly tipped white and faintly cross-rayed. *Below,* chin, breast and belly white; flanks, vent and under tail-coverts fulvous. Sexes alike.

STATUS AND HABITAT: Rare. Presumably resident between 2000 ft. (as in Bhutan) and 6000 ft. elevation. Affects tree forest with moss- and lichen-covered trunks and boughs.

DISTRIBUTION OUTSIDE SIKKIM: Bhutan, Assam hills north and south of Brahmaputra River; Manipur, Burma, Shan States. The species extends to Thailand, N. Tonkin, S. Yunnan.

GENERAL HABITS: Arboreal. Small parties keep to the canopy foliage in tall trees. The birds creep along the branches or clamber on the trunks like a nuthatch, occasionally head downwards, searching crevices of the bark and under the moss and lichens for insect food. The call note has been described as a clear single whistle.

NESTING: Not specifically recorded in Sikkim. *Season*—May-June. *Nest*—a neat, compact cup of moss and leaves lined with root fibres. Placed 8 to 20 ft. up in the fork of an outhanging branoh. *Eggs*—2 or 3, variable. Commonest type pale bluish or greenish grey, blotched and smeared with reddish brown, with spots and short wavy lines here and there, and secondary smudges of pale lavender or pale brown. Size about 22×16 mm.

RACIAL CHARACTERISTICS, MEASUREMENTS, ETC: The Fauna gives the measurements as: ♂♀ Wing 75-80; bill 15-16; tarsus *c.* 24; tail 85-87 mm.

Iris brownish; bill black yellow at base of lower mandible; tarsus and toes wax yellow; claws brownish.

## THE BLACKHEADED SIBIA

*Heterophasia capistrata bayleyi* (Kinnear)

*Leioptila capistrata bayleyi* Kinnear, 1939, *Ibis*: 752—Taktoo, near Sakdan, E. Bhutan.

F.B.I. I: 296

LOCAL NAMES: Sambriak-pho (Lepcha); Sesigona (Bhutia); Sibya (Nepali).

SIZE: Bulbul+, with proportionately long tail.

FIELD CHARACTERS: A handsome, black-crested, rufous, bulbul-like bird, with a conspicuous white patch in the black wings in flight. Above and below bright rufous with only the upper back ('saddle') greyish brown. Whole head, including a full crest and sides of neck, glossy black. Edges of closed wings bluish grey; a white patch near shoulder. Tail rufous and black, tipped with bluish grey; tips of the central pair of rectrices broad and with a black subterminal band. Sexes alike.

STATUS AND HABITAT: Resident. Common between about 2000 and 9000 ft. elevation (Martam, Kewzing, Temi, Gangtok, Chungthang, Lachen, Manshitang, etc.) with considerable altitudinal movement seasonally. Affects tall forest, and dense secondary growth.

DISTRIBUTION OUTSIDE SIKKIM: Eastern Nepal, Bhutan, Assam hills north of Brahmaputra River. Other races in central Nepal and western Himalayas.

GENERAL HABITS: Strictly arboreal. Small noisy flocks in winter; pairs in summer. Commonly amongst the mixed itinerant hunting parties. Very active and lively. Hunts in the foliage canopy and on moss covered tree-trunks with tit-like acrobatics, hanging upside down on sprigs to peer under the leaves and in crevices. Sometimes flies out to catch an insect on the wing. Berries and seeds are also eaten. A regular visitor to *Salmalia* (=*Bombax*) and rhododendron flowers for insects and nectar. Hops swiftly from branch to branch like a laughing thrush or scimitar babbler. Flight like tree pie's, from tree-top to tree-top; also reminiscent of the minivet's. Has a clear, rather mournful whistling song *tee-riri-reeri-reeri*, like the jingling of a tiny silver bell, repeated every half minute or so. In the distance this sometimes sounds like the strident 'music' of a large cicada.

NESTING: *Season*—April to July. *Nest*—a deep cup of moss, grass and roots in a high bush or small tree, 8 to 20 ft. up. *Eggs*—2 or 3, pale bluish grey, clouded, spotted and lined with various shades of brown. Size about 25×19 mm.

RACIAL CHARACTERISTICS, MEASUREMENTS, ETC: The adjoining Nepal race *nigriceps* is paler and more cinnamon coloured, with a suffusion of olive (instead of clove) in the greyish brown saddle. The west Himalayan race, *capistrata*, is the palest and largest of the three.

Three specimens collected by the Sikkim Survey measure:

| | Wing | Bill | Tarsus | Tail |
|---|---|---|---|---|
| 2 ♂♂ | | 22-22.5 | 30-30.5 | 102.5-103.5 mm. |
| 1 ♀ | 92 | 21 | 27.5 | 97.5 mm. |

Twenty adults in the Schäfer Sikkim collection have Wing 89 (♀) to 101 (♂) against the Fauna's '91-96' mm. (Stresemann).

Iris brown; bill black; legs and feet brownish flesh colour; claws horny brown.

## THE LONGTAILED SIBIA

*Heterophasia picaoides picaoides* (Hodgson)

*Sibia picaoides* Hodgson, 1839, *Jour. Asiat. Soc. Bengal* 8: 38—Nepal.

F.B.I. 1: 295

LOCAL NAME: Matcheo-pho (Lepcha).

SIZE: Bulbul, with a long tail.

FIELD CHARACTERS: A long-tailed greyish brown bulbul-like bird with black forehead, a white patch on the wings, and white-tipped graduated tail. *Above*, deep slaty brown. *Below*, ashy grey; slaty brown on throat and breast, whitish on abdomen. Sexes alike.

STATUS AND HABITAT: Resident at fairly low elevations, from the base of the hills to about 3000 ft. where Stevens found it breeding. The Survey only came across it at Rangpo and Singtam, between 1200 and 1800 ft. Frequents rather open scrub forest interspersed with large trees such as *Salmalia* (=*Bombax*).

DISTRIBUTION OUTSIDE SIKKIM: Eastern Nepal, Bhutan, Assam hills north of the Brahmaputra. Other races in Burma, Thailand, Indo-china, Malaya, Indonesia.

GENERAL HABITS: Arboreal. In small parties or flocks of up to 20. Very partial to the large red flowers of the Silk Cotton tree (*Salmalia*), feeding on the nectar in company with such habitués as Haircrested Drongos and Black Bulbuls. Also eats insects, flower-buds and seeds. A rich whistling call of thrush quality is constantly uttered. It consists of six notes ending *wheet-wheew*, recalling in cadence the song of the Quaker Babbler (*Alcippe poioicephala*), but much louder. While the birds hop among the branches the long tail is frequently swung about and cocked over the back as in the Himalayan Tree Pie.

NESTING: Stevens took nests in the Rungbong Valley at *c.* 3000 ft. elevation. *Season*—April to June. *Nest*—a cup of green and brown moss lined with moss roots. Placed among tufts of needles high up in Chir pines, and almost invisible from below. *Eggs*—5 (?), pale grey-green, finely marked all over with small blotches of light reddish brown, more densely at the broad end. Some eggs are erythristic, i.e. pale pinkish white marked with pale red instead of reddish brown. Size about 25×18 mm.

RACIAL CHARACTERISTICS, MEASUREMENTS, ETC: ♂♀ Wing 120-125; bill *c.* 24; *c.* 30; tail 210-220 mm.

Iris red or crimson, occasionally brown; bill black or horny black; legs dusky grey; claws horny brown. (Stuart Baker.)

## *Subfamily* SYLVIINAE: Warblers

### THE SLATYBELLIED WREN[1]

*Tesia cyaniventer* Hodgson

*Tesia cyaniventer* Hodgson, 1837, *Jour. Asiat. Soc. Bengal* **6**: 101—Nepal.

F.B.I. **1**: 463

LOCAL NAMES: Tisi (Nepali); Samtit-tammong (Lepcha).

SIZE: Sparrow —. Same as the Brown Wren (p. 157).

FIELD CHARACTERS: At first glimpse a tiny, plump, tailless, dark grey wren. Two distinct forms (or species?):

(a) *olivea: Above,* forehead, crown and nape glistening golden olive; lores, and a broad stripe from eye to nape black; back, edges to wings, upper tail-coverts and tail olive-green. *Below,* sides of head and underparts slate-blue. Sexes alike.

(b) *cyaniventer: Above,* head olive-green concolorous with rest of upper parts. A diffuse yellowish supercilium above the black post-orbital streak. *Below,* ashy suffused with white. Sexes alike.

STATUS AND HABITAT: Fairly common. There is suggestive evidence from the adjoining Bhutan area that (a) and (b) may be altitudinal forms, the darker (*olivea*) breeding up to about 6000 ft., and the paler (*cyaniventer*) higher up—a case parallel with that of the Brown and Scalybreasted Wrens (*Microura*). Proof in the shape of actually breeding birds is not yet available. All the three examples obtained by the Sikkim Survey were at *c.* 1000 ft. elevation (Rangpo, Singtam) in December, and belong to the paler form *cyaniventer*, presumably a winter visitor from the higher altitudes. I have examined a ♂ of the dark, golden headed *olivea* taken in January between Rorathang and Rongli, in the Chicago Museum of Natural History.

Affects tangled humid undergrowth of ferns, weeds and nettles in forest.

DISTRIBUTION OUTSIDE SIKKIM: Garhwal (?), Nepal, Assam hills north and south of Brahmaputra River; Naga Hills, Manipur, Burma, N. Thailand, N. Yunnan, Indochina, S. China. The species extends to Java.

GENERAL HABITS: Very similar to those of the Brown Wren (p. 157). Keeps singly on or near the ground, skulking amongst the rank herbage. Prances ceaselessly among fern and weed stalks, now clambering up one, now hopping to the next and back again, now up and down the same stem like some clockwork toy, but all so lightly that hardly a leaf stirs to mark its position. Usually a fairly loud *chirik-chirik* gives the only indication of its presence. This is apparently not so much an alarm call as merely a sign of awareness of an intruder's proximity, and of its own extreme inquisitiveness. Has a lively wren-like song, described as a clear, rippling, whistling *pip-pipi-pip-pipeti-pip.*

NESTING: *Season*—chiefly May to June. *Nest*—a ball of vivid green moss, compactly lined with fine moss roots. Placed about a

[1] Preferably 'Slatybellied Ground Warbler' as 'Wren' is a misnomer.

foot from the ground in low brushwood or among boulders on a steep bank, hidden in moss and weeds. *Eggs*—usually 4, pale pink profusely and densely stippled with bright brick-red, with variations. Size about 18×13 mm.

RACIAL CHARACTERISTICS, MEASUREMENTS, ETC: The Sikkim Survey specimens measure:

| | Wing | Bill | Tarsus | Tail |
|---|---|---|---|---|
| 1 ♂ | 50 | 14.5 | 24 | 19 mm. |
| 1 ♀ | 49 | 13 | 23 | 19.5 mm. |
| 1 o? | 51 | 14 | 24 | 17 mm. |

Iris brown; upper mandible blackish brown, lower yellow to deep orange with horny brown tip; legs, feet and claws brownish flesh with slight olive tinge.

## THE CHESTNUT-HEADED WREN

***Tesia castaneocoronata castaneocoronata*** **(Burton)**

*Sylvia? castaneocoronata* Burton, 1836, *Proc. Zool. Soc. London:* 152—Himalayas (=Nepal).

**Plate 18, fig. 3 (facing p. 209)**

F.B.I. 1: 465

LOCAL NAMES: Tisi (Nepali); Samtit-pho (Lepcha).

SIZE: Sparrow−. Same as the Brown and Slatybellied Wrens.

FIELD CHARACTERS: A tiny, tailless, bright coloured wren. *Above*, forehead, crown, and nape bright chestnut. Rest of upper plumage including wings and diminutive tail dark olive-green. *Below*, bright yellow. Sexes alike.

STATUS AND HABITAT: Not common, but found from low elevations (Rangpo, Singtam, Singhik, Lingtam) up to 10,000 ft. or more according to Blanford, with perhaps some seasonal altitudinal movement. In Bhutan, Ludlow frequently met with it at 10,000 to 11,000 ft. A specimen was collected by Polunin at 13,000 ft. in central Nepal in August/September (*JBNHS* 52:890). Affects similar facies to the Slatybellied Wren—dense, low brushwood and nettles etc. in humid forest, especially in ravines and bordering streams.

DISTRIBUTION OUTSIDE SIKKIM: The Himalayas from Kulu eastward, including the Assam hills north and south of Brahmaputra River. Burma, Yunnan. The species extends to Tonkin.

GENERAL HABITS: Restless, skulking—similar to the Slatybellied Wren, though perhaps oftener seen hopping among weed stems and seedlings a foot or two above ground, and on rocks in fern-scrub and brushwood. In addition to the inquisitive, chattering, wren-like *chiruk-chiruk*, it is described as having a loud and piercing *seek-seek* note (Whistler), a single distinctive alarm note *wee* repeated at intervals of several seconds (Ripley), and a shrill call of four notes resembling that of the Greyheaded Flycatcher, *Culicicapa ceylonensis*, uttered at intervals (Osmaston)—none of which I have heard.

NESTING: *Season*—May to July. *Nest* (a ball of moss), and *eggs*, in size and colour, indistinguishable from those of the Slatybellied Wren. A cuckoo's egg was taken from a nest at Tonglu (10,000 ft., Darjeeling Dist.) by Mr C. M. Inglis.

RACIAL CHARACTERISTICS, MEASUREMENTS, ETC: The distinctive juvenile is not described in the Fauna. It is 'dark olive-green with a brownish tint above, and chestnut below' (*Ibis*, 1957: 261).

Two specimens collected by the Sikkim Survey (♀, ♂?) measure: Wing 48-49, bill 11; tarsus 21-22; tail 21.5-22 mm.

Eleven Sikkim specimens collected by Stevens, now in the Chicago Museum of Natural History, have Wing 5 ♂♂ 48-50 (av. 49); 6 ♀♀ 45-50 (av. 47) mm.

Iris brown; upper mandible horny brown, lower yellowish with brownish tip; legs, feet and claws brownish flesh with an olive tinge.

## THE RUFOUSCAPPED BUSH WARBLER

*Cettia brunnifrons brunnifrons* (Hodgson)

*Prinia brunnifrons* Hodgson, 1845, *Proc. Zool. Soc. London:* 29—Nepal.

F.B.I. 2: 512

LOCAL NAME: Lik-lik-pho (Lepcha).

SIZE: Sparrow—.

FIELD CHARACTERS: *Above*, forehead, crown, and nape chestnut-brown shading to rufous olive-brown on rest of upper plumage including exposed portions of wings and tail. A pale buff supercilium. Lores and a line behind eye blackish. *Below*, chin, throat and breast grey. Flanks darker grey, shading into ochraceous on thighs and under tail-coverts. Centre of breast and abdomen white. Sexes alike.

STATUS AND HABITAT: Common resident. Breeding at *c.* 10,000-12,000 ft. (Lachung, Singalila Ridge); descending to *c.* 3500 ft. or lower in winter. Schäfer collected specimens in October, November, February, March and July between *c.* 5000 and 13,500 ft. (Chungthang, Gangtok, Lachen, Lachung, Thangu, Changu).

In Bhutan, Ludlow found it 'very common indeed' between 9000 and 13,000 ft. in summer, and collected several juveniles, July to September.

Affects bamboo clumps, rhododendron scrub, and bramble and grass thickets in forest clearings.

DISTRIBUTION OUTSIDE SIKKIM: Nepal to Bhutan and Assam. The adjoining western Himalayas, from Garhwal to the Pir Panjal Range, are occupied by the paler and brighter race *whistleri*. Eastward, the species stretches into Yunnan.

GENERAL HABITS: Like its congeners, a great skulker. The alarm note is described as a shrill piercing whistle. Another call which is constantly repeated 'consists of ordinary chirping notes, followed by a curious grating mouse-like sound, twice repeated and of a ventriloquistic nature' (Osmaston).

NESTING: *Season*—May-June. *Nest*—a domed oval of moss, dry grass and bamboo leaves scantily lined with fine grass and feathers, and with a circular opening near the top. Placed low down in thick bushes *c.* 2 ft. from the ground. *Eggs*—3 or 4, variable, pale to very deep terra cotta red with a darker cap at the broad end. Size about 18×13 mm.

RACIAL CHARACTERISTICS, MEASUREMENTS, ETC: Stresemann found two of Schäfer's specimens of 10 September moulting feathers of the back and all tail feathers simultaneously, but not the wing feathers. Dr Ripley also collected a specimen in west Nepal, *c.* 500 ft. in January, with all the tail feathers missing, which suggests that this may well be the characteristic pattern of moult in this species. Minus tail, and in its scrubby environment, the last looked deceptively like a *Tesia*!

Schäfer's good series from Sikkim measures: Wing 6 ♂♂ 48-51 (av. 48.7); 3 ♀♀ 45, 47, 47 mm. (Stresemann).

Iris hazel; upper mandible black, lower fleshy yellow; legs and feet fleshy white, darker on joints and toes.

## THE LARGE BUSH WARBLER

*Cettia major major* (Moore)

*Horeites major* Moore, 1854, Cat. Birds Mus. E. I. Co. 1: 323—Nepal.

F.B.I. 2: 510

LOCAL NAME:

SIZE: Sparrow—.

FIELD CHARACTERS: Differs from all other Sikkim bush warblers in having the crown contrastingly coloured with the back.

*Above*, crown of head deep rich chestnut-brown. Line of forehead and supercilium paler, more rufous. Lores and a line behind eye blackish. Upper plumage including exposed portions of tail and wings dark olive-brown, the last tinged rufous. *Below*, chin, throat and breast greyish white. Rest of lower parts dull white suffused with brown excepting on centre of abdomen. Sexes alike.

STATUS AND HABITAT: Resident. Recorded as breeding at *c.* 9000 ft. (Lachung), and doubtless breeds at still higher elevations. Sikkim specimens collected in April, May, June, August and October are in the British Museum, but without altitudinal data. In Bhutan, where this bird is apparently more plentiful than in Sikkim or Nepal, Ludlow found it at higher altitudes than any other bush warbler. He procured it up to 13,500 ft. between July and September. Its favourite habitat was dense rhododendron jungle in silver fir forest. The habitat in Sikkim is unrecorded, but will presumably be the same.

DISTRIBUTION OUTSIDE SIKKIM: Nepal, Bhutan, Szechwan.

GENERAL HABITS: Typical of this group.

NESTING: *Season*—(June)-July. *Nest* and *eggs* indistinguishable from those of *C. fortipes* (p. 220), the eggs measuring about 18×14 mm.

RACIAL CHARACTERISTICS, MEASUREMENTS, ETC: The Fauna gives for ♂♀ Wing 57-67; bill 11; tarsus 24-25; tail 44-51 mm.

Iris brown; bill horny brown, yellowish on lower mandible and commissure; legs and feet 'tan-brown'.

## BLANFORD'S BUSH WARBLER

*Cettia pallidipes pallidipes* (Blanford)

*Phylloscopus pallidipes* Blanford, 1872, *Jour. Asiat. Soc. Bengal* **41** (2), pl. vii, fig. 1—Sikkim.

**Plate 22, fig. 4** (facing p. 273)

F.B.I. **2**: 508

LOCAL NAME:

SIZE: Sparrow−.

FIELD CHARACTERS: Differs from the Strongfooted Bush Warbler (p. 220) in being olive-brown above with only the edges of the flight feathers tinged rufous. Also in the under tail-coverts being brownish white, and the legs fleshy white. Sexes alike.

STATUS AND HABITAT: Resident; recorded breeding between *c.* 4000 and 5000 ft. altitude. Apparently descends to lower levels in winter. The British Museum has Sikkim specimens collected in March, May and August (elevations ?), and others from the Bhutan duars, January and April. Ludlow did not procure it in higher Bhutan. Affects scrub growth in forest.

DISTRIBUTION OUTSIDE SIKKIM: Dehra Dun and western Nepal (Osmaston, Ripley) to E. Assam, north and south of the Brahmaputra River; Manipur, N. Burma. The species extends to Yunnan and the Andamans.

GENERAL HABITS: Typical of the bush warblers: skulking in undergrowth and difficult to observe. It has a very insistent 4-noted call (Osmaston).

NESTING: *Season*—May-June. *Nest* and *eggs* indistinguishable from those of the bush warblers described, the latter both as to colour and size.

RACIAL CHARACTERISTICS, MEASUREMENTS, ETC: The Fauna gives the measurements as: ♂♀ Wing 47-54; bill 10-11; tarsus *c.* 20; tail 40-49 mm.

Iris brown; bill pale horny, darker on culmen; legs and feet yellowish white or fleshy white.

## THE STRONGFOOTED BUSH WARBLER

*Cettia fortipes fortipes* (Hodgson)

*Horornis fortipes* Hodgson, 1845, *Proc. Zool. Soc. London:* 31—Nepal.

F.B.I. 2: 506

LOCAL NAME:

SIZE: Sparrow —.

FIELD CHARACTERS: *Above,* including exposed portions of wings and tail, dark rufous olive-brown. A narrow buff supercilium to nape. Lores and a line through eye brown. *Below,* buffish brown, paler on chin and throat, white on centre of abdomen. Sexes alike.

STATUS AND HABITAT: Fairly common and resident at elevations between *c.* 3500 and 6500 ft. (Chungthang, Kewzing, Gangtok)—November to April. In Bhutan, where it is apparently the commonest bush warbler, Ludlow procured specimens between 6500 and 8000 ft. —July to October. Affects bamboo jungle, bramble thickets and grass-and-bracken scrub in forest.

DISTRIBUTION OUTSIDE SIKKIM: Nepal, Bhutan, Assam, Manipur, N. Burma. The species extends to the Indochinese and Malaysian subregions.

GENERAL HABITS: Keeps singly to undergrowth, hopping about amongst the branches in search of insect food, seldom showing itself, and only rarely ascending to moderate heights in trees. Its distinctive call, usually the only indication of its presence, is an amazingly loud series of explosive notes preceded by a thin long-drawn whistle.

NESTING: *Season*—May to July. *Nest*—domed, similar to that of the next. *Eggs*—3 to 5, also deep chestnut-chocolate like those of Hume's Bush Warbler, measuring about 17×13 mm.

RACIAL CHARACTERISTICS, MEASUREMENTS, ETC: On an unobstructed view, may be differentiated in the field from the last (*C. pallidipes*) by the colour of the upper plumage (more rufous-brown instead of olive-brown) and of the legs (brownish instead of whitish).

Schäfer's Sikkim specimens (2 ♂♂) have Wing 56, 57 mm. The Fauna gives the range (♂♀) as: Wing 50-57; bill 10-11; tarsus 21-22; tail 41-51 mm. (Bill '♂ 13-15 mm.'—Kinnear).

Iris dark brown; bill horny brown, paler below; legs and feet pale fleshy brown to brown.

## HUME'S BUSH WARBLER

*Cettia acanthizoides brunnescens* (Hume)

*Horeites brunnescens* Hume, 1872, *Ibis:* 109—Darjeeling.

F.B.I. 2: 505

LOCAL NAME:

SIZE: Sparrow —.

FIELD CHARACTERS: *Above,* rufous-brown, brighter rufous on exposed portions of wings and tail. A broad buffy yellow supercilium.

Lores and behind eye dark brown. Cheeks and ear-coverts mottled brown and yellowish. *Below*, greyish buff, browner on flanks. Sexes alike.

STATUS AND HABITAT: Stevens procured it at *c.* 10,000 ft. (above Karponang), in March, 'in dense "prong" bamboo thickets, a habitat similarly frequented by *Conostoma aemodium*'. The British Museum has Sikkim skins collected by Mandelli in January, February, April and November, but without data as to localities or heights. Neither Schäfer nor the recent Survey obtained it in Sikkim. Ludlow found it at *c.* 9000 ft. in Bhutan.

DISTRIBUTION OUTSIDE SIKKIM: Nepal; Bhutan to E. Assam north and south of Brahmaputra River; Manipur, Lushai Hills. The species extends to western China.

GENERAL HABITS: Skulks singly in shrubbery at high elevations. B. B. Osmaston describes its call as a series of four long-drawn whistles, each higher than the last, followed by a quick series of up and down notes.

NESTING: *Season*—May-June, between *c.* 9500 and 10,500 ft. *Nest*—domed; of bamboo leaves and grass, densely lined with feathers, with entrance hole near the top. Placed in ringal bamboo bushes within *c.* 2 ft. of the ground. *Eggs*—2 or 3, deep rich terra cotta red with a darker cap at the broad end. Size about 17×13 mm.

RACIAL CHARACTERISTICS, MEASUREMENTS, ETC: The several birds of this group occurring in Sikkim are superficially very alike in appearance and habits and difficult to differentiate in the field. Therefore, unless confirmed by specimens, sight records are not completely dependable.

The Fauna gives the measurements (♂♀) as: Wing 50-54; bill *c.* 9; tarsus 21-22; tail 40-49 mm.

Iris brown; bill horny brown, lower mandible fleshy brown tipped darker; legs and feet fleshy or yellowish brown.

## THE ABERRANT WARBLER

*Cettia flavolivaceus flavolivaceus* (Hodgson)

*Neornis flavolivacea* Hodgson, 1845, in Blyth, *Jour. Asiat. Soc. Bengal* 14: 590—Nepal.

F.B.I. 2: 502

LOCAL NAME:

SIZE: Sparrow—.

FIELD CHARACTERS: A sober coloured little bird superficially very like a leaf warbler (*Phylloscopus*), with no wing-bar. *Above*, including exposed portions of wings and tail, dull olive-green. A narrow yellow supercilium from nostril to nape. A brown line from lores through eye. *Below*, fulvous yellow, suffused with brown on sides of breast and flanks. Sexes alike.

STATUS AND HABITAT: Stevens records it at 3500 ft. elevation in February (Rungbong Valley) and at 10,000 ft. in May (Sikkim-Nepal frontier). Not met with by the Survey, but Schäfer collected an adult and a juvenile at 9200 ft. on 27 August (Lachen) which shows that it breeds at that altitude. Ludlow found it common between 7000 and 12,000 ft. in Bhutan—July to October—and collected adults as well as juveniles up to 12,750 ft.

Affects mixed tall grass-and-bracken scrub at the edge of forest.

DISTRIBUTION OUTSIDE SIKKIM: The Himalayas from the Tons Valley in W. Garhwal eastward through Nepal to W. Assam. The species, in other races, extends through Assam to Burma and W. China.

GENERAL HABITS: Said to be an inquisitive bird, and not very shy. Skulks and hops about amongst the undergrowth, rarely if ever ascending into trees. The normal call note is a *tsik* or *chek* rather like a Whitethroat's. Heinrich describes its song as a short, extraordinarily high and thin whistle.

NESTING: *Season*—May-June, from 3500 ft. to at least 9000. *Nest*—globular, of bamboo leaves and grass lined with feathers, with entrance hole near the top. Placed on the ground or a few inches above it, in grass and scrub. *Eggs*—3, deep dull claret colour with a dark zone or cap at the broad end. Size about 18×13 mm.

RACIAL CHARACTERISTICS, MEASUREMENTS, ETC: The Fauna gives the measurements of ♂♀ as: Wing 53-56; bill 10-11; tarsus *c.* 22; tail 48-56 mm.

Schäfer's Sikkim skins have Wing ad. ♀ 52; juv. ♀ 52 mm. On 7 August the former was in post-nuptial moult with primaries 7, 8 and 9 (counting inward) in quill. The young bird had not yet commenced post-juvenal moult. (Stresemann.)

Iris hazel; bill horny, paler yellowish brown on lower mandible; legs and feet pale yellowish brown.

## THE BROWN BUSH WARBLER

*Bradypterus luteoventris luteoventris* (Hodgson)

*Tribura luteoventris* Hodgson, 1845, *Proc. Zool. Soc. London:* 30—Nepal.

F.B.I. 2: 406

LOCAL NAME:

SIZE: Sparrow−.

FIELD CHARACTERS: *Above*, including closed wings and tail, rufous-brown; the tail darker and cross-rayed. A narrow pale buff supercilium, and sometimes a ring of whitish feathers round eye. Sides of head and neck rufous, the first with faint white shaft-stripes. *Below*, chin, throat, middle of lower breast and abdomen white. Upper breast, flanks, vent, and under tail-coverts rufous; the last more or less scalloped with white. Sexes alike.

STATUS AND HABITAT: Obtained at Phalut (*c.* 11,500 ft., Darjeeling Dist.) in summer by C. M. Inglis. Status probably more or less same as of the next species, but not recorded by the Sikkim Survey nor by Schäfer. In adjoining Bhutan Ludlow collected specimens between 8000 and 11,000 ft. in June and July, but did not meet with it as high up as *B. thoracicus*. Affects open grass and bush country on hillsides; also undergrowth in pine forest.

DISTRIBUTION OUTSIDE SIKKIM: Nepal, Bhutan, Assam hills north and south of Brahmaputra River; Chin Hills, N. Burma. Other races in Burma, Thailand, and the Indochinese subregion.

GENERAL HABITS: Similar to the Spotted Bush Warbler (below). Keeps to tall grass and bushes, mounting a stem now and again to expose itself momentarily. Its song is described as very like the chirping of a large grasshopper. Stuart Baker likens it to that of a 'common Reed Warbler' (species?) but much softer and lower. Its alarm notes, *tek . . . tek*, are reminiscent of a Whitethroat's.

NESTING: Not specifically recorded in Sikkim. *Nest* and *eggs* similar to those of the foregoing.

RACIAL CHARACTERISTICS, MEASUREMENTS, ETC: For diagnosis see under *B. thoracicus*.

The Fauna gives for ♂♀ Wing 52-58; bill 10-11; tarsus 19-20; tail 55-66 mm. Ludlow's Bhutan skins measure Wing 3 ♂♂ 53; 1 ♀ 52 mm.

'Iris yellowish brown to bright hazel; bill: above dark horny brown or blackish, lower mandible and commissure fleshy yellow or light horny, more yellow at the mouth; legs flesh colour, fleshy yellow to dark fleshy brown.'

## THE SPOTTED BUSH WARBLER

*Bradypterus thoracicus thoracicus* (Blyth)

*Dumeticola thoracica* Blyth, 1845, *Jour. Asiat. Soc. Bengal* **14**: 584—Nepal.

**Plate 18, fig. 7** (facing p. 209)

F.B.I. **2**: 405

LOCAL NAME:

SIZE: Sparrow –.

FIELD CHARACTERS: A skulking plain brown bird of scrub and bushes. *Above*, rufous-brown including closed wings and tail. A supercilium from bill to nape, white anteriorly, grey behind eye. A small blackish line under eye. Sides of head, and ear-coverts, ashy brown, the latter with pale shafts. *Below*, chin and upper throat bufty white; foreneck and upper breast ashy brown, boldly spotted with blackish; lower breast ashy. Flanks, vent and under tail-coverts dull rufous-brown, the last scalloped with white. Sexes alike.

STATUS AND HABITAT: Resident, moving altitudinally with season. ? Uncommon. The British Museum contains specimens collected in the Sikkim Himalayas (Darjeeling Dist.) in 1875 or thereabouts by Mandelli and Gammie who found it breeding between 5000 and 10,000 ft. In recent years obtained at Phalut 9000 ft. by C. M. Inglis in summer. In adjoining Bhutan, Ludlow procured it between July and September at 11,000 to 13,000 ft. and as high as 14,500 ft., in dwarf juniper.

Affects open ground under mixed grass and bracken bushes and low scrub.

DISTRIBUTION OUTSIDE SIKKIM: *Summer* (breeding), Central Asia; the Himalayas from Kashmir to Bhutan; possibly also the mountains of N. Assam. *Winter,* lower elevations and foothills.

GENERAL HABITS: Insectivorous; non-gregarious; keeping to bushes and low undergrowth. According to Ludlow it is not a great skulker and shows itself up freely while it weaves its way through the shrubbery. The only note recorded is a loud *tchik tchik.*

NESTING: *Season*—May-June. *Nest*—deep cup-shaped or domed, of coarse grass, rough and loose on the outside, compact within, usually with just one or two feathers as token lining. Well concealed amongst low bracken and grass tufts, on or near the ground. *Eggs*—3 or 4, pale pinkish, densely specked and freckled with pinkish red. Size about 18×14 mm.

RACIAL CHARACTERISTICS, MEASUREMENTS, ETC: In this and the last species, *Bradypterus luteoventris,* the feathers are of a soft silky texture. Tail much rounded, with the feathers rather pointed. First primary in both about half the length of the second, but throat in *thoracicus* ashy, spotted with black, as against unspotted white in the other.

Specimens collected by Ludlow in Bhutan give Wing 5 ♂♂ 51-55; 4 ♀♀ 52.5-55 mm. (Kinnear).

'Iris dark brown; bill dark horny brown to black above, lower mandible fleshy or pale horny; mouth and edges of gape yellow; tarsus pale wax yellow or fleshy yellow; toes darker and claws horny brown.' (Fauna.)

## TICKELL'S LEAF WARBLER

### *Phylloscopus affinis* (Tickell)

*Motacilla offinis* [*sic*] Tickell, 1833, *Jour. Asiat. Soc. Bengal* 2: 576—Borabhúm.

F.B.I. 2: 454

LOCAL NAME: Ani chin (Tibetan).

SIZE: Sparrow—.

FIELD CHARACTERS: A ground-feeding leaf warbler with no trace of a wing-bar. *Above,* dark olive-green with a bright yellow supercilium. *Below,* clear bright yellow. Legs pale coloured. Sexes alike.

STATUS AND HABITAT: Breeds at high elevations in the Tibetan plateau facies of northern Sikkim where Schäfer collected specimens, including juveniles, in July 1938 (Thangu, Gyagong). Apparently only a passage migrant in central and southern Sikkim. Blanford (*Jour. Asiat. Soc. Bengal,* 1872: 54) shot two or three examples in the Lachen and Lachung Valleys at 8000-9000 ft. about 26 September (1870) which he believed were on passage from their breeding grounds in Tibet. Schäfer also obtained it at Lachen in October and November, and Ludlow at Gangtok, 30 April.

DISTRIBUTION OUTSIDE SIKKIM: *Summer* (breeding), the alpine and Tibetan facies of the Himalayas and beyond, between 8000 and

1. Rufousbreasted Accentor (*Prunella s. strophiata*) 2. Allied Grosbeak (*Mycerobas affinis*) 3. Redheaded Bullfinch (*Pyrrhula erythrocephala*) 4. Goldenheaded Black Finch (*Pyrrhoplectes epauletta*) 5. Scarlet Finch (*Haematospiza sipahi*) 6. Sikkim Whitebrowed Rosefinch (*Carpodacus t. thura*) 7. Sikkim Large Rosefinch (*Carpodacus e. rubicunda*) 8. Nepal Dark Rosefinch (*Carpodacus n. nipalensis*) 9. Redbrowed Finch (*Callacanthis burtoni*)—see Appendix 10. Tibetan Siskin (*Carduelis t. thibetana*) 11. Hodgson's Mountain Finch (*Leucosticte n. nemoricola*)

PLATE 19

1. Nepal Crimsonwinged Laughing Thrush (*Garrulax p. phoeniceus*) 2. Sikkim Redheaded Laughing Thrush (*Garrulax e. nigrimentum*) 3. Coralbilled Scimitar Babbler (*Pomatorhinus f. ferruginosus*) 4. Sikkim Striated Laughing Thrush (*Garrulax s. sikkimensis*) 5. Sikkim Rufousnecked Scimitar Babbler (*Pomatorhinus r. godwini*) 6. Rufouschinned Laughing Thrush (*Garrulax r. rufogularis*) 7. Sikkim Greysided Laughing Thrush (*Garrulax c. caerulatus*) 8. Whitespotted Laughing Thrush (*Garrulax o. ocellatus*) 9. Bluewinged Laughing Thrush (*Garrulax squamatus*) 10. Slenderbilled Scimitar Babbler (*Xiphirhynchus s. superciliaris*)

PLATE 20 [*c.* × ½]

15,000 ft., from Gilgit to NW. Kansu. *Winter*, practically all India and Burma.

GENERAL HABITS: Affects scrub-covered treeless country, feeding largely on the ground. Flicks wings nervously and utters a feeble sparrow-like *tsip* as it hops about. Usually single, but sometimes several loosely together. *Food:* tiny insects. *Song:* (in breeding season) a single note repeated quickly four to six times preceded by a high-pitched *pick*, thus *pick . . . whiw-whiw-whiw-whiw* etc. delivered from a bush.

NESTING: *Season*—June-July. *Nest*—an untidy ball of coarse grass well lined with feathers. Placed low down in a dwarf juniper or furze bush. *Eggs*—4 or 5, pure china white, sometimes faintly marked at the large end with scanty red specks. Size about 15×12 mm.

RACIAL CHARACTERISTICS, MEASUREMENTS, ETC: Specimens collected in Sikkim and S. Tibet by Schäfer give Wing 5 ad. ♂♂ 60-62; 4 ad. ♀♀ 54-59 mm. (Stresemann).

Iris dark brown; upper mandible brown, lower mandible and gape horny yellow; legs and feet horny olivaceous or pale horny brown; soles dingy yellow.

## THE SMOKY LEAF WARBLER

*Phylloscopus fuligiventer fuligiventer* (Hodgson)

*Horornis? fuligiventer* Hodgson, 1845, *Proc. Zool. Soc. London:* 31—Nepal.

F.B.I. 2:460

LOCAL NAME:

SIZE: Sparrow—.

FIELD CHARACTERS: No trace of a wing-bar. *Above*, including wings and tail, dark sooty brown, with an ill-defined dusky yellow supercilium. *Below*, dusky oil-green; centre of breast dull yellow. Sexes alike.

STATUS AND HABITAT: Blanford collected a specimen in rhododendron scrub at *c.* 14,000 ft. (Momé Samdong) in September 1870, and Schäfer another at 13,000 ft. (Thangu) on 16 July 1938. In winter, Meinertzhagen procured one near Teesta Bridge (1000 ft.) just south of the Sikkim frontier (28 December 1925). The recent Sikkim Survey failed to record it between November and May.

In Bhutan, Ludlow notes it as affecting rocks and boulders in open ground in and above the rhododendron-scrub zone, *c.* 14,000 ft., in August.

DISTRIBUTION OUTSIDE SIKKIM: *Winter*, 'Lower elevations in the eastern Himalayas and their foothills; Nepal; (Sikkim); Bhutan; the Duars east to Sadiya north of the Brahmaputra River, west to Darbhanga' (Ticehurst). Rarely also south of the Brahmaputra.

NESTING: Unknown, but probably breeds at high elevations in N. Sikkim.

RACIAL CHARACTERISTICS, MEASUREMENTS, ETC: Ticehurst gives the measurements as:

| | Wing | Bill | Tarsus | Tail |
|---|---|---|---|---|
| ♂♂ | 56.5-61.5 | 12.5-14 | 21.5-22 | 45-51 mm. |
| ♀♀ | 52-58 | | | 43-48 mm. |

Iris brown; upper mandible black; lower mandible brown, yellowish at base; legs and feet greenish brown.

## THE DUSKY LEAF WARBLER

*Phylloscopus fuscatus fuscatus* (Blyth)

*Phyllopneuste fuscata* Blyth, 1842, *Jour. Asiat. Soc. Bengal* **11**: 113—Calcutta.

**Plate 18, fig. 8 (facing p. 209)**

F.B.I. 2: 461

LOCAL NAME:

SIZE: Sparrow—.

FIELD CHARACTERS: No trace of a wing-bar. 'Upper parts fairly warm grey-brown, darkest on head, wings and tail . . . Conspicuous pale superciliary stripe above dark brown line from bill through eye. Underparts pale grey, tinged with buff; sides warm buff (but variable). Legs brown.

'Keeps close to the ground, sometimes skulking hidden among roots etc., at other times coming into the open. . . The phylloscopine flicking of wings and tail (especially tail) incessant. Tail square, less forked than in, for example, the Siberian Chiffchaff (*P. collybita tristis*). Call note *tack* or *tek*, rather like the Lesser Whitethroat's (*Sylvia curruca*), but softer' (H. G. Alexander).

STATUS: Winter visitor. Sight records of leaf warblers are by themselves unreliable, but Dr Ticehurst has examined winter specimens from low elevations in Sikkim. The bird has also been obtained by Dr Dillon Ripley in Nepal and by Mr F. Ludlow in Bhutan.

RACIAL CHARACTERISTICS, MEASUREMENTS, ETC: Ticehurst gives as follows:

| | Wing | Bill | Tarsus | Tail |
|---|---|---|---|---|
| ♂♂ | 60-70, mostly 61-66 | 12-13.5 | 21-23 | 50-56 mm. |
| ♀♀ | 53.5-61, mostly 55-58 | | | 44-50.5 mm. |

Iris brown; upper mandible and tip of lower dusky brown, yellowish flesh at base of lower mandible; legs and feet brownish flesh, yellowish brown, or olivaceous brown.

## THE GREYFACED LEAF WARBLER

*Phylloscopus maculipennis maculipennis* (Blyth)
*Abrornis maculipennis* Blyth, 1867, *Ibis:* 27—Nepal or Sikkim.

F.B.I. 2: 468
LOCAL NAME:
SIZE: Sparrow—.

FIELD CHARACTERS: With two conspicuous yellowish wing-bars. Head brownish grey with a broken central mesial band (like 'centre parting'), and a long, well-defined whitish supercilium, bordered below by a blackish line. Grey throat contrasting with yellow breast. 'The diminutive size, yellow rump, grey head and throat, and white in the outer tail feathers at once distinguish this from any other *Phylloscopus*. Only two others have yellow rumps (both occurring in Sikkim): *proregulus* (p. 229) which has no white in the tail, and *pulcher* (p. 228) which is larger and has not a grey head and throat, and has orange, not yellowish wing-bars'. (Ticehurst.) Sexes alike.

STATUS AND HABITAT: One of the commonest leaf warblers in winter between 1000 and 7000 ft. elevation (Singtam, Chungthang, Rinchinpong, Kewzing, Manshitang, Gangtok, Pemionche). Fairly common at 9000-10,000 ft. in last week April (Lachen, Thangu), then apparently in, or working up to, its breeding grounds. Schäfer collected two examples at this elevation (near Laohen) on 11 September in post-juvenal moult.

Affects the foliage canopy and middle storey in forest.

DISTRIBUTION OUTSIDE SIKKIM: E. Nepal, Bhutan to E. Assam; Manipur, Burma, Yunnan. The paler race *virens* occupies the Punjab Himalayas to W. Nepal. Ripley has recently described an intermediate race, *centralis*, from west and central Nepal. Overall breeding and winter ranges imperfectly known.

GENERAL HABITS: Several invariably present amongst the mixed hunting flocks of 'tinies' in the canopy foliage. Sometimes also feeds singly. Exceedingly active and restless, and never still for a moment. Incessantly flicks wings and white-margined tail as it flutters and hovers in front of sprigs. The call note, constantly repeated, is a *tsip*, indistinguishable from that of *P. proregulus*.

RACIAL CHARACTERISTICS, MEASUREMENTS, ETC: Distinguished from the Greyheaded Flycatcher-Warbler (*Seicercus xanthoschistos*, p. 237)—also with double yellow wing-bars, yellow rump, and prominent white outer tail feathers—by shorter tail, iron grey (not blue grey) head with superciliary, and almost uniform pale yellow (not bright yellow) underparts.

The Survey specimens, together with others from Sikkim in the Chicago Museum of Natural History, measure:

| | Wing | Bill | Tarsus | Tail |
|---|---|---|---|---|
| 6 ♂♂ | 48-52 | 9-10.5 | 17-19 | 29-36.5 mm. |
| 1 ♀ | 48 | 10 | 18 | 34 mm. |

Schäfer's Sikkim specimens give Wing 9 ♂♂ 49-52 (av. 50.4); 4 ♀♀ 44.5-48 (av. 46.3) mm. (Stresemann).

Iris brown; bill horny brown; legs and feet horny brown with yellow tinge; claws horny brown.

## THE ORANGEBARRED LEAF WARBLER

*Phylloscopus pulcher pulcher* Blyth

*Phylloscopus pulcher* Blyth, 1845, *Jour. Asiat. Soc. Bengal* **14**: 592—Nepal.

**Plate 18, fig. 9** (facing p. 209)

F.B.I. **2**: 464

LOCAL NAME:

SIZE: Sparrow −.

FIELD CHARACTERS: Larger size, orange (not yellowish) double wing-bars, and all-yellow underparts, without the contrasting grey throat, distinguish it from *P. maculipennis*, the only other *Phylloscopus* with the combination of yellow rump-band and white outer tail feathers. (See Field Characters, p. 227.) Sexes alike.

STATUS AND HABITAT: Fairly common in winter between *c.* 4000 and 7000 ft. elevation. Meinertzhagen found it even at 11,100 ft. (Phalut) in mid-winter. Generally at higher elevations in summer; evidently breeding at *c.* 13,000 ft. (Thangu) where Schäfer collected a specimen on 13 July. Blanford procured it at 13,000 ft. in Chola Range (E. Sikkim) in September 1870, and notes: 'doubtless a resident'.

A bird of the conifer and conifer-dwarf rhododendron association, keeping to the foliage canopy.

DISTRIBUTION OUTSIDE SIKKIM: E. Nepal, Bhutan to E. Assam; Manipur, Burma, Yunnan. The race *kangrae*—more yellowish olive above and paler on head and underparts—occupies the NW. Himalayas, Kashmir to Garhwal. Birds from western and central Nepal are intermediate in coloration and recognized by Ripley as *erochroa*.

GENERAL HABITS: Very similar to *P. maculipennis*. Arboreal; usually in the mixed hunting parties of 'tinies' in lofty foliage canopy. *Call:* a loud sharp *tsip* or *twick*, constantly repeated; sometimes said to run quickly, sounding rather like a flowerpecker's twitter.

NESTING: Not recorded in Sikkim. *Season*—presumably June-July as in the western race. *Nest*—(in *kangrae*) domed, with side entrance, of green moss, lichen, strips of bark, etc., lined with feathers. Placed 8 to 15 ft. off ground. *Eggs*—3 or 4, variable, unmarked white, or white densely speckled with red. Size about 15×11 mm.

RACIAL CHARACTERISTICS, MEASUREMENTS, ETC: Ticehurst gives the range as:

| | Wing | Bill | Tarsus | Tail |
|---|---|---|---|---|
| ♂♂ | 56.5-63.5 | 12-13 | 17.5-18.5 | 40-46.5 mm. |
| ♀♀ | 52.5-57 | | | 37-41 mm. |

Three ♂♂ collected in Sikkim by Schäfer have Wing 58, 59, 61 mm.

Iris brown; bill brownish black, base of lower mandible yellowish; legs and feet horny brown.

## PALLAS'S HIMALAYAN LEAF WARBLER

*Phylloscopus proregulus newtoni* Gaetke

*Phylloscopus newtoni* Gaetke, 1889, *Ibis:* 579—India (=Darjeeling. Ticehurst).

F.B.I. 2: 466

LOCAL NAME:

SIZE: Sparrow—.

FIELD CHARACTERS: Very like *P. maculipennis* and *P. pulcher*, also with two wing-bars (yellowish), yellow band across rump and mesial coronal band, but easily distinguished from both by absence of white outer feathers in tail. Sexes alike. (See Field Characters, p. 227.)

STATUS AND HABITAT: Fairly common in winter (mid-October to April) between *c.* 1000 and 9000 ft. elevation (Singtam, Rinchinpong, Manshitang, Gangtok, Penlom La, between Lachen and Zemu, Lachen). Schäfer also obtained specimens at 13,000 ft. (Thangu) in the first week of July, evidently on their breeding ground. There is a Stevens specimen from Gnatong *c.* 12,500 ft. in the Chicago Museum of Natural History.

Affects foliage canopy of tall trees in forest.

DISTRIBUTION OUTSIDE SIKKIM: E. Nepal, Bhutan, SE. Tibet, Manipur. The adjoining, intermediate race *chloronotus* occurs in central and western Nepal. The better known *simlaensis*—with upper parts brighter, more yellowish green, and underparts paler yellow—ranges westward thence through Garhwal and Kashmir to the Afghan frontier. Eastward, the species extends to Yunnan.

GENERAL HABITS: Not appreciably different from *P. maculipennis* or *P. pulcher*. When characteristically fluttering against a sprig or at the end of a fir branch, the yellow rump, coronal streak and wing-bars show up clearly, and the absence of white in the tail furnishes a diagnostic clue. *Call:* (winter) a soft double note *tsip-tsip*.

NESTING: Once recorded on Singalila Ridge (Sikkim-Darjeeling Dist. frontier) at 10,000 ft. *Season*—July. *Nest*—a neat, domed structure of compactly interwoven bark, moss, lichen, etc., profusely lined with feathers. Placed in a tree at a moderate height. *Eggs*—3 or 4, white, sparsely scattered over with deep chestnut-red specks, more densely to form a zone at the broad end. Size about 14×11 mm.

RACIAL CHARACTERISTICS, MEASUREMENTS, ETC: Dr Ripley, who has recently made extensive collections in Nepal, feels that Nepal birds are sensibly less dark than Sikkim-E. Himalayan *newtoni*, and since Gray's name *chloronotus* was already available for them he has resuscitated it.

Two ♂♂ collected by the Survey measure: Wing 50.5-55; bill 10; tarsus 17-17.5; tail 38-40 mm.

Schäfer's fine series from Sikkim gives Wing 9 ♂♂ 52-56 (av. 53.9); 11 ♀♀ 48-52 (av. 50.4) mm.

Iris brown; bill horny brown, paler (yellowish) at base of lower mandible; legs, feet and claws horny brown.

## THE YELLOWBROWED LEAF WARBLER

*Phylloscopus inornatus inornatus* (Blyth)
*Regulus inornatus* Blyth, 1842, *Jour. Asiat. Soc. Bengal* **11**: 191—near Calcutta.

LOCAL NAME:
SIZE: Sparrow—.
FIELD CHARACTERS: Small size with relatively short tail. Conspicuous double yellowish white wing-bars. No yellow on rump. *Above*, olive-green with brown wings and tail, and a very faint incomplete pale coronal band. A broad yellow supercilium with dark line below it behind eye. *Below*, yellowish white. Sexes alike.

Characteristic call *weest*, as against *tisyip* or *chilip* in the more familiar west Himalayan race *humei*.

Breeds in the Palaearctic Region. Under 'Winter Range' Ticehurst gives 'Sikkim to 4700 ft.' The only Sikkim specimen examined by me is a female collected by the Survey at Rinchinpong (*c.* 5000 ft.) on 1.i.1953: Wing 55; bill 10; tarsus 17; tail 37 mm.

Possibly less rare than appears, as I have sight records (unconfirmed) also from Singhik and Chungthang in February.

## THE DULL GREEN LEAF WARBLER

*Phylloscopus trochiloides trochiloides* (Sundevall)
*Acanthiza trochiloides* Sundevall, 1838, *Fysiogr. Sällskap. Tidskr.* **1**: 76—Calcutta.

**Plate 18, fig. 10 (facing p. 209)**

F.B.I. **2: 478**
LOCAL NAME:
SIZE: Sparrow—.
FIELD CHARACTERS: A large leaf warbler with a single wing-bar; rarely also with traces of a second. No yellow on rump. No coronal stripe. *Above*, including edges of wings and tail, dark olive. A yellowish white supercilium with dark olive-brown lores and a line behind eye. *Below*, dirty yellowish white. Lower mandible yellow. Sexes alike.

STATUS AND HABITAT: *Summer*, fairly common and breeding at the higher altitudes, 10,000-14,000 ft. *Winter*, at lower elevations, mostly on passage to the foothills and northern plains.

(Specimens: Dentam, 4600 ft., 9 January (Meinertzhagen); Gangtok, 6000 ft., 30 April; Changu, 11,000 ft., 11 May (Ludlow); Thangu, 14,000 ft., 18 May; Yumthang, 13,000 ft., 22 June (Stevens); Thangu, 13,000 ft., 1-10 July, 1-10 October; Lachen, 9200 ft., 14 September (Schäfer); Chola Range and Lachung Valley, 10,000-14,000 ft., September (Blanford).

Affects forest.

DISTRIBUTION OUTSIDE SIKKIM: *Summer*, Nepal, Bhutan, SE. Tibet (Himalayan facies); N. Burma, Yunnan, Szechwan. *Winter*, Nepal and Sikkim terai, Bhutan duars, Bengal, Assam, Manipur, etc. Represented by other races in the W. Himalayas.

GENERAL HABITS: Typically phylloscopine. Arboreal; keeps to foliage canopy.

NESTING: Stevens took a nest with eggs on Singalila Ridge on 22 May (1912). Schäfer collected a juvenile with wings and tail in quill on 7 July at Thangu, and another in juvenile plumage on 14 September. *Season*—May to July. *Nest*—on ground: cup-shaped when built amongst exposed roots of a tree; domed when not within such a hollow. Of moss and fine bents, lined with feathers and hair. *Eggs*—3 or 4, pure white. Size about 16×12 mm.

RACIAL CHARACTERISTICS, MEASUREMENTS, ETC: Almost indistinguishable in the field from *P. magnirostris* (next species) except by colour of legs (brown instead of slate grey), and lower mandible (yellow instead of brown). The latter also has very distinctive call notes.

A large series collected in Sikkim by Schäfer gives Wing 13 ♂♂ 62-66 (av. 64.0); 10 ♀♀ 57-62 (av. 59.5) mm.—Stresemann. Tail ♂♂ 50-57; ♀♀ 47-51.5 mm.—Ticehurst.

Iris brown; bill brown, lower mandible yellow; legs and feet fleshy horn to horny brown.

## THE LARGEBILLED LEAF WARBLER

*Phylloscopus magnirostris* Blyth

*Phylloscopus magnirostris* Blyth, 1843, *Jour. Asiat. Soc. Bengal* 12: 966—Calcutta.

F.B.I. 2: 476

LOCAL NAME:

SIZE: Sparrow –.

FIELD CHARACTERS: A large leaf warbler with a single wing-bar, often indistinct, very similar to and easily confused with *P. t. trochiloides* (above). May be differentiated by colour of lower mandible (brown instead of yellow), and legs (slate grey instead of brown), but most reliably by its very distinctive call note, a mousy, interrogative *whee-chi?* or *dir-tee?* with the second syllable somewhat higher in key. Also in summer by its clear tinkling five-noted song *tee . . . titi-titi*. Sexes alike.

STATUS AND HABITAT: *Summer*, common (evidently breeding) at elevations between *c.* 8000 and 13,000 ft. (Lachen, Thangu) as Ludlow also found in Bhutan and SE. Tibet. Possibly higher. No winter record traceable for Sikkim. Affects forest.

DISTRIBUTION OUTSIDE SIKKIM: *Summer*, the Himalayan facies from the Afghan frontier through Kashmir and Nepal; Bhutan, SE. Tibet, Kansu, Szechwan, etc. *Winter*, at lower elevations and in the Indian plains south to Travancore. Ceylon, Andaman Islands.

GENERAL HABITS: Keeps to forest in the neighbourhood of rushing streams, usually up in the canopy foliage. Its presence is revealed by the constantly uttered, distinctive call-note and/or song. The latter closely resembles the song of the Whitethroated Fantail Flycatcher (*Rhipidura albicollis*).

NESTING: Unrecorded in Sikkim, though it doubtless breeds here as elsewhere in its high summer range. In Bhutan, Ludlow found a nest with c/4 at 9000 ft. on 13 June. *Nest*—normally on the ground, similar to that of *P. trochiloides* but apparently never lined with feathers. *Eggs*—4 or 5, pure white, about 18×13 mm.

RACIAL CHARACTERISTICS, MEASUREMENTS, ETC: Ticehurst gives the range of measurements as:

| | Wing | Bill | Tarsus | Tail |
|---|---|---|---|---|
| ♂♂ | 68-75 | 14.5-16 | 18-19.5 | 51-56.5 mm. |
| ♀♀ | 63-69 | | | 48-51.5 mm. |

A ♂ collected by Schäfer (Lachen, 6 Sept.) has Wing 69 mm.

Iris brown; upper mandible horny brown, lower slaty plumbeous or brown, pale fleshy at base; legs and feet bluish slate or greyish brown.

## BLYTH'S CROWNED LEAF WARBLER

*Phylloscopus reguloides reguloides* (Blyth)

*Phyllopneuste reguloides* Blyth, 1842, *Jour. Asiat. Soc. Bengal* 11: 191—Calcutta (=Darjeeling. Ripley, Synopsis).

F.B.I. 2:481 (=*Acanthopneuste trochiloides trochiloides*)

LOCAL NAME:

SIZE: Sparrow—.

FIELD CHARACTERS: With two broad yellow wing-bars; a pale mesial coronal streak. No yellow rump band; relatively short tail. *Above*, yellowish olive-green, with dark brown wings and tail. Distinct yellowish mesial streak on crown, bordered on either side by dark olive bands. A well-defined yellow supercilium. Lores and a line under supercilium dark olive. Cheeks and ear-coverts yellowish. *Below*, including throat, uniform greyish white, tinged and faintly streaked with yellow. Sexes alike.

STATUS AND HABITAT: Obtained by the Survey between 1500 and 3000 ft. (Singtam, Martam) in December; by Schäfer at 6000 ft. (Gangtok) on 16 June, and 9200 ft. (Lachen), 4-12 September. One on the latter date was a young bird just commencing post-juvenal moult. Ludlow collected specimens in Bhutan at 7500 and 9500 ft. in July, evidently also in their breeding grounds. On 24 June he took a nest at 11,200 ft. in SE. Tibet.

Affects forest.

DISTRIBUTION OUTSIDE SIKKIM: *Summer*, Nepal, Bhutan, SE. Tibet, *c.* 6000 to 12,000 ft. *Winter*, at lower elevations; also in the terai and duars. Other races in the western Himalayas; Assam, Yunnan, Szechwan, etc.

GENERAL HABITS: Keeps to the foliage canopy in forest, commonly in the mixed hunting flocks of 'tinies'.

NESTING: *Season*—May to July. *Nest*—on the ground in forest; in a hollow or among loose stones of a retaining wall, and the like. Usually a flimsy domed or roofed structure of moss and grass, mixed with hair and wool. *Eggs*—4 or 5, white, about 15×12 mm.

RACIAL CHARACTERISTICS, MEASUREMENTS, ETC: In the hand a good diagnostic clue is the narrow white edging (1-2 mm.) to the inner webs of the two outer tail feathers on either side.

The specimens collected by the Sikkim Survey measure:

| | Wing | Bill | Tarsus | Tail |
|---|---|---|---|---|
| 1 ♂ | 59 | 12.5 | 17.5 | 42 mm. |
| 2 ♀♀ | 53-57.5 | 10.5-11.5 | 17.5-18 | 36-41 mm. |

Schäfer's Sikkim skins give Wing 3 ♂♂ 58, 58, 59; 4 ♀♀ 53, 54, 54, 54 mm.

Iris brown; upper mandible horny brown, lower yellowish flesh colour; legs and feet greyish brown with an olive tinge; claws horny brown.

The following two leaf warblers, superficially resembling each other closely, have also been obtained in Sikkim. They may best be distinguished by the different contrasts in their lower plumage: yellow throat with whitish underparts in *Phylloscopus cantator*, yellow under tail-coverts with whitish underparts in *P. o. coronatus*.

## TEMMINCK'S CROWNED LEAF WARBLER

*Phylloscopus occipitalis coronatus* (Temminck & Schlegel)

*Ficedula coronata* Temminck & Schlegel, 1847, Siebold's Fauna Japon., Aves: 48, (pl. 18)—Japan.

F.B.I. 2: 480

LOCAL NAME:

SIZE: Sparrow−.

FIELD CHARACTERS: Upper parts olive-brown, with a single narrow yellowish wing-bar. No yellow rump band. A faint yellowish grey mesial coronal streak, bordered by dark olive lateral bands. A well-marked yellowish supercilium, with a dark olive line below it, continued on lores. Under tail-coverts bright yellow, contrasting with whitish underparts.

STATUS: Winter visitor? Meinertzhagen obtained a specimen at Rangpo (2100 ft.) and another at Gangtok (6400 ft.) on 26 and 15 December respectively.

MEASUREMENTS: 'Wing ♂♂ 60.5-66, one 68; ♀♀ 57, 58.5-61.5 mm.' (Ticehurst).

## TICKELL'S, or THE BLACKBROWED, LEAF WARBLER

*Phylloscopus cantator* (Tickell)

*Motacilla cantator* Tickell, 1833, *Jour. Asiat. Soc. Bengal* 2: 576—Borabhúm, Lower Bengal.

F.B.I. 2: 492

LOCAL NAME:

SIZE: Sparrow−.

FIELD CHARACTERS: With one distinct yellow and one faint rudimentary wing-bar. A well-marked greenish yellow mesial coronal streak bordered by dark olive lateral bands. Throat yellow, contrasting with white breast and greyish white underparts. Otherwise as in *coronatus*.

STATUS: Possibly breeding at the higher elevations? Schäfer collected a specimen (♂ Wing 56 mm.) at Gangtok (6200 ft.) on 13 June. Sight recorded by H. G. Alexander at Rangpo (1000 ft.), end November.

MEASUREMENTS: 'Wing ♂♂ 53-58; ♀♀ 48.5-52 mm.' (Ticehurst).

## THE SIKKIM GOLDCREST

*Regulus regulus sikkimensis* R. & A. Meinertzhagen

*Regulus regulus sikkimensis* Meinertzhagen, 1926, *Bull. Brit. Orn. Cl.* 46: 97—Native Sikkim.

**Plate 18, fig. 5 (facing p. 209)**

F.B.I. 8: 647

LOCAL NAME:

SIZE: Sparrow−.

FIELD CHARACTERS: A tiny *Phylloscopus*-like bird. *Male: Above*, dull olive-green, brighter and more yellowish on rump and upper tail-coverts. Two yellowish white wing-bars. A golden orange stripe along centre of crown, bordered on either side by black. Face uniform greenish grey. No pale supercilium; no dark streak through eye. *Below*, fulvous white tinged with olive on flanks and sides of breast.

*Female:* similar, but with crown-stripe yellow, not orange. Young birds lack the crown-stripe.

STATUS AND HABITAT: Resident. Sparse but not uncommon between *c.* 5000 and 10,000 ft. elevation—November to May—(Kewzing, Lachen, Lachung, Phalut). Meinertzhagen obtained it at Thangu (12,800 ft.) in November, and the Suydam Cutting Expedition at Gnatong (*c.* 12,500 ft.) in March.

Affects tall forest.

DISTRIBUTION OUTSIDE SIKKIM: E. Nepal, Bhutan, Dafla and Abor hills. The western Himalayas, from W. Nepal through Kashmir and into Afghanistan, are populated by the paler race *himalayensis*. The species extends widely both east and west of the above areas.

GENERAL HABITS: Restless, active, and very similar to the leaf warblers (*Phylloscopus*) with which it commonly associates in the mixed hunting parties. Keeps to the canopy foliage of rhododendron, oak, deodar and other conifers, usually in family groups. Has a distinctive, continuous, high-pitched, mouse-like squeaking—*tsi-tsi-tsi*—which reveals its presence among a mixed band of small insectivorous birds where it is otherwise apt to be overlooked.

NESTING: Little known, and not specifically recorded from Sikkim. *Season*—(in W. Himalayas) May to July. *Nest*—a neatly felted hanging pouch of green moss, lichens, spiders' egg-cases, etc. at the tip of a branch, fairly high up. *Eggs*—5 to 7 (?), pinky buff to white, often speckled with reddish brown. Size about 14×11 mm.

RACIAL CHARACTERISTICS, MEASUREMENTS, ETC: The Sikkim race is intermediate in depth of coloration between the adjacent *himalayensis* and the darker eastern form, *yunnanensis*.

A specimen collected in Sikkim (♂?) measures: Wing 56; bill 10; tarsus 19; tail 36 mm.

A series of *sikkimensis* recently obtained by Ludlow in SE. Tibet gives Wing 4 ♂♂ 55-58; 4 ♀♀ 51-53 mm.

Iris brown; bill blackish brown; legs, feet and claws pale horny brown.

## THE ALLIED FLYCATCHER-WARBLER

*Seicercus affinis* (Hodgson)

*Abrornis affinis* Hodgson, 1854, *in* Horsfield & Moore. Cat. Birds Mus. E. I. Co. 1: 341—Nepal.

F.B.I. 2: 486

LOCAL NAME:

SIZE: Sparrow—.

FIELD CHARACTERS: A tiny restless *Phylloscopus*-like bird, olive-green and deep yellow overall, with a prominent yellow wing-bar. Crown and nape black with a broad bluish grey mesial band. Supercilium and sides of head bluish grey with a distinct white ring round eye. Inner webs of two outer pairs of tail feathers largely white. Sexes alike.

STATUS AND HABITAT: Recorded from the Teesta Valley up to *c.* 6000 ft. Neither the Survey nor Schäfer procured it in Sikkim, though Ludlow collected specimens in Bhutan at 6000 and 7500 ft. in June and July, and at 4000 ft. in November. He describes it as 'an inhabitant of dense leech-infested forest at no great altitude'.

DISTRIBUTION OUTSIDE SIKKIM: Bhutan to E. Assam, north and south of Brahmaputra River; N. Burma to Annam.

GENERAL HABITS: Very similar to the leaf warblers. Keeps singly or among the mixed hunting parties of 'tinies' in the foliage of trees and bushes, flitting about tirelessly, nervously flicking wings, and fluttering and hovering in front of sprigs to pick insects.

NESTING: Doubtless breeds in Sikkim, but no specific records.

RACIAL CHARACTERISTICS, MEASUREMENTS, ETC: Confusable, and probably often is, with the next, *Seicercus burkii*, but which has the eye-ring yellow instead of white, and sides of head yellowish instead of bluish grey.

The Fauna gives for ♂♀ Wing 52-58; tail 42-45 mm.

Iris brown; upper mandible dark brown, lower yellow; legs and feet yellow; claws browner.

## THE BLACKBROWED FLYCATCHER-WARBLER

*Seicercus burkii burkii* (Burton)

*Sylvia burkii* Burton, 1836, *Proc. Zool. Soc. London:* 153—Himalayas (=Sikkim. Ticehurst).

**Plate 22, fig. 1 (facing p. 273)**

F.B.I. 2: 487

LOCAL NAME:

SIZE: Sparrow—.

FIELD CHARACTERS: Overall olive-green and deep yellow. Similar to *S. affinis* but with yellow ring round eye instead of white; coronal band and sides of head greyish green instead of bluish grey. Sexes alike.

STATUS AND HABITAT: Resident. Stevens records it as common on the Singalila Ridge at 10,000 ft. in April and May. In Nepal also it is 'extremely common from 10,000 to 12,000 ft.' in May (Mrs Proud). In Bhutan, Ludlow found it breeding at *c.* 10,000 ft. in June, and met it up to 12,500 ft. in July. Common at lower altitudes, *c.* 1000 to 6000 ft. in winter (Rangpo, Singtam, Martam, Dikchu, Singhik, Rinchinpong, Chungthang, Gangtok, Lachen).

Affects the middle storey in forest, and shrubby growth.

DISTRIBUTION OUTSIDE SIKKIM: Nepal, Bhutan to E. Assam. The paler race *whistleri* occupies the W. Himalayas from Kashmir to Garhwal and N. Kumaon. Other races extend the species through N. Burma and Thailand to Yunnan.

GENERAL HABITS: Very common and abundant in its winter range. Singly in undergrowth, as well as several in association with the mixed hunting parties of small babblers, flycatchers and leaf warblers. Actions and behaviour typically phylloscopine. Utters a sharp single note, *chiw*, every few seconds while working through the shrubbery. The short *Leiothrix*-like song heard in the breeding season is reminiscent of that of the more familiar *S. xanthoschistos*, but unmistakable once known.

NESTING: Certainly breeds up to 9000 ft., where Schäfer collected juveniles in August (Lachen). *Season*—June-July. *Nest*—ball-shaped, of bamboo leaves, root fibres, moss, etc., lined with moss and lichen. Placed on the ground on a sloping bank, in thick growth of weeds and bracken, or amongst the exposed roots of a tree, in forest. *Eggs*—4 or 5, pure white; about 16×12 mm.

RACIAL CHARACTERISTICS, MEASUREMENTS, ETC: The Survey specimens

(3 ♂♂, 2 o?) measure: Wing 54-60; bill 11.5-13; tarsus 19-20; tail 43.5-51 mm.

Schäfer's large series gives Wing 9 ♂♂ 55-60 (av. 57.9); 10 ♀♀ 51-56 (av. 53.2) mm. (Stresemann).

Iris brown; upper mandible horny brown, lower yellow or orange-yellow; legs, feet and claws yellowish brown.

## THE GREYHEADED FLYCATCHER-WARBLER

*Seicercus xanthoschistos xanthoschistos* (Gray)

*Phyllopneuste xanthoschistos* 'Hodgson'=Gray, 1846, Cat. Mamms. Birds Nepal: 65, 151—Nepal.

F.B.I. 2: 489

LOCAL NAME:

SIZE: Sparrow−.

FIELD CHARACTERS: *Above*, ashy grey and yellowish olive-green. Crown dark ashy grey with an ill-defined paler mesial band. Sides of head and neck grey. A prominent long white supercilium and a blackish line through eye. Tail brown, edged with green, with the inner webs of the outer pair of feathers on either side white. *Below*, bright yellow. Sexes alike.

STATUS AND HABITAT: Common between *c.* 1000 and 7000 ft. elevation, with a slight seasonal altitudinal movement (Dikchu, Singhik, Kewzing, Rinchinpong, Gangtok, Pemionche). Affects the lower and middle storey in forest, and also foliage canopy of tall trees.

DISTRIBUTION OUTSIDE SIKKIM: Nepal, Bhutan. The Himalayas west of Nepal and up to the Afghan border are occupied by the paler race *albo-superciliaris*; east of Bhutan the darker and more slaty race *flavogularis* occurs in the Mishmi Hills. The species extends to N. Burma.

GENERAL HABITS: Active and restless; similar to other flycatcher-warblers and to the leaf warblers. Like them, commonly associates with the mixed hunting parties in forest. Has a distinctive high-pitched call-note, and in the breeding season a pleasing and lively but monotonous little song.

NESTING: *Season*—April-May. *Nest*—a domed structure of moss, lined with vegetable down etc. Placed on the ground in a pocket in a sloping bank, or among the exposed roots of a tree. *Eggs*—3 or 4, pure white, about 16×12 mm.

RACIAL CHARACTERISTICS, MEASUREMENTS, ETC: Two ♂♂ collected by the Survey measure: Wing 55-58; bill 11-12; tarsus 19; tail 39.5-40 mm.

Seven specimens in Schäfer's Sikkim collection have Wing 49 (♀) to 55 (♂) mm. (Stresemann).

Iris brown; upper mandible horny brown, lower orange-yellow; legs and feet brownish flesh with a yellow tinge; claws pale flesh colour.

## THE GREYCHEEKED FLYCATCHER-WARBLER

*Seicercus poliogenys* (Blyth)

*Culicipeta poliogenys* Blyth, 1847, *Jour. Asiat. Soc. Bengal* 16: 441—Darjeeling.

F.B.I. 2: 491

LOCAL NAME:

SIZE: Sparrow−.

FIELD CHARACTERS: Differs from *S. xanthoschistos* chiefly in the lower plumage being not wholly bright yellow, but with chin and lower cheeks pale grey. The white in the tail applies to three outer feathers on each side instead of two.

General colour scheme like the Greyheaded Flycatcher, *Culicicapa ceylonensis* (p. 146) but with a white ring round eye as conspicuous as in the White-eye, *Zosterops*. Sexes alike.

STATUS AND HABITAT: No specimens collected in Sikkim by the Survey or Schäfer. According to Stevens, occurs in moderate numbers at *c*. 4700 in the Rungbong Valley; also observed sparingly at *c*. 10,000 ft. on Singalila Ridge in April and May. In Bhutan, Ludlow obtained it at 3000 and 6000 ft. in November.

DISTRIBUTION OUTSIDE SIKKIM: Nepal, Bhutan to extreme E. Assam north and south of the Brahmaputra; Manipur, Yunnan.

GENERAL HABITS: Phylloscopine; typical of this group of tiny birds aptly named 'flycatcher-warblers'.

NESTING: No authentic record for Sikkim. *Nest* and *eggs* similar to the last.

RACIAL CHARACTERISTICS, MEASUREMENTS, ETC: The Fauna gives for ♂♀ Wing 50-55; tail 40-42 mm.

Iris dark brown; upper mandible dark brown, lower yellow; legs and feet pale yellowish brown.

## THE CHESTNUT-HEADED FLYCATCHER-WARBLER

*Seicercus castaniceps castaniceps* (Hodgson)

*Abrornis castaniceps* Hodgson, 1845, in Blyth, *Jour. Asiat. Soc. Bengal* 14: 593—Nepal.

Plate 22, fig. 2 (facing p. 273)

F.B.I. 2: 492

LOCAL NAME:

SIZE: Sparrow−.

FIELD CHARACTERS: The only *Seicercus* in Sikkim that is not mainly bright yellow on the underparts. Differs from *S. xanthoschistos* (p. 237) in having the chin, throat and upper breast bluish grey instead of the entire underparts yellow. Forehead and crown bright chestnut, bordered from above eye to nape by black lateral bands with a narrow white line below them. A conspicuous white ring round eye. Upper back greyish olive-green, changing to bright yellow on rump and upper tail-coverts. Two yellow wing-bars. Sexes alike.

STATUS AND HABITAT: Fairly common up to *c.* 6500 ft., November to April (Rangpo, Singtam, Martam, Singhik, Gangtok). Schäfer obtained it at 6300 ft. (Gangtok) also on 16 June. In Bhutan, Ludlow found it locally distributed, and as high as 8000 ft. on 1 September. Collected in Nepal in February in the terai, and at 7500 ft. in April (Ripley).

Affects forest of oak and rhododendron, usually the foliage canopy.

DISTRIBUTION OUTSIDE SIKKIM: Nepal, Bhutan, Assam, Manipur, N. Burma. The species extends to S. China and Malaysia.

GENERAL HABITS: As of the genus. Usually seen in the mixed hunting parties of small babblers, nuthatches, flycatchers, leaf warblers, etc. The normal call note is described as a 'quite distinctive, very loud, wren-like *tsik*'.

NESTING: *Season*—May-June, at *c.* 6000 ft. and above. *Nest*—on the ground, dome-shaped, similar to those described. *Eggs*—4 or 5, pure white, about 15×12 mm. The nests are commonly parasitized by the Emerald Cuckoo, *Chalcites maculatus*.

RACIAL CHARACTERISTICS, MEASUREMENTS, ETC: Specimens collected by the Sikkim Survey (5 ♀♀, 1 o?) measure: Wing 47-50; bill 9.5-10; tarsus 17-17.5; tail 35.5-37.5 mm.

Schäfer's Sikkim skins give Wing 1 ♂ 52, 1 ♀ 48 mm.

Iris brown; upper mandible horny brown; lower yellowish flesh colour; legs and feet yellowish brown or olive-brown; claws horny brown.

## THE YELLOWBELLIED FLYCATCHER-WARBLER

*Abroscopus superciliaris albigularis* (Blyth)

*Abrornis albigularis* Blyth, 1861, *Proc. Zool. Soc. London:* 200—Sikkim.

F.B.I. 2: 494

LOCAL NAME:

SIZE: Sparrow—.

FIELD CHARACTERS: *Above*, forehead brownish, changing to oily green on crown and rest of upper parts. A broad white supercilium from nostril to nape. A dark brown line under it from lores to behind eye. Tail brown, edged outwardly with olive-green and inwardly with cinnamon. *Below*, chin, throat, and upper breast white; rest of lower plumage bright yellow. Sexes alike.

STATUS AND HABITAT: Met with by the Survey only at low elevations, 1000 to 3500 ft., between November and April (Rangpo, Singtam, Martam), as also recorded by Stevens. In the foliage canopy and middle storey in mixed bamboo forest.

DISTRIBUTION OUTSIDE SIKKIM: Bhutan to E. Assam, north of the Brahmaputra River. Mishmi Hills birds are darker and attributed to the race *drasticus*. The species, in other races, ranges to Burma, Yunnan, Malaysia.

GENERAL HABITS: Not different from those of *Seicercus*, nor appreciably from *Phylloscopus*.

NESTING: In spite of the close superficial similarity in appearance, habits, and behaviour of this genus with *Seicercus* (from which it differs only in possessing ten tail feathers against twelve) the nests and eggs of the two are quite different. The only nesting record of this species in 'Sikkim' (Gammie) is at 1800 ft. elevation on 15 June. The nest, of bamboo leaves and soft fibres, was placed inside a hollow bamboo stem with the bird's entrance through a notch hacked by some villager. It contained 3 eggs, dull pinky white, freckled or mottled with brownish or purplish red, more densely at the broad end forming a cap or zone. Size about 16×11 mm.

RACIAL CHARACTERISTICS, MEASUREMENTS, ETC: Specimens collected by the Survey (1 ♂, 1 o?) measure: Wing 52.5-54; bill 12; tarsus 18.5-20; tail 42.5-44 mm.

Iris brown; bill horny brown, pinky plumbeous at base of lower mandible; legs and feet brownish flesh colour.

## THE BLACKFACED FLYCATCHER-WARBLER

*Abroscopus schisticeps schisticeps* (Gray)

*Culicipeta schisticeps* Gray, 1846, Cat. Mamms. Birds Nepal: 67, 153—Nepal.

**Plate 22, fig. 3 (facing p. 273)**

F.B.I. 2: 496

LOCAL NAME:

SIZE: Sparrow—.

FIELD CHARACTERS: *Above*, line of forehead, lores, and around eye black. Upper forehead, and broad supercilium to nape bright deep yellow. Crown to upper back slaty grey-blue; rest of upper plumage olive-green, yellower on rump. Wings and tail brown edged with green: the latter with white inner webs to the two outermost feathers on each side. *Below*, bright yellow, paling to whitish on centre of abdomen and vent. Sexes alike.

STATUS AND HABITAT: According to Stevens generally distributed in the Sikkim Himalayas up to about 5500 ft. elevation, but uncommon. Neither the Survey nor Schäfer procured specimens. Affects the foliage canopy in heavy forest.

DISTRIBUTION OUTSIDE SIKKIM: Nepal. Birds from Bhutan go better with the east Himalayan race *flavimentalis*. The species, in other races, is found in Assam, Manipur, N. Burma, Yunnan.

GENERAL HABITS: As of the genus. Usually seen high up in the foliage canopy amongst the mixed hunting parties of tinies. In this restless activity, as Stevens points out, it may, on colour alone, be quite easily confused with the diminutive Yellowbellied Fantail Flycatcher (*R. hypoxantha*)—also a very regular ingredient.

NESTING: The only nest taken in Sikkim was by Gammie at *c.* 5500 ft. on 29 May, containing 5 hard-set eggs. In a natural cavity in a small tree, 5 ft. above ground, lined with bamboo leaves, and with a small entrance. The eggs, similar to the last, measured about 15×11 mm.

RACIAL CHARACTERISTICS, MEASUREMENTS, ETC: Differs from the Bhutan and east Himalayan population in having the canary yellow of the throat extending on breast and flanks. In *flavimentalis* the yellow is restricted to the throat and upper breast only, making the underparts look much whiter.

The Fauna gives the measurements (♂ ♀) as: Wing 46-48; tail 40-42 mm.

Iris dark brown; bill dark horny brown, paler on lower mandible; legs and feet pale yellowish brown.

## THE BROADBILLED FLYCATCHER-WARBLER

*Abroscopus hodgsoni hodgsoni* (Moore)

*Abrornis? hodgsoni* Moore, 1854, *in* Horsfield & Moore, Cat. Birds Mus. E. I. Co. 1: 412—Nepal.

F.B.I. 2: 500

LOCAL NAME:

SIZE: Sparrow—.

FIELD CHARACTERS: A tiny, brightly coloured bird very like *Seicercus* in appearance but with a bigger, blunter bill, and with long hairs extending from its base beyond the tip (reminiscent of the barbets), though hardly noticeable except in a specimen in the hand.

*Above,* olive-green, yellowish on rump, chestnut on forehead and crown. Lores and sides of head grey, with a paler grey short supercilium. Inner webs of the two outermost tail feathers on each side white. *Below,* chin, throat, and breast grey; rest of lower plumage bright yellow. Sexes alike.

STATUS AND HABITAT: Not collected by the Sikkim Survey or by Schäfer. Stevens records it between 3800 ft. (July) and 6000 ft. (March), but in the Chicago Museum of Natural History there is a specimen collected by him at Jeluk, *c.* 9000 ft., on 11 April.

Affects undergrowth at the edge of forest.

DISTRIBUTION OUTSIDE SIKKIM: Besides Sikkim apparently only known from Mt Victoria (Chin Hills), Burma.

GENERAL HABITS: Unlike *Seicercus* and other species of *Abroscopus* keeps mostly to thick undergrowth and not to the foliage canopy of trees, nor normally with the mixed hunting parties. Hops about singly in shrubbery in the manner of the Tailor Bird or the bush-warblers (pp. 217 sqq.). *Call:* described by Osmaston as a single, long-drawn, very shrill whistle, followed after a short pause by two notes, the second of which is lower. The song according to Heinrich consists of a sharp, thin warble.

NESTING: The only nest known was taken by B. B. Osmaston at *c.* 6800 ft. in Sikkim on 6 June, in a thicket of saplings in lofty forest. *Nest*—roughly egg-shaped, of dry bamboo leaves lined with black rhizomorphs and softer bamboo leaves, with a tiny entrance hole near the top. It contained 3 eggs, pale claret, spotted, streaked and speckled with darker claret markings, chiefly at the broad end. Size about 16×12 mm.

RACIAL CHARACTERISTICS, MEASUREMENTS, ETC: Stevens gives the measurements of his two Sikkim skins as: ♂ Wing 47.5; bill 8.5 mm.; ♀ Wing 46.5; bill 10 mm.

I measured a ♂ collected by Stevens at Jeluk, now in the Chicago Museum, as: Wing 46; bill 12; tarsus 21; tail 44 mm.

Iris brown; bill horny brown, paler and more yellow at base of lower mandible; legs pale yellow or fleshy horn.

## THE GOLDENHEADED TAILOR BIRD

*Orthotomus cucullatus coronatus* Blyth

*Orthotomus coronatus* Blyth, 1861, *Proc. Zool. Soc. London:* 200—Sikkim.

**Plate 22, fig. 5** (facing p. 273)

F.B.I. **2**: 516 (=*Phyllergates coronatus*)

LOCAL NAME:

SIZE: Sparrow−.

FIELD CHARACTERS: General effect very like the familiar tailor bird of the plains. *Above*, olive-green, yellower on rump and upper tail-coverts. Forehead and crown chestnut; sides of head, neck and nape dark ashy grey. A short yellow supercilium. Lores and a line behind eye dark brown. *Below,* cheeks silvery white; chin, throat and breast pale ashy white. Rest of lower plumage bright pale yellow. Sexes alike.

STATUS AND HABITAT: Resident, probably at low and medium elevations as elsewhere in its range. Sikkim specimens in the British Museum do not give the heights. Not met with by the Loke-Sálim Ali Survey, nor recorded by Schäfer or other recent collectors.

DISTRIBUTION OUTSIDE SIKKIM: Bhutan (?), Assam, Manipur, Burma, N. Thailand.

GENERAL HABITS: Actions and behaviour strongly reminiscent of *Orthotomus sutorius*. A great skulker. Keeps to thick undergrowth and bamboo jungle, singly or in small parties. Impossible to distinguish in the field from *Abroscopus hodgsoni* except by its distinctive song. Smythies describes this as a four-noted whistle, 'the first two notes on the same pitch, the third a trill (three or four notes uttered very rapidly), and the fourth either higher or lower in pitch than the first two, the whole repeated in a remarkable number of different keys both high and low'.

NESTING: Not recorded in Sikkim. The nest is of the tailor bird type, and the eggs are also similar.

RACIAL CHARACTERISTICS, MEASUREMENTS, ETC: In the hand this tailor bird can be readily told from the superficially similar *Abroscopus hodgsoni* by its longer and finer pointed bill and by the absence of the extraordinarily long hairs over it extending beyond its tip. Both species have some white on the inner webs of the two outermost pairs of rectrices: in *A. hodgsoni* the entire inner webs are white; in *O. c. coronatus* the white is restricted as a narrow edge to the inner webs. The measurements of the two species are almost overlapping. For this tailor bird the Fauna gives ♂♀ Wing 43-47; bill 13-15; tarsus *c.* 20; tail 34-41 mm.

Iris brown; upper mandible horny black, lower fleshy horn; legs and feet fleshy or pale yellowish.

## THE TAILOR BIRD

*Orthotomus sutorius patia* Hodgson

*Orthotomus patia* Hodgson, 1845, *Proc. Zool. Soc. London:* 29—Nepal.

F.B.I. 2: 412

LOCAL NAME: Patia (Nepali).

SIZE: Sparrow –.

FIELD CHARACTERS: A restless little bird of shrubbery. *Above*, olive-green with deep rufous forehead and crown and dark ashy nape. Pointed, graduated tail olive-green, carried cocked as in the Magpie Robin, with two elongated pin-shaped central feathers in breeding plumage. *Below*, buffy white. Bill straight and thin; legs comparatively long. Sexes alike, but female lacks the long central tail 'pins'.

STATUS AND HABITAT: Resident. Fairly common at the lower altitudes, up to *c.* 3000 ft. Sparingly also up to 5000 or 6000 ft. (Rangpo, Martam, Dikchu, Pakyong, Rinchinpong, Gangtok). Affects open shrubbery, hedges, etc. in the neighbourhood of habitations, in resthouse compounds and the like.

DISTRIBUTION OUTSIDE SIKKIM: Nepal, Bhutan, Assam, East Pakistan, Burma. In many other races the species stretches from India to Thailand, China and Malaysia.

GENERAL HABITS: Keeps singly or in pairs, hopping about in low bushes or on the ground at their base searching for food; rarely high up in trees. *Food:* caterpillars, moths and other insects and their eggs. Also flower nectar. *Call:* a distinctive *towit-towit-towit* or *pitchik-pitchik-pitchik*, unexpectedly loud for its size, which makes it oftener heard than seen. In addition to these normal calls I found some notes of Sikkim birds to be particularly loud and quite unlike any heard in the plains.

NESTING: *Season*—May to July. *Nest*—a rough cup of soft fibres and vegetable down placed within a funnel or cone formed by folding over and stitching along the edges a large broad leaf, or several smaller leaves together; normally under 3 ft. from the ground. The stitching material is cotton wool or vegetable down, cleverly twisted into yarn and knotted to prevent the sewing becoming undone. *Eggs*—3 or 4, reddish or bluish white, usually spotted with brownish red. Size about 16×11 mm.

RACIAL CHARACTERISTICS, MEASUREMENTS, ETC: This race is much darker than the adjoining west Himalayan (and all-Indian) *guzurata*, being more olive-green, less yellowish green, above. The forehead and crown are deep rufous instead of chestnut, and the nape a darker ashy.

The Sikkim Survey specimens, all collected in December/January, measure:

| | Wing | Bill | Tarsus | Tail |
|---|---|---|---|---|
| 2 ♂♂ | 48-49 | 16 | 20-20.5 | 44-45 mm. |
| 2 ♀♀ | 49-50 | 14.5-16.5 | 20-20.5 | 37.5-41.5 mm. |

Iris orange-brown; upper mandible horny brown, lower flesh colour; legs and feet brownish flesh; claws horny brown.

## THE RUFOUS WREN-WARBLER

*Prinia rufescens rufescens* Blyth

*Prinia rufescens* Blyth, 1847, *Jour. Asiat. Soc. Bengal* **16**: 456—Arakan.

F.B.I. **2**: 427

LOCAL NAME:

SIZE: Sparrow—.

FIELD CHARACTERS: A slim, skulking wren-warbler, with longish partly-cocked tail. *Above*, forehead, crown and nape ashy brown. A white line from nostril over eye. Rest of upper plumage rufous-brown, brighter and more rufous on wings and tail. Tail feathers tipped with black and rufescent white. *Below*, pale fulvous. Sexes alike.

STATUS AND HABITAT: Met with by the Sikkim Survey only up to *c.* 3000 ft. elevation (Rangpo, Singtam, Martam) in November/December. Affects low herbage on openly wooded hillsides.

In Bhutan, Ludlow collected specimens at 2000-3000 ft. in November, 3250 ft. in June, and 4000 ft. in October.

DISTRIBUTION OUTSIDE SIKKIM: The Himalayas, up to moderate elevations, from Kumaon through Nepal and Bhutan to E. Assam, north and south of the Brahmaputra. Also peninsular India, Burma, Thailand, Yunnan, Annam.

GENERAL HABITS: Keeps singly or in twos and threes to heavy low *Eupatorium* and other scrub on openly forested and terrace-cultivated hillsides. A great skulker; seldom shows itself except for momentary glimpses as it makes short jerky flights of a few yards to dive into the undergrowth again. Thereafter its presence is revealed only by the slight movement of the herbage which marks its hidden progress through the stems and rootstocks. Occasionally it may also be found with hunting parties of small undergrowth-skulking babblers such as *Stachyris*. I found it very silent, but its notes are described as similar to those of Franklin's Wren-Warbler, as indeed are most of its actions and behaviour.

NESTING: Presumably breeds in Sikkim, but no authentic record.

RACIAL CHARACTERISTICS, MEASUREMENTS, ETC: Specimens collected by the

Sikkim Survey (2 ♀♀, 1 o?) measure: Wing 43-45; bill 12.5-13; tarsus 19-20.5; tail 47-54 mm.

Iris orange-brown; upper mandible horny brown, lower pale flesh colour; legs and feet pale brownish flesh; claws horny brown.

## THE BLACKTHROATED HILL WARBLER

*Prinia atrogularis atrogularis* (Moore)

*Suya atrogularis* Moore, 1854, *in* Horsfield & Moore, Cat. Birds Mus. E. I. Co. 1: xviii, 326—Darjeeling.

F.B.I. 2: 523

LOCAL NAME:

SIZE: Sparrow—; with a long tail *c.* 4 inches.

FIELD CHARACTERS: A small, streaked, brown warbler, with a long, pointed tail. *Summer: Above,* dark olive-brown, darker and greyer on head and nape. Wings and tail rufous-brown. A distinct white cheek-stripe. No supercilium. *Below,* chin, throat and upper breast black. Lower breast and abdomen white, spotted and streaked with black. Rest of lower plumage fulvous, more ochraceous on flanks, thighs and under tail-coverts. *Winter: Above,* paler, streaked with blackish. A whitish supercilium. Lores and a band behind eye blackish. *Below,* throat and breast whitish streaked with black. Sexes alike.

STATUS AND HABITAT: Resident. Fairly common between *c.* 4500 and 8500 ft. elevation (Dentam, Rinchinpong, Chungthang, Penlom La, Gangtok, Lachung). Affects open hillsides with grass and scrub, sites of old hill cultivation, etc.

DISTRIBUTION OUTSIDE SIKKIM: Eastern Nepal, Bhutan, SE. Tibet. The race *khasiana* inhabits Assam and the Chin Hills.

GENERAL HABITS: Skulks in tall grass and scrub, singly or in pairs, clambering among the stems and occasionally showing itself at the top. Flight feeble and jerky, typical of the wren-warblers. When alarmed shoots down a steep hillside with great velocity, wings pulled in and the long tail doubled over the back. *Call:* a loud *p'ty, p'ty, p'ty* like that of the Jungle Wren-Warbler of the plains. *Song:* a monotonous, wheezy, reeling *tsee-tswee-tsee-tswee* etc. uttered from a bush-top. During the breeding season the male indulges in a series of extravagant steeply undulating nose dives and wave crests in the air. *Food:* tiny insects.

NESTING: *Season*—May-June. *Nest*—globular, of grass, with a lateral entrance. Placed low down in a bush on a scrub-and-grass covered hillside. *Eggs*—very variable; white to salmon-pink or blue, blotched and speckled with reddish brown, usually with an ill-defined ring round the broad end. Size about 17×13 mm.

RACIAL CHARACTERISTICS, MEASUREMENTS, ETC: Differs from the Assam race *khasiana* in having the upper plumage dark olive-brown instead of bright ferruginous-brown.

A specimen (♂) collected by the Survey measures: Wing 51; bill 13.5; tarsus 21; tail (winter) 101 mm. Schäfer's Sikkim specimens (7 ♂♀) have Wing 45 (♀) to 52 (♂) mm.

In summer (breeding) plumage the male's tail is longer than the female's.

Iris greyish brown; bill horny brown; legs and feet brownish flesh colour; claws horny brown.

## *Subfamily* TURDINAE: Chats, Robins, Thrushes

### THE INDIAN BLUE CHAT

*Erithacus brunneus brunneus* (Hodgson)

*Larvivora brunnea* Hodgson, 1837, *Jour. Asiat. Soc. Bengal* **6**: 102—Nepal.

F.B.I. **2**: 14

LOCAL NAME: Manzil-pho (Lepcha).

SIZE: Sparrow—.

FIELD CHARACTERS: *Male: Above,* lores, sides of head and neck black with a conspicuous long broad white supercilium. Rest of upper plumage including exposed portions of closed wings and tail, dark blue. *Below,* point of chin white, continued backwards as a narrow underline to the black cheeks. Chin, throat, breast and flanks bright chestnut; rest of underparts white.

*Female: Above,* olive-brown, tinged with russet on rump and upper tail-coverts. Wings and tail brown edged with fulvous rufous. *Below,* bright fulvous.

STATUS AND HABITAT: Breeding at between 8000 and 11,000 ft. elevation in summer (Lachung, Lachen); absent in winter. Frequents dense undergrowth in forest.

DISTRIBUTION OUTSIDE SIKKIM: *Summer,* throughout the Himalayas from Kashmir to Bhutan. *Winter,* Himalayan foothills; Eastern and Western Ghats; Ceylon.

GENERAL HABITS: Keeps singly or in separated pairs, flitting about or skulking in heavy undergrowth of brambles etc. Hops mostly on ground, but also mounts into lower branches. Expands and jerks up tail from time to time, uttering a soft *chr-r-r* or *chick-chick* like a flycatcher. At intervals also a squeak, repeated about once a second. *Song:* a loud *peep, peep, peep,* slowly and deliberately repeated in ascending scale, followed by an explosive trill of 4 or 5 quick-repeated sweet notes (reminiscent of the song of the British Robin) ending abruptly. *Food:* insects and their larvae.

NESTING: *Season*—May-June. *Nest*—a pad of dead leaves, weeds, moss, roots, etc. lined with hair and a few feathers. Placed on ground in deep jungle, in the side of an earth bank or at the roots of a bramble or bracken bush. *Eggs*—3 to 5, deep 'Hedge-Sparrow' blue. Size about 20×15 mm.

RACIAL CHARACTERISTICS, MEASUREMENTS, ETC: ♂♀ Wing 73-78; bill 15-16; tarsus *c.* 28; tail 45-50 mm.

Iris dark brown; bill blackish brown, pale flesh colour at gape and chin; legs, feet and claws brownish flesh colour.

## THE EAST HIMALAYAN RUBYTHROAT

*Erithacus pectoralis confusus* (Hartert)

*Luscinia pectoralis confusa* Hartert, 1909, Vögel paläark. Fauna 1: 740—Sikkim.

F.B.I. 2: 93

LOCAL NAME:

SIZE: Sparrow.

FIELD CHARACTERS: A skulking, robin-like, ground-hopping bird. *Male: Above,* forehead and short supercilium white; forecrown blackish; sides of head black; rest of upper parts dark slaty grey. Tail slaty blackish brown with the lateral feathers broadly white at base, and tipped with white. *Below,* chin and throat bright crimson; sides of crimson patch and breast black, fringed with olive-brown or ashy brown; rest of underparts white or whitish.

*Female: Above,* olive-brown with short dingy white supercilium; tail brown, without white except on tips. *Below,* chin and throat dull white; breast fulvous brown fading to fulvous white on abdomen.

STATUS AND HABITAT: ? Not met with by the Survey, nor apparently by Meinertzhagen or Schäfer. Blanford (in 1870) recorded it as common on the Chola Range, less abundant in N. Sikkim, in August-September at 12,000 ft., usually above the limit of forest.

DISTRIBUTION: 'Nepal, Sikkim, Bhutan in the transition zone between Himalayan and Tibetan facies. In winter Nepal terai, lower elevations in Sikkim, 3500-5000 ft. and probably lower, the Duars and N. Bengal' (Ticehurst, *Ibis* 1940: 330). The adjoining west Himalayan (typical) race *pectoralis* stretches westward to Afghanistan. Visits many parts of peninsular India and a great part of SE. Asia in winter. The breeding range of the species includes Siberia, Kamchatka, N. China.

GENERAL HABITS: A great skulker. Keeps on the ground under bushes, or amongst boulders on screes and moraines. Normally tail cocked up jauntily, with wings drooping at sides, and twitched up from time to time. When aware of being watched, runs furtively, with swift mincing steps—almost glides—from bush to bush, head lowered and tail slightly raised. Utters a harsh *ke* like *Turdoides*, sometimes followed by a short snatch of song. *Song* (in breeding season): short, pleasant, of Accentor quality, very like Pied Bushchat's, of three or four seconds' duration, repeated almost without intermission for half to one hour at a time from a bushtop. *Food:* insects.

NESTING: Little known. Nearest record from north of Chumbi Valley, *c.* 14,000 ft., 22 June. *Nest*—described as semi-domed, of grass, in slight hollow in ground under a bush. *Eggs*—3 or 4, dull green, faintly freckled with reddish. Size about 23×15 mm.

RACIAL CHARACTERISTICS, MEASUREMENTS, ETC: *Male* differs from west Himalayan *pectoralis* in having the upper parts deep blackish slate, and the white forehead broader. *Females* of the two races not always separable.

The Fauna gives Wing (♂♀) as 68-75 mm.; according to Hartert up to 77 mm.

Iris brown; bill black, lighter at tip; legs and feet brown, fleshy brown or plumbeous brown.

## THE TIBET RUBYTHROAT

*Erithacus pectoralis tschebaiewi* (Przevalski)

*Calliope tschebaiewi* Przevalski, 1876, Mongol. i Str. Tangut 2: 44—Kansu Mountains.

F.B.I. 2: 94

LOCAL NAME:

SIZE: Sparrow.

FIELD CHARACTERS: *Male* distinguished from *E. p. confusa* by presence of a broad white moustache. White at base of tail less extensive; white forehead less broad, i.e. not broader than supercilium. *Female* difficult to differentiate satisfactorily.

This rubythroat is believed to be the Tibetan facies representative of the Himalayan species. It was obtained from 'Native Sikkim' by Mandelli in March 1878 and *may* breed at the highest altitudes in northern Sikkim. Meinertzhagen did not come across it there in winter.

## THE COMMON RUBYTHROAT

*Erithacus calliope* (Pallas)

*Motacilla calliope* Pallas, 1776, Reise Russ. Reichs 3: 697—Yenesei.

Plate 14, fig. 6 (facing p. 145)

F.B.I. 2: 91

LOCAL NAME:

SIZE: Sparrow.

FIELD CHARACTERS: *Male* distinguished from the Himalayan Rubythroat by its *olive-brown* upper parts, a white cheek-stripe in addition to the more conspicuous long white supercilium, and absence of white in the tail. Underparts dirty whitish. Scarlet throat-patch enclosed by a thin black loop.

STATUS: Blanford saw this species in northern Sikkim occasionally in the latter part of September and more frequently in October—apparently on southward passage. He procured a specimen at Mome Shamdong, *c.* 15,000 ft., in Tibetan facies, on 19 September.

According to Stevens 'it occurs in limited numbers throughout the cold weather in suitable haunts on the Outer Ranges . . . . Apparently neither Meinertzhagen nor Schäfer came across it in high northern Sikkim in winter. The recent Loke-Sálim Ali Survey, which worked up to *c.* 13,500 ft. (November to May), also failed to meet with it.

## THE GOLDEN BUSH ROBIN

*Erithacus chrysaeus chrysaeus* (Hodgson)

*Tarsiger chrysaeus* Hodgson, 1845, *Proc. Zool. Soc. London:* 28—Nepal.

**Plate 14, fig. 7** (facing p. 145)

F.B.I. 2: 95

LOCAL NAME: Manshil-pho (Lepcha).

SIZE: Sparrow—.

FIELD CHARACTERS: *Male: Above,* lores, cheeks, ear-coverts, around eye, and line of forehead, black. Forehead to hindneck, and down middle of back, olive. Supercilium, sides of back, rump, and upper tail-coverts, bright orange-yellow. Tail orange-yellow, broadly banded at tip with black; central rectrices black with yellow bases to outer webs. Wings black, margined with dull olive. *Below,* bright orange-yellow.

*Female: Above,* olive-green; yellowish around eye and with faint olive-yellow supercilium. *Below,* yellow and olivaceous.

Male, female and juvenile often met in puzzling intermediate plumages. In all phases, colour pattern of tail diagnostic.

STATUS AND HABITAT: Breeds at elevations of *c.* 10,000 ft. to the limit of rhododendron scrub, *c.* 13,000-14,000 ft. (Thangu, Karponang). In winter down to between 7000 and 2500 ft. (Temi, Gangtok, Penlom-la). Affects thick bush jungle.

DISTRIBUTION OUTSIDE SIKKIM: Nepal, Bhutan, SE. Tibet; Naga Hills, Manipur. NE. Burma, Yunnan, Tonkin, Szechwan. The adjoining paler west Himalayan race *whistleri* stretches to Hazara.

GENERAL HABITS: Unobtrusive; of robin-like bearing and movements. Hops about quietly under dense undergrowth in search of insect food; occasionally mounts to a bush-top. Has a harsh croak which betrays its presence; sometimes of several syllables, likened to 'the subdued grinding of a few stones of an old-fashioned watchman's rattle'. Said to have a 'beautiful song' in the breeding season; no details.

NESTING: *Season*—May to July. A nest taken by Hickley as low as *c.* 8000 ft. (above Gangtok). *Nest*—a cup or pad of moss, lined with wool and hair. Placed in a niche in an earth-bank amongst rhododendron scrub etc. *Eggs*—3 or 4, pale verditer blue. Size about 20×15 mm.

RACIAL CHARACTERISTICS, MEASUREMENTS, ETC: The Fauna gives:

| | Wing | Bill | Tarsus | Tail |
|---|---|---|---|---|
| ♂♂ | 65-69 | 11 | 29-30 | 49-53 mm. |
| ♀♀ | 62-68 | 11 | 29-30 | 49-50 mm. |

Stresemann measures a series collected by Schäfer in Sikkim: Wing 8 ad. ♂♂ 67-73 (av. 69.3); 7 ♀♀ and imm. ♂♂ 63-68 (av. 64.4) mm.

Iris dark brown; bill black, yellow on lower mandible and along commissure, legs and feet fleshy.

## THE REDFLANKED BUSH ROBIN

*Erithacus cyanurus rufilatus* (Hodgson)

*Nemura rufilata* Hodgson, 1845, *Proc. Zool. Soc. London:* 27—Nepal.

F.B.I. 2: 99

LOCAL NAME: Mangzhil-pho (Lepcha).

SIZE: Sparrow.

FIELD CHARACTERS: *Male: Above*, forehead, broad supercilium, rump, and upper tail-coverts bright ultramarine blue. Ear-coverts, lores, and around eye black. Rest of upper parts including exposed portions of wings, deep purplish blue. Tail black, suffused with deep blue. *Below*, sides of head, throat, neck, and breast deep purplish blue. Chin, throat, and rest of underparts white, sullied with ashy brown on breast. Sides of body orange-chestnut.

*Female: Above*, rufous olive-brown; wing-coverts and flight feathers edged with rufous. Rump greenish blue; upper tail-coverts deep blue. Tail dark brown, the feathers edged with blue. *Below*, sides of head and neck, and whole breast ochraceous brown; chin and throat narrowly white down the middle. Abdomen white; rest of underparts ochraceous; sides of body orange-chestnut. Around eye white.

STATUS AND HABITAT: Fairly common. Breeding up to *c.* 14,000 ft. altitude; in winter down to between 7000 and 3500 ft. (Rinchinpong, Chungthang, Gangtok, Pemionche, Lingtam, Lachung, Thangu, Gnatong, Karponang, Yumthang, Chola Range, etc.).

Affects undergrowth of seedlings etc. in tall forest on hillsides—laurel, oak, rhododendron and conifers.

DISTRIBUTION OUTSIDE SIKKIM: E. Nepal, Bhutan, S. Tibet and across to the Mishmi Hills. Assam hills and Manipur (winter only?); Burma, Yunnan, Kansu. The species ranges widely in Siberia (breeding); SE. Asia (winter).

The adjoining paler west Himalayan race, *pallidiora*, stretches westward to Kashmir and the Afghan boundary, and perhaps beyond.

GENERAL HABITS: Active; unobtrusive; typically robin-like. Usually seen in pairs in undergrowth of seedlings in forest, hopping in search of food. Sometimes mounting a low bush, whence it makes short flycatcher-like sorties in the air after winged insects. Incessantly flicks wings, and rapidly expands and closes tail. *Call:* a plaintive *pheeou*. Song poor, of three notes—the first and third being the same, the middle note a tone lower.

NESTING: *Season*—May-June. *Nest*—a rough cup of moss, grass, roots and leaves, lined with wool and hair. Placed under the exposed roots of a large tree, or in a hollow on a steep hillside, sheltered under herbage. *Eggs*—3 to 5, chalky white, unmarked or faintly freckled with pale pink forming an ill-defined ring at the broad end. Size about 18×14 mm. Both sexes feed the young.

RACIAL CHARACTERISTICS, MEASUREMENTS, ETC: The Survey specimens measure:

| | Wing | Bill | Tarsus | Tail |
|---|---|---|---|---|
| 1 ♂ | 81 | 12.5 | 24.5 | 60 mm. |
| 2 ♀♀ | 80-82 | 13 | 24-26 | 62-64 mm. |

Stresemann measures a series collected by Schäfer in Sikkim: Wing 6 ad. ♂♂ 81-85 (av. 84.0); 12 ♀♀ and imm. ♂♂ 78-83 (av. 80.9) mm.

Iris brown; bill horny brown or black; legs, feet and claws blackish brown; soles of feet whitish.

## THE WHITEBROWED BUSH ROBIN

*Erithacus indicus indicus* (Vieillot)

*Sylvia indica* Vieillot, 1817, Nouv Dict. d'Hist. Nat., nouv. éd., **11**: 267—India (=Darjeeling).

**Plate 14, fig. 8 (facing p. 145)**

F.B.I. 2: 102

LOCAL NAME:

SIZE: Sparrow.

FIELD CHARACTERS: *Male: Above*, dull slate-blue with a diagnostic broad white supercilium from bill to nape. Lores, in front of and below eye, black; sides of head blackish blue. Tail black, suffused with blue. Wing quills blackish brown edged with olive-yellow. *Below*, orange-rufous, whitish on middle of abdomen.

*Female: Above*, olive-brown with partially concealed white supercilium to nape. Wings and tail brown, edged with rufous olive-brown. *Below*, ochraceous—deepest on breast, whitish on abdomen.

STATUS AND HABITAT: Not common. Normally between *c.* 1000 and 11,000 ft. elevation. Met with by me at 11,000 ft. (Phalut) even at the end of December, and by Schäfer at 12,500 ft. (Changu) in February. As a population, however, probably has a lower ceiling in winter (Gangtok, Chungthang, Lachen, Lachung). Affects similar facies to that of the Redflanked Bush Robin—tall forest on steep hillsides with undergrowth of seedlings, bracken and low bushes.

DISTRIBUTION OUTSIDE SIKKIM: Garhwal (?); Nepal, Bhutan, Khasia Hills, N. Cachar. The species extends to Chwanben, Szechwan, Yunnan and Tonkin.

GENERAL HABITS: Robin-like and similar to the two described; but little known. Baker has recorded it mounting into large leafy trees to feed on insects, making occasional sallies into the air after them.

NESTING: No record for Sikkim. *Season*—elsewhere May-June. *Nest*—an untidy loose cup or pad of soft dry grass and dry moss, lined with fine fern-roots. Placed on the ground among the exposed roots of a tree or in a hollow under a stone. *Eggs*—3 or 4, indistinguishable from those of the Redflanked Bush Robin. Size about 18×14 mm.

RACIAL CHARACTERISTICS, MEASUREMENTS, ETC: A Survey specimen (♂) measures Wing 79; bill 14; tarsus 28; tail 64 mm. Schäfer's skins from Sikkim give Wing 3 ♂♂ 79, 80, 82; 1 ♀ 77 mm.

Iris brown; bill brownish black; legs and feet greyish brown; claws horny brown.

## THE RUFOUSBELLIED BUSH ROBIN

*Erithacus hyperythrus* (Blyth)

*Ianthia hyperythra* Blyth, 1847, *Jour. Asiat. Soc. Bengal* **16**: 132—Darjeeling.

F.B.I. **2**: 103

LOCAL NAME:

SIZE: Sparrow.

FIELD CHARACTERS: *Male:* Readily distinguished from the Redflanked Bush Robin by the sides of the body being uniformly coloured with the rest of underparts. *Above,* forehead continued behind as supercilium, upper tail-coverts, and patch at shoulder of wing bright ultramarine blue. Lores, in front of eye, and ear-coverts black. Rest of upper plumage, with sides of head and neck, deep purplish blue. Wing quills and tail black edged with purplish blue. *Below,* orange-chestnut; only vent and under tail-coverts white.

*Female: Above,* rufous olive-brown; sides of head tinged fulvous. Short supercilium, and rump slaty blue; upper tail-coverts deep blue. *Below,* rich ochraceous—browner on breast, brightest at sides of abdomen; white on vent and under tail-coverts.

STATUS AND HABITAT: Rare and little known. Has been recorded between 4000 and 12,000 ft. altitude (Singhik, Toong, Gangtok, Karponang, Changu, Phalut) in scrub undergrowth of dwarf rhododendron etc. on forested hillsides.

DISTRIBUTION OUTSIDE SIKKIM: Known only from Nepal and some Assam hills (Abor, Miri and Khasia).

GENERAL HABITS: Similar to other bush robins, but little specifically recorded.

RACIAL CHARACTERISTICS, MEASUREMENTS, ETC: The Fauna gives for ♂♀ Wing 75-79; bill 10; tarsus *c.* 24; tail 52-55 mm. Against this 3 ♂♂ in the Schäfer Sikkim collection have Wing 79, 80, 81 (Stresemann).

Iris brown; bill black; legs and feet horny brown.

## THE WHITETAILED BLUE BUSH ROBIN

*Cinclidium leucurum* (Hodgson)

*Muscisylvia leucura* Hodgson, 1845, *Proc. Zool. Soc. London:* 27—Nepal.

F.B.I. 2: 106

LOCAL NAME: Mangshia (Lepcha).

SIZE: Sparrow +.

FIELD CHARACTERS: *Male: Above,* black suffused with blue. Forehead, supercilium, and a patch on wing-shoulder bright cobalt blue. Lores, and sides of head and neck black; a concealed white patch on each side of neck. Wings black, with bluish edges. Tail largely white on basal portions of all except middle and outermost pairs of feathers which are black. *Below,* deep black, a few feathers on abdomen blue-fringed. Posterior flanks and under tail-coverts fringed with white.

*Female:* Rufescent brown. Wings and tail brown, edged with ferruginous; the latter with the basal white patches smaller.

The conspicuous white patches in the tail of both sexes are diagnostic.

STATUS AND HABITAT: Fairly common at moderate altitudes, *c.* 3500 to 8000 ft. (Rishap, Lebong, Gangtok, Pemionche). Affects undergrowth of low bushes in shady forest, especially at the edge of mule paths, firelines and streams.

DISTRIBUTION OUTSIDE SIKKIM: Nepal, Bhutan (?), Dafla Hills, Assam, Manipur, Burma, N. Thailand, Yunnan, Indochina, S. China.

GENERAL HABITS: Shy and silent. Keeps singly. Hops on ground in search of insects and flies up into lower branches when disturbed, like Blueheaded Rock Thrush. There slowly expands its conspicuous white-and-black tail, and presently descends to the ground again. The male has a fine song in the breeding season.

NESTING: *Season*—May-June. *Nest*—a compact deep cup, or domed structure with side entrance, of fine roots intermixed with leaves, and with a little moss on the outside. Placed in a crack or hole in the face of a vertical rock, or hollow in earth bank or roadside cutting. *Eggs*—3 or 4, pale cream or buff, densely and minutely stippled all over with pale reddish clay colour, producing a pinky overall appearance. Size about 24 × 17 mm.

RACIAL CHARACTERISTICS, MEASUREMENTS, ETC: A Sikkim Survey specimen (♂) measures: Wing 97; bill 18; tarsus 27.5; tail 81. A Schäfer ♂ has Wing 93 mm.

Iris brown; legs and feet black.

## THE BLUEFRONTED ROBIN

### *Cinclidium frontale frontale* Blyth

*Cinclidium frontale* Blyth, 1842, *Jour. Asiat. Soc. Bengal* **11**: 181—Sikkim.

**Plate 23, fig. 3** (facing p. 288)

F.B.I. 2: 107

LOCAL NAME:

SIZE: Bulbul.

FIELD CHARACTERS: Sex for sex very like the Whitetailed Blue Bush Robin (p. 253) and easily mistakable for it; but absence of white patches in tail diagnostic.

STATUS AND HABITAT: Rare and little known. Not met with by Stevens, Meinertzhagen or Schäfer, nor by the recent Sikkim Ornithological Survey. In the British Museum there are old skins collected in Sikkim, without proper data. Described as a forest bird, 'apparently between 6000 and 10,000 feet'.

DISTRIBUTION OUTSIDE SIKKIM: Not known from adjoining Nepal or Bhutan, or from elsewhere in the Himalayas. Recorded from farther south-east, in Tonkin and Laos.

GENERAL HABITS: From its long tarsus, presumably robin-like, but nothing specifically recorded.

NESTING: Unknown.

RACIAL CHARACTERISTICS, MEASUREMENTS, ETC: Tail graduated and longer than in *C. leucurum*. Tarsus also much longer. The Fauna gives the measurements (from Sikkim specimens in the British Museum) as:

| | Wing | Bill | Tarsus | Tail |
|---|---|---|---|---|
| ♂♂ | 83-91 | 14-15 | 37-38 | 75-80 mm. |
| ♀♀ | 81-82 | 13 | — | 78 mm. |

Bill black; legs and feet brown.

## HODGSON'S GRANDALA

### *Grandala côelicolor côelicolor* Hodgson

*Grandala côelicolar* [*sic*] Hodgson, 1843, *Jour. Asiat. Soc. Bengal* **12**: 447—Nepal.

**Plate 23, fig. 2** (facing p. 288)

F.B.I. 2: 89

LOCAL NAME:

SIZE: Between Bulbul and Myna.

FIELD CHARACTERS: Reminiscent of a rock thrush at rest; of a starling in flight.

Adult *Male:* Entire plumage *above* and *below* glistening, silky, bright purple-blue, brighter on rump and upper tail-coverts. Wings and tail black.

*Female: Above,* brown, streaked with fulvous white, with slight blue tinge on rump and upper tail-coverts. Wings and tail brown, the former with a prominent white wing-spot or 'mirror'; some of the secondaries tipped white. *Below*, chin dull fulvous; rest brown, streaked with pale fulvous.

STATUS AND HABITAT: Resident at very high altitudes, *c.* 15,000 to 17,000 ft., hardly descending in winter unless forced down temporarily by heavy snowfalls and severe weather, and then not below *c.* 9000 ft. (Lachen, Lachung, Thangu, Yumthang, Gyagong, Natu La, Phalut). Affects mountainous country in the high alpine zone just below the snow-line; rocky slopes with *Hippophae* bushes, at its lowest winter limit (Lachen and Lachung valleys).

DISTRIBUTION OUTSIDE SIKKIM: Kashmir, Spiti, Garhwal, Nepal, Bhutan. N. Burma, Chwanben, Szechwan to N. Kansu.

GENERAL HABITS: Gregarious. Keeps in close-packed flocks, sometimes (in winter) of several hundred birds together—in one instance (Lachen, February 1952) estimated at 1000+. This swarm kept circling high over the valley in a massed 'cloud', chiefly gliding, with occasional wing beats. The cloud appeared as though wafted here and there by the wind. From time to time the birds would drop steeply like rain more or less in unison to settle on tall leafless trees, covering the top branches in dense clusters like starlings at the roost. Every little while, for no apparent reason, the swarm would suddenly take wing, circle aloft and tumble again into another tree in a restricted 'beat' of rocky mountainside. A nervous restlessness seemed to pervade the swarm, and for the several days it was under observation the same behaviour prevailed. When settled on a tree the birds could be approached quite closely, which showed that the restlessness was unconnected with our intrusion. Their taking off suddenly, flying in a close-packed rabble and circling back to the tree reminded me of the behaviour of a flock of Greyheaded Mynas (*Sturnus malabarica*) feeding on a flowering *Bombax*. The long pointed wings, slightly forked tail, style of flight, and the habit of clustering on bare tree-tops are distinctly starling-like. The general shape, while at rest, is reminiscent of the rock thrush (e.g. *Monticola solitaria*), and a peculiar prolongation of the posterior part of the body heightens the resemblance.

This swarm, and other smaller flocks at Lachen, were feeding exclusively on the abundant, sour, juicy berries of *Hippophae salicifolia* Don. Certain patches on the mountainside were favoured, while equally laden thickets in neighbouring ravines were ignored. A circling flock would suddenly tumble into a food tree jostling and crowding in on the fruit-bearing branches, devour the berries ravenously for a brief spell—sometimes just three or four berries hurriedly and in great apparent nervousness—then they would as suddenly take to wing and resume the interminable circling around. From a cluster of birds in a tree-top three or four to a dozen would launch out in the air every now and again like an *Artamus* or *Merops* —to circle back to the perch, literally tumbling into the tree when a few feet above. Definitely not hawking insects though the actions are clearly suggestive of this.

The great preponderance of adult males over ♀-plumaged birds in the flocks was very marked. The same disparity was also noted by Schäfer in eastern Tibet, though Meinertzhagen found some flocks composed entirely of ♀-plumaged birds in N. Sikkim (December 1925). Meinertzhagen has recorded that (on the ground) 'they hop, and are fond of jumping chat-like on to a rock'.

*Voice* and *call:* In winter an occasional short *twit* was uttered by individuals, but on the whole very silent. In the breeding season, according to Schäfer, the male has a ringing, finch-like, scolding call *diu-di di diu*, and the female a shrill *dee dee dee*. *Food:* insects (moths), and berries (*Hippophae, Vaccinium,* etc.).

NESTING: No record for Sikkim, and very little known. Apparently flocks do not break up into pairs for breeding, neither do they nest in colonies. The meagre records suggest the season as May to July. Seven ♂♂ (including one in ♀ plumage) in the Chicago Museum of Natural History, collected by V. S. La Personne at Thangu, '18,000 ft.' (?), 21-23 May 1931, have the testes sketched on their labels as *c.* 9×6 mm., therefore presumably ready to breed. Four ♀♀ with the same data, however, are shown with no gonadal development.

RACIAL CHARACTERISTICS, MEASUREMENTS, ETC: A series collected by the Sikkim Survey measures:

| | Wing | Bill | Tarsus | Tail | |
|---|---|---|---|---|---|
| 6 ♂♂ ad. | 146-152 | 19.5-21 | 28.5-31 | 84-91 | mm. |
| 3 ♀♀ | 140-147 | 19.5-20 | 28.5-30 | 77.5, 81, 87 | mm. |

Iris hazel; bill black, yellow at gape; inside mouth (both sexes) bright lemon yellow; legs and feet black.

## HODGSON'S SHORTWING

*Hodgsonius phoenicuroides phoenicuroides* (Gray)

*Bradypterus phaenicuroides* [*sic*] Gray, 1846, Cat. Mamms. Birds Nepal: 70, 153—Nepal.

F.B.I. 2: 21

LOCAL NAME:

SIZE: Bulbul.

FIELD CHARACTERS: *Male:* General effect reminiscent of the Magpie Robin. Head, entire upper parts, throat and breast slaty blue; tail blue-black with a conspicuous chestnut patch on either side near base. Abdomen white. A white patch near base of primaries (on bastard wing) conspicuous in flight and when wings drooped.

*Female: Above,* olive-brown with rufous tinge on margins of wings and tail, the latter with the chestnut patch near base, as in male. *Below,* ochraceous, suffused with brown on breast and flanks; abdomen whitish.

STATUS AND HABITAT: Apparently rare. Stevens records it in the Sikkim Himalayas between *c.* 3000 and 5000 ft. elevation (September to February), but it doubtless goes higher in summer, as in the western Himalayas (7500 to 11,000 ft.). Affects undergrowth of moderately high shrubs on open hillsides and outskirts of forest.

DISTRIBUTION OUTSIDE SIKKIM: The Himalayas from the Khagan Valley and Kashmir to Bhutan (and NE. Assam); Yunnan. The species extends to Szechwan, Kansu, Kuku Nor. Also recorded from Indochina.

GENERAL HABITS: Shy and retiring. Keeps singly, mostly on the ground in scrub and undergrowth, hopping or running about in search of insect food. Utters a harsh metallic *trick-trick-trick*. Tail usually carried spread out and depressed, with the wings partially drooping at the sides. In this position the chestnut patches on the tail, as also the white patch on the wing, are prominent and diagnostic. Tail sometimes flicked up momentarily and cocked over the back. Sings from the centre of bushes or higher trees, with tail held up vertically and fanned out. *Song:* a somewhat mournful, whistling soliloquy *pe-pee-pit* (accent on the middle syllable), reminiscent of snatches of the Magpie Robin's song. Distinctive, but intriguing until definitely placed. Sings early mornings and late evenings; often even in moonlight.

NESTING: *Season*—not recorded in Sikkim. In the western Himalayas, June-July. *Nest*—cup-shaped, of coarse grass, dead leaves, etc. lined with fine grass, feathers or fur. Usually placed in low bushes up to 3 ft. from the ground. *Eggs*—3, exceptionally beautiful, deep greenish blue (dark jade). Size about 23×16 mm. Both parents feed the young, but whether, and to what extent, they share in nest-building and incubation is undetermined.

RACIAL CHARACTERISTICS, MEASUREMENTS, ETC: Has the typical short rounded wings and long tarsus of other shortwings (*Brachypteryx*), but differs in possessing a comparatively long tail. Measurements: ♂♀ Wing 73-77; bill *c.* 15; tarsus *c.* 30; tail 75-82 mm. (Fauna).

Iris brown; bill plumbeous olive, paler on lower mandible and yellowish at gape; legs and feet plumbeous olive.

## THE BLUEFRONTED REDSTART

*Phoenicurus frontalis* (Vigors)

*Phoenicura frontalis* Vigors, 1832, *Proc. Zool. Soc. London:* 172—Himalayas.

F.B.I. 2: 69

LOCAL NAME: Tak-tirriri-pho (Lepcha).

SIZE: Sparrow.

FIELD CHARACTERS: *Male: Above,* forehead and supercilium bright blue; rest of head, and back, dark blue; rump orange-chestnut; tail largely chestnut with black terminal band. *Below*, chin and throat dark blue; rest of underparts orange-chestnut.

*Female: Above,* fulvous brown; tail as in male. *Below,* throat and breast fulvous brown, paler on chin; rest of underparts orange-brown.

STATUS AND HABITAT: A common high-elevation redstart, breeding up to at least 15,000 ft. In winter down to between *c.* 9000 and

3000 ft. (Dikchu, Singhik, Chungthang, Kewzing, Rinchinpong, Gangtok, Lachen, Lachung, Yumthang, Thangu, Manshitang, Gyagong). Hardly ever descends to the plains. Frequents rocky grass-covered slopes, rhododendron and juniper scrub, yak pastures and rock moraines near or above the tree-line in summer.

DISTRIBUTION OUTSIDE SIKKIM: *Summer*, throughout the high Himalayas from Afghanistan and Gilgit, through Kashmir, to SE. Tibet. *Winter*, lower elevations in the same; also Assam hills, Naga Hills, Manipur, NE. Burma, N. Yunnan, Szechwan, Kansu, etc.

GENERAL HABITS: Keeps singly or in widely separated pairs. Perches upright; constantly flicks tail jerkily up and down in the manner of the Whitecapped Redstart—not shivered or flirted as in the Common Redstart (*P. ochruros*). Descends to ground from boulder or bush from time to time to pick up an insect, and flies off to another perch nearby within its feeding area. Occasionally takes winged insects in the air. Utters a low, clicking *prit-prit*. Male has a sweet song during the breeding season when he becomes pugnacious and intolerant of others of his kind.

NESTING: *Season*—May-June. *Nest*—a shallow cup, or pad, of moss, grass, etc. lined with moss, feathers and hair. Placed near the ground in hollows in rocks, or under stones and boulders. *Eggs*—3 or 4, pinkish café-au-lait with a zone of confluent markings and a few grey specks near the broad end. Size about 19×15 mm.

RACIAL CHARACTERISTICS, MEASUREMENTS, ETC: In all redstarts (*Phoenicurus*) sexes dissimilar and tail largely chestnut. *P. frontalis* readily distinguished from others by all tail feathers being abruptly tipped with black, except middle pair. Summer plumage darker, with purer colours due to loss by abrasion of brown fringes to feathers. The Sikkim Survey specimens measure:

| | Wing | Bill | Tarsus | Tail |
|---|---|---|---|---|
| 3 ♂♂ | 88-90 | 13.5-15.5 | 24-25 | 65-67 mm. |
| 1 ♀ | 86.5 | 14.5 | 23 | 70 mm. |

For Schäfer's large series from Sikkim, Stresemann gives Wing 16 ♂♂ 84-90 (av. 87.7); 9 ♀♀ 80-85 (av. 82.2) mm.

Iris brown; bill black; legs, feet and claws blackish brown.

## THE WHITETHROATED REDSTART

*Phoenicurus schisticeps schisticeps* (Gray)

*Ruticilla schisticeps* Gray, 1846, Cat. Mamms. Birds Nepal: 69, 153—Nepal.

**Plate 16, fig. 8** (facing p. 161)

F.B.I. **2**: 70

LOCAL NAME:

SIZE: Sparrow.

FIELD CHARACTERS: *Male: Above*, forehead and crown cobalt blue; back black with fulvous edges and some chestnut on scapulars; wings black with a white patch, particularly conspicuous in flight; rump and upper tail-coverts chestnut; tail largely black and chestnut.

*Below*, chin and throat black with a white patch in centre; rest of underparts chestnut, albescent on abdomen.

Fulvous edges to feathers of upper parts lost by wear in summer.

*Female: Above*, head and back brown; rump and upper tail-coverts chestnut; tail as in male, but dull rufous replacing chestnut; wings brown with small ashy patch. *Below*, brown fringed with ashy; abdomen whitish; large white throat-patch.

STATUS AND HABITAT: Fairly common locally at high elevations. *Summer*, between 10,000 and 14,000-15,000 ft.; *winter*, down to between 5000 and 11,000 (Toong, Chungthang, Gangtok, Lachen, Lachung, Yumthang, Thangu, Changu). Affects open, sparsely scrub-covered hillsides, with boulders and rock outcrops.

DISTRIBUTION OUTSIDE SIKKIM: Nepal, Bhutan, Chumbi Valley, extending to N. Yunnan, Chwanben, Kuku Nor, Kansu, Szechwan, etc.

GENERAL HABITS: Typical of the redstarts. *Food:* insects; also seeds and berries in winter. Voice and calls unrecorded. In Sikkim I always found it inordinately wild.

NESTING: Not recorded within Indian limits, but will probably be found to breed at high altitudes in Nepal and Sikkim.

RACIAL CHARACTERISTICS, MEASUREMENTS, ETC: Large white throat-patch in both sexes diagnostic.

The Sikkim Survey specimens measure:

| | Wing | Bill | Tarsus | Tail | |
|---|---|---|---|---|---|
| 1 ♂ | 85 | 15 | 23.5 | 70 | mm. |
| 2 ♀♀ | 81-85 | 15.5-16 | 22.5-23.5 | 64-73 | mm. |

Three Schäfer skins have Wing ♂ 85, 85; ♀ 81 mm.

Iris brown; bill, legs, feet and claws black.

## HODGSON'S REDSTART

### *Phoenicurus hodgsoni* (Moore)

*Ruticilla hodgsoni* Moore, 1854, *in* Horsfield & Moore, Cat. Birds Mus. E. I. Co. 1: 303—Bootan, Nepal.

F.B.I. 2: 74

LOCAL NAME: Thar-capni (Nepali).

SIZE: Sparrow.

FIELD CHARACTERS: *Male:* Like the Common Redstart (*P. ochruros*), but with practically no black on upper parts. *Above*, crown white or nearly white, this extending to over eye; mantle ashy grey; a conspicuous white patch in wing.

*Female: Above*, greyer, less brown than female *ochruros*. *Below*, ashy; whitish on abdomen. Distinguished in the field from female *frontalis* by much paler overall coloration and absence of terminal black bar to tail.

STATUS AND HABITAT: Local and uncommon winter visitor to low and moderate elevations *c.* 5500 to 1000 ft. (Rangpo, Martam, Dentam, Dikchu, Chungthang, Gangtok, Lachen). Breeds in the Tibetan facies at 8000-12,000 ft. altitude. In its winter quarters, affects the vicinity of streams and dry river beds, and open, rocky, scrub-and-bush country.

DISTRIBUTION OUTSIDE SIKKIM: Nepal, Bhutan, Assam hills N. and S. of the Brahmaputra; Naga Hills, plains of N. Assam, Manipur, NE. Burma. Breeds in Kansu, Szechwan, Kuku Nor, Chwanben.

GENERAL HABITS: Typical of the genus. On streams, actions and behaviour very like the Plumbeous Redstart's. Keeps in widely separated pairs. Shivers or flirts tail like *P. ochruros.* Utters *prit, prit* like Bluefronted Redstart. Song unrecorded.

NESTING: Not recorded in Sikkim.. Possibly breeds at high elevations in the Tibetan facies of extreme northern Sikkim?

RACIAL CHARACTERISTICS, MEASUREMENTS, ETC: The Sikkim Survey specimens measure:

| | Wing | Bill | Tarsus | Tail |
|---|---|---|---|---|
| 3 ♂♂ | 86-87 | 15-16 | 24-25 | 65-67 mm. |
| 1 ♀ | 84 | 14.5 | 24.5 | 66.5 mm. |

Iris brown; bill, legs, feet and claws black or blackish brown.

## THE DAURIAN REDSTART

*Phoenicurus auroreus leucopterus* (Blyth)

*Phoenicura leucoptera* Blyth, 1843, *Jour. Asiat. Soc. Bengal* 12: 962—Malay Peninsula.

F.B.I. 2: 71 (*auroreus*)

LOCAL NAME:

SIZE: Sparrow.

FIELD CHARACTERS: *Male: Above,* forehead whitish; crown, neck and mantle slaty grey; back black; rump chestnut; prominent white wing-patches (as in Blueheaded Rock Thrush). *Below,* sides of head and neck, throat, and upper breast black; rest chestnut.

*Female: Above,* olive-brown; a whitish ring of feathers round eye; chestnut rump; white wing-patches as in male. *Below,* fulvous brown.

STATUS AND HABITAT: Not met with by Stevens in the Sikkim Himalayas, nor by the recent Loke-Sálim Ali Survey. Meinertzhagen came across a small party in Natu La (14,100 ft.) on 21.xii.1926, 'doubtless on passage', and secured two adult males.

DISTRIBUTION: 'Native Sikkim', Bhutan, Duars, Assam hills N. and S. of the Brahmaputra, Assam Valley; Manipur, Burma. Breeds from SE. Siberia south to Kansu, Szechwan, Chwanben, N. Yunnan. In winter extends to N. Thailand and Indochina.

MEASUREMENTS: The Fauna gives for ♂♀ Wing 70-77; bill 10-11; tarsus 23; tail 58-60 mm.

## THE BLACK REDSTART

*Phoenicurus ochruros rufiventris* (Vieillot)

*Œnanthe rufiventris* Vieillot, 1818, Nouv. Dict. d'Hist. Nat., nouv. éd., 21: 431—S. Africa *in errore*=Bengal.

F.B.I. 2: 77

LOCAL NAME:

SIZE: Sparrow.

FIELD CHARACTERS: *Male* (winter): *Above*, forehead, sides of head and neck black, the feathers fringed with grey; crown, nape, hindneck and back ashy grey; rump and upper tail-coverts bright chestnut; tail chestnut and brown. *Below*, chin, throat and breast black; rest deep orange-brown.

In summer the grey edges to feathers of back, throat, and breast wear off, leaving these parts a deeper black.

*Female: Above*, pale fulvous brown; rump and tail as in male; a ring of pale feathers round eye. *Below*, buffy brown.

STATUS AND HABITAT: Rare. Only a passage migrant in autumn and spring (?) between its breeding grounds on the high Tibetan plateau and the Indian plains. Schäfer collected specimens in the Tibetan plateau facies of N. Sikkim at 14,000 to 16,000 ft. altitude (Gyagong etc.) between July and October, and at Lachen (*c.* 7500 ft.) on 3 November (1938). Blanford noted it abundant on passage in the Lachen and Lachung valleys in September, and one in the Teesta Valley at *c.* 4000 ft. in October. Meinertzhagen did not meet with this species in Sikkim in winter, neither did Stevens before him nor myself since, except for the only sight record of a solitary example at Chungthang *c.* 5000 ft. (22.ii.1952).

DISTRIBUTION: *Summer*, SE. Tibet, Kuku Nor, Kansu. *Winter*, peninsular India east of a line from *c.* Jhansi to Khandesh, south to about Madras City and foot of the Nilgiris. Also Bengal, Assam, Manipur, Burma. The species has a wide Palaearctic distribution through Europe and Asia.

GENERAL HABITS: Characteristic of the redstarts. Shivers or oscillates chestnut tail as if fixed on a spring wire, and dips forepart of body from time to time.

RACIAL CHARACTERISTICS, MEASUREMENTS, ETC: In the adjoining race *phoenicuroides* (western Himalayas, through Kashmir to Afghanistan, Turkestan, Iran) the male has the black upper parts almost obscured in winter by heavy ash-grey and ash-brown fringes, particularly on the crown. Its wing is also somewhat smaller—80-86 mm. (majority *under* 85), as against 86-93 mm. in *rufiventris* (majority *over* 85).

## GÜLDENSTÄDT'S REDSTART

*Phoenicurus erythrogaster grandis* (Gould)

*Ruticilla grandis* Gould, 1850, *Proc. Zool. Soc. London:* 112—Afghanistan and Tibet.

**Plate 16, fig. 9 (facing p. 161)**

F.B.I. 2: 78

LOCAL NAME:

SIZE: Bulbul—.

FIELD CHARACTERS: Adult *Male* superficially like the Whitecapped Redstart in general aspect, but larger. Summer: *Above*, crown, nape and hindneck white; forehead, sides of head and neck, back and wings black, the last with a large white patch (or 'mirror'); tail deep chestnut with brown-tipped central feathers. *Below*, chin, throat and breast black; rest deep chestnut-red.

In winter, white feathers of crown, and black portions of plumage fringed with grey.

*Female: Above*, pale ashy brown; rump and tail like male's but paler chestnut. *Below*, fulvous grey, rufous-tinged on under tail-coverts.

STATUS AND HABITAT: An extreme high altitude redstart. Blanford met it between 14,000 and 16,500 ft. (Dongkya La, Kangra Lama La) in September and October. Schäfer collected specimens in the Tibetan facies of N. Sikkim at Gyaokong (Gyagong) *c.* 15,000-16,000 ft., June to August, including juveniles. Meinertzhagen procured it in the same locality, and also at Momé Shamdong, in November and December. The Loke-Sálim Ali Expedition got it in January near Lachung, at *c.* 10,500 ft. and three days later even as low as Chungthang, *c.* 5000 ft. Here many birds kept loosely together, doubtless having been forced down temporarily by the sudden bad weather and heavy snowfalls above, which also brought down other high elevation birds, e.g. *Eremophila* larks.

Affects the neighbourhood of streams in barren, sparsely scrubbed country and rocky moraines above tree-line.

DISTRIBUTION OUTSIDE SIKKIM: Afghanistan, Chitral, Gilgit, Baltistan, Ladakh, Chamba, Bhutan, Tibet, Kansu. The species is widely distributed in central Asia.

GENERAL HABITS: Lives at very high elevations even in winter, at which season it feeds largely on *Hippophæ* berries. Actions and behaviour typically redstart. Descends to ground to pick up beetles, ants, etc.; also captures winged insects in the air. In the breeding season the male has a short, clear song delivered from a boulder, or during his pretty display flight with outstretched quivering wings (Schäfer).

RACIAL CHARACTERISTICS, MEASUREMENTS, ETC: The Sikkim Survey specimens measure:

| | Wing | Bill | Tarsus | Tail |
|---|---|---|---|---|
| 3 ♂♂ | 108-115 | 17-18 | 28-30 | 70-75 mm. |
| 4 ♀♀ | 103-105 | 15-17 | 27-28 | 71-75.5 mm. |

The Fauna gives: Wing ♂ 102-111; ♀ 95-99 mm.
Iris brown; bill, legs, feet and claws brownish black to black.

## THE BLUEHEADED ROBIN

*Phoenicurus caeruleocephalus* (Vigors)

*Phoenicura coeruleocephala* [*sic*] Vigors, 1831, *Proc. Zool. Soc. London*: 35—Himalayas.

**Plate 23, fig. 1 (facing p. 288)**

F.B.I. 2: 104

LOCAL NAME:

SIZE: Sparrow.

FIELD CHARACTERS: *Male:* A black robin-like bird with a dull whitish (grey-blue) crown and nape, a broad white wing-bar, and whitish abdomen and vent.

*Female:* Rich brown with paler (ashy brown) underparts, and ferruginous rump.

At a distance, and without binoculars, could easily be confused, sex for sex, with the Pied Bushchat (*Saxicola caprata*); the female also with the Rufoustailed Flycatcher (*Muscicapa ruficauda*).

STATUS AND HABITAT: Recorded by Stevens at 11,500 ft. altitude on the Sikkim-Nepal frontier in February (1912), inside pine forest with the ground in places heavily covered with snow. Normally avoids heavy forest. Not met with since by Meinertzhagen or Schäfer, nor by the recent Loke-Sálim Ali Survey.

DISTRIBUTION OUTSIDE SIKKIM: Turkestan, Afghanistan, and eastward through the Himalayas as far as about Bhutan.

GENERAL HABITS: Typical of the Black and other redstarts, with a dash of the bush robins. Shakes rather than shivers tail. Its preferential habitat is more wooded country than redstarts', and it keeps to higher branches than they. Also occurs in open scrub of *Berberis* etc. on the edge of forested hill-slopes. Constantly utters *tik, tik*, much like a British Robin's. A. E. Jones describes the song in the breeding season as strongly reminiscent of the Eastern Meadow Bunting's (*Emberiza c. stracheyi*) with some of the notes more sustained. *Food:* insects.

NESTING: Not recorded in Sikkim (or Nepal). *Season*—in W. Himalayas, May to July. *Nest*—cup-shaped, of grass and moss, lined with hair and some feathers. Well concealed in a hollow in a bank, or under a stone or exposed roots of a tree. *Eggs*—3 or 4, pale grey-green to pale dull creamy buff, faintly speckled with light red. Size about 20×15 mm.

RACIAL CHARACTERISTICS, MEASUREMENTS, ETC: The Fauna gives for ♂♀ Wing 77-80; bill 11; tarsus 22; tail 58-64 mm.

Iris dark brown; bill blackish brown; legs and feet black.

## THE WHITECAPPED REDSTART

*Chaimarrornis leucocephalus* (Vigors)

*Phoenicura leucocephala* Vigors, 1831, *Proc. Zool. Soc. London:* 35—Himalayas.

F.B.I. 2: 79

LOCAL NAMES: Mati-tap-pho (Lepcha): Chulia-mati (Chubia ?) (Bhutia).

SIZE: Sparrow +.

FIELD CHARACTERS: A sprightly robin-like black and chestnut bird. *Above*, crown and nape white; sides of head, back and wings glossy blue-black; rump, upper tail-coverts, and tail bright chestnut—the last with a broad black terminal band. *Below*, chin, throat and breast black; rest bright orange-chestnut. Sexes alike.

STATUS AND HABITAT: Common. *Summer*, resident between 6000 and 16,000 ft. altitude; *winter*, from *c.* 8000 ft. down to plains level; commoner below 5000 (Rangpo, Singtam, Martam, Gangtok, Chungthang, Lachung, Lachen, Yumthang, Thangu, Gyagong, Penlom La, Karponang). Affects rocky streams and torrents, and their proximity.

DISTRIBUTION OUTSIDE SIKKIM: The Himalayan system from Afghanistan to extreme NE. Assam; Manipur, Burma, Yunnan, Tonkin, Kuku Nor, Kansu, SE. Turkestan. In many of these, and at the lower levels, a winter visitor only.

GENERAL HABITS: Singletons, or widely separated pairs, in staked-out stretches of stream, on rocks amidst raging torrent, or banks. Captures tiny insects borne along on the swirling current or cast up by the wavelets. Also flies out over the torrent and zigzags in aerial pursuit of midges, returning to its base on outstretched rapidly vibrating wings. When perched, and also upon alighting, wags expanded tail jerkily and deliberately up and down, with wings drooping on either side, from cocked position, as in robin, till its tip almost touches the ground. Tail-wagging often accompanied by bend-stretch curtseying. These sudden movements frequently employed for stampeding lurking insects. Also eats berries. *Call:* a loud, shrill, plaintive *tseee*; no song.

NESTING: Between 6000 and 16,000 ft. elevation. *Season*—May to July. *Nest*—a bulky cup of moss, leaves, etc., lined with wool, hair and roots. Placed in a crevice or hollow of rock or bank, or under the exposed roots of a tree near a stream. *Eggs*—3 or 4, pale sea-green profusely spotted with dark reddish- or rusty brown, more densely at the broad end. Size about 25×17 mm. Both parents feed the young.

RACIAL CHARACTERISTICS, MEASUREMENTS, ETC: A Sikkim Survey specimen (♂) measures Wing 102; bill 19; tarsus 33; tail 78 mm.

A series of 18 adult ♂♀ in Schäfer's Sikkim collection gives Wing 89 (♀)-103 (♂) mm.

Iris deep brown; bill, legs, feet and claws black.

## THE PLUMBEOUS REDSTART

*Rhyacornis fuliginosus fuliginosus* (Vigors)

*Phoenicura fuliginosa* Vigors, 1831, *Proc. Zool. Soc. London:* 35—Himalayas.

F.B.I. 2: 81

LOCAL NAMES: Suradum parbo-pho (Lepcha); Chubbia nakki (Bhutia).

SIZE: Sparrow.

FIELD CHARACTERS: *Male: Above* and *below*, slaty blue; upper and under tail-coverts, vent, and tail bright chestnut.

*Female: Above,* dull bluish brown; tail-coverts and tail white, the latter broadly tipped brown. *Below,* ashy white squamated with brown. Expanded tail shows up a brown triangle with end of tail as its base.

STATUS AND HABITAT: Common, and with a wide altitudinal range: *summer, c.* 2000 to 12,000-13,000 ft.; *winter,* from *c.* 7000 ft. or above, down to plains level (Rangpo, Martam, Gangtok, Dikchu, Lachen, Lachung, Thangu, Yatung and elsewhere on all affluents of the Teesta, Great Rangeet, and other rivers). Strictly confined to mountain streams and torrents.

DISTRIBUTION OUTSIDE SIKKIM: The Himalayas from Chitral eastward through Kashmir to extreme NE. Assam; Naga and Khasia hills; Manipur, NE. Burma, N. Thailand, Yunnan, N. China, Hainan. The species extends to Formosa.

GENERAL HABITS: Singletons, or widely separated pairs, on staked-out stretches of streams—'spheres of influence'—which, though shared with Whitecapped Redstarts and dippers, are jealously guarded against encroachment by its own kind. Demonstrates threateningly by craning neck forward, tail fully fanned out and depressed, uttering a sharp, angry, prolonged *kreee*, and chases intruder off. Extremely active. Flits from stone to stone amidst rushing torrent. Makes short arc-like aerial sallies on rapidly vibrating wings over water after midges; springs up in air above the foam and spray to capture one, or hovers momentarily to scoop up an insect borne along on the wavelets. Constantly flicks tail open and closed with a rhythmic wagging scissors-like action, as in the Little Forktail; also fans it out from time to time and lowers it till almost touching the ground. In the female, the 'twinkling' of the black-and-white pattern in the tail harmonizes to perfection with the foam of tumbling water. *Song* of male: sharp, creaky and metallic, of about five seconds' duration, exactly like a cricket's chirping, and similarly rising in pitch.[1] Succeeded quickly by another burst. No movement of tail while singing.

NESTING: Between *c.* 2000 ft. ( Martam! ) and 12,000-13,000—mostly under 7000 ft. *Season*—March/April to June/July. *Nest*—a compact cup of moss, roots and leaves, lined with fibres, wool and hair.

[1] My description of it as like the song of the Whitethroated Fantail Flycatcher, *Rhipidura albicollis* (Indian Hill Birds: 61) is incorrect.

Placed in hollows in earth banks or under exposed roots of trees alongside streams. *Eggs*—4 or 5, pale greenish, speckled and blotched with reddish brown. Size about 18×14 mm. Both sexes share in nest building and feeding young. Apparently female alone incubates.

RACIAL CHARACTERISTICS, MEASUREMENTS, ETC: A specimen collected by the Sikkim Survey (♂) measures Wing 72 (?); bill 13; tarsus 23; tail 51 mm.

Seven ♂♂ in Schäfer's Sikkim collection give Wing 77-80 mm.; 2 ♀♀ 72, 73 mm.

Iris dark brown; bill, legs, feet and claws blackish brown.

## THE MAGPIE ROBIN

*Copsychus saularis saularis* (Linnaeus)

*Gracula saularis* Linnaeus, 1758, Syst. Nat., 10th ed. 1: 109—Asia (=Bengal).

F.B.I. 2: 113

LOCAL NAME: Zannid-pho (Lepcha).

SIZE: Bulbul.

FIELD CHARACTERS: A familiar, trim black-and-white bird with cocked tail and drooping wings.

*Male:* Head, neck, back, throat and breast black. Rest of underparts white. Tail black, with white outer feathers. Wings black with a conspicuous long white shoulder-patch.

*Female* slaty grey where male black; white portions sullied.

STATUS AND HABITAT: Not common, but frequent at low elevations; in summer up to *c.* 5500 ft. (Rangpo, Singtam, Martam and elsewhere in the Teesta and Great Rangeet valleys; Gangtok). Affects lightly wooded open country around villages and cultivation.

DISTRIBUTION OUTSIDE SIKKIM: The greater part of India and both Pakistans. The species ranges widely in SE. Asia to the Philippines.

GENERAL HABITS: Shy and silent in winter, skulking in shrubbery, only uttering a plaintive *swee-eet* and harsh *chur-r.* Conspicuous during breeding season when male sings lustily from exposed perches. Song cheerful and spirited, of thrush pattern but thin and less rich, consisting of refrains repeated to the point of monotony, frequently interlarded with calls of other birds. Keeps to branches of trees, but hops about and feeds on ground, mainly on insects. Also fond of nectar of *Erythrina* and *Salmalia* flowers. Flight undulating, with tail flicked open at every dip. In the dusk, against the dark background of forest, this flickering of the white rectrices is very arresting.

NESTING: *Season*—April to June. *Nest*—a pad of grass, rootlets, hair, etc. in a hole in tree-trunk or bough, 5 to 20 ft. up. *Eggs*—3 to 5, pale blue-green, blotched and mottled with reddish brown. Size about 22×17 mm. The female does most of the incubating, but the male shares equally in all other domestic chores.

RACIAL CHARACTERISTICS, MEASUREMENTS, ETC: A specimen (♀?) collected by the Survey measures: Wing 93; bill 21; tarsus 29; tail 83 mm. Three ♂♂ in the Schäfer Sikkim collection have Wing 99, 99, 100 mm.

Iris brown; bill, legs, feet and claws horny black.

THE SHAMA, *Copsychus malabaricus indicus* (Baker), doubtless occurs in the lower foothills as it does in Nepal and Bhutan, but has not been specifically recorded. It is an unmistakable cousin of the Magpie Robin, more confined to a forest biotope. Tail black-and-white, graduated and longer; underparts chestnut instead of white. A large white rump-patch, which, together with the white outer rectrices, is conspicuous in flight and diagnostic.

## THE TIBETAN BLACKBIRD

*Turdus merula maximus* (Seebohm)

*Merula maxima* Seebohm, 1881, Cat. Birds Brit. Mus. 5: 405—Cashmere. Restricted to Gulmarg.

F.B.I. 2: 123

LOCAL NAME:

SIZE: Between Myna and Pigeon.

FIELD CHARACTERS: Adult *Male:* Deep glossy black, with yellow bill. Plumage with a slight brown tinge when worn.

*Female* dark brown, tinged with slaty above.

STATUS AND HABITAT: A high altitude thrush, found by Meinertzhagen only in *Lenoa* and *Grandala* biotope above tree-level—open scrub and grass covered hills—to the east of Yumthang, between 14,000 and 15,500 ft. in winter.

DISTRIBUTION OUTSIDE SIKKIM: The Himalayas from W. Pakistan to Bhutan, north and south of the main range; SE. Tibet.

GENERAL HABITS: Excessively shy and wary. Feeds on juniper berries, hips of wild rose, and also on the ground on insects, small lizards, etc. Has a powerful flight. Collects in large flocks in winter. Call, uttered from time to time, harsh and unpleasant. Song also poor, lacking in quality and variety, with none of the rich fluty notes typical of the thrushes.

NESTING: Not recorded in Sikkim. Elsewhere breeds in May and June. *Nest*—a massive structure of herbage and grass mixed with a little earth, and thickly lined with fine grass. Placed on a ledge of rock, sometimes quite unconcealed. *Eggs*—3 or 4, pale greenish, boldly blotched with red-brown. Size about 33×23 mm.

MEASUREMENTS, ETC: ♂♀ Wing 150-157 (160 according to Hartert); bill 24.5-29.5; tarsus 38; tail 107-120 mm.

Iris brown; bill orange-yellow (♂), dull greenish yellow (♀); legs and feet black or dark brown.

## THE WHITECOLLARED BLACKBIRD

*Turdus albocinctus* Royle

*Turdus albocinctus* Royle (=*albicollis* Royle), 1831, Ill. Bot. Himalayas, pl. lxxvii—Himalayas.

F.B.I. 2: 129

LOCAL NAME:

SIZE: Between Myna and Pigeon.

FIELD CHARACTERS: *Male:* Entire plumage blackish brown with a broad pure white collar. Chin and throat white streaked with brown; under tail-coverts blackish brown streaked with white.

Whitecollared Blackbird
About one-third

*Female:* Collar as in male, but ashy white. Rest of plumage *above*, rufous-brown; *below*, paler, the feathers pale-fringed, producing a scaly effect.

STATUS AND HABITAT: Not common, but frequent between *c.* 5500 and 10,000 ft. in winter (Gangtok, Chungthang, Lachen, Lachung, Karponang). Recorded up to 13,500 ft. in summer by Blanford (Chola Range) and F. N. Betts (Yumthang, Thangu). Affects open oak, rhododendron and conifer forest.

DISTRIBUTION OUTSIDE SIKKIM: The Himalayas from Kangra to Garhwal, and through Nepal and Bhutan to the Dafla Hills. Chumbi Valley (S. Tibet). In winter, straggles into Assam, Manipur, N. Burma.

GENERAL HABITS: Pairs in summer; parties or often large flocks in winter, sometimes associated with other thrushes as *T. r. atrogularis* and *T. boulboul.* Has the typical harsh chuckling *chuck-chuck* alarm note in winter; a fine, rich, mellow song in the breeding season.

Feeds in trees as well as on the ground, digging in the turf or rummaging among fallen leaves. *Food:* berries and insects.

NESTING: *Season*—May-June. *Nest*—a massive cup of moss, grass, roots and leaves, lined with dried grass. Placed on a moss-covered branch, 5 to 12 ft. from the ground. *Eggs*—3, greyish green, heavily blotched with chestnut or reddish brown, with secondary blotches of pinkish lavender. Size about 31×22 mm.

RACIAL CHARACTERISTICS, MEASUREMENTS, ETC: The Fauna gives the measurements as:

| | Wing | Bill | Tarsus | Tail |
|---|---|---|---|---|
| ♂♂ | 142-151 | 23 | 35 | 101-109 mm. |
| ♀♀ | 131-143 | 22 | 35 | 100-104 mm. |

Schäfer's Sikkim specimens give Wing 1 ♂ 145; 4 ♀♀ 133, 136, 138, 140 mm.

Iris brown; bill yellow, dusky at tip; legs and feet dark ochraceous yellow.

## THE GREYWINGED BLACKBIRD

*Turdus boulboul* (Latham)

*Lanius boulboul* Latham, 1790, Index Orn. 1: 80—India=Darjeeling.

F.B.I. 2: 130

LOCAL NAMES: Phoyiong-pho (Lepcha); Chemam or Chomam (Bhutia).

SIZE: Between Myna and Pigeon.

FIELD CHARACTERS: Adult *Male: Above*, black, with a prominent silver-grey patch on wing. *Below*, brownish black paling towards abdomen and vent.

*Female:* Brownish ashy with olivaceous tinge. Grey wing-patch of male replaced by rufous.

STATUS AND HABITAT: Frequent, but not common, from the lowest elevations up to *c.* 6000 ft. in winter; *c.* 9000 ft. in summer (Gangtok, Temi, Kewzing, Pemionche, Chacung, Chungthang, Karponang). Affects forest of oak, rhododendron, deodar, etc., and is partial to neighbourhood of streams.

DISTRIBUTION OUTSIDE SIKKIM: The outer Himalayas in Kashmir, and from Murree eastward through Nepal and Bhutan probably to the Miri and Abor hills (breeding). Assam hills south of the Brahmaputra; Manipur, Burma, S. Yunnan to N. Tonkin (winter only ?).

GENERAL HABITS: Typical of the thrushes. Perhaps one of the finest songsters among Indian birds. Song rich and fluty, of great variety and mellowness. Delivered during the breeding season at all hours of the day, principally in the mornings and late afternoons till well into dusk. At this season very pugnacious and intolerant towards others of its kind. *Food:* fruits and berries, insects, earthworms, etc.

NESTING: *Season*—May-June. *Nest*—a bulky cup of grass-roots and leaves, covered outside with moss; lined with finer roots and grass, sometimes mixed with a little mud. Placed in a crutch or horizontal fork of branches, 10-20 ft. up. Gammie found the stumps of pollarded *Ficus* trees a favourite site in Sikkim. *Eggs*—3 or 4, similar to those of the Whitecollared species, pale grey-green, blotched all over with pale red-brown and with lavender-pink secondary blotches. Size about 29×21 mm.

RACIAL CHARACTERISTICS, MEASUREMENTS, ETC: The Survey specimens measure:

| | Wing | Bill | Tarsus | Tail |
|---|---|---|---|---|
| 1 ♂ | 145 | 25 | 35 | 109 mm. |
| 1 ♀ | 138 | 26 | 36 | 108 mm. |

Schäfer's Sikkim birds give Wing 12 ♂♂ 139-146; 4 ♀♀ 133-140 mm.

Iris brown; fine rim round eye yellow; bill reddish orange (♂), brownish orange (♀); legs and feet horny brown with yellowish or orange tinge; claws horny brown.

## THE GREYHEADED THRUSH

### *Turdus rubrocanus rubrocanus* Hodgson

*Turdus rubrocanus* 'Hodgson' *in* Gray, 1846, Cat. Mamms. Birds Nepal: 81—Nepal.

F.B.I. 2: 132

LOCAL NAME:

SIZE: Between Myna and Pigeon.

FIELD CHARACTERS: *Male:* Head, neck and throat dark grey; rest of plumage above and below chestnut, paler on abdomen. Tail black.

*Female:* Similar to male, but paler.

STATUS AND HABITAT: Rare. Winter visitor? The only specimen the Sikkim Survey came across was one collected by Dr B. Biswas of the Zoological Survey of India, at Kewzing, *c.* 5500 ft., on 7 January 1953. Stevens obtained a female on 3 May 1912 at Kalo Pokhari, Singalila Ridge (10,000 ft.—Darjeeling Dist.) on the western boundary of Sikkim. In Nidification (vol. ii, 119) Baker says this was 'in breeding condition', but Stevens himself is much less assertive in his original note (*Jour. Bombay Nat. Hist. Soc.* 30: 358). Meinertzhagen and Schäfer did not come across the species in Sikkim, nor Ludlow in Bhutan.

DISTRIBUTION OUTSIDE SIKKIM: Breeding mainly in the NW. Frontier Province (perhaps also Afghanistan), Kashmir, Garhwal, W. Nepal (?) between 5000 and 10,000 ft.—in a higher zone than *Turdus boulboul.*

GENERAL HABITS: Similar to other thrushes with which it consorts in flocks in winter to feed on various berries. Has a delightful song in the breeding season, delivered from the tip of a tall fir or similar tree.

NESTING: No record for Sikkim. Nest similar to that of the Grey-winged Blackbird.

MEASUREMENTS, ETC: The Fauna gives for ♂♀ Wing 130-142; bill 21; tarsus 33; tail 95-98 mm.

Iris brown; bill, legs, feet and eyelids wax yellow to dusky yellow.

## PRZEVALSKI'S THRUSH

*Turdus kessleri* Przevalski

*Turdus kessleri* Przevalski, 1876, Mongol. i Str. Tangut: 62—Kansu.

F.B.I. 2: 134

LOCAL NAME:

SIZE: Between Myna and Pigeon.

FIELD CHARACTERS: *Male:* Whole head, neck and extreme upper breast black. Mantle and breast dull rufous white or cream changing to dull dark rufous or chestnut on lower back, rump, upper tail-coverts, flanks and abdomen. Wings and tail black.

*Female:* Head, neck, wings and tail dark brown. Rest of plumage ashy grey, more rufescent below and darker and browner on upper tail-coverts.

STATUS AND HABITAT: A winter straggler within our limits. Mandelli's skin, recorded as from near Darjeeling (*c.* 9000 ft.—November 1876) was actually obtained in Tibet close to the Sikkim border. Meinertzhagen saw a party of four near Changu (12,100 ft.) on 21 December 1925, of which a male was secured. This, therefore, is the first and only record of its occurrence in India.

GENERAL HABITS: *Song:* short, like that of *Turdus viscivorus* abbreviated. *Flight:* characteristic, low over the ground, 10 to 15 strong beats alternating with glides.

NESTING: Breeds in Kansu and E. Kuku Nor at 12,000 to 14,000 ft. in rhododendron and juniper forest.

## THE REDTHROATED THRUSH

*Turdus ruficollis ruficollis* Pallas

*Turdus ruficollis* Pallas, 1776, Reise Russ. Reichs 3: 694—Dauria.

F.B.I. 2: 136

LOCAL NAME:

SIZE: Myna+.

FIELD CHARACTERS: Adult *Male: Above,* supercilium chestnut; rest of upper plumage pale ashy brown. Tail rufous, tipped with dark brown. *Below,* cheeks, chin, throat and breast chestnut. A few black specks down each side of chin and throat. Rest of underparts white; sides of breast and flanks mottled with dark ashy.

Under tail-coverts ashy and chestnut; in winter the chestnut feathers fringed with whitish.

*Female:* Chestnut of breast etc. paler, more mottled with white, less heavily spotted with black.

STATUS AND HABITAT, ETC.: See under next species.

## THE BLACKTHROATED THRUSH

*Turdus ruficollis atrogularis* Jarocki

*Turdus atrogularis* Jarocki, 1819, Spis Ptaków Król. Warszawa: 14—Poland.

F.B.I. 2: 137

LOCAL NAME:

SIZE: Myna+.

FIELD CHARACTERS: *Male: Above,* grey-brown, the crown with blackish centres; lores black. Wings and tail dark brown. *Below,* cheeks, chin, throat, sides of neck and upper breast black with narrow white margins. Rest of underparts white, the sides suffused with ashy.

*Female:* Sides of head and neck greyish brown like upper plumage. *Below,* chin and throat whitish, streaked with dark brown. Upper breast ashy grey, tinged with rufous and spotted with black. Rest of underparts white, suffused with grey.

Both these thrushes are superficially very similar. The rufous tail and more pronounced chestnut throat and breast will usually distinguish *ruficollis.* Intermediates have been recorded.

STATUS AND HABITAT: Winter visitors. Not uncommon between November and April at elevations between about 4000 and 14,000 ft. (Chungthang, Kewzing, Lachen, Karponang, Manshitang, Penlom La, Phalut). On open ground, grassy slopes, stubbles and pastures in the vicinity of habitations and cultivation. Partial to damp spots and water meadows. Meinertzhagen found huge flocks of *atrogularis* feeding on berries in SW. Sikkim in January between 3000 and 4500 ft.

DISTRIBUTION OUTSIDE SIKKIM: *ruficollis: Summer,* breeds in central and SE. Altai, Sayan Mountains and NW. Mongolia. *Winter,* Afghanistan; the Himalayas, rare in the west, commoner in the east; Assam hills; Manipur, Burma, Szechwan, Kansu, Chwanben, N. Yunnan, S. Tibet.

*atrogularis: Summer,* breeds in N. Urals to Yenesei, south to Kusnetz and Altai; Tarbagatai. *Winter,* from Iran and Afghanistan, through Kashmir, along the Himalayas to the extreme NE. Frontier; Assam hills N. and S. of the Brahmaputra; Manipur, Burma, E. Pakistan, etc. N. Yunnan, Kansu, S. Tibet.

GENERAL HABITS: Highly gregarious in winter, often in mixed scattered flocks, but also in small parties. Shy and silent. Call note similar to that of the European Blackbird, a thin *tick, tick.* Song not heard in winter quarters. *Food:* earthworms, energetically dug out of the soft ground; also beetles and larvae, berries and flower nectar, e.g. of the silk cotton tree.

NESTING: Records of *atrogularis* breeding within Indian limits, including Sikkim, quite unreliable and not confirmed.

1. Nepal Goldenheaded Babbler (*Stachyris c. chrysaea*) 2. Firetailed Myzornis (*Myzornis pyrrhoura*). Male 3. Chestnut-throated Shrike-Babbler (*Pteruthius m. melanotis*) 4. Stripedthroated Yuhina (*Yuhina g. gularis*) 5. Goldenbreasted Babbler (*Alcippe c. chrysotis*) 6. Sikkim Blackthroated Babbler (*Stachyris n. nigriceps*) 7. Assam Redfronted Babbler (*Stachyris r. ambigua*) 8. Nepal White-eyed Quaker Babbler (*Alcippe n. nipalensis*) 9. Yellownaped Ixulus (*Yuhina f. flavicollis*) 10. Whitebrowed, or Hume's, Staphida (*Yuhina c. rufigenis*) 11. Chestnut-headed Babbler (*Alcippe c. castaneceps*) 12. Sikkim Fulvetta (*Alcippe v. chumbiensis*)

PLATE 21 [c. × $\frac{5}{8}$]

1. Blackbrowed Flycatcher-Warbler (*Seicercus b. burkii*) 2. Chestnut-headed Flycatcher-Warbler (*Seicercus c. castaniceps*) 3. Blackfaced Flycatcher-Warbler (*Abroscopus s. schisticeps*) 4. Blanford's Bush Warbler (*Cettia p. pallidipes*) 5. Goldenheaded Tailor Bird (*Orthotomus c. coronatus*) 6. Firetailed Yellowbacked Sunbird (*Aethopyga i. ignicauda*) 7. Mrs Gould's Yellowbacked Sunbird (*Aethopyga g. gouldiae*) 8. Blackbreasted Sunbird (*Aethopyga s. saturata*) 9. Firebreasted Flowerpecker (*Dicaeum i. ignipectus*)

PLATE 22

MEASUREMENTS, ETC: Specimens collected by the Sikkim Survey measure:

| | Wing | Bill | Tarsus | Tail |
|---|---|---|---|---|
| *ruficollis* 1 ♂ | 143 | 23 | 34 | 100 mm. |
| *atrogularis* 1 ♀ | 136 | 22.5 | 34 | 93 mm. |

Schäfer's Sikkim skins give Wing:

*ruficollis* 4 ♂♂ 131, 140, 140, 141; 2 ♀♀ 138, 138 mm.

*atrogularis* 2 ♂♂ 136, 140; 3 ♀♀ 130-138 mm. (Stresemann).

Iris brown; bill horny brown, yellow at base of lower mandible; legs and feet brownish flesh colour; claws horny brown.

## THE ORANGEHEADED GROUND THRUSH

*Zoothera citrina citrina* (Latham)

*Turdus citrinus* Latham, 1790, Index Orn. 1: 350—India, Cachar.

F.B.I. 2: 148

LOCAL NAME:

SIZE: Myna.

FIELD CHARACTERS: *Male:* Head, neck and underparts bright orange-chestnut. Back dark blue-grey. Wings and tail brown, edged with blue-grey. A prominent white patch on wings. Vent and under tail-coverts white.

*Female:* Like male but with upper plumage olive-brown instead of blue-grey.

STATUS AND HABITAT: Resident between *c.* 3000 and 6000 ft. altitude (Pakyong, Temi, Chungthang, Gangtok). Affects undergrowth and shrubbery in open forest and ravines.

DISTRIBUTION OUTSIDE SIKKIM: Throughout the lower Himalayas from Murree eastward to Assam, Bengal, Burma, Thailand. The white-cheeked race *cyanotus* inhabits southern peninsular India. The species extends to Malaysia.

GENERAL HABITS: Usually seen singly. Hops on ground under bushes, quietly rummaging amongst dry leaves and mulch for insects. Also eats berries and ripe fruit. Flies up into trees when disturbed, soon descending again to resume its search. Only utters an occasional high-pitched *kree-ee* in winter. Has a loud, rich, typically thrush song in the breeding season, delivered from a branch with tail held low and wings drooping at the sides. Heard chiefly in the mornings and at dusk.

NESTING: *Season*—May-June. *Nest*—a shallow cup of moss, roots, leaves, etc., lined with finer roots and grass; sometimes with a little mud incorporated. Placed in a small bushy tree, 4 to 15 ft. up. *Eggs*—normally 4, pale bluish or creamy white blotched and freckled with pale reddish, sometimes more at the broad end. Size about 26×20 mm. Both sexes share in all the domestic chores.

RACIAL CHARACTERISTICS, MEASUREMENTS, ETC: The Fauna gives Wing ♂ 109-121; ♀ 100-106; bill 19-20; tarsus 33; tail 67-69 mm.

Two adults (sex ?) collected by Schäfer in Sikkim have Wing 114, 120 mm.

Iris hazel to deep brown; bill dark horny brown; legs and feet creamy yellow to flesh pink.

## THE SMALLBILLED MOUNTAIN THRUSH

*Zoothera dauma dauma* (Latham)

*Turdus dauma* Latham, 1790, Index Orn. 1: 362—India.

**Plate 23, fig. 6 (facing p. 288)**

F.B.I. 2: 158

LOCAL NAME:

SIZE: Myna+.

FIELD CHARACTERS: A pale golden brown, rather short-tailed thrush, with small black crescent-shaped markings on the back. Underparts fulvous white, barred with crescentic black spots. A pale wingbar conspicuous in flight. Sexes alike.

Coloration very obliterative on ground amongst dry leaves.

STATUS AND HABITAT: Resident at moderate elevations—up to *c.* 9000 ft., with some downward movements in winter (Singtam, Temi, Dikchu, Toong, Penlom La, Chungthang, Gangtok). Affects dense jungle with undergrowth of seedlings, bracken, etc.

DISTRIBUTION OUTSIDE SIKKIM: Throughout the outer Himalayas from the Afghan frontier to Assam, at moderate elevations; Burma, Malaya, Thailand. A race in the Nilgiris and another in Ceylon. The species extends through Indochina to Japan.

GENERAL HABITS: Solitary, shy, and largely terrestrial. Hops and walks about on the ground, flicking aside the dry leaves in quest of insects and windfallen berries etc. Wags hind part of body violently and flicks open tail with a sudden opening and shutting of wings in order to stampede lurking insects. When disturbed, flies silently up into a tree and sits motionless, soon descending to resume its hunt. Flight swift and direct, reminiscent of the hawk-cuckoo, with an upward sweep before settling in a tree. The male has a fine loud song in the breeding season of several clear musical phrases, some reiterated rather as in the British Song Thrush.

NESTING: Not specifically recorded for Sikkim. *Season*—elsewhere in the Himalayas April to June. *Nest*—a substantially built cup of moss, twigs, roots and fern stalks lined with fine roots. Placed in the fork of a tree 6 to 20 ft. up. *Eggs*—3 or 4, variable, commonly pale yellowish- or greenish grey to dull clay brown, finely freckled and feebly blotched with pale reddish. Size about 31×23 mm.

RACIAL CHARACTERISTICS, MEASUREMENTS, ETC: Readily distinguished from the rather similar *Zoothera mollissima* and *Z. dixoni* by the bold crescentic black bars on its back, which in them is plain coloured. The Sikkim Survey specimens measure:

| | Wing | Bill | Tarsus | Tail |
|---|---|---|---|---|
| 2 ♂♂ | 147-149 | 29-29.5 | 34-36.5 | 91-101 mm. |
| 2 ♀♀ | 142-148 | 26-26.5 | 34-35 | 97-100 mm. |

Two examples collected by Schäfer (sex ?) have very small Wing—131, 140 mm.]

Iris brown; bill horny brown, paler (yellowish horn) at base of lower mandible; legs and feet brownish flesh colour; claws horny brown.

## THE PLAINBACKED MOUNTAIN THRUSH

*Zoothera mollissima mollissima* (Blyth)

*Turdus mollissimus* Blyth, 1842, *Jour. Asiat. Soc. Bengal* 11: 188. No locality=Darjeeling.

F.B.I. 2: 162

LOCAL NAMES: Phanniok-kiok-pho (Lepcha); Telia kanrim (Bhutia).

SIZE: Between Myna and Pigeon.

FIELD CHARACTERS: *Above*, rich rufescent olive-brown. A ring of fulvous feathers round eye. Wings dark brown, edged with olive-brown. Two pale wing-bars conspicuous in flight. Tail olive-brown and dark brown, tipped with white on all except four middle feathers. Below, ochraceous white (changing to pure white on abdomen) with black crescentic spots. Sexes alike.

STATUS AND HABITAT: Presumably resident, with apparently a higher summer ceiling than *Z. dauma*—up to *c.* 12,000 ft., Changu (Schäfer). Fairly common in winter between *c.* 4000 and 9000 ft. (Temi, Kewzing, Chungthang, Zemu, Manshitang, Lachen, Gangtok). Affects less-forested biotope than *Z. dauma.* Often met with in open bush country about fallow cultivation on hillsides and stream valleys, and along mule paths etc.

DISTRIBUTION OUTSIDE SIKKIM: Nepal, Bhutan to east Assam; Burma, Thailand, Yunnan. The Himalayas west of Nepal are inhabited by two other races.

GENERAL HABITS: Very similar to *Z. dauma* but less solitary. Commonly seen in small scattered parties. Feeds quietly on the ground in shady spots, flying up almost perpendicularly into overhanging branches when disturbed, and there sitting absolutely motionless. Its colour pattern obliterates it in a remarkable way amongst the filigree of the foliage.

NESTING: Very little specific data for Sikkim. Osmaston found a nest above Darjeeling (this or *dixoni* ?) at *c.* 11,000 ft. altitude on 10th June. Built of moss and dried grass in a cleft of rock *c.* 5 ft. from the ground, in dense forest. It contained 2 eggs, white, densely covered with specks, spots and blotches of blood red and reddish brown, and clouds of pale purple. Size about 32×21 mm.

RACIAL CHARACTERISTICS, MEASUREMENTS, ETC: In spite of the fact that Stuart Baker does not recognize the longer-tailed *dixoni* as different from *mollissima*, there seems no doubt that these two are distinct species. They occur side by side at the appropriate elevations in Sikkim and Bhutan, also during the breeding season. Though usually impossible to tell apart in the field, the Tail/Wing index[1] is diagnostic in the hand, being on the average *c.* 70 in the case of *mollissima* and *c.* 80 in *dixoni.* This characteristic is clearly shown by the Survey specimens as well as by the good series of both species collected by Schäfer in Sikkim and analysed by Prof. E. Stresemann.

Specimens of *mollissima* collected by the Survey measure:

| | Wing | Bill | Tarsus | Tail |
|---|---|---|---|---|
| 3 ♂♂ | 141-146 | 25.5-26 | 37.5-39.5 | 98-99 mm. |
| 2 ♀♀ | 139-144 | 24.5-26 | 36-36.5 | 91-96 mm. |

Iris brown; bill brownish black, dusky yellow at base of lower mandible; legs and feet brownish flesh colour; claws horny brown.

## THE LONGTAILED MOUNTAIN THRUSH

### *Zoothera dixoni* (Seebohm)

*Geocichla dixoni* Seebohm, 1881, Cat. Birds Brit. Mus. 5: 161—Himalayas (Nepal).

F.B.I. 2: 161 (included with *mollissima*)

LOCAL NAMES: Same as for *mollissima.*

SIZE: Between Myna and Pigeon.

FIELD CHARACTERS: Difficult to distinguish from *mollissima* in the field except for its relatively longer tail. With binoculars, large and distinct fulvous tips to greater and medium wing-coverts diagnostic, especially when side-by-side comparison with *mollissima* possible.

STATUS AND HABITAT: Obtained by the Sikkim Survey as well as by Schäfer between 5000 and 9000 ft. elevation, November to April (Temi, Gangtok, Chungthang, Lachen). Also a juvenile by Schäfer at Lachen in September indicating breeding in that area. Both species in the same biotope, sometimes feeding together.

DISTRIBUTION OUTSIDE SIKKIM: Near Mussooree (Blanford); Nepal, Bhutan, Naga Hills, Manipur, N. Burma, Thailand (?). Range imperfectly known.

GENERAL HABITS: Same as of the Plainbacked species.

NESTING: No precise data.

RACIAL CHARACTERISTICS, MEASUREMENTS, ETC: The longer tail of this species as against *mollissima* (Tail/Wing index[1] *c.* 80) is a constant and reliable diagnostic feature. Two ♂♂ collected by the Survey measure: Wing 140, 140; bill 24, 26; tarsus 38, 39; tail 107, 115 mm.

Schäfer's Sikkim skins give:

| | Wing | Tail |
|---|---|---|
| 1 ♂ | 139 | 112 mm. |
| 5 ♀♀ | 134-144 | 108-116 mm. (Stresemann) |

Colours of soft parts as in *mollissima.*

[1] $\frac{\text{Tail} \times 100}{\text{Wing}}$

## THE LARGE BROWN THRUSH

### *Zoothera monticola monticola* Vigors

*Zoothera monticola* Vigors, 1832, *Proc. Zool. Soc. London:* 172—Himalayas.

F.B.I. 2: 166

LOCAL NAME:

SIZE: Pigeon—.

FIELD CHARACTERS: *Above,* dark slaty brown including wings and tail. Sides of head streaked and spotted with fulvous. *Below,* chin and middle of throat white. Sides of throat and breast fulvous olive-brown, narrowly barred with blackish. Lower breast and abdomen white, heavily spotted with blackish. Bill long, stout, strongly curved near tip. Sexes alike.

STATUS AND HABITAT: Generally distributed though not common, with a wide altitudinal range at all seasons. Stevens records one in the Teesta Valley at 2500 ft. in October. Meinertzhagen and Schäfer found it at Singhik, *c.* 4000 ft., in October and December; the former also at Rinchinpong, *c.* 5600 ft., in January. Blanford obtained it in the Lachung Valley at *c.* 10,000 ft. in September, and Dr Biswas took one at *c.* 11,000 ft. (Phalut) on 29 December. Affects dense damp forest.

DISTRIBUTION OUTSIDE SIKKIM: Throughout the Himalayas east of Kulu Valley; Assam; Manipur; N. Burma.

GENERAL HABITS: Largely crepuscular. Lives in damp spots in densely shaded forest, preferably near small mountain streams. The bird's coloration obliterates it completely in its natural habitat, and only movement gives it away. Hops about on the ground, digging into the damp soil with its powerful bill for insects, snails, etc.; also eats berries. The feet and bills of specimens are usually covered with wet mud. Flies up into branches when disturbed. Mostly silent, but said to have a beautiful mellow whistle.

NESTING: Not specifically recorded in Sikkim. *Season*—elsewhere May to July. *Nest*—a large untidy cup of fresh damp moss on the outside, lined with roots, lichens and rhizomorphs. Placed 10 to 20 ft. up in a small tree or on a boulder in forest. *Eggs*—3 or 4, variable, pale grey-green or sea-green to dull pale olive-green, with specks, freckles and blotches of reddish- or purplish brown. Size about 30×22 mm.

RACIAL CHARACTERISTICS, MEASUREMENTS, ETC: The Fauna gives for ♂♀ Wing 134-145; bill 34-38; tarsus *c.* 36; tail 83-89 mm.

A specimen (♂) collected by Schäfer has Wing 138 mm.

Iris dark brown; bill dark brown to almost black; legs and feet light horny brown.

## THE LESSER BROWN THRUSH

*Zoothera marginata marginata* Blyth

*Zoothera marginata* Blyth, 1847, *Jour. Asiat. Soc. Bengal* **16**: 141—Arracan.

Lesser Brown Thrush, about one-third

F.B.I. 2: 168

LOCAL NAME:

SIZE: Myna+.

FIELD CHARACTERS: *Above*, rufous olive-brown with faint scaly pattern on back and cross-raying on tail. Primaries and their coverts edged pale rufous. *Below*, chin and middle of throat white, irregularly barred with dark brown. Sides of throat, breast and flanks dark olive-brown; paler on abdomen with scale-like olive-brown markings. Bill long, stout and strongly curved near tip.

STATUS AND HABITAT: A bird of lower elevations than the last; normally met with under 6000 ft. Meinertzhagen obtained it at 2600 and 5900 ft. in Darjeeling Dist. in December, and at 4700 ft. at Chacung (W. Sikkim) in January. Affects the vicinity of mountain streams, and damp spots in shady forest recesses.

DISTRIBUTION OUTSIDE SIKKIM: Bhutan and eastward to Assam; Manipur; Burma. The species extends to Thailand and Yunnan.

GENERAL HABITS: Shy, silent, and largely crepuscular and terrestrial —very similar to those of its larger relative. Voice and call (or song) unrecorded.

NESTING: *Season*—May to July. *Nest*—not different from that of *Z. monticola*. *Eggs*—3 or 4, variable, small replicas of those of the last species. Size about 27×20 mm.

RACIAL CHARACTERISTICS, MEASUREMENTS, ETC: The smaller size and rufous olive-brown upper plumage readily distinguish it from *Z. monticola* which is dark slaty brown above. The Fauna gives for ♂♀ Wing 121-129; bill 28-29; tarsus 29-30; tail 75-79 mm.

Iris hazel; bill dark brown to blackish; legs and feet plumbeous with olive tinge.

## THE CHESTNUTBELLIED ROCK THRUSH

*Monticola rufiventris* (Jardine & Selby)

*Petrocincla rufiventris* Jardine & Selby, 1833, Illustr. Orn. 3, pl. 129—Himalayas.

**Plate 23, fig. 5 (facing p. 288)**

F.B.I. 2: 170

LOCAL NAME: Ningri-pho (Lepcha).

SIZE: Myna.

FIELD CHARACTERS: *Male: Above*, including tail, brilliant cobalt blue. Wing quills blackish, edged with cobalt blue. Lores, sides of head and neck black. *Below*, chin and throat black. Rest dark chestnut-maroon.

*Female: Above*, olive-brown with dark crescentic bars, more defined on rump. A fulvous ring round eye. Ear-coverts blackish. *Below*, chin, throat, and faint moustachial streaks buff. Rest buff, barred with black.

STATUS AND HABITAT: Resident between *c.* 5000 and 10,000 ft. altitude; in winter down *c.* 2000 ft. (Martam, Dentam, Rinchinpong, Gangtok, Lachen, Manshitang, Penlom La). Affects forest on hillsides.

DISTRIBUTION OUTSIDE SIKKIM: The Himalayas from Chamba in the west to eastern Assam; Manipur, Burma, Thailand, Cochinchina, etc.

GENERAL HABITS: Reminiscent of the redstarts. Solitary, arboreal and usually wild. Perches on tops of tall trees or dead trunks near openings in forest or along mule paths, constantly jerking up its tail to the cocked position. Descends to ground from time to time to pick up a snail or grasshopper or small lizard. Sometimes springs up into the air like a flycatcher to capture a winged insect. Has a pleasant warbling song in the breeding season. On alarm a short, low *tick* is uttered at intervals, and a harsh jay-like note when angry.

NESTING: *Season*—May-June. *Nest*—an untidy cup of moss, grasses, etc., lined with soft material like roots and fibres. Placed in a crevice of rock or hollow in earth bank, in forest. *Eggs*—4 to 6, pale yellowish cream to deep buff, finely freckled with reddish. Size about 27×20 mm. Both sexes build and feed the young. Apparently the female does most of the incubating.

RACIAL CHARACTERISTICS, MEASUREMENTS, ETC: No white patch in wing. ♂ upper tail-coverts and tail blue; lower plumage chestnut, with black chin and throat. ♀ upper plumage olive-brown; back and rump barred.

A specimen (♂) collected by the Survey measures: Wing 124; bill 24; tarsus 27.5; tail 96 mm. Schäfer's Sikkim series gives: Wing 3 adult ♂♂ 125, 128, 128; 3 ad. ♀♀ 116, 118, 122 mm. (Stresemann).

Iris brown; bill, legs, feet and claws blackish brown; angle of gape cream colour.

## THE BLUEHEADED ROCK THRUSH

*Monticola cinclorhynchus* (Vigors)

*Petrocincla cinclorhyncha* Vigors, 1832, *Proc. Zool. Soc. London:* 172—Himalayas.

F.B.I. **2**: 171

LOCAL NAME: Krishen-patti (Nepali).

SIZE: Bulbul.

FIELD CHARACTERS: *Male: Above,* head, nape and lesser wing-coverts cobalt blue; back and scapulars black; tail black, edged with blue. Wings black, with a broad white patch conspicuous at rest and in flight. *Below,* chin and throat cobalt blue; rest chestnut.

*Female: Above,* olive-brown, barred with dull black on upper tail-coverts. *Below,* white, barred with blackish from breast down; scalloped on under tail-coverts.

STATUS AND HABITAT: Not met with by the Survey between November and April. According to Stevens 'entirely absent from the hills' in winter, but with a similar breeding range to the Chestnutbellied Rock Thrush in the outer ranges, namely *c.* 5000-10,000 ft. altitude. Schäfer collected three specimens, including a juvenile, at Gangtok in mid-June. Usually keeps to a lighter, more open type of forest than *rufiventris.*

DISTRIBUTION OUTSIDE SIKKIM: *Summer,* throughout the Himalayas from the Afghan boundary to eastern Assam and N. Burma. *Winter,* practically all India and E. Pakistan; Burma.

GENERAL HABITS: Very similar to those of *rufiventris.* In the breeding season delivers a loud, clear but monotonous song from tops of trees and also during its pretty volplaning display flight. Sometimes descends to ground to pick up an insect and returns to the perch like a bushchat, but finds most of its insect food on the trunks and branches of trees.

NESTING: *Season*—May-June. *Nest*—an untidy shallow pad or cup of moss, grass and roots. Placed in a hollow in a steep bank or hillside, or amongst the exposed roots of a tree clinging to a cliff. *Eggs*—3 to 5, like those of *rufiventris,* creamy white to deep buff, densely covered with tiny reddish freckles, sometimes thickly at the broad end. Size about 24×18 mm. Both sexes share in all the domestic chores.

RACIAL CHARACTERISTICS, MEASUREMENTS, ETC: *Male* readily distinguished from all other rock thrushes by its blue chin and throat, and large white wing-patches; *female* by the plain olive-brown back with barring confined to rump. The Fauna gives the measurements as:

| | Wing | Bill | Tarsus | Tail |
|---|---|---|---|---|
| ♂♂ | 100-104 | 18-19 | 24-25 | 65-68 mm. |
| ♀♀ | 93-105 | — | — | 65-69 mm. |

Schäfer's Sikkim skins have Wing: 1 adult ♂ 103; 1 ad. ♀ 103 mm. Iris brown; bill black; legs and feet greyish brown.

## THE BLUE ROCK THRUSH

*Monticola solitarius pandoo* (Sykes)

*Petrocincla pandoo* Sykes, 1832, *Proc. Zool. Soc. London:* 87—Ghauts, Dukhun.

F.B.I. 2: 174

LOCAL NAME: Ningri-pho (Lepcha).

SIZE: Bulbul.

FIELD CHARACTERS: *Male: Above* and *below*, bright leaden- or indigo blue.

*Female: Above*, greyish brown with a pale wing-bar. *Below*, whitish, cross-barred with dark brown.

STATUS AND HABITAT: Met with by the Survey only at Rangpo (*c.* 1000 ft.) in December. According to Stevens, has been obtained in winter in the Teesta Valley at elevations between 1100 and 3500 ft. I can trace no record of its occurrence or status in summer in E. Nepal, Sikkim or Bhutan except for the one bird seen at *c.* 4500 ft. in the Darjeeling Dist. on 9.vi.1944 (Lister, *Jour. Bombay Nat. Hist. Soc.* 52:41). Avoids forest. Affects dry shingly river beds with large boulders, rock cliffs, stone quarries, etc.

DISTRIBUTION OUTSIDE SIKKIM: *Summer*, breeding in the W. Himalayas between *c.* 6000 and 9000 ft. or higher, from Kashmir to Garhwal. According to Baker (F.B.I. and Nidification ii:152) also 'East to Tibet, Sikkim, and hills of N. Assam'. *Winter*, practically all India, both Pakistans, Ceylon, Burma. The species is widely distributed in S. Europe and Asia.

GENERAL HABITS: Solitary and locally sedentary. Keeps to favoured spots in its winter quarters day after day throughout the season. Perches bolt upright on a rock or ledge, bows jerkily and flirts its tail like a redstart. Sallies down to pick up crawling prey, whacking it on the ground, if too large or protesting, before swallowing it. Sometimes springs up in the air from its perch to capture winged termites or other flying insects. *Food:* dragonflies, grasshoppers, centipedes, lizards, etc., also berries. Breeding males have a short pleasant whistling song delivered from a perch or during the volplaning display flight.

NESTING: No data for Sikkim. *Season*—in W. Himalayas, chiefly April to June. *Nest*—a rough pad of moss, grass, leaves, etc. in a hole in a cliff or bank. *Eggs*—3 to 5, pale blue, sometimes faintly freckled with light reddish at the broad end. Size about 26×19 mm. Both sexes feed the young.

RACIAL CHARACTERISTICS, MEASUREMENTS, ETC: ♂ all blue; without white wing-patch. ♀ bluish- or greyish brown, as against olive-brown in *rufiventris* and *cinclorhynchus*.

A specimen (o?) collected by the Sikkim Survey measures: Wing 123; bill 26; tarsus 30; tail 90 mm.

Iris brown; bill black, yellow at gape; legs and feet black.

## THE COLLARED BUSHCHAT

*Saxicola torquata indica* (Blyth)

*Pratincola indica* Blyth, 1847, *Jour. Asiat. Soc. Bengal* **16**: 129—India, restricted to Calcutta.

**Plate 16, fig. 7** (facing p. 161)

F.B.I. **2**: **28**

LOCAL NAME:

SIZE: Sparrow.

FIELD CHARACTERS: *Male:* In summer (breeding) plumage distinctly pied, resembling Pied Bushchat from behind or on a fleeting glimpse. *Above*, head black; back brown, heavily black-streaked; most of wings and tail black; rump and upper tail-coverts white; conspicuous white patches on sides of neck ('collar'), and on shoulders. *Below,* throat black; breast reddish orange; abdomen whitish. In winter, black feathers of head, throat and back, broadly fringed with fulvous, greatly altering appearance.

*Female:* Fulvous brown overall, with dark-streaked upper parts and pale rusty rump.

STATUS AND HABITAT: Not common. Met with at moderate elevations, *c.* 4000 to 9000 ft. (Temi, Pakyong, Arita, Chungthang, Gangtok, Lachen, Penlom La). Also down in the foothills and plains in winter. Meinertzhagen procured a male of the migrant Turkestan-Tibet breeding race *przevalskii* at Dentam, 4600 ft., in January (1926).

Affects open, sparsely scrubbed hillsides, often in the neighbourhood of terraced cultivation.

DISTRIBUTION OUTSIDE SIKKIM: Throughout the Himalayas from Kashmir to Bhutan. Other races are found in Assam, Burma, Thailand, and practically all Europe, Asia, and Africa.

GENERAL HABITS: Active. Perches on a bushtop; constantly flicks open tail and jerks it loosely up and down, uttering *check, check.* Descends to ground to pick up insects; returns to same perch or flies low across to another within its well-defined beat or feeding area. Also captures winged insects in the air like a flycatcher. *Song:* short but lively, often interlarded with mimicked calls of other birds. Delivered from a perch or in slow display flight, with wings 'clapping' over back as in a pigeon, but noiselessly.

NESTING: *Season*—April to June, but not specifically recorded. *Nest*—a shallow cup or pad of grass, hair and wool. Placed in a hole in an earth-bank or under a stone. *Eggs*—4 to 6, pale bluish white, speckled and blotched with reddish brown. Size about 17×14 mm. Only female incubates. Male shares in nest-building and feeding young.

RACIAL CHARACTERISTICS, MEASUREMENTS, ETC: The migrant race *przevalskii* has a larger wing (nearly always over 71 mm.). Often impossible to differentiate from *indica* in its winter quarters.

Two specimens (♂ ♀) of *indica* obtained by the Sikkim Survey measure: Wing 66, 66; bill 13.5, 13; tarsus 21, 21; tail 46, 44 mm.

Five adults in the Schäfer Sikkim collection give Wing 2 ♂♂ 67, 71; 3 ♀♀ 63, 65, 67 mm.

Iris brown; bill, legs, feet and claws brownish black in male, paler in female.

The large, distinctive, Central Asian-breeding HODGSON'S BUSHCHAT, *Saxicola insignis* Gray, of a more or less similar colour scheme to *indica* but with considerably more white in the wing (83-92 mm.), was recorded by Mandelli over 80 years ago from the 'lower hills of Sikkim'—presumably meaning the terai. It has not been met with in Sikkim proper.

## THE DARK-GREY BUSHCHAT

*Saxicola ferrea* Gray

*Saxicola ferrea* Gray, 1846, Cat. Mamms. Birds Nepal: 71, 153—Nepal.

F.B.I. 2: 36

LOCAL NAME: Sarrak-chak-pho (Lepcha).

SIZE: Sparrow.

FIELD CHARACTERS: An unmistakable cousin of the Collared Bushchat. *Male*, winter: *Above*, dark grey and black, with a conspicuous white supercilium and a broad black streak through and below eye. Wings black, with a white band across. *Below*, chin and throat white; rest ashy white, darker on breast and flanks. Summer: General effect pied black and white. *Above*, almost black, with white patch on wing. *Below*, pure white.

*Female: Above*, russet brown with broad dark streaks; a pale grey supercilium; tail rufous, with dark chestnut upper coverts. *Below*, chin and throat white; rest ashy rufous, darkest on breast.

STATUS AND HABITAT: Fairly common between 6000 and 9000 ft. in summer; descends to foothills in winter (Rangpo, Martam, Dentam, Rinchinpong, Gangtok). Stuart Baker mentions eggs received by him from Gnatong (12,500 ft.), surely a very exceptional altitude. One of the most familiar species in Gangtok town from March to May, singing lustily from the overhead electric wires everywhere. Affects open scrub-covered hillsides, particularly in the neighbourhood of terraced cultivation.

DISTRIBUTION OUTSIDE SIKKIM: The entire Himalayas from the Afghan border to extreme east Assam; Manipur, Burma, N. Thailand, N. Yunnan, Szechwan, Indochina, S. China.

GENERAL HABITS: Very similar to those of the Collared Bushchat. Usually seen in widely separated pairs. The male sings in the vicinity of the nest from the top of a tall tree on a hillside or telegraph wire, or in the air during his display flight. *Song:* a short, pleasant but feeble trill *sisiri-swir-r*, the final syllable a rolling whistle.

NESTING: *Season*—April-May. *Nest* and *eggs* (4 or 5) similar to those of the Collared Bushchat, the latter slightly deeper in ground colour and larger. Size about 18×15 mm. Only the female incubates.

RACIAL CHARACTERISTICS, MEASUREMENTS, ETC: Three specimens collected by the Survey (♂ ♀) measure: Wing 67-68; bill 14-14.5; tarsus 22-23; tail 59-60 mm. A large series obtained by Schäfer in Sikkim gives Wing 11 ♂♂ 66-70 (av. 68.1) mm.; 8 ♀♀ 64-68 (av. 66.1) mm.

Iris brown; bill, legs, feet and claws brownish black or blackish brown.

## GOULD'S SHORTWING

*Brachypteryx stellata* Gould

*Brachypteryx* (*Drymochares*) *stellatus* Gould, 1868, *Proc. Zool. Soc. London:* 218—Nepal.

**Plate 23, fig. 4 (facing p. 288)**

F.B.I. 2: 16

LOCAL NAME:

SIZE: Sparrow.

FIELD CHARACTERS: A dark, stub-tailed ground-skulker, chestnut above with the iron-grey underparts distinctly bespangled with small white stars.

*Above*, bright chestnut with black lores, a narrow grey supercilium, and white-spotted slaty grey rump. *Below*, chin, throat and breast slaty grey suffused with rufous-brown on abdomen and flanks, vermiculated throughout with fine grey and black bars, and with triangular white spots on the lower portions. Sexes alike.

STATUS AND HABITAT: Secretive and apparently uncommon. Normally at high elevations, *c.* 9000 to 14,000 ft. (Yumthang, Zemu-Lhonak, Gnatong, Changu), but Schäfer obtained a specimen as low down as *c.* 1800 ft. (Dikchu) in February. Affects dense undergrowth of bamboo, dwarf rhododendron, etc.

DISTRIBUTION OUTSIDE SIKKIM: Nepal; Bhutan and adjoining areas of S. Tibet. The westernmost record is from Dhodi Tal, *c.* 11,000 ft., 70 miles N. of Mussooree (*Jour. Bombay Nat. Hist. Soc.* 53 (3): 468).

GENERAL HABITS: Little known, though apparently rather similar to those of the undergrowth-haunting wrens, e.g. *Pnoepyga*. Meinertzhagen records it as running on the ground in and out of roots and fallen branches just like a mouse—not hopping—and mounting on to stumps etc. Ludlow (in Bhutan) found the birds 'on the tops of rhododendron bushes and not skulking on the ground as is the custom of the genus'. *Food:* larvae, grubs and tiny beetles. Alarm note described as a *tik-tik*; song unknown.

NESTING: Unknown.

RACIAL CHARACTERISTICS, MEASUREMENTS, ETC: Wing short and rounded; tail very short; tarsi very long and slender. The chestnut upper plumage is diagnostic. The Fauna gives for ♂ ♀ Wing 72-77; bill 12; tarsus 30; tail 45-47 mm.

Two Schäfer Sikkim skins (♂, o?) have Wing 73, 76 mm., and Kinnear measures Ludlow's Bhutan skins Wing 3 ♂♂ 75-76; 2 ♀♀ 70-72 mm.

Iris dark brown; bill black; inside mouth black; legs and feet fleshy horn.

## THE RUSTYBELLIED SHORTWING

*Brachypteryx hyperythra* Jerdon & Blyth

*Brachypteryx hyperythra* Jerdon & Blyth, 1861, *Proc. Zool. Soc. London*: 201—Darjeeling.

F.B.I. 2: 17

LOCAL NAME:

SIZE: Sparrow.

FIELD CHARACTERS: *Male: Above,* lores and in front of eye black. Short, concealed supercilium silky white. Sides of head, neck, and whole upper plumage including exposed parts of wings and tail deep blue. *Below,* bright ferruginous, darker on flanks. Easily mistakable for the Blue Chat (*Erithacus brunneus*, p. 246), but white supercilium markedly less conspicuous.

*Female: Above,* olive-brown. No supercilium. *Below,* pale ferruginous; abdomen whitish, suffused with olive-brown on the sides.

STATUS AND HABITAT: Very rare and little known. Stevens observed a male in dense bamboo growth at Tonglu (9700 ft.—Darjeeling Dist.) in January.

DISTRIBUTION OUTSIDE SIKKIM: Dafla Hills; Naga Hills (?).

GENERAL HABITS: Presumably like the other shortwings, but nothing recorded.

NESTING: Unknown.

RACIAL CHARACTERISTICS, MEASUREMENTS, ETC: Key to the species: ♂ upper plumage blue; chin and throat chestnut. ♀ upper plumage brown; chin and throat chestnut. The Fauna gives the measurements as:

| | Wing | Bill | Tarsus | Tail |
|---|---|---|---|---|
| ♂ | 63-64 | 11 | 29 | *c.* 45 mm. |
| ♀ | *c.* 62 | 11 | 28 | 38 mm. |

'Iris brown; bill black, more or less fleshy at the base and on the mandible during the non-breeding season; legs fleshy to light horny brown.'

## THE WHITEBROWED SHORTWING

*Brachypteryx montana cruralis* (Blyth)

*Calliope? cruralis* Blyth, 1843, *Jour. Asiat. Soc. Bengal* 12: 929, 933—Darjeeling.

F.B.I. 2: 17

LOCAL NAME:

SIZE: Sparrow.

FIELD CHARACTERS: *Male* (adult): Overall plumage deep indigo blue. Lores, frontal band, and over eye velvety black; a conspicuous long white supercilium from forehead to ear-coverts. Centre of abdomen ashy; under tail-coverts blue, narrowly margined with ashy.

*Female* (adult): *Above,* lores, ring round eye and frontal line golden ferruginous; a concealed white supercilium. Rest of upper parts including exposed portion of wings and tail olive-brown tinged with rusty, especially on head. *Below*, ashy brown, paler and more yellowish on abdomen, rufescent on vent and under tail-coverts.

Immature (or dimorphic ?) *male:* Like the adult female but with the white supercilium prominent, and rather more chestnut wings and tail. Occasionally with some blue feathers intermixed on breast and mantle.

STATUS AND HABITAT: Comparatively common, with a wide altitudinal range. Between 1000 and at least 8000 ft. in winter; 5000 to at least 11,000 in summer (Rangpo, Lachen, Lachung). Affects dense humid undergrowth and brushwood in mossy forest.

DISTRIBUTION OUTSIDE SIKKIM: (Kumaon; Garhwal ?); Nepal, Bhutan, Assam hills north and south of the Brahmaputra; N. Thailand, Tonkin. The species extends to Yunnan and south China.

GENERAL HABITS: A skulker in undergrowth like the other shortwings. Dashes from bush to bush along the ground like a rat when pressed, and reluctant to fly. The song has been described as short, pretty, thrush-like, of a few notes ending abruptly. *Food:* insects and larvae.

NESTING: *Season*—June-July. *Nest*—a domed structure of moss, lined with fine roots, with a lateral entrance. Built close to the ground in damp shady forest, against the face of a moss-covered vertical rock or tree-trunk, incorporated into and blending perfectly with the surrounding moss. *Eggs*—2 or 3, pure white. Size about 23×16 mm.

RACIAC CHARACTERISTICS, MEASUREMENTS, ETC: Key to the species: ♂ upper plumage blue; chin and throat indigo blue; abdomen barred with ashy. ♀ upper plumage brown; chin and throat ashy brown.

Two ♂♂ collected in Sikkim have Wing 70, 72 mm. In one of these, bill 15.5; tarsus 34; tail 48.5 mm.

Iris brown; bill black; legs, feet and claws horny brown.

## THE NEPAL SHORTWING

*Brachypteryx leucophrys nipalensis* Hodgson

*Brachypteryx nipalensis* Hodgson, 1854, *in* Horsfield & Moore, Cat. Birds, Mus. E. I. Co. 1: 397, *ex* Hodgson MS.—Nepal.

F.B.I. 2: 19

LOCAL NAME:

SIZE: Sparrow—.

FIELD CHARACTERS: *Male* (adult): *Above,* lores and under eye dusky blue; short, partially concealed white supercilium; sides of head and neck, and all upper parts including exposed portions of wings and tail, dark slate-blue. *Below,* chin, throat, centre of abdomen and under tail-coverts white; rest smoky grey.

*Female: Above,* ferruginous brown with a concealed white eyebrow. *Below,* dull white; flanks, sides of breast and a diffuse band across it fulvous.

Immature (or dimorphic ?) *male:* brown like female.

STATUS AND HABITAT: Rare. According to Stevens found above *c.* 5000 ft. elevation in the Sikkim Himalayas at the nesting season. Affects low dense undergrowth in humid forest.

DISTRIBUTION OUTSIDE SIKKIM: Nepal; (Bhutan), Assam hills north and south of the Brahmaputra; E. Manipur, parts of Burma. The species extends to Thailand, Malaya, Indonesia, Indochina, Yunnan, Szechwan, S. China.

GENERAL HABITS: Similar to those of other shortwings. Keeps to dense forest undergrowth in damp shady glens etc., creeping about amongst fallen leaves, moss or rotting fallen tree-trunks, searching insect food. Flies little and seldom. *Call:* a soft, single *seep.* Male recorded as having a loud, sweet song in the breeding season.

NESTING: *Season*—mainly May-June. *Nest*—a compact, oval ball of bamboo leaves etc. bound together with roots and strands of moss. Well concealed on or near the ground in thick bushes or moss-covered fallen decaying tree-trunks. *Eggs*—3 or 4, pale olive or sea-green, normally densely covered with light reddish brown specks and freckles. Size about 19×14 mm. Both sexes share in nest building and incubation.

RACIAL CHARACTERISTICS, MEASUREMENTS, ETC: Key to the species: ♂ upper plumage blue; chin and throat white. ♀ upper plumage brown; chin and throat dull white.

The Fauna gives the measurements as ♂♀ Wing 58-64; bill 11.5-13; tarsus *c.* 26; tail 27-32 mm.

Iris dark brown; bill dark brown, yellowish horn on lower mandible, yellowish white at gape; legs and feet whitish- to purplish flesh.

## THE HIMALAYAN WHISTLING THRUSH

*Myiophoneus caeruleus temminckii* (Vigors)

*Myiophoneus temminckii* Vigors, 1832, *Proc. Zool. Soc. London:* 171—Himalayas.

F.B.I. 2:180

LOCAL NAMES: Chamong-pho (Lepcha); Tetiman (Bhutia).

SIZE: Pigeon.

FIELD CHARACTERS: A large blue-black thrush with bright deep blue forehead, wings and tail. Breast and flanks with round and elongated spots of glistening blue. Median wing-coverts with white tips. Sexes alike.

STATUS AND HABITAT: Resident and fairly common. Met with, even in mid-winter, at all elevations between *c.* 1000 and 9000 ft. (Rangpo, Singtam, Martam, Dikchu, Gangtok, Chungthang, Lachen, Lachung, Singhik, Toong). Schäfer collected it at Thangu, *c.* 12,000 ft., in July. Affects all rocky hill streams and rivers, neighbourhood of water meadows, and edge of damp forest.

DISTRIBUTION OUTSIDE SIKKIM: Throughout the Himalayas from the

Afghan frontier to extreme eastern Assam, north and south of the Brahmaputra; Arakan. Other races in Burma, China, Indonesia.

GENERAL HABITS: Mostly terrestrial. Solitary and shy. Progresses on ground in long hops, or runs in spurts with short mincing steps. Digs into wet mud with its stout bill for food. Every now and again does a violent 'bend-stretch' on its legs and raises and lowers tail slowly and deliberately. It is fully fanned out on the downward movement when its tip almost scrapes the ground—a movement reminiscent of the similarly torrent-haunting Whitecapped Redstart. *Food:* snails, crabs, and aquatic insects. Also windfallen fruit. Utters a sharp *kreee* and creaky *kich-kich-kich-kich* as it flies—calls of the identical pattern to those of the similarly torrent-haunting Spotted Forktail. Has a loud fine whistling song of considerable range to which the tumult of the waters provides romantic accompaniment.

NESTING: *Season*—chiefly May-June. *Nest*—a massive cup of moss and lichens mixed with mud, and lined with moss- and fern-roots. Placed on a ledge of rock near or overhanging a mountain stream. *Eggs*—3 to 5, pale clay colour, sparsely covered with faint pale reddish freckles, spots and blotches, more numerously at the broad end. Size about 36×25 mm. Both sexes share the domestic chores.

RACIAL CHARACTERISTICS, MEASUREMENTS, ETC: A Sikkim Survey specimen (♀) measures: Wing 173; bill 34; tarsus 55; tail 126 mm. A series of 17 adults in the Schäfer collection gives Wing 155 (♀) to 187 (♂) mm.

Iris brown; bill yellow, culmen except commissure horny brown; legs, feet and claws black.

## THE PURPLE THRUSH

*Cochoa purpurea* Hodgson

*Cochoa purpurea* Hodgson, 1836, *Jour. Asiat. Soc. Bengal* 5: 359—Nepal.

**Plate 23, fig. 7** (facing p. 288)

F.B.I. **2**: 184

LOCAL NAMES: Lo-nyum-pho (Lepcha); Cocho (Nepali).

SIZE: Between Myna and Pigeon.

FIELD CHARACTERS: *Male:* Overall aspect of plumage brownish purple, darkest on chin and throat. Crown lavender blue; lores, supercilium and sides of head black. Wing-coverts and bars on secondaries lavender purple. Wing quills black, with a broad band of lavender grey at base. Tips of secondaries black. Tail lavender purple with black tip.

*Female* differs from male in having the purple parts replaced by reddish brown.

STATUS AND HABITAT: Undetermined. Very rare. Blanford obtained it on the Chola Range (Kapup ?) at 10,000 ft. altitude on 28 August 1870. Schäfer collected two specimens at Gangtok and one at

1. Blueheaded Robin (*Phoenicurus caeruleocephalus*) 2. Hodgson's Grandala (*Grandala c. coelicolor*) 3. Bluefronted Robin (*Cinclidium f. frontale*) 4. Gould's Shortwing (*Brachypteryx stellata*) 5. Chestnutbellied Rock Thrush (*Monticola rufiventris*) 6. Smallbilled Mountain Thrush (*Zoothera d. dauma*) 7. Purple Thrush (*Cochoa purpurea*) 8. Green Thrush (*Cochoa viridis*)

PLATE 23

1. Blackfronted Parrotbill (*Paradoxornis n. humii*) 2. Fulvousfronted Parrotbill (*Paradoxornis f. fulvifrons*) 3. Sultan Tit (*Melanochlora s. sultanea*). Male 4. Lesser Redheaded Parrotbill (*Paradoxornis a. oatesi*) 5. Yellowbrowed Tit (*Parus m. modestus*) 6. Himalayan Cole-Tit (*Parus a. aemodius*) 7. Brown Crested Tit (*Parus d. dichrous*) 8. Rufousfronted Tit (*Ægithalos iouschistos*)

PLATE 24 [c. × 1]

Chungthang on 17 and 24 June 1938. Neither Meinertzhagen nor the recent Survey came across it in Sikkim between November and May. According to Stuart Baker (Nidification, ii: 160) it breeds 'above 3500 ft., certainly up to 6000, and probably up to 8000 ft., haunting evergreen forest with lofty trees and heavy wet undergrowth'.

DISTRIBUTION OUTSIDE SIKKIM: The Himalayas from Simla to eastern Assam, north and south of Brahmaputra River; Manipur, Burmese hills to Tenasserim, Thailand.

GENERAL HABITS: Little known besides that it keeps solitary, is silent, and feeds on fruits, berries and insects as much on the ground as in trees.

NESTING: Not recorded in Sikkim. *Season*—elsewhere, May to July. *Nest*—a shallow untidy cup of moss, compactly lined with lichens, fine moss and roots. Built in a small tree *c.* 6 to 12 ft. up, in an evergreen wooded ravine. *Eggs*—3, rarely 4, typically thrush-like, pale sea-green blotched with bright reddish brown. Size about 32×22 mm. Both sexes incubate.

RACIAL CHARACTERISTICS, MEASUREMENTS, ETC: The Fauna gives for ♂♀ Wing 140-144; bill 14-15; tarsus *c.* 28; tail 95-105 mm.

Schäfer's skins, all ad. ♂♂, have Wing 144, 144, 145 mm.

Iris crimson-brown or reddish brown; orbital skin lavender blue; bill black; legs and feet slaty black.

## THE GREEN THRUSH

*Cochoa viridis* Hodgson

*Cochoa viridis* Hodgson, 1836, *Jour. Asiat. Soc. Bengal* 5: 359-360—Nepal.

**Plate 23, fig. 8 (facing p. 288)**

F.B.I. 2: 185

LOCAL NAME:

SIZE: Between Myna and Pigeon.

FIELD CHARACTERS: *Male:* Overall aspect of plumage deep rich bronzy green. Crown, nape and hindneck brilliant cobalt blue; lores and a short supercilium black; ear-coverts indigo blue. Tail blue, slightly graduated, broadly tipped and narrowly margined with black. Wing-coverts green and pale blue, tipped with black. Wings black, with a broad band of pale blue near bases of the quills.

*Female* only differs in having the edges of greater wing-coverts and tips of secondaries marked with yellowish brown instead of blue.

STATUS AND HABITAT: Undetermined. Very rare. Stevens refers to specimens from the Sikkim Himalayas in the British and Tring Museums, collected at 'Gokh, Rammam Valley', 2500-3000 ft., 24 July 1870. Schäfer obtained a specimen at Singhik on 23 June (1938). Not met with by Meinertzhagen or the recent Sikkim Ornithological Survey between November and May, but I have examined a skin labelled '♂ 4.v.1931 Toong, 6000 ft.. coll. V. S. La Personne' now in the Chicago N. H. Museum (No. 85148).

DISTRIBUTION OUTSIDE SIKKIM: The Himalayas from Kumaon and Garhwal to eastern Assam; Manipur, hills of Burma to Tenasserim, Thailand, and eastward to W. China.

GENERAL HABITS: Little known. Apparently similar to those of the Purple Thrush.

NESTING: Somewhat doubtfully recorded from 10,000-11,000 ft. in Sikkim in June. Breeds in other areas (e.g. Assam hills) at much lower levels, 2500-5000 ft., May to July. *Nest*—similar to that of the Purple Thrush, in moderate sized trees in dense wet forest. *Eggs*—3, rarely 4, indistinguishable from those of *C. purpurea*. Size about 31×22 mm.

RACIAL CHARACTERISTICS, MEASUREMENTS, ETC: The Fauna gives for ♂♂ Wing 135-145; bill 12.5-13.5 (?); tarsus 25-26; tail 98-117 mm. The Toong ♂ in Chicago measures: Wing 145; bill 23; tarsus 27; tail 120 mm.

Schäfer's specimen (adult ♀) has Wing 147 mm.

Iris brownish orange to deep crimson or maroon-brown (duller in ♀); bill black, the gape and orbital skin pink; legs and feet fleshy brown to horny brown.

## THE EASTERN SPOTTED FORKTAIL

*Enicurus maculatus guttatus* Gould

*Enicurus guttatus* Gould, 1865, *Proc. Zool. Soc. London:* 664—Sikkim=Darjeeling.

F.B.I. 2:58

LOCAL NAMES: Oong-sam ching-pho (Lepcha); Chubia- (Chuka-) leka (Bhutia).

SIZE: Between Bulbul and Myna.

FIELD CHARACTERS: A graceful, spotted, black and white bird, rather like a wagtail in general aspect and deportment, with a long, deeply forked white tail. *Above*, forehead and anterior crown white; rest black with small round white spots on hindneck and mantle, sparse or absent on lower back; rump and upper tail-coverts white; wings black with a white bar of dense stippling. *Below*, throat, neck and breast black; rest white. Sexes alike.

STATUS AND HABITAT: Fairly common between 2000 and 8500 ft. elevation (Dikchu, Singhik, Chungthang, Gangtok, Lachen). Affects rocky mountain streams in damp heavy jungle.

DISTRIBUTION OUTSIDE SIKKIM: E. Nepal; Bhutan, Assam hills north and south of the Brahmaputra; Manipur, Burma, N. Yunnan, N. Tonkin. The species extends to Indochina and south China. The adjoining (typical) race *maculatus* stretches westward to the Afghan frontier.

GENERAL HABITS: Seen singly or in pairs tripping over rocks amidst or on the edge of clear, shady mountain streams. Tail held horizontally off the ground and swayed gently up and down, as the bird pivots facing this way and that. Utters a sharp *kree* in flight very like a Whistling Thrush's. Also a sharp, creaky *cheek-chik-chik-chik-chik* almost identical with one of the familiar calls of the Blue Magpie. *Food:* aquatic insects and their larvae. The spangled plumage completely obliterates the bird in its native setting of rushing water, black rocks and foamy spray with dappled sunlight filtering through the leaves; and its modulated movements harmonize with the torrent to heighten the invisibility.

NESTING: *Season*—April to June. *Nest*—a thick-sided cup of moss, moss-roots, hair, etc., lined with skeleton leaves and rootlets. The moss is often deliberately soaked at the water's edge to make it pliant for plastering on to the nest. Placed near water in a niche or hollow in a stream bank, overhung with ferns and roots. *Eggs*—3 or 4, pale buff or pale grey-green, freckled and spotted with light reddish brown. Size about 25×18 mm. Both sexes share in nest building, incubation and feeding young.

RACIAL CHARACTERISTICS, MEASUREMENTS, ETC: In the somewhat larger west Himalayan race *maculatus*, the spots on the back are larger, and more crescent-shaped on lower back. Also its black breast is spotted with white.

The Fauna gives for ♂♀ Wing 96-103; bill 18-19; tarsus 28-30; tail 118-132 mm. Stresemann measures the Wing of six adult ♂♀ in Schäfer's Sikkim collection: 95, 95, 96, 97, 100, 103 mm.

Iris dark brown; bill black; legs and feet white, pinkish at the joints.

Eastern Spotted Forktail
About two-fifths

## THE SLATYBACKED FORKTAIL

*Enicurus schistaceus* (Hodgson)

*Motacilla (Enicurus) schistaceus* Hodgson, 1836, *Asiat. Res.* **19**: 189—Nepal.

F.B.I. **2**: 59

LOCAL NAME:

SIZE: Between Bulbul and Myna.

FIELD CHARACTERS: Very similar to the last, but with back slaty grey, plain and unspotted, and breast white (only chin and throat black).

*Above*, narrow forehead and supercilium white. Lores, cheeks and ear-coverts black. Crown and back slaty blue, tipped with white only on the scapulars. Wings black with two broad white bands. Rump and upper tail-coverts white. Tail largely white. *Below*, only chin and throat black; rest white, washed with slaty on flanks. Sexes alike.

STATUS AND HABITAT: Fairly common at the lower elevations *c.* 1000 to 2500 ft.; sparingly up to 6000 ft. (Rangpo, Singtam, Martam, Dikchu, Gangtok). Affects more open rocky streams; often even little trickles by mule paths and along the motor road—favourite haunts of the Grey Wagtail.

DISTRIBUTION OUTSIDE SIKKIM: From Kumaon eastward to the extreme NE. frontier, Naga Hills, Manipur, Burma, N. Thailand, Malaya, Yunnan, Indochina. The species extends to S. China.

GENERAL HABITS: Very similar to the last, and to other forktails. It will sometimes leap up into the air from a rock amidstream to capture a winged insect. Flight undulating, like a wagtail's. When disturbed, flies swiftly up or down stream uttering the characteristic sharp *kree*, and often takes momentary refuge in a low branch.

NESTING: *Season*—March-April to June-July. *Nest*—similar to the last: a deepish cup of moss, in a herbage-overhung hollow in a stream bank. *Eggs*—3 or 4, similar to those of the Spotted Forktail, somewhat more variable. Size about 22×17 mm. Both sexes share in nest building, incubation and feeding young.

RACIAL CHARACTERISTICS, MEASUREMENTS, ETC: The Sikkim Survey specimens measure:

| | Wing | Bill | Tarsus | Inner tail | Outer tail | |
|---|---|---|---|---|---|---|
| 2 ♂♂ | 97-99 | 21 | 29 | 43-44 | 128.5-139 | mm. |
| 1 ♀ | 98 | 20 | 29.5 | 48 | 125 | mm. |

Three Schäfer skins from Sikkim have Wing 1 ♂ 99; 2 ♀♀ 91, 92 mm. Iris dark brown; bill black; legs, feet and claws fleshy white.

Two other pied forktails of a generally similar size and appearance also occur at lower altitudes in the foothills, between *c.* 1000 ft. (or lower) and 4500 ft. (Teesta and Great Rangeet valleys):

1. THE BLACKBACKED FORKTAIL, *Enicurus immaculatus* (Hodgson). Forehead, supercilium, and round the back of eye white. Rest of

head and upper back black, plain and unspotted. Chin and throat black; rest of underparts white. Wing ♂♀ 85-94 mm. In open forest or outskirts, on rocky streams lined with dense undergrowth of bracken etc. (Dentam, *c.* 4000 ft.).

2. THE BLACKBREASTED FORKTAIL, *Enicurus leschenaulti indicus* Hartert. Forehead and anterior crown white. Rest of head and upper back black, plain and unspotted. Chin, throat and upper breast black; lower breast and rest of underparts white. Wing ♂♀ 98-114 mm.

The largest and blackest of the forktails.

On overgrown streams and rocky ravines in dense forest.

GENERAL HABITS (of both): As described above.

## THE LITTLE FORKTAIL

*Enicurus scouleri* Vigors

*Enicurus scouleri* Vigors, 1832, *Proc. Zool. Soc. London:* 174—Himalayas.

Little Forktail, about one-half

F.B.I. 2: 65

LOCAL NAME: Oong-sumbrek-pho (Lepcha).

SIZE: Sparrow.

FIELD CHARACTERS: A stub-tailed miniature of the Spotted Forktail. *Above*, forehead and forecrown white; rest of head, neck and back black. Wings black, spotted with white at shoulder, and with a broad triangular white bar. Rump and upper tail-coverts white, the former with a broad black band across it. *Below*, throat and upper breast black; rest of underparts white. Tail short, slightly forked, of the same black-and-white pattern as in female Plumbeous Redstart. Sexes alike.

STATUS AND HABITAT: Fairly common and with a wide overall altitudinal range, between *c.* 1000 and 10,000 ft. (Singtam, Martam, Dikchu, Singhik, Toong, Chungthang, Lachen, Lachung). Affects rocky, torrential mountain streams, and nullahs with cascades and waterfalls.

DISTRIBUTION OUTSIDE SIKKIM: SE. Turkestan and Altai Mountains; throughout the Himalayas from Gilgit and Chitral through Kashmir to extreme east Assam north and south of Brahmaputra River; Naga Hills, NE. Burma, S. Tibet, N. Yunnan, Tonkin. The species extends to S. China and Formosa.

GENERAL HABITS: Typical of the forktails. On a rock amidst the torrent, wags stub tail slowly up and down, and rapidly opens and shuts it with a smooth rhythmic scissors-like motion flicking the black-and-white pattern. This exactly resembles the foam of water tumbling over roughnesses of rock and often renders the bird completely invisible. Silent. *Food:* aquatic and dipterous insects and their larvae, taken at the water's edge or by flying out over the rapids in pursuit, very like the Plumbeous Redstart.

NESTING: *Season*—May-June. *Nest*—a miniature of that of the Spotted Forktail: a deep cup of moss, lined with moss-roots, skeleton leaves, etc. Placed in a hole or cleft of rock near or under a waterfall, or in the bank of a stream. *Eggs*—3, white, sparsely speckled with light reddish brown. Size about 20×15 mm. Apparently, as in other forktails, both sexes share the domestic duties.

RACIAL CHARACTERISTICS, MEASUREMENTS, ETC: The Fauna gives for ♂♀ Wing 73-79; bill 12; tarsus *c.* 24-26; tail 41-49 mm. Six adult ♂♀ in the Schäfer Sikkim collection have Wing 72, 73, 74, 76, 78, 79 mm.

Iris dark brown; bill black; legs and feet fleshy white.

## *Subfamily* TROGLODYTINAE: Wrens

### THE NEPAL WREN

*Troglodytes troglodytes nipalensis* Blyth

*Troglodytes nipalensis* Blyth, 1845, *Jour. Asiat. Soc. Bengal* **14**: 589, *ex* Hodgson MS.—Nepal.

F.B.I. 1: 445

LOCAL NAME: Marchek-pho (Lepcha).

SIZE: Sparrow—.

FIELD CHARACTERS: A diminutive, stub-tailed, dark rufous-brown bird with the lower back, wings and tail closely barred with black. *Below*, slightly paler and tinged fulvous, closely black-barred except on chin, throat, and breast. Some white spots on under tail-coverts. The short tail is jauntily cocked up like a robin's. Sexes alike.

STATUS AND HABITAT: Resident. Common at high elevations up to, and above the tree line, between *c.* 8000 and 16,000 ft., even in winter (Lachen, Lachung, Phalut, Zemu, Thangu, Manshitang, Karponang, Gnatong, Changu, etc.). Affects glacier moraines, rocky gulleys and boulder-strewn nullahs with fallen tree-trunks and brushwood, piled stone parapet walls surrounding hill cultivation, etc.

DISTRIBUTION OUTSIDE SIKKIM: Garhwal, Nepal, Bhutan, Chumbi Valley, parts of S. Tibet, Dafla Hills. The adjoining W. Himalayan race, *neglectus*, extends to Kashmir and the Afghan border. The species has a wide overall distribution in Europe and Asia.

GENERAL HABITS: Terrestrial; restless. Hops about lithely amongst boulders, creeping in and out of crevices and rotting tree-trunks and brushwood in search of food. Utters a soft *chiruk, chiruk.* When disturbed, bobs up and down ('bend-stretch') like a dipper (*Cinclus*), with wings partially drooped and stub tail erect, before disappearing into cover. *Food:* small spiders and insects. In summer, has a lively, high pitched jumble of a song, astonishingly loud and piercing, delivered from the top of a boulder or some other exposed situation.

NESTING: *Season*—May-June. *Nest*—a large domed structure of moss, grass and leaves, thickly lined with feathers. Placed in the fissure of a birch tree or rock, or in the stone walls of a derelict shepherd's hut. *Eggs*—5 or 6, white, faintly and sparsely stippled with red, with a few specks at the larger end. Size about 18 × 13 mm.

RACIAL CHARACTERISTICS, MEASUREMENTS, ETC: In the west Himalayan race, *neglectus*, the upper plumage is a much paler rufous-brown.

Specimens collected by the Sikkim Survey measure:

| | Wing | Bill | Tarsus | Tail |
|---|---|---|---|---|
| 2 ♂♂ | 52.5-53.5 | 13-15 | 20-20.5 | 30-31.5 mm. |
| 2 ♀♀ | 49-50 | 12.5-13 | 19-19.5 | 29.5-30 mm. |

Ten Sikkim skins in the Schäfer collection give Wing 49(♀)-54(♂) mm. (av. 52.2)—Stresemann.

Iris brown; bill, legs, feet and claws horny brown.

Nepal Wren
About two-thirds

## *Subfamily* CINCLINAE: Dippers

### THE WHITEBREASTED ASIATIC DIPPER

*Cinclus cinclus cinclus* (Linnaeus)[1]

*Sturnus cinclus* Linnaeus, 1758, Syst. Nat., 10th ed., 1: 168—Sweden.

Whitebreasted Asiatic Dipper, about three-eighths

F.B.I. 2: 2
LOCAL NAME:
SIZE: Myna.

FIELD CHARACTERS: A dumpy, stub-tailed, thrush-like bird, slaty and chocolate brown with glistening white throat and breast. Sexes alike.

STATUS AND HABITAT: A high elevation species, occupying a higher zone than the Brown Dipper (*C. pallasii*). Meinertzhagen came across it in the Tibetan Plateau country of northern Sikkim at Gyagong (15,700 ft.) and Changu Lake (12,300 ft.), and there are five skins in the Chicago Museum collected by Stevens at Gnatong (12,500 ft.) and Gyagong. Its normal range is between 9000 and 15,000 ft. The surveys came across it only at Thangu (*c.* 13,000 ft., N. Sikkim). Affects clear, swift mountain torrents; also glacier lakes and tarns, even though partially frozen.

DISTRIBUTION OUTSIDE SIKKIM: Bhutan; Chumbi Valley (S. Tibet). Most of Palaearctic Europe and Asia. The paler race *cashmeriensis* occurs in Kashmir and Ladakh. Several other races are recognized over its wide range.

GENERAL HABITS: Usually solitary, or in widely separated pairs. Stands on a rock in the middle of a clear snow-fed torrent, cocking its stub tail and bobbing up and down, partly flexing and stretching its legs, and turning its head from side to side. Takes a headlong plunge into the icy water from time to time, remaining submerged for a half minute or more in search of food. On emerging floats like a bobbing cork on the surface, jumps on to a stone again, shakes off the water from its plumage and resumes bowing and curtseying.

[1] According to Vaurie, C., (Bds. Pal. Fauna: 198) Sikkim birds are intermediate between the races *cashmeriensis* and *przevalskii*.

In flight, the short rounded wings vibrate rapidly with slight intermittent pauses. When on a black rock with the swirling torrent breaking into foam around it, the bird's colour scheme completely obliterates it from view. This is also the case when the bird courses along a foot or two above the foam-flecked wavelets. *Call:* a shrill *dzchit, dzchit* uttered in flight. Also has a bright, rather loud, wren-like song in the breeding season. *Food:* chiefly aquatic insects and their larvae.

NESTING: *Season*—April to June, at 5000 to 14,000 ft. altitude. *Nest*—a large, untidy ball of grass, leaves, weed stalks, etc., looking like a natural accumulation of flotsam debris. Placed on a ledge or in a crevice of rock on the bank of a torrent or islanded in it. *Eggs*—3 or 4, pure white. Size about 26×18 mm.

RACIAL CHARACTERISTICS, MEASUREMENTS, ETC: Sikkim birds are darker than the Kashmir population, and go better with the typical Palaearctic race. The mutant (or colour dimorph ?) *sordidus*, formerly considered a distinct species,—with throat and breast brown like head—has been recorded from *c.* 15,000 ft. in Sikkim.

A Sikkim specimen measures: Wing 100; bill 22; tarsus 27; tail 53 mm.

Iris hazel; bill black or brownish black; legs, feet and claws blackish slaty brown.

## THE BROWN DIPPER

*Cinclus pallasii tenuirostris* Bonaparte

*Cinclus tenuirostris* Bonaparte, 1850, Consp. Gen. Av. 1: 252, *ex* Gould MS. for Gould, Century of Birds, pl. 24—Himalayas.

F.B.I. 2: 4

LOCAL NAMES: Nambong-karriak (Lepcha); Chubia nakka (Bhutia).

SIZE: Myna.

FIELD CHARACTERS: A sober, squat, chocolate-brown bird with small wings and stumpy tail; reminiscent of a large wren. Sexes alike.

STATUS AND HABITAT: Moderately common on all the larger streams and torrents from *c.* 1000 to 9000 ft. elevation, even in winter (Rangpo, Martam, Gangtok, Chungthang, Lachen, Lachung). Above this altitude replaced by the white-breasted species.

DISTRIBUTION OUTSIDE SIKKIM: Nepal and the western Himalayas to Kashmir, Gilgit, Afghanistan. Chumbi Valley birds intergrade with *dorjei* of Bhutan, Assam hills north of the Brahmaputra, N. Burma, N. Thailand. Another race in Formosa.

The species has a wide Palaearctic range in Europe and Asia.

GENERAL HABITS: Similar to those of the Whitebreasted Dipper. Usually solitary or separated pairs, on boulders or driftwood in clear mountain streams. Upon alighting on a rock, jerkily droops wings and tail and does a quick bend-stretch on its legs. Dips into swirling torrent or miniature cascade and disappears for fifteen seconds or more, often walking along the bottom thus submerged. Surfaces and floats like a tiny moorhen, sometimes whirled around like a coracle by the eddies. Frequently dives again from floating position like a dabchick. Jumps on to a rock, shakes the water off its plumage, bobs, curtseys and pivots. *Call:* a harsh, shrill *dzchit, dzchit* heard above the roar of the water. A short, full and rich song in breeding season. *Flight:* reminiscent of quail, on rapidly vibrating wings, low over the stream. *Food:* aquatic insects and larvae.

NESTING: *Season*—March-April or earlier. *Nest*—globular, of green moss lined with leaves etc., with lateral entrance. Placed in a cleft of rock or on an overhung ledge in a stream, close above spray. *Eggs*—4 or 5, white. Size about 27×18 mm.

RACIAL CHARACTERISTICS, MEASUREMENTS, ETC: The adjoining race *dorjei* of Bhutan and eastward is considerably darker.

The Fauna gives the measurements as: ♂♀ Wing 93-101; bill 18-19; tarsus *c.* 28; tail 55-60 mm.

Iris dark brown; bill black; legs and feet pale brown; soles yellow.

## *Family* PRUNELLIDAE: Accentors

### THE EASTERN ALPINE ACCENTOR

*Prunella collaris nipalensis* (Blyth)

*Accentor nipalensis* Blyth, 1843, *Jour. Asiat. Soc. Bengal* **12**: 958, *ex* Hodgson—Nepal.

F.B.I. **2**: 188

LOCAL NAME:

SIZE: Between Sparrow and Bulbul.

FIELD CHARACTERS: A fine-billed but otherwise sparrow-like brown and chestnut bird with greyish crown, narrowly barred white throat, and conspicuously white-tipped tail.

*Above*, greyish brown, more rufous on back and with broad black centres to feathers, producing a scaly pattern. Rump and upper tail-coverts rufous. Tail dark brown, tipped with rufous and white. Wing-coverts greyish brown and dark brown, spotted with white. Wing quills dark brown, narrowly edged and tipped paler. *Below*, chin and throat white, closely barred with black. Sides of head and neck, and breast greyish brown. Rest of underparts deep chestnut; middle of abdomen rufous-grey; under tail-coverts scalloped with white. Sexes alike.

STATUS AND HABITAT: A high elevation species, recorded by Schäfer from *c.* 16,000 ft. in July and August (Gyagong). During winter months sometimes as low as *c.* 8000 ft., but seldom below (Lachen, Lachung, Karponang, Phalut, Sandakphu, Thangu, Gnatong, Changu). Affects rocky forest at high altitudes, and alpine country with rock outcrops above the tree-line.

DISTRIBUTION OUTSIDE SIKKIM: Nepal, Bhutan, SE. Tibet. Other races in the western Himalayas, Tibet, Yunnan, Szechwan, NW. China.

GENERAL HABITS: Keeps singly or in small loose parties of 5 or 6, quietly hopping on the ground like a house-sparrow, picking up insects and seeds. Usually very tame and confiding. In winter commonly seen amidst village houses and about the piled stone parapets separating adjacent back yards and orchards, e.g. at Lachen, flying on to ledges of the roofs or window sills etc. when disturbed. Normally silent, but utters a low *chit-chittur* when in parties. Song not adequately described, but said to be like that of the English Hedge-Sparrow or Dunnock.

NESTING: *Season*—July-August. *Nest*—a well made cup of moss and grass, sometimes lined with a little fur. Placed under a rock or stone slab on a steep hillside, or in a crevice low down in a cliff-face. *Eggs*—3, beautiful deep blue, unmarked. Size about 23×16 mm.

RACIAL CHARACTERISTICS, MEASUREMENTS, ETC: The species *P. collaris* is differentiated from the next, *P. himalayana*, by its uniformly greyish brown breast as against rufous (with the feathers edged white) in the latter.

The adjoining W. Himalayan race *whymperi* is paler than *nipalensis*, and less rufous.

A specimen (♂) collected by the Survey measures: Wing 97; bill 15; tarsus 25; tail 66.5 mm. Schäfer's Sikkim series gives Wing 6 ♂♂ 97-104 (av. 97.6); 4 ♀♀ 93-98 (av. 95.2) mm.

Iris dark brown; bill black, bright yellow at base and gape; legs and feet brownish flesh colour.

Eastern Alpine Accentor
About one-half

## THE ALTAI, or RUFOUSBREASTED, ACCENTOR

*Prunella himalayana* (Blyth)

*Accentor himalayanus* Blyth, 1842, *Jour. Asiat. Soc. Bengal* **11**: 187—Himalayas.

F.B.I. **2**: 191

LOCAL NAME:

SIZE: Sparrow.

FIELD CHARACTERS: *Above*, forehead to hindneck greyish brown with dark streaks; a narrow pale grey supercilium. Back black with rufous edges to the feathers; rump pale greyish brown. Tail dark brown, edged with pale rufous and tipped with white. Wing-coverts black and rufous, tipped with white. Wing quills blackish, broadly edged with pale rufous on secondaries. *Below*, chin, throat and foreneck white, spotted with brown at sides, bordered below by an indefinite short black collar; sides of neck greyish brown. Rest of underparts ferruginous, the feathers edged with white, broadly on flanks and under tail-coverts; middle of abdomen whitish. Sexes alike.

STATUS AND HABITAT: A high altitude species. Meinertzhagen obtained it at 11,650 ft. (Yumthang) in December (1925); there is a specimen in the Chicago Museum of Natural History collected by the Suydam Cutting Sikkim Expedition at Gnatong, *c.* 12,500 ft., in March (1931), and it breeds at even higher elevations. Does not normally descend below 8000 ft. in winter, but I once came across a flock of about 50 birds at 6800 ft. (between Chungthang and Lachung)—18 January 1953—which had doubtless been forced down temporarily by the severe snowstorms at higher levels during the previous 2 or 3 days. (Lachen, Lachung, Karponang, Jeluk). Affects open stony country with dwarf rhododendron scrub etc.

DISTRIBUTION OUTSIDE SIKKIM: The Altai Mountains, Turkestan, Afghanistan and eastward through Kashmir and Nepal to the Miri Hills and SE. Tibet. Ludlow did not come across it in Bhutan.

GENERAL HABITS: In winter often forms large close-packed flocks which hop about and feed among the stones, flying up all at once when disturbed and perching close together in bare tree-tops like starlings at a roost. From here the flock launches into the air every now and again to wheel around and return to the perch in a way reminiscent of grandalas. The flock, whether in a tree or on the ground, keeps up a constant warbling twitter. Also reported to utter 'very sweet notes on the wing'.

NESTING: The nearest records (2) are from Yatung (14,000 ft.), 7 May and 4 July. *Nest*—an untidy cup of grass, leaves, roots, etc., lined with wool. Placed at the base of a low bush, or in a hollow under a rock. *Eggs*—deep blue, unmarked. Size about 23×16 mm.

RACIAL CHARACTERISTICS, MEASUREMENTS, ETC: The rufous breast of this accentor, scalloped with white, distinguishes it readily from *P. collaris* in which the breast is a uniform greyish brown.

The Survey specimens measure:

| | Wing | Bill | Tarsus | Tail |
|---|---|---|---|---|
| 2 ♂♂ | 94-97 | 13.5-14 | 22-22.5 | 55-57 mm. |
| 2 ♀♀ | 91-94 | 13.5 | 22 | 54-56 mm. |

Iris pale claret; bill blackish brown, yellow on commissure at gape; legs and feet orange-brown; claws horny brown.

Below each joint of the toes is a curious pimple-like pad such as is also present in the Mountain Finch (*Leucosticte nemoricola*). Possibly an insulating mechanism for hopping on snow?

## THE MAROONBACKED ACCENTOR

*Prunella immaculata* (Hodgson)

*Accentor immaculatus* Hodgson, 1845, *Proc. Zool. Soc. London:* 34—Nepal, ex *Zool. Miscell.:* 83, 1844, *nom. nud.*

F.B.I. 2: 193

LOCAL NAME:

SIZE: Sparrow.

FIELD CHARACTERS: *Above,* forehead, crown and nape dark ashy, scalloped with white on forehead. Lores black; ear-coverts slaty brown. Upper back rufous olive-brown, changing to maroon on lower back and rump. Upper tail-coverts rufous olive-brown. Tail greyish brown. Wing quills largely blackish, edged with grey. *Below,* ashy brown; lower abdomen, vent and under tail dark chestnut; thighs slaty. Sexes alike.

STATUS AND HABITAT: A high altitude species. According to Stevens 'sparingly distributed and of irregular occurrence at elevations from 7000 to 8000 ft. during winter'. Meinertzhagen obtained a single specimen at Phalut, 12,100 ft., on 9 January (1926), and during the Survey Dr Biswas got another a thousand feet lower in the same locality on 29 December (1952). In summer up to 15,000 ft. or higher. Affects rhododendron and conifer forest interspersed with open grassy patches and rock outcrops.

DISTRIBUTION OUTSIDE SIKKIM: Nepal, Bhutan, SE. Tibet, Yunnan, W. China.

GENERAL HABITS: Gregarious in winter. Ludlow writes that it is 'not only a ground bird but also a restless inhabitant of the summits of conifers where it utters an oft-repeated monotonous two-syllabled call. It is a strong flier.' (*Ibis,* 1944: 192).

NESTING: I cannot trace any specific breeding record for Sikkim though Stuart Baker (Nidification, ii: 166) says 'it breeds in Sikkim at elevations of 10,000 ft. and upwards . . .' and he is doubtless correct. *Season*—May to July. *Nest*—the typical untidy cup of grass, leaves, etc., lined with goat's hair and wool. Built on or near the ground, at the base of a furze bush. *Eggs*—3 or 4, rarely 5, deep blue, unmarked. Size about 20×15 mm.

RACIAL CHARACTERISTICS, MEASUREMENTS, ETC: The unstreaked maroon upper plumage of this accentor is diagnostic.

Three specimens (♀♀) collected in E. Nepal by Dr Dillon Ripley measure: Wing 78-81; bill 12.5-13; tail 49.5-57 mm.

'Iris orange with a white inner ring; bill black; legs and feet pale brownish flesh.'

## THE ROBIN ACCENTOR

*Prunella rubeculoides* (Horsfield & Moore)

*Accentor rubeculoides* Horsfield & Moore, 1854, Cat. Birds Mus. E. I. Co. 1: 361—Nepal.

F.B.I. 2: 193

LOCAL NAME: Phoo-ching-pho (Lepcha).

SIZE: Sparrow.

FIELD CHARACTERS: *Above,* forehead, crown, nape and sides of neck brown. Back and rump rufous-brown, the feathers with broad black centres. Upper tail-coverts olive-brown. Tail brown with pale edges. Wing-coverts brown, tipped with white; wing quills blackish, edged paler. *Below,* chin, throat, and sides of neck mottled ashy brown; breast dark ferruginous. Rest of underparts whitish, the sides of abdomen and under tail streaked with rufous-brown. Sexes alike.

STATUS AND HABITAT: A high altitude species. Found by Meinertzhagen at between 13,000 and 16,000 ft. (Thangu, Yumthang, Gyagong) even in winter—November, December. Schäfer collected a large series including juveniles at *c.* 16,000 ft. (Gyagong) in July and August; also a specimen at 4000 ft. (Singhik) in October, which is an abnormally low limit for this bird. The Sikkim Survey obtained an example at 8500 ft. (Lachen) in February. Affects barren hillsides and typical windswept Tibetan plateau country in N. Sikkim, dotted with rounded furze (*Caragana*) bushes or 'hedgehogs'.

DISTRIBUTION OUTSIDE SIKKIM: The high Himalayas from the Afghan boundary and Garhwal through Nepal and Bhutan; Tibet, Hsifan Mountains to northern Nan-shan; Szechwan, Kansu, etc.

GENERAL HABITS: Gregarious in winter like other accentors, but in smaller flocks. Usually fearless and confiding. Hops on ground stiffly like a sparrow, picking up seeds and insects. During the breeding season the only 'song' heard by me was a pleasant but feeble *tilili*. Whether the 'sweet little song' mentioned in the Fauna is a reference to the same or another is not clear.

NESTING: *Season*—June-July. *Nest*—an untidy cup of grass, weed stems, etc. lined with hair. Placed on or near the ground within a furze 'hedgehog', or in a hollow in a bank. *Eggs*—normally 3, deep turquoise—or 'hedge-sparrow' blue. Size about 20×16 mm.

RACIAL CHARACTERISTICS, MEASUREMENTS, ETC: The species is readily distinguished from the other rufous-breasted accentor, *P. strophiata*, by the absence of a supercilium. Birds from Kashmir and the W. Himalayas are somewhat paler than those from Nepal and Sikkim.

Stresemann measures Schäfer's N. Sikkim series as: Wing 15 ♂♂ 75-84; 7 ♀♀ 72-76 mm.

'Iris whitey brown to clear pale brown; bill black; legs and feet fleshy brown to horny reddish brown; claws darker.'

## THE RUFOUSBREASTED ACCENTOR

*Prunella strophiata strophiata* (Blyth)

*Accentor strophiatus* Blyth, 1843, *Jour. Asiat. Soc. Bengal* **12**: 959, *ex* Hodgson MS.—Nepal.

**Plate 19, fig. 1** (facing p. 224)

F.B.I. **2**: 196

LOCAL NAME: Phoo-ching-pho (Lepcha).

SIZE: Sparrow.

FIELD CHARACTERS: *Above*, rufescent brown, boldly streaked with blackish. Sides of face dark brown; a conspicuous broad rufous supercilium (whitish anteriorly), bordered above with black. Sides of neck ashy, with blackish streaks. Tail brown. Wing quills brown, edged with rufous: coverts white-tipped, forming a narrow wing-bar. *Below*, chin and throat white, with black spots at sides and base. Breast deep ferruginous, paling on flanks, and to whitish on abdomen and under tail. Sides of breast, flanks and abdomen boldly streaked with black. Sexes alike.

STATUS AND HABITAT: In winter sparingly between *c.* 5500 and 9000 ft. (Chungthang, Lachen, Lachung, Gangtok). Schäfer procured it in February (1938) at *c.* 12,000 ft. (Changu) and the Suydam Cutting Expedition at 12,500 ft. (Gnatong) in March (1931). Blanford recorded it at 12,000 ft. in the Chola Range in September (1870). Schäfer collected adults and juveniles at 13,000 ft. (Thangu), July-August. Breeds up to c. 16,000 ft. Affects forested hillsides as well as opener scrub growth of dwarf rhododendron, juniper, etc. in summer—a wetter biotope than other accentors.

DISTRIBUTION OUTSIDE SIKKIM: Garhwal, Nepal, Bhutan, SE. Tibet. The adjoining race *jerdoni* stretches westward through Kashmir to the Afghan boundary. The species extends to the mountains of Szechwan, Kansu, etc.

GENERAL HABITS: Keeps in pairs or small parties in summer to dwarf rhododendron and juniper covered hillsides. Forms larger flocks in winter, then affecting opener country dotted sparsely with *Berberis, Lonicera* and such-like bushes, and the neighbourhood of fallow hill cultivation. The bird hops about quietly at the base of bushes, picking up seeds and insects. When disturbed it works its way with great speed through the tangles of thorny branches, and hops across to the next bush. When flushed it dives into cover abruptly after a short hedge-hopping flight. Normal note, a rather high-pitched *tr-r-r.* In the breeding season the male delivers a short pretty wren-like song, but less loud or penetrating.

NESTING: *Season*—May to July. *Nest*—a rather untidy cup of grass, moss and lichen neatly lined with fine dry grass, wool or feathers. Usually placed in a low bush. *Eggs*—3 or 4, beautiful turquoise or 'hedge-sparrow' blue. Size about 19×14 mm. Both sexes incubate and feed the young.

RACIAL CHARACTERISTICS, MEASUREMENTS, ETC: The combination of rufous breast with prominent supercilium is diagnostic of this species. The W. Himalayan race *jerdoni* has a paler rufous breast, and greyish brown upper parts as against rufous-brown.

The Sikkim Survey specimens measure: 2 ♂♂ Wing 70-73; bill 13, 13; tarsus 20.5-22.5; tail 60, 60 mm.

Schäfer's Sikkim skins give Wing 1 ♂ 69; 3 ♀♀ 64, 65, 66 mm.

Iris dark orange-brown; bill horny brown, pale at chin and commissure at base of lower mandible; legs and feet dusky orange-brown; claws horny brown.

## *Family* MOTACILLIDAE: Wagtails Pipits

### THE KANSU TREE-PIPIT

*Anthus hodgsoni berezowskii* Zarudny[1]

*Anthus maculatus berezowskii* Zarudny, 1909, *Orn. Monatsb.* 17: 41—SW. Kansu.

F.B.I. 3: 283

LOCAL NAME:

SIZE: Sparrow.

FIELD CHARACTERS: A slim, sober-coloured, wagtail-like bird. *Above*, olive-brown, broadly dark-streaked, and with a prominent fulvous and white supercilium. Two narrow wing-bars. *Below*, fulvous white, streaked with black on throat and breast. Sexes alike.

Pipits are all superficially very alike and the different species not easily or satisfactorily identified in the field. In the present case, moreover, three races evidently occur together in Sikkim in winter. Sight records as to subspecies, if unsupported by specimens, are therefore valueless.

STATUS AND HABITAT: This, as determined by Stresemann, is the breeding race of Sikkim and Bhutan. Schäfer collected a large series, including juveniles, on its breeding grounds at c. 13,000 ft. (Thangu) between 1 and 17 July. Also at Lachen (9000 ft.) in August; Chungthang (5000 ft.) in November; and Gangtok (6300 ft.) in December and January. The Sikkim Survey collected ten specimens between November and February between 1000 and 6500 ft. (Rangpo,

[1] Vaurie (1959, The Birds of the Palaearctic Fauna: 68) considered the race *berezowskii* of questionable validity. Since then Ripley has also altered his view and merged this race with nominate *hodgsoni* in his Synopsis of the Birds of India and Pakistan.

Singtam, Temi, Rinchinpong and above Chungthang) comprising the other two races, namely *hodgsoni* and *yunnanensis*, which are abundant as passage migrants and winter visitors, first arriving in September. Schäfer also procured *hodgsoni* at Lachen (September), Thangu (1 October) and Gangtok (10 December, 31 January, 2 and 18 February, 1 March). Meinertzhagen found *hodgsoni* abundant in suitable country in Sikkim between 5000 and 6000 ft. altitude, November to January. This appears to be the position in Sikkim—but far from clear. (For diagnosis of the races, their ranges and other details see Ripley, *Jour. Bombay Nat. Hist. Soc.* 47 (4): 622-627—1948, but see footnote above).

GENERAL HABITS: Very wagtail-like. Loose parties or flocks affect upland pastures, fallow cultivation, mule paths and openings in forest, running about on the ground to capture tiny insects, flying up into trees when disturbed. *Call:* a sharp single *tseep* from time to time. In the breeding season the male rises a short distance in the air on quivering wings from a bare tree-top and volplanes back to his perch with wings and tail outspread, singing a pretty but wheezy lark-like song.

NESTING: *Season*—May to July. *Nest*—a shallow cup of grass, roots and leaves, lined with finer grasses. Placed in a depression at the base of a grass tuft or boulder. *Eggs*—3 or 4, variable, pinkish- or yellowish stone, or greyish, profusely speckled with reddish brown. Size about 22×16 mm.

RACIAL CHARACTERISTICS, MEASUREMENTS, ETC: Hind claw not exceeding hind toe in length; pale tip of inner web of penultimate tail feather very small—white; upper plumage greenish, streaked.

Schäfer's skins measure:

| | | | |
|---|---|---|---|
| *berezowskii* | Wing | 20 ♂♀ | 78-86 (av. 82.7) mm. |
| *hodgsoni* | | 12 ♂♂ | 81-90 (av. 85.0) mm. (Stresemann). |

The Sikkim Survey specimens measure:

| | | Wing | Bill | Tarsus | Tail |
|---|---|---|---|---|---|
| *A. h. hodgsoni* | 5 ♂♀ | 82-86 | 13-14 | 21-22.5 | 55-64 mm. |
| *A. h. yunnanensis* | 5 ♂♀ | 84-88 | 13-15 | 21-22 | 58-64 mm. |

Iris brown; bill horny brown, paler on lower mandible; legs and feet brownish flesh colour; claws horny brown.

## THE VINACEOUSBREASTED, or HODGSON'S, PIPIT

### *Anthus roseatus* Blyth

*Anthus roseatus* Blyth, 1847, *Jour. Asiat. Soc. Bengal* 16: 437, *ex* Hodgson MS.—Nepal.

F.B.I. 3: 295

LOCAL NAME:

SIZE: Sparrow.

FIELD CHARACTERS: *Summer* (breeding): *Above*, black, each feather edged with olive-brown. A broad vinous pink supercilium. *Below*,

20

chin, throat and breast vinous pink; rest of lower plumage fulvous. Sides of breast, and flanks, boldly streaked with black. Sexes alike. In winter the vinous pink is paler.

STATUS AND HABITAT: Breeds in the alpine zone in N. Sikkim between *c.* 12,000 and 16,500 ft. (Yumthang, Thangu, Gnatong, Gyag-ong, 'Kiang-Lager'). Mostly on passage at lower levels, September/October and March/April, but some apparently stay behind even near the highest levels well into or throughout the winter. Obtained between October and April at Chungthang, Lachen, Gangtok, Karponang. In summer affects upland pastures, glacier valleys, boggy meadows recently under snow, and moors above the tree-line.

DISTRIBUTION OUTSIDE SIKKIM: *Summer* (breeding), central Asia, Afghanistan and throughout the high Himalayas, east to Kansu, Yunnan, etc. *Winter*, practically throughout N. India, Assam, N. Burma.

GENERAL HABITS: On its alpine breeding grounds rather similar to *A. h. berezowskii*, including the aerial nuptial display and song.

NESTING: *Season*—mainly June-July. *Nest* and *eggs*—typical of the pipits, similar to those described; the latter also with the same wide range of variations. Size about 22×15 mm.

RACIAL CHARACTERISTICS, MEASUREMENTS, ETC: Hind claw exceeding hind toe in length; sides of body coarsely streaked with black; axillaries and under wing-coverts primrose yellow.

Schäfer's Sikkim series measures: Wing 10 ♂♂ 85-95 (av. 88.8); 3 ♀♀ 83, 87, 87 mm.

Iris brown; bill horny black, paler on lower mandible; legs and feet brownish flesh colour; claws darker.

Schäfer collected 7 examples of BLYTH'S PIPIT, *Anthus godlewskii* (Taczanowski) = *striolatus* Blyth, at Lachen (9000 ft.) between 4 and 18 September 1938, evidently on southward passage from its breeding grounds in Transbaikalia over Tibet to Assam and Burma. Stresemann measures these (♂♀) as: Wing 88-97 (over 90 mm. in 5); tarsus 25-28; hind toe 11-12; hind claw 10-12 (once 14) mm.

Blanford found this pipit common in clearings a little below 7000 ft. in early September, and also at Phalung, above 15,000 ft. (N. Sikkim) in the beginning of October (*c.* 1870).

RECOGNITION: *Above*, brown with broad dark centres to the feathers. *Below*, fulvous, faintly streaked on breast and anterior flanks. Hind toe about equal in length to hind claw.

## HODGSON'S PIED WAGTAIL

*Motacilla alba alboides* Hodgson

*Motacilla alboides* Hodgson, 1836, *Asiat. Res.* 19: 191—Nepal.

F.B.I. 3: 262

LOCAL NAME:

SIZE: Sparrow; with longer tail.

FIELD CHARACTERS: A slim, handsome, black-and-white bird seen on rocks and shingle beds in streams, constantly wagging its tail up and down. Sexes more or less alike.

*Summer: Above*, forehead broadly white; crown, ear-coverts and rest of upper parts black, with a broad white wing-band. Tail black with outer pair of feathers white. *Below*, chin, throat and breast black; rest of lower plumage white.

*Winter: Above*, dark grey; ear-coverts black. *Below*, chin and throat white or mottled with white. The broad wing-band usually prominent.

In winter plumage difficult to tell from the Masked Wagtail (*M. a. personata*) which *may* turn up in Sikkim on passage. Less easily confused with the Indian White Wagtail (*M. a. dukhunensis*)—also a possible passage migrant—the ear-coverts of the latter being consistently white at all seasons.

STATUS AND HABITAT: Sparing winter visitor to the lower reaches of the Teesta and other rivers, *c*. 1000 ft. (Rangpo, Singtam). Blanford obtained it at *c*. 12,000 ft. altitude (Lachung Valley) in September. Schäfer collected specimens July to November in N. Sikkim between *c*. 9000 and 16,500 ft. (Lachen, Thangu, Gyagong), including juveniles in July and August. Betts observed Pied Wagtails, presumably this species, at 12,000 ft. (Yakthang) in May—pairs occupying territories and evidently about to breed.

DISTRIBUTION OUTSIDE SIKKIM: *Summer* (breeding): the high Himalayas from Gilgit through Kashmir, Nepal and Bhutan to E. Tibet; Szechwan, Kansu, etc.

GENERAL HABITS: Pairs, or small scattered parties (in winter), affect rocks and shingle banks in and along stretches of clear mountain streams where comparatively placid. The birds run about with quick mincing steps, wagging their tails, picking up tiny insects and molluscs cast up by the spray and ripples; sometimes wading in, and occasionally springing up a few feet in the air to capture winged prey. *Flight:* characteristic of the wagtails, a series of dipping curves produced by a few rapid wing beats alternated with a short pause. It is accompanied by sharp *chichip, chichip* notes.

NESTING: Not specifically recorded in Sikkim, but season evidently from mid-May to July. *Nest*—a fairly bulky cup of grass, roots, etc. lined with wool or hair. Placed in a hole or pocket under a boulder, or amongst flotsam washed up on an islet amid stream. *Eggs*—4 or 5, white, freckled and spotted with reddish brown, more densely at the broad end. Size about 22×16 mm.

RACIAL CHARACTERISTICS, MEASUREMENTS, ETC: Schäfer's specimens from N. Sikkim measure: Wing 5 ad. ♂♂ 89-97 (av. 94.0); 3 ♀♀ 84, 86, 86 mm.

Iris brown; bill, legs, feet and claws black.

Schäfer procured specimens of SWINHOE'S WHITE WAGTAIL (*Motacilla alba baicalensis* Swinhoe) in N. Sikkim, at Lachen (9000 ft.) and 'Kiang-Lager' (16,500 ft.) in September and October, evidently on passage from their E. Siberian breeding grounds to their winter quarters in S. China etc. They measure: Wing 3 ♂♂ 90, 95, 98; 2 ♀♀ 88, 89 mm. (Stresemann).

This race is superficially very close to *M. a. personata* Gould (grey-backed, with black ear-coverts), but in summer plumage always retains the white chin, and the white forecrown extends further back to almost behind the eyes. The two are indistinguishable in the field in winter.

## THE LARGE PIED WAGTAIL

*Motacilla maderaspatensis* Gmelin

*Motacilla maderaspatensis* Gmelin, 1789, Syst. Nat. 1 (2): 961—India (=Madras).

Large Pied Wagtail

Hodgson's Pied Wagtail

About two-thirds

F.B.I. 3: 263

LOCAL NAME:

SIZE: Bulbul.

FIELD CHARACTERS: Similar to Hodgson's Pied Wagtail, but somewhat larger. The black of the crown extends in a narrow point down the forehead to base of bill, parting the broad white supercilia. (In *a. alboides* the forehead is broadly white, unbroken in the middle). The white wing-band is narrower and less arresting. In the female the black portions are duller and browner.

STATUS AND HABITAT: Not common. Met with only on the Teesta River at Rangpo, *c.* 1200 ft.—November to April; no data thereafter. Presumably resident at low altitudes.

DISTRIBUTION OUTSIDE SIKKIM: Throughout the Himalayas up to *c.* 2000 ft. elevation, and the entire Indian Union excepting Assam.

GENERAL HABITS: Non-migratory. Normally keeps in pairs to clear, rocky, placid streams, tanks, and reservoirs. Has a number of pleasing whistling calls, and a sweet Magpie Robin-like song in the breeding season. Food etc. as of other wagtails.

NESTING: Not recorded in Sikkim. *Nest*—a cup-shaped pad of rootlets, hair, wool, etc. under a projecting rock or girders of a bridge, or among the rafters of a dwelling house—always near water. *Eggs*—3 or 4, greyish-, brownish-, or greenish white blotched and streaked with various shades of brown. Size about 22×16 mm.

RACIAL CHARACTERISTICS, MEASUREMENTS, ETC: The Fauna gives the measurements (♂♀) as: Wing 97-103; bill 14-15; tarsus 25-28; tail 95-105 mm.

Specimens collected by Dr Biswas at Rangpo give Wing 2 o? 90, 95 mm.

Iris brown; bill, legs, feet and claws black.

## THE EASTERN GREY WAGTAIL

*Motacilla caspica caspica* (Gmelin)

*Parus caspicus* Gmelin, 1744, Reise d. Russ. 3, pl. 20, fig. 2: 104—Enzeli on the southern shore of the Caspian Sea.

F.B.I. 3: 265

LOCAL NAME:

SIZE: Sparrow; slimmer, with longer tail.

FIELD CHARACTERS: *Male* (winter): *Above*, blue-grey with olive tinge. Faint whitish supercilia and moustachial streaks. Rump greenish yellow. Tail largely white and black. *Below*, chin, throat, breast and underparts buffy white, yellow on vent and under tail-coverts. Sexes alike in winter plumage.

*Male* (summer): *Above*, darker and more slaty grey. Supercilia and moustachial streaks whiter and more prominent. A white wing-patch at base of inner secondaries. *Below*, chin, throat, and upper breast black; rest of underparts bright yellow.

*Female* (summer): Supercilia and moustachial streaks less prominent. Black of chin and throat mottled with white. Yellow underparts less bright than in male.

STATUS AND HABITAT: Apparently not breeding in Sikkim. An uncommon passage migrant in small numbers southward in September, returning in April, though a few may overwinter at moderate elevations. Schäfer obtained specimens at Lachen (9000 ft.) on 14 and 17 September, and at Gangtok (6300 ft.) on 20 and 30 December and 15 January. Between November and April the Sikkim Survey only came across a single example at Martam (*c.* 2000 ft.—21 December) at a seepage trickle along the motor road.

DISTRIBUTION OUTSIDE SIKKIM: *Summer* (breeding), eastern N. Asia south to Afghanistan and the Himalayas, at least in Kashmir and Garhwal. *Winter*, hilly biotope throughout the Indian Union, both Pakistans, Burma, Ceylon, the Andamans and Malaysia.

GENERAL HABITS: Like other wagtails, but solitary and unsociable. Normally met with singly, widely separated from the next of its kind, and not in association with other wagtails.

RACIAL CHARACTERISTICS, MEASUREMENTS, ETC. Schäfer's Sikkim specimens measure: Wing/tail 1 ♂ 83/88; 4 ♀♀ 79/85; 80/90; 80/92; 82/92 mm. (Stresemann).

Iris brown; bill horny brown, paler at chin and commissure; legs and feet brownish flesh colour; claws dusky.

## THE BLACKBACKED YELLOWHEADED WAGTAIL

### *Motacilla citreola calcarata* Hodgson

*Motacilla calcarata* Hodgson, 1836, *Asiat. Res.* 19: 190—Nepal.

F.B.I. 3: 274

LOCAL NAMES: Ane-kegah; Ani-chepta (Tibetan).

SIZE: Sparrow; slimmer, with longer tail.

FIELD CHARACTERS: *Male* (summer): *Above,* head and neck bright lemon yellow. Rest of upper plumage deep black, with some white in wings and tail. *Below,* bright lemon yellow or canary yellow.

*Female:* similar but paler overall. Upper plumage brownish black; yellow parts sometimes almost whitish.

*Male* (winter): *Above,* forehead, a broad supercilium and sides of head yellow; crown dark olive; back grey. A dusky line through eye. *Below,* yellow; breast more or less mottled with dusky.

*Female:* similar in general but duller. Yellow forehead very narrow making the whole head dark olive with a yellow tinge.

Various other species of yellow wagtails are likely to occur as passage migrants in Sikkim. In winter plumage they are difficult to identify in the field.

STATUS AND HABITAT: Breeds at high altitudes. Schäfer collected a good series in N. Sikkim at *c.* 16,000 ft. (Gyagong) on 10 August. Also specimens at 'Kiang-Lager' (16,500 ft.) on 1 October, and at Lachen (9000 ft.) on 11 September and 14 and 15 October. All the August specimens were in breeding plumage; the others in winter or juvenile dress.

Not met with by the Survey or other investigators between November and April, so it evidently does not overwinter in Sikkim.

DISTRIBUTION OUTSIDE SIKKIM: *Summer* (breeding), central Asia, Iran, Afghanistan, and the Himalayas eastward to Sikkim, and Tibet. *Winter,* N. India south to Kutch, east to extreme E. Assam. Also Burma.

GENERAL HABITS: A water wagtail, keeping in pairs to swamps and little streams meandering through grassy upland meadows. Otherwise not different from other wagtails.

NESTING: *Season*—June to July/August. *Nest*—a neat cup of grass and roots, thickly lined with wool and hair. Placed at the base of a small bush or in soft lush grass on a waterlogged meadow. *Eggs*—3 to 5, greyish stone or pale khaki, with darker stippling. Size about 21×15 mm.

RACIAL CHARACTERISTICS, MEASUREMENTS, ETC: Dr Stresemann remarks on the possibility that the breeding population of high Sikkim may be diluted in autumn by passage migrants of the E. Siberian nominate race. In winter plumage, this is difficult to differentiate save maybe by its slightly longer wings and tail, and relatively somewhat shorter tarsus. Thus he considers it possible that 3 of Schäfer's mid-October skins may belong to true *citreola*.

Schäfer's Sikkim series measures:

| | Wing | Bill | |
|---|---|---|---|
| 10 ad. ♂♂ | 82-84 (av. 83.3) | 13-15 (av. 13.8) | mm. |
| 4 ad. ♀♀ | 73, 76, 76, 78 | 13-13.5 | mm. |

Iris dark brown; bill, legs, feet and claws black.

## *Family* LANIIDAE: Shrikes

### THE BROWN SHRIKE

**_Lanius cristatus cristatus_ Linnaeus**

*Lanius cristatus* Linnaeus, 1758, Syst. Nat., 10th ed., 1: 93—Bengal.

F.B.I. 2: 300

LOCAL NAME:

SIZE: Bulbul.

FIELD CHARACTERS: Adult: *Above,* reddish brown with white forehead and supercilium. A black line from lores through eyes to ear-coverts. Tail rufous-brown. Wings brownish black, edged rufous; without white 'mirror'. *Below,* chin, throat and cheeks white. Rest pale fulvous, richest on flanks. Sexes alike.

STATUS AND HABITAT: Uncommon. According to Stevens a winter visitor to the hills and valleys of the Sikkim Himalayas at moderate elevations, chiefly on passage to the Indian plains. The Sikkim Survey came across it only once at Rinchinpong, *c.* 5000 ft., in January. Not recorded by Meinertzhagen or Schäfer.

DISTRIBUTION OUTSIDE SIKKIM: *Summer,* throughout Siberia from Lake Baikal to Kamchatka. *Winter,* peninsular India, Ceylon, Burma, Thailand, etc. Together with other races, ranges widely over SE. Asia in winter.

GENERAL HABITS: Typical of the shrikes. Rather crepuscular.

RACIAL CHARACTERISTICS, MEASUREMENTS, ETC: The only Sikkim Survey specimen (♀) measures Wing 88; bill 17; tarsus 25.5; tail 84.5 mm.

Iris brown; upper mandible horny brown, flesh coloured at gape; lower mandible flesh coloured, horny brown at tip; legs, feet and claws dark horny brown.

## THE GREYBACKED SHRIKE

*Lanius tephronotus tephronotus* (Vigors)

*Collurio tephronotus* Vigors, 1831, *Proc. Zool. Soc. London:* 43—Himalayas. Restricted by Stuart Baker, 1924, to Gyantse, Tibet (F.B.I. 2: 297); corrected by Mayr, 1947, to 'Foothills of the Himalayas near Darjeeling where breeding birds of the Gyantse district may be expected in winter'. (*Jour. Bombay Nat. Hist. Soc.* 47: 127.)

**Plate 14, fig. 1** (facing p. 145)

F.B.I. 2: 297

LOCAL NAMES: Sakrik-pho (Lepcha); Totem (Bhutia); Bhadraya or Bagaha-tentha (Nepali).

SIZE: Between Bulbul and Myna.

FIELD CHARACTERS: *Above*, forehead and a broad band through eyes to ear-coverts black. Crown, nape, hindneck and back dark leaden grey. Rump and upper tail-coverts rufous. Tail chestnut-brown. Wings black, rarely with a small white patch or 'mirror'. *Below*, rufous; paler on abdomen. Sexes alike.

STATUS AND HABITAT: A high elevation shrike, breeding at 10,000 to 15,000 ft. in the Tibetan facies of N. Sikkim. Descends lower in winter. Recorded, November to April, at Rangpo, Singtam, Martam, Chungthang, Gangtok, Lachung. Schäfer collected specimens, including juveniles, at Chungthang, Lachen, Thangu—June to September (1938). Blanford found it common at Lachung, 8000-9000 ft., at the beginning of September (1870) but absent three weeks later.

Affects open scrub and secondary growth in and about abandoned hill cultivation clearings.

DISTRIBUTION OUTSIDE SIKKIM: Garhwal through Nepal and Bhutan to SE. Tibet, Yunnan, Szechwan, Koko Nor. The high Himalayas west of Garhwal, and W. Tibet, are occupied by the paler race *lahulensis.*

GENERAL HABITS: Keeps singly or in widely separated pairs, in feeding territories where intrusion by others of its kind is actively resented. Usually excessively wary and difficult to approach. When disturbed, drops from its bushtop, flies with rapid wing beats flat along the ground, and sweeps upward to perch on another vantage point some distance away. Has the typical harsh cries, mimicry, song and behaviour.

NESTING: *Season*—May-June. *Nest*—a deep, untidy, bulky cup of thorny twigs and grass mixed, matted and neatly lined with hair, wool, etc. Placed in a small tree or fair-sized bush. *Eggs*—3 to 6, variable, mostly greenish white spotted with purplish brown, especially at the broad end. Size about 25×19 mm.

RACIAL CHARACTERISTICS, MEASUREMENTS, ETC: The western race *lahulensis* has the rufous in the upper parts more extensive, and the grey paler. A white wing mirror is almost always present.

The Sikkim Survey specimens (1 ♂, 1 o?) measure: Wing 95-101; bill 21-23; tarsus 28-29.5; tail 102-111 mm.

Schäfer's series from N. Sikkim and S. Tibet give:

| | Wing | Bill |
|---|---|---|
| 8 ♂♂ | 97-105 | 105-119 mm. |
| 5 ♀♀ | 98-104 | 110-112 mm. |

Iris brown; bill horny brown or black, paler at base of lower mandible; legs, feet and claws horny black.

## THE BLACKHEADED SHRIKE

### *Lanius schach tricolor* (Hodgson)

*Collurio tricolor* Hodgson, 1837, *Ind. Review* 1: 446—Restricted to Kathmandu, Nepal Valley.

F.B.I. 2: 292

LOCAL NAME: Sakrik-pho (Lepcha).

SIZE: Between Bulbul and Myna, with a relatively longer tail.

FIELD CHARACTERS: General aspect suggestive of a miniature hawk. Typical stout, hook-tipped shrike bill. A small white patch or 'mirror' on blackish wings, particularly conspicuous in flight. *Above*, crown, sides of head, nape and hindneck black. Upper back ashy, changing to light chestnut on rest of upper plumage. Tail black, tipped and margined with rufous. *Below*, cheeks, chin, and throat white shading to pale rufous on breast and to bright rufous on rest of lower plumage, excepting abdomen which is whitish. Sexes alike.

STATUS AND HABITAT: Resident. Not common. Recorded by the Sikkim Survey at elevations between 4000 and 6000 ft. in winter—November to April (Temi, Dentam, Chungthang, Gangtok). Col. Meinertzhagen also found it at Lachung, *c.* 7000 ft., in December. Affects open scrub country in and about terraced cultivation.

DISTRIBUTION OUTSIDE SIKKIM: The Himalayas from Garhwal to eastern Assam; Manipur, Burma, N. Thailand, Yunnan. The species is widely distributed over the Indian, Indochinese and Malaysian subregions.

GENERAL HABITS: Shy and very vigilant. Keeps singly, perched upright on a bushtop maintaining a sharp look-out for crawling prey—grasshoppers, lizards, young mice, etc. Swoops to the ground and carries it off in its bill to the same or another perch nearby, where it is held down underfoot and torn to pieces with the hooked bill before being devoured. Utters harsh grating notes. Has a pretty, rambling song in the breeding season, delivered from a bush in the nature of a soliloquy. Is also a very accomplished mimic of other birds' calls.

NESTING: *Season*—May-June. *Nest*—a large massive cup of feathery grasses, grass stems, thorny twigs, etc. lined with grass, roots and fibres. Placed in shrubs, bamboo clumps or small trees up to about 20 ft. from the ground. *Eggs*—4 to 6, variable, pink to buff or pale green, blotched and spotted with grey-brown, reddish brown or purplish brown, more densely at the broad end. Size about 24×18 mm.

RACIAL CHARACTERISTICS, MEASUREMENTS, ETC: A specimen (♂) collected by the Sikkim Survey measures: Wing 96; bill 21; tarsus 29; tail 118 mm.

Schäfer's Sikkim specimens give:

| | Wing | Tail |
|---|---|---|
| 3 ♂♂ | 95-99 | 117-122 mm. |
| 2 ♀♀ | 92-93 | 114 (1) mm. |

Iris brown; bill black, flesh coloured at base of lower mandible; legs, feet and claws brownish black.

## *Family* ARTAMIDAE: Swallow-Shrikes

### THE ASHY SWALLOW-SHRIKE

*Artamus fuscus* Vieillot

*Artamus fuscus* Vieillot, 1817, Nouv. Dict. d'Hist. Nat., nouv. éd., 17: 297—Bengal.

F.B.I. 2: 348

LOCAL NAME: Silliangchi-pho (Lepcha).

SIZE: Bulbul. Dumpier.

FIELD CHARACTERS: A sleek, dark slaty grey bird with paler (almost whitish) rump and underparts. Tail short, square-ended, slaty black tipped with white. Wings long, pointed, reaching to end of tail when closed. Heavy, somewhat sparrow-like, bluish bill. Sexes alike.

STATUS AND HABITAT: According to Stevens, a summer visitor to the Sikkim Himalayas up to about 5500 ft. elevation—arriving in the Rungbong Valley in late March or early April, and departing in the first week or later in October. Between November and May the Sikkim Survey came across it only once at *c.* 4500 ft. (between Kewzing and Pemionche) on 30 March—a party of about 15 hawking over terraced cultivation.

DISTRIBUTION OUTSIDE SIKKIM: Ceylon, and all India east of a line from Godhra (in Gujarat) to Simla; Assam, Burma, Thailand to Yunnan and W. China.

GENERAL HABITS: Parties perch on bare tree-tops, often huddled together, and launch out in the air singly, in twos and threes, or all together, to hawk winged insects like bee-eaters, returning to the foraging base in a wide circle. *Flight:* rapid wing beats followed by a graceful glide; very swallow-like. While perched, tail constantly moved up and down slowly and screwed from side to side. *Call:* a harsh, shrike-like *chek-chek-chek*. *Food:* winged insects, largely butterflies.

NESTING: Gammie found it breeding in 'Sikkim' at 3500 ft.

*Season*—April-May. *Nest*—a loosely built cup of grass, roots and fibres, on a horizontal bough, or in a depression in the stump of a tall dead tree, 30 to 40 ft. up. *Eggs*—2 or 3, greenish white spotted with light brown chiefly at the broad end. Size about 23×17 mm.

RACIAL CHARACTERISTICS, MEASUREMENTS, ETC: The Fauna gives for ♂♀ Wing 126-138; bill 18-19, tarsus 17-18; tail 53-64 mm.

Iris brown; bill bluish grey, black at tips of both mandibles; legs and feet slaty; claws black.

## *Family* DICRURIDAE: Drongos

### THE HIMALAYAN GREY DRONGO

*Dicrurus leucophaeus hopwoodi* Baker

*Dicrurus leucophaeus hopwoodi* Baker, 1918, *Novit. Zool.* 25: 294—Dacca.

F.B.I. 2: 362 (=*stevensi*)

LOCAL NAMES: Sahim or Sahim-pho (Lepcha); Che-chum (Bhutia).

SIZE: Bulbul+, with a longer tail.

FIELD CHARACTERS: A slim and agile, glossy steel grey bird with a long deeply forked tail. If otherwise in doubt, the ruby-red iris is diagnostic. Sexes alike.

STATUS AND HABITAT: Fairly common. Resident up to *c.* 9000 ft. in summer, with a slight seasonal altitudinal movement (Rangpo, Martam, Singhik, Dentam, Rinchinpong, Kewzing, Gangtok, Lachen). Affects open forest.

DISTRIBUTION OUTSIDE SIKKIM: The eastern Himalayas from Darjeeling (where it intergrades with the W. Himalayan-Indian *longicaudatus*), Bhutan to Assam, Burma, Thailand, etc. The species, in several races, is widespread in the Indochinese and Malaysian subregions.

GENERAL HABITS: Arboreal and insectivorous. Keeps singly or in scattered pairs, perched on bare tree-tops and other points of vantage, on the look-out for insects. Numbers collect where food is plentiful, as for example where there is a hatch of winged termites emerging. Takes prey mostly in the air like a flycatcher; sometimes swoops with great agility and gives determined chase to a locust or moth. Commonly associates with the mixed hunting parties in forest. Rather crepuscular; often hunts till well after sundown. Very fond of flower nectar, and commonly seen at *Erythrina* and crimson *Rhododendron* flowers. Has a variety of harsh challenging notes, as well as some pleasant musical ones. It is also a very good mimic of other birds' calls.

NESTING: *Season*—April to June. *Nest*—a lightly built saucer of grass and weed-stems etc. bound with cobwebs. Cradled in a horizontal fork of a branch or bamboo stem, 10 to 30 feet up. *Eggs*—3 or 4, variable, chiefly whitish spotted with brownish red. Size about 26×18 mm.

RACIAL CHARACTERISTICS, MEASUREMENTS, ETC: 'Paler above and below than *longicaudatus*, tail averages a little shorter and less deeply forked' (Vaurie). A Sikkim Survey specimen (♂) measures: Wing 148; bill 29; tarsus 20; inner tail 104; outer tail 153 mm.

Schäfer's Sikkim skins give Wing/Outer tail 8 ♂♂ 138/154, 140/160, 141/153, 141/155, 141/153, 143/168, 145/160, 145/165; 3 ♀♀ 129/129; 130/129, 132/— mm.

Iris crimson; bill, legs, feet and claws black.

## THE BRONZED DRONGO

### *Dicrurus aeneus aeneus* Vieillot

*Dicrurus aeneus* Vieillot, 1817, Nouv. Dict. d'Hist. Nat., nouv. éd., 9: 586; based on Levaillant, Ois. Afr., pl. 176—Bengal.

F.B.I. 2: 368

LOCAL NAME: Chaptia (Nepali).

SIZE: Bulbul; with longer tail.

FIELD CHARACTERS: A small black drongo, highly glossed all over with bronzy green and blue. Very like the familiar Black Drongo of the Indian plains, but appreciably smaller and with the tail less deeply forked. Bill broad and flattened like a flycatcher's. Sexes alike.

STATUS AND HABITAT: Fairly common. Resident up to at least 6000 ft. (Rangpo, Martam, Dentam, Kewzing, Rinchinpong, Gangtok). Affects evergreen forest.

DISTRIBUTION OUTSIDE SIKKIM: The Himalayas from about Mussooree east through Nepal and Bhutan to E. Assam; Manipur, Burma, Thailand, etc. Patchily in the wetter forests of peninsular India from Khandala (W. Ghats) to Bastar (Madhya Pradesh), Orissa, and Andhra south to Kerala.

GENERAL HABITS: Typical of the drongos as described under the foregoing. Essentially a forest bird, keeping singly to the neighbourhood of trails and similar openings. Partial to flower nectar and commonly seen in attendance on *Erythrina* and *Salmalia* (=*Bombax*) blossoms. Has a large repertoire of loud musical calls, and is an accomplished mimic.

NESTING: *Season*—April-May. *Nest*—like the other drongos', a neat shallow cup of fibres etc. bound with cobwebs. Secured in the fork of a slender horizontal branch 10 to 15 feet from the ground. *Eggs*—3 or 4, whitish pink to salmon pink, with a ring or cap of tiny reddish pink spots at the broad end. Size about 21×16 mm. Both sexes share all the domestic chores.

RACIAL CHARACTERISTICS, MEASUREMENTS, ETC: A Sikkim Survey specimen (ad. ♀) measures: Wing 119; bill 21.5; tarsus 13; tail 89/124 mm. A female in juvenile plumage obtained by Schäfer at Gangtok (20 July) has

Wing 120 mm. The Fauna gives the Wing range of this race (♂♀) as 115-132 (av. *c.* 124) mm.

Iris brown; bill, legs, feet and claws black.

## THE HAIRCRESTED, or SPANGLED, DRONGO

*Dicrurus hottentottus hottentottus* (Linnaeus)

*Corvus hottentottus* Linnaeus, 1766, Syst. Nat., ed. 12, 1: 155—Cape of Good Hope (*errore*). Restricted to Chandernagor by Stresemann, 1952, *Ibis* 94: 517, 521.

F.B.I. 2: 370 (part)

LOCAL NAMES: Povong-pho (Lepcha); Kesya, Jobraj (Nepali).

SIZE: Myna; with longer tail.

FIELD CHARACTERS: A highly metallic green-glossed and spangled black drongo with very slightly forked (almost square-cut) tail, curled upward on its lateral extremities. A flimsy tuft of a few hair-like feathers from forehead lying backward over hindcrown and upper back (visible with binoculars). Bill long, pointed and conspicuously downcurved. Sexes alike.

STATUS AND HABITAT: The commonest drongo at low and medium elevations. Resident up to about 6000 ft. (Rangpo, Martam, Rongli, Dikchu, Kewzing, Rinchinpong, Gangtok). Affects open forest, particularly about terraced cultivation in valleys.

DISTRIBUTION OUTSIDE SIKKIM: The Himalayas from about Murree eastward through Nepal and Bhutan to E. Assam and NW. Yunnan. Peninsular India in the Western Ghats, Madhya Pradesh, Orissa, Chota Nagpur, Andhra, Madras, Mysore, Kerala, East Pakistan. The species, in numerous other races, has a wide range: Burma, Thailand, Malaysia, China, Philippines and across to New Guinea and Australia.

GENERAL HABITS: Typical, but it is pre-eminently a nectar eater. Invariably present, sometimes in numbers, at flowers of *Erythrina*, *Salmalia*, and numerous other species, and plays an important part in their cross-pollination. Besides nectar, it eats large insects. Has the usual loud calls, some harsh, others musical, and it is also an excellent mimic.

On one occasion a close-packed gathering of 20 or more of these drongos was observed mobbing a marten up in the forest canopy, dogging his movements from branch to branch with an agitated, creaky swearing which sounded like shrieks of the Blossomheaded Parakeet. Having put the marten to rout, the birds flew off in a flock like grackles, and later dispersed in ones and twos. Such a large assemblage must have collected from over a very wide area, perhaps 'snowballing' as they went.

NESTING: *Season*—May-June. *Nest*—a largish shallow cup of fibres, grasses and fine twigs loosely cemented together with cobweb. Placed in the end fork of a horizontal branch or on the upper surface of a bough, 15 to 30 ft. up. *Eggs*—3 or 4, pale creamy to salmon colour, covered with longitudinal reddish blotches. Size about 30×22 mm.

RACIAL CHARACTERISTICS, MEASUREMENTS, ETC: Himalayan birds are slightly larger in every measurement than southern populations. Four ♂♂ collected by the Sikkim Survey measure: Wing 163-173; bill 41-43; tarsus 26.5-29; inner tail 118-124; outer tail 131-156 mm.

Stresemann gives for Schäfer's Sikkim skins Wing/Inner tail 3 ♂♂ 162/117, 167/—, 168/125; 1 ♀ 168/129 mm.

Iris brown; bill, legs, feet and claws horny black.

Haircrested, or Spangled, Drongo
About one-fifth

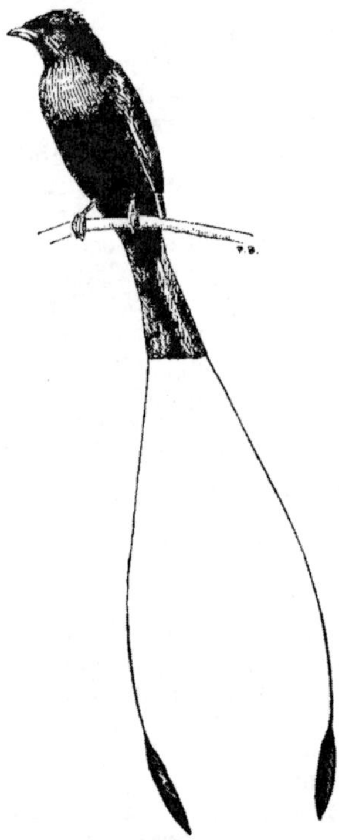

Indian Lesser Racket-tailed Drongo
About one-fifth

## THE INDIAN LESSER RACKET-TAILED DRONGO

*Dicrurus remifer tectirostris* (Hodgson)
*Bhringa tectirostris* Hodgson, 1836, *Ind. Rev.* 1: 325—Nepal.

F.B.I. 2: 375

LOCAL NAMES: Nambong punnong (Lepcha); Poyadi yapo (Bhutia).

SIZE: Myna; with a long tail.

FIELD CHARACTERS: A highly purple-and-green glossed black, uncrested drongo with two wire-like streamers in the tail, ending in broadened paddle-shaped 'rackets'. Lores, cheeks, and a frontal tuft of feathers (from forehead over bill) velvety black. Sexes alike.

STATUS AND HABITAT: Fairly common. The Sikkim Survey as well as Stevens and Schäfer found it only at elevations up to about 3000 ft. between November and May (Rangpo, Singtam, Martam, Dikchu). Gammie, in the 70's, took a nest at Rashap in the Teesta Valley at 4800 ft., which must be about its highest limit in Sikkim. Affects forest in the hot, moist valleys.

DISTRIBUTION OUTSIDE SIKKIM: E. Nepal; Bhutan (?) to E. Assam, north and south of Brahmaputra River; Manipur, Eastern Pakistan, Burma, Thailand, Yunnan. The species extends to the Indochinese and Malaysian subregions.

GENERAL HABITS: Similar to the other forest drongos, with the same range of calls and mimicry. Met with singly, or in twos and threes, commonly as members of the roving bands of mixed insectivorous birds in forest.

NESTING: *Season*—May-June. *Nest*—a broad, shallow cup of roots etc., bound with cobweb and lined with finer roots. Slung hammock-wise in the horizontal fork of a small branch, 15 to 25 ft. up. *Eggs*—3 or 4, pale pink to rich salmon-pink or terracotta, usually with blurred blotches or freckles of brownish red, more dense at the broad end. Size about 26×18 mm. Both sexes take part in all domestic chores.

RACIAL CHARACTERISTICS, MEASUREMENTS, ETC: Specimens collected by the Sikkim Survey measure:

| | Wing | Bill | Tarsus | Inner tail | Racket |
|---|---|---|---|---|---|
| 1 ♂ | 140 | 28.5 | 22 | 130 | — mm. |
| 1 ♀ | 136 | 26 | 21 | 125 | 361 mm. |

Stresemann measures Wing/Racket feather of 3 ad. ♂♂ in Schäfer's Sikkim collection as 143/402, 136/362, 144/407 mm.

Iris brown to brownish crimson; bill, legs, feet and claws black or brownish black.

# *Family* ORIOLIDAE: Orioles

## THE MAROON ORIOLE

*Oriolus traillii traillii* (Vigors)

*Pastor traillii* Vigors, 1832, *Proc. Zool. Soc. London:* 175—Himalayas, Darjeeling.

**Plate 14, fig. 4** (facing p. 145)

F.B.I. 3: 14

LOCAL NAMES: Melambok (Lepcha); Tania-pia (Bhutia).

SIZE: Myna.

FIELD CHARACTERS: *Male:* Glossy crimson-maroon with black head, neck and wings, and chestnut-maroon tail.

*Female* has the lower plumage greyish white, streaked with blackish. Juvenile ♂ coloured like adult ♀.

In overhead flight, against the sky, appears as a dark bird with square cut claret-crimson tail.

STATUS AND HABITAT: Resident. Fairly common in the foothills and up to *c.* 7000 ft. elevation (Singtam, Martam, Rinchinpong, Pemionche, Gangtok, Singhik, Chungthang). Affects dense forest.

DISTRIBUTION OUTSIDE SIKKIM: Throughout the Himalayas from the Sutlej Valley to E. Assam; Manipur, hilly tracts of Burma, Thailand, Annam.

GENERAL HABITS: Keeps to the tree-tops in thick forest, singly or in pairs, often in association with drongos, minivets, nuthatches, etc. *Food:* fruits, berries, flower nectar and insects. *Calls:* a harsh *kee-ah*, usually followed by rich liquid musical whistles like *pi-lo-lo*. Indistinguishable from the calls of the more familiar Golden Oriole (*O. o. kundoo*) of the NW. Himalayas and the plains.

NESTING: *Season*—April-May. *Nest*—a massive deep cup of bast fibres bound with cobwebs, suspended hammock-wise in the horizontal fork of a branch 12 to 30 ft. up, in thick jungle. *Eggs*—2 or 3, pinkish white, spotted with black or reddish brown. Size about 30×20 mm. Both sexes share all the domestic chores.

RACIAL CHARACTERISTICS, MEASUREMENTS, ETC: The Sikkim Survey specimens measure:

| | Wing | Bill | Tarsus | Tail |
|---|---|---|---|---|
| 2 ♂♂ | 141-147 | 31-32 | 24.5-26 | 99-104.5 mm. |
| 1 ♀ | 146 | 33 | 25.5 | 105 mm. |

Four ad. ♂♂ collected by Schäfer have Wing 142, 145, 148, 150 mm.

Iris biscuit colour to creamy white; bill pale bluish grey; legs and feet plumbeous; claws horny brown.

## THE YELLOWBILLED BLUE MAGPIE

*Kitta flavirostris flavirostris* (Blyth)

*Psilorhinus flavirostris* Blyth, 1846, *Jour. Asiat. Soc. Bengal* 15: 28—Darjeeling.

Plate 25, fig. 3 (facing p. 336)

F.B.I. 1: 43

LOCAL NAMES: Tying jongring (Lepcha); Pianging-jabring (Bhutia).

SIZE: Pigeon; with tail 15-17 inches long.

FIELD CHARACTERS: A conspicuous, long-tailed, purplish blue bird with black head, neck and breast, and pale primrose-yellow underparts. Bill yellow; legs bright orange. Sexes alike. Pairs or parties in open forest.

STATUS AND HABITAT: Resident between about 5500 and 11,000 ft. elevation, descending to at least 3000 ft. in winter.

DISTRIBUTION OUTSIDE SIKKIM: From eastern Nepal across to Bhutan and the north Assam and N. Burma hills. Replaced in the W. Himalayas by the paler race *cucullata* with white underparts.

GENERAL HABITS: Affects open oak and rhododendron forest, secondary jungle, fruit orchards and the neighbourhood of terraced cultivation. In pairs or family parties of 5 to 7 birds; occasionally more. Omnivorous and chiefly arboreal. Hunts for caterpillars, etc. in the foliage of trees. Sometimes descends to the ground and hops about with cocked-up tail in search of food—fallen fruits, insects, carrion, etc. Has a large repertoire of loud, harsh grating calls and chattering, reminiscent of the tree pies, as well as a number of not unpleasant whistles. Is a good mimic of other birds' calls, e.g. Serpent Eagle, Shikra.

The parties fly about from one patch of forest to another in follow-my-leader fashion with the long graduated tail spread out and the streamers trailing behind. Flight typical of the pies—a few rapid flaps followed by a glide, sometimes by a curious butterfly-like 'delayed action' of the wings which almost clap over the back.

NESTING: *Season*—May-June. *Nest*—a shallow cup of sticks lined with rootlets etc. 15 to 18 ft. up in a tree. *Eggs*—3 or 4, pale cream coloured, blotched with bright reddish brown with sparse secondary blotches of neutral tint. Size about 33×23 mm. Nests and eggs have rarely been taken in Sikkim.

RACIAL CHARACTERISTICS, MEASUREMENTS, ETC: Differs from its sympatric red-billed congener, *K. erythrorhyncha occipitalis*, in the colour of the bill, and in having the white nuchal patch not reaching to the end of the black hindneck.

In life, and in freshly killed specimens, underparts, tips of all rectrices except central pair, wing margins and lower back strongly suffused with primrose-yellow. This fades in museum skins.

A ♂ collected by the recent Sikkim Survey measures: Wing 195; bill 28.5; tarsus 50.5; tail 410 mm. For 12 Schäfer skins from Sikkim (♂♀) Stresemann gives Wing 175-195; tail 345-420 mm.

The Fauna (1: 43) gives Wing 178-190; tail up to 470 mm. Females slightly smaller than males.

Iris dark brown to yellow; bill orange-yellow; legs and feet yellowish orange, claws horny brown with yellowish tinge.

THE REDBILLED BLUE MAGPIE, *Kitta erythrorhyncha occipitalis* Blyth, of the western Himalayas, extends through Nepal into western Sikkim, but is rare. It occupies lower altitudes than the yellow-billed species. It has not been recorded in central or eastern Sikkim, Bhutan, etc. Further east, in Yunnan, the typical race *erythrorhyncha* occurs.

THE BLACKRUMPED MAGPIE, *Pica pica bottanensis* Delessert.

Stuart Baker (F.B.I. 1: 40) gives the distribution as 'Sikkim, Bhutan and Eastern Tibet to Kansu' and says it breeds in Sikkim between 10,000 and 15,000 ft. Since 1873, when two specimens were collected in 'Sikkim' by Mandelli's collectors, and another in 1874 on the 'Tibetan frontier' (exact localities unstated), there is no record of this magpie from Sikkim. The recent Loke-Sálim Ali expeditions did not come across it, nor did Stevens, Meinertzhagen or Schäfer previously. Meinertzhagen suspects, perhaps rightly, that the old records for Sikkim actually refer to southern Tibet.

In Bhutan, Ludlow (1937) found it rare and confined only to the neighbourhood of Bumthang, *c.* 10,000 ft. (c. 27° 30′×90° 40′), which is some 75 miles east of the eastern frontier of Sikkim.

## THE HIMALAYAN TREE PIE

*Dendrocitta formosae himalayensis* Blyth

*Dendrocitta himalayensis* Blyth, 1865, *Ibis:* 45—Himalayas (=Sikkim).

F.B.I. 1: 52

LOCAL NAMES: Karrio-pho (Lepcha); Karriah-ban (Bhutia).

SIZE: Myna; with a 10″-long tail.

FIELD CHARACTERS: A long-tailed grey and sooty-brown bird with the longest tail feathers (blunt and spatulate) ashy and broadly black-tipped. Black forehead; ashy nape, upper back and upper tail-coverts; a conspicuous white spot in the black wings; and chestnut under tail-coverts are additional distinguishing points. Underparts largely rusty brown and whitish. Sexes alike.

STATUS AND HABITAT: Resident. Common. Foothills and up to 7000 ft. elevation (e.g. Pemionche). Frequents forest and well wooded country in the neighbourhood of terrace cultivation.

DISTRIBUTION OUTSIDE SIKKIM: The race *himalayensis* occurs east of about Almora (Kumaon) across to Assam and the Burmese hills.

GENERAL HABITS: A sociable bird, largely arboreal and omnivorous, often associating with laughing thrushes in hunting parties. *Food:* caterpillars, moths, grasshoppers and other large insects, lizards, eggs and nestling birds, as well as flower-nectar (of *Salmalia, Erythrina,* etc.), fruits and grain. The cob-like seeds encased in a hairy epicarp, known locally as 'kutas', are a favourite food item. Large gatherings are sometimes seen feeding energetically on these trees in fruit, fluttering amongst the foliage, flying off from the tree and back again with much noisy whirring of the wings. In the winter months considerable assemblages occasionally collect in harvested terraced paddy fields, hopping about on the ground with cocked-up tails, picking food. Flight undulating—a few rapid noisy flaps, followed by a glide. When alarmed or agitated, these undulations become curiously syncopated and steeply 'saw-edged' with the bird shooting down rocket-like on closed wings at every dip. It has a variety of loud calls, some raucous and grating, others quite melodious. One commonly heard is *kokila-ka-ka.* A throaty *kr-r-r* is sometimes uttered by a solitary bird from a tree-top, reminiscent of the soliloquy of a jungle crow when at ease.

NESTING: *Season*—May to July. *Nest*—a shallow saucer of twigs, tendrils, roots and leaves, with a slight central depression lined with softer material. Gammie, in Sikkim, found nests from 8 to 20 ft. up in shrubs and bamboos interspersed amid clear cultivated tracts. *Eggs*—normally 3 or 4, pale bluish, or yellowish stone colour, boldly blotched with dark brown or reddish brown with some secondary inky markings. Size about 29×20 mm.

RACIAL CHARACTERISTICS, MEASUREMENTS, ETC: This race differs from the west Himalayan *occidentalis* in being somewhat smaller, and from *sarkari* of the Vaisakhapatnam Ghats in having a larger bill.

Eight adult Sikkim specimens (♂♀) collected by myself and Dr Schäfer have Wing 142-148 mm. (av. about 145).

Iris brownish crimson; bill horny black; legs, feet and claws blackish brown.

## THE BLACKBROWED TREE PIE

*Dendrocitta frontalis* Horsfield

*Dendrocitta frontalis* Horsfield, 1840, *Proc. Zool. Soc. London:* 163—Assam.

**Plate 25, fig. 4 (facing p. 336)**

F.B.I. 1: 54

LOCAL NAMES: Hamshi-bon (Lepcha); Kolio-ko (Bhutia).

SIZE: Myna; with a 10″-long tail.

FIELD CHARACTERS: A pale grey and chestnut tree pie with very white nape, black face, throat and foreneck, and heavy bowed black bill. Readily distinguished from the Himalayan species by the tail being entirely black and the absence of the large white wing-patch. Sexes alike.

STATUS AND HABITAT: Uncertain. Apparently very rare and local. Not met with by the Loke-Sálim Ali expeditions, nor by Stevens, Schäfer or other recent investigators, but recorded from Sikkim at 5000 ft. elevation. Affects dense evergreen jungle and bamboos.

DISTRIBUTION OUTSIDE SIKKIM: Dafla Hills; N. Cachar; E. Assam; Upper Burma. A race described from Tonkin.

GENERAL HABITS: Similar to those of the Himalayan Tree Pie. Keeps in small parties. Has the usual range of discordant and musical, metallic call notes though distinct enough to be recognizable from those of other members of the genus. Said to be less noisy, and shy. *Food:* fruit, seeds, insects. Has been observed to hawk winged termites in the air from tops of bamboos after the manner of drongos.

NESTING: *Season*—May to July. *Nest*—like that of *D. f. himalayensis*, of twigs etc., more compact, lined with fern roots and softer material. Up in bamboo clumps or tall thorny bushes at edge of forest. *Eggs*—3 or 4, like those of the Himalayan species, rather more profusely marked. Size about 25×19 mm.

RACIAL CHARACTERISTICS, MEASUREMENTS, ETC: A smaller bird than the Himalayan Tree Pie with Wing (*vide* Fauna) 120-126 mm.; tail 245-255 mm.

Iris reddish brown; bill, legs, feet and claws black.

# HUME'S GROUND CHOUGH

*Podoces humilis* Hume

*Podoces humilis* Hume, 1871, *Ibis:* 408—Sanju Pass, Yarkand.

F.B.I. 1: 71

LOCAL NAME: Day-day (Tibetan).

SIZE: Between Sparrow and Myna.

FIELD CHARACTERS: A greyish sandy brown bird with brown wings, a whitish collar (broad on hindneck), and a dark streak through the eyes. Square-ended tail largely sandy white with central feathers brown. Slightly curved black bill. Sexes alike.

Colour pattern reminiscent of a miniature Grey Babbler (*Turdoides malcolmi*); general effect of a Wheatear.

STATUS AND HABITAT: So far only recorded from extreme northern and eastern Sikkim—Gyagong, 14,800-15,750 ft. (Meinertzhagen, Schäfer); Thangu, 14,300 ft. (Hingston, Bailey). Affects flat, open Tibetan plateau country, above the tree line, with dwarf rhododendron and furze bushes.

DISTRIBUTION OUTSIDE SIKKIM: Central Asia—Yarkand, S. Tibet, Kansu, Kuku Nor.

GENERAL HABITS: Mainly terrestrial. Keeps singly or in pairs or family parties. Active and sprightly. Rummages amongst shingle, 'pick-axes' energetically with its bill in the earth like a Jungle Babbler for food—ground beetles and other insects—peers under stones and probes into crevices of boulders, etc. Very obliteratingly coloured in its natural biotope. Often invisible when motionless, only the momentary flicker of the whitish tail feathers giving it away. Moves on the ground stiffly erect, in long hops, bouncing like a rubber ball. Mounts a stone every now and again to bob violently a couple of times like a chat. Flicks open tail, and also wings, particularly when bobbing. Ordinary flight shrike-like; when flying to nest-hole, with a rapid vibrating action of the wings. Call reminiscent of the Yelloweyed Babbler (*Chrysomma sinensis*): a plaintive whistling *chip* (slight pause) *cheep-cheep-cheep-cheep* (quickly repeated). Also utters a feeble *cheep* like a munia's but more prolonged.

NESTING: Unrecorded in Sikkim, but specimens collected above Thangu and at Gyagong (16,000-18,000 ft.), now in the Chicago Museum of Natural History, had their gonads in full breeding condition in May and June. Elsewhere, *season*—May to July. *Nest*—a large untidy pad of sheep's wool and hair on a foundation of moss, grass and fibres in a widened chamber at the end of a tunnel some 3 inches in diameter and 4 to 6 ft. long, excavated by the birds in an earth bank. *Eggs*—4 to 6, white, unmarked, with a pinkish translucence when fresh. Average size of a c/6 taken by me in W. Tibet 23.6×16.75 mm.

RACIAL CHARACTERISTICS, MEASUREMENTS, ETC: Sikkim birds, according to Stresemann, agree well with his race *saxicola* (type locality NW. Kansu). For 12 examples collected by Schäfer in N. Sikkim between 18 June and 10 August, he gives Wing 9 ♂♂ 86-95 (av. 89.8); 3 ♀♀ 81-88 (av. 85.3) mm.

Six specimens from N. Sikkim in the Chicago Museum of Natural History measure:

| | Wing | Bill | Tarsus | Tail |
|---|---|---|---|---|
| 3 ♂♂ | 88-90 | 21.5-23 | 28-30 | 58-60 mm. |
| 3 ♀♀ | 85-92 | 21-24 | 26.5-28 | 51.5-56 mm. |

A breeding ♀ collected by me in W. Tibet measured (in the flesh) Wing 94; bill 24; tarsus 34; tail 64 mm.

Iris brown; bill, legs, feet and claws brownish black.

## THE EAST HIMALAYAN NUTCRACKER

*Nucifraga caryocatactes macella* Thayer & Bangs

*Nucifraga hemispila macella* Thayer & Bangs, 1909, *Bull. Mus. Comp. Zool.* 52: 150—Hsien-shan-hsien, Hupeh, China, 7000 ft.

East Himalayan Nutcracker
About one-third

F.B.I. 1: 66

LOCAL NAMES: Lho-kariyo-pho (Lepcha); Lek-bhali (Paharia).

SIZE: House Crow.

FIELD CHARACTERS: A chocolate and umber brown bird, streaked and spotted with white above and below, with a stout, wedge-shaped, woodpecker-like bill. Wings black. Tail largely, under tail-coverts wholly, white. In flight the last two are conspicuous features. Sexes alike.

STATUS AND HABITAT: Resident between 9000 and 10,000 ft. elevation; recorded from 13,000 ft. (Thangu). Affects tall rhododendron, fir, spruce and deodar forest where interspersed with open glades and alpine meadows.

DISTRIBUTION OUTSIDE SIKKIM: Central Nepal east; Bhutan, SE. Tibet, Dafla and Mishmi hills (Assam), Yunnan in the zone of spruce and pines.

GENERAL HABITS: Usually seen singly or in widely separated pairs—sometimes family parties of 5 or 6—moving among lofty tree-tops or winging its way across a valley. Perches restlessly on the tip of a tall deodar or similar tree and constantly flicks open the white outer tail feathers. A noisy bird, invariably advertising its presence by loud guttural calls *kraak* or *kraak-kraak-kraak*, sometimes prefaced by a nasal bleat, as of a goat kid. Flight straight, direct and crow-like by slow deliberate flaps of the rounded wings. Sometimes the wings have a curious hesitating or 'delayed action' effect recalling the jays and Blue Magpies. When alarmed or suspicious, the birds become fussy and noisy, flying about from tree to tree, peering down at the intruder and uttering their grating calls. The food consists almost entirely of spruce and pine seeds and the bird's distribution is closely linked with the occurrence of these trees. Occasionally insects are also eaten.

NESTING: An early breeder. Our nearest record is only from the north of the Chumbi Valley. *Season*—March to May. *Nest*—a compact platform of twigs with some lichen intermingled, lined with dry grass, moss, etc., 20 to 50 ft. up in a deodar or similar tree. *Eggs*—4, pale bluish white speckled and blotched with dull brown and inky brown, somewhat more densely at the broad end. Size about 35×26 mm. Both sexes incubate.

RACIAL CHARACTERISTICS, MEASUREMENTS, ETC: Differs from the larger-spotted W. Pakistan Himalayas race, *N. c. multipunctata*, in having the rump and upper tail-coverts chocolate brown, *not* marked with white. In *N. c. hemispila* of the Indian west Himalayas the bill is less heavy than in *macella* (usually under 13 mm. wide). The white spots on breast and back are larger, and the plumage less dark than in Sikkim birds.

Specimens collected by Dr Biswas at Lamteng and Lachen measure: 2 ♂o? Wing 208, 210; bill —, 47.5; tarsus 41, 42.5; tail 139, — mm.

Nineteen Schäfer skins from Sikkim examined by Stresemann have Wing ♂♀ 202, 210-227 (av. 215.8) mm.

Iris rich brown; bill and mouth black; legs and feet black.

## THE HIMALAYAN YELLOWBILLED, or ALPINE, CHOUGH

*Pyrrhocorax graculus digitatus* Hemprich & Ehrenberg

*Pyrrhocorax alpinus* var. *digitatus* Hemprich & Ehrenberg, 1833, Symb. Phys. fol. 2—Syria.

F.B.I. 1: 70

LOCAL NAME:

SIZE: Slightly smaller than the Redbilled Chough (next).

FIELD CHARACTERS: Differs from the Redbilled Chough chiefly in its bill which is yellow, shorter and not curved. Sexes alike.

STATUS AND HABITAT: Less common than the Redbilled Chough and normally resident at higher altitudes. Not extending trans-Himalaya into the dry mountainous Tibetan country, or very rarely. Observed flying at 28,000 ft. on Mt Everest by Sir Edmund Hillary and Dr Charles Evans (1953).

DISTRIBUTION OUTSIDE SIKKIM: Throughout the Himalayan Range at high altitudes, often coincident with the Redbilled Chough. The nominate race occurs in C. and W. Asia and S. Europe.

GENERAL HABITS: Very similar to the next species, with which it sometimes associates, but is perhaps bolder and more omnivorous. Enters mountaineers' and traders' camps for kitchen scraps and refuse; has also been recorded eating carrion. Juniper berries and hips and haws of the wild rose are favourite food items. The voice too is somewhat different. The call *quee-ah* or *cree-ah* and *chak-chak* is harsher and shriller.

NESTING: Unrecorded in Sikkim. Differs little from the Redbilled Chough, except that the nests are perhaps more inaccessible. It is doubtful also if they are ever built in houses (monasteries etc.). The eggs of the two choughs are indistinguishable, but in this species they average slightly smaller: about 39×29 mm.

RACIAL CHARACTERISTICS, MEASUREMENTS, ETC: The Himalayan race *digitatus* is larger than the typical European *graculus*. Ticehurst (*Jour. Bombay Nat. Hist. Soc.* 31: 491, 1926) measures: ♂♂ Wing 275-298, bill 35-38 mm.; ♀♀ Wing 262-266, bill 34-35 mm.

Iris dark brown; bill yellow; mouth livid greenish yellow, bluish slate posteriorly; legs and feet dull coral red.

## THE HIMALAYAN REDBILLED CHOUGH

*Pyrrhocorax pyrrhocorax himalayanus* (Gould)

*Fregilus himalayanus* Gould, 1862, *Proc. Zool. Soc. London:* 125—Kumaon.

F.B.I. 1: 68

LOCAL NAME: Chumboo (Lepcha).

SIZE: Jungle Crow; slenderer.

FIELD CHARACTERS: A glossy jet black crow with bright red legs and bill, the latter slender and slightly curved. Sexes alike.

STATUS AND HABITAT: Resident. In summer to about 18,000 ft. elevation; in winter down to at least 9000 ft. (Lachen, Lachung). Affects cliffs, open steep rocky hillsides and alpine pastures.

DISTRIBUTION OUTSIDE SIKKIM: Practically throughout the Himalayan Range at high altitudes. Other races in N. Asia, Europe, N. Africa.

GENERAL HABITS: Keeps in flocks of 20 or 30, and even up to a hundred birds, in the neighbourhood of crags, steep rocky slopes, alpine pastures and uplands cultivation. Quite tame near villages, grubbing in fields. *Food:* principally wire-worms, grubs of beetles, crickets, etc. dug up by probing in the soil as the birds saunter about.

Occasionally damages newly sown and ripened crop of barley by beating out the grain from the ears by blows of the beak.

Choughs have the characteristic habit of disporting themselves high up in the air or around steep crags and precipices, rising on the thermal currents or eddies and circling gracefully in a close-packed rabble on motionless wings for long periods. The sailing is punctuated by a variety of spectacular aerobatics, the birds tumbling in the air, side-slipping and nose-diving, obviously in pure fun. They utter a shrill, rather musical plaintive *chiaow, chiaow* which I have noted as something between the cawing of a jackdaw and the screeching call of the large parakeet.

NESTING: No specific record for Sikkim. In the nearby Chumbi Valley, *season*—March to May. *Nest*—a pad of sticks lined with wool, placed in a hole or fissure, usually in an inaccessible cliff, either singly or in a small colony. Occasionally in houses and monasteries etc. *Eggs*—3 or 4, pale greenish white, or bluish- or pinkish white, blotched with light reddish brown or umber to dark brown. There are fainter lavender or inky grey markings scattered thickly over the entire surface. Size about 42×29 mm.

RACIAL CHARACTERISTICS, MEASUREMENTS, ETC: The Himalayan race is larger than the typical race of Europe in which the Wing in males seldom exceeds 300 mm.

Two ♂♂ collected in Sikkim by Col. R. Meinertzhagen (*Ibis*, 1927, p. 372) have Wing 330-332; 1 ♀ 309 mm.

Iris dark brown; bill coral red; mouth orange-salmon; legs and feet darker coral red.

## THE HOUSE CROW

*Corvus splendens splendens* Vieillot

*Corvus splendens* Vieillot, 1817, Nouv. Dict. d'Hist. Nat. 8: 44—Bengal.

F.B.I. 1: 33

LOCAL NAME: Kag or kak (Bengali).

SIZE: Slightly larger than the Pigeon (17").

FIELD CHARACTERS: Smaller than the Jungle Crow (next), and distinguished by its dusky grey neck. Sexes alike.

STATUS AND HABITAT: Resident and local vagrant. Sparse and local in Gangtok town and as yet only in a few of the larger villages on the countryside at lower elevations, e.g. Gezing, Kewzing (W. Sikkim); Pakyong, Arita (E. Sikkim). Gangtok, *c.* 5800 ft., is the highest altitude at which we recorded an established population of House Crows in Sikkim, but in May 1943 F. N. Betts observed a vagrant pair in Lachung village as high as *c.* 8900 ft.

GENERAL HABITS: Omnivorous, and as elsewhere, a scavenger and commensal of man in urban areas.

NESTING: Season and other details lacking for Sikkim; elsewhere chiefly April to July. *Nest* and *eggs*—Similar to the Jungle Crow's; the eggs slightly smaller, averaging about 37×27 mm.

RACIAL CHARACTERISTICS, MEASUREMENTS, ETC: In Sikkim birds (*splendens*) the grey parts of the plumage contrast more strongly with the black parts than in the Ceylon race *protegatus*. In birds inhabiting the drier areas of NW. India (*zugmayeri*) the grey parts are markedly paler—almost whitish. Schäfer's specimens from Gangtok measure: Wing 1 '♀' ad. 273, 1 o? imm. 255 mm.

## THE JUNGLE CROW

(a) *Corvus macrorhynchus intermedius* Adams
(b) *Corvus macrorhynchus levaillanti* Lesson (? or *macrorhynchus*)

F.B.I. 1: 28

LOCAL NAMES: Ulakpho (Lepcha); Ulak (Bhutia); Kak (Paharia).

SIZE: Larger than the House Crow.

FIELD CHARACTERS: An all-black crow with purplish sheen and heavy bill, and with a hoarser deeper caw than the House Crow's. Sexes alike.

STATUS AND HABITAT: The common crow of Sikkim as a whole. In a large series collected by Schäfer, Stresemann found that birds from Gangtok, *c.* 6000 ft. elevation, belonged to the lower level race *levaillanti* (? or *macrorhynchus*), while birds from Lachen (*c.* 9000 ft.) and upwards to 14,000 ft. in 'Tibetan plateau' country were of the high elevation form *intermedius*.

DISTRIBUTION OUTSIDE SIKKIM: *levaillanti* (? or *macrorhynchus*): Bengal, Assam. *intermedius:* the Himalayas from Afghanistan to Bhutan, above about 8000 ft.

GENERAL HABITS: More sophisticated than the Raven. A scavenger in and about Gangtok, and round villages and gompas on the countryside. In ones and twos, and small parties. As elsewhere, destructive to the eggs and young of other birds. In the high mountains fond of spiralling aloft on thermal currents for sport, like Chough. *Call:* a deep caw; in *intermedius* noticeably different from that of low level birds—often bell-like and reminiscent of the Raven's. Also has a variety of croaks and gurgles expressive of various emotions, uttered during intervals of rest.

NESTING: *Season*—late February to May. *Nest*—an untidy twig-platform lined with soft roots, fibres, etc., 20 to 60 ft. up in a tree, preferably near a hamlet. *Eggs*—4 to 6, pale blue-green, spotted and blotched with brown. Size about 45×32 mm.

RACIAL CHARACTERISTICS, MEASUREMENTS, ETC: *intermedius* is a large bird with a comparatively weak bill. Plumage comparatively dull greyish black with little gloss on the hindneck and lower parts. Grey bases of the nape feathers usually whiter than in other Indian races. Stresemann gives Wing of 12 Schäfer birds from N. Sikkim (11 ♂♂, 1 ♀) as 328-368 (av. 345.6) mm.

Three specimens of *levaillanti* from Gangtok measured: Wing 1 ♀ ad. 292; 2 juv. o? 306+, 314+ mm. In addition to its smaller size, *levaillanti* is distinguished from *intermedius* by the bases of the nape feathers being a darker grey.

## THE TIBET RAVEN

*Corvus corax tibetanus* Hodgson

*Corvus tibetanus* Hodgson, 1849, *Ann. Mag. Nat. Hist.* 3 (2): 203—Tibet.

F.B.I. 1: 23

LOCAL NAME: Neka-wak (Tibetan).

SIZE: Kite.

FIELD CHARACTERS: A large heavy edition of the familiar all-black Jungle Crow, with a hoarse wooden bell-like call. Sexes alike. Singly or in pairs at high elevations on barren mountainsides with cliffs etc.

STATUS AND HABITAT: Resident, normally between 13,000 and 16,000 ft. above the tree-line in typical 'Tibetan Plateau' country in N. Sikkim. Normally a trans-Himalayan species, but in winter sometimes occurs south of the main axis (Lachen 9000 ft.). Often seen scavenging around nomadic encampments and along the trade routes to Tibet.

DISTRIBUTION OUTSIDE SIKKIM: Throughout the Himalayas from Kashmir eastward to and including Bhutan and N. Assam. Tibet.

GENERAL HABITS: Omnivorous, but living largely on carrion and the young of birds and mammals. Much given to soaring aloft in circles on thermal currents like Choughs. Indulges in spectacular aerobatics around cliffs, obviously in play. *Call:* a hoarse wooden bell-like *pruk-pruk*, and a guttural *kreeuk*.

NESTING: Not recorded in Sikkim. *Season* elsewhere—February-March. *Nest*—a rough platform of sticks lined with wool or hair, on a ledge or hole in a precipitous cliff. *Eggs*—3 to 5, pale lavender to inky or greenish grey, profusely marked with brown. Size about 52×35 mm.

RACIAL CHARACTERISTICS, MEASUREMENTS, ETC: The largest of the three races found within our limits. Wing normally between 490 and 510 mm., bill 80-85 mm. (F.B.I.)

## *Family* STURNIDAE:

### *Subfamily* STURNINAE: Starlings, Mynas

### THE SPOTTEDWINGED STARE

*Saroglossa spiloptera* (Vigors)
*Lamprotornis spilopterus* Vigors 1831, *Proc. Zool. Soc. London:* 35—Himalayas.

**Plate 14, fig. 5** (facing p. 145)

F.B.I. 3: 25
LOCAL NAME:
SIZE: Bulbul.
FIELD CHARACTERS: A dainty, spruce little myna. *Male: Above,* brownish grey, scalloped with black. *Below,* rusty white with the chin and throat deep chestnut-rufous. A prominent white patch in the wings, as in the Blueheaded Rock Thrush.

*Female: Above,* sooty brown; sides of head dark brown. *Below,* pale fulvous ashy brown scalloped with white, especially on chin and throat. White wing-patch as in male.

Pointed blackish wings with the conspicuous white patch, and typical starling flight in flocks, diagnostic.

STATUS AND HABITAT: ? Resident. Recorded by Stevens up to 3800 ft. elevation in the Sikkim Himalayas (Teesta Valley). Not met with by the Survey, nor by other recent investigators. Affects open forest.

DISTRIBUTION OUTSIDE SIKKIM: Throughout the Himalayas from the Kangra Valley to E. Assam.

GENERAL HABITS: Strongly reminiscent of the Greyheaded Myna (*Sturnus malabaricus*) of the plains and Himalayan foothills: arboreal, gregarious, frugivorous. Also eats insects and is particularly fond of flower nectar. On a flowering *Bombax* tree it often plays dog-in-the-manger in the blustering, bullying manner of the Rosy Pastor, attacking and driving away other bird visitors from the flowers although satiated itself. From time to time, for no apparent reason, a flock will suddenly dive from a leafless flowering *Bombax* and indulge in lightning twists and gyrations in the air as if to dodge some invisible devil in pursuit! After wheeling round the tree at top speed a couple of times, the birds re-settle in the branches and resume feeding. In the breeding season the male utters a twittering warble.

NESTING: Not recorded in Sikkim. In the W. Himalayas *season*—April to June. *Nest*—a pad of leaves and rubbish in a natural tree hollow or old barbet's hole, 20-30 ft. up. *Eggs*—3 or 4, pale stone colour or pale blue with small reddish brown specks and blotches. Size about 26×18 mm.

RACIAL CHARACTERISTICS, MEASUREMENTS, ETC: The Fauna gives for ♂♀ Wing 101-110; bill 17-18; tarsus 21-22; tail 53-59 mm.

Iris lemon yellow to white; bill black, horny red at base, yellowish at gape; legs, feet and claws black.

## THE COMMON MYNA

*Acridotheres tristis tristis* (Linnaeus)

*Paradisea tristis* Linnaeus, 1766, Syst. Nat., 12th ed. 1: 167—Calcutta.

F.B.I. 3: 53

LOCAL NAME:

SIZE: Between Bulbul and Pigeon (= *c.* 9 inches).

FIELD CHARACTERS: A familiar, perky, dark vinous brown bird with glossy black head, neck and breast, and white vent and lower abdomen. Tail broadly white-tipped. A large white patch in the wings conspicuous in flight. Bright yellow legs, bill, and bare skin round the eyes. Sexes alike.

STATUS AND HABITAT: Common, and even locally abundant, in and about villages along the motor road from Rangpo to Gangtok. Also in eastern and western Sikkim. 7500 ft. is the highest elevation at which it was observed between November and May. Resident in Gangtok town with perhaps a slight general downward movement in winter. The process of penetrating into the interior and to higher elevations continues, and every new habitation of any size attracts prospecting pioneers, who under favourable conditions establish themselves in commensalism with the human population.

DISTRIBUTION OUTSIDE SIKKIM: Overall, from Afghanistan and Turkestan in the west to Indochina in the east, and steadily expanding. All India, locally up to *c.* 9000 ft. in the Himalayas. The darker race *melanosternus* in Ceylon.

GENERAL HABITS: Tame; confiding; omnivorous. Pairs or family parties, usually in the neighbourhood of villages and cultivation. Has a variety of loud shrieks and chatter, a scolding *rádio, rádio, rádio* being one of the commoner calls. Also has a characteristic, rather pleasant 'song'—*keek-keek-keek, kok-kok-kok, churr-churr*, etc. delivered with the plumage frowzled and a ludicrous bobbing of the head.

NESTING: *Season*—May to ? August. *Nest*—a collection of twigs, roots, paper and rubbish in a hole in a tree, or in the wall or ceiling of an occupied house, even amidst a noisy bazaar (e.g. in Gangtok). *Eggs*—4 or 5, glossy turquoise-blue. Size about 31×22 mm. Both sexes share all the domestic chores.

RACIAL CHARACTERISTICS, MEASUREMENTS, ETC: Specimens collected by Schäfer at Gangtok have Wing 5 ♂♂ 140-147; 1 ♀ 136 mm.

Iris brown or greyish brown stippled with white; orbital skin bright yellow; bill yellow with sides of base of lower mandible brownish green; legs, feet and claws yellow like bill, paler than orbital skin.

## THE NORTH INDIAN GRACKLE

*Gracula religiosa intermedia* A. Hay

*Gracula intermedia* A. Hay, 1844, *Madras Jour. Lit. Sci.* 13 (2): 157—Cachar.

North Indian Grackle, about one-fourth

F.B.I. 3: 19

LOCAL NAME:

SIZE: Between Myna and Pigeon.

FIELD CHARACTERS: A large jet black myna, highly glossed with purple and green, with a white patch on the wings particularly conspicuous in flight. Bill and legs yellow. Naked patches and wattles on nape and sides of head bright orange-yellow. Sexes alike.

STATUS AND HABITAT: Presumably resident. Confined to low elevations. The Sikkim Survey came across it only at Rangpo (*c.* 1000 ft.) where a flock of 25-30 birds was observed in three different years between November and March (1951, 1953, 1955). The only recent specimen collected in Sikkim (by Schäfer) also comes from the same locality (23.ii.1939). Affects forest.

DISTRIBUTION OUTSIDE SIKKIM: The Himalayan foothills from Almora to Assam. Other races are found in the Orissa area, SW. India and Ceylon. The species extends through Burma and Thailand to Indochina and Malaysia.

GENERAL HABITS: Arboreal, gregarious, and frugivorous. Also eats flower nectar and insects. Extremely noisy, especially in the mornings and evenings. Has a wide range of loud creaky shrieks, whistles and chuckles. *Flight:* swift and direct; accompanied by a

1. Green Magpie (*Kitta c. chinensis*) 2. Sikkim Redcrowned Jay (*Garrulus g. interstinctus*) 3. Yellow-billed Blue Magpie (*Kitta f. flavirostris*) 4. Blackbrowed Tree Pie (*Dendrocitta frontalis*) 5. Great Parrot-bill (*Conostoma aemodium*)

PLATE 25 [*c.* $\times \frac{1}{3}$]

Ibisbill (*Ibidorhyncha struthersii*) on nest.

PLATE 26

whirring sound of wings as in green pigeons. This race enjoys the reputation of being a much better talker in captivity than the smaller birds from SW. India. Whether there is any justification for this belief is not known, but it certainly commands an inordinately higher price from bird fanciers.

NESTING: Not recorded in Sikkim. *Nest*—a collection of grass, leaves, feathers and rubbish in a natural hollow or enlarged woodpecker-hole in the trunk of a lofty tree, 30 or 40 ft. up. *Eggs*—2 or 3, bright blue, sparsely blotched and spotted with reddish brown or chocolate. Size about 36 × 26 mm.

RACIAL CHARACTERISTICS, MEASUREMENTS, ETC: Whistler gives the measurements of *intermedia*, the largest of the Indian races, as: (♂♂) Wing 169-176.5; bill 30.5-33; tail 78-84 mm. Schäfer's Sikkim specimen (ad. ♂) has Wing 169 mm.

Iris brown; bill orange-red, coral red at tip and on culmen; wattles and naked skin at nape yellow to orange-yellow; infra-orbital patch livid bluish; legs and feet yellow; claws brownish.

## *Family* PARIDAE: Tits

### *Subfamily* PARINAE: True Tits

### THE GREENBACKED TIT

*Parus monticolus monticolus* Vigors

*Parus monticolus* Vigors, 1831, *Proc. Zool. Soc. London:* 22—Himalayas (Simla).

F.B.I. 1: 80

LOCAL NAME: Sarak-chak-pho (Lepcha).

SIZE: Sparrow.

FIELD CHARACTERS: An uncrested, greenish yellow and black tit with prominent white cheeks, and whitish patch on nape. Head, breast, and broad black band down centre of abdomen glossy black. Rest of underparts bright yellow. Sexes alike.

STATUS AND HABITAT: Common. Resident between 1500 and 9000 ft. elevation, with slight up and down seasonal movement. Affects open wooded country, orchards and cultivation.

DISTRIBUTION OUTSIDE SIKKIM: Throughout the Himalayas, west to east. Assam hills, N. Burma, Manipur, Yunnan.

GENERAL HABITS: Chiefly arboreal. Sociable, restless and sprightly. Tame and confiding near human habitations. Pairs or family parties; frequently in the mixed hunting flocks of various insectivorous species. Hunts energetically for insects and their eggs and caterpillars amongst the foliage of trees, clinging to sprigs sideways or upside down in the search. Also eats fruits and berries. The loud, clear, joyous whistling song of the male is heard in the breeding season: *whitee, whitee, whitee* . . . repeated 4 to 6 times.

NESTING: *Season*—mainly April to June. *Nest*—a pad of fur, wool, moss and feathers in holes in tree-stumps, stone walls, ceilings of bungalows and outhouses, etc., at moderate heights. *Eggs*—5 to 8, white or pinkish white, spotted and speckled with reddish brown. Size about 17×13 mm.

RACIAL CHARACTERISTICS, MEASUREMENTS, ETC: Sikkim birds were separated by Meinertzhagen as his race *lepcharum* on the basis of darker coloration above and below. The difference is so slight and inconsistent that it does not seem worthwhile recognizing them as different from the typical race of the W. Himalayas.

Four specimens collected by the Loke-Sálim Ali Survey measure: ♂♀ 64-69; bill 10.5-11; tarsus 18-19; tail 49-55 mm.

Twenty-four skins in Schäfer's Sikkim collection have Wing 61(♀) to 68(♂).

Iris brown; bill black; legs and feet plumbeous; claws horny brown.

## THE HIMALAYAN COLE-TIT

*Parus ater aemodius* Hodgson

*Parus aemodius* Hodgson, 1844, *in* Blyth, *Jour. Asiat. Soc. Bengal* 13: 943—Nepal.

**Plate 24, fig. 6** (facing p. 289)

F.B.I. 1: 84

LOCAL NAME:

SIZE: Sparrow—.

FIELD CHARACTERS: A small crested tit, bluish grey above, ferruginous (=pale rusty red) below. Head, throat and crest black. Cheeks and a patch on nape white. Two white bars on wing. Sexes alike.

STATUS AND HABITAT: Resident at high elevations, between about 9000 and 12,500 ft. (Lachung, Lachen, Thangu, Gnatong, etc.) even in winter. Not rare where occurring. Partial to conifer forests.

DISTRIBUTION OUTSIDE SIKKIM: Nepal, Bhutan, N. Burma. Other races are found in Yunnan, Szechwan, Kansu; Europe, NW. Africa and N. Asia.

GENERAL HABITS: Parties, sometimes of 50 or more in winter, usually met with in association with tree creepers, goldcrests, etc. hunting up among the spruce and deodars even when shrouded in snow. The birds keep up a thin cheeping *tsi, tsi* as they search the foliage for insect prey in the energetic and acrobatic manner typical of the family.

NESTING: Unrecorded in Sikkim. Very little is known concerning the Himalayan race. Stuart Baker records a nest 'with some eggs' —a pad of rats' fur in a hole in an oak tree between 10,000 and 11,000 ft. elevation—on 13 June. The locality is not mentioned.

The eggs are described as similar to those of European birds, white, stippled with light reddish brown.

RACIAL CHARACTERISTICS, MEASUREMENTS, ETC: The Crested Black Tit (*Parus melanolophus*), common in the W. Himalayas, which also has a double row of white spots on the wing, is differentiated by its somewhat larger size, and by the colour of the abdomen which is iron grey, not ferruginous.

Six specimens collected by the Loke-Sálim Ali Sikkim Survey measure:

| | Wing | Bill | Tarsus | Tail |
|---|---|---|---|---|
| 4 ♂♂ | 59-62 | 8.5-9.5 | 16-18 | 40-41 mm. |
| 2 ♀♀ | 58-61 | 8.5-9.5 | 16.5-17 | 40-42 mm. |

Iris brown; bill black; legs and feet plumbeous blue; claws horny brown.

## THE SIKKIM BLACK TIT

*Parus rubidiventris beavani* (Jerdon)

*Lophophanes beavani* 'Blyth'=Jerdon, 1863, Birds of India 2: 275—Mount Tonglo, Sikkim.

Sikkim Black Tit, about one-half

F.B.I. 1: 86

LOCAL NAME: Liho Tasso (Lepcha).

SIZE: Sparrow.

FIELD CHARACTERS: A black-crested tit, blue grey above, greenish grey below, with rusty buffish cheeks. Remainder of head and upper breast black. A white spot on nape. Under tail-coverts chestnut. Sexes alike.

STATUS AND HABITAT: A bird of high elevations, 9000-14,000 ft. (Lachung, Yumthang, Changu, Thangu, Gnatong, etc.) in pine forest. Even found above the tree limit in dwarf rhododendron scrub. Its seasonal altitudinal movement seems to be insignificant.

DISTRIBUTION OUTSIDE SIKKIM: E. Nepal, Bhutan, S. Tibet, N. Burma, W. China.

GENERAL HABITS: Typical of the tits. The song, commonly heard in the high pine and juniper forests in summer, is a cheerful musical double whistle *whiwhee, whiwhee, whiwhee, whiwhee* (usually repeated four times). Insects and their eggs and larvae form the staple diet, but berries are also eaten. Kernels are extracted from their hard shells by persistent hammer blows of the bill while they are held down under foot.

NESTING: The only Sikkim record is from 'above Gangtok' at about 10,000 ft. elevation in 'open forest of stunted oak and other trees'—19 May. The nest was 'a pad of moss and fur placed in a hole at the roots of a tree on a mossy sloping bank'. It contained 2 eggs, pure white blotched with reddish, measuring 18.8×14.0 and 18.5×13.8 mm. (Nidification 1:68).

RACIAL CHARACTERISTICS, MEASUREMENTS, ETC: Differs from the W. Himalayan race *rufonuchalis* in having the nuchal spot pure white (unmixed with rusty), and in the black of the breast not extending to the abdomen. From the Crested Black Tit (*P. melanolophus*) of the W. Himalayas it differs in being slightly larger and darker coloured, and in the absence of the two rows of whitish spots which show up as wing-bars.

Three ♂♂ collected by the Sikkim Survey measure: Wing 69-75; bill 10-10.5; tarsus 20-21; tail 47.5-51 mm.

For 12 adults collected by Schäfer in Sikkim, Stresemann gives Wing 67(♀)-73(♂) mm.

Iris brown; bill black; legs and feet brownish plumbeous; claws horny brown.

## THE BROWN CRESTED TIT

*Parus dichrous dichrous* Hodgson

*Parus dichrous* Hodgson, 1844, *in* Blyth, *Jour. Asiat. Soc. Bengal* 13: 943—Nepal.

**Plate 24, fig. 7** (facing p. 289)

F.B.I. 1: 87

LOCAL NAME:

SIZE: Sparrow.

FIELD CHARACTERS: Greyish brown above with an erect pointed crest; tawny below. A conspicuous buff-coloured interrupted collar on hindneck looping forward under the cheeks to base of bill—like the head straps in a horse's bridle. Sexes alike. Rather similar in general effect to the Yellownaped Ixulus (p. 202).

STATUS AND HABITAT: A high elevation tit, fairly common between 9000 and 13,000 ft. (Lachen, Thangu, Changu, etc.) but not abundant. Affects oak, rhododendron and juniper forest.

DISTRIBUTION OUTSIDE SIKKIM: Nepal, Bhutan, S. Tibet (Himalayan facies), N. Burma. A paler race, *kangrae*, occurs in the W. Himalayas from S. Kashmir to Garhwal. Other races in W. China.

GENERAL HABITS: Often found in company with the Cole and Black Tits, tree creepers and other small birds; usually not more than a pair or so in every hunting party. Keeps to low or moderate heights in trees. In winter feeds a good deal on the ground, often in snow, amongst dwarf rhododendron scrub. Otherwise a typical tit in all its habits and behaviour. I have not heard its call, neither has it been recorded.

NESTING: No specific record for Sikkim. In W. Himalayas the *season* is April, May, and possibly June. *Nest*—a pad of moss lined with fur or hair and a few feathers, in a hole in the trunk or derelict stump of a tree, fairly low down. *Eggs*—4 or 5, pure white, spotted with reddish, more densely at the broad end. Size about 17×13 mm.

RACIAL CHARACTERISTICS, MEASUREMENTS, ETC: The west Himalayan race *kangrae* (Whistler) is altogether paler.

A Sikkim Survey specimen (♂) measures: Wing 71; bill 10; tarsus 20; tail 48 mm.

For 6 adult Sikkim examples in the Schäfer collection, Stresemann gives Wing 68(♀)-73(♂) mm.

Iris orange-brown; bill black; legs and feet plumbeous; claws horny brown.

## THE BLACKSPOTTED YELLOW TIT

### *Parus xanthogenys spilonotus* Bonaparte

*Parus spilonotus* Bonaparte, 1850, Consp. Gen. Av. 1: 228, new name for *Parus xanthogenys* Blyth, 1847, *Jour. Asiat. Soc. Bengal* 16: 444—Himalaya (*nec P. xanthogenys* Vigors, 1831). Restricted by Stuart Baker (F.B.I. i: 89) to N. Cachar, 1922.

F.B.I. 1: 89

LOCAL NAME: Muchetink-pho (Lepcha).

SIZE: Sparrow.

FIELD CHARACTERS: A handsome, erect-crested yellow and black tit, with bright yellow forehead, supercilium, sides of head and neck, and underparts. Rest of head and throat, and a broad band down centre of underparts to the vent, black. Back and scapulars yellow, each feather laterally margined with black, producing a black-spotted overall effect. Prominent white spots on black upper wing-coverts. Sexes alike.

STATUS AND HABITAT: Resident at medium elevations from 4000 to 8000 ft. (Gangtok); Meinertzhagen collected it at 12,000 ft. (Changu) in December. Local and sparse. Inhabits wooded country—forest as well as neighbourhood of cultivation.

DISTRIBUTION OUTSIDE SIKKIM: Nepal, Bhutan (?), hill ranges of Assam, Manipur and N. Burma. The species extends to Thailand, Indochina and Yunnan.

GENERAL HABITS: Pairs or family parties, frequently associated with the restless mixed hunting flocks of small insectivorous birds. Habits not different from other tits'. The song, delivered from a high tree top, is one of the earliest bird calls at dawn. It is loud and spirited and has been well syllabified as *did-he-do-it, did-he-do-it, no-he-didn't.*

NESTING: No record for Sikkim. Elsewhere, *season* April to June. *Nest*—a pad of grass, moss, wool, feathers, etc., in a hole in a tree-trunk, less often in a stone wall, fairly low down. *Eggs*—4-6, white, spotted and blotched with reddish or purplish brown. Size about 18×14 mm.

RACIAL CHARACTERISTICS, MEASUREMENTS, ETC: Differentiated from the rather similar Yellowcheeked Tit (*Parus x. xanthogenys*) by the forehead and lores being bright yellow instead of black; spots on wings white instead of yellow; rump grey (tinged with yellow of the upper parts) instead of olive green; feathers of mantle and scapulars yellow, laterally margined with black. The Yellowcheeked Tit is common in the Himalayas west of the Nepal Valley at 4000-7000 ft., but may possibly occur in W. Sikkim.

Two specimens collected by Schäfer at Gangtok have Wing: ♂ 81, ♀ 76 mm.

Iris brown; bill dark plumbeous horn; legs and feet bluish plumbeous.

## THE YELLOWBROWED TIT

*Parus modestus modestus* (Burton)

*Sylviparus modestus* Burton, 1836 (1835), *Proc. Zool. Soc. London:* 154—Himalayas. Restricted by Stuart Baker (Handlist: 8) to Nepal.

**Plate 24, fig. 5 (facing p. 289)**

F.B.I. 1: 88

LOCAL NAME:

SIZE: Sparrow—.

FIELD CHARACTERS: A small leaf warbler-like bird, olive green above, pale yellow below, with an indistinct ring of yellow feathers round the eye and a short yellow eyebrow. Bright yellow edge to closed wing. A short crest sometimes raised. Sexes alike.

STATUS AND HABITAT: Incompletely known. Apparently resident between 6500 and 9500 ft. elevation, in rhododendron, oak and conifer forests; descending somewhat lower in winter, e.g., below Chungthang where a specimen was collected at about 5000 ft. in January.

DISTRIBUTION OUTSIDE SIKKIM: Nepal, Bhutan, Naga Hills, Manipur, N. Burma and eastward to China. A paler and brighter race (*simlaensis*) inhabits the W. Himalayas.

GENERAL HABITS: The old name *Sylviparus* for this little tit was particularly apt since the bird's habits closely resemble both the tits' and the warblers'. It moves about busily among the trees, hanging in acrobatic positions on sprigs in search of insects like a tit, or flits restlessly in the foliage, nervously flicking its wings like a leaf warbler (*Phylloscopus*). Usually keeps amongst the mixed hunting parties of small insectivorous birds and is easily mistaken for a leaf warbler without wing-bars. In life the yellow eyebrow normally remains concealed, except perhaps when the bird is displaying or as a warning signal to rivals. However, this needs to be investigated. Its note has been described as very like that of the British Blue Tit.

NESTING: Curiously enough nothing is known regarding the season, site or structure of this tit's nest, not only in Sikkim but also elsewhere in its extensive range. Its eggs remain undescribed.

RACIAL CHARACTERISTICS, MEASUREMENTS, ETC: In the hand the bird can be immediately distinguished from a leaf warbler by its longer and stouter, tit-like tarsi. The yellow eyebrow and ring round the eye can only be seen if the concealing feathers are raised. The yellow eyebrow becomes much paler in worn plumage.

A specimen (♀) collected by the Sikkim Survey measures: Wing 55; bill 8; tarsus 15; tail 32.5 mm. Two ♂♂ in the Schäfer collection have Wing 61-64 mm.

Iris brown; bill horny brown; legs and feet plumbeous; claws horny brown.

## *Subfamily* AEGITHALINAE: Longtailed Tits

### THE SIKKIM REDHEADED TIT

*Ægithalos concinnus rubricapillus* (Ticehurst)

*Ægithaliscus concinna rubricapillus* Ticehurst, 1925, *Bull. Brit. Orn. Cl.* 46: 22—Sikkim.

F.B.I. 8: 597

LOCAL NAME: Pyiong-samyi (Lepcha).

SIZE: Sparrow—. About that of a sunbird.

FIELD CHARACTERS: A diminutive, uncrested tit, blue grey above, ferruginous (=pale rusty) below. Forehead, crown and nape chestnut; a broad white eyebrow; a black patch on upper breast ('bib'); a broad black band enclosing the eyes. White moustachial streaks. Some white in the outer rectrices, conspicuous when tail spread in alighting. Sexes alike.

STATUS AND HABITAT: Resident between 4000 and 8000 ft. elevation, in fairly open broad-leaved forest with *Rubus* thickets.

DISTRIBUTION OUTSIDE SIKKIM: Nepal, Bhutan, and eastward to the Mishmi and Miri hills. The race *iredalei* occupies the W. Himalayas. Other races extend the species to Manipur, Burma and SW. China.

GENERAL HABITS: Very sociable. Invariably seen in fussy flocks, usually in the mixed itinerant parties of 'tinies', or small insectivorous birds, which hunt energetically in the canopy foliage and 'flow on' rapidly, in disorderly follow-my-leader fashion, from tree to tree. Also feeds largely on wild raspberries (*Rubus* spp.), clinging sideways or upside down on the bunches and pecking vigorously at the ripe fruit. A shrill, pleasant *tweet* is constantly uttered while feeding, and also on the wing.

NESTING: No record from Sikkim. In W. Himalayas, *season* March to May. *Nest*—a beautiful oval ball, about 5″×4″, of green moss, lichens, fine roots, spiders' egg cases, and feathers, neatly bound together with cobweb and thickly lined with wool and vegetable down.

Suspended between several twigs, or wedged into the fork of a bush, 3 to 6 feet up, where it is well camouflaged. *Eggs*—3-6, white or pinkish white, freckled with pinkish red, more densely and forming a ring at the broad end. Size about 14×11 mm.

RACIAL CHARACTERISTICS, MEASUREMENTS, ETC: The Sikkim race differs from the west Himalayan in being more blue on the back, with the head and flanks a darker chestnut. It is also somewhat smaller, thereby agreeing with the general tendency in Himalayan birds to decrease in size from west to east.

Specimens collected by the Sikkim Survey measure:

| | Wing | Bill | Tarsus | Tail |
|---|---|---|---|---|
| 1 ♂ | 50 | 7.5 | 16 | 48.5 mm. |
| 1 ♀ | 49 | 7.5 | 17 | 45 mm. |

For 9 examples in the Schäfer collection, Stresemann gives Wing 45(♀)-52(♂). Sikkim skins in the Chicago Museum of Natural History measure: Wing 3 ♂♂ 49-51; 2 ♀♀ 46-48 mm.

Iris brown; bill black; legs and feet yellowish brown; claws horny brown.

## THE RUFOUSFRONTED TIT

*Ægithalos iouschistos iouschistos* (Hodgson)

*Parus iouschistos* Hodgson, 1844, *in* Blyth, *Jour. Asiat. Soc. Bengal* 13: 943—Nepal.

**Plate 24, fig. 8** (facing p. 289)

F.B.I. 1: 99

LOCAL NAME:

SIZE: Sparrow—.

FIELD CHARACTERS: A small uncrested tit, ashy olive above with dark ferruginous underside and cheeks. Head black with a broad pinkish grey forehead and medial stripe ('centre parting') extending backward to the nape. Sides of neck and a broad collar on upper back also pinkish grey (fawn colour). Chin and throat silvery white, stippled with black. Sexes alike.

STATUS AND HABITAT: A high altitude tit. Resident between 9000 and 12,000 ft., descending to 8000 ft. or so in severe winters. Affects mixed deciduous and conifer forests, but particularly the rhododendron zone below the pines, and scrubby growth on mountainsides flanking hill streams.

DISTRIBUTION OUTSIDE SIKKIM: Nepal, Bhutan, Chumbi Valley (S. Tibet). Its western boundary in Nepal is presumably the Arun-Kosi River.

NESTING: Nothing recorded. Betts observed one carrying nesting material into the upper branches of a large fir tree (Lachen *c.* 9000 ft., 23 May 1943) but apparently did not see it building there. Ludlow obtained an oviduct egg from a specimen shot in Bhutan at 11,000 ft. elevation on 24 May (1933).

RACIAL CHARACTERISTICS, MEASUREMENTS, ETC: According to Stresemann, this species together with *Æ. niveogularis* of the W. Himalayas and *Æ. bonvaloti* of the Chin Hills, Yunnan and western China etc., constitute an 'Artenkreis' or Superspecies.

Twenty-two specimens collected by Schäfer at Lachen and Lachung in N. Sikkim measure: Wing 54 (♀)-59 (♂) mm.

Iris brown; bill black; legs yellowish brown (Jerdon). Iris yellow (Blanford).

## THE SULTAN TIT

*Melanochlora sultanea sultanea* (Hodgson)

*Parus sultaneus* Hodgson, 1837, *Indian Review* 2 (1): 31—Nepal.

**Plate 24, fig. 3** (facing p. 289)

F.B.I. 1: 101

LOCAL NAME: Bon-tylia-pho (Lepcha).

SIZE: Bulbul.

FIELD CHARACTERS: A showy, crested, black and yellow arboreal bird. *Male:* Deep black above, including tail; also sides of head, neck, chin, throat and breast. Rest of underparts, forehead, crown and long crest bright yellow. *Female:* Similar, but with upper parts blackish brown, and chin and throat heavily washed with olive-yellow. In overhead flight, silhouetted against the sky, looks very like Redvented Bulbul.

STATUS AND HABITAT: Resident. Not uncommon in the hot, steamy valleys from plains level up to about 3500 ft. elevation. Between 1200 and 2500 ft. seems to be the optimum zone. (Four skins in the Schäfer collection are labelled 'Gangtok, 1900 m.', i.e. 6000 ft., which is unusually high!) Affects open deciduous forest and large trees bordering terrace cultivation, roads, etc.

DISTRIBUTION OUTSIDE SIKKIM: The lower Himalayas from Nepal to NE. Assam. The species extends through the lower hills of Assam, Manipur and Burma south to Tenasserim and Thailand.

GENERAL HABITS: Goes about in pairs or small parties. Actions and behaviour essentially tit-like. Hunts systematically for insects in the foliage canopy of lofty trees or under the bark, clinging to the sprigs and tree-trunks in all manner of acrobatic positions, and peering into crevices and under leaves. The birds flit lightly from branch to branch on hovering wings, reminiscent of the Iora's parachuting display or of a foraging party of wood shrikes (*Tephrodornis*). *Food:* mainly insects, but also fruits and seeds. *Song:* a musical *tew-r-r, tew-r-r, tew-r-r* usually repeated three times. A harsh rolling *krikrew*, like the alarm note of some laughing thrush, is uttered from time to time. A short, rather nasal conversational *chick* helps a foraging party to maintain contact.

NESTING: In spite of its being a common bird, very few records exist, and none from Sikkim. *Season*—April-May. *Nest*—a thick pad of moss heavily lined with cotton down, built in a hole or crevice in a tree-trunk. *Eggs*—6-7, white, thickly scattered over with bold brownish red spots and underlying ones of pinkish grey and light neutral tint. Size about 20×16 mm.

RACIAL CHARACTERISTICS, MEASUREMENTS, ETC: 3 ♀♀ collected by the Sikkim Survey measure: Wing 95-105; bill 16-16.5; tarsus 22-24.5; tail 85-92 mm.

Four Schäfer skins have Wing 2 ♂♂ 107-109; 2 ♀♀ 99-103 mm.

Iris brown; bill brownish black; legs and feet bluish plumbeous; claws horny brown.

## *Subfamily* REMIZINAE: Penduline Tits

### THE SIKKIM FIRECAPPED TIT-WARBLER

*Cephalopyrus flammiceps olivaceus* Rothschild[1]

*Cephalopyrus flammiceps olivaceus* Rothschild, 1923, *Novit. Zool.* **30**: 263—Vicinity of Tengyueh.

**Plate 18, fig. 6** (facing p. 209)

F.B.I. **2**: 545

LOCAL NAME:

SIZE: Sparrow.

FIELD CHARACTERS: A brightly coloured, dumpy little flowerpecker-like bird with a comparatively short tail, and two yellow wing-bars, the lower broader and more prominent. *Above*, forehead orange-scarlet; head and back olive-orange. *Below*, chin and throat orange-scarlet; breast golden yellow; underparts paler yellow.

*Female* duller and paler.

STATUS AND HABITAT: Rather uncommon. Was met with only at fairly low levels, 1000 to 4500 ft. (Rangpo, Dentam) between November and May, but doubtless goes higher in summer as in the western Himalayas—up to 10,000 ft. Affects forest.

DISTRIBUTION OUTSIDE SIKKIM: E. Nepal, Bhutan, SE. Tibet, Yunnan. The Himalayas from western Nepal to Afghanistan are inhabited by the paler nominate race.

GENERAL HABITS: Restless and very like flowerpeckers'. Moves about singly or in small scattered parties (in winter) from tree to tree, clinging upside down and sideways, in the manner of tits, to the ends of leafy twigs in search of insect food. Also flicks wings nervously like a leaf warbler. The male has a pretty song in the breeding season resembling that of the goldfinch, but more subdued.

NESTING: Not recorded in Sikkim. In the W. Himalayas, 5000-10,000 ft., *season*—April to June. *Nest*—a natural hollow in a branch or an old barbet's hole, usually between 20 and 40 ft. up, lined with grass and feathers. *Eggs*—normally 4, unmarked blue-green. Size about 16×12 mm. The female is a close sitter and, like tits, hisses at intruders.

RACIAL CHARACTERISTICS, MEASUREMENTS, ETC: Sikkim birds are darker than west Himalayan *flammiceps*. The Fauna gives the measurements as ♂♀: Wing 57-60; bill *c.* 9; tarsus *c.* 17; tail 28-31 mm.

[1] *C. f. saturatus* Whistler.

Iris dark brown; bill plumbeous or horny grey; legs and feet plumbeous or slaty brown.

## *Family* SITTIDAE:

### *Subfamily* TRICHODROMADINAE: Wall Creeper, Spotted Grey Creeper

### THE WALL CREEPER

*Tichodroma muraria nepalensis* Bonaparte (Linnaeus)

*Tichodroma nepalensis* Bonaparte, 1850, Consp. Gen. Av. 1: 225—Central Asia.

**Plate 15, fig. 8 (facing p. 160)**

F.B.I. 1: 441

LOCAL NAME: Sag-gorsa-lamdong-pho (Lepcha).

SIZE: Sparrow.

FIELD CHARACTERS: General colour French grey. Wings bright crimson with white spots conspicuous in flight. Chin and throat black in summer, pure white in winter. Tail comparatively short, rounded, black, tipped with ashy and white. A long, slender black bill. Sexes alike, but in summer dress black of chin and throat less in female.

STATUS AND HABITAT: Not common and rather sporadic, to 12,000 ft. elevation and higher in summer; down to 1000 ft. or lower in winter (Rangpo, Toong, Chungthang, Dentam, Lachung). Affects boulders and rocky sides of streams and gorges, cliffs, etc.

DISTRIBUTION OUTSIDE SIKKIM: Throughout the Himalayas from Kashmir eastward. Nepal, Bhutan, Assam hills north of Brahmaputra River. The species ranges through Europe and Asia to China.

GENERAL HABITS: Solitary, or in widely separated pairs. Clambers up vertical surfaces in jerky spurts, flicking open and shut the broad crimson wings from time to time to stampede insects and spiders lurking amongst lichens and in the crevices and unevennesses of the rock. Flight curiously reminiscent of a large butterfly: flap . . . pause (with wings closed) . . . flap . . . pause, and so on. Also rather hoopoe-like. Voice and call unrecorded in our limits.

NESTING: Breeds at high altitudes, 12,000-16,000 ft. No record for Sikkim. Elsewhere in the Himalayas: *Season*—May-June. *Nest*—a pad of wool, grass, etc., wedged between boulders in a precipitous cliff-face. *Eggs*—4-6, dull white, speckled and spotted at the larger end with black or deep red-brown. Size about 22×15 mm.

RACIAL CHARACTERISTICS, MEASUREMENTS, ETC: The Fauna gives for ♂♀ Wing 94-102; bill 27-32; tarsus 25-27; tail *c.* 50-54 mm.

A Sikkim Survey ♂ measures Wing 103.5; bill 29; tarsus 24; tail 55.5 mm. Iris brown; bill brownish black; legs, feet and claws blackish brown.

## *Subfamily* SITTINAE: Nuthatches

### THE WHITETAILED NUTHATCH

*Sitta himalayensis himalayensis* Jardine & Selby

*Sitta himalayensis* Jardine & Selby, 1835, Illustr. Orn. 3, pl. 144—Himalayas (Simla).

F.B.I. 1: 122

LOCAL NAME: Siddyi-phip (Lepcha).

SIZE: Sparrow—.

FIELD CHARACTERS: A short and square-tailed slaty blue bird with pale fulvous and chestnut underparts and longish straight pointed bill. Forehead black continued behind in a black line through the eye down sides of neck to the shoulder. Under tail-coverts chestnut. Its chief distinguishing mark from other nuthatches is the white patch at the base of the tail feathers. In overhead flight a white patch on the otherwise blackish underwing, conspicuous. Sexes alike; female somewhat duller and paler.

STATUS AND HABITAT: Resident between 5000 and 11,000 ft. (August), descending as low as about 3000 ft. in winter (March). Partial to oak and rhododendron forest.

DISTRIBUTION OUTSIDE SIKKIM: Himalayas from Kangra and Chamba eastward to Bhutan and the Aka Hills (north of Brahmaputra River). Also at the higher elevations of the N. Cachar and Manipur hills, and N. Burma.

The species extends to Tonkin.

GENERAL HABITS: Pairs or scattered family parties, often amongst the hunting bands of small insectivorous birds that rove the forest. Creeps jerkily along the upper or under side of moss-covered boughs or up and around tree-trunks with astonishing agility, prying into crevices in the bark or under the moss in search of lurking insects, presently flying off to another tree nearby—occasionally in low shrubs—to resume the hunt. The birds maintain contact with one another by a feeble, mousy *chip-chip*. At the onset of the nesting season a clear, spirited, tit-like, whistling song *wheet-wit-wit-wit-wit*—quickly repeated 6 to 8 times—is delivered by the male with neck partially upstretched, from a perch in a tree. *Food:* mainly insects, but also kernels of nuts and seeds. The nut is fixed in a suitable hollow in a branch and hacked open by determined hammer blows of the pointed bill.

NESTING: An early breeder. *Season*—March to May. *Nest*—a pad of green moss and moss roots in some natural hollow in a tree trunk or bough, at any height between 5 and 25 ft. The opening is plastered up with clay leaving a neat round entrance hole about 1½ inches in diameter. *Eggs*—5 to 7, white, thickly blotched and spotted with red, more profusely at the broad end. Size about 19×14 mm.

RACIAL CHARACTERISTICS, MEASUREMENTS, ETC: Two ♀♀ collected at Chungthang measure: Wing 68-74; bill 14-15; tarsus 17-18; tail 33.5-38 mm.

For 30 specimens in the Schäfer Sikkim collection (Gangtok, Chungthang, Lachen, Manshitang, Penlom-la, Karponang) Stresemann gives Wing 68(♀)-76(♂).

Iris brown; upper mandible blackish brown, lower pale plumbeous with horny brown tip; legs, feet and claws pale horny brown.

## THE CINNAMONBELLIED NUTHATCH

*Sitta castanea cinnamoventris* Blyth

*Sitta cinnamoventris* Blyth, 1842, *Jour. Asiat. Soc. Bengal* **11**: 459, *ex* Tickell MS.—Darjeeeling.

F.B.I. **1**: 125

LOCAL NAME: Siddyi-phip (Lepcha).

SIZE: Sparrow.

FIELD CHARACTERS: *Male:* Slaty blue above, including crown and nape; chestnut red below. A black streak from the nostril backward through the eye to the shoulder. Cheeks, ear-coverts and chin white, sharply defined. Under tail-coverts white, fringed with bright chestnut. White patches near tip of outer tail feathers. In overhead flight a white patch visible under wing at base of primaries.

*Female:* White on face less sharply defined. Lower plumage cinnamon brown, paler on throat and breast. Easily confused with Whitetailed Nuthatch; for diagnosis see below.

STATUS AND HABITAT: Resident and common between about 1000 ft. elevation (or lower) and about 5500 ft. (Rangpo, Martam, Gangtok, Singhik, Dentam, Rinchinpong, etc.). Affects openly wooded country with large trees.

DISTRIBUTION OUTSIDE SIKKIM: Nepal (up to 6500 ft.—Ripley); Bhutan to extreme east Assam north and south of the Brahmaputra; Manipur; Chittagong Hill Tracts (E. Pakistan). The species in other races is widely distributed in S. Europe and Asia, including the greater part of India and Burma.

GENERAL HABITS: Similar to those of the white-tailed species. Often seen in association with the Velvetfronted Nuthatch, which, however, it treats as a food competitor and invariably chases off if on the same branch. Occasionally descends to the ground to feed on termites etc. The male's breeding call is a single loud and clear whistle, *chwhee*, repeated about once in two or three seconds.

NESTING: *Season*—April to June. *Nest*—not different from that of the species described, except perhaps in that the moss is often capped by mammal fur for the eggs to lie on. An unusual nest found in Sikkim by Gammie was placed 20 ft. up in the internode section of a decaying bamboo and consisted of several alternate layers of green moss and pieces of tree bark piled one over the other. *Eggs*—5 to 7, white, less boldly spotted with dark red than in the white-tailed species. Size about 19×14 mm.

RACIAL CHARACTERISTICS, MEASUREMENTS, ETC: Both sexes differ from corresponding sexes of the race *castanea*, found over most of India, (1) in possessing a blunter, longer, and heavier bill; (2) the crown and nape are concolorous with the back, not paler; (3) chestnut-fringed under tail-coverts white, not slaty blue; (4) underparts of male a brighter redder chestnut, not dark chestnut bay.

Female *cinnamoventris* may be differentiated in the field from *Sitta himalayensis* by (1) absence of white patch at base of tail; (2) its slightly larger size and darker chestnut underparts; (3) its chestnut-fringed *white* under tail-coverts, not pale chestnut as in that species.

Three ♂♂ collected by the Loke-Sálim Ali Survey measure: Wing 83-86; bill 21-22; tarsus 20; tail 40-42.5 mm. A Sikkim ♀ in the Schäfer collection has Wing 83 mm.

Iris brown; upper mandible horny black except ridge of culmen (for about 10 mm. posteriorly) which is pale plumbeous; lower mandible pale plumbeous except tip and commissure which are black; legs and feet plumbeous; claws brown.

## THE BEAUTIFUL NUTHATCH

*Sitta formosa* Blyth

*Sitta formosa* Blyth, 1843, *Jour. Asiat. Soc. Bengal* 12: 938—Darjeeling.

**Plate 15, fig. 6 (facing p. 160)**

F.B.I. 1: 131

LOCAL NAME: Tishe kuyi gumbo (Lepcha).

SIZE: Bulbul—.

FIELD CHARACTERS: A large, handsome, black and blue nuthatch, unmistakable for any other bird. Forehead black. Crown, nape and mantle black streaked with cobalt blue. Sides of neck and back black streaked with bluish white. Rest of upper parts blue. Flight and tail feathers black, more or less edged with blue. Tail tipped bluish white. Sides of head, chin, and throat white, shading into the dull chestnut lower plumage. In flight a white patch on the black underwing, at base of primaries, conspicuous from below. Sexes alike.

STATUS AND HABITAT: Very rare and local. In recent years obtained only by Meinertzhagen at 1100 ft. elevation (Rangpo) in December, and again at 6400 ft. (Rangiroon, Darjeeling Dist.) in the same month. Evidently, therefore, it occupies a wide altitudinal range (seasonal ?).

DISTRIBUTION OUTSIDE SIKKIM: Bhutan and the eastern Himalayas to our extreme NE. frontier. Assam hills south of Brahmaputra River; Manipur; N. Burma.

GENERAL HABITS: Very little recorded. Keeps in pairs or parties of 4 or 5. Not shy. Its actions and behaviour while creeping up and down boughs and tree-trunks in search of food are characteristic of the genus but slower, resembling those of a woodpecker. Flight fast. *Call:* typical of the nuthatches; described as lower and sweeter in tone.

NESTING: No record for Sikkim. *Season* (in Assam)—April to June.

*Nest*—a pad of rodents' fur in a tree-hole 8 to 25 ft. up, walled up with clay, leaving a neat round entrance. *Eggs*—4 to 6, white with small dark red specks and spots. Size about 21×16 mm.

RACIAL CHARACTERISTICS, MEASUREMENTS, ETC: The Fauna gives the measurements as: ♂♀ Wing 114-118; bill *c.* 17; tarsus *c.* 21; tail *c.* 58-60 mm.

Against the above, Dr Ripley measures 2 ♀♀ collected in the Mishmi Hills as: Wing 98-99.5; bill 20-21.5.

Iris dark brown; bill blackish; legs and feet greenish horn. (Whistler MS.)

## THE VELVETFRONTED NUTHATCH

*Sitta frontalis frontalis* Swainson

*Sitta frontalis* Swainson, 1820, Zool. Illustr., series 1, pt. *i*, pl. 2—Ceylon.

F.B.I. 1: 132

LOCAL NAME:

SIZE: Sparrow—.

FIELD CHARACTERS: A small purplish blue nuthatch with pale lilac grey underparts, velvety black forehead, and coral red bill. A white spot at base of black primaries visible from below. *Male* with a black stripe (supercilium) above eye, extending to nape; *female* without.

STATUS AND HABITAT: Stevens records it up to 2500 ft. elevation in the Teesta Valley. In Sikkim, according to him, it nowhere approaches 5000 ft. as given by Oates for the Himalayas. The Loke-Sálim Ali Survey found the species commonest between 1000 and 2000 ft., but also came across it at about 4500 ft. (Singhik) and between 5500 and 6500 ft. (Gangtok) in February and December 1952 and April 1955. Affects broad-leaved forest.

DISTRIBUTION OUTSIDE SIKKIM: Practically all India, Pakistan and Burma excepting the arid areas. Plains, and up to about 6000 ft. elevation.

GENERAL HABITS: Very similar to those of the Whitetailed and other nuthatches. Pairs or family parties usually seen amongst mixed hunting associations of small insectivorous birds. *Call:* a loud cheeping whistle of the quality and volume of a sunbird's. Members of a party maintain contact with one another by a variety of mousy cheeps. The male has a trilling 'song' in the breeding season.

NESTING: *Season*—April to June. *Nest*—a pad of moss lined with fur, and sometimes a few feathers. Placed in a small tree-hole usually under 20 ft. (but up to 40 ft.). On account of the smallness of the hole normally selected, plastering up with clay as in other nuthatches is seldom necessary. *Eggs*—4 or 5, white, densely speckled and blotched with red and purplish. Size about 17×13 mm.

RACIAL CHARACTERISTICS, MEASUREMENTS, ETC: A ♂ collected in Sikkim measures: Wing 73; bill 14.5; tarsus 16.5; tail 40 mm.

Measurements of series from Nepal, Naga Hills, etc. show the difference in size between south Indian and north Indian birds to be so insignificant that it seems pointless to recognize the northern race *corallina*, separated on the character of smallness. This conclusion agrees with Vaurie's recent revison of the Asiatic nuthatches (*Amer. Mus. Novitates*, No. 1472: 12. 1 Nov. 1950).

## *Family* Certhiidae: Tree Creepers

### THE NEPAL TREE CREEPER

*Certhia familiaris mandellii* Brooks

*Certhia mandellii* Brooks, 1874, *Jour. Asiat. Soc. Bengal* 42 (2): 256—Sikkim.

**Plate 15, fig. 7** (facing p. 160)

F.B.I. **1**: 433 (=*nipalensis*)

LOCAL NAME:

SIZE: Sparrow—.

FIELD CHARACTERS: A small, mottled, dark brown bird with bright ferruginous rump and upper tail-coverts, and a longish, pointed, woodpecker-like, reddish brown tail. An oblique fulvous band across wings. Chin, cheeks, throat and breast white; under tail-coverts fulvous. Slender, slightly curved bill. Sexes alike.

STATUS AND HABITAT: Resident. Not uncommon at the higher elevations, usually between *c.* 7500 and 13,500 ft. (Lachen, Lachung, Thangu, Gnatong, Karponang, Sandakphu), but also noted at *c.* 5500 ft. (Kewzing). Affects silver fir, deodar and rhododendron forest.

DISTRIBUTION OUTSIDE SIKKIM: Eastern Nepal, Bhutan, S. Tibet. Another race (*hodgsoni*) occurs in the western Himalayas, from NW. Kashmir to W. Nepal.

GENERAL HABITS: Entirely arboreal, though occasionally seen on moss-covered rocks. Partial to conifers. Pairs or family parties, almost invariably amongst the mixed hunting parties of tits, flycatchers, etc. Clings to moss- and lichen-covered tree trunks, creeps up in short spurts, directly or in irregular spirals, and searches the crevices and under the bark for hiding insects. After working up to near the top of a tree, flies off to another, alighting on the trunk near its base and scuttling upward in the same way. Has a number of squeaky, mouse-like notes.

NESTING: *Season*—chiefly May-June. *Nest*—a shapeless mass of feathers, straw, etc. wedged in a crevice or bulge of loose outflaking bark of a deodar, 4 to 40 ft. from the ground. *Eggs*—4 or 5, pale pinkish white, heavily spotted and speckled with reddish brown, more densely at the broad end to form an irregular cap or zone. Size about 16×12 mm.

RACIAL CHARACTERISTICS, MEASUREMENTS, ETC: White underparts, slightly shorter bill, and faintness or absence of cross-rays in the tail, distinguish this species (*familiaris*) from *himalayana*.

The W. Himalayan race *hodgsoni* differs in being paler brown above, with only a tinge of fulvous on lower back and rump.

The Survey specimens measure:

| | Wing | Bill | Tarsus | Tail |
|---|---|---|---|---|
| 2 ♀♀ | 63-64.5 | 14.5-15.5 | 17-17.5 | 55-57 mm. |
| 1 o? | 64 | 13 | 17.5 | 54.5 mm. |

Four Sikkim ♂♂ in the Chicago Museum of Natural History have Wing 65-67; 4 ♀♀ 63-66 mm.

Iris brown; upper mandible horny brown, lower pinkish flesh colour; legs, feet and claws horny brown.

## THE SIKKIM TREE CREEPER

### *Certhia discolor discolor* Blyth

*Certhia discolor* Blyth, 1845, *Jour. Asiat. Soc. Bengal* **14**: 580—Darjeeling.

F.B.I. 1: 435

LOCAL NAME: Saddyer-pho (Lepcha).

SIZE: Sparrow—.

FIELD CHARACTERS: Similar to the Nepal Tree Creeper, but with the entire lower plumage earthy brown; under tail-coverts ferruginous; bill a little longer and more curved. Sexes alike.

STATUS AND HABITAT: Resident. Fairly common, and on the whole seems to occupy a lower zone than the Nepal Tree Creeper at least in winter (4000 to 6000 ft., Rinchinpong, Temi). But Meinertzhagen also found it higher up, 9000 to 12,000 ft., in late December (Karponang, Changu), so the ranges of the two species evidently overlap. Affects deciduous oak forest at the lower levels, and conifers and rhododendrons at higher elevations.

DISTRIBUTION OUTSIDE SIKKIM: Nepal, Bhutan, Assam hills north and south of Brahmaputra River, Naga Hills, W. Manipur. Other races extend the species through E. Manipur to Burma, Yunnan, Thailand, Tonkin, Annam.

GENERAL HABITS: Similar to those of the Nepal Tree Creeper. A pair or so almost invariably amongst the mixed hunting parties of tits and other tinies, creeping jerkily on moss- and lichen-covered trunks and boughs.

NESTING: Not recorded in Sikkim. *Season*—in Assam hills, April-May. *Nest* and *eggs* very similar to those of *mandellii*, but perhaps the eggs are more densely marked with tiny blotches and freckles of a deeper red-brown, and with a lesser tendency to form a ring or cap at the broad end. Size about 16×12 mm.

RACIAL CHARACTERISTICS, MEASUREMENTS, ETC: Sikkim Survey specimens measure:

| | Wing | Bill | Tarsus | Tail |
|---|---|---|---|---|
| 3 ♂♂ | 67-70 | 18 | 17-18 | 73.5-80 mm. |
| 1 ♀ | 68 | 16 | 16.5 | 73 mm. |
| 1 o? | 68 | 16 | 15.5 | 71 mm. |

Iris brown; upper mandible horny brown, lower flesh coloured; legs, feet and claws pale horny brown.

## STOLICZKA'S TREE CREEPER

*Certhia nipalensis* Blyth

*Certhia nipalensis* 'Hodgson'=Blyth, 1845, *Jour. Asiat. Soc. Bengal* 14: 581—Nepal.

F.B.I. 1: 438

LOCAL NAME:

SIZE: Sparrow—.

FIELD CHARACTERS: Like the Nepal and Sikkim Tree Creepers, with the conspicuous buff wing bar, but *above* black, streaked with fulvous; *below,* chin and throat white, rest of underparts including under tail-coverts ferruginous (rusty red). Sexes alike.

STATUS AND HABITAT: Stevens records it from 6500 to 10,000 ft. in winter; Meinertzhagen also obtained specimens between 5200 and 10,500 ft. elevation (Rinchinpong, Chungthang, Lachen, Changu), November to January, and found it not uncommon. Its biotope overlaps that of the other two tree creepers. The Sikkim Ornithological Survey apparently overlooked it.

DISTRIBUTION OUTSIDE SIKKIM: E. Nepal, Bhutan to E. Assam. Possibly also Naga Hills and Manipur.

GENERAL HABITS: Same as of the two previous species, but according to Meinertzhagen oftener met with by itself, singly or in pairs, than in the mixed hunting parties of tits etc. He also describes it as being more silent, slower and more deliberate in its movements, and keeping largely to lower rotten and mossy trees, seldom ascending high up into the branches.

NESTING: Unknown.

RACIAL CHARACTERISTICS, MEASUREMENTS, ETC: The Fauna gives the measurements (♂ ♀) as: Wing 67-74; bill *c.* 13-18, generally *c.* 16; tarsus *c.* 18; tail 64-71 mm.

Soft parts as in the other tree creepers.

# *Family* DICAEIDAE: Flowerpeckers

## THE FIREBREASTED FLOWERPECKER

*Dicaeum ignipectus ignipectus* (Blyth)

*Myzanthe ignipectus* 'Hodgson'=Blyth, 1843, *Jour. Asiat. Soc. Bengal* 12: 983—Nepal.

**Plate 13, fig. 4** (facing p. 144)
**Plate 22, fig. 9** (facing p. 273)

F.B.I. 3: 427

LOCAL NAME: Sangti-pro-pho (Lepcha).

SIZE: Sparrow—.

FIELD CHARACTERS: A restless, brilliant, stub-tailed little bird, very like a sunbird but with a shorter bill. *Male: Above,* deep glossy metallic greenish black. *Below,* rich buff washed with greenish on the flanks. A bright crimson patch on breast, and a black patch below this, sometimes down to centre of abdomen.

*Female: Above,* olive-green with a contrasting yellowish rump. *Below,* as in male but without the crimson or black patches.

STATUS AND HABITAT: The commonest flowerpecker in Sikkim. Met with between *c.* 2500 and 6500 ft. (Temi, Kewzing, Rinchinpong, Dikchu, Singhik, Manshitang, Gangtok). According to Stevens, 'generally distributed between 3500 and 10,000 ft.' in the Sikkim Himalayas. Stuart Baker even says 'it certainly breeds up to 12,000 ft. in Sikkim', though he does not give his authority. On *Loranthus* clumps parasitizing forest trees.

DISTRIBUTION OUTSIDE SIKKIM: Throughout the lower Himalayas from the Sutlej Valley to NE. Assam. Also rest of Assam, Manipur, Burma, Thailand. The species ranges to S. China, the Philippines and Malaysia.

GENERAL HABITS: Arboreal. Inseparable from the parasitic *Loranthus* clumps so abundant on the tall forest trees, its staple food being the ripe berries of this plant. It plucks and revolves a berry between its mandibles to strip off and swallow the epicarp, wiping the viscous seed on a neighbouring branch where it quickly sprouts and starts a fresh infestation. Or sometimes it will swallow the entire berry and void the seed in due course on a different tree, thus spreading the mischief farther afield. Much rivalry prevails between individuals feeding amongst the *Loranthus* clumps and intruders are chased off with persistence and determination. Nectar, small insects and spiders are also eaten.

Utters a sharp *chik-chik-chik* as it hops restlessly amongst the parasitic clusters, or dashes from tree to tree.

NESTING: *Season*—April-May. *Nest*—a beautiful little pear-shaped pouch with a lateral entrance hole, of soft felted vegetable down, occasionally draped on the outside with some green moss. Hung from a twig 12 to 20 ft. from the ground. *Eggs*—2 or 3, white, measuring about 15×10 mm.

RACIAL CHARACTERISTICS, MEASUREMENTS, ETC: The Sikkim Survey specimens measure: 4 ♂♂ Wing 49-53; bill 9-10; tarsus 12-13; tail 24.5-27 mm.

Schäfer's Sikkim skins give Wing 3 ♂♂ 49, 50, 51; 2 ♀♀ 47, 48 mm.

Iris brown; bill black, or with lower mandible plumbeous horn; legs, feet and claws blackish brown.

## THE YELLOWBELLIED FLOWERPECKER

*Dicaeum melanozanthum* (Blyth)

*Pachyglossa melanozantha* 'Hodgson' = Blyth, 1843, *Jour. Asiat. Soc. Bengal* 12: 1010—Nepal.

F.B.I. 3: 439

LOCAL NAME:

SIZE: Sparrow—.

FIELD CHARACTERS: *Male: Above,* including sides of neck and breast, velvety black. Two outer pairs of tail feathers with a white patch on inner web near tip. *Below,* middle of chin, throat and breast white. Rest of lower plumage bright yellow.

*Female:* Like the male, but black replaced by greenish brown, paler on sides of head, neck, and breast. Middle of chin and throat greyish white. Abdomen and under tail-coverts yellow.

STATUS AND HABITAT: Rare. In the Chicago Museum there is a good series collected by Stevens from 5500 to 6000 ft. elevation (Lingtam) in January and February 1931. Schäfer obtained 4 examples at *c.* 9000 ft. (Lachen) between 6 and 12 Sept. 1939.

DISTRIBUTION OUTSIDE SIKKIM: Kumaon and through Nepal and Bhutan (?) to E. Assam.

GENERAL HABITS: Said to be typical of the flowerpeckers, but little known.

NESTING: Unknown.

RACIAL CHARACTERISTICS, MEASUREMENTS, ETC: Schäfer's Sikkim specimens have Wing 2 ♂♂ 70, 75; 2 ♀♀ 63, 66 mm.

Iris red; bill black; legs and feet dark plumbeous (Fauna).

## *Family* NECTARINIIDAE: Sunbirds

The genus *Aethopyga* is characterized by the males possessing, in addition to brilliant metallic plumage, a bright yellow rump and long graduated tails with elongated central feathers narrowing to a point. The females have shorter, less graduated tails (without the lengthened central feathers), and are conspicuously greenish tinged on the underparts. The bill, as in other sunbirds, is slender and downcurved, well adapted for probing into tubular flowers.

## THE FIRETAILED YELLOWBACKED SUNBIRD

*Aethopyga ignicauda ignicauda* (Hodgson)

*Cinnyris ignicauda* Hodgson, 1836, *Ind. Review* 1 (7): 273—Nepal.

**Plate 13, fig. 3** (facing p. 144)
**Plate 22, fig. 6** (facing p. 273)

F.B.I. 3: 383

LOCAL NAME:

SIZE: Sparrow−.

FIELD CHARACTERS: *Male* (breeding): *Above*, forehead, crown, and sides of chin and throat metallic blue. Rest of upper parts crimson except rump which is bright yellow, and long pointed tail which is largely crimson brick-red. *Below*, chin and throat metallic purple; breast yellow, suffused with scarlet-crimson. Rest of lower plumage dull greenish yellow.

After breeding the male moults into a dull, rather female-like eclipse plumage, with the tail, though much duller and shorter, still retaining its pointed shape. Head, chin and throat grey; crown streaked darker. Scarlet on breast much reduced, but rest, including yellow rump and scarlet upper tail-coverts, as in the breeding plumage.

*Female: Above*, ashy green; rump and tail-coverts fringed with yellow, but no distinct yellow rump-band. Tail blackish, tinged with ashy green and obsoletely pale-tipped; the central feathers golden brown. *Below*, blackish ashy green changing to greenish yellow on abdomen and posterior flanks.

STATUS AND HABITAT: The Sikkim sunbird with the highest altitudinal ceiling. Normally resident between *c.* 4500 and 13,000 ft., moving down slightly from its highest levels in severe winters (Dentam, Rinchinpong, Pemionche, Gangtok, near Manshitang, Lachung, Yumthang, Thangu). Blanford recorded it at 11,000 ft. in the Chola Range in August. According to Stevens occasionally found at 2000 ft. or lower in winter. Affects forest of oak, rhododendron and conifers.

DISTRIBUTION OUTSIDE SIKKIM: Kumaon, Garhwal, Nepal, Bhutan, SE. Tibet (Himalayan facies); Assam, Manipur. The species extends to Mt Victoria, NE. Burma, Yunnan.

GENERAL HABITS: Arboreal. Restless and active. Flits about the tree-tops glittering like a living gem against the dark foliage. Hangs sideways or upside down on a cluster of rhododendron blossoms nervously twitching its wings, and probes into the flower tubes for nectar. Hovers momentarily in front of sprigs on rapidly vibrating wings—like a hawk-moth—in search of insects and spiders which also form a large part of its diet. Its song has not been recorded.

NESTING: *Season*—April-May. *Nest*—an oblong pouch of moss mixed with fine grass, roots and vegetable down, with an entrance hole near the top. Suspended from the tip of a ringal bamboo branch or bush, 3 ft. or so from the ground, in silver fir and rhododendron forest frequently at altitudes of 10,000-12,000 ft. *Eggs*—2, variable, white to pale violet-white or pale brick-red, freckled with purplish or reddish brown. Size about 16×12 mm.

RACIAL CHARACTERISTICS, MEASUREMENTS, ETC: Specimens collected by the Sikkim Survey in January (eclipse plumage) measure: 2 ♂♂ Wing 58-59; bill 22-24; tarsus 16, 16; tail 48-48.5 mm. In breeding plumage the tail is '108-118 mm.' (Fauna).

Schäfer's Sikkim series, including males in breeding as well as eclipse plumage, gives Wing 15 ♂♂ 56-60 (av. 57.6); 2 ♀♀ 52, 55 mm. (Stresemann).

Iris brown; bill, legs, feet and claws horny brown.

## THE BLACKBREASTED SUNBIRD

*Aethopyga saturata saturata* (Hodgson)

*Cinnyris saturata* Hodgson, 1836, *Ind. Review* 1 (7): 273—Nepal.

**Plate 13, fig. 2** (facing p. 144)
**Plate 22, fig. 8** (facing p. 273)

F.B.I. 3: 388

LOCAL NAME:

SIZE: Sparrow–.

FIELD CHARACTERS: *Male:* Very dark, almost black in the distance, with long pointed tail. *Above,* forehead, crown, nape, hindneck, and a broad moustachial streak metallic bluish purple. Upper back very dark crimson-maroon, changing to dull black lower; a narrow and inconspicuous yellow rump-band; rump, tail-coverts and tail largely glistening steel blue. *Below,* sides of head and neck, chin, throat and breast black; rest of lower plumage dull grey-green. There is no eclipse plumage.

*Female:* Confusingly like female *ignicauda,* but with upper plumage light green and a distinct yellow band across the rump. Tail, excepting central feathers, broadly tipped with dull white.

STATUS AND HABITAT: A fairly common resident at the lower elevations, up to *c.* 6500 ft. (Singtam, Martam, Dikchu, Chungthang, Gangtok). Affects fringes of dense evergreen forest, and secondary jungle.

DISTRIBUTION OUTSIDE SIKKIM: Garhwal, Nepal, Bhutan, SE. Tibet (Himalayan facies). The species extends through Assam, Manipur and Burma to Yunnan and Tonkin.

GENERAL HABITS: Typical of the sunbirds as described under *Ae. ignicauda.* Perhaps less bursting with energy than many of its congeners, often remaining hopping about in one flower-laden bush for minutes instead of flashing ceaselessly from bush to bush. The flowers of a species of *Holmskjoldia,* common within its altitudinal range, form an irresistible attraction to this and other sunbirds.

NESTING: Not specifically recorded in Sikkim. *Season* elsewhere—May to July. *Nest*—a compact oblong pouch of fibres and moss, lined copiously with fine cotton down, with a porched lateral entrance. Attached to a thin twig or creeper stem usually under 4 ft. from the ground. *Eggs*—2 or 3, white, spotted and blotched with inky black and inky grey, more densely at the broad end. Size about 15×12 mm.

RACIAL CHARACTERISTICS, MEASUREMENTS, ETC: Specimens collected by the Sikkim Survey measure: 2 ♂♂ Wing 55-58; bill 23-23.5; tarsus 14-16; tail 74-76 mm.

Schäfer's Sikkim skins give Wing 10 ♂♂ 53-57 (av. 55.4); 1 ♀ 47 mm.

Iris brown; bill brownish black; legs, feet and claws dark horny brown.

Curiously enough, as reflected also by the specimens collected, males of this sunbird and the Firetailed species in Sikkim appear vastly to outnumber the females—in the proportion of something like 10 : 1—and this in spite of a special look-out being kept for the latter.

## THE SIKKIM YELLOWBACKED SUNBIRD

*Aethopyga nipalensis koelzi* Ripley

*Aethopyga nipalensis koelzi* Ripley, 1948, *Proc. Biol. Soc. Washington* 61: 106—Mishmi Hills, N.E. Assam.

F.B.I. 3: 391 (part)

LOCAL NAME:

SIZE: Sparrow—.

FIELD CHARACTERS: *Male: Above,* forehead to hindneck metallic green. Sides of neck and upper back deep crimson-maroon. Lower back olive-green; rump bright yellow. Tail-coverts and central tail largely metallic green; rest of tail black. *Below,* chin and throat metallic green; breast golden yellow, finely streaked with scarlet. Rest of lower plumage olive-yellow.

*Female:* Difficult to tell with certainty. Overall olive-green and olive-grey. No yellow band across rump. Under tail-coverts yellowish.

STATUS AND HABITAT: Fairly common resident from *c.* 1000 to 9000 ft. altitude (Singtam, Martam, Dikchu, Singhik, Lingtam, Chungthang, Lachen, Manshitang, Gangtok). Schäfer procured a specimen at Changu, *c.* 12,000 ft., in February.

DISTRIBUTION OUTSIDE SIKKIM: Assam north and south of Brahmaputra River, westward through SE. Tibet and Bhutan to E. Nepal. The species extends further west to Garhwal and Kumaon. Also found in Burma.

GENERAL HABITS: Similar to the foregoing.

NESTING: *Season*—May-June. *Nest*—typical of the sunbirds, an oval pouch of moss mixed with roots, lined with vegetable down, and with a lateral entrance hole near the top; no projecting porch over it. Suspended at the end of a twig of a low bush, 2 to 4 ft. from the ground. *Eggs*—usually 2, white, sometimes with a little reddish mottling at the broad end. Size about 16×11 mm.

RACIAL CHARACTERISTICS, MEASUREMENTS, ETC: The race *koelzi* of Sikkim and the E. Himalayas is larger in size than the W. Himalayan *nipalensis,* with the scarlet streaking on the breast much richer. The Survey specimens measure:

| | Wing | Bill | Tarsus | Tail |
|---|---|---|---|---|
| 2 ♂♂ | 53-54 | 23-24 | 16-17 | 56-60 mm. |
| 2 ♀♀ | 50-50 | 22-23.5 | 13.5-15 | 41-42 mm. |

A large series collected by Schäfer in Sikkim gives Wing 20 ♂♂ 53-56, 58 (av. 54.4); 14 ♀♀ 48-51 (av. 49.3) mm. (Stresemann).

Iris brown; bill brownish black; legs, feet and claws horny brown.

MRS GOULD'S YELLOWBACKED SUNBIRD, *Aethopyga gouldiae gouldiae* (Vigors)—**Plate 13, fig. 1; Plate 22, fig. 7**—is uncommon in Sikkim, with an indeterminate local status. Stevens says, 'Found at all elevations from 4000 to 10,000 ft. (in the Sikkim Himalayas) according to season.' I came across it only once at *c.* 6500 ft. (below Lachen), 24 February. Schäfer collected two males at 9000 ft. (Lachen), 29 June. Wing 55, 57 mm.

RECOGNITION: *Male:* Crimson above, yellow below. Forehead, crown, chin, throat, and a spot on either side of breast deep metallic purple-blue. Rump bright yellow. Upper tail-coverts and central tail metallic purple-blue.

*Female:* Overall olive grey-green with a yellow band across rump. Indistinguishable in the field from female of *saturata;* in the hand its smaller bill is a clue.

## THE INDIAN STREAKED SPIDERHUNTER

*Arachnothera magna magna* (Hodgson)

*Cinnyris magna* Hodgson, 1836, *Ind. Review* 1 (7): 272—Nepal.

F.B.I. 3: 414

LOCAL NAMES: Dom-siriok-pho (Lepcha); Yedong-pichang (Bhutia).

SIZE: Sparrow+.

FIELD CHARACTERS: A dumpy, short-tailed, flower-haunting bird with a long, slender, curved bill and stout, yellow legs. Overall olive-yellow, heavily streaked with black. Tail olive-yellow with pale yellowish tips and broad blackish subterminal bands. Sexes alike.

STATUS AND HABITAT: Not common or abundant, but frequent at elevations between *c.* 1500 and 5000 ft. (Singtam, Martam, Dikchu, Chungthang). Closely associated with wild banana plants (*Musa* sp.), in tropical foothills forest.

DISTRIBUTION OUTSIDE SIKKIM: The lower Himalayas from the Sutlej Valley to extreme NE. Assam. Assam, Manipur, Chittagong Hill Tracts (E. Pakistan), Burma. The species extends to Yunnan and Indochina.

GENERAL HABITS: Arboreal. Active and energetic. Keeps singly or in pairs, visiting a large variety of flowering trees, shrubs and parasitic *Loranthus* clumps in quest of nectar and the attendant insects which comprise its food. Sometimes hovers for several seconds at a time in front of a sprig of leaves to take a spider from its web. Inseparable from wild banana plants whose flowers form a perfect sheath for its bill and which, in return for the nectar, it must largely serve to pollinate. Utters a sharp, metallic *kikikik*, rather reminiscent of the Five-striped Squirrel's call, both whilst feeding and on the wing.

NESTING: *Season*—April-May. *Nest*—a neatly finished inverted dome of skeleton leaves compactly felted together with cobwebs and lined with similar but finer material. Sewn by means of vegetable down, like a tailor bird's nest, on the underside of a banana or similar large drooping leaf, keeping a small opening for entrance at the top. *Eggs*—2 or 3, variable, mostly sepia, chocolate, or some other shade of brown, with a darker zone at the broad end. Size about 23×16 mm. Both sexes share all the domestic chores. In spite of its structure and unsteady site the nest is commonly parasitized by several species of cuckoos. It is difficult to conceive how the eggs are introduced within unless it be by the bill of the parasite. Gammie recorded a full-fledged Indian Cuckoo (*Cuculus micropterus*) being fed by a pair of these spiderhunters in Sikkim in September (*S.F.* 5: 386).

RACIAL CHARACTERISTICS, MEASUREMENTS, ETC: The Fauna gives the measurements (♂♀) as: Wing 85-96; bill 34-41; tarsus 19-22; tail 46-64 (?) mm.

A female collected by Schäfer in Sikkim has Wing 85 mm.

Iris brown; bill horny brown or black, orange along edge of lower mandible; legs and feet chrome yellow (yellowish orange).

Indian Streaked Spiderhunter
About two-thirds

# *Family* ZOSTEROPIDAE: White-eyes

## THE INDIAN WHITE-EYE

*Zosterops palpebrosa palpebrosa* (Temminck)

*Sylvia palpebrosa* Temminck, Planch. Color. d'Ois., livre 49, pl. 293, fig. 3—Bengal=Cuttack, Orissa.

F.B.I. 3: 358

LOCAL NAME:

SIZE: Sparrow−.

FIELD CHARACTERS: A tiny, square-tailed, warbler-like bird, greenish yellow above, bright yellow and greyish white below, with a conspicuous white ring round the eye. Slender, pointed, slightly curved blackish bill. Sexes alike.

STATUS AND HABITAT: Fairly common. Resident at low and moderate elevations, up to at least 6500 ft. (Rangpo, Singtam, Martam, Pakyong, Gangtok). Affects secondary forest, and groves of trees near habitations.

DISTRIBUTION OUTSIDE SIKKIM: Northern India (up to *c.* 7000-8000 ft. in the Himalayas) from the extreme north-west, through Nepal, Bhutan and Assam. Also a large part of peninsular India, the rest being covered by two other races. The species stretches across to S. China and over Malaysia.

GENERAL HABITS: Arboreal; sociable; largely insectivorous and nectar-eating. Flocks of 5 to 20 birds or more hunt energetically amongst the foliage of trees and bushes for insects and spiders; or cling upside down and in all manner of acrobatic positions on *Loranthus* clumps and flowering bushes (such as *Woodfordia*) to probe with their bills into the flower-tubes for nectar. The fleshy pulp of fruits and berries is also eaten. The members of the flock maintain contact with one another by feeble conversational *cheeps*. In the breeding season the male has a pretty jingling song reminiscent of the Verditer Flycatcher's. It begins almost inaudibly, grows louder and again fades out as it began.

NESTING: *Season*—May-June, and perhaps later. *Nest*—a tiny cup of fibres, neatly bound and plastered with cobweb. Hung hammock-wise in the fork of an outhanging twig, normally 5 to 10 ft. up. *Eggs*—2 or 3, beautiful unmarked blue, sometimes with a deeper blue cap at the broad end. Size about 15×12 mm.

RACIAL CHARACTERISTICS, MEASUREMENTS, ETC: The races differ mainly in the extent and depth of the greenish and yellow in the plumage.

A specimen (♀) collected by the Sikkim Survey measures: Wing 51; bill 13; tarsus 15.5; tail 34 mm.

Two ♂♂ procured by Schäfer have Wing 51, 51 mm.

Iris brown; bill horny brown, plumbeous on underside at base of lower mandible; legs and feet plumbeous; claws horny brown.

# *Family* Ploceidae: Weaver Finches

## *Subfamily* Passerinae: House and Rock Sparrows

### THE CINNAMON TREE SPARROW

*Passer rutilans schäferi* Stresemann[1]

*Passer rutilans schäferi* Stresemann, 1939, *Orn. Monatsb.* 47: 176—Shigatse, S. Tibet.

F.B.I. 3: 180

LOCAL NAME: Kang-chigo-ma (Tibetan).

SIZE: House Sparrow.

FIELD CHARACTERS: Sexes dissimilar. *Male: Above,* rather like the Tree Sparrow (next), but with bright chestnut-red or cinnamon crown and upper parts and no black spot on the white ear-coverts. Two white wing-bars, the upper more prominent. *Below,* chin and throat black. Sides of head and rest of lower plumage sulphur-tinged grey, yellower on abdomen, vent and under tail-coverts. *Female: Above,* a broad fulvous-white supercilium; a dusky line through eye. Rest of upper plumage brown, rufous-tinged on tail-coverts. Double wing-bar as in male. *Below,* including sides of head, pale ashy yellow.

STATUS AND HABITAT: Uncertain. Not met with by the Survey, November to April. Stevens also failed to come across it in Sikkim but suggests that 'it may pass over the hills at moderate elevations when on migration'—presumably to and from Tibet. Meinertzhagen collected four examples in Sikkim in January, and Schäfer three (including a juvenile!) at Gangtok in September.

DISTRIBUTION OUTSIDE SIKKIM: Nepal, Bhutan, SE. Tibet. The Himalayas from Nepal westward to Afghanistan are occupied by the smaller race *cinnamomeus.* Other races extend the species eastward through NE. Assam, Manipur, N. Burma, Yunnan and Szechwan to Japan and Formosa.

GENERAL HABITS: A forest-dwelling sparrow, sometimes found in the neighbourhood of habitations and terraced cultivation. Gregarious in winter when it migrates to lower levels and the foot-hills. Gleans seeds and grain on the ground. *Call: chilp . . . chilp,* similar to the House Sparrow's, but softer and more musical. Also a *swee . . . swee* of the timbre of the Indian Robin's notes.

NESTING: Not recorded in Sikkim. *Nest*—a collection of grass, feathers, etc. in a tree-hole. *Eggs*—4 to 6, very like those of the House and Tree Sparrows. Size about 19×14 mm.

RACIAL CHARACTERISTICS, MEASUREMENTS, ETC: This race, *schäferi,* differs from the more familiar *cinnamomeus* of the W. Himalayas in its slightly larger size: Wing ♂♂ 77-82 mm.[1]

[1] This has since been synonymized with *cinnamomeus* (Gould) by Ripley—Synopsis Bds. India Pakistan.

Specimens collected by Schäfer in Gangtok (September) have the Wing 1 ♂ ad. 73; 1 ♀ ad. 69 mm., which seems rather small, but Meinertzhagen measures his 4 Sikkim ♂♂ as 76-80, which falls within the range of *schäferi*.

Iris brown; bill black in summer, horny brown above, yellowish below in winter (♂ only); legs and feet dark horny brown.

## THE TREE SPARROW

*Passer montanus malaccensis* Dubois

*Passer malaccensis* Dubois, 1885, Fauna Ill. Vert. Belg., Ois. 1: 572—Malacca.

F.B.I. 3: 177

LOCAL NAME:

SIZE: House Sparrow.

FIELD CHARACTERS: Differs from the familiar House Sparrow (cock) chiefly in the crown and nape being chestnut instead of ashy grey, and in having a black spot on the white cheeks. The black bib is smaller and does not cover the upper breast. Sexes alike.

STATUS AND HABITAT: Resident. Common in Gangtok town and many of the older established villages throughout Sikkim, up to about 9000 ft. elevation (Damthang, Pakyong, Dentam, Mangan, Chungthang, Lachen, Lachung). Seen further afield, in cultivation, during summer.

DISTRIBUTION OUTSIDE SIKKIM: The lower Himalayas from Kashmir to E. Assam. The species, in other races, stretches over practically the whole of Europe and Asia. Not in peninsular India.

GENERAL HABITS: Takes the place of the House Sparrow, freely occupying the thatch of huts and outhouses and the space between the ceiling and corrugated roofs of tenanted bungalows, bazaar shops, gompas, etc. In Gangtok there is a flourishing colony in the roofs and rafters of the General Hospital and its outhouses. Also in the gompa near the Government Secretariat. Usually keeps on the outside of buildings. *Call:* the typical sparrow chirp, but pleasanter and more musical than the House Sparrow's. *Food:* grain and seeds, leaf-buds, kitchen scraps, and insects.

NESTING: *Season*—May to (?) August, during which at least two broods are raised. *Nest*—an accumulation of grass, feathers, tow, etc. in holes in walls among eaves and rafters, or in the thatching. Sometimes in holes in trees and earth banks. *Eggs*—4 to 6, like the House Sparrow's, variable, chiefly pale greenish white, speckled with brown. Size about 19×14 mm.

RACIAL CHARACTERISTICS, MEASUREMENTS, ETC: Specimens collected by Col. Meinertzhagen in Sikkim give Wing 6 ♂♂ 67-73; 5 ♀♀ 66-72 mm. 13 ad. ♂♀ in Schäfer's Sikkim collection measure Wing 66-71 (av. 69.8) mm.—Stresemann.

Iris brown; bill black, paler in non-breeding season especially at base; legs and feet brownish flesh.

The Loke-Sálim Ali Survey did not come across the HOUSE SPARROW (*Passer domesticus*) anywhere in Sikkim although according to Stevens it occurs capriciously up to *c.* 4500 ft elevation in the Rungbong Valley.

The snow finches (genus *Montifringilla*), of which the following species have been obtained in Sikkim, are characterized by the tail being quite square-cut at the end and by the great amount of white in both wings and tail. The outer rectrices are largely white with a broad blackish terminal bar or spot. The sexes are practically alike.

## THE TIBET SNOW FINCH

*Montifringilla adamsi adamsi* Adams

*Montifringilla adamsi* Adams, 1859 (1858), *Proc. Zool. Soc. London*: 428, *ex* Moore MS.—Ladak.

F.B.I. 3: 187
LOCAL NAME: Richi-kya-shok (Tibetan).
SIZE: Sparrow+.

1 ad., 5 juvs., Gayamthashana Tso, 16,300 ft., 15-24 August 1938 (Schäfer). A large series from S. Tibet, including the above Sikkim adult, measures: Wing 16 ♂♂ 109-117 (av. 112.5); 15 ♀♀ 106-113 (av. 110.3) mm.

## THE REDNECKED SNOW FINCH

*Montifringilla ruficollis* Blanford

*Montifringilla ruficollis* Blanford, 1871, *Proc. Asiat. Soc. Bengal*: 227—Lachen Valley, N. Sikkim.

F.B.I. 3: 189
LOCAL NAMES: Abyé; Reb-che-har-pho (Tibetan).
SIZE: Sparrow.

Kangra Lama and Phalung, N. Sikkim, 15,000-10,000 ft., September (Blanford). Natu La, E. Sikkim, 14,100 ft., 21 December 1925 (Meinertzhagen).

## BLANFORD'S SNOW FINCH

*Montifringilla blanfordi blanfordi* Hume

*Montifringilla blanfordi* Hume, 1876, *Stray Feathers* 4: 487—Tibet.

F.B.I. 3: 190
LOCAL NAME: Abyé-pho (Tibetan).
SIZE: Sparrow.

At 15,200 ft., N. Sikkim, May(?). first Mt Everest Expedition. Natu La, E. Sikkim, 14,100 ft., 21 December 1925 (Meinertzhagen).

Gyagong; Gayamthashana Tso 16,000-16,500 ft., N. Sikkim, 20 July-1 October 1938.

Wing ad. ♂♂ *c.* 90-96 mm.

FIELD CHARACTERS: Overall effect of all the above three brown or greyish brown above; white below. A broad white patch or bar on the wings and much white in the tail feathers, particularly conspicuous in flight.

KEY FOR IDENTIFICATION

| | |
|---|---|
| Sides of neck pale fulvous; lores pale; no black marks on head ... | *adamsi* |
| Sides of neck cinnamon-buff or ferruginous; lores black ... | either *ruficollis* or *blanfordi* |
| Chin and throat white; black moustachial streaks; no black on forehead ... | *ruficollis* |
| Chin and throat black; no moustachial streaks; black streaks on white forehead ... | *blanfordi* |

NESTING: Not recorded in Sikkim. All these snow finches commonly utilize the disused burrows of mouse-hares as nest sites.

A fourth species, the MONGOLIAN SNOW FINCH, *Montifringilla davidiana potanini* (Sushkin), has recently been added to the Indian and Sikkim list by a specimen secured by Col. R. Meinertzhagen at Lachen, *c.* 9000 ft., 4 March 1952—a single bird mixed up in a large flock of Brandt's Mountain Finches. Wing 86 mm. (*Jour. Bombay Nat. Hist. Soc.* **51**(1):273.)

This small snow finch differs from *blanfordi* in having the throat as well as entire forehead black, unstreaked with white.

## *Subfamily* ESTRILDINAE: Munias

### THE SPOTTED MUNIA

*Lonchura punctulata punctulata* (Linnaeus)

*Loxia punctulata* Linnaeus, 1758, Syst. Nat., ed. 10, 1: 173—Asia=Calcutta.

F.B.I. 3: 91

LOCAL NAME:

SIZE: Sparrow—.

FIELD CHARACTERS: *Above,* forehead and sides of head rich chocolate-brown. Rest of upper parts dull chocolate-brown except rump which is barred with white and blackish, and upper tail-coverts and tail which are golden fulvous. *Below,* chin and throat rich chocolate-brown; rest white, speckled with black except on abdomen.

Non-breeding plumage like immature, more or less plain brown. Sexes alike.

STATUS AND HABITAT: Same as the next. Schäfer obtained it at Gangtok, *c.* 6300 ft.

DISTRIBUTION OUTSIDE SIKKIM: Throughout the lower Himalayas, up to *c.* 6000 ft., from Dalhousie to W. Assam; also practically all India and Ceylon. The species extends through Assam to Burma, Thailand, Malaysia and W. China.

GENERAL HABITS: Same as the next. Sometimes seen in large flocks of a hundred to two hundred or more birds.

NESTING: In general, similar in all respects to Hodgson's Munia.

RACIAL CHARACTERISTICS, MEASUREMENTS, ETC: Two ♂♂, 1 ♀ collected by Schäfer at Gangtok (June) have Wing 55, 58, 58 mm.

Iris orange-brown; bill slaty black, blue-grey at base of lower mandible; legs and feet bluish slate; claws brown.

## HODGSON'S MUNIA

*Lonchura striata acuticauda* (Hodgson)

*Munia acuticauda* Hodgson, 1836, *Asiat. Res.* 19: 153—Nepal.

Hodgson's Munia, about two-thirds

F.B.I. 3: 84

LOCAL NAMES: Samprek-pho (Lepcha); Namprek (Bhutia).

SIZE: Sparrow—.

FIELD CHARACTERS: A tiny, social, thick-billed, pointed-tailed, black and white finch. Forehead, face, chin, upper throat, wings and tail black. Rump white. Rest of plumage chocolate-brown except lower breast, abdomen and flanks which are greyish white streaked with brown. Sexes alike.

STATUS AND HABITAT: Resident. The Sikkim Survey came across this munia only at low elevations, *c.* 1000 to 3000 ft. (Rangpo, Singtam, Martam), but Stevens records it up to *c.* 6000 ft. in the Rungbong Valley. Affects the neighbourhood of cultivation.

DISTRIBUTION OUTSIDE SIKKIM: The Himalayan terai and foothills from Garhwal to E. Assam; Bihar, East Pakistan, N. Burma,

N. Thailand. Other races in peninsular India, Malaya, and the Indo-chinese subregion.

GENERAL HABITS: Very sociable. Keeps in flocks of 10 to 15, occasionally larger. Feeds mostly on the ground gleaning paddy grains and grass- and weed-seeds in and around harvested terraced fields. The flocks fly about in a disorderly undulating rabble, uttering feeble cheeps and chirrups.

NESTING: *Season*—chiefly May to August. *Nest*—a large, loosely woven globular structure of coarse grass and bamboo leaves, lined with soft feathery grass, with a lateral entrance hole. Placed in a dense bush 5 to 10 ft. up; sometimes several nests close together. *Eggs*—5 to 7, pure white, measuring about 15×11 mm. Both sexes share all the domestic chores. The nests are used by the entire family as dormitories long after the young have flown.

RACIAL CHARACTERISTICS, MEASUREMENTS, ETC: This race differs from nominate *striata* of the plains in having the abdomen streaked with brown; in the latter the abdomen is plain white. Specimens collected by the Sikkim Survey measure:

| | Wing | Bill | Tarsus | Tail |
|---|---|---|---|---|
| 2 ♂♂ | 53-55 | 12 | 14 | 38-43 mm. |
| 1 ♀ | 54 | 11.5 | 14 | 40 mm. |

Iris brown; upper mandible horny brown, lower bluish horn; legs and feet brownish plumbeous; claws horny brown.

# *Family* FRINGILLIDAE: Finches

## *Subfamily* EMBERIZINAE: Buntings

### THE CRESTED BUNTING

*Melophus lathami subcristatus* (Sykes)

*Emberiza subcristata* Sykes, 1832, *Proc. Zool. Soc. London:* 93—Dukhun.

F.B.I. 3: 221 (=*melanicterus*)

LOCAL NAME:

SIZE: Sparrow+.

FIELD CHARACTERS: *Male:* Glistening black with chestnut wings, of more or less the colour scheme of the crow-pheasant, but with tail also largely chestnut. A prominent pointed crest. *Female:* Also crested; dark brown with cinnamon colour in wings and tail.

STATUS AND HABITAT: A summer visitor, breeding up to *c.* 6000 ft. Largely absent in winter when the majority are down in the plains. Gammie found it breeding between 2000 and 4000 ft. in the Teesta Valley in May; C. M. Inglis at *c.* 5000 ft. (Dentam) in early August. Schäfer obtained specimens at Gangtok, *c.* 6300 ft., on 13 and 27 June and also on 15 and 25 February. Affects open grassy hillsides.

DISTRIBUTION OUTSIDE SIKKIM: The Himalayas up to *c.* 6000 ft. from Kashmir through Nepal and Bhutan to E. Assam. Resident in the peninsular Indian hills south to about Mahableshwar, and widespread in winter. The species extends to China.

GENERAL HABITS: Keeps in pairs or small scattered parties gleaning seeds and grain on the ground, and flying up into trees when disturbed. Partial to newly burnt stony 'jhoom' hillsides where its coloration is particularly obliterative in the charred surroundings. *Call: pink, pink* like a munia's, but louder. *Song* (of breeding male): spirited, reminiscent of the Pied Bushchat's: *which . . . which . . . which-whi-whee-which* (accent on *whee*).

NESTING: *Season*—May to July/August. *Nest*—a deep cup of grass lined with fine rootlets etc., in a pocket in an earth-cutting, or under a stone or grass tuft. *Eggs*—3 or 4, pale greenish grey freckled with purplish brown, densely at the broad end. Size about 20×15 mm. Both sexes share all the domestic chores.

RACIAL CHARACTERISTICS, MEASUREMENTS, ETC: Four ♂♂ collected by Schäfer in Sikkim measure Wing 83-85 mm.

Iris dark brown; bill dull orange-brown; legs and feet purplish brown; claws horny brown.

## THE LITTLE BUNTING

### *Emberiza pusilla* Pallas

*Emberiza pusilla* Pallas, 1776, Reise Russ. Reichs 3: 697—Transbaikalian Alps.

F.B.I. 3: 200

LOCAL NAME:

SIZE: Sparrow—.

FIELD CHARACTERS: A slim, sparrow-like bird with rufous and black head and black-streaked white underparts. White in outer tail feathers conspicuous in flight.

*Male: Above,* crown black with a rich rufous central band from forehead to nape; a pale rufous supercilium; a black line behind eye looping round rich rufous ear-coverts. Upper parts rufous and fulvous, broadly streaked with black. Wings dark brown with rufous edges. Tail dark brown; the inner webs of the two outermost pairs of rectrices largely white. *Below,* chin, cheeks and sides of throat rufous. Rest of lower plumage white, finely streaked with black on foreneck, breast and flanks. In winter, black and rufous of head duller and obscured by pale edges; chin and sides of throat white.

*Female:* Similar to winter ♂.

STATUS AND HABITAT: According to Stevens an irregular passage migrant in the Sikkim Himalayas to and from the eastern Indian plains. The Survey came across it only in early January between *c.* 4800 and 6500 ft. (Temi, Kewzing), and Schäfer procured four specimens at Gangtok, *c.* 6300 ft., between 30 December and 3 February. In the Bombay Natural History Society's collection there is a pair (♂♀) labelled 'Sikkim, May 1904, E. C. Stuart Baker'.

DISTRIBUTION OUTSIDE SIKKIM: *Summer* (breeding): Across N. Europe and N. Asia to Manchuria and Mongolia. *Winter:* Bengal, Bihar, Assam, Manipur, Burma, Thailand, Indochina, S. China.

GENERAL HABITS: Seen feeding on the ground at the edge of fallow terraced fields in small parties in association with tree pipits, flying up with them into tall bare tree-tops when disturbed.

MEASUREMENTS: The specimens collected by the Survey measure: 2 o? Wing 73; bill 11.5-12; tarsus 17-17.5; tail 58-58.5 mm. Schäfer's skins give Wing 1 ♂ 70; 3 ♀♀ 69, 70, 72 mm.

Iris brown; bill horny brown, paler on lower mandible; legs and feet brownish flesh or brownish yellow; claws horny brown.

Meinertzhagen obtained 3 ♂♂ of the rare YANGTSE BLACKFACED BUNTING, *Emberiza spodocephala sordida* Blyth, at Karponang (9000 ft.) on 19 December 1925 from a small, obviously migrating flock. This species has not been recorded from Sikkim before or since. It breeds in the Yangtse Valley and NW. China.

*Male: Above,* face black, shading into olive-green on head, neck and breast. Upper parts largely rufous-brown. *Below,* bright yellow.

*Female:* Like male but with a supercilium, cheeks and throat pale yellow. Brown spots on sides of throat and breast; the latter streaked with brown, as also are the flanks.

## *Subfamily* CARDUELINAE: Rosefinches, Goldfinches, etc.

### THE TIBETAN SISKIN

*Carduelis thibetana thibetana* (Hume)

*Chrysomitris thibetana* Hume, 1872, *Ibis:* 107—borders of Sikkim and Thibet.

**Plate 19, fig. 10** (facing p. 224)

F.B.I. **3**: 162

LOCAL NAME:

SIZE: Sparrow—.

FIELD CHARACTERS: A small yellow-green and brownish finch with a small, sharply pointed bill and slightly forked tail.

*Male: Above,* an ill-defined supercilium and collar bright yellow. Upper parts olive-yellow, the mantle faintly brown-streaked. Rump brighter yellow. Tail feathers brown, edged with yellow. A yellow wing-bar. *Below,* deep yellow, washed with olive on sides of neck and flanks.

*Female:* Like ♂ but duller and streaked with brown above and below, excepting throat and upper breast. Immature like ♀, but more heavily streaked, and with the abdomen whitish.

STATUS AND HABITAT: Uncommon. Observed or taken only in

winter, December to February, between *c.* 5000 and 10,000 ft. altitude (Temi, Lachen, Lingtam, Changu). In Nepal also it has been recorded as low as the Kathmandu Valley in winter in several recent years. In SE. Tibet, Ludlow found the birds paired off in May and June and affecting *Tsuga*, birch and *Abies* forest with an undergrowth of rhododendrons, several thousand feet below the snow-line.

DISTRIBUTION OUTSIDE SIKKIM: Nepal, SE. Tibet, NE. Burma (Yunnan border).

GENERAL HABITS: Gregarious and rather similar to those of the Greenfinch. Has a soft twittering note when in flock. Song not described.

NESTING: Not recorded in Sikkim, and almost unknown.

RACIAL CHARACTERISTICS, MEASUREMENTS, ETC: Specimens collected by Dr Biswas at Temi measure:

| | Wing | Bill | Tarsus | Tail |
|---|---|---|---|---|
| 2 ♀♀ | 66.5-69 | 13.5-14 | 14-14 | 40-41 mm. |
| 1 o? | 67 | 13 | 14 | 42 mm. |

Stevens's skins from Lingtam in the Chicago Museum of Natural History have Wing 7 ♂♂ 67-72.5 (av. 69.3); 2 ♀♀ 67, 68 mm.

Iris brown; bill pinkish grey; legs and feet fleshy grey.

## THE HIMALAYAN GREENFINCH

*Carduelis spinoïdes spinoïdes* Vigors

*Carduelis spinoïdes* Vigors, 1831, *Proc. Zool. Soc. London:* 44—Himalayas (=Simla-Almora District).

F.B.I. 3: 160

LOCAL NAME:

SIZE: Sparrow.

FIELD CHARACTERS: A handsome black-and-yellow finch with a slender, pointed bill. *Male: Above*, forehead, round the eye, short broad supercilium, sides of neck (meeting in an indistinct collar on hindneck), and rump bright yellow. Rest of upper plumage greenish brown, darkest on cap. Wings and tail blackish, variegated with bright yellow. A broad yellow wing-patch conspicuous in flight. *Below*, bright yellow.

*Female:* Like male, but duller. Immature birds heavily streaked blackish on the under side.

STATUS AND HABITAT: Resident. Not uncommon but rather local and sporadic. In winter (November to March) between *c.* 5000 and 9000 ft. altitude (Gangtok, Penlom La, Lachen, Lachung); higher in summer. The first Mt Everest Expedition obtained it at 12,500 ft. in May, and there is a breeding specimen from Yumthang, 12,800 ft., in the Chicago Natural History Museum, 20 June 1931. Affects forested hillsides of oak, rhododendron and conifers, frequently about cultivation.

DISTRIBUTION OUTSIDE SIKKIM: Throughout the Himalayas from

the Afghan frontier through Kashmir, Garhwal, Nepal, Bhutan. A very dark race, *heinrichi*, occurs in Manipur and Mt Victoria.

GENERAL HABITS: Gregarious at all seasons. Feeds chiefly on weed seeds; also millet in cultivated fields. Flocks frequently seen in the gardens and outskirts of Gangtok town questing for sunflower seeds; those of the wild hemp also being specially favoured. Has a number of soft twittering call notes uttered in flight which draw attention to a flock going overhead. A long-drawn *beez*, rather like the Goldfinch's, is uttered by the male from a tree-top.

NESTING: *Season*—May to July. *Nest*—a compact cup of grass, roots, moss, etc. lined with roots, feathers and hair. Placed on a horizontal branch of pine or deodar, sometimes several nests in a restricted area. *Eggs*—normally 4, greenish white or pale blue, lightly speckled with black and reddish, more densely at the broad end. Size about 19×14 mm.

RACIAL CHARACTERISTICS, MEASUREMENTS, ETC: The Yumthang specimen (♀) in the Chicago Museum measures Wing 77; bill 12.5; tail 45 mm. A large series collected by Schäfer in Sikkim gives Wing 8 ♂♂ ad. 77-81 (av. 79.1); 7 ♀♀ ad. 74-80 (av. 76.9) mm. (Stresemann).

Iris brown; bill fleshy or yellowish horn, darker on culmen and tip; legs and feet fleshy.

Mountain finches are sparrow-like birds of high altitudes, found chiefly in the treeless alpine country near the snow-line and in the Tibetan plateau facies of the Sikkim Himalayas and across the main range. Well adapted to living permanently under severe climatic conditions, and seldom descending lower than about 10,000 ft. even in winter except temporarily when driven down by abnormally freakish weather. They live in flocks and feed on the ground on seeds of various mountain plants, often on the edge of melting snow fields. Insects are also eaten.

The mountain finches (genus *Leucosticte*) differ from the snow finches (*Montifringilla*, p. 365), of similar habits, in having a distinctly forked tail and practically no white in their plumage. They are represented in Sikkim by the following two:

## THE SIKKIM MOUNTAIN FINCH

*Leucosticte brandti audreyana* Stresemann

*Leucosticte brandti audreyana* Stresemann, 1939, *Orn. Monatsb.* 47: 177—N. Sikkim.

F.B.I. 3: 194 (part)

LOCAL NAME:

SIZE: Sparrow—.

FIELD CHARACTERS: A blackish- and sandy brown finch with rosy rump. *Above*, forehead, round the eyes and anterior crown black.

Rest of upper parts dark brown, scalloped paler (sandy). Greyer on lower back and largely rosy on rump. Two whitish wing-bars, the upper one rose-tinged. *Below*, chin, throat and breast dark ashy brown, scalloped paler. Rest of lower plumage pale ashy. Sexes alike.

In late winter the pale edges to the feathers (scalloping) wear off, making the bird look very dark.

STATUS AND HABITAT: Resident at extreme altitudes up to *c.* 18,000 ft. and seldom found below *c.* 12,000 ft., an elevation at which Ludlow came across it in early May (Changu). Blanford recorded it above 15,000 ft. on the Kangra Lama Pass in September. The first Mt Everest Expedition obtained it up to 17,500 ft. in May (?). Meinertzhagen found it common in large flocks at 15,750 ft. (Gyagong) in the third week of November 'confining themselves to the bleakest situations'. Schäfer collected a large series in N. Sikkim (Gyagong between 17 July and 10 August and at Yabuk, Zemu Glacier, *c.* 13,000 ft., on 1 November—types of *L. b. audreyana*).

DISTRIBUTION OUTSIDE SIKKIM: North Sikkim; S. Tibet. The species overall is found in the mountains of central Asia from the Tian Shan in the north to the Himalayas in the south; west to the Pamirs, east to W. China.

GENERAL HABITS: Not appreciably different from the next (*nemoricola*) except that it is partial to wet or boggy ground such as by lakes and streams, and along the margins of melting snow fields. The birds run along the water's edge like sandpipers, picking up seeds etc. thrown up by the ripples.

RACIAL CHARACTERISTICS, MEASUREMENTS, ETC: This race is much darker than the west Himalayan *haematopygia*.

Schäfer's fine series from N. Sikkim and S. Tibet gives Wing 19 ♂♂ 112-122 (av. 116.9); 13 ♀♀ 109-117 (av. 115.8) mm.

Iris brown; bill (in breeding season) black, paler in ♀; legs and feet black.

From amongst a large vagrant flock of these mountain finches that had evidently been driven down by adverse weather, Meinertzhagen obtained a specimen of the very pale North Tibetan race *pallidior*, near Lachen (*c.* 9000 ft.) on 4.iii.1952. *Jour. Bombay Nat. Hist. Soc.* 51(1): 273.

## HODGSON'S MOUNTAIN FINCH

*Leucosticte nemoricola nemoricola* (Hodgson)

*F.(ringalauda) Nemoricola* Hodgson, 1836, *Asiat. Res.* **19**: 158—Nepal.

**Plate 19, fig. 11** (facing p. 224)

F.B.I. 3: 191

LOCAL NAME:

SIZE: Sparrow+.

FIELD CHARACTERS: A slim, dark, hen sparrow-like finch with a finer bill. *Above*, dark brown, scalloped with rufous; rump dark ashy grey; tail-coverts broadly white-tipped. Two narrow whitish wing-bars and a faint supercilium. *Below,* dull sooty brown, paler on abdomen. Breast and flanks streaked with blackish. Sexes alike.

STATUS AND HABITAT: Resident at high altitudes. Locally common and abundant. Breeding at 13,000-16,000 ft. and seldom descending below *c.* 9000 ft. even in winter (Lachen, Lachung, Thangu, Yumthang, Phalut, Changu, Karponang, Gyagong, etc.). Affects open mountain-tops, forest clearings, fallow or freshly sown barley fields, and edge of melting snow patches.

DISTRIBUTION OUTSIDE SIKKIM: Nepal, Bhutan, S. Tibet to Kansu. The adjoining W. Himalayas, through Kashmir to Afghanistan, are occupied by the race *altaica.*

GENERAL HABITS: Highly gregarious, even in the breeding season. Large flocks of up to 200 birds or more in winter, feeding on the ground, moving about like pipits. Every now and again the birds take wing and fly around in an undulating rabble. They resettle for a minute or two of feeding; then the nervous restlessness is resumed. The birds often alight on the bare branches of trees in starling-like clusters. *Call:* a soft, lively twitter. *Food:* seeds and insects.

NESTING: Not recorded in Sikkim. *Nest*—an untidy pad of grass and feathers hidden in a (rat-) hole in the ground or under a rock, in desolate wastes of rock and scree. *Eggs*—3 to 5, white, measuring about 20×15 mm.

RACIAL CHARACTERISTICS, MEASUREMENTS, ETC: The nominate race (*nemoricola*) is distinguished in the hand by its yellow axillaries as against grey in the W. Himalayan *altaica.*

Specimens collected by the Sikkim Survey measure:

| | Wing | Bill | Tarsus | Tail |
|---|---|---|---|---|
| 5 ♂♂ | 96-101 | 12.5-14 | 19.5-21.5 | 65-72 mm. |
| 5 ♀♀ | 95-101 | 12-13.5 | 20.5-21.5 | 64-69 mm. |

A large series taken by Schäfer in N. Sikkim and S. Tibet gives Wing 15 ♂♂ 94-103 (av. 98.8); 12 ♀♀ 91-98 (av. 94.2) mm.

Iris orange-brown; bill horny black, yellow at base of both mandibles; legs, feet and claws dark horny brown; soles of feet primrose yellow.

## BLANFORD'S ROSEFINCH

*Carpodacus rubescens* (Blanford)

*Procarduelis rubescens* Blanford, 1872 (1871), *Proc. Zool. Soc. London:* 694, pl. 74—Sikkim.

F.B.I. **3**: 148

LOCAL NAME:

SIZE: Sparrow—.

FIELD CHARACTERS: *Male* differs from ♂ *nipalensis* (next) chiefly in having the crown and nape crimson, practically concolorous with the forehead and supercilium.

*Female* differs from ♀ *nipalensis* in having the rump and upper tail-coverts not all brown but suffused with crimson.

STATUS AND HABITAT: Evidently rare. Recorded at elevations of 10,000 ft. and higher in summer, and as low as Gangtok in March, and 4500 ft. in the Sikkim Himalayas in winter (Stevens). The Chicago Natural History Museum has specimens collected by Stevens at Gnatong, *c.* 12,500 ft., in March 1931.

In Bhutan, Ludlow obtained two specimens in conifer and birch forest, 10,500-11,000 ft., in August and June respectively. Later, in SE. Tibet, he found the bird quite common between 10,500 and 12,000 ft. April to September.

DISTRIBUTION OUTSIDE SIKKIM: E. Nepal, Bhutan, SE. Tibet. A darker race is found in Yunnan.

GENERAL HABITS: Little known. According to Ludlow it has a peculiar and persistent clacking note which attracts attention, and but for which it would easily be overlooked in the sombre foliage of the firs.

NESTING: Unknown.

RACIAL CHARACTERISTICS, MEASUREMENTS, ETC: See under *C. nipalensis.* The Sikkim specimens in the Chicago Museum measure:

| | Wing | Bill | Tail |
|---|---|---|---|
| 1 ♂ | 80 | 14 | 49 mm. |
| 3 ♀♀ | 78-79 | 13-15 | 49-52 mm. |

'Iris dark brown; bill pale horny brown, the lower mandible paler and yellowish; legs light brown' (Fauna).

## THE NEPAL DARK ROSEFINCH

*Carpodacus nipalensis nipalensis* (Hodgson)

*C.(arduelis) Nipalensis* Hodgson, 1836, *Asiat. Res.* **19**: 157—Nepal.

**Plate 19, fig. 8 (facing p. 224)**

F.B.I **3**: 146

LOCAL NAME: Ka-biya (Lepcha).

SIZE: Sparrow.

FIELD CHARACTERS: *Male: Above,* forehead, forecrown and broad supercilium rosy crimson. A broad streak through eye, blackish crimson. Crown and nape deep velvety crimson. Rest of upper plumage deep brown washed with crimson. *Below,* rosy red, excepting upper breast and flanks which are crimson-brown, and under tail-coverts which are brown scalloped with pinkish white.

*Female: Above,* dark brown faintly scalloped with ochraceous, and with double wing-bars. *Below,* ochraceous brown; under tail-coverts scalloped paler.

STATUS AND HABITAT: Fairly common between *c.* 5000 and 9000 ft. altitude, November to May (Temi, Kewzing, Dentam, Gangtok, Lachen). Other records: Yumthang, 11,500 ft., (June); Sandakphu and Phalut, *c.* 12,000 ft. (August); Chola Range, 13,000-14,000 ft.

(end August). Affects rhododendron, oak and silver fir forest; also hill-slopes with stunted thorn bushes and weeds, and alpine pastures.

In Bhutan, Ludlow found it common in summer between 10,000 and 14,000 ft. altitude.

DISTRIBUTION OUTSIDE SIKKIM: The Himalayas from Kashmir through Garhwal and Nepal to the Assam hills north of Brahmaputra River. The species extends to Yunnan and the Shan States.

GENERAL HABITS: Gregarious in the non-breeding season. Flocks feed on berries in bushes and shrubs; also from rhododendron flowers (nectar ?).

NESTING: Not recorded in Sikkim, and not authentically known.

RACIAL CHARACTERISTICS, MEASUREMENTS, ETC: The straight, slender, pointed bill as in the Goldfinch, and the unstreaked plumage of the female characterize this rosefinch and the previous species *C. rubescens*. Specimens collected by the Sikkim Survey measure:

| | Wing | Bill | Tarsus | Tail |
|---|---|---|---|---|
| 2 ♂♂ | 90-93 | 13.5-15 | 23 | 61.5-64 mm. |
| 2 ♀♀ | 83.5-85.5 | 13-13.5 | 22 | 56.5-58 mm. |

Iris brown; bill horny brown, paler on lower mandible; legs, feet and claws horny brown.

Schäfer obtained four specimens of the large *Carpodacus rubicilla* (Güldenstädt) at *c.* 15,800 and 16,500 ft. altitude in the Tibetan Plateau facies of N. and E. Sikkim (Gyagong and 'Kiang-Lager') in July, August and October. Stresemann considers these as near the race *severtzovi* Sharpe, SEVERTZOV'S ROSEFINCH, but darker and possibly belonging to an unnamed race which, according to Schäfer, extends eastward to the upper reaches of the Yangtse River.

SIZE: Bulbul. *Male:* Crown, nape, ear-coverts and sides of head, chin and throat bright pink, each feather narrowly streaked with white. Upper parts pinky fulvous grey with the mantle practically unstreaked; lower plumage scalloped rosy pink. Wing 1 ♂ ad. 122; 2 ♂♂ imm. 113, 116 mm.

A vagrant specimen (♂) was collected by Dr Biswas at Chungthang, 5200 ft., on 24.i.1953 after a spell of inclement weather and heavy snowfall at the higher altitudes which had also driven down horned larks (*Eremophila*) to this level. Wing 121; bill 20; tarsus 24; tail 88 mm.

In the same area as Schäfer's (Gyagong *c.* 16,000 ft.) Col. Meinertzhagen obtained a ♂ and ♀ of the similar species but with a heavily dark-streaked mantle, namely the GREAT ROSEFINCH, *Carpodacus rubicilloides lucifer* R. & A. Meinertzhagen, on 21 November 1925, which suggests that the two species overlap in N. Sikkim, at least in winter. The Chicago Museum of Natural History has a ♂ 18.iii.1931 Thangu, 14,500 ft., coll. V. S. La Personne.

Wing 10 ♂♂ 108-115.5 mm. (Kinnear).

## THE COMMON ROSEFINCH

*Carpodacus erythrinus roseatus* (Blyth)

*Pyrrhula roseata* 'Tickell'=Blyth, 1842, *Jour. Asiat. Soc. Bengal* **11**: 461—Chyebassa.

F.B.I. **3**: 135

LOCAL NAMES: Phulin-pho (Lepcha); Amonga-tuti (Nepali); Do-di-ma-mo (Tibetan).

SIZE: Sparrow+.

FIELD CHARACTERS: *Male: Above,* forehead, crown and nape deep crimson. A rufous-brown line through eye. Rest of upper parts lighter crimson, edged with light olive-brown; rump and lower back crimson. *Below,* chin, cheeks, throat and upper breast bright crimson; rest paler, fading to pinkish white on abdomen. *Female: Above,* olive-brown streaked with dark brown. *Below,* dull olive-white, streaked with brown on throat and breast.

In both sexes the slightly forked tail and pale double wing-bars (pink in ♂, ochraceous in ♀) are conspicuous features.

STATUS AND HABITAT: Not met with by the Sikkim Survey between November and April when it is widespread over the Indian plains. According to Stevens 'occurs on the upward migration at moderate elevations'. He mentions specimens collected in March and April between 4250 and *c.* 4700 ft., and one out of a small party at 4800 ft. in November. F. N. Betts saw a male, evidently this species, at Yumthang (11,500 ft.) on 17 May 1943, and Schäfer took an example at Thangu (13,000 ft.) on 4 July 1938.

In Bhutan, Ludlow obtained it in June at 10,000 ft. and in October at 12,500 ft.

DISTRIBUTION OUTSIDE SIKKIM: *Summer* (breeding): The high Himalayas, from Kashmir through Garhwal and Nepal to Yunnan etc. *Winter:* Practically throughout India barring desert areas. The species stretches across to Asia Minor and Turkestan and on to Russia and northern Asia.

GENERAL HABITS: One of the non-skulking rosefinches, seen in flocks in the non-breeding season, feeding on millet and other crops, and flower nectar. *Call:* a pleasant interrogative whistling *tooee? Song:* (of male) 'a bright cheery refrain of 5 to 8 notes repeated at intervals from a tree or bush not far from the nest' (Osmaston).

NESTING: Not recorded in Sikkim. In Garhwal, *season*—June to August. *Nest*—a cup of grass, lined with fine roots and hair; placed in a rose or similar bush, 2 to 6 ft. up. *Eggs*—3 or 4, blue, spotted and speckled with blackish and light red. Size about 21×14 mm.

RACIAL CHARACTERISTICS, MEASUREMENTS, ETC: The west Asian (typical) race is paler than *roseatus*, above and below, with the rose colour of the underparts confined to chin, throat and breast.

The Fauna gives for ♂♀: Wing 83-87; bill 9-10; tarsus *c.* 17; tail 55-60 mm. Schäfer's skin from Thanku (♂ ad.) has Wing 84 mm.

Iris dark brown or hazel brown; bill horny brown, paler at base; legs and feet dusky brown.

## THE SIKKIM LARGE ROSEFINCH

*Carpodacus edwardsii rubicunda* (Greenway)
*Erythrina edwardsii rubicunda* Greenway, 1933, *Bull. Mus. Comp. Zool.* Harvard 74: 163—Su-Wa-Tong, Tibet, Salween-Irrawaddy Divide.

**Plate 19, fig. 7 (facing p. 224)**

F.B.I. 3: 131

LOCAL NAME:

SIZE: Sparrow+.

FIELD CHARACTERS: *Male: Above,* forehead mixed pink and crimson-brown. A broad glistening pink supercilium. Crown and nape deep crimson-brown with black shaft-lines. Rest of upper parts blackish, edged with rufous-brown and washed with crimson. Rump unstreaked rufous-brown with faint crimson flush. *Below,* cheeks, chin and throat pink with black shaft-streaks. Rest rosy brown; bright rosy pink on abdomen and vent.

*Female: Above,* ashy ochre-brown with broad dark streaks. An ill-defined ochre-buff supercilium. *Below,* buff, finely streaked with brown.

STATUS AND HABITAT: Not common but frequent between *c.* 8000 and 13,000 ft. elevation in practically all seasons (Lachung, Thangu, Karponang, Changu, Zemu). Affects low jungle of dwarf rhododendron and rose bushes or ringal bamboo, and opener mountainsides with *Berberis* and thorn scrub lining nullahs.

DISTRIBUTION OUTSIDE SIKKIM: Nepal, Bhutan and SE. Tibet to E. Assam. The species stretches to Kansu and Szechwan, possibly a different race.

GENERAL HABITS: A skulker like most of its congeners. Seen in small scattered parties feeding in bushes or on the ground.

NESTING: Not recorded in Sikkim, and imperfectly known.

RACIAL CHARACTERISTICS, MEASUREMENTS, ETC: Specimens collected by the Sikkim Survey measure:

| | Wing | Bill | Tarsus | Tail |
|---|---|---|---|---|
| 2 ♂♂ | 83-84 | 14-15 | 24 | 61.5-64 mm. |
| 1 ♀ | 82 | 15 | 24 | 66 mm. |

Schäfer's Sikkim specimens have Wing 1 ♂ ad. 80; 1 ♂ imm. 79; 2 ♀♀ 77, 78 mm.

Iris dark brown or dark orange-brown; bill horny brown, paler at chin; legs and feet brownish flesh, or horny brown.

## THE PINKBROWED ROSEFINCH

*Carpodacus rhodochrous* (Vigors)

*Fringilla rodochroa* (*sic*) Vigors, 1831, *Proc. Zool. Soc. London:* 23—Himalayas (=Simla-Almora District).

F.B.I. 3: 129

LOCAL NAME:

SIZE: Sparrow.

FIELD CHARACTERS: *Male: Above,* forehead and supercilium pale rosy red. Crown of head and a broad band behind eye brownish crimson. Rump rosy red. Rest of upper plumage pale brown suffused with dark rose and broadly streaked with blackish. *Below,* rose-red; sides of head paler and more glistening.

*Female: Above,* ashy rufous-brown with broad blackish streaks. Rump ochraceous buff with the streaks obsolete. *Below,* ochraceous buff, paler on chin and throat, streaked with blackish except on centre of abdomen.

STATUS AND HABITAT: Rare. Stevens and Meinertzhagen both obtained it only at Tonglu (*c.* 10,000 ft.) on the Sikkim side of the E. Nepal border in January.

DISTRIBUTION OUTSIDE SIKKIM: The high Himalayas, 10,000-17,000 ft., from Kashmir through Nepal.

GENERAL HABITS: Not different from the next species. *Call:* described as a canary-like note *sweet.*

NESTING: Not recorded in Sikkim. *Nest* and *eggs* similar to those of the Beautiful Rosefinch (next).

RACIAL CHARACTERISTICS, MEASUREMENTS, ETC: The Fauna gives for ♂♀ Wing 71-75; bill *c.* 10-11; tarsus *c.* 19-20; tail 58-62 mm.

Iris reddish brown; bill dark brown, paler on lower mandible; legs and feet dark brown.

## THE BEAUTIFUL ROSEFINCH

*Carpodacus pulcherrimus pulcherrimus* (Moore)

*Propasser pulcherrimus* Moore, 1855, *Proc. Zool. Soc. London:* 216—Nepal.

F.B.I. 3: 126

LOCAL NAME:

SIZE: Sparrow.

FIELD CHARACTERS: *Male: Above,* forehead and broad supercilium rosy pink and brown, with *no* white shaft-lines as in *C. thura.* Upper plumage ashy brown streaked with blackish; rump rosy red. *Below,* rosy red with black streaks on breast and abdomen. Flanks brown, streaked darker.

*Female: Above,* fulvous brown, broadly streaked with blackish, and with an ill-defined broad fulvous supercilium. *Below,* fulvous white, streaked with dark brown.

STATUS AND HABITAT: Found locally in winter (December to March) between c. 8000 and 12,000 ft. elevation (Lachung, Tonglo, Phalut). The first Mt Everest Expedition obtained it at 14,800 ft. (May?). Affects scrub on fairly open hill slopes.

DISTRIBUTION OUTSIDE SIKKIM: Garhwal, Kumaon, Nepal, Bhutan, SE. Tibet (south of the main range). Other races extend the species from Tibet to W. China.

GENERAL HABITS: As of other rosefinches. Keeps in small parties of 3 or 4 in bushes, and likely to be overlooked on account of its skulking and quiet disposition. 'Harsh bleating notes' by a party of males recorded by B. E. Smythies.

NESTING: Not recorded in Sikkim. In Garhwal, *season*—July-August. *Nest*—cup-shaped, of strips of bark and grass, lined with fine rootlets, wool and hair. Placed low down in bushes. *Eggs*—normally 4, greenish blue, sparsely blotched and spotted with black round the broad end. Size about 19×14 mm.

RACIAL CHARACTERISTICS, MEASUREMENTS, ETC: The Fauna gives for ♂♀ Wing 76-80; bill 10-11; tarsus c. 20; tail 62-64 mm.

Iris dark brown; bill horny brown, paler on lower mandible; legs and feet pinkish flesh or pinkish horn.

## THE SIKKIM WHITEBROWED ROSEFINCH

*Carpodacus thura thura* Bonaparte & Schlegel

*Carpodacus thura* Bonaparte & Schlegel, 1850, Monogr. Loxiens: 21, pl. 23—Sikkim.

**Plate 19, fig. 6** (facing p. 224)

F.B.I. 3: 123

LOCAL NAME:

SIZE: Sparrow+.

FIELD CHARACTERS: All rosefinches of the genus *Carpodacus* are distinguished by the overall rose-coloured plumage of the males, and the streaked brown plumage of the females without any pronounced green or yellow in it.

*Male: Above,* lores and face crimson; forehead, broad supercilium and ear-coverts pale glistening (silky) pink with white shaft streaks. Hind end of supercilium white. Crown, nape and back brown broadly streaked with black; rump rosy pink. Wing and tail feathers brown, margined dull pinkish. *Below,* chin and throat silky pink like forehead; rest of underparts bright rosy pink.

*Female: Above,* dark brown streaked with black. Feathers of rump and upper tail-coverts edged golden yellow. Forehead and a broad supercilium buff. *Below,* chin, throat, breast and flanks pale rufous, abdomen greyish white—all streaked with black. Mature males frequently keep in female plumage.

STATUS AND HABITAT: A high elevation rosefinch, resident between 10,000 and 14,000 ft. at all seasons and seldom found below 8000 ft.

even in winter (Lachen, Lachung, Thangu, Gnatong, Karponang, Changu, Sandakphu, Phalut, Pemionche). Blanford got it at 12,000 ft. in the Chola Range in August, and Schäfer at *c.* 6300 ft. (Gangtok) in May. Affects juniper scrub, dwarf rhododendron and ringal bamboo-covered slopes near and above the tree-line. Also open hillsides with *Berberis* and other thorn scrub.

DISTRIBUTION OUTSIDE SIKKIM: Garhwal, Nepal, Bhutan. The species stretches from the Afghan frontier in the west, through Kashmir and the above, to SE. Tibet; Yunnan Szechwan.

GENERAL HABITS: Keeps in small scattered parties, feeding in bushes or hopping on the ground—in winter often in deep snow. *Food:* seeds of blackberry and raspberry (*Rubus*), and also of various weeds. *Call:* 'a soft conversational *wid-wid*' (A. E. Jones).

NESTING: Not recorded in Sikkim, but Mandelli took a nest with c/3 in Nepal at 12,000 ft. elevation on 1 August—a compact cup of fine grasses, coated outside with brown moss and lined with hair. Placed 6 ft. up in a thorny bush. *Eggs*—rather like those of the Scarlet Finch (p. 385). Size about 22×16 mm.

RACIAL CHARACTERISTICS, MEASUREMENTS, ETC.: The west Himalayan race *blythi* (Garhwal, Kashmir, etc.) is a much duller rose-pink below with a strong purple tint.

Specimens collected by the Sikkim Survey measure:

| | Wing | Bill | Tarsus | Tail |
|---|---|---|---|---|
| 1 ♂ (brown) | 85 | 14 | 25 | 75 mm. |
| 1 ♀ ad. | 83 | 13.5 | 25 | 65 mm. |

Schäfer's large series from Sikkim gives Wing 5 ad. ♂♂ 85-86; 11 imm. ♂♂ and ♀♀ 81-86 mm.

Iris dark brown; bill pale horn colour; legs and feet fleshy grey.

## THE REDBREASTED ROSEFINCH

*Carpodacus puniceus puniceus* (Blyth)

*Pyrrhospiza punicea* 'Hodgson'=Blyth, 1845 (1844), *Jour. Asiat. Soc. Bengal* 13: 953—Himalayas (=Nepal).

F.B.I. 3: 120

LOCAL NAME:

SIZE: Bulbul—.

FIELD CHARACTERS: *Male: Above,* forehead and short broad supercilium glistening crimson. A brown streak through the eye. Rest of upper parts brown, scalloped paler. *Below,* cheeks, chin, throat and upper breast crimson, mottled with white. Abdomen ashy brown, streaked with blackish.

*Female: Above,* dark brown scalloped with pale yellowish brown, and on rump with yellowish green. *Below,* fulvous buff, streaked with dark brown. Mature males frequently keep in female plumage.

STATUS AND HABITAT: Rare. An extreme high elevation rosefinch. The first Mt Everest Expedition recorded it between 16,000 and

17,500 ft. in summer. Blanford obtained it on the Chola Range at *c.* 14,000 ft. in August 1870, Col. Meinertzhagen in Natu La (E. Sikkim) at 14,350 ft. in mid-winter (21 December 1925), and Schäfer at Thangu, 13,000 ft. and Gyagong, 16,000 ft., in July 1938.

Meinertzhagen describes its typical habitat—shared with *Grandala* and *Lerwa*—as the steep high-level country above tree-limit, clothed in dwarf vegetation (rhododendron-juniper scrub), which forms the transition zone between the true Himalayan and the true Tibetan Plateau facies.

DISTRIBUTION OUTSIDE SIKKIM: Nepal, Bhutan, SE. Tibet, Assam hills north of Brahmaputra River. The paler race *humii* inhabits the western Himalayas from Garhwal through Kashmir to Gilgit. The species extends to Szechwan and NW. Kansu.

GENERAL HABITS: Pairs or small parties. Shy. Addicted to bare, precipitous country with sparse dwarf vegetation where it hops about on the ground in search of food: petals and buds of various flowers, and seeds. For the west Himalayan race Whitehead describes the call-note as sounding like *'are you quite ready?'*.

NESTING: Nothing known. The W. Himalayan race builds a shallow cup of roots etc. in a scrubby thorn bush close to the ground, or on a ledge of rock.

RACIAL CHARACTERISTICS, MEASUREMENTS, ETC: This race differs from *humii* of Garhwal, Kashmir, etc. in being much darker, especially on the upper parts. The Fauna gives the measurements (♂♀) as: Wing 102-117; bill 14-15; tarsus 23-24; tail 74-83 mm.

Schäfer's skins from N. Sikkim give Wing 4 ♂ 106, 109, 110, 113; 1 ♀ 111 mm.

'Iris brown; bill horny to dark brown; legs and feet brown, generally with a fleshy tinge' (Fauna).

## THE REDHEADED ROSEFINCH

*Propyrrhula subhimachala* (Hodgson)

*Corythus ? subhimachalus* Hodgson, 1836, *Asiat. Res.* 19: 152—Nepal.

F.B.I. 3: 119

LOCAL NAME:

SIZE: Bulbul.

FIELD CHARACTERS: *Male: Above,* forehead, supercilium and cheeks crimson; crown, nape and back dull crimson; rump and upper tail-coverts bright crimson. *Below,* chin, throat and upper breast crimson, mottled paler on the last. Rest of lower plumage greyish brown, paler on abdomen.

*Female:* Rather like ♀ Scarlet Finch (p. 385)—brownish olive-yellow overall, with forehead, supercilium, and upper breast brighter and more yellowish, and a noticeably longer tail. Rump like upper breast, not bright yellow as in *H. sipahi.*

STATUS AND HABITAT: A dweller at high altitudes, 10,000 to

12,000 ft. or higher, winter and summer (Singalila Ridge, Tonglo, Sandakphu). Partial to patches of dwarf rhododendron.

In Bhutan, Ludlow collected specimens at 12,500 and 13,500 ft. between May and August, and met it up to 14,000 ft. in dwarf juniper.

DISTRIBUTION OUTSIDE SIKKIM: Nepal, Bhutan, SE. Tibet to Yunnan. The higher Assam hills and Manipur (in winter).

GENERAL HABITS: Little known. Shy, skulking and silent. Meinertzhagen records a sparrow-like chirruping but quite melodious note. Stomachs examined by him contained no trace of seeds, but only green food.

NESTING: Not authentically recorded.

RACIAL CHARACTERISTICS, MEASUREMENTS, ETC: The Fauna gives for ♂♀ Wing 92-104; bill 12-13; tarsus 21-22; tail 74-79 mm.

'Iris hazel brown; bill, upper mandible blackish horny, lower mandible pale horny, darker at tip; tarsus brownish horny' (Stevens).

## THE HIMALAYAN CROSSBILL

*Loxia curvirostra himalayensis* Blyth

*Loxia himalayensis* 'Hodgson'=Blyth, 1845 (1844), *Jour. Asiat. Soc. Bengal* 13: 952—Nepal.

Himalayan Crossbill, about natural size

F.B.I. 3: 115

LOCAL NAME:

SIZE: Sparrow.

FIELD CHARACTERS: Easily recognized by the peculiar structure of the bill in which the tips of the two mandibles cross each other. *Male:* Scarlet crimson, brighter on rump, with brown wings and tail. *Female:* Greyish olive-green, with the rump more yellow.

Strong flight and twittering calls reminiscent of the Greenfinch (*Carduelis spinoïdes*).

STATUS AND HABITAT: A rare and erratic vagrant of unaccountable dispersal and wandering movements. Normally at high elevations in the fir, spruce and larch zone, but has been obtained as low as 5200 ft. in the Sikkim Himalayas in December. Sikkim specimens in the British Museum collected by Mandelli's Lepcha collectors, January to March, and May, lack precise localities or altitudes. The Survey came across it only at Phalut, *c.* 11,000 ft., where Dr Biswas of the Zoological Survey of India secured specimens. In the Chicago Natural History Museum there is one collected by V. S. La Personne at Lachen, *c.* 9000 ft., on 14 May 1931, where Schäfer also obtained it in November 1938.

Ludlow did not meet with it in Bhutan, but he collected specimens in SE. Tibet between 9500 and 13,500 ft.

DISTRIBUTION OUTSIDE SIKKIM: The Himalayas from Lahul in the west to SE. Tibet; NE. Burma, Yunnan.

GENERAL HABITS: A restless finch of erratic occurrences, seen in small flocks frequenting the tops of spruce, larch and other conifers, with parrot-like movements when feeding. *Food:* mainly seeds of coniferous trees, to extract which from the cones the bill is specially adapted. Stevens records shooting a specimen clinging to and pecking at the face of a boulder, whose stomach contained minute pieces of white quartz!

NESTING: Not recorded.

RACIAL CHARACTERISTICS, MEASUREMENTS, ETC: There is a wide variation in the wing and bill lengths of Sikkim birds, but evidently they all belong to the one race *himalayensis* and are not composed of a resident and a migrant population as has been suggested. Two ♂♂ shot together by Schäfer from the same flock have Wing 82 and 89 mm.

Dr Biswas's Phalut specimens measure:

| | Wing | Bill | Tarsus | Tail |
|---|---|---|---|---|
| 4 ♂♂ | 82-85 | 17.5-19 | 15-16 | 50-55 mm. |

Iris hazel brown; upper mandible dark horny, lower tinged greenish; legs and feet horny brown; claws darker.

## THE GOLDENHEADED BLACK FINCH

*Pyrrhoplectes epauletta* (Hodgson)

*Pyrrhula ? Epauletta* Hodgson, 1836, *Asiat. Res.* **19**: 156—Nepal.

**Plate 19, fig. 4** (facing p. 224)

F.B.I. **3**: **114**

LOCAL NAME: Lho-sampreh-pho (Lepcha).

SIZE: Sparrow.

FIELD CHARACTERS: *Male:* Entire plumage black except hindcrown and nape, which are golden orange. Middle of abdomen orange-buff. Inner webs of tertiaries white, showing as a white line on the wing.

*Female:* Head and neck yellowish ashy grey. Rest of plumage chestnut-brown, paler on underparts. White line in wing as in male.

STATUS AND HABITAT: A high elevation finch; not uncommon locally. In summer up to *c.* 14,000 ft.; apparently not descending lower than *c.* 5000 ft. in winter. Blanford obtained it at 11,000 ft. on the Chola Range in August; Meinertzhagen at 8800 ft. (Lachen) in November, and at 11,900 ft. (Changu) in December. There is a June specimen from Yumthang, 11,000 ft., in the Chicago Natural History Museum.

In Bhutan, and the Himalayan facies of SE. Tibet, Ludlow found it plentiful between 9000 and 13,000 ft.—May to October—affecting bamboo and rhododendron undergrowth.

GENERAL HABITS: Hops about in low scrub and dense thickets. Feeds on weed seeds, mostly on the ground, and keeps very still when thus occupied. *Call:* described as a low musical pipe; also as a rather squeaky whistling note not unlike that of the European Bullfinch.

NESTING: Nothing recorded.

RACIAL CHARACTERISTICS, MEASUREMENTS, ETC: Bill smaller and less swollen than in the bullfinches. Rump of same colour as back—not contrasty white. The pure white inner webs of the tertiaries (inner secondary wing quills) in both sexes, are a distinctive feature of this finch. The Sikkim specimen (♂) in the Chicago Museum measures: Wing 77; bill *c.* 12 (damaged); tarsus 18.5; tail 59.5 mm. According to the Fauna the Wing (♂♀) ranges between 75 and 79 mm.

Iris brown or black; bill horny brown, blacker on culmen; legs and feet brown or olive-brown.

## THE SCARLET FINCH

*Haematospiza sipahi* (Hodgson)

*Corythus* ? *Sipahi* Hodgson, 1836, *Asiat. Res.* 19: 151—Nepal.

Plate 19, fig. 5 (facing p. 224)

F.B.I. 3: 117

LOCAL NAMES: Phanying-pho-biu (Lepcha); Labbia mapho (Bhutia).

SIZE: Bulbul—.

FIELD CHARACTERS: *Male:* Overall brilliant deep scarlet.

*Female: Above,* brownish olive-yellow with a bright yellow rump (conspicuous in flight); *Below,* brown, scalloped with yellowish grey.

STATUS AND HABITAT: Resident (?) between *c.* 2000 and 6500 ft. elevation. Not uncommon, but local and patchy (Dikchu, Singhik, Temi, Penlom La, Gangtok). Affects forest.

DISTRIBUTION OUTSIDE SIKKIM: Nepal, Bhutan, Assam hills north and south of Brahmaputra River; NE. Burma, Mt Victoria, Yunnan.

GENERAL HABITS: Social. Small parties and scattered flocks of 25-30 birds keep to the tree-tops in forest, feeding on various seeds and berries, and searching under the moss on the branches for insects. *Flight:* typically finch-like, strong and dipping, with rapid wing beats. *Call:* a pleasant *too-eee,* reminiscent in a way of the Large Cuckoo-Shrike (*Coracina*) but rather softer and higher pitched.

NESTING: Not recorded in Sikkim and little known. *Nest*—bulky, cup-shaped, of twigs and roots. *Eggs*—blue, blotched with reddish brown. Size about 23×18 mm.

RACIAL CHARACTERISTICS, MEASUREMENTS, ETC: Specimens collected by the Sikkim Survey measure:

| | Wing | Bill | Tarsus | Tail |
|---|---|---|---|---|
| 3 ♂♂ | 101-102 | 18-19 | 19-21.5 | 63.5-64 mm. |
| 1 ♀ | 99 | 19 | 21.5 | 60 mm. |

Schäfer's Sikkim skins give Wing 4 ♂♂ 100, 103, 104, 108; 5 ♀♀ 95, 99, 99, 99, 102 mm. *Contra* the suggestion in the Fauna, the relative tail-length in both sexes is equal (Stresemann).

Iris brown or hazel brown; bill ♂ brownish flesh colour with a pale crimson flush when fresh, ♀ without flush; legs, feet and claws horny brown.

## THE BROWN BULLFINCH

*Pyrrhula nipalensis nipalensis* Hodgson

*P.(yrrhula) Nipalensis* Hodgson, 1836, *Asiat. Res.* 19: 155—Nepal.

F.B.I. 3: 112

LOCAL NAME:

SIZE: Sparrow.

FIELD CHARACTERS: The short, abrupt, swollen bill, white rump (particularly conspicuous in flight), and metallic black wings and tail —the latter distinctly forked—readily distinguish all Sikkim bullfinches. *Male* differs from the Redheaded and Beavan's bullfinches in having the band round base of bill (also a narrow ring round eye) dark brown instead of velvety black. Crown, nape and back ashy brown; upper rump black, lower white. Wings and tail metallic purplish black. A pale ashy wing-bar. Outer web of innermost secondary edged with crimson. A white patch under and behind eye. *Below,* ashy vinous brown, turning to whitish on abdomen and to white on under tail-coverts.

*Female* differs only in the edge of the innermost secondary being yellow instead of crimson.

STATUS AND HABITAT: Rare. Has been obtained by Inglis at Tonglo, 10,000 ft., in June and by Blanford in the Lachen Valley, 10,000 ft., in September. I have examined specimens in the Chicago Natural History Museum collected by the Suydam Cutting Expedition at Lachung (9000-10,000 ft.) in June 1931. More recently Schäfer got it at Thangu, 13,000 ft., in July and at Gangtok, *c.* 6000 ft., in March.

DISTRIBUTION OUTSIDE SIKKIM: Throughout the Himalayas from Gilgit in the west to E. Assam, and on into China. Also Mt Victoria in Burma.

GENERAL HABITS: Similar to those of the Redheaded Bullfinch except for the call note which is described as more melodious—a whistling twitter.

NESTING: Not authentically known.

RACIAL CHARACTERISTICS, MEASUREMENTS, ETC: Sikkim specimens in the Chicago Museum measured by me:

| | Wing | Bill | Tarsus | Tail |
|---|---|---|---|---|
| 2 ♂♂ | 89 | 12.5-13 | 17-17.5 | 72.5-77 mm. |
| 1 ♀ | 85 | 12 | — | 70.5 mm. |

An ad. ♂ in Schäfer's Sikkim collection has Wing 88 mm.

Iris brown; bill greenish horn with black tip; legs and feet fleshy brown.

## BEAVAN'S BULLFINCH

### *Pyrrhula erythaca erythaca* Blyth

*Pyrrhula erythaca* Blyth, 1862, *Ibis:* 389--Sikkim.

F.B.I. 3: 111

LOCAL NAME: Kobyu (Lepcha).

SIZE: Sparrow.

FIELD CHARACTERS: *Male* differentiated from the Redheaded Bullfinch by the crown being ashy grey like the back, instead of red Upper rump black; lower rump white. *Below,* throat ashy grey; breast, upper abdomen and flanks orange-red. Lower abdomen grey, paling to white on under tail-coverts.

*Female:* Similar but browner and duller, and without red on the breast.

STATUS AND HABITAT: Very rare. Meinertzhagen is the only recent investigator who has collected it in Sikkim almost since it was first described thence, over 80 years previously—♂ 9.i.1926, Phalut, 10,700 ft. Ludlow did not obtain it during his first Bhutan expedition, but in SE. Tibet he found it common and abundant in the basin of the Subansiri, north of the main Himalayan range (between long. 92° 30′ and 94°), and collected a large series between 7000 and 13,500 ft. elevation—May to October. He concludes that the real home of this bullfinch lies east of Bhutan, and that its rarity in Bhutan and Sikkim is simply due to these areas being on the westernmost fringe of its distribution. Affects mixed conifer and rhododendron forest.

DISTRIBUTION OUTSIDE SIKKIM: Bhutan; SE. Tibet. The species extends to Yunnan, Szechwan and Kansu.

GENERAL HABITS: Not different from those of the Redheaded Bullfinch, including the calls. Feeds largely on the catkins of willow and buds of buckthorn trees. Frequently also on the ground.

RACIAL CHARACTERISTICS, MEASUREMENTS, ETC: Ludlow's specimens from Bhutan and SE. Tibet give Wing 11 ♂♂ 81-86; 12 ♀♀ 79-83 mm.

'Iris brown to dark brown; legs and feet fleshy brown to horny brown' (Ludlow).

## THE REDHEADED BULLFINCH

*Pyrrhula erythrocephala* Vigors

*Pyrrhula erythrocephala* Vigors, 1832, *Proc. Zool. Soc. London:* 174—Himalayas (=Simla-Almora District).

**Plate 19, fig. 3 (facing p. 224)**

F.B.I. 3: 110

LOCAL NAME: Kobyu (Lepcha).

SIZE: Sparrow.

FIELD CHARACTERS: *Male: Above,* a broad velvety black forehead band encircling base of bill and narrowly masking it at the chin. Crown, nape and hindneck vermilion or deep orange-chestnut. Back ashy grey; rump white; tail and wings metallic black. An ashy grey wing-bar. *Below,* pale dull red fading to white on lower abdomen and under tail-coverts.

*Female:* Like male but yellowish green on crown and nape, and greyish brown and whitish on underparts.

STATUS AND HABITAT: Fairly common but rather sporadic. In summer up to *c.* 13,000 ft.; in winter some birds down to 4000 ft. while others still at the highest limits (Chola Range, Sandakphu, Tonglo, Thangu, Lachen, Lachung, Yumthang, Gangtok, Singhik). Affects secondary growth in the rhododendron and conifer facies.

DISTRIBUTION OUTSIDE SIKKIM: Throughout the Himalayas from Kashmir to Bhutan and SE. Tibet.

GENERAL HABITS: Sociable. Usually in small flocks in bushes and shrubs, but frequently also on the ground. *Food:* mainly weed seeds and leaf-buds. *Call:* a soft plaintive whistle *phew-phew,* indistinguishable from that of the European Bullfinch.

NESTING: Not recorded in Sikkim. In the western Himalayas (9000-12,000 ft.) *season*—(? July)-August. *Nest*—cup-shaped, of thin twigs, lined with coarse grass and beard-moss. *Eggs*—3 or 4, dull grey-white with specks and blotches of reddish brown, and faint grey and lavender markings. Size about 21×15 mm.

RACIAL CHARACTERISTICS, MEASUREMENTS, ETC: The Fauna gives for ♂♀ Wing 77-80; bill 9-10; tarsus 18-19; tail 60-64 mm.

A large series collected by Schäfer in Sikkim has Wing 9 ♂♂ 77-80 (av. 78.5); 10 ♀♀ 76-80 (av. 77.7) mm. (Stresemann).

Iris brown or hazel; bill black; legs and feet pale flesh colour or fleshy brown.

## THE SPOTTEDWINGED GROSBEAK

*Mycerobas melanozanthos* (Hodgson)

*Coc.(cothraustes) Melanozanthos* Hodgson, 1836, *Asiat. Res.* 19: 150—Nepal.

F.B.I. 3: 105

LOCAL NAME: Maltam-pho (Lepcha).

SIZE: Myna.

FIELD CHARACTERS: *Male: Above,* including wings and tail, slaty black or blackish brown. Wings with oval yellow spots on the tertiaries, and a conspicuous white spot at the base of several primaries. *Below,* chin and throat dark brown; rest deep yellow.

*Female: Above,* black, each feather edged with yellow; more yellow on forehead and crown. A broad black band through the eye. *Below,* yellow, streaked with black on the sides. White wing-spot as in male.

The disproportionately large and heavy bluish bill, and the comparatively short distinctly forked tail are diagnostic features.

STATUS AND HABITAT: Resident; apparently uncommon. Schäfer obtained specimens at Gangtok, *c.* 6000 ft., in January and June 1939, and Elwes at Yumthang, 11,000 ft., in September (*c.* 1870). In Bhutan, Ludlow found it up to 12,000 ft. in summer in the conifer and birch zone, and down to 2000 ft. in winter in thick tropical forest.

DISTRIBUTION OUTSIDE SIKKIM: Throughout the Himalayas at appropriate altitudes, from Hazara in the west to E. Assam. Manipur, N. Burma, N. Thailand, Szechwan.

GENERAL HABITS: Ludlow remarks that in Bhutan these grosbeaks collect into flocks with the approach of autumn and become very noisy, especially in the mornings and evenings. They descend to lower altitudes with the advance of winter. *Food:* mainly kernels of the wild cherry and other nuts, to crack the hard shells of which its powerful bill is specially adapted. The cracking sound of cherry stones and nuts can be heard a good distance away and often provides the first indication of a feeding flock in the vicinity. *Calls:* a harsh *krrr,* and a parakeet-like note. In summer, a loud creaky song of half to one minute's duration—with occasional bulbul-like musical notes, frequently repeated.

NESTING: No record in Sikkim. *Season* elsewhere (at high altitudes), May to July. *Nest*—bulky, cup-shaped, of moss, fern-stems, roots, etc., up in a pine tree. *Eggs*—2 or 3, very pale grey-green, feebly ringed at the broad end with grey-brown or reddish freckles. Size about 30×20 mm.

RACIAL CHARACTERISTICS, MEASUREMENTS, ETC: The Fauna gives for ♂♀ Wing 126-135; bill 23-25; tarsus 23-24; tail 74-79 mm. An adult ♂ in Schäfer's Sikkim collection has Wing 130 mm.

Iris brown; bill bluish plumbeous; legs and feet leaden grey.

## THE WHITEWINGED GROSBEAK

*Mycerobas carnipes carnipes* (Hodgson)

*Coc.(cothraustes) Carnipes* Hodgson, 1836, *Asiat. Res.* **19**: 151—Nepal.

F.B.I. **3**: 104

LOCAL NAME:

SIZE: Myna.

FIELD CHARACTERS: *Male: Above,* including tail black; rump greenish yellow. Wings black with a conspicuous broad white band near base of primaries. Flight feathers tipped and edged with yellow. *Below,* chin, throat and breast black; rest of underparts greenish yellow or dull olive-orange.

*Female* similar but duller, with the black portions largely replaced by ashy brown.

STATUS AND HABITAT: Resident and fairly common between *c.* 8500 and 14,000 ft. elevation, even in winter (Lachung, Thangu, Gnatong, Phalut, Changu, Karponang). A bird of high elevations, especially partial to juniper forest and scrub.

DISTRIBUTION OUTSIDE SIKKIM: The high Himalayas from Garhwal through Nepal, Bhutan, and SE. Tibet to E. Assam. The species extends westward to Afghanistan and N. Iran.

GENERAL HABITS: Similar to those of the Allied Grosbeak (next). Goes about in large flocks in winter. Meinertzhagen describes it as noisy and restless, with a rasping call-note and a clumsy dipping flight. *Food:* mostly juniper berries.

NESTING: Not recorded in Sikkim, but Schäfer took a juvenile specimen at Thangu, 13,000 ft., in July.

RACIAL CHARACTERISTICS, MEASUREMENTS, ETC: Meinertzhagen, who examined a large series of Sikkim skins, comments upon the inordinately large variation in the wing length, ranging between 103 and 123 mm. Schäfer's Sikkim specimens have Wing 3 ad. ♂♂ 118, 120, 123; 1 ♀ 117 mm. (Stresemann). As these were collected in July, along with a juvenile, they obviously represent the resident population and are not migrants from the hills of W. China or E. Tibet as Meinertzhagen suggested the larger Sikkim birds (with Wing above *c.* 115 mm.) *may* be.

Iris brown; bill: 'upper mandible horny brown, lower mandible almost white; legs pale fleshy brown to fleshy pink. The bill apparently has no seasonal change of colour' (Fauna). Stevens describes the legs as 'plumbeous brown'.

# THE ALLIED GROSBEAK

*Mycerobas affinis* (Blyth)

*Hesperiphona affinis* Blyth, 1855, *Jour. Asiat. Soc. Bengal* **24**: 179—Alpine Punjab.

Plate 19, fig. 2 (facing p. 224)

F.B.I. 3: 103

LOCAL NAME:

SIZE: Myna.

FIELD CHARACTERS: A large, heavy-billed finch. *Male:* Black and deep golden- or orange-yellow of more or less the colour pattern of the Blackheaded Oriole.

*Female:* Head, chin and throat ashy grey. Rest of plumage olive-green above, yellower on rump; olive-yellow below. Wings and tail black.

STATUS AND HABITAT: According to Stevens 'occurs sparingly on the Singalila Ridge during the winter months and evidently does not descend to a lower limit than about 9000 ft. on either side of the Nepal-Sikkim frontier'. He obtained specimens at Tonglo, 9500-9900 ft., in January and February. Meinertzhagen records it at Darjeeling, 6600 ft., on 17 January 1926. The Sikkim Survey came across this grosbeak only at Thangu, *c.* 13,000 ft., in April. In Bhutan, Ludlow collected it between 10,500 and 14,000 ft. in June and July. A bird of high oak and conifer forests.

DISTRIBUTION OUTSIDE SIKKIM: The high Himalayas from Hazara in the west through Garhwal, Nepal, Bhutan and SE. Tibet to W. China.

GENERAL HABITS: Keeps in pairs or flocks, sometimes quite large ones, to tall fir and deodar trees, biting into the cones with its powerful bill to extract the seeds which are its chief food. Also takes berries from shrubs, and insects etc. on the ground. *Calls:* 'a sharp alarm note, *kurr*, like two stones struck together, and a musical call of seven notes *te-de-le-li-di-li-um*' (A. E. Osmaston). In Sikkim I recorded in April a loud creaking song, punctuated by musical bulbul-like notes, lasting about 30 seconds and constantly repeated.

NESTING: Has not been observed in Sikkim, nor apparently elsewhere within its Indian range.

RACIAL CHARACTERISTICS, MEASUREMENTS, ETC: Differs from the very similar but better known Black-and-Yellow Grosbeak (*M. icterioïdes*) of the western Himalayas in having the thighs yellowish instead of black in the ♂, and breast and abdomen olive-yellow instead of ashy grey and buff in the ♀.

The Fauna gives the measurements as: Wing ♂ 126-136, ♀ 122-128; bill 23-25; tarsus 28-29; tail 88-97 mm.

For a ♀ Stevens records: iris brown; bill greenish blue (sea green); tarsus fleshy; claws horny.

# APPENDIX

Birds recorded as occurring, or having occurred, in 'Sikkim' including the terai, foothills, mountains, and the Tibetan Plateau facies, of which either the status is indeterminate or no recent or sufficient data are available:

## *Family* PHALACROCORACIDAE: Cormorants

Indian Shag (*Phalacrocorax fuscicollis*)

## *Family* ARDEIDAE: Herons, Egrets

Giant Heron (*Ardea goliath*)
Cattle Egret (*Bubulcus ibis*)
Little Green Heron (*Butorides striatus*)

## *Family* ANATIDAE: Ducks, Geese

Pintail (*Anas acuta*)
Wigeon (*Anas penelope*)
Gadwall (*Anas strepera*)
Common Teal (*Anas crecca*)
Brahminy Duck (*Tadorna ferruginea*)
Barheaded Goose (*Anser indicus*)

## *Family* ACCIPITRIDAE: Vultures, Hawks

Blyth's Baza (*Aviceda jerdoni*)
Blackcrested Baza (*Aviceda leuphotes*)
Honey Buzzard (*Pernis ptilorhynchus*)
Rufousbellied Hawk-Eagle (*Lophotriorchis kienerii*)
Whitebacked Vulture (*Gyps bengalensis*)
Longbilled Vulture (*Gyps indicus*)
Fulvous Vulture (*Gyps fulvus*)
Cinereous Vulture (*Aegypius monachus*)
Osprey (*Pandion haliaetus*)

## *Family* FALCONIDAE: Falcons

Redlegged Falcon (*Falco amurensis*)
Hobby (*Falco subbuteo*)
Indian Hobby (*Falco severus*)

## *Family* TURNICIDAE: Bustard Quails, Button Quails

Bustard Quail (*Turnix suscitator*)
Little Button Quail (*Turnix sylvatica*)
Yellowlegged Button Quail (*Turnix tanki*)

*Family* RALLIDAE: Rails, Waterhens, etc.

Ruddy Crake (*Amaurornis fuscus*)
Moorhen (*Gallinula chloropus*)
Purple Coot, or Gallinule (*Porphyrio porphyrio*)

*Family* CHARADRIIDAE: Plovers

Whitetailed Lapwing (*Chettusia leucura*)
Redwattled Lapwing (*Hoplopterus indicus*)
Golden Plover (*Pluvialis dominica*)
Little Ring Plover (*Charadrius dubius*)
Wood Snipe (*Gallinago nemoricola*)
Pintail Snipe (*Gallinago stenura*)

*Family* PTEROCLIDIDAE: Sandgrouse

Tibetan Sandgrouse (*Syrrhaptes tibetanus*)
Lhonak Valley, May. Also between Gyagong and Tso Chomo, 17,000 ft. (Matthews).

*Family* PSITTACIDAE: Parrots

Large Indian Parakeet (*Psittacula eupatria*)
Blossomheaded Parakeet (*Psittacula cyanocephala*)
Lorikeet (*Loriculus vernalis*)

*Family* CUCULIDAE: Cuckoos

Hawk-Cuckoo, or 'Brainfever Bird' (*Cuculus varius*)
Redwinged Crested Cuckoo (*Clamator coromandus*)
Pied Crested Cuckoo (*Clamator jacobinus*)
Sirkeer Cuckoo (*Taccocua leschenaulti*)
Crow-Pheasant (*Centropus sinensis*)
Lesser Crow-Pheasant (*Centropus toulou (bengalensis)*)

*Family* STRIGIDAE: Owls

Hawk-Owl (*Ninox scutulata*)
Scops Owl (*Otus scops*)
Brown Fish Owl (*Bubo zeylonensis*)
Tibet Owlet (*Athene noctua ludlowi*)
Specimen ♂ (Wing 179 mm.) Gayamtashana Tso, *c.* 16,000 ft., N. Sikkim, 28.viii.1938 (Schäfer).

*Family* APODIDAE: Swifts

Alpine Swift (*Apus melba*)

*Family* MEROPIDAE: Bee-eaters

Redheaded Bee-eater (*Merops leschenaulti*)
Common Green Bee-eater (*Merops orientalis*)

*Family* CORACIIDAE: Rollers

Roller, or Blue Jay (*Coracias benghalensis*)

Pied Hornbill, about one-fifth

Family BUCEROTIDAE: Hornbills

Pied Hornbill (*Anthracoceros malabaricus*) (see figure above)

Family CAPITONIDAE: Barbets

Lineated Green Barbet (*Megalaima lineata*)
Blue-eared Barbet (*Megalaima australis*)

Family PICIDAE: Woodpeckers

Wryneck (*Jynx torquilla*)

Family PITTIDAE: Pittas

Indian Pitta (*Pitta brachyura*)
A specimen picked up dead, Gangtok, May 1953 (J. S. Lall).

Greenbreasted Pitta (*Pitta cucullata*)
A breeding specimen, Great Rangeet Valley, *c.* 1200 ft. (Jerdon)

Family HIRUNDINIDAE: Swallows, Martins

Crag Martin (*Hirundo rupestris*)
Sand Martin (*Riparia paludicola*)

Family CAMPEPHAGIDAE: Cuckoo-Shrikes, Minivets

Large Grey Cuckoo-Shrike (*Coracina novaehollandiae*)
Rosy Minivet (*Pericrocotus roseus*)

Family IRENIDAE: Fairy Bluebird, Chloropses, Ioras

Common Iora (*Aegithina tiphia*)

Family PYCNONOTIDAE: Bulbuls

Redwhiskered Bulbul (*Pycnonotus jocosus*)

Crowbilled Drongo
About one-fourth

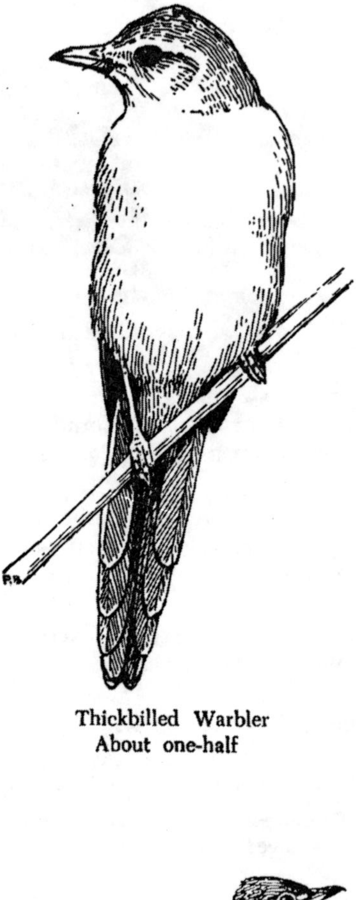

Thickbilled Warbler
About one-half

Pied Bushchat
About one-half

Layard's Flycatcher
About two-thirds

*Family* MUSCICAPIDAE:

*Subfamily* MUSCICAPINAE: Flycatchers

Blacknaped Blue Flycatcher (*Monarcha azurea*)
Layard's Flycatcher (*Muscicapa muttui*) (see figure opposite)
Brooks's Flycatcher (*Muscicapa poliogenys*)

*Subfamily* TIMALIINAE: Babblers

Abbott's Babbler (*Trichastoma abbotti*)
Jungle Babbler (*Turdoides striatus*)

*Subfamily* SYLVIINAE: Warblers

Ashy Wren-Warbler (*Prinia socialis*)
Brown Hill Warbler (*Prinia polychroa criniger*)
Whitethroated Flycatcher-Warbler (*Abroscopus albogularis*)
Thickbilled Warbler (*Phragamaticola aëdon*) (see figure opposite)
Grasshopper Warbler (*Locustella naevia*)

*Subfamily* TURDINAE: Thrushes, Robins, Chats

Pied Ground Thrush (*Turdus wardi*)
Salvadori's Thrush (*Turdus obscurus*)
Dusky Thrush (*Turdus eunomus*)
Pied Bushchat (*Saxicola caprata*) (see figure opposite)

*Family* PRUNELLIDAE: Accentors

Brown Accentor (*Prunella fulvescens*)

*Family* MOTACILLIDAE: Pipits, Wagtails

Water Pipit (*Anthus spinoletta*)
Indian Pipit (*Anthus novaeseelandiae*)
Rock Pipit (*Anthus similis*)
Forest Wagtail (*Motacilla indica*)

*Family* DICRURIDAE: Drongos

Black Drongo (*Dicrurus adsimilis* (=*macrocercus*))
Crowbilled Drongo (*Dicrurus annectans*) (see figure opposite)

*Family* ORIOLIDAE: Orioles

Blacknaped Oriole (*Oriolus chinensis*)

*Family* CORVIDAE: Crows, Pies, etc.

Tree Pie (*Dendrocitta vagabunda*)

*Family* DICAEIDAE: Flowerpeckers

Thickbilled Flowerpecker (*Dicaeum agile*)
Yellowvented Flowerpecker (*Dicaeum chrysorrheum*)
Scarletbacked Flowerpecker (*Dicaeum cruentatum*)

## *Family* NECTARINIIDAE: Sunbirds

Purple Sunbird (*Nectarinia asiatica*)
Indian Yellowbacked Sunbird (*Aethopyga siparaja seheriae*)

## *Family* FRINGILLIDAE: Buntings, Sparrows, Finches, Weavers

Chestnut Bunting (*Emberiza rutila*)
Yellowbreasted Bunting (*Emberiza aureola*)
Greyheaded Bunting (*Emberiza fucata*)
Tibetan Twite (*Carduelis flavirostris rufostrigata*)
Specimen Natu La, 14,000 ft., 21.xii.1925 (Meinertzhagen). Abundant in Bhutan north of main range, *c.* 15,000 ft. (Ludlow).
Redbrowed Finch (*Callacanthis burtoni*) (Plate 19, fig. 9)
Specimens: Tonglo, 10,000 ft., and Singalila Ridge (Stevens). Normally W. Himalayas east to Kumaon.

# INDEX

**Main entries are indicated by page numbers in bold type**


*abbotti, Trichastoma*, 397
*Abroscopus*, **241**
Accentor, Altai, or Rufousbreasted, **300**
  Brown, 397
  Eastern Alpine, **298**
  Maroonbacked, **301**
  Robin, **302**
  Rufousbreasted, **303**
Accipitridae, **2**, 393
*acuta, Anas*, 393
*acuticauda, Lonchura striata*, **367**
*acutirostris, (Calandrella acutirostris)*, **105**
*adamsi, (Montifringilla)*, **366**
  *Montifringilla adamsi*, **365**
*adsimilis* (=*macrocercus*), *Dicrurus*, 397
*aëdon, Phragamaticola*, 397
Aegithalinae, **343**
*aemodium, Conostoma*, 165, 221
*aemodius, Parus ater*, **338**
*aeneus, Dicrurus aeneus*, **316**
*aestigma, Muscicapa superciliaris*, **136**
*Aethopyga*, **356**
*affinis, Accipiter virgatus*, 4, **6**
  *(Apus affinis)*, **73**, **74**
  *Ithaginis cruentus*, **24**
  *Mycerobas*, 391
  *(Pericrocotus brevirostris)*, **116**
  *P.(ericrocotus) b.(revirostris)*, 117
  *Phylloscopus*, **224**
  *Seicercus*, **235**, **236**
*agile, Dicaeum*, 397
*agricola, Streptopelia orientalis*, **44**, 45
Alaudidae, **104**
*albicollis, Rhipidura*, 232, 265
  *Rhipidura albicollis*, **148**
  *Yuhina flavicollis*, 203
*albigularis, Abroscopus superciliaris*, **239**
*albiventer, Microura albiventer*, **156**
*albocinctus, Turdus*, **268**
*albogularis, Abroscopus*, 397
  *Garrulax albogularis*, **172**
*alboides, Motacilla alba*, **307**, 308
*albonotatus, Caprimulgus macrurus*, **69**
*albo-superciliaris, (Seicercus xanthoschistos)*, **237**
Alcedinidae, **75**
*altaica, (Leucosticte nemoricola)*, 374
*Amaurornis*, **104**
*ambigua, (Hirundo rustica)*, 108
  *Stachyris rufifrons*, **160**
*amurensis, Falco*, 393
Anatidae, **1**, 393
*annectans, Dicrurus*, 397
*annectens, Heterophasia annectens*, **212**
*apicauda, Treron apicauda*, **37**
Apodidae, **70**, **394**
Apodinae, **70**
*aquilonifer, Tetraogallus tibetanus*, **21**, 22
*Arachnothera*, **56**
*argentauris, Leiothrix argentauris*, **187**
Ari (Arita), xxviii
*arquata, Numenius*, 37
Artamidae, **314**
*Artamus*, 17, **255**
Arun-Kosi River, xxiv
*arvensis, Alauda*, **105**
*asiatica, Megalaima asiatica*, **85**
  *Nectarinia*, 398
*asiaticus, Caprimulgus*, 31
*athertoni, Nyctyornis athertoni*, **77**
*atrifrons, Charadrius mongolus*, **30**
*atrogularis, Prinia atrogularis*, **245**
  *Turdus ruficollis*, 268, **272**, 273
*atrosuperciliaris, P.(aradoxornis) a.(trosuperciliaris)*, 169
*audreyana, Leucosticte brandti*, **372**, 373
*aureola, Emberiza*, 398
*aureus, Gypaëtus barbatus*, **13**, 15
*aurifrons, Chloropsis aurifrons*, **119**
*austerum, (Glaucidium cuculoides)*, **64**
*australis, Megalaima*, 395
*azurea, Monarcha*, 397

Babbler, Abbott's, 397
  Assam Redfronted, **160**
  Bengal Redcapped, **164**
  Chestnut-headed, **208**
  Chestnut-throated Shrike-, **193**
  Coralbilled Scimitar, **153**
  Dusky Green, or Yellowthroated, **208**
  Goldenbreasted, **207**
  Green Shrike-, **192**
  Grey, 327
  Jungle, 126, 397
  Longbilled Wren-, **155**

Babbler, Nepal Goldenheaded, **162**
Nepal White-eyed Quaker, **211**
Quaker, 202, 214
Redcapped, **164**
Redheaded, **161**
Redwinged Shrike-, **191**
Rufousbellied Shrike-, **190**
Sikkim Blackthroated, **163**
Sikkim Rufousnecked Scimitar, **151**
Sikkim Rustycheeked Scimitar, **152**
Sikkim Spotted, **149**
Slatyheaded Scimitar, **150**
Slenderbilled Scimitar, **154**
Whiteheaded Shrike-, **194**
Yellowbreasted, **164**
Yelloweyed, 170, 327
Yellowthroated, **208**
Babblers, **149**, 397
*badius, Accipiter*, **5**
*baicalensis, Motacilla alba*, **308**
Bailey, Col. F. M., xxvi
*baileyi, (Yuhina flavicollis)*, **203**
*bakeri, Cuculus canorus*, 51, **52**, 53, 54, 55
*(Garrulax phoeniceus)*, **186**
*(Paradoxornis ruficeps)*, **170**
*Yuhina*, **201**
Barbet, Blue-eared, 395
Bluethroated, **85**
Goldenthroated, **84**
Great Assam, **83**
Green, **86**
Large Green, **78**
Lineated Green, 395
Barbets, **83**, 395
Barheads, 2
Barwing, Nepal, **195**
Sikkim Hoary, **196**
*bayleyi, Heterophasia capistrata*, **213**
Baza, Blackcrested, 393
Blyth's, 393
*beavani, Parus rubidiventris*, **339**
Bee-eater, Bluebearded, **77**
Common Green, 394
Redheaded, 394
Bee-eaters, **77**, 394
*bengalensis, Alcedo atthis*, **76**
*(bengalensis), Centropus toulou*, 394
*bengalensis, Gyps*, 393
*Pycnonotus cafer*, **123**
*Timalia pileata*, **164**
*benghalensis, Coracias*, 394
*berezowskii, Anthus hodgsoni*, **304**, 305
*besra, (Accipiter virgatus)*, **4**
*bethelae, Garrulax affinis*, **184**
*biddulphi, (Strix aluco)*, **66**
*bispecularis, (Garrulus glandarius)*, **321**
Biswas, Dr Biswamoy, xxx
Blackbird, Greywinged, **269**
Tibetan, **267**
Whitecollared, **268**
Blanford, (William Thomas), xxvi
*blanfordi, (Montifringilla)*, 366
or *ruficollis, (Montifringilla)*, 366
*Montifringilla blanfordi*, **365**
Bluebird, Fairy, **119**, 395
Sikkim Fairy, **121**
Blue Jay, or Roller, 394
Jays, **78**
*blythi, (Carpodacus thura)*, 381
*bonvaloti, Æ.(githalos)*, 344
*bottanensis, Pica pica*, **324**
*boulboul, Turdus*, 268, 269, 270
*Brachypteryx*, 257
*brachyura, Pitta*, 395
'Brainfever Bird,' or Hawk-Cuckoo, 394
*brevirostris, Collocalia brevirostris*, **70**
*(Pericrocotus)*, 116, 117
*Pericrocotus brevirostris*, **116**
Broadbill, Hodgson's, or Nepal Collared, **101**, 191
Longtailed, **102**
Broadbills, **101**
*brodiei, Glaucidium brodiei*, **63**
*brunnescens, Cettia acanthizoides*, **220**
*brunneus, Erithacus brunneus*, **246**, 285
*brunnifrons, Cettia brunnifrons*, **217**
Bucerotidae, **81**, 395
Bulbul, Black, **124**
Blackcrested Yellow, **122**
Browneared, **127**
Himalayan Black, **128**
Redvented, **123**
Redwhiskered, 395
Rubythroated, 122
Rufousbellied, **126**
Striated Green, **124**
Whitecheeked, **122**
Whitethroated, **125**
Bulbuls, **122**, 395
Bullfinch, Beavan's, **387**
Brown, **386**
Redheaded, **388**
Bunting, Chestnut, 398
Crested, **368**
Eastern Meadow, 263
Greyheaded, 398
Little, **369**
Yangtse Blackfaced, **370**
Yellowbreasted, 398
Buntings, **368**, 398
*Burhinus*, 30
*burkii, Seicercus*, 236
*Seicercus burkii*, 236

*burmanicus*, *Buteo buteo*, 7
*burtoni*, *Callacanthis*, 398
Bushchat, Collared, 282
Dark-Grey, 283
Hodgson's, 283
Pied, 247, 263, 397
Bustard Quails, 393
Buzzard, Honey, 393
Japanese Desert, 7
Longlegged, 6

*cacabata*, *Muscicapa sibirica*, 129
*caerulatus*, *Garrulax caerulatus*, 179
*caeruleocephalus*, *Phoenicurus*, 263
*caerulescens*, *Microhierax caerulescens*, 16
*calcarata*, *Motacilla citreola*, 310
*calidus*, (*Falco peregrinus*), 18
*calipyga*, *Leiothrix lutea*, 188
*calliope*, *Erithacus*, 248
*calochrysea*, *Culicicapa ceylonenis*, 146
*calvus*, *Torgos*, 11
Campephagidae, 111, 395
*canescens*, (*Rhipidura albicollis*), 149
*canorus*, (*Cuculus canorus*), 53
*cantator*, *Phylloscopus*, 233, 234
*capensis*, *Pelargopsis capensis*, 77
*capistrata*, (*Heterophasia capistrata*), 213
*capitalis*, *Hemipus picatus*, 111
Capitonidae, 83, 395
*caprata*, *Saxicola*, 263, 397
Caprimulgidae, 68
Carduelinae, 370
*carnipes*, *Mycerobas carnipes*, 390
*Carpodacus*, 380
*cashmeriensis*, (*Cinclus cinclus*), 296
*Delichon urbica*, 110
*caspica*, *Motacilla caspica*, 309
*castanea*, (*Sitta castanea*), 350
*castaneceps*, *Alcippe castaneceps*, 208
*castaneocoronata*, *Tesia castaneocoronata*, 216
*castaniceps*, *Seicercus castaniceps*, 238
*cathpharius*, *Dendrocopos cathpharius*, 96
*caudacuta*, (*Chaetura*), 72
*caudatus*, *Spelaeornis*, 158
*centralis*, (*Phylloscopus maculipennis*), 227
(*Tetraogallus tibetanus*), 22
Certhiidae, 352
*ceylonensis*, *Culicicapa*, 216, 238
(*Culicicapa ceylonensis*), 146
Champion, H. G., xxix
Changu (Chhanggu, or Tsomgo), xxviii
Charadriidae, 29, 394
Charadriinae, 29

Chat, Blue, 285
Indian Blue, 246
Chats, 246, 397
*cheela*, *Spilornis cheela*, 15
*chersonesus*, (*Chrysocolaptes lucidus*), 100
Chho Lhāmo Lake, xxiii
Chiffchaff, Siberian, 226
*chinensis*, *Kitta chinensis*, 322
*Oriolus*, 397
*chlorolophus*, *Picus chlorolophus*, 92
*chloronotus*, (*Phylloscopus proregulus*), 229
Chloropses, 119, 395
Chloropsis, Goldfronted, 119, 120
Orangebellied, 120
*chloropus*, *Gallinula*, 394
Chough, Alpine, 329
Himalayan Redbilled, 330
Himalayan Yellowbilled, or Alpine, 329
Hume's Ground, 327
Redbilled, 330
*chrysaea*, *Stachyris chrysaea*, 162
*chrysaeus*, *Erithacus chrysaeus*, 249
*Chrysomma*, 170
*chrysotis*, *Alcippe chrysotis*, 207
*chrysorrheum*, *Dicaeum*, 397
Chumbi Valley, xxiii
*chumbiensis*, *Alcippe vinipectus*, 209, 210
Chumthang (Chungthang), xxviii
Chungthang, xxiii
(Chumthang), xxviii
Cinclinae, 296
*cinclorhynchus*, *Monticola*, 280, 281
*Cinclus*, 295
*cinclus*, *Cinclus cinclus*, 296
*cinerea*, *Alcippe*, 208
*cinnamomeus*, (*Passer rutilans*), 363
*cinnamoventris*, *Sitta castanea*, 349, 350
*citreola*, (*Motacilla citreola*), 311
*citrina*, *Zoothera citrina*, 273
*cochinchinensis*, (*Chaetura caudacuta*), 72
*côelicolor*, *Grandala côelicolor*, 254
*collaris*, (*Prunella*), 299, 300
*collini*, *Muscicapa westermanni*, 135
*coltarti*, *Alcedo meninting*, 76
Columbidae, 37
*concinnus*, *Æ.*(*githaliscus*), 197
*confusus*, *Erithacus pectoralis*, 247
*Conostoma*, 166
*continentalis*, *Ceryle lugubris*, 75
Coot, Purple, or Gallinule, 394
*Coracias*, 40
Coraciidae, 78, 394
*Coracina*, 385

*corallina*, (*Sitta frontalis*), 351
Cormorants, 393
*coromanda*, *Halcyon coromanda*, 77
*coromandus*, *Clamator*, 394
*coronatus*, *Orthotomus cucullatus*, 242, 243
*Phylloscopus occipitalis*, 233, 234
Corvidae, 321, 397
Crake, Ruddy, 394
*crecca*, *Anas*, 393
Creeper, Nepal Tree, 352, 354
Sikkim Tree, 353, 354
Spotted Grey, 347
Stoliczka's Tree, 354
Wall, 347
Creepers, Tree, 352
*criniger*, *Prinia polychroa*, 397
*cristatus*, *Lanius cristatus*, 311
Crossbill, Himalayan, 383
Crow, House, 331
Jungle, 332
Crow-Pheasant, 394
Crows, 321, 397
*cruentatum*, *Dicaeum*, 397
*cruentus*, (*Ithaginis cruentus*), 24
*cruralis*, *Brachypteryx montana*, 285
Cuckoo, Baybanded, 55
Emerald, 56, 239
Haircrested, 102
Hawk-, or 'Brainfever Bird', 394
Himalayan, 53
Hodgson's Hawk-, 50
Indian, 51, 361
Indian Plaintive, 55
Khasia Hills, 51, 52
Large Hawk-, 49
Pied Crested, 394
Redwinged Crested, 394
Sirkeer, 394
Small, 54
Cuckoo-Dove, Bartailed, 43
Cuckoos, 49, 394
Cuckoo-Shrike, Dark Grey, 114
Large, 385
Large Grey, 395
Cuckoo-Shrikes, 111, 395
Cuculidae, 49, 394
*cucullata*, (*Kitta flavirostris*), 323
*Pitta*, 395
*cuculoides*, *Glaucidium cuculoides*, 64
*Culicicapa*, 194
*cuprea*, (*Ducula badia*), 39
Curlew, 37
Stone, 30
*curruca*, *Sylvia*, 226
Cutia, Nepal, 189
*cyaneus*, *Circus cyaneus*, 15
*cyanicollis*, *Eurystomus orientalis*, 78
*cyaniventer*, *Tesia*, 157, 215
*cyanocephala*, *Psittacula*, 394
*cyanotus*, (*Zoothera citrina*), 273
*cyanouroptera*, *Minla cyanouroptera*, 199

*daflaensis*, (*Actinodura nipalensis*), 197
*dalhousiae*, *Psarisomus dalhousiae*, 102
*darjellensis*, *Dendrocopos darjellensis*, 96, 97
*dauma*, *Z.*(*oothera*), 275
*Zoothera dauma*, 274
Densappa, Rai Bahadur, xxx
Dentam, Great Rangeet Valley, xxviii
Dicaeidae, 354, 397
*dichrous*, *Parus dichrous*, 340
Dicruridae, 315, 397
*dicruroïdes*, *Surniculus lugubris*, 57
*digitatus*, *Pyrrhocorax graculus*, 329, 330
Dikchu, xxviii
Dipper, Brown, 296, 297
Whitebreasted Asiatic, 296
Dippers, 296
*discolor*, *Certhia discolor*, 353
*dixoni*, *Zoothera*, 274, 275, 276
Dollar Bird, or Broadbilled Roller, 78
*domesticus*, *Passer*, 365
*dominica*, *Pluvialis*, 394
Dongkia Mountain, xxiii
*dorjei*, (*Cinclus pallasii*), 297, 298
Dove, Emerald, 46
Indian Spotted, 46
Rufous Turtle, 44
Doves, 37
*drasticus*, (*Abroscopus superciliaris*), 240
Drongo, Black, 397
Bronzed, 316
Crowbilled, 397
Haircrested, or Spangled, 317
Himalayan Grey, 315
Indian Lesser Racket-tailed, 319
Drongo-Cuckoo, Indian, 57
Drongos, 315, 397
*Dryocopus*, 91
*dubius*, *Charadrius*, 394
Duck, Brahminy, 393
Ducks, 1, 393
*dukhunensis*, *Calandrella cinerea*, 105
*M.*(*otacilla*) *a.*(*lba*), 307
*duvaucelii*, *Vanellus spinosus*, 29

Eagle, Black, 10
Bonelli's Hawk-, 9
Booted Hawk-, 9
Crested Serpent, 15
Himalayan Hawk-, 8
Pallas's Fishing, 11

Eagle, Ringtailed, or Pallas's Fishing, 11
Rufousbellied Hawk-, 393
*egertoni, Actinodura egertoni*, 195
Egret, Cattle, 393
Egrets, 393
*Elanus*, 17
*elwesi, Eremophila alpestris* 106, 107
Emberizinae, 368
*epauletta, Pyrrhoplectes*, 384
*epops, (Upupa epops)*, 80
*Eremophila*, 262, 376
*erithacus, Ceyx erithacus*, 77
Erpornis, Whitebellied, 206
*erythaca, Pyrrhula erythaca*, 387
*erythrocephala, Pyrrhula*, 388
(*Streptopelia orientalis*), 45
*erythrocephalus*, (*Garrulax erythro cephalus*), 185
(*Harpactes erythrocephalus*), 75
*erythrogenys*, (*Pomatorhinus erythrogenys*), 153
*erythropterus, Pteruthius e.(rythropterus)*, 191
*erythropygia*, (*Hirundo daurica*), 109
*erythrorhyncha*, (*Kitta erythrorhyncha*), 324
Estrildinae, 366
*ethologus, P.(ericrocotus) e.(thologus)*, 116, 117
*eunomus, Turdus*, 397
*eupatria, Psittacula*, 394
*eurhinus, Tringa totanus*, 31, 32
Eurylaimidae, 101

Fairy Bluebird, 119, 395
Falcon, Redlegged, 393
Shahin, 17
Falconet, Himalayan, 16
Falconidae, 16, 393
Falcons, 16, 393
*familiaris*, (*Certhia*), 352
*fasciata, Psittacula alexandri*, 47
*fasciatus, Nisaëtus fasciatus*, 9
*fastuosa*, (*Muscicapa sundara*), 140
*ferrea, Saxicola*, 283
*ferrugilatus*, (*Pomatorhinus erythrogenys*), 153
*ferruginea, Muscicapa*, 130
*Tadorna*, 393
*ferruginosus, Pomatorhinus ferruginosus*, 153
Finch, Blanford's Snow, 365
Goldenheaded Black, 384
Hodgson's Mountain, 373
Mongolian Snow, 366
Mountain, 301
Redbrowed, 398
Rednecked Snow, 365
Finch, Scarlet, 385
Sikkim Mountain, 372
Tibet Snow, 365
Finches, 368, 398
Weaver, 363
*finschii*, (*Psittacula himalayana*) or (*Psittacula*), 48, 49
*flammeus, Asio flammeus*, 67
*flammiceps*, (*Cephalopyrus flammiceps*), 346
*flavalus, Hypsipetes flavalus*, 127
*flaveolus, Criniger flaveolus*, 125
*flavicollis, Yuhina flavicollis*, 202, 203
*flavimentalis*, (*Abroscopus schisticeps*), 240, 241
*flavinucha, Picus flavinucha*, 91
*flavipes, Bubo*, 62
*flavirostris, Kitta flavirostris*, 323
*Paradoxornis flavirostris*, 171, 172
*flaviventris, Pycnonotus melanicterus*, 122
*flavogularis*, (*Seicercus xanthoschistos*), 237
*flavolivaceus, Cettia flavolivaceus*, 221
*flavulus, Hypsipites flavulus*, 127
Flowerpecker, Firebreasted, 354
Scarletbacked, 397
Thickbilled, 397
Yellowbellied, 356
Yellowvented, 397
Flowerpeckers, 354, 397
Flycatcher, Blacknaped Blue, 397
Bluethroated, 143
Brooks's, 397
Ferruginous, 130
Greyheaded, 146, 216, 238
Layard's, 397
Little Blue-and-White, 136
Little Pied, 135
Nepal Sooty, 129
Orangegorgetted, 131, 134
Pale Blue, 142
Pigmy Blue, 145
Redbreasted Blue, or Slatybacked, 134
Rufousbreasted Blue, 133
Rufoustailed, 135, 137
Sapphireheaded, 138
Sikkim Whitegorgetted, 132
Slaty Blue, 137
Slatybacked, or Redbreasted Blue, 134
Tickell's Redbreasted Blue, 143
Verditer, 142, 144, 362
Whitethroated Fantail, 148, 232
Yellowbellied Fantail, 147
Flycatchers, 129, 397
Flycatcher-Shrike, Brownbacked Pied, 111

Forktail, Blackbacked, 292
  Blackbreasted, 293
  Eastern Spotted, 290
  Little, 293
  Slatybacked, 292
  Spotted, 292
*formosa, Sitta*, 350
*formosus, Spelaeornis*, 159
*forresti, (Xiphirhynchus superciliaris)*, 155
*fortipes, C.(ettia)*, 218
  *Cettia fortipes*, 220
*franklinii, Megalaima franklinii*, 84
*fraterculus, (Pericrocotus flammeus)*, 115
Fringillidae, 368, 398
Frogmouth, Hodgson's, 67
Frogmouths, 67
*frontale, Cinclidium frontale*, 254
*frontalis, Dendrocitta*, 326
  *Phoenicurus*, 257, 258, 259
  *Sitta frontalis*, 351
*fucata, Emberiza*, 398
*fugax, Cuculus*, 50
*fuliginosus, Rhyacornis fuliginosus*, 265
*fuligiventer, Phylloscopus fuligiventer*, 225
*fuligula, Aythya*, 2
*fulvescens, Gyps*, 12
  *Prunella*, 397
Fulvetta, Sikkim, 209
*fulvifrons, Paradoxornis fulvifrons*, 167
*fulvus, Gyps*, 393
*fuscatus, Phylloscopus fuscatus*, 226
*fuscicollis, Phalacrocorax*, 393
*fuscus, Amaurornis*, 394
  *Artamus*, 16, 314

Gadwall, 393
Gallinule, or Purple Coot, 394
*ganeesa, (Hypsipetes madagascariensis)*, 128
Gangtok, xxiii, xxviii
*Garrulax* spp., 160
Gayamtashana Tso (Gayum Chhona), xxviii, 394
Geese, 1, 393
Gezing, xxviii
Giaogang (Gyagong, or Gyaokong), xxviii
*glareola, Tringa*, 37
Gnatong (Nāthang), xxviii
*godlewskii=striolatus, Anthus*, 306
*godwini, Pomatorhinus ruficollis*, 151, 152
Goldcrest, Sikkim, 234
Goldfinches, 370
*goliath, Ardea*, 393
Goosander, Eastern, 1
Goose, Barheaded, 393
Goshawk, Crested, 6
  Eastern, 3
*gouldiae, Aethopyga gouldiae*, 360
*govinda, Milvus migrans*, 2, 3
Grackle, North Indian, 336
*graculus, (Pyrrhocorax graculus)*, 330
*gradaria, (Columba leuconota)*, 40, 41
*Grandala*, 267, 382
Grandala, Hodgson's, 254
*grandis, Muscicapa grandis*, 139
  *Phoenicurus erythrogaster*, 262
*grantia, Gecinulus grantia*, 94
Great Rangeet, xxiii
Greenfinch, 383
  Himalayan, 371
Grosbeak, Allied, 391
  Black-and-Yellow, 391
  Spottedwinged, 389
  Whitewinged, 390
*grosvenori, (Garrulax rufogularis)*, 177
*gularis, Paradoxornis gularis*, 170
  *P.(ycnonotus)*, 122
  *Yuhina gularis*, 203
*gulgula, (Alauda)*, 106
*gulmergi, (Muscicapa sibirica)*, 129, 130
*guttacristatus, Chrysocolaptes lucidus*, 100
*guttaticollis, (Paradoxornis flavirostris)*, 172
*guttatus, Enicurus maculatus*, 290
*guttulata, (Ceryle lugubris)*, 75, 76
*gutturalis, Hirundo rustica*, 108
*guzurata, (Orthotomus sutorius)* 244
Gyagong (Giaogang, or Gyaokang) xxviii
*gyldenstolpei, Picus canus*, 90

*haematopygia, (Leucosticte brandti)*, 373
*haliaetus, Pandion*, 393
*Haliastur*, 9
*hardwickii, Chloropsis hardwickii*, 120
*haringtoni, Pomatorhinus erythrogenys*, 152, 153
Harrier, Hen, 15
Hawk-Cuckoo, or 'Brainfever Bird' 394
  Hodgson's, 50
  Large, 49
Hawk-Eagle, Bonelli's, 9
  Booted, 9
  Himalayan, 8
  Rufousbellied, 393
Hawk-Owl, 394
Hawks, 2, 393
*hazarae, Caprimulgus indicus*, 68, 69
*heinrichi, (Carduelis spinoïdes)*, 372

*helenae*, (*Harpactes erythrocephalus*), 75
*hemispila*, *N.*(*ucifraga*) *c.*(*aryocatactes*), 329
*hercules*, *Alcedo*, 76
Heron, Giant, 393
Little Green, 393
Herons, 393
*himalayana*, (*Certhia*), 352
*Prunella*, 299, 300
*P.*(*sittacula*), 47
*Psittacula himalayana*, 48, 49
*himalayanus*, *Pyrrhocorax pyrrhocorax*, 330
*himalayensis*, *Dendrocitta formosae*, 324, 325, 326
*Gyps*, 11
*Loxia curvirostra*, 383, 384
(*Regulus regulus*), 234, 235
*Sitta himalayensis*, 348, 350
*T.*(*etraogallus*), 22
Hirundinidae, 108, 395
Hobby, 393
Indian, 393
Hodgson, Brian, xxvi
*hodgsoni*, *Abroscopus*, 242, 243
*Abroscopus hodgsoni*, 241
(*Anthus hodgsoni*), 304, 305
*Batrachostomus hodgsoni*, 67
(*Certhia familiaris*), 352
*Muscicapella hodgsoni*, 145
*Phoenicurus*, 259
*hodgsonii*, *Columba*, 42
*Harpactes erythrocephalus*, 74, 75
*Muscicapa*, 134
(*Muscicapa*), 133, 137
*homrai*, *Buceros bicornis*, 81
Honeyguide, Yellowbacked, 86
Honeyguides, 86
Hooker, Sir J. D., xxix
Hoopoe, Tibetan, 79
Hoopoes, 79
*hopwoodi*, *Dicrurus leucophaeus*, 315
Hornbill, Great, 81
Pied, 395
Rufousnecked, 81
Hornbills, 81, 395
*hottentottus*, *Dicrurus*, 102
*Dicrurus hottentottus*, 317
*humei*, (*Micropternus brachyurus*), 89, 90
(*Phylloscopus inornatus*), 230
*Sphenocichla humei*, 160
*humii*, (*Carpodacus puniceus*), 382
*P.*(*aradoxornis*) *n.*(*ipalensis*), 167
*Paradoxornis nipalensis*, 168, 169
*humilis*, *Podoces*, 327
*hyperythra*, *Brachypteryx*, 285
*Dumetia*, 161
*hyperythra*, (*Muscicapa*), 137
*Muscicapa hyperythra*, 133
*hyperythrus*, *Erithacus*, 131, 252
*Hypopicus hyperythrus*, 95
*hypoleucos*, *Tringa*, 33
*hypoxantha*, *Rhipidura*, 147, 194, 240

*icterioides*, *M.*(*ycerobas*), 391
*ignicauda*, *Ae.*(*thopyga*), 358
*Aethopyga ignicauda*, 357
*ignipectus*, *Dicaeum ignipectus*, 354
*ignotincta*, *Minla ignotincta*, 197
*immaculata*, *Prunella*, 301
*immaculatus*, *Enicurus*, 292
*impejanus*, *Lophophorus*, 26
*indica*, *Chalcophaps indica*, 46
*Motacilla*, 397
*Saxicola torquata*, 282
Indicatoridae, 86
*indicus*, *Accipiter trivirgatus*, 6
*Anser*, 2, 393
(*Caprimulgus*), 69
(*Caprimulgus indicus*), 69
*Copsychus malabaricus*, 267
*Enicurus leschenaulti*, 293
*Erithacus indicus*, 251
*Gyps*, 393
*Hoplopterus*, 394
*indranee*, (*Strix leptogrammica*), 65
*indus*, *Haliastur*, 7
*innominatus*, *Picumnus innominatus*, 87
*inopinata*, (*Alauda arvensis*), 105
*inornatus*, *Phylloscopus inornatus*, 230
*insignis*, *Ducula badia*, 39
*Saxicola*, 283
*intermedia*, *Gracula religiosa*, 336, 337
*intermedius*, *Corvus macrorhynchus*, 332
*interstinctus*, *Falco tinnunculus*, 18
*Garrulus glandarius*, 321
*intextus*, (*Xiphirhynchus superciliaris*), 155
Iora, Common, 395
Ioras, 119, 395
*iouschistos*, *Ægithalos iouschistos*, 344
*iredalei*, (*Ægithalos concinnus*), 343
Irenidae, 119, 395
Ixulus, Chestnut-headed, or White-naped, 201
Yellownaped, 202

*jacobinus*, *Clamator*, 394
Jay, Sikkim Redcrowned, 321
Jays, Blue, 78
Jelep La, xxiii
*jerdoni*, *Aviceda*, 393
(*Prunella strophiata*), 303, 304
Jeyluk (Jeluk), xxviii

*jocosus, Pycnonotus*, **395**
Junglefowl, Red, **28**
Junnoo, xxiii

Kabru, xxiii
Kalimpong, xxiii
*kangrae, (Parus dichrous)*, 340, 341
*(Phylloscopus pulcher)*, 228
*kanoi, A.(pus) p.(acificus)*, 73
Kapup (Kupup), xxviii
Karponang, xxviii
*kashmirensis, (Accipiter virgatus)*, 4
*kelaarti, (Spizaëtus nipalensis)*, 8
*kessleri, Turdus*, **271**
Kestrel, Himalayan, **18**
Kewzing (Sosing), xxviii
*khasiana, (Prinia atrogularis)*, 245
'Kiang-Lager' (Schäfer's camp), xxviii
*kienerii, Lophotriorchis*, 393
Kinchinjhau, xxiii
Kinchinjunga, xxiii
Kingfisher, Assam Blue-eared, **76**
Blyth's, **76**
Brownheaded Storkbilled, **77**
Common Indian, **76**
Indian Ruddy, **77**
Threetoed Forest, **77**
West Himalayan Pied, **75**
Whitebreasted, **77**
Kingfishers, **75**
Kite, Blackeared, or Large Indian, **2**
Blackwinged, 17
Brahminy, 7
Large Indian, **2**
Pariah, **2**
*koelzi, Aethopyga nipalensis*, **359**
Kongra La Pass, xxiii
*kumaonensis, (Picus flavinucha)*, 92
*kundoo, O.(riolus) o.(riolus)*, 320
Kupup (Kapup), xxviii

*laetus, Pericrocotus ethologus*, **116**, 117
*lahulensis, (Lanius tephronotus)*, 312
Lall, John S., xxix
Laniidae, **311**
Lark, Crested, 107
Elwes's, or Tibetan, Horned, **106**
Longbilled Calandra, **107**
Rufous Short-toed, **105**
Tibetan, or Elwes's, Horned, **106**
Tibetan Short-toed, **104**
Larks, **104**
*lathami, (Lophura leucomelana)*, 28
Leiothrix, Redbilled, or 'Pekin Robin', **188**
*lepcharum, (Parus monticolus)*, 338
*lerwa, Lerwa*, **20**
*leschenaulti, Merops*, 394
*Taccocua*, 394
*lettia, Otus bakkamoena*, **60**
*leucocephalus, Chaimarrornis*, **264**
*leucogenys, Pycnonotus leucogenys*, **122**
*leucolophus, Garrulax leucolophus*, **176**
*leucomelana, (Lophura leucomelana)*, 28
*leucomelanura, (Muscicapa leucomelanura)*, 135
*Muscicapa leucomelanura*, **137**
*leuconota, Columba leuconota*, **40**
*leuconyx, Apus pacificus*, 72, 73
*leucopterus, Phoenicurus auroreus*, **260**
*leucoryphus, Haliaëtus*, **11**
*Leucosticte*, 372
*leucotis, (Pycnonotus leucogenys)*, 123
*leucura, Chettusia*, 394
*leucurum, Cinclidium*, **253**, **254**
*leuphotes, Aviceda*, 393
*levaillanti (? or macrorhynchus), Corvus macrorhynchus*, 332
Lhasa, xxiii
Lhonak Valley, 394
*lineata, Megalaima*, 395
*lineatus, (Garrulax lineatus)*, 181
*Milvus migrans*, **2**, 3
Lingtam, xxviii
Loke Wan Tho, xxx
*longicaudatus, (Dicrurus leucophaeus)*, 315, 316
*longirostris, (Eremophila alpestris)*, 106, 107
Lorikeet, 394
*lucifer, Carpodacus rubicilloides*, **376**
Ludlow, Frank, xxvi
*ludlowi, Athene noctua*, 394
*luteoventris, Bradypterus*, 224
*Bradypterus luteoventris*, **222**

*macei, Dendrocopos macei*, **97**
*macella, Nucifraga caryocatactes*, **328**, 329
*macgrigoriae, Muscicapa*, **141**
*maculatus, Chalcites*, **56**, 239
*(Enicurus maculatus)*, 290, 292
*maculipennis, P.(hylloscopus)*, 228, 229
*Phylloscopus maculipennis*, **227**
*maderaspatensis, Motacilla*, 308
*magna, Arachnothera*, 51
*Arachnothera magna*, **360**
*magnifica, Megalaima virens*, **83**
*magnirostris, Phylloscopus*, 149, **231**
Magpie, Blackrumped, **324**
Green, **322**
Redbilled Blue, **324**
Yellowbilled Blue, **323**
Magpies, Blue, **322**

Maharajkumar of Sikkim, Hon. Lt.-Col. P. T. Namgyal, P.V., O.B.E., xxx
*major*, *Cettia major*, **218**
*malabarica*, *Sturnus*, 255
*malabaricus*, *Anthracoceros*, 395
*malaccensis*, *Passer montanus*, 364
*malacoptilus*, *Rimator malacoptilus*, **155**
*malcolmi*, *Turdoides*, 327
Malkoha, Large Himalayan Greenbilled, **58**
Martam, xxviii
*mandellii*, *Arborophila*, **23**
*Certhia familiaris* 352, 353
*Pellorneum ruficeps*, **149**, 150
Manshitang, xxviii
*marginata*, *Zoothera marginata*, **278**
*marshalli*, (*Hypopicus hyperythrus*), 96
*marshallorum*, (*Megalaima virens*), 84
Martam, xxviii
Martin, Crag, 395
Kashmir House, **110**
Nepal House, **110**
Sand, 395
Martins, **108**, 395
*maxima*, *Melanocorypha maxima*, **107**
*maximus*, *Turdus merula*, **267**
*mcclellandi*, *Hypsipetes virescens*, **126**
(*Pomatorhinus erythrogenys*), 153
*meena*, (*Streptopelia orientalis*), **45**
Meinertzhagen, Col. R., xxvi
*melanolophus*, *Parus*, 339, 340
*melanosternus*, (*Acridotheres tristis*), 335
*melanota*, *Lophura leucomelana*, **27**
*melanotis*, *Garrulax pectoralis*, **174**
*Pteruthius melanotis*, **193**
*melanozanthos*, *Mycerobas*, **389**
*melanozanthum*, *Dicaeum*, **356**
*melaschista*, *Coracina melaschista*, **114**
*melaschistos*, *Accipiter nisus*, **5**, 6
*melba*, *Apus*, 394
*merganser*, (*Mergus merganser*), **2**
Meropidae, **77**, 394
*Merops*, 255
Mesia, Silvereared, **187**
*micropterus*, *Cuculus*, 361
*Cuculus micropterus*, **51**
*Microura*, 55, 215
Minivet, Scarlet, **115**
Shortbilled, **116**
Sikkim Longtailed, **116**
Yellowthroated, **118**
Minivets, **111**
Minla, Redtailed, **197**
*minor*, (*Pycnonotus melanicterus*), **122**
*mitchellii*, (*Dendrocopos canicapillus*), 98, 99
*modestus*, *Parus modestus*, **342**
*mohun*, *Mulleripicus pulverulentus*, **95**
*mollissima*, *Zoothera*, 274, 276
*Zoothera mollissima*, **275**
*monachus*, *Aegypius*, 393
Monal, **26**
*mongolus*, *C.*(*haradrius*), 31
*monileger*, *Muscicapa monileger*, **132**
*moniligerus*, *Garrulax*, **174**
*Garrulax moniligerus*, **173**
*monticola*, *Z.*(*oothera*), 278
*Zoothera monticola*, **277**
*monticolus*, *Parus monticolus*, **337**
*Montifringilla*, **365**, 372
Moorhen, **394**
Motacillidae, **304**, 397
Mountain Finch, Hodgson's, **373**
Sikkim, **372**
*multipunctata*, *N.*(*ucifraga*) *c.*(*aryocatactes*), **329**
Munia, Hodgson's, **367**
Spotted, **366**
Munias, **366**
*murghi*, *Gallus gallus*, **28**
Muscicapidae, **129**, 397
Muscicapinae, **129**, 397
*muttui*, *Muscicapa*, 397
Myna, Common, **335**
Greyheaded, 255
Mynas, **334**
Myzornis, Firetailed, **189**

*naevia*, *Locustella*, 397
Namgyal, Hon. Lt.-Col. P. T., P.V., O.B.E., Maharajkumar of Sikkim, xxx
Natu La, xxiii
Nectariniidae, **356**, 398
*neglectus*, (*Troglodytes troglodytes*), **295**
*nemoricola*, *G.*(*allinago*) [read *nemoricola C.*(*apella*)], 34
*Gallinago*, 394
*Leucosticte*, 301
*Leucosticte nemoricola*, **373**, 374
*nepalensis*, *Tichodroma muraria*, **347**
*newarensis*, *Strix leptogrammica*, **65**
*newtoni*, *Phylloscopus proregulus*, **229**
Nightjar, Common, 31
Himalayan Jungle, **68**
Longtailed, **69**
Nightjars, **68**
*nigriceps*, (*Heterophasia capistrata*), **213**
*S.*(*tachyris*), 162
*Stachyris nigriceps*, **163**
*nigrimenta*, *Yuhina* 201
*Yuhina nigrimenta*, **205**

*nigrimentum, Garrulax erythrocephalus*, **185**
Niltava, Large, **139**, **140**
Rufousbellied, **140**
Small, **141**
*nipalensis, Aceros*, **81**
(*Actinodura nipalensis*), **197**
(*Aethopyga nipalensis*), 359
*Alcippe*, 209
*Alcippe n.(ipalensis)* 208
*Alcippe nipalensis*, **211**
*Apus affinis*, **73**
*Brachypteryx leucophrys*, **286**
*Bubo nipalensis*, **61**
(*Carpodacus*), 374, 375
*Carpodacus nipalensis*, **375**
*Certhia*, **354**
*Cutia nipalensis*, **189**
*Delichon*, 110
*Delichon nipalensis*, **110**
*Hirundo daurica*, 73, **109**
(*Paradoxornis nipalensis*), 168
*Pitta*, **103**
*Prunella collaris*, **298**, 299
*Pyrrhula nipalensis*, **386**
*Spizaëtus nipalensis*, **8**
*Troglodytes troglodytes*, **294**
*nisicolor, Cuculus fugax*, **50**
*nisosimilis*, (*Accipiter nisus*), **5**, **6**
*niveogularis*, *Æ.(githalos)*, 344
*nivicola, Strix aluco*, **66**
*novaehollandiae, Coracina*, 395
*novaeseelandiae, Anthus*, 397
*nudipes, Chaetura caudacuta*, **71**, **72**
Nutcracker, East Himalayan, **328**
Nuthatch, Beautiful, **350**
Cinnamonbellied, **349**
Velvetfronted, **351**
Whitetailed, **348**
Nuthatches, **348**

*oatesi, Paradoxornis atrosuperciliaris*, **169**
*obscurus, Turdus*, 397
*occidentalis*, (*Dendrocitta formosae*), 325
(*Pteruthius xanthochloris*), 193
*occipitalis, Kitta erythrorhyncha*, 323, 324
*Y.(uhina)*, 203, 204
*Yuhina occipitalis*, **204**
*ocellatus, Garrulax ocellatus*, **178**
*ochracea, Sasia ochracea*, **88**, **89**
*ochropus, Tringa*, **32**
*ochruros, P.(hoenicurus)*, 258, 259, 260
*olivaceus, Cephalopyrus flammiceps*, **346**
*olivea*, (*Tesia cyaniventer*), 215

*orientalis, Mergus merganser*, **1**, **2**
*Merops*, 394
(*Streptopelia orientalis*), **45**
Oriole, Blacknaped, 397
Golden, 124, 320
Maroon, **320**
Orioles, **320**, 397
Oriolidae, **320**, 397
*Orthotomus*, 164, 192
Osmaston, B. B., xxvii
Osprey, 393
Owl, Brown Fish, 394
Eastern Spotted Scops, **61**
Forest Eagle-, **61**
Hawk-, 394
Himalayan Brown Wood, **65**
Himalayan Collared Scops, **60**
Himalayan Wood, **66**
Scops, 394
Shorteared, **67**
Sikkim Bay, 59
Tawny Fish, **62**
Owlet, Collared Pigmy, **63**
Himalayan Barred, **64**
Tibet, 394
Owls, 59, 394

Pakhyong (Pakyong), xxviii
Pakyong (Pakhyong), xxviii
*pallasii, C.(inclus)*, **296**
*pallidior*, (*Leucosticte brandti*), **373**
(*Microura albiventer*), **156**, **157**
*pallidiora*, (*Erithacus cyanurus*), 250
*pallidipes, C.(ettia)*, 220
*Cettia pallidipes*, **219**
*palpebrosa, Zosterops palpebrosa*, **362**
*paludicola, Riparia*, 395
Pandim, xxiii
*pandoo, Monticola solitarius*, **281**
*Paradoxornis*, 166
Parakeet, Blossomheaded, 394
Himalayan Slatyheaded, **48**
Indian Redbreasted, **47**
Large Indian, 394
Paridae, **337**
Parinae, **337**
Parrotbill, Blackbrowed, 169
Blackfronted, **168**
Brown, **166**
Fulvousfronted, **167**
Gould's, **171**
Great, **165**
Greyheaded, **170**
Lesser Redheaded, **169**
Redheaded, **169**
Parrots, **47**
Partridge, Blyth's, or the Rufousthroated Hill, **23**
Common Hill, **22**

Partridge, Redbreasted Hill, 23
Rufousthroated Hill, 23
Snow, 20
Partridges, 20
Passerinae, 363
*passerinus, Cacomantis merulinus*, 55
*patia, Orthotomus sutorius*, 243
*patkaicus, (Garrulax leucolophus)*, 176
*pectoralis, (Erithacus pectoralis)*, 247, 248
*Garrulax*, 173
*pelvica, Tephrodornis virgatus*, 113
Pemayangtse (Pemionche), xxviii
Pemionche (Pemayangtse), xxviii
*penelope, Anas*, 393
Penlom La (Penlong La), xxviii
Penlong La (Penlom La), xxviii
*pennatus, Hieraëtus*, 9
*peregrinator, Falco peregrinus*, 17
*Pericrocotus*, 102
*perniger, Ictinaëtus malayensis*, 10
*personata, M.(otacilla) a.(lba)*, 307, 308
*phaioceps, Micropternus brachyurus*, 89
Phalacrocoracidae, 393
Phasianidae, 20
Pheasant, Blackbacked Kaleej, 27
Blood, 24
Crimson Horned, or Satyr Tragopan, 25
Impeyan, or Monal, 26
Pheasants, 20
*phoeniceus, Garrulax phoeniceus*, 186
*phoenicuroides, Hodgsonius phoenicuroides*, 256
*(Phoenicurus ochruros)*, 261
*Phoenicurus*, 258
*Phylloscopus*, 54, 55, 145, 156, 221, 227, 228, 235, 240, 342
*picaoides, Heterophasia picaoides*, 214
Picidae, 87, 395
Piculet, Himalayan Speckled, 87
Rufous, 88
Pie, Blackbrowed Tree, 326
Himalayan Tree, 324, 326
Tree, 397
Pies, 321, 397
Pigeon, Ashy Wood, 43
Blue Rock, 41
Hodgson's Imperial, or the Nepal Maroonbacked, 39
Kokla Green, 38
Nepal Maroonbacked Imperial, 39
Pintailed Green, 37, 39
Snow, 40
Speckled Wood, 42
Turkestan Hill, 41
Wedgetailed Green, 38
Pigeons, 37
Pintail, 393
Pipit, Blyth's, 306
Hodgson's, 305
Indian, 397
Kansu Tree-, 304
Rock, 397
Vinaceousbreasted, or Hodgson's, 305
Water, 397
Pipits, 304, 397
Pitta, Bluenaped, 103
Greenbreasted, 395
Indian, 395
Pittas, 103, 395
Pittidae, 103, 395
Ploceidae, 363
Plover, Golden, 394
Little Ring, 394
Pamirs Lesser Sand, 30
Spurwinged, 29
Plovers, 29, 394
*plumipes, (Otus bakkamoena)*, 60, 61
*Pnoepyga*, 284
Pochard, Tufted, 2
Podargidae, 67
*poioicephala, Alcippe*, 202, 214
*poliocephalus, Cuculus poliocephalus*, 54
*poliogenys, Muscicapa*, 397
*Seicercus*, 238
*porphyrio, Porphyrio*, 394
*potanini, Montifringilla davidiana*, 366
*proregulus, (Phylloscopus)*, 227
*protegatus, (Corvus splendens)*, 332
Prunellidae, 298, 397
*przevalskii, (Cinclus cinclus)*, 296
*(Saxicola torquata)*, 282
*psaroïdes, Hypsipetes madagascariensis*, 128
Psittacidae, 47, 394
Pteroclididae, 394
*ptilorhynchus, Pernis*, 393
*puella, (Irena puella)*, 121
*pulcher, (Phylloscopus)*, 227, 229
*Phylloscopus pulcher*, 228
*pulcherrimus, Carpodacus pulcherrimus*, 379
*pulchricollis, Columba*, 43
*punctulata, Lonchura punctulata*, 366
*puniceus, Carpodacus puniceus*, 381
*purpurea, Cochoa*, 288, 290
*pusilla, Emberiza*, 369
*Microura pusilla*, 157, 159
Pycnonotidae, 122, 395
*pyrrhothorax, (Dendrocopos cathpharius)*, 97
*pyrrhotis, Blythipicus pyrrhotis*, 99
*pyrrhoura, Myzornis*, 189

Quail, Bustard, 393
Little Button, 393
Yellowlegged Button, 393
Quails. 20

*radcliffii*, (*Indicator xanthonotus*), 86
Rails, 394
Raja of Sikkim, xxix
Rallidae, 394
Rangeet, Great, xxiii
Rangpo, xxiii, xxviii
Ratong (River), xxvi
Raven, Tibet, 333
Redshank, 31
Redstart, Black, 261
Bluefronted, 257
Common, 258, 259
Daurian, 260
Güldenstädt's, 262
Hodgson's, 259
Plumbeous, 265
Whitecapped, 264
Whitethroated. 258
*reguloides*, *Phylloscopus reguloides*, 232
*reichenowi*, (*Sasia ochracea*), 88, 89
Remizinae, 346
*rhodochrous*, *Carpodacus*, 379
Rinchinpong, xxviii
Ripley, Dr S. Dillon, xxx
Robin, Bluefronted, 254
Blueheaded, 263
Golden Bush, 249
Magpie, 266
'Robin, Pekin', or Redbilled Leiothrix, 188
Robin, Redflanked Bush, 250
Rufousbellied Bush, 252
Whitebrowed Bush, 251
Whitetailed Blue Bush, 253, 254
Robins, 246, 397
Roller, 40
Broadbilled, or Dollar Bird, 78
Rollers or Blue Jays, 78, 394
Rongli, xxiii
*roseatus*, *Anthus*, 305
*roseatus*, *Carpodacus erythrinus*, 377
Rosefinch, Beautiful, 379
Blanford's, 374
Common, 377
Great, 376
Nepal Dark, 375
Pinkbrowed, 379
Redbreasted, 381
Redheaded, 382
Sikkim Large, 378
Sikkim Whitebrowed, 380
Rosefinches, 370
*roseus*, *Pericrocotus*, 395
*rubeculoides*, *Muscicapa rubeculoides*, 143
*Prunella*, 302
*rubescens*, *Carpodacus*, 374
*rubicilla*, *Carpodacus*, 376
*rubicunda*, *Carpodacus edwardsii*, 378
*rubricapilla*, *Macronous gularis*, 161, 162, 164
*rubricapillus*, *Ægithalos concinnus*, 343
*rubrocanus*, *Turdus rubrocanus*, 270
*rubropygius*, *Serilophus*, 191
*Serilophus lunatus*, 101
Rubythroat, Common, 248
East Himalayan, 247
Tibet, 248
*rufescens*, *Prinia rufescens*, 244
*ruficauda*, *Muscicapa*, 135, 137, 263
*ruficeps*, *Paradoxornis*, 169, 171
*Paradoxornis ruficeps*, 169
(*Pellorneum ruficeps*), 150
*S.*(*tachyris*), 160
*Stachyris ruficeps*, 161
*ruficollis*, *Garrulax*. 180
or *blanfordi*, (*Montifringilla*), 366
*Montifringilla*, 365, 366
*Turdus ruficollis*, 271, 272, 273
*rufifrons*, *S.*(*tachyris*) *r.*(*ufifrons*). 162
*rufigenis*, *Yuhina castaniceps*, 200
*rufilatus*, *Erithacus cyanurus*, 250
*rufinus*, *Buteo rufinus*, 6, 7
*rufiventer*, *Pteruthius rufiventer*, 190
*rufiventris*, *Monticola*, 279, 280, 281
*Phoenicurus ochruros*, 261
*rufogularis*, (*Arborophila*), 23
*Arborophila rufogularis*, 23
*Garrulax rufogularis*, 177
*rufonuchalis*, (*Parus rubidiventris*), 340
*rufostrigata*, *Carduelis flavirostris*, 398
*rufulus*, *Gampsorhynchus rufulus*, 194
*rupestris*, *Hirundo*, 395
*rusticola*, *Scolopax rusticola*, 34
Rustomjee, K. R., xxx
*rutila*, *Emberiza*, 398

*saliens*, (*Rhopodytes tristis*), 59
*sálimalii*, *Apus pacificus*, 73
Sandgrouse, 394
Tibetan, 394
Sandpiper, Common, 33
Green, 32
Spotted, 37
Sandpipers, 31
*sanguiniceps*, (*Picus canus*), 90, 91
*sapphira*, *Muscicapa*, 138
*sarkari*, (*Dendrocitta formosae*). 325
*saturata*, *Aethopyga saturata*, 358
*Upupa epops*, 79, 80

*saturatus*, *C.(ephalopyrus) f.(lammiceps)*, 346
*Cuculus saturatus*, 53, 55
(=*interstinctus*), *Falco tinnunculus*, 19
*Phodilus badius*, 59
*satyra*, *Tragopan*, 25
*saularis*, *Copsychus saularis*, 266
*saxicola*, (*Podoces humilis*), 327
Schäfer, Dr Ernst, xxvi
*schäferi*, *Passer rutilans*, 363
*schistaceus*, *Enicurus*, 292
*schisticeps*, *Abroscopus schisticeps*, 240
*Phoenicurus schisticeps*, 258
*Pomatorhinus schisticeps*, 150
*schvedowi*, *Accipiter gentilis*, 3
Scolopacinae, 31
*scops*, *Otus*, 394
*scouleri*, *Enicurus*, 293
*scutulata*, *Ninox*, 394
*seheriae*, *Aethopyga siparaja*, 398
*Seicercus*, 54, 55, 238, 240, 241
*semicoronatus*, *Dendrocopos canicapillus*, 98
*setafer*, *Garrulax lineatus*, 181
*severtzovi*, (*Carpodacus rubicilla*), 376
*severus*, *Falco*, 393
Shag, Indian, 393
Shama, 267
Shikra, 5
*shorii*, *Dinopium shorii*, 93
Shortwing, Gould's, 284
Hodgson's, 256
Nepal, 286
Rustybellied, 285
Whitebrowed, 285
Shrike, Ashy Swallow-, 16, 314
Blackheaded, 313
Brown, 311
Brownbacked Pied Flycatcher-, 111
Dark Grey Cuckoo-, 114
Greybacked, 312
Large Grey Cuckoo-, 395
Nepal Wood, 113
Shrikes, 311
Cuckoo-, 111
Swallow-, 314
Sibia, Blackheaded, 213
Longtailed, 214
Sikkim Chestnutrumped, 212
Sikkim Ornithological Survey, xxx
*sikkimensis*, *Garrulax striatus*, 175
*Irena puella*, 121
*Regulus regulus*, 234, 235
*similis*, *Anthus*, 397
*simlae*. (*Picus chlorolophus*), 92, 93
*simlaensis*, (*Minla strigula*), 199
(*Parus modestus*), 342
(*Phylloscopus proregulus*), 229
*simlaensis*, (*Picumnus innominatus*), 88
Simvo, xxiii
*sinensis*, *Centropus*, 394
*Chrysomma*, 327
Singalila Ridge or Spur, xxiii
Singhik, xxviii
Singtam, xxviii
Siniolchu, xxiii
*sipahi*, *Haematospiza*, 382, 385
Siskin, Tibetan, 370
Sittidae, 347
Sittinae, 348
Siva, Barthroated, 198
Nepal Bluewinged, 199
Skylark, 105
*smyrnensis*, *Halcyon smyrnensis*, 77
Snipe, 31
Common, 34
Eastern Solitary, 33
Pintail, 394
Wood, 34, 394
Snowcock, Sikkim, 21
Tibetan, 22
*socialis*, *Prinia*, 397
*solaris*, *Pericrocotus solaris*, 118
*solitaria*, *Capella solitaria*, 33
*solitaria*. *Monticola*. 255
*somervillei*, *Turdoides*, 126
*sonneratii*, *Cacomantis s.(onneratii)*, 55
*sordida*, *Emberiza spodocephala*, 370
*sordidus*, (*Cinclus*), 297
Sosing (Kewzing), xxviii
Sparrow, Cinnamon Tree, 363
House, 364, 365
Tree, 364
Sparrow-Hawk, Besra, 4
Indian, 5
Sparrows, 398
House and Rock, 363
*sparverioïdes*, *Cuculus sparverioïdes*, 49, 50
*speciosus*, *Pericrocotus flammeus*, 115
*sphenura*, *Treron sphenura*, 38
Spiderhunter, Indian Streaked, 360
Spiderhunters, Streaked, 51
*spilocephalus*, *Otus spilocephalus*, 61
*spilonotus*, *Parus xanthogenys*, 341
*spiloptera*, *Saroglossa*, 334
*spinoïdes*, *Carduelis spinoïdes*, 371
*spinoletta*, *Anthus*, 397
*splendens*, *Corvus splendens*, 331, 332
*squamatus*, *Garrulax*, 182
*Stachyris*, 164, 244
*stanleyi*, (*Rhipidura albicollis*), 149
Staphida, Whitebrowed, or Hume's, 200
Stare, Spottedwinged, 334
Starlings, 334

*stellata, Brachypteryx,* **284**
*stenura, Gallinago,* 394
Stevens, Herbert, xxvi
Stint, Temminck's, **36**
*stracheyi, Emberiza c.(ia),* **263**
*strepera, Anas,* 393
Stresemann, Prof. Erwin, xxvii
*striata, (Lonchura striata),* **368**
*striatus, Butorides,* 393
  *(Garrulax striatus),* 175
  *Pycnonotus striatus,* **124**
  *Turdoides,* 397
Strigidae, **59**, 394
Striginae, **60**
*strigula, Minla strigula,* **198**, 199
*striolatus, Anthus godlewskii=,* **306**
*strophiata, Muscicapa strophiata,* **131**
  *P.(runella),* 302
  *Prunella strophiata,* **303**
*struthersii, Ibidorhyncha,* **36**
Sturnidae, **334**
Sturninae, **334**
*subbuteo, Falco,* 393
*subcristatus, Melophus lathami,* **368**
*subhimachala, Propyrrhula,* **382**
*subunicolor, Garrulax subunicolor,* **183**
*sultanea, Melanochlora sultanea,* **345**
*sultaneus, (Chrysocolaptes lucidus),* 100
Sunbird, Blackbreasted, **358**
  Firetailed Yellowbacked, **357**
  Indian Yellowbacked, 398
  Mrs Gould's Yellowbacked, **360**
  Purple, 398
  Sikkim Yellowbacked, **359**
Sunbirds, **356**, 398
*sundara, Muscicapa sundara,* **140**
*superciliaris, Xiphirhynchus superciliaris,* **154**, 155
*suratensis, Streptopelia chinensis,* **46**
*suscitator, Turnix,* 393
*sutorius, Orthotomus,* 242
Suydam Cutting Expedition, xxx
Swallow, Eastern, **108**
  Himalayan Striated, **109**
  Striated, 73
Swallows, **108**, 395
Swallow-Shrike, Ashy, 16, **314**
Swallow-Shrikes, **314**
Swift, Alpine, 394
  Blyth's Whiterumped Spinetail, **72**
  Nepal House, **73**
  Whiterumped Spinetail, **72**
  Whitethroated Spinetail, **71**
Swiftlet, Himalayan Plainrumped, **70**
Swifts, **70**, 394
*sylvatica, Chaetura,* **72**
  *Turnix,* 393
*sylvicola, (Tephrodornis virgatus),* 113
Sylviinae, **215**, 397
*Sylviparus,* **342**

Tailor Bird, **243**
  Goldenheaded, **242**
Talung, xxiii
Tangkar La, xxiii
*tanki, Turnix,* 393
Teal, Common, 393
*tectirostris, Dicrurus remifer,* **319**
Teesta River, xxiii
  Valley, xxiii
Temi, xxviii
*temminckii, Calidris,* **36**
  *Myiophoneus caeruleus,* **287**
*tenuirostris, Cinclus pallasii,* **297**
*Tephrodornis,* 345
*tephronotus, Lanius tephronotus,* **312**
*terrignotae, (Tringa totanus),* 32
*thalassina, Muscicapa,* 142
  *Muscicapa thalassina,* **144**
Thangu (Thanggu), xxviii
Thanggu (Thangu), xxviii
*thibetana, Carduelis thibetana,* **370**
*thoracicus, B.(radypterus),* 223, 224
  *Bradypterus thoracicus,* **223**
Thrush, Blackfaced Laughing, **184**
  Blackgorgetted Laughing, **174**
  Blackthroated, **272**
  Blue Rock, **281**
  Blueheaded Rock, **280**
  Bluewinged Laughing, **182**
  Chestnutbellied Rock, **279**
  Dusky, 397
  Green, **289**
  Greyheaded, **270**
  Himalayan Whistling, **287**
  Himalayan Whitecrested Laughing, **176**
  Large Brown, **277**
  Lesser Brown, **278**
  Longtailed Mountain, **276**
  Necklaced Laughing, **173**
  Nepal Crimsonwinged Laughing, **186**
  Orangeheaded Ground, **273**
  Pied Ground, 397
  Plainbacked Mountain, **275**
  Plaincoloured Laughing, **183**
  Przevalski's, **271**
  Purple, **288**
  Redthroated, **271**
  Rufouschinned Laughing, **177**
  Rufousnecked Laughing, **180**
  Salvadori's, 397
  Sikkim Greysided Laughing, **179**
  Sikkim Redheaded Laughing, **185**
  Sikkim Striated Laughing, **175**
  Smallbilled Mountain, **274**

Thrush, Streaked Laughing, 181
Whitespotted Laughing, 178
Whitethroated Laughing, 172
Thrushes, 246, 397
*thura, C.(arpodacus)*, 379
*Carpodacus thura*, 380
*tibetana, Calandrella acutirostris*, 104, 105
*tibetanus, Corvus corax*, 333
*(Ithaginis cruentus)*, 24
*Syrrhaptes*, 394
*T.(etraogallus)*, 22
*(Tetraogallus tibetanus)*, 22
Tichodromadinae, 347
*tickelliae, Muscicapa*, 143
Timaliinae, 149, 397
*tinnunculus, (Falco tinnunculus)*, 19
*tiphia, Aegithina*, 395
Tit, Blackspotted Yellow, 341
Brown Crested, 340
Crested Black, 339, 340
Greenbacked, 337
Himalayan Cole-, 338
Redheaded, 197
Rufousfronted, 344
Sikkim Black, 339
Sikkim Redheaded, 343
Sultan, 345
Yellowbrowed, 342
Yellowcheeked, 342
Tits, 337
Longtailed, 343
Penduline, 346
True, 337
*torqueola, Arborophila torqueola*, 22, 23
*torquilla, Jynx*, 395
Tragopan, Satyr, or Crimson Horned Pheasant, 25
*traillii, Oriolus traillii*, 320
*transfluvialis, (Paradoxornis gularis)*, 171
*tricolor, Lanius schach*, 313
*tristis, Acridotheres tristis*, 335
*P.(hylloscopus) collybita*, 226
*Rhopodytes tristis*, 58, 59
*trochiloides, Phylloscopus trochiloides*, 230, 231
Troglodytinae, 294
Trogon, Redheaded, 74
Trogonidae, 74
Trogons, 74
*tschebaiewi, Erithacus pectoralis*, 248
Tso Chomo, 394
Turdinae, 246, 397
*Turdoides*, 247
*turkestanica, Columba rupestris*, 41
Turnicidae, 393
*tusalia, Macropygia unchall*, 43
Twite, Tibetan, 398
Tytoninae, 59

*unicolor, M.(uscicapa)*, 144
*Muscicapa unicolor*, 142
*Paradoxornis unicolor*, 166
Upupidae, 79

*vagabunda, Dendrocitta*, 397
*validirostris, Pteruthius flaviscapis*, 191
*varius, Cuculus*, 394
*vernalis, Loriculus*, 394
*vibex, (Garrulax striatus)*, 175
*vinctura, Actinodura nipalensis*, 196, 197
*vinipectus, (Alcippe vinipectus)*, 210
*virens, M.(egalaima)*, 85
*(Megalaima virens)*, 84
*(Phylloscopus maculipennis)*, 227
*viridis, Cochoa*, 289
*viscivorus, Turdus*, 271
Vulture, Bearded, 13
Black, or King, 11
Cinereous, 393
Fulvous, 12, 393
Himalayan Griffon, 11
King, 11
Lämmergeier, or Bearded, 13
Longbilled, 393
Whitebacked, 393
Vultures, 2, 393

Wagtail, Blackbacked Yellowheaded, 310
Eastern Grey, 309
Forest, 397
Hodgson's Pied, 307
Indian White, 307
Large Pied, 308
Masked, 307
Swinhoe's White, 308
Wagtails, 304, 397
Warbler, Aberrant, 221
Allied Flycatcher-, 235
Ashy Wren-, 397
Blackbrowed Flycatcher-, 236
Blackfaced Flycatcher-, 240
Blackthroated Hill, 245
Blanford's Bush, 219
Blyth's Crowned Leaf, 232
Broadbilled Flycatcher-, 241
Brown Bush, 222
Brown Hill, 397
Chestnut-headed Flycatcher-, 238
Dull Green Leaf, 230
Dusky Leaf, 226
Grasshopper, 397
Greycheeked Flycatcher-, 238

Warbler, Greyfaced Leaf, 227
Greyheaded Flycatcher-, 227, 237
Hume's Bush, 220
Large Bush, 218
Largebilled Leaf, 149, 231
Orangebarred Leaf, 228
Pallas's Himalayan Leaf, 229
Rufous Wren-, 244
Rufouscapped Bush, 217
Sikkim Firecapped Tit-, 346
Slatybellied Ground, 215
Smoky Leaf, 225
Spotted Bush, 223
Strongfooted Bush, 220
Temminck's Crowned Leaf, 233
Thickbilled, 397
Tickell's, or Blackbrowed Leaf, 234
Tickell's Leaf, 224
Yellowbellied Flycatcher-, 239
Yellowbrowed Leaf, 230
Warblers, 215, 397
*wardi, Turdus*, 397
Waterhens, 394
Weavers, 398
*whistleri, (Cettia brunnifrons)*, 217
*(Erithacus chrysaeus)*, 249
*(Garrulax albogularis)*, 173
*(Seicercus burkii)*, 236
White-eye, 238
Indian, 362
White-eyes, 362
Whitethroat, Lesser, 226
*whymperi, (Prunella collaris)*, 299
Wigeon, 393
Woodcock, 31, 34
Woodpecker, Assam Blacknaped, 90
Black, 91
Crimsonbreasted Pied, 96
Darjeeling Pied, 97
East Himalayan Small Yellownaped, 92
Fulvousbreasted, 97
Great Slaty, 95
Himalayan Goldenbacked Threetoed, 93
Woodpecker, Large Yellownaped, 91
Northern Rufous, 89
Paleheaded, 94
Pigmy Pied, 98
Redeared Bay, 99
Rufousbellied, 95
Tickell's Goldenbacked, 100
Woodpeckers, 87, 395
Wren, Brown, 157, 159
Chestnut-headed, 216
Hume's Wedgebilled, 160
Nepal, 294
Scalybreasted, 156
Slatybellied, 215
Spotted, 159
Tailed, 158
Wrens, 294
Wryneck, 395

*xanthochloris, Pteruthius xanthochloris*, 192
*xanthogenys, Parus x.(anthogenys)*, 342
*xanthonotus, Indicator xanthonotus*, 86
*xanthoschistos, Seicercus*, 227, 236, 238
*xanthoschistos, Seicercus xanthoschistos*, 237

Yeumthang (Yumthang), xxviii
Yuhina, Blackchinned, 205
Rufousvented, 204
Slatyheaded, or Rufousvented, 204
Stripedthroated, 203
Yumthang (Yeumthang), xxviii
*yunnanensis, (Anthus hodgsoni)*, 305
*(Minla strigula)*, 199
*(Regulus regulus)*, 235

*zantholeuca, Yuhina zantholeuca*, 206
Zemu, xxiii
*zeylonensis, Bubo*, 394
Zosteropidae, 362
*Zosterops*, 144, 238
*zugmayeri, (Corvus splendens)*, 332